J. N. (Johan Nikolai) Madvig, Thomas Kerchever Arnold

Syntax of the Greek Language

Especially of the Attic Dialect

J. N. (Johan Nikolai) Madvig, Thomas Kerchever Arnold

Syntax of the Greek Language
Especially of the Attic Dialect

ISBN/EAN: 9783743394742

Manufactured in Europe, USA, Canada, Australia, Japa

Cover: Foto ©Paul-Georg Meister /pixelio.de

Manufactured and distributed by brebook publishing software (www.brebook.com)

J. N. (Johan Nikolai) Madvig, Thomas Kerchever Arnold

Syntax of the Greek Language

SYNTAX

OF

THE GREEK LANGUAGE,

ESPECIALLY OF THE ATTIC DIALECT,

For the Use of Schools:

BY

DR. J. N. MADVIG,

PROFESSOR IN THE UNIVERSITY OF COPENHAGEN.

TRANSLATED FROM THE GERMAN

BY THE REV.

HENRY BROWNE, M.A.

AND EDITED BY THE REV.

THOMAS KERCHEVER ARNOLD, M.A.

LATE RECTOR OF LYNDON,

AND FORMERLY FELLOW OF TRINITY COLLEGE, CAMBRIDGE.

TOGETHER WITH AN

APPENDIX ON THE GREEK PARTICLES, BY THE TRANSLATOR.

SECOND EDITION.

RIVINGTONS,

London, Oxford, and Cambridge.

1873.

CONTENTS.

PART I.

PART II.

PART III.

APPENDIX (BY THE TRANSLATOR).

ON THE USE AND MEANING OF THE PARTICLES.

PART I.

ON THE CONNEXION OF WORDS IN SENTENCES.

CHAPTER I.

On the agreement of the Subject and Predicate; of the Substantive and Adjective:—and on the Impersonal form of expression.

a) The verb of the predicate conforms to the subject in person § 1.
and number. But with a plural *subject* of the neuter gender, the (211)
verb stands in the singular. With a dual subject of the masculine or feminine gender, the verb not unfrequently stands in the plural, when no stress is laid on the fact of there being precisely *two*. (The first person of the dual is not used in prose.) Τὼ ξένω τώδε σοφὼ καὶ φίλω ἐστὸν ἐμώ (*Pl. Gorg.* 487). Ὦ Λάχης καὶ Νικία, εἴπατον ἡμῖν, τίνι δὴ δεινοτάτῳ συγγεγόνατον περὶ τῆς τῶν νεῶν τροφῆς (*Pl. Lach.* 186). Γένος καὶ μέρος οὐ ταὐτόν ἐστον (*Pl. Pol.* 263).—Ὅπλα οὐ πάρεστιν. Τὰ καλὰ τὴν ψυχὴν εὐφραίνει.—Δότε παράδειγμα ἡμῖν, ὦ Λάχης καὶ Νικία, τίνας ἐκ φαύλων καλούς τε καὶ ἀγαθοὺς ἐποιήσατε (*Pl. Lach.* 187). Οὕτω διάκεισθον σύ τε καὶ ὁ ἀδελφός, ὥσπερ εἰ τὼ χεῖρε, ἃς ὁ θεὸς ἐπὶ τῷ συλλαμβάνειν ἀλλήλαιν ἐποίησεν, ἀφεμένω τούτου τράποιντο ἐπὶ τὸ διακωλύειν ἀλλήλω (*Xen. Mem.* 2, 3, 18). Θερσαγόρας καὶ Ἐξήκεστος ᾤκουν ἐν Λέσβῳ (*Dem.* 23, 143). Οὐ χρώμεθα τούτοις ἐγὼ καὶ ὁ ἀδελφός (*Pl. Euthyd.* 273).

Rem. 1. The occurrence of a plural verb with a plural subject of the neuter gender is a rare exception: Φανερὰ ἦσαν καὶ ἵππων καὶ ἀνθρώπων ἴχνη πολλά (*Xen. Anab.* 1, 7, 17). Τὰ τέλη Λακεδαιμονίων (the Lacedæmonian *authorities*) Βρασίδαν ἐξέπεμψαν (*Thuc.* 4, 88).

Rem. 2. Now and then we meet with the plural of a substantive with reference to *two* objects: e. g. Δύο ἄνδρας ἔχω (*Xen. Anab.* 4, 1, 22). Δυοῖν ὀνόμασι χρώμεθα (*Pl. Soph.* 244), ἀμφοτέρω τὼ παῖδε and οἱ στρατηγοὶ ἀμφότεροι, and then a plural subject of this kind may take its verb either in the dual or in the plural (or, if it be of the neuter gender, in the singular): Δύο ταῦτα ἐστον (Pl. Pol. 282). Ἔστι δύο ταῦτα κακὼ ἐν τῇ ψυχῇ γένη (Pl. Soph. 228[1]).

REM. 3. In the poets, the plural of the first person is sometimes used instead of the singular: in prose this occurs only when a writer speaks of himself as an *author*: Οἱ Ἑλλήνων, ἐν δόμοις, ἐστερήμεθα Helen, Eur. Tr. 904. Ὅσα ἐπυθόμεθα περὶ Κύρου, ταῦτα πειρασόμεθα διηγήσασθαι (Xen. Cyr. 1. 1. 6). (In the masculine gender, even of a female, since there is no longer an accurate specification of the individual): Οἰκ ἄν ὡς ἐπαινούμενοι μεγάλως ἤλθες Hecuba. Eur. Hec. 511.

6. The adjective or participle of the predicate conforms to the subject in number, gender, and case: in the same way every adjective (participle) conforms to the substantive to which it is, whether *attributively* or *predicatively*, attached: Τω ἄνδρε τούτω (Κριτίας καὶ Ἀλκιβιάδης) ἐφύσει φιλοτιμοτάτω πάντων Ἀθηναίων ἐγενέσθην (Xen. Mem. 1, 2. 14). Πανσόμεθα ὡς ἐπιδείξοντε καὶ διδάξοντε, ἐὰν τις ἐθέλῃ μανθάνειν (Pl. Euthyd. 274). Χρήματα ἄνευ νοῦ βλαβερὰ γίγνεται. Πάντα κάλλιω γίγνεσθαι φιλεῖ θεραπείας τυγχάνοντα.

REM. 1. With dual subjects a participle, as *apposition* or *predicate* (but not as *attributive*), sometimes stands in the plural: Ἐγελασάτην ἄμφω βλέψαντες εἰς ἀλλήλους (Pl. Euthyd. 273).

REM. 2. With a dual subject of the feminine gender there is sometimes found a participle of the masculine: δύο τινὲ ἰδέα ἄρχοντε καὶ ἄγοντε (Pl. Phæd. 237 D).

REM. 3. A masculine or feminine subject, or a neuter subject in the plural number, may take a *predicative* adjective in the neuter of the singular, when it denotes, in a general way, the *essence* of a certain *class* of objects: Πονηρὸν ὁ συκοφάντης ἀεί (Dem. 18. 242). Ἀσθενέστερον γυνὴ ἀνδρός (Pl. Rep. 5. 455). Οἱ τοιοῦτοι ἄνθρωποι χρησιμώτερον νομίζουσι χρήματα ἢ ἀδελφούς (Xen. Mem. 2, 3, 1).

REM. 4. When a neuter adjective with the verb ἐστί is predicated of an infinitive, it sometimes (especially in the *older* writers) stands in the plural: Θέρους δι' ἀνυδρίαν ἀδύνατα ἦν ἐπιστρατεύειν ταῖς Αἰόλου νήσοις (Thuc. 3, 88). Also in impersonal expressions, especially with the *verbals* in -τέος, the adjective is sometimes used in the plural of the neuter gender: πολεμητέα ἐστίν (Thuc. 1, 88).

REM. 5. Instead of a predicative noun with εἰμί, γίγνομαι, a demonstrative or relative pronoun of the neuter gender may also be used, to indicate a preceding predicate: for this, ἀμφότερον, οὐδέτερον, ἀμφότερα, οὐδέτερα may also be used: Ὁ μὲν δίκαιος φρόνιμός τε καὶ ἀγαθός, ὁ δὲ ἄδικος οὐδέτερα (Pl. Rep. 1. 349). The words last mentioned may also be referred to verbs: λέγειν ἢ γράφειν ἢ ἀμφότερα (or both).

REM. 6. The verb εἶναι is connected, not only with *local* adverbs (e. g. μακρὰν εἶναι, *to be far off or away*, χωρὶς εἶναι, *to be apart, by itself*), but also with the

---

[1] Ἔστι καὶ ἐν ταῖς ἄλλαις πόλεσιν ἄρχοντές τε καὶ δῆμος (Pl. Rep. 5. 463; *there are* —). So in a few instances ἔστι, γίγνεται, in the poets also ἦν, before a masculine or feminine subject in the plural.

[2] For the dual forms of the article and certain pronouns that are common to the masculine and feminine gender, see the Accidence.

adverb *μάτην*, e. g. *μάτην ἐστὶ τὸ μεμνῆσθαι περὶ τούτων* (*Isocr. Paneg.* 5). (*Ἅλις ἐστίν.*) In the same way the impersonal *ἐστίν*, *it is* = *it is going on* (*well, ill*, &c.) is used with adverbs, e. g. *καλῶς ἔσται*, *ὁποτέρως ἔσται*. With *local* adverbs *γίγνεσθαι* also is used, e. g. *ἐγγύτερον γίγνεσθαι*, *to come nearer*, *χωρὶς γ.*, *δίχα γίγνεσθαι*, *to separate* (to come into the state of being found at two places). [§ 1.]

a) When two or more subjects of different persons are spoken of together, they are connected with the first or second person of the plural [with the *first*, if any one of them is of that person]: *Τὴν τέχνην ταύτην ἐγώ τε καὶ ὁ πατὴρ ἀσκοῦμεν. Καὶ σὺ καὶ οἱ ἀδελφοὶ παρῆστε*, except when peculiar prominence is to be given to the nearest subject (by making the verb conform to it): *Ταῦτα καὶ σὺ καὶ πάντες οἱ τότε παρόντες ἴσασιν.* (*Σύ τε Ἕλλην εἶ καὶ ἡμεῖς.* *Xen. Anab.* 2, 1, 16.) § 2. (212, 213)

b) When several connected subjects of the singular number are *living* creatures, especially *persons*, they usually take the predicate in the plural; two in the dual: if they are of different genders, the predicate, if capable of distinction of sex, is masculine: *Κριτίας καὶ Ἀλκιβιάδης Σωκράτει ὡμιλείτην* (*Xen. Mem.* 1, 2, 40). *Καὶ ἡ γυνὴ καὶ ὁ ἀνὴρ ἀγαθοί εἰσιν* (*Pl. Men.* 73). The singular, however, is also used when the predicate is a single verb and *precedes* the subjects, only the nearest subject being then regarded: *Ἴσως ἀναβήσεται καὶ συνερεῖ τῇ βουλῇ Φίλιππος καὶ Ἀντιγένης καὶ ὁ ἀντιγραφεύς* (*Dem.* 22, 38). *Ἧκεν ὁ Θερσαγόρας καὶ ὁ Ἐξήκεστος εἰς Λέσβον καὶ ᾤκουν ἐκεῖ* (*Dem.* 23, 143). (*Ἐκ τῶν πατρῴων θρέψεται* (*ὁ τύραννος*) *αὐτός τε καὶ οἱ συμπόται τε καὶ ἑταῖροι καὶ ἑταῖραι*, *Pl. Rep.* 8, 568.)

c) If the connected subjects are *things* and impersonal notions, then the predicate may either conform only to the nearest subject (so that all the subjects are conceived as one, or, it may be, the nearest is rendered prominent), or be placed in the plural, the *plurality* and *distinction* being both alike regarded. (For several subjects of the neuter gender, the *verb* always stands in the singular, according to § 1, a.) *Τῶν ἡμετέρων κακῶν ἡ τῶν πολιτῶν στάσις καὶ ὁ πόλεμος αἴτιός ἐστιν. Οἱ ἐμοὶ πόνοι καὶ ταλαιπωρίαι καὶ τὰ πολλὰ ψηφίσματα τοῦτο ἀπειργάσατο* (*Dem.* 18, 218). *Σοφία καὶ νοῦς ἄνευ ψυχῆς οὐκ ἄν ποτε γενοίσθην* (*Pl. Phil.* 30). If, in the last case, the predicate is such a verb as expresses no independent notion, with an adjective or participle, if the subjects are of different genders, the predicate is always *neuter*: if they are of the same gender (masculine or feminine) it is most commonly neuter (the subjects in general being regarded as *things, objects*), and then the verb also stands in the singular: *Πόλεμος καὶ στάσις ὀλέθρια ταῖς πόλεσίν ἐστιν. Κάλλος καὶ ἰσχὺς δειλῷ*

[§ 2.] καὶ κακῷ ξυνοικοῦντα ἀπρεπῆ φαίνεται (*Pl. Men.* 246). Φθόνος καὶ ἔρως ἐναντία ἐστίν. (Less commonly: φθόνος καὶ ἔρως ἐναντίοι[1].)

d) If several plural subjects of different genders are connected, then, with respect to the gender of the predicate, the rule given under *b* and *c* holds good: Εἶδον νέους τε καὶ νέας ὁμιλοῦντας φιλοφρόνως ἀλλήλοις (*Pl. Legg.* 9, 835). Τῶν δυνατῶν καὶ οἱ φθόνοι καὶ οἱ ἔρωτες δεινοί. Πολεμοι καὶ στάσεις ὀλέθρια ταῖς πόλεσιν. Also, when the subjects are of the same gender (masculine or feminine), the predicate *may* be neuter (denoting *things*, in a general way, according to *c*): Ταραχαὶ καὶ στάσεις ὀλέθρια ταῖς πόλεσιν (*are ruinous things*).

Rem. 1. When of several subjects the *nearest* (to the verb), is in the singular (or in the plural, but of the neuter gender), the rest in the plural, then the predicate may conform either to the nearest alone, or to all of them: Ἀθήνησι καὶ οἱ πένητες καὶ ὁ δῆμος πλέον ἔχει τῶν γενναίων καὶ τῶν πλουσίων (*Xen. Ath. Pol.* 1, 2). Σάρκες καὶ νεῦρα ἐξ αἵματος γίγνεται (*Pl. Tim.* 82). Αἱ τῶν Λακεδαιμονίων ἁμαρτίαι καὶ παρασκευὴ ὑπὸ τῆς ὕλης οὐ δῆλα ἦν τοῖς Ἀθηναίοις (*Thuc.* 4, 29). (Now and then the predicate conforms to a more remote subject, which is at the same time the most important one: Βασιλεὺς καὶ οἱ σὺν αὐτῷ εἰσπίπτει εἰς τὸ Κύρειον στρατόπεδον, *Xen. Anab.* 1, 10, 1.)

Rem. 2. If the subjects are connected by the disjunctive ἤ, the predicate, as a general rule, conforms only to the nearest; sometimes, however, it is referred to both. With ἤ—ἤ, οὔτε—οὔτε, the predicate *nearly always* conforms only to the nearest subject.

§ 3. (215) Sometimes the natural quality and character of the predicate is more regarded, than the grammatical form of the word employed.

a) In the case of a *collective*, denoting living beings, the predicate sometimes refers to the *individuals* comprehended under it, and stands in the plural, and in the *natural* gender (i. e. that of the objects designated): Ἀθηναίων τὸ πλῆθος Ἵππαρχον οἴονται ὑφ᾽ Ἁρμοδίου καὶ Ἀριστογείτονος τύραννον ὄντα ἀποθανεῖν (*Thuc.* 1, 20). Πολὺ γένος ἀνθρώπων τοῖς μὲν ἐκ τῆς γῆς φυομένοις εἰς τροφὴν οὐ χρῶνται, ἀπὸ δὲ βοσκημάτων γάλακτι καὶ τυρῷ καὶ κρέασι τρεφόμενοι ζῶσι (*Xen. Anab.* 4, 3, 10). So also a participle, added *appositively*, stands in the plural: Τὸ στράτευμα ἐπορίζετο σῖτον, ὅπως ἐδύνατο, ἐκ τῶν ὑποζυγίων, κόπτοντες τοὺς βοῦς καὶ ὄνους (*Xen. Anab.* 2, 1, 6).

b) If persons are denoted figuratively by neuter substantives, or men by feminine substantives, the predicate (or a participle as *apposition*) is sometimes added in the plural: Ἔδοξε τοῖς Λακεδαιμονίοις, τὰ τέλη (that *the authorities*) καταβάντας ἐς τὸ στρατόπεδον βουλεύειν (*Thuc.* 4, 15). Πεντήκοντα τριήρεις τῶν Ἀθηναίων πλέουσαι εἰς Αἴγυπτον ἴσχον (*landed*) κατὰ τὸ Μενδήσιον κέρας, οὐκ εἰδότες τῶν γεγενημένων οὐδέν (*Thuc.* 1, 110). (Ἀλκιβιάδης ἑώρα τὴν πόλιν ἑαυτῷ εὔνουν οὖσαν καὶ στρατηγὸν αὐτὸν ᾑρημένους, *Xen. Hell.* 1, 4, 12, — *and that they*, namely, the Athenians, —.)

c) A subject in the singular, to which another personal name is attached by σύν or μετά, is sometimes considered as a *plural* subject, when stress is to be laid

---

[1] Ἡ καλλίστη πολιτεία τε καὶ ὁ κάλλιστος ἀνὴρ λοιπά ἐστιν ἡμῖν διελθεῖν, *Pl. Rep.* 8, 562 (a non-personal notion and a person).

on the *community* of action: Δημοσθένης μετὰ τῶν ξυστρατηγῶν σπένδονται [§ 3.] Μαντινεῦσιν (*Thuc.* 3, 109).

When the predicate consists of a substantive (or a word used substantively), with *εἰμί, γίγνομαι,* or any of the other verbs that cannot express a complete predicate, the verb nearly always conforms to the substantive, and is generally *placed* close by it: Οἱ σοφισταὶ φανερά ἐστι λώβη τε καὶ διαφθορὰ τῶν συγγιγνομένων (*Pl. Men.* 91). Αἴτιον ἐγένετο τῆς ἀποστολῆς τῶν νεῶν οἱ πολλοὶ τῶν Χίων οὐκ εἰδότες τὰ πρασσόμενα (*Thuc.* 8, 9, *the reason of the ships being sent was*—). Τὸ χωρίον τοῦτο πρότερον ἐννέα ὁδοὶ ἐκαλοῦντο (*Thuc.* 4, 102). Πάντα, ὅσα ὑπὸ ποιητῶν λέγεται, διήγησις οὖσα τυγχάνει ἢ γεγονότων ἢ ὄντων ἢ μελλόντων (*Pl. Rep.* 3, 392). Τὴν ἡδονὴν διώκετε ὡς ἀγαθὸν ὄν (*Pl. Prot.* 354). § 4. (216)

A more special distinction by means of the words ἄλλος, ἄλλο (ἄλλοθεν, &c.), ὁ μὲν — ὁ δὲ, ἕκαστος (of *two*, ἑκάτερος) is often attached to a plural subject without exerting any influence upon the predicate; sometimes, however, the predicate conforms to this *apposition* (only, however, when it follows it): Ὡς εἶδόν μ' εἰσιόντα, εὐθὺς, πόῤῥωθεν ἠσπάζοντο ἄλλος ἄλλοθεν (*Pl. Charm.* 153). Ἐγώ τε καὶ σὺ μακρὸν λόγον ἑκάτερος ἀπετείναμεν (*Pl. Prot.* 361).—Πελοποννήσιοι πάντες ἰσόψηφοι ὄντες καὶ οὐχ ὁμόφυλοι τὸ ἐφ' ἑαυτὸν ἕκαστος σπεύδει (*Thuc.* 1, 141). Οὗτοι ἄλλος ἄλλα λέγει (*Xen. Anab.* 2, 1, 15). (Cf. on the partitive gen. § 50, a. REM. 3.) § 5. (217, R. 2)

REM. When one subject is appended to another by the *comparative* particle ἤ, the predicate often conforms to the appended subject: Τῶν κοινῶν οὐδὲν σὺ μᾶλλον ἤ τις ἄλλος ἔχει (*Pl. Theæt.* 209).

a) The subject is usually omitted in Greek, when it would be the personal pronoun of the first or second person, without any peculiar emphasis or opposition to other notions (but: ὡς καὶ ἡμεῖς λέγομεν καὶ ὑμεῖς ὁμολογεῖτε [1]); so also always, when it is *that* third person, who has hitherto been the subject of discourse, and is sufficiently known from the context (whereas, by the use of a demonstrative pronoun, the subject is rendered prominent, and distinguished from other notions in a marked way, or even opposed to them). § 6. (208, R. 2)

REM. Sometimes, by a less careful mode of expression, the third person of a verb without a pronoun is so placed, that we must understand it to be spoken of some other subject (sufficiently implied by the context), than that of another verb in the third person, which preceded it: Αἰσθόμενοι οἱ Ἀθηναῖοι τοὺς Λακεδαιμονίους διὰ κατάγνωσιν ἀσθενείας σφῶν (*because they considered the Athenians weak*) παρασκευαζομένους, δηλῶσαι βουλόμενοι, ὅτι οὐκ ὀρθῶς ἐγνώκασιν (namely, οἱ Λακεδαιμόνιοι), ἀλλ' οἷοί τε εἰσί (namely, οἱ Ἀθηναῖοι), μὴ κινοῦντες τὸ ἐπὶ Λέσβῳ ναυτικόν, καὶ τὸ ἀπὸ Πελοποννήσου ἐπιὸν ῥαδίως ἀμύνεσθαι, ἐπλήρωσαν ναῦς ἑκατόν (*Thuc.* 3, 16). Ἀφανῆ τὸν Γύγην γενέσθαι φασὶν τοῖς παρακαθημένοις καὶ διαλέγεσθαι (namely, αὐτοὺς, τοὺς παρακαθημένους) ὡς περὶ οἰχομένου (*Pl. Rep.* 306). Some-

---

[1] Οἱ ἄλλοι σκηνοῦμεν ὑπαίθριοι (*Xen. Anab.* 5, 5, 21,—*we others: the rest of us*). Θεμιστοκλῆς ἥκω παρὰ σέ (*Thuc.* 1, 137).

[§ 6.] times, by an inaccuracy, the expression passes over from a whole class, denoted by a plural substantive, to the singular, denoting one of the individuals contained in the class: *οἱ τύραννοι*, and then *τίνων γὰρ ἔτι ἄρξει;* namely, *ὁ τύραννος* (*Xen. Hier.* 6, 14).

(208, R. 3) *b*) The third person of a verb in the plural is sometimes found without a subject expressed, when it is to be understood of men in general; especially when the thing spoken of is the common opinion or common talk of men; or when particular men are intended, who are easily known from the context: *Τοὺς εὖ παθόντας, ὅταν δυνάμενοι χάριν ἀποδοῦναι μὴ ἀποδῶσιν, ἀχαρίστους καλοῦσιν* (*Xen. Mem.* 2, 2, 1). *Ὁ Νικίας* (*ὅπερ πάσχουσιν ἐν τοῖς μεγάλοις ἀγῶσι*) *πάντα τε ἔργῳ ἔτι ἐνδεᾶ εἶναι ἐνόμιζε καὶ λόγῳ οὔπω ἱκανὰ εἰρῆσθαι* (*Thuc.* 7, 69). (Often *φασί*, *they say, people say; it is said.*) *Τῷ ποταμῷ γέφυραι οὐκ ἔπεισιν, διαβαίνουσι δὲ ἐπὶ σχεδιῶν* (namely, *the inhabitants* of the country).

(211 a, R. 370) *c*) The second person of the verb is used, in some kinds of sentences, to denote an assumed indefinite subject: *Οὐδὲ βουλόμενος ἂν εὗρες ῥᾳδίως τὸν νύκτωρ πορευόμενον* (*Xen. Cyr.* 4, 5, 6, *would you have found*, i. e. *would* a person, anybody, *have found*).

Rem. The second person stands in this way only in hypothetical sentences with *ἄν*, of what would have shown itself to be the case in a certain assumed state of things; and, in subjunctive subordinate sentences, with *ἐάν* or a relative word with *ἄν*. *Ὁρῶν ταῦτα ἡγήσαιο ἂν Λακεδαιμονίους μόνους τῷ ὄντι τεχνίτας τῶν πολεμικῶν εἶναι* (*Xen. Pol. Lac.* 13, 5). *Οἱ ἀνοήτως φοβούμενοι, ὅσῳ ἂν μᾶλλον αὐτοῖς θαρρεῖν παρακελεύῃ, τοσούτῳ ἐν δεινοτέροις ἡγοῦνται εἶναι* (*Xen. Cyr.* 5, 2, 34). (In Herodotus and the poets also the second person of the future in the indicative, e. g. Herod. 1, 139.)

§ 7. (207, R. 1) *a*) The third person plural of several active verbs stands without any substantive (or substantivized word) as subject (*impersonally*), e. g. *ὕει*, *it rains*, *ἔξεστι* (*ἰέναι*), *it is permitted*, = *one* (*you*, &c.) *may* (licet), *ἐδήλωσε*, *it was plain*.

In this way are used in Greek:

1) Verbs that denote a state of the weather, or certain natural phenomena: as *ὕει, νίφει, βροντᾷ, ἀστράπτει, χειμάζει, συσκοτάζει* (*it is growing dark*), *ἔσεισε* (*there was an earthquake: a shock was felt*). With these verbs some indefinite being is regarded as the agent who causes the event (*ὁ θεὸς ὕει*, *Herod.* 2, 13; *ἔσεισεν ὁ θεός*, *Xen. Hell.* 4, 7, 4; *Ζεὺς βροντᾷ*).

2) The verbs which denote generally the propriety or possibility of an action, and have for their subject an infinitive, or *acc. cum infin.*, as *δεῖ, χρή, προσήκει, πρέπει, ἔξεστι, ἐγχωρεῖ, ἐνδέχεται*, and also *συμβαίνει*, *it happens*. In certain phrases, *ἔχει* stands in the same way, as: *φύσιν ἔχει*, *it is natural*, *δίκην ἔχει*, *it is just.*

3) The verbs *δοκεῖ* (*it seems;* and with an infinitive; *it seems good*, *it is resolved*), *ἔοικε*, and in some connexions *δηλοῖ* and *δείκνυσι* (*ἐδήλωσε, δηλώσει*, *it was manifest, will be manifest*, *δείξει*), with which the thing intended must be mentally supplied.

4) Verbs which (in certain connexions) denote generally the state and progress of circumstances, as *εὖ* (*καλῶς, οὕτως, ἄλλως*) *ἔχει*, *δεῖ* (*πολλοῦ, ὀλίγου*), *προχωρεῖ*

(μοι), *it is going on* (successfully), *I am succeeding* (in any thing): εἰς τοῦτ' ἦλθεν, *it has come to this*, and a few others. (Of relations of *time*: Ἦν ἀμφὶ ἀγορὰν πλήθουσαν, *it was about the time when the market-place fills*.) Further μέλει (*curæ est*) and μεταμέλει (μοι, *pœnitet me*). [§ 7.]

5) Some verbs which denote the action of persons appointed to perform it, when the occurrence of the action is the thing contemplated, without any thought of the personal agent: especially, σημαίνει, *a signal is given* (ἐπειδὰν σημήνῃ), σαλπίζει (*the trumpet sounds*), κηρύττει (*proclamation is made*): (ἐκηρύξε). (Ἀναγνώσεται, *he shall read*, in the orators, of the *clerk* who was present for the purpose.)

b) In other instances, the action is denoted impersonally by the third person singular of intransitive or intransitively-used verbs: Λέγεται, τοὺς θεοὺς ὑπὸ Διὸς βασιλεύεσθαι (*Isocr. Nic.* 26). Συρακούσιοι τοὺς Μεγαρεῖς τοὺς ἐν τῇ Σικελίᾳ ἀνέστησαν, ὥσπερ καὶ πρότερόν μοι εἴρηται (*Thuc.* 6, 94). Οὐκ ἄλλως αὐτοῖς πεπόνηται (*Pl. Phæd.* 232). Ἐπειδὴ παρεσκεύαστο τοῖς Κορινθίοις, ἀνήγοντο ὡς ἐπὶ ναυμαχίαν (*Thuc.* 1, 48). Ὧν ἂν καταψηφισθῇ, ἀποκτείνειν δεήσει (*Pl. Pol.* 299). (Δέδοκται, *it is resolved*).

Rem. 1. This use is, however, for the most part, restricted to verbs that denote to *say* (λέγειν, ὁμολογεῖν), and to the perfect and pluperfect of other verbs, with an appended dative of the agent (see on Dat. § 38, g), of the completed action, and what has been effected. (On the other hand, the Latin practice, of using *impersonally* in the passive voice verbs which govern the dat., e.g. invidetur, invidebatur mihi, is not customary in Greek.)

Rem. 2. Now and then we meet with a general impersonal expression (without a sentence for its subject), with a neuter adjective (sometimes in the plural, § 1, b. R. 4), to denote a relation that exists, and a certain state of affairs, e.g. ἕτοιμά ἐστιν, γίγνεται (*Thuc.* 2, 3; *it is ready* = *things are in readiness*, or *all is ready*); βάσιμα ἦν, ἄβατα ἦν (*Xen. Anab.* 3, 4, 49); εὐ ἐπίθετον ἦν ἐνταῦθα (*Xen. Anab.* 3, 4, 20; here it was easy to attack = *here was a convenient opportunity for attacking*). On the Gerundive, see Chap. VII.

Rem. 3. Observe, that the Greeks occasionally use a personal expression with a definite substantive (or *substantivized*) subject, where in English we use a neuter adjective with *it is*, &c., having a sentence for its subject: as in the case of the adjectives φανερός, δῆλος (see on the Participle, § 177, b. R. 2), and δίκαιος (see on Infin. § 165, a. R.).

CHAPTER II.

On the use of the Article.

The Greek article (like the English definite article, *the*) represents the substantive before which it is placed, as the name or designation of a certain definite and known object (as opposed to a representation of *some one or other* indefinite object amongst several of the same kind). It stands, therefore, 1) before the generic names § 8.

CHAP. II.

of objects which are, in their own nature, isolated and definite[1]; 2) before substantives which denote the whole class designated by the substantive (or substantive with its adjective), not any individual object; 3) before the names of persons or things, *a*) which are sufficiently distinguished from others by some appended specification (adjective, participle, genitive, preposition with its case), or *b*) which have been already mentioned, or follow immediately from what has been said, or *c*) of which it is easily understood, from the circumstances under which they are spoken of, that they, and no others, are the objects intended: Ὁ οὐρανός, ἡ γῆ, ὁ ἥλιος, ἡ θάλασσα.—Οἱ ἱππεῖς. Τὰ θηρία. Οἱ ἵπποι καλλίους τῶν ὄνων εἰσίν. Ὁ συκοφάντης (*the sycophant*, as a class[2]). Οἱ σοφοὶ ἄνδρες. Αἱ καλαὶ γυναῖκες. Οἱ ἄλλοι ἄνθρωποι. (Ἀγαθοὶ ἄνδρες, *good men*, ἄλλοι ἄνθρωποι, *other men*.)—Ὁ πρεσβύτερος ἀδελφός. Οἱ προτεταγμένοι ἱππεῖς. Ἡ ἐπὶ τῷ ποταμῷ πόλις. Ἡ τοῦ πατρὸς οἰκία.—Ὁ ἀνὴρ οὔπω ἥκει. Ποῦ οἱ ἵπποι (*the horses*, which have been spoken of, and are here meant). Κῦρος ἀναβὰς ἐπὶ τὸν ἵππον τὰ παλτὰ εἰς τὰς χεῖρας ἔλαβεν (*Xen. Anab.* 1, 8, 3, *the* javelins = *his* javelins, it being supposed a *known* thing, that javelins made a part of his equipment). Οἶνος ἐν τῷ πίθῳ οὐκ ἔστιν (in *the* cask, *the* cask in use). Ξέρξης ἀγείρας τὴν ἀναρίθμητον στρατιὰν ἦλθεν ἐπὶ τὴν Ἑλλάδα (*Xen. Anab.* 3, 2, 13, *the* well-known, numerous *army*).

Rem. 1. The article stands more frequently than in English, to denote an object that is defined by its relation to another (subject, object, or relational-object in the sentence): in such cases we generally use a possessive pronoun in English: Οἱ πλούσιοι τοῖς χρήμασιν ἐξωνοῦνται τοὺς κινδύνους (*Lys.* 24, 17). Τοὺς τοιούτους πατέρας οὐδὲ οἱ παῖδες αἰδεῖσθαι δύνανται. Ἴσμεν ὑμᾶς εἰθισμένους τοῖς εὐεργέταις μεγίστην χάριν ἀποδιδόναι (*Isocr. Plat.* 1).

Rem. 2. With certain words in certain connexions (without an adjective) the article is *occasionally* omitted in Greek (as in some similar instances in English), although a definite notion is denoted, some peculiarity in the nature or conception of the notion having caused, in particular instances, the retention of the old manner of expression, when the use of the article was not yet become general, and firmly established. Such words are:

a) The names of the large and peculiar portions of external nature (οὐρανός, γῆ, θάλασσα, ὠκεανός, ἥλιος), especially when a particular point or particular manifestation of them is contemplated: Ἐπὶ θαλάττῃ, *on* the *sea*. Ὕδωρ ἐξ οὐρανοῦ πολύ. Ἥλιος ἀνατέλλει, ἥλιος ἐδύετο, περὶ ἡλίου δυσμάς (*at sunset* = *the* setting of the sun); further, sometimes θεοί and ἄνθρωποι, when it is precisely the *generic term*, that is to be made prominent: Τὰ ἐν ἀνθρώποις (*Xen. Cyr.* 2, 2, 7), *human affairs and institutions*. Τῶν ὄντων ἀγαθῶν καὶ καλῶν οὐδὲν ἄνευ πόνου καὶ

[[1] Bp. Middleton's '*monadic* nouns.'—T. K. A.]

[[2] Where, however, our idiom allows us to say 'a sycophant,' taking one as the type of the class.—T. K. A.]

ἐπιμελείας θεοὶ διδόασιν ἀνθρώποις (*Xen. Mem.* 2, 1, 28), and the names of naturally-defined *times* (*ἅμα ἕῳ*, *at day-break; with* the *dawn; at* the *break of day;* even when a particular day is meant; but also *ἅμα τῇ ἕῳ*). [§ 8.]

b) The term *βασιλεύς*, when the Persian king is intended (*βασιλεὺς ὁ μέγας*). *Οἱ πρόγονοι οἱ βασιλέως.* (Here the article is nearly always omitted.)

c) The names of *virtues, vices, sciences, arts, and occupations*, when they are considered as general conceptions, which may be exhibited in a different form in different persons: *Πάντα τὰ καλὰ καὶ ἀγαθὰ ἀσκητά ἐστιν. οὐχ ἥκιστα δὲ σωφροσύνη* (*Xen. Mem.* 1, 2, 23, *moderation*, or *temperance*). *Οὐδέποτ' ἄρα λυσιτελέστερον ἀδικία δικαιοσύνης* (*Pl. Rep.* 1, 354, but also *λυσιτελέστερον ἡ ἀδικία τῆς δικαιοσύνης*, *Pl. ib.* as a single definite notion). *Ἀνδρὶ καλῷ τε κἀγαθῷ ἐργασία καὶ ἐπιστήμη κρατίστη γεωργία* (*Xen. Œc.* 6, 8).

d) *Πόλις, ἄστυ, ἀγρός, ἀγορά, τεῖχος, πεδίον*, and other *local* designations, when they denote oppositions between the parts of a given and presupposed principal locality, and are governed by prepositions[1]: *Ἑσπέρας γενομένης ἡ διαδοχὴ τῇ πρόσθεν φυλακῇ ἔρχεται ἐκ πόλεως* (*Xen. Cyr.* 1, 3, 17). *Δοκεῖτέ μοι πρὸς ἄστυ ὡρμῆσθαι* (*Pl. Rep.* 1, 327, *to the city*, Athens, from the Piræus; but shortly before *ἀπῇμεν πρὸς τὸ ἄστυ*). *Ἔξω Ἰσθμοῦ* (*Thuc.* 1, 62, *beyond the Isthmus* of Corinth, but in the same chap. *ἐν τῷ Ἰσθμῷ*). *Ἐκτὸς τείχους* and *ἐκτὸς τοῦ τείχους* (of *the* wall of the city). In the same way sometimes also *στρατός, στρατιά, στράτευμα, στρατόπεδον* (and with adjectives as one word, *δεξιὸν κέρας, εὐώνυμον κέρας, the right, the left wing: Κορινθίοις τὸ μὲν δεξιὸν κέρας αἱ Μεγαρίδες νῆες εἶχον καὶ αἱ Ἀμπρακιώτιδες, εὐώνυμον δὲ κέρας αὐτοὶ οἱ Κορίνθιοι εἶχον*, *Thuc.* 1, 48). (*Ἀπὸ δεξιᾶς*, &c.)

e) Names of *relationship* in certain connexions with an emphatic prominence given to the generic term of the relationship: *Οὔτε πατρὸς οὔτε μητρὸς φείδεται. Οἱ Καρδοῦχοι ἔχοντες γυναῖκας καὶ παῖδας*[2] *ἔφευγον ἐπὶ τὰ ὄρη* (*Xen. Anab.* 4, 18, with their wives and children).

f) And in general, the article is sometimes omitted when, by the combination of two or more opposed members, the expression of the whole is brought out with a certain emphasis[2]: *Λύσις καὶ χωρισμὸς ψυχῆς ἀπὸ σώματος* (*Pl. Phæd.* 67, as in English, *body and soul;* but, 64: *ἡ τῆς ψυχῆς ἀπὸ τοῦ σώματος ἀπαλλαγή*. *Παυσανίας συγκαλέσας πολεμάρχους καὶ πεντηκοστῆρας ἐβουλεύετο* (*Xen. Hell.* 3, 5, 22). *Ἀπὸ τελευτῆς ἐπ' ἀρχήν*[3] [cf. note 1].)

Rem. 3. A superlative (or other adjective) with a predicative noun, or a superlative standing alone as the predicate, never takes the article in Greek: nor does it stand with a substantive and the 'superlative of eminence' (denoting only a *very high* degree, and therefore not distinguishing any particular object as belonging to *the highest degree* of all): *Ἀνδρὶ καλῷ κἀγαθῷ ἐργασία κρατίστη ἐστὶ γεωργία* (*Xen. Œc.* 6, 8). (*Οὗτοι φανερά ἐστι διαφθορὰ τῶν συγγιγνομένων, are evidently* the ruin *of —*: *Pl. Men.* 91, c.) *Πάντων φιλομαθέστατος Κῦρος ἦν. Οἱ Φασηλῖταί εἰσι πονηρότατοι ἀνθρώπων καὶ ἀδικώτατοι* (*Dem.* 35, 2). (*Τοῦτο βαρύ-*

[[1] Bp. Middleton considers government by a preposition to favour the omission of the article generally.—T. K. A.]

[[2] This belongs to Bp. Middleton's head of *enumeration*.—T. K. A.]

[3] *Ὁ ὁπλίτης δραχμὴν ἐλάμβανε τῆς ἡμέρας* (*Thuc.* 3, 17, *received a drachma a day = every day*); but also *δέκα, εἷς ἀπὸ φυλῆς* (*Xen. Hell.* 2, 4, 24, *ten, one from each Phyle*), *εἷς ἀπὸ πόλεως* (*ib.* 4, 2, 8).

CHAP. II.]

[§ 8.] τατόν ἐστι τοῦ στρατεύματος, *Xen. Cyr.* 5, 3, 37, *the most heavily-armed division.* Διὰ βραχυτάτων, *in the shortest way* I can.)

Rem. 4. The Attic poets often omit the article where it must have stood in prose, as well before substantives undefined by any added specification, as before such as have a genitive or adjective (possessive pronoun) with them: e. g. Θύματος ἐπιστάτης ἐπέστη τοῦδε παῖς Ἀχιλλέως (*Eur. Hec.* 224). Παῖδα σὴν κτενοῦσιν. Πέμπουσί με δισσοὶ Ἀτρεῖδαι (*Eur. Hec.* 510). Ἑκάβη κεῖται κόνει φύρουσα δύστηνον κάρα (*Eur. Hec.* 496). In the old poets (Homer, Hesiod) the usage is still more fluctuating.

§ 9. *a*) The adjective or participle by which the substantive is defined, stands, with any appended notion dependent on it, either between the article and its substantive, or, with the article repeated, after the substantive: Ὁ ἀγαθὸς ἀνήρ. Ὁ πάντων κάλλιστος καὶ πᾶσι φίλτατος ἀνήρ. Οἱ στρατηγικοὶ νομιζόμενοι ἄνδρες. Αἱ ἄρισται δοκοῦσαι εἶναι φύσεις (*Xen. Mem.* 4, 1, 3).—Αἱ τιμαὶ αἱ πολιτικαί. Οἱ στρατηγοὶ οἱ ταῦτα βεβουλευκότες. (Τὰς μεγάλας ἡδονὰς καὶ τὰ ἀγαθὰ τὰ μεγάλα ἡ πειθὼ καὶ ἡ καρτερία καὶ οἱ ἐν καιρῷ πόνοι παρέχονται. *Xen. Cyr.* 3, 3, 8.)

The latter position, that with the article repeated, is, however, the more rare, especially in the Attic writers, and is usually employed only when the object is first mentioned, as a notion sufficiently defined in and by itself, and then has a nearer specification added to it besides: Τὸ τεῖχος περιεῖλον τὸ καινόν (*Thuc.* 4, 51). Ἐπὶ τῆς νεὼς τῆς διαφθαρείσης (*Dem.* 34, 2).

Rem. 1. When the participle has itself a specification (by means of dependent words), it not uncommonly happens, that only this nearer specification, or only the participle itself, is placed between the article and its substantive: Αἱ πρὸ τοῦ στόματος (*before the mouth of the harbour*) νῆες ναυμαχοῦσαι (*Thuc.* 7, 23). Αἱ ὑπ' Αἰσχίνου βλασφημίαι εἰρημέναι (*Dem.* 18, 126). Ὁ κατειληφὼς κίνδυνος τὴν πόλιν (*Dem.* 18, 220[1]).

Rem. 2. The adjective may stand as an *apposition*, either before the article or after the substantive, without repetition of the article, see § 12. Otherwise Ὁ ἀνὴρ καλός or καλὸς ὁ ἀνήρ signifies (with ἐστίν omitted) *the man is handsome.*

Rem. 3. Sometimes the article makes its first appearance before the *following* adjective (participle) or prepositional expression, the object being first placed as an undefined notion, and then more closely defined: Ἀρετῆς ἕνεκα καὶ προθυμίας τῆς ἐν ἐκείνοις τοῖς κινδύνοις γενομένης (*Thuc.* 2, 71). Σκεπτέον, πῶς ποτε ἡ ἄκρᾱτος δικαιοσύνη πρὸς ἀδικίαν τὴν ἄκρατον ἔχει (*Pl. Rep.* 8, 535, *is related to*).

b) A preposition with its case is connected *attributively* with a substantive by means of an article, in the same way as an adjective: Ἡ ἐπὶ τῷ ποταμῷ πόλις. Αἱ ἀπὸ Ἀθηνῶν νῆες. Οἱ στρατιῶται οἱ ἐν

---

[1] Μετὰ τὸν ὕστερον πόλεμον τῆς καθαιρέσεως τῶν Ἀθήνησι τειχῶν (*Xen. Hell.* 5, 1, 35. The specification of an adjective appended to it after the substantive). The placing of a secondary specification before the article is a rare and poetical construction: Τούτων τὰ ἐναντία ἐπιφημίσματα (*Thuc.* 7, 75 = τὰ ἐν. τούτων ἐπιφημ.) (Ὅστις γὰρ ἦν ἐκεῖνον ὁ κτανών, *Soph. Œd. T.* 139.)

τῇ πόλει. Τὸ τεῖχος τὸ παρὰ τὸν ποταμόν. This is also the case with [§ 9.]
adverbs of *time* and *place*, of what manifests itself *at* the *time* or *place* expressed: Οἱ πάλαι ἄνθρωποι, *the men of former days; of the olden time.* Ἡ τότε ταραχή. (Completely: Ἡ τότε ταραχὴ γενομένη.) Ἡ Αἰσχίνου τότε μισθαρνία (*Dem.* 18, 50). Ἡ ἄνω πόλις. Ἡ πρότερον ἀπραγμοσύνη (*your former*, or *previous, inactivity*; ἡ προτέρα, *the former*, of *two*). Οἱ ἄρχοντες οἱ Ἀθήνησι. Ἡ πόλις ἡ ὑπὸ τῷ ὄρει. In this way ἄγαν and λίαν are also used (ἡ ἄγαν ἐπιθυμία. *Thuc.* 6. 24) with πάνυ (ὁ πάνυ Περικλῆς, *the celebrated Pericles*): as are also a few other isolated adverbs, when no corresponding adjective exists, or with a peculiar meaning: Τὰ καταλογάδην συγγράμματα (*Isocr. ap. Nic.* 7, *prose writings*). Τὸ ἀληθῶς φῶς (*Pl. Phæd.* 109, *the light which is truly light*). (Also Ὁ γόνῳ πατήρ, *Lys.* 13, 91, *the natural father.*)

Rem. Now and then a specification which would be properly attached to the substantive by an article, is referred less accurately to the verb: ὅσοι τῶν πραγμάτων πρὸς τοὺς Ἀθηναίους μάλιστα μετέσχον (*Thuc.* 4, 74).

The article stands in Greek with substantives that are defined by § 10.
an appended genitive, either of a generic term with the article, or of a proper name: Ἡ τοῦ πατρὸς οἰκία, ἡ τοῦ ὑπὲρ τῶν Ἠλείων ὄρους κορυφή (*Xen. Hell.* 7, 4, 13), (οἱ Σόλωνος νόμοι), ἡ οἰκία τοῦ πατρός, ἡ οἰκία ἡ τοῦ πατρός. Of these forms the first (that of the genitive in the middle) is the most common; the second (the genitive following the substantive) is also common: the third (the genitive following the substantive with its article repeated, by means of which the specification is, as it were, returned for and appended with emphasis) is less common. Fourthly, the genitive may also precede, when it stands with emphasis on account of an opposition, or in a transition: Τῶν παλαιῶν ἡ φιλοσοφία (*Pl. Prot.* 343). Τοῦ χωρίου ἡ ἀπορία (*Thuc.* 4, 29). (Τὸ τῆς τοῦ ξαίνοντος τέχνης ἔργον, *Pl. Rep.* 381, after the first form. Περὶ τοῦ μισθοῦ τῆς ἀποδόσεως, *Thuc.* 8, 85, after the fourth [1].)

Rem. 1. The partitive genitive very frequently precedes, and with this genitive the article can never be repeated: cf. § 50, Rem. 1.

Rem. 2. A substantive which governs a genitive with the article, itself stands without the article, when, in spite of the appended genitive, the object is *undefined* (especially in the case of the partitive and objective genitives; e.g. μέρος τῆς πόλεως ἐπὶ βλάβῃ τῆς πόλεως (*Thuc.* 8, 72, *for injury to the city* [though *we* should say, *to* the *injury of the city*] μεγάλαι δαπάναι τῶν τε τριηράρχων καὶ τῆς πόλεως (*Thuc.* 6, 31), *great outlays on the part of the trierarchs and the state*): sometimes also, when it is wished to express a notion that in itself is definite, in a general and indefinite way: ἐν ἀρχῇ τοῦ λόγου (*Dem.* 37, 28). ὑπὸ πλήθους τῶν ἐπικειμένων νεῶν (*Thuc.* 8, 105). The article is always omitted, when the governing substantive is the *predicate* with εἰμί or γίγνομαι, or belongs to the predicate as an appo-

---

[1] But αἱ ἴδιαι ἡμῶν ἑκάστων πόλεις (*Isocr. Plat.* 8), and ἡ δοκοῦσα ἡμῶν πρότερον σωφροσύνη (*Thuc.* 1, 32), where the genitive attaches itself to another specification (Rem. 6).

[§ 10.] sition[1]: Ἡ τῶν πολεμίων βλάβη κέρδος τῆς πόλεως γίγνεται. Σωτὴρ γενοῦ τῆς πατρίδος. Μεγάλων κακῶν ἄγγελοι ἥκομεν. (Νόμοι πόλεως, *laws of a state*; περὶ ἀρίστου ὥραν, *Thuc.* 7, 81.)

Rem. 3. Now and then the article does not stand with the substantive itself, but is not placed till before the following genitive[2]: Ἐπὶ σκηνὴν ᾔεσαν τὴν Ξενοφῶντος (*Xen. Anab.* 9, 2, 19). Τισσαφέρνης ᾔδει τοὺς Μιλησίους ἐς τὴν Λακεδαίμονα πορευομένους ἐπὶ καταβοῇ τῇ αὐτοῦ μάλιστα (*Thuc.* 8, 85).

Rem. 4. With respect to the position of the article with the governing substantive, the genitive of a personal or possessive pronoun has the same effect as the genitive of a substantive with the article. The genitive of the personal pronoun stands either before the article or after the substantive (enclitically). Ἡμῶν ἡ πόλις, ἡ πόλις ἡμῶν. Τοῦτό σοι δίδωμι ὅτι μου τὴν μητέρα (τὴν μητέρα μου) τιμᾷς. The genitive of a demonstrative or reflexive pronoun either stands in the middle, or follows with the article repeated: ὁ τούτου ἀδελφός, ὁ ἀδελφὸς ὁ τούτου (*Dem.* 35, 15). Τὴν ἑαυτῶν συκοφαντίαν δηλοῦσιν. Παρὰ τὸν τρόπον τὸν ἑαυτῶν (*Thuc.* 5, 63). (Partitively also: Ἑαυτῶν τοὺς βελτίστους αἱροῦνται, and τοὺς βελτίστους αἱροῦνται ἑαυτῶν.)

Rem. 5. In the case of substantives with possessive pronouns, the article stands as in the case of substantives with adjectives: Ὁ ὑμέτερος πατήρ. ὁ πατὴρ ὁ σός. Τοὺς οἴκους τοὺς ὑμετέρους αὐτῶν, or τοὺς ὑμετέρους αὐτῶν οἴκους ἀσφαλῶς κεκτῆσθαι βούλεσθε. (But δοῦλος ὑμέτερος, *one of your slaves; a slave of yours.* Σοὶ δοῦλοί ἐσμεν.)

Rem. 6. When two specifications are appended to a substantive (adjective, participle, preposition, adverb, or genitive), the one of which bears such a relation to the other, that *the two* are blended into *one* (complex) specification, they are usually comprehended under *one article*: when, however, they are taken, each by itself, as two co-ordinated specifications, the article is used with each: and this is sometimes done even in the first case, especially if both are adjectives, particularly in the instance of ἄλλος: Τὰ ἐν τῇ ἠπείρῳ Αἰολικὰ πολίσματα (*Thuc.* 4, 52). Ὁ Ἀλκιβιάδου τούτου νεώτερος ἀδελφός (*Pl. Prot.* 320). Μέμνησθε τῆς ἐν Σαλαμῖνι πρὸς τὸν Πέρσην ναυμαχίας (*Æsch.* 2, 74). Εἰς τὰς ἄλλας Ἀρκαδικὰς πόλεις (*Xen. Hell.* 7, 4, 38). Αἱ ἀπὸ τῆς Σικελίας Πελοποννησίων ἑκκαίδεκα νῆες (*Thuc.* 8, 13). Τὰ ἐκ τῆς Ἰάσου μεγάλα χρήματα διαρπασθέντα (*Thuc.* 8, 36; the participle removed according to § 9, a. Rem. 1).—Ἡ σεμνὴ αὕτη, ἡ τῆς τραγῳδίας ποίησις (*Pl. Gorg.* 502). Ἡ ἄνω ἡ πρὸς τῷ τείχει ἀπόληψις τῶν ὁπλιτῶν (*Thuc.* 7, 51). Αἱ πέντε καὶ εἴκοσι νῆες τῶν Κορινθίων αἱ τοῖς Ἀθηναίοις ἀνθορμοῦσαι (*Thuc.* 7, 31). Τὸ ἐν Ἀρκαδίᾳ τὸ τοῦ Διὸς τοῦ Λυκαίου ἱερόν (*Pl. Rep.* 8, 565). Κατὰ τὴν Ἀττικὴν τὴν παλαιὰν φωνήν (*Pl. Crat.* 398). Τεκμαίρομαι ἐκ τοῦ ἄλλου τοῦ ὑμετέρου τρόπου (*Pl. Rep.* 2, 368). (Also where the other adjective or participle stands substantively: Οἱ ἄλλοι οἱ παρόντες τῶν στρατιωτῶν, *Xen. Anab.* 6, 4, 7.) (It is seldom that one of the specifications follows without the repeated article: ἡ τῆς πόλεως ἀνάλωσις δημοσία, *Thuc.* 6, 31. Μετὰ τὴν τῶν τυράννων κατάλυσιν ἐκ τῆς Ἑλλάδος, *Thuc.* 1, 18. Τὸν πρεσβύτατον υἱὸν ἑαυτοῦ, *Xen. Mem.* 2, 2, 1.)

§ 11. The article stands with substantives (appellatives), that are connected with a demonstrative pronoun, οὗτος, ὅδε, or ἐκεῖνος. The

[1] [So, often, αἴτιος, αἴτιον, &c., used substantively in the *predicate*, = the *cause*.]
[2] [Observe that in both the instances substantives are under the government of *prepositions*.]

demonstrative stands before the article or after the substantive: [§ 11.] Οὗτος ὁ ἀνήρ. Ἥδε ἡ πόλις. Κατὰ τοὺς νόμους ἐκείνους. Ἐκτῶντο τὴν τιμὴν ταύτην (*Isocr. Phil.* 107). If, however, besides the pronoun, an adjective or the like is also added, the pronoun may either attach itself to this (the more usual case), or retain its own peculiar position: Ἡ στενὴ αὕτη ὁδός (*Xen. Anab.* 4, 2, 6). Αἱ πρὸς τοὺς τυράννους αὗται λίαν ὁμιλίαι (*Dem.* 6, 21).—Οἱ ἀλαζόνες λόγοι ἐκεῖνοι (*Pl. Rep.* 8, 560). Ἐκείνη ἡ ὑψηλοτάτη πλάτανος (*Pl. Phæd.* 229). (Αὐτός, *self*, has no influence on the use of the article[1].)

REM. 1. The article is omitted, when the substantive is properly a predicative noun, or an apposition (connected with the predicate) to the pronoun, which last, instead of standing independently, conforms in gender, according to the Greek practice, to the substantive (is *attracted* by it): Αὕτη ἐστὶν ἀνδρὸς ἀρετή (*Pl. Men.* 71, *this is the virtue of a man*). Κίνησις αὕτη μεγίστη τοῖς Ἕλλησιν ἐγένετο (*Thuc.* 1, 1). Ταύτην τέχνην ἔχει (*Lys.* 6, 7). Ταύτῃ ἀπολογίᾳ χρῆται (*Dem.* 49, 63, *he uses this as an excuse*). Ὡς οἱ περὶ Κλεόμβροτον ἐκράτουν τῇ μάχῃ, σαφεῖ τούτῳ τεκμηρίῳ γνοίη ἄν τις (*Xen. Hell.* 6, 4, 13; *from this as from a certain indication*, or *proof*); and in the same way, where the pronoun refers to something following, by which the notion is defined for the first time: Οὗτοι, οὓς ὁρᾶτε, βάρβαροι, πολέμιοι ἡμῖν ἔσονται (*Xen. Anab.* 1, 5, 16). Μενεκλῆς ἐδεῖτο ὑμῶν δοῦναι χάριν ταύτην αὐτῷ, ἐκδοῦναι ἄλλῳ τὴν ἀδελφήν (*Isæ.* 1, 14; *to have the kindness to* —). (In the poets, the article is omitted with demonstratives in other cases; especially in the case of ὅδε, a thing of rare occurrence in prose, with a definite *pointing out* of the object, '*here*': Φέρε λαβὼν χιτῶνας τουτουσὶ τοῖς τῶν δορυφόρων ἡγεμόσι, κασᾶς δὲ τούσδε τοὺς ἐφιππείους τοῖς τῶν ἱππέων ἡγεμόσι, καὶ τῶν ἁρμάτων τοῖς ἡγεμόσι ἄλλους τούσδε χιτῶνας, *Xen. Cyr.* 8, 3, 6.)

REM. 2. In the same way, ἑκάτερος, ἄμφω, ἀμφότεροι are always accompanied by the article: Ἀμφοῖν τοῖν χεροῖν. With ἕκαστος it may be either expressed or omitted: Κατὰ τὴν ἡμέραν ἑκάστην and καθ' ἡμέραν ἑκάστην. Ἐν ἑκάστῃ τῇ πόλει and ἐν ἑκάστῃ πόλει.

REM. 3. With the adjectives τοιοῦτος, τοιόσδε, τοσοῦτος (τηλικοῦτος, τηλικόσδε) the article *may* stand (*before* them, as in the case of other adjectives), when the notion of a definite class of such a kind is to be rendered prominent: Τί οὐκ ἂν πράξειεν ὁ τοιοῦτος ἀνήρ; (*Dem.* 34, 29, *such a man = the man who acts in this way.*) (Τὸ τοιόνδε λέγω, *Pl. Gorg.* 476, *I mean the following relation.*)

REM. 4. Πᾶς, *every*, stands without the article (Πᾶσα πόλις. Πᾶς ἀνήρ); but πάντες, *all*, usually with the article (of a definite class): Πάντα τὰ ἀγαθά. (Πᾶν τὸ καλῶς ἔχον, *Pl. Rep.* 2, 381, *all that is good.*) Ἡ Σπάρτη πασῶν τῶν πόλεων ἀρετῇ διαφέρει (*Xen. Pol. Lac.* 10, 4). Πᾶσαι αἱ καλαὶ πράξεις (not after the article), but also without it: Πάντα ἀγαθά, *all good things*. Πασῶν πόλεων Ἀθῆναι μάλιστα πεφύκασιν ἐν εἰρήνῃ αὔξεσθαι (*Xen. de Vect.* 5, 2). (Πάντες θεοί, πάντες ἄνθρωποι.) Πᾶς, *whole*, stands with the article, usually *on the outside* of the article and its substantive; that is to say, either before the article or after the substantive (as apposition, cf. § 12): Πᾶσα ἡ πόλις, ἡ πόλις πᾶσα (*the whole*

---

[1] Ἡμεῖς οἱ στρατηγοί. Ἐγὼ ἡ τάλαινα.

[§ 11.] *city*, the latter properly, *the city, all of it*), so also ὅλος (ὅλη ἡ πόλις, ἡ πόλις ὅλη). (Without the article ὅλη πόλις, πόλις ὅλη, seldom πόλις πᾶσα, *an entire city, the whole of a city*.) Πᾶς, however, and especially ὅλος, also stands after the article, like other adjectives: Ἡ πᾶσα Σικελία (*Thuc.* 4, 61, *the whole of Sicily, Sicily as a whole*). Ἡ σύμπασα Ἑλλάς (*Isoc. Paneg.* 8, 3). Τὸ πᾶν πλῆθος τῶν ὁπλιτῶν (*Thuc.* 8, 93). Τὸ ὅλον πρόσωπον (*Pl. Prot.* 329). Τὸ ὅλον γένος (*Pl. Crat.* 392). In the same way we also meet with in the plural: Τὰ πάντα μέρη, *all the portions together*, οἱ πάντες ἄνθρωποι (*Xen. Anab.* 5, 6, 7), μόνη τῶν πασῶν πόλεων (*Dem.* 8, 64), and always οἱ πάντες. = *in all*, e.g. δέκα ταῖς πάσαις ναυσίν. (Ξύμπαντες ἑπτακόσιοι ὁπλῖται, *in all; together*, *Thuc.* 4, 129.)

Rem. 5. The article also stands with the interrogative pronominal adjective ποῖος, to denote that the inquiry is made about the property of an object named or otherwise indicated: Τὴν ποίαν κατάστασιν πολιτείας ὀλιγαρχίαν λέγεις; (*Pl. Rep.* 8, 550). Θέλω σοι πάνυ μεγαλόφρονα τῆς γυναικὸς ἔργα διηγήσασθαι. Τὰ ποῖα; (*Xen. Œc.* 10, 1.)

Rem. 6. Where parts of a whole are stated in numbers, the article is sometimes prefixed to the numeral (to denote the definiteness of the relation): Αἱ ἑκκαίδεκα τῶν νεῶν (*Thuc.* 1, 116). Τὰ δύο μέρη. In like manner it is said: Ἀμφὶ τοὺς εἴκοσι, *about twenty*. (But on the other hand: ὑπὲρ ἥμισυ[1] τοῦ στρατεύματος, *Xen. Anab.* 5, 10, 10, *above half*, or *the half*.)

§ 12. The article stands in Greek with substantives to which an adjective is added as an *apposition* (*outside* of the article) and belonging to the *predicate*, to intimate that the notion of the *substantive* follows of itself, and is *assumed* (as something *given* and existing), so that the only question is about the *property*. (In English we usually put the substantive with the adjective indefinitely: but if we wish to express the definiteness of the substantive, we give the words a different turn, or have recourse to a periphrasis.) Οἱ ἄνθρωποι ὑπὸ τοῦ ἡλίου καταλαμπόμενοι τὰ χρώματα μελάντερα ἔχουσιν (*Xen. Mem.* 4, 7, 7, *acquire a darker hue*, or, *come to have their hue darker*, or, *their hue becomes darker*). Πόσον ἄγει τὸ στράτευμα; (*Xen. Cyr.* 2, 1, 2, *how great is the army which he leads?*) Τὸ σῶμα θνητὸν ἅπαντες ἔχομεν (*Isocr. Phil.* 134). Ἀπ' ὀρθῆς καὶ δικαίας τῆς ψυχῆς τὰ πάντα μοι πέπρακται (*Dem.* 18, 298, *with an upright and honest mind; in the uprightness and integrity of my mind*). (Αὐτὸς ἀγαθὸς σὺν ἀγαθοῖς τοῖς παρ' ἐμοί, *Xen. Cyr.* 8, 6, 12, *with those about me good, with good people about me.*) Οἱ παρ' ἐμοί, substantively, cf. § 14, b[2]. (Ὁ λιμὴν τὸ στόμα εἶχε ὀκτὼ σταδίων, *Thuc.* 7, 59, with the descriptive genitive.)

Rem. The same position (outside the article) is also taken by the adjective and participle in other cases, when they are in apposition (i.e. used, not *attributively*, but *appositively*): Οἱ Κερκυραῖοι ἐνέπρησαν τὰς σκηνὰς ἐρήμους (*Thuc.* 1, 49, *left with none to defend them*). Ὁ ποταμὸς διὰ μέσης τῆς πόλεως ῥεῖ (*Xen. Cyr.* 7, 5, 8). Ἄκραις ταῖς χερσίν. Ἅμα τῷ ἦρι ἀρχομένῳ. On the adjective, see § 86, and on the participle, § 181, R. 7.

§ 13. *a*) Proper names do not require the article (which is accordingly omitted even where a demonstrative is annexed: οὑτοσὶ Ἀπατούριος, *this A. here*); but they *may* take it, if the person or

---

[[1] Cf. note 1, p. 9.—T. K. A.]

[2] Τίνας λέγεις, τὰς τέσσαρας πολιτείας; (*Pl. Rep.* 8, 544, *what are the four polities you are speaking of?*)

object is made prominent, as having been previously named, and as being essential to the matter in hand, or as being so generally known and presupposed, that the scope of the discourse naturally leads one to expect the mention; sometimes without any particular emphasis: Ταῦτα λαβὼν ὁ Παυσανίας τὰ γράμματα πολλῷ μᾶλλον ἦρτο (*Thuc.* 1, 130, in the continuation of an account of Pausanias.)—Καὶ ἐκ τοῦ Βυζαντίου βίᾳ ἐκπολιορκηθεὶς (Παυσανίας) ἐς μὲν τὴν Σπάρτην οὐκ ἀνεχώρει. ἐς δὲ Κολωνὰς τὰς Τρωϊάδας ἱδρύθη (*Thuc.* 1, 131; *Byzantium*, mentioned before as the place where Pausanias was residing; *Sparta*, his well-known home. But shortly afterwards: ἀνεχώρει ἐς Σπάρτην). Ἐν δὲ τῇ Πύλῳ—ἐν δὲ ταῖς Ἀθήναις (*Thuc.* 4, 26, 27, the narrative now passing on to these before-mentioned cities). Ἡ Θεμιστοκλέους ἀρετή, ἡ ἀρετὴ ἡ Θεμιστοκλέους (by § 10), but not ἡ ἀρετὴ Θεμιστοκλέους (though it may be ἡ ἀρετὴ τοῦ Θεμιστοκλέους with the article, and ἡ ἀρετὴ ἡ τοῦ Θεμ.). Εὕρημα Θεμιστοκλέους, *an invention of Themistocles.* [§ 13.]

Rem. Ὁ μέγας Ἀλέξανδρος, Θῆβαι αἱ ἐν Βοιωτίᾳ, Ἀλέξανδρος ὁ Μακεδών, for distinction from others of the same name. Ὁ Σιλανὸς ὁ Ἀμβρακιώτης (*Xen. Anab.* 6, 4, 13). (the before-mentioned) *S. the Ambraciote* (who is recalled to one's thoughts here; otherwise Σιλ. ὁ Ἀμβρ.). When, to describe a person more exactly, the name of the father is added in the genitive, the governing word may take an article after it before the genitive, which makes the addition more prominent: Κλέων ὁ Κλεαινέτου, Περίβοια ἡ Ἀλκάθου, but also without the article: Κλέων Κλεαινέτου (in the business-style). (With appended designation of birth-place and district: Κάλλιππος ὁ Φίλωνος ὁ Αἰξωνεύς, or Καλλικλῆς Ἐπιτρέφους Θριάσιος, *Dem.* 50, 47 [1].)

b) For names of nations, the same rule holds good, when they are used of the whole nation. (But always *οἱ* Ἕλληνες, in contradistinction to *οἱ βάρβαροι* [2].) Ὁ Ἀθηναίων δῆμος, ὁ δῆμος ὁ Ἀθηναίων (in public transactions this is the most usual) and ὁ δ. τῶν Ἀθηναίων. (Rarely Ὁ δῆμος ὁ τῶν Ἀθηναίων.) When some of a nation are spoken of, it is οἱ Ἀθηναῖοι, οἱ Ἕλληνες, and Ἀθηναῖοι, Ἕλληνες, according to the general rules for the article. Ἕλληνές ἐσμεν. So Ἀθηναῖος and ὁ Ἀθηναῖος.

§ 14. *a*) In the same manner as with substantives, the article stands with adjectives or participles when they are used substantively of persons or things (definite individuals or classes): Ὁ καλός, τὸ ἀγαθόν. Οἱ καλοί, τὰ ἀγαθά. Τὰ ἐν ἀνθρώποις ἀγαθά. (Οἱ πολλοί, *the many; the multitude, the popular party*: οἱ ὀλίγοι, *the oligarchical party*). Οἱ πολεμοῦντες. Ὁ βουλόμενος, *whoever will.* Οἱ πρῶτοι ἐρχόμενοι. Ὁ ἄκων ἁμαρτάνων. Πᾶν τὸ καλῶς ἔχον (*Pl. Rep.* 381). Οἱ κινδυνεύειν

---

[1] Ὁ Μαίανδρος ποταμός (with different genders: ἐπὶ τῇ Αἴτνῃ τῷ ὄρει, or ἐπὶ τῷ ὄρει τῇ Αἴτνῃ), more rarely μέχρι Μαιάνδρου ποταμοῦ.

[2] Μόνος Ἑλλήνων καὶ βαρβάρων, *of Greeks and barbarians*, § 8, R. 2, f.

[§ 14.] *ἐθέλοντες* or *οἱ ἐθέλοντες κινδυνεύειν*. Ὁ *τὸ τεῖχος ἑλών*. Ὁ *ἑλὼν τὸ τεῖχος*.

REM. 1. Where such a participle has a predicate nominative, this is usually placed between the article and the participle (*ὁ φαῦλος νομιζόμενος*), more rarely after the participle (*ὁ νομιζόμενος φαῦλος*). A case governed by the participle is rarely (by reason of special emphasis) placed before the article: Καὶ *τὴν σοφίαν ὡσαύτως τοὺς ἀργυρίου πωλοῦντας σοφιστὰς ἀποκαλοῦσιν* (*Xen. Mem.* 1, 6, 12).

REM. 2. The Greeks sometimes put a participle substantively with the article, where we say indefinitely *people who* or *people to—*, see § 186, b. R. 1.

REM. 3. Some such substantative expressions formed of the article with a neuter adjective, and denoting a relation of time, or an extent or amount, are used (in the accusative) as adverbs, e. g. *τὸ ἀρχαῖον, τὸ παλαιόν*, *of old*, *τὸ πρῶτον* (*τὸ δεύτερον, πέμπτον*, etc.), *for the first time*. *τὸ τελευταῖον*, *lastly*, *at last*, *τὸ ὅλον*, *τὸ ξύμπαν*, *on the whole*, *τὸ μέγιστον*, *for the greatest part*, *τὰ πολλά*, *mostly*, *τὸ πλέον*, *τὰ πλείω*, *for the more part* (in Thucyd. sometimes *τὸ πλέον* for the mere adverb *πλέον*), *τὸ λοιπόν*, *τὰ λοιπά*, *for the future*, *τἆλλα*, *for the rest*, *τὰ τελευταῖα* (*Thuc.* 1, 24), *lastly*.

b) In the same way, the article without a substantive is prefixed to a preposition and its case, or to an adverb of time or place (§ 9 b), to denote persons or things (definite individuals or classes), which are in the situation or relation assigned by the preposition or adverb: *Οἱ ἐν τῇ πόλει*, *the people in the city*, *οἱ παρὰ Νικίου* (*the persons sent from N.*), *οἱ ἐφ' ἡμῶν, ἐμοῦ* (*our, my, contemporaries, people in our times*), *οἱ ἐπὶ τῶν πραγμάτων* (*Dem.*, *those over the affairs*, i. e. *those who are at the head of them*). Ὁ *ἐν τῷ πλοίῳ* (*the men in the ship*, of a person lately mentioned). *Οἱ νῦν, οἱ ἐνθάδε, οἱ ἐκεῖ*. *Οἱ ἐγγυτάτω* (*γένους*), *the next of kin*. *Τὰ εἰς τὸν πόλεμον*, *what belongs to war*, *the preparations for war*. *Τὰ ἐφ' ἡμῖν*, *what is in our power*. *Τὰ κατὰ Σικελίαν*, *the Sicilian affairs*. *Τὰ ἐνθάδε*, *the affairs here*[1].

REM. 1. In the singular of the neuter gender, some such expressions, governed by a preposition, serve to mark time and place. *Ἐν τῷ τότε*, *at that time*, *ἐν τῷ πρὸ τοῦ*, *in the time preceding*, *ἐκ τοῦ ἐπὶ θάτερα*, *ἐκ τοῦ ἐπ' ἀριστερά*, *from the opposite side*, *from the left side*, *τὰ ἐν τῷ ἐπέκεινα τῆς ἄκρας γιγνόμενα* (*Thuc.* 8, 104), *what was doing on the other side of the promontory*.

REM. 2. Some such expressions, formed with the neuter article and a preposition, are used (in the accusative) as adverbs to denote a certain compass or extent, thus: *τὸ ἀπὸ τοῦδε*, *from this time forth*, *τὸ ἐπ' ἐμοί*, *as far as it depends on me*, *for my part*, *τὸ καθ' ἑαυτόν*, *for his own part*, *as regards oneself*, *τὸ πρὸ τούτου*, *in former times*. The article stands in this way even before adverbs of time, to denote a certain extent of time: *τὸ πρίν*, *of yore*, *τὸ τήμερον*, *τὸ νῦν*, *τὰ νῦν*

[1] Rarely *τὸ σφόδρα*, *τὸ φανερῶς*, and the like, with an infinitive understood: *the putting it strongly*, *the vehement form*, *the speaking openly*.

(τονῦν, τανῦν), *now* (τὰ νῦν τάδε), τό τε παραυτίκα καὶ τὸ ἔπειτα (*Thuc.*), *both* [§ 14.]
for the instant and for the future. (Τὰ μάλιστα, *in the highest degree.*)

c) The article in the plural masculine is put with the genitive of the name of a person to denote that person's people, train, troops, &c.: Κλέαρχος ἤλαυνεν ἐπὶ τοὺς Μένωνος (*Xen. An.* 1, 5, 13). But especially the article is put in the neuter with the genitive, and conveys a general substantive notion of that which belongs to, or arises from, or concerns a person or thing: Τὰ τῶν πολεμίων. Τὰ τῆς πόλεως, *the concerns* or *affairs of the city.* Ἡ Δίκη πάντα τὰ τῶν ἀνθρώπων ἐφορᾷ (*Dem.* 25, 11). Τὸ τῆς ἐπιτροπῆς ἐλέλυτο (*Dem.* 33, 19, *the affair of the guardianship*). Τὰ τῆς τύχης, *the dispensations, dealings, of fortune.* Τὰ τῶν Ἀθηναίων φρονεῖν, *to think that which is for the interest of the Athenians*, i. e. *to take part with the Athenians.* Τὸ τοῦ Θεμιστοκλέους (*Pl. Rep.* 1, 329, *the expression of Th., what Th. said*). Δοκεῖς μοι τὸ τοῦ Ἰβυκείου ἵππου πεπονθέναι (*Pl. Parm.* 136, *what befell the horse of Ibycus*). (Sometimes little more than a mere periphrasis: Ἦν ἄδηλα τὰ τῆς σωτηρίας Χαριδήμῳ, *Dem.* 23, 163. Τὸ τῶν πρεσβυτέρων ἡμῶν. *Pl. Legg.* 2, 657, *we elders, as for us elders.* Τὰ βαρβάρων γὰρ δοῦλα πάντα πλὴν ἑνός, *Eur. Hel.* 276.)

a) The article is put with infinitives to mark that the notion of the § 15.
action is conceived as a substantive (τὸ λέγειν, *the speaking*, τὸ κολάζεσθαι, *the being punished*); see on the Infinitive, § 154 f. Further, it is put with any other not substantive word which is used *materialiter* as substantive; and so, with a set of connected words. Τὸ ὑμεῖς, *the word* ὑ. Τὸ λέγεται. Τὸ γνῶθι σαυτόν. Ὑπερέβη τὸ "καὶ ἐὰν ἁλῷ φόνου" (*Dem.* 23, 220; *he left out the words* —). Ἰσχόμαχος ἐγέλασεν ἐπὶ τῷ "Τί ποιῶν καλὸς κἀγαθὸς κέκλησαι;" (*Xen. Œc.* 7, 3).

b) The article stands before a whole proposition in indefinite form (acc. with inf.), to denote that the matter of the proposition is conceived as a substantive; *the circumstance that—, the fact of—*, &c. See under Inf. § 170.

Rem. 1. Even the substance of a dependent proposition is sometimes put definitely by the article, and thereby brought into connexion with the primary sentence, especially in dependent interrogative propositions: Οὐ περὶ τοῦ ἐπιτυχόντος ὁ λόγος, ἀλλὰ περὶ τοῦ, ὅντινα τρόπον χρὴ ζῆν (*Pl. Rep.* 1, 352, *but about the question, how—*). Τὸ γὰρ ὡς τὰ ἄριστά τε ἔπραττον καὶ διὰ παντὸς εὔνους εἰμί, ἱκανῶς ἐκ τῶν εἰρημένων δεδηλῶσθαί μοι νομίζω (*Dem.* 18, 110).

Rem. 2. A short relative expression may be attached to a substantive by the article, even so as to obtain an adjective sense: Οὐ τὴν ὥσπερ ἐπὶ τοῦ δίφρου ἕδραν ἐπαινοῦμεν (*Xen. Hipp.* 7, 5, of a rider: *a way of sitting upon a horse, as one would upon a chair*). Ἀνδροτίων τῆς ὅπου βούλεσθε ὀλιγαρχίας ἀσελγέστερος γέγονεν (*Dem.* 22, 52, *more insolent than an oligarchy be it where you will;—than any, oligarchy*). Σόλων ἐμίσει τοὺς οἷος οὗτος (ἐστὶν) ἀνθρώπους (*Dem.* 19, 254. Cf. § 106, R. 2).

a) Where the same substantive (or word put substantively) with the article ought to be put twice (or oftener) with different adjuncts, it is sufficient merely to repeat the article: Ὁ τῶν ἰδιωτευόντων βίος αἱρετώτερος ἢ ὁ τῶν τυραννευόντων (*Isocr. ad Nic.* 4). Ἔχομεν Μοῦσαν τῆς τῶν χορῶν καλλίω καὶ τῆς ἐν τοῖς κοινοῖς θεάτροις (*Pl. Legg.* 2, 667). Ὑπὸ τῶν πεττεύειν δεινῶν οἱ μὴ (viz. πεττεύειν δεινοί) τελευτῶντες ἀποκλείονται (*Pl. Rep.* 6, 487). Καὶ παρὰ τῶν ὑμετέρων στρατιωτῶν καὶ παρὰ τῶν ἐνθάδε. Πολὺ κρείττων ἐστὶν ὁ τῆς ψυχῆς ἢ ὁ τοῦ σώματος ἔρως (*Xen. Symp.* 8, 12) [1]. In like manner: Ἀνὴρ δόκιμος ὁμοῖα τῷ μάλιστα, viz. δοκίμῳ, *Hdt.* 7, 118. Σέβομαί τι ὁμοῖα τῷ μάλιστα, viz. σεβομένῳ, *Hdt.* 3, 8.

b) When two notions coupled by '*and*' so closely cohere that they together make one notion, or may be comprised under one head, the article is sometimes put only once: Οἱ στρατηγοὶ καὶ λοχαγοί (*Xen. An.* 3, 1, 29, (*the chief officers*, to wit) *generals and captains*: in other passages οἱ στρ. καὶ οἱ λοχ.). Ὁ ἥλιος καὶ σελήνη καὶ ἄστρα (*Pl. Phæd.* 111, *the heavenly bodies*, to wit). Τό τε δίκαιον καὶ τὸ ἄδικον καὶ καλὸν καὶ αἰσχρὸν καὶ ἀγαθὸν καὶ κακόν (*Pl. Euthyph.* 7, *these moral conceptions, one and all*). Ἔν τε τοῖς Ἀργείοις καὶ τοῖς ξυμμάχοις (*Thuc.* 5, 61). (Τῆς τε Ἰταλίας καὶ Σικελίας, *Thuc.* 1, 36, with two proper names, *the west*, viz. *It. and Sic.*)

In certain expressions, the article is put elliptically with an adjective or similar defining adjunct, a particular substantive being understood, from which the article takes its gender. (Usually in the feminine, because the masculine article suggests only the general notion of a *person*; the neuter, that of a *thing*.) Ἡ ἡμετέρα (γῆ), ἐν τῇ τῶν πολεμίων, ἐν τῇ βασιλέως (*Pl. Alcib.* i. 121). Ἡ αὔριον (ἡμέρα). Κατὰ τὴν ἐμήν (γνώμην). Τὴν ἐπὶ Βαβυλῶνος ἰέναι (ὁδόν). Τὴν ἐπὶ θανάτῳ ἄγειν τινά (*to lead one to execution*), and similar expressions denoting the direction of a motion. (Of the Adjectives see the further § 87 b.)

(Appendix to Chap. 2 [2].) *a*) The Greeks are more regular than we in their use of the plural of substantives, in speaking of a number of individuals and of things which each of these individuals possesses (e. g. ψυχαί, σώματα).

Rem. Sometimes however the singular is used, so that the notion is given in a merely general way: Τὸν πηλὸν ἐπὶ τοῦ νώτου ἔφερον (*Thuc.* 4, 4). Τὰς πρῴρας καὶ τῆς νεὼς ἄνω ἐπὶ πολὺ (*a good bit*) κατεβύρσωσαν (*Thuc.* 7, 65); especially

---

[1] Μεγάλη τις δύναμις ἡ τῶν εὖ λεγόντων, with the substantive drawn over to the predicate.

[2] Strictly speaking this does not come under the Syntax.

without the article, distributively: Δώδεκα ψιλοὶ ξὺν ξιφιδίῳ καὶ θώρακι (*Thuc.* 3, 22). [§ 18.]

b) Even substantives denoting abstract and other general conceptions to which the notion of number does not apply, are put in the plural to mark the occurrence of the condition, affection, or the like, in different forms, with different subjects or at different times, or with some special modification, e. g. ψύχη καὶ θάλπη, αὐχμοί, πλοῦτοι, δυναστεῖαι, ἔνδειαι, ταπεινότητες, γέλωτες (γέλωτες ἐξαίσιοι), μέσαι νύκτες, *midnight*, κρέα (conceived as pieces), πυροί, κριθαί (*wheat, barley*, as masses), ἅλες.

c) Conversely, certain words, denoting individual objects which admit of being numbered, sometimes stand in the singular, to denote the genus and a multitude, *e.g.* πλίνθος, *bricks*, or *tiles*. Note especially the figurative use of ἀσπίς, to signify *a host of heavy-armed* (poetically, λόγχη), and of ἵππος (ἡ) for *the cavalry*, with the numerals χιλία and μυρία in the singular: Herodotus has even ἡ κάμηλος, denoting *a troop of camels*.

CHAPTER III.

The Cases. Nominative and Accusative.

In Greek, an apposition is often attached to the subject or object of a proposition, sometimes even to a case governed by a preposition, to denote in what quality, to what end, the person or thing appears in the action: Ἥκεις μοι σωτήρ. Τίνος διδάσκαλοι ἥκετε; (*Pl. Euthyd.* 287). Οὐ χείρους βοηθοί σοι παραστησόμεθα ἢ εἰ παῖδας ἐκέκτησο (*Xen. Cyr.* 5, 3, 19). Τοὺς φίλους μάρτυρας παρέχω. Τὰ περιττὰ χρήματα πράγματα ἔχουσιν (*Xen. Cyr.* 8, 2, 21; *as a burden*, i. e. *in their superfluous wealth they have only an incumbrance*). Ἴσως τάχα τοὺς Θηβαίους ἄλλους Λακεδαιμονίους εὑρήσετε (*Xen. Hell.* 7, 1, 24). Σὺν σοὶ φίλῳ καὶ ταῦτα διαπράξομαι[1]. § 19.

Rem. 1. Such an apposition is rarely found with objects which are not in the accusative, except with χρῶμαι (dative: Χρῶμαι τοῖς φίλοις βοηθοῖς) and τυγχάνω (genitive: Ἐρωτᾶτε τοὺς Τραπεζουντίους, ὁποίων τινῶν ἡμῶν ἔτυχον, *Xen. An.* 5, 5, 15, *what sort of people they found us*). (Θρασυμήδης οὐδὲν ᾔδει, οἵοις θηρίοις ἐπλησίαζε τοῖς ἀνθρώποις τούτοις, *Dem.* 35, 8, *with what monsters he associated, in having to do with these men.*)

Rem. 2. In a numerical statement of breadth, length, height, weight, or value, the general term is often put as an apposition (100 feet as *length*, i. e. in length): and so, in speaking of a sum of money, the more special description of the way in which it is applied (30 *talents as reward* = *for reward*, as we also say, 30 *t.*

---

[1] On the other hand a relation of time is never denoted (as it is in Latin) by the apposition of a substantive or adjective (without the participle ὤν). *When*, or, *as consul*, is ὑπατεύων, *as a child*, παῖς ὤν. See § 174 b. R.

[§ 19.] *reward*). Τὸ ἄγαλμα τεσσαράκοντα τάλαντα σταθμὸν εἶχε χρυσίου ἀπέφθου (*Thuc.* 2, 13). Ἀρχέβιος καὶ Λυσιθείδης ἔχουσι χρήματα Ναυκρατικά, τίμημα τάλαντα ἐννέα καὶ τριάκοντα μνᾶς (*Dem.* 24, 11). Ἐπὶ μισθῷ τριάκοντα ταλάντοις (*Hdt.* 8, 4). Ἐμοὶ ὁ πατὴρ κατέλιπε τριάκοντα μνᾶς ἀπὸ τοῦ ἐργαστηρίου τὴν πρόσοδον (*Dem.* 27, 18, *as the produce, the profits, of the workshop*).

Rem. 3. An entire proposition may have a description of its purport, or of its predicate, annexed to it in the form of an apposition. In an active proposition, this apposition attaches itself to the object; in a passive one, to the subject; but in prose it consists only of an adjective or a similar expression in the neuter: Τὸ δὲ πάντων μέγιστον καὶ κάλλιστον, τὴν μὲν σὴν χώραν αὐξανομένην ὁρᾷς, τὴν δὲ τῶν πολεμίων μειουμένην (*Xen. Cyr.* 5, 5, 24). Παρμενίδης μοι φαίνεται, τὸ τοῦ Ὁμήρου, αἰδοῖός τε ἅμα δεινός τε (*Pl. Theæt.* 183, *P. seems to me, Homer's expression, both—*, i. e. *as Homer has it*). Πανωλεθρίᾳ δή, τὸ λεγόμενον, καὶ πεζὸς καὶ νῆες καὶ οὐδὲν ὅ,τι οὐκ ἀπώλετο (*Thuc.* 7, 87, *as the saying is*). In like manner the nature of the predicate is premised in the form of an apposition by such expressions as δυοῖν θάτερον, *one or other of these two*: (Τοιαῦτα ἐροῦμεν, ἐξ ὧν, δυοῖν θάτερον, ἢ μεταστήσομεν τὰς γνώμας αὐτῶν ἢ τὰς κατηγορίας ἐλέγξομεν ψευδεῖς οὔσας, *Isocr. Antid.* 197), ἀμφότερα (τοὺς ἀμφότερα ταῦτα, καὶ εὔνους τῇ πόλει καὶ πλουσίους, *Dem.* 18, 171). οὐδέτερον, ταὐτὸν τοῦτο, πᾶν τοὐναντίον, &c. (Hence ταὐτὸν τοῦτο, *in the same way, likewise*, τοὐναντίον, *on the contrary*, as adverbs.)

Rem. 4. With the verb λέγω, *I mean*, either the foregoing case is repeated, or the more exact specification is attached, as object, to λέγω: Πάντες οἱ στρατηγοὶ παρ' ὧν ἂν ἕκαστοι δύνωνται, τούτων τῶν τὴν Ἀσίαν οἰκούντων λέγω, χρήματα λαμβάνουσιν (*Dem.* 8, 24). Προσέκρουσα ἀνθρώπῳ πονηρῷ, ᾧ τελευτῶσα ὅλη προσέκρουσεν ἡ πόλις, Ἀνδροτίωνα λέγω (*Dem.* 24, 6).

§ 20. (221) In the *nominative* stands (1) the subject; the predicate; and (3) an apposition to the subject: Κῦρος πάντων κράτιστος ἐνομίζετο. Κῦρος στρατηγὸς ἀπεδείχθη. Γωβρύας ψευδὴς φαίνεται (*Xen. Cyr.* 5, 2, 4). Ὁ ἀδελφός μοι ζημία μᾶλλον ἢ ὠφέλειά ἐστιν (*Xen. Mem.* 2, 3, 6). Ὄνομα τῷ μειρακίῳ Ἀγάθων ἐστίν [1].

Rem. 1. [*Verbs of imperfect predication.*] The verbs which in themselves do not form a complete predicate, and therefore require a predicate noun, are in Greek (besides εἰμί) ὑπάρχω, γίγνομαι, and certain passives (see § 24), πέφυκα, *I am by nature*. (Λαγχάνω, *become by lot*: Δημοσθένης οὔτ' ἔλαχε τειχοποιὸς οὔτ' ἐχειροτονήθη, *Æsch.* 3, 28. Δοκῶ with εἶναι omitted.)

Rem. 2. When a *participle* has a *predicative-noun* or an *apposition*, the predicate or apposition follows the case of the subject and of the participle: Ὁ φαῦλος νομιζόμενος, τῶν φαύλων νομιζομένων (*of those who are accounted vile*). Τοῖς ἄκουσιν ἁμαρτάνουσι μέτεστι συγγνώμης (*Dem.* 24, 49). Ἀντισθένην Ἀθηναῖοι εἵλοντο στρατηγόν, τὸν οὐδὲ ὁπλίτην πώποτε στρατευσάμενον (*Xen. Mem.* 3, 4, 1, *who had never even served as a hoplite*). Τῶν Λακεδαιμονίων προτέρων ἐλθόντων, οἱ Ἀθηναῖοι ἀπετράποντο.

Rem. 3. In comparisons with ὡς, ὥσπερ, and καθάπερ, there is often a nominative to which we must supply a verb in the indicative, which stands in the principal

---

[1] In Latin, "Damno magis quam utilitati;" and most frequently, "Nomen adolescenti Agathoni est."

member of the sentence either as participle in a different case, or as infinitive [§ 20.] (accusative with infinitive): Ἄξιον κολάζειν τοὺς παραβαίνειν τολμῶντας τὰς συνθήκας, ἄλλως τε καὶ τοὺς ὥσπερ Καλλίμαχος βεβιωκότας (*Isocr. Call.* 47). Πέπεισμαί σε μᾶλλον ἀποθανεῖν ἂν ἑλέσθαι ἢ ζῆν ὥσπερ ἐγώ (*Xen. Mem.* 1, 6, 4). Ἐν ἀνδράσιν οὕτως ἀνοήτοις ὥσπερ οἱ παῖδες (*Pl. Gorg.* 464, where εἰσίν is understood from the adjective). But the noun after the ὥσπερ may also pass, by attraction, into the case of the preceding noun, although the verb by which that case is governed, has nothing to do with the comparative clause: Ἀστυάγης τῷ Κύρῳ ἥδετο οὐ δυναμένῳ σιγᾶν ὑπὸ τῆς ἡδονῆς, ἀλλ' ὥσπερ σκύλακι γενναίῳ ἀνακλάζοντι (*Xen. Cyr.* 1, 4, 15). (Cf. § 98 on the Comparative.)

REM. 4. In the vague infinitive sentence, subject and predicate stand in the accusative: Ἤκουσα ὄνομα αὐτῷ εἶναι Ἀγάθωνα (*Pl. Prot.* 315). See under *Infinitive.*

The *accusative* is the case of the object of transitive verbs (whether § 21.
in the active, middle, or passive-deponent form): *Οἱ Ἕλληνες τοὺς* (222)
Πέρσας ἐνίκησαν. (In the passive: *Οἱ Πέρσαι ἐνικήθησαν ὑπὸ τῶν Ἑλλήνων.*) *Τὴν ἀσπίδα προβάλλομαι. Νικίας τοὺς ἄλλους στρατηγοὺς μετεπέμψατο* (*sent for*; in the passive: *Παρῆσαν μεταπεμφθέντες ὑπὸ Νικίου*). *Οἱ Ἀθηναῖοι τοὺς τῶν Συρακουσίων ἱππέας ἐφοβήθησαν.* (On the forms of the verb see chap. 7.)

REM. 1. The active subject is usually expressed in the passive by ὑπό. Of the use of the dative and of the prepositions πρός, ἐξ, ἀπό, under certain circumstances, see under *Dative* (§ 38, g) and the *Prepositions.*

REM. 2. In the transitive verbs which take the *accusative*, the relation of the action to the object is so conceived, that the object is the passive recipient or the result of the action. Distinct from these are the verbs in which the action or state is conceived, as having merely a reference to an object which is expressed by the *dative*; and also those in which the relation is conceived as a connexion with or a proceeding from an object which is denoted by the *genitive*. These latter come nearest to the properly transitive verbs.

a) In many verbs the view of the relation of the action to the § 22.
object is somewhat different in the Greek from that which underlies (223)
the corresponding English and Latin words by which they are commonly rendered, whence they are construed in a different way, viz., transitively. This must be learnt in detail by practice, and from the Lexicon. For example, these verbs in Greek are transitive: εὐλαβοῦμαί (τι), εὐεργετῶ (τινα), κακουργῶ, ἐπιτροπεύω, δορυφορῶ (τινα), λανθάνω (*escape the observation of some one*), τιμωροῦμαί (τινα, *avenge myself on some one*, and *punish him*), αἰσχύνομαι (*feel myself ashamed*, or *awed, before some one*, e. g. τοὺς στρατιώτας [1]).

[1] The learner must especially be on his guard against supposing that the particular mode of conception which appears in certain Latin verbs, and the (dative) construc-

[§ 22.] *b*) Sundry usually intransitive verbs sometimes obtain a transitive signification in certain connexions, e. g. *θαῤῥῶ* (*μάχας, θάνατον*), *δυσχεραίνω* (*τὴν ἀδικίαν*), *ὄμνυμι* (*τοὺς θεούς*), *πλέω* (*τὴν θάλασσαν*), *ἀποδιδράσκω* (*τὸν δεσπότην*), *εἶμι, πορεύομαι* (*ὁδόν*), *εἰσέρχομαι* (*γραφήν*, as *we say, enter a complaint before the judges*), *εἴσειμι* (*τυράννους, act* [*the part of*] *sovereigns on the stage*), *πρεσβεύω* (*εἰρήνην, negotiate a peace as ambassador*[1]).

REM. 1. The passive, however, of such verbs, is, for the most part, never used.

REM. 2. The poets often go much greater lengths in ascribing transitive signification to intransitive verbs: such poetical expressions are, e. g. *χορεύω θεόν* (*celebrate with dancing*), *ἀΐσσω χεῖρα, παραβαίνω τὸν ἕτερον πόδα, ἧμαι* (*κεῖμαι, θάσσω, πηδῶ*) *τόπον τινά, διφρηλατῶ τὸν οὐρανόν. Τοὺς εὐσεβεῖς θεοὶ θνήσκοντας οὐ χαίρουσιν* (*Eur. Hipp.* 1339). (In the passive: *Πᾶν μέλαθρον αὐλεῖται, Eur. Iph.* 367, *is filled with the music of the flute.*)

§ 23. *a*) In particular it must be remarked, that many intransitive verbs,
(224) which denote a motion, on composition with a preposition (especially *διά, μετά, παρά, περί, ὑπέρ, ὑπό*) assume a transitive signification, partly proper, partly metaphorical, e. g. *διαβαίνω* (*ποταμόν*), *διέρχομαι, δίειμι, διέξειμι, διεξέρχομαι, go through* (*in discourse and writing*), *διαπλέω, μετέρχομαι, prosecute in revenge and punishment, παραβαίνω, transgress, πάρειμι, παρέρχομαι, pass by, περίειμι* (*τὴν Ἑλλάδα*), *περιΐσταμαι* (*λόφον, ἄνθρωπόν τινα*), *ὑπερβαίνω, overstep, exceed, transgress, ὑπέρχομαί* (*τινα, flatter; we* say, *come over*), *ὑφίσταμαι* (*κινδύνους*), *ὑποδύομαι* (*πόνον, submit to a labour*).

REM. 1. In some verbs, not metaphorically used, the preposition is occasionally repeated, e. g. *διαπορεύομαι διὰ τῆς χώρας.*

REM. 2. In verbs compounded with other prepositions, the transitive signification is more rare, and usually is found only in the metaphorical sense, e. g. in *εἴσειμι* (*εἰσῄει με ἔλεος, Pl. Phæd.* 58; but also *εἰσέρχεταί μοι δέος, Pl. Rep.* 1, 330), *ἐκβαίνω, exceed* (*τὰ τριάκοντα ἔτη*), *ἐξίσταμαι, ὑπεξίσταμαι* (*κίνδυνον, evade*: = declinare); or poetical, e. g. *εἰσπίπτω συμφοράν.* (Cf. § 36, b. R. 1.)

b) *Κατά* forms from intransitive verbs transitives expressive of destruction, annihilation, as brought about by the action assigned by the simple verb, e. g. *καταναυμαχῶ, καταπολεμῶ, καταπολιτεύομαί τινα—κατοψοφαγῶ, καθιπποτροφῶ τὴν οὐσίαν* (*waste my property by keeping horses*).

---

tion thence resulting, holds also in the Greek. These verbs, for instance, in Greek, are simple transitives:

ἀδικῶ, βλάπτω, πείθω, κολακεύω,
οἰκτείρω, ἐλεῶ, ὠφελῶ, ἐνεδρεύω.

[1] *Τεθνάναι τῷ φόβῳ τοὺς Θηβαίους* (*Dem.* 19, 81), *ἔξαρνον εἶναι* (*γίγνεσθαι*) *τὴν δίαιταν* (*Isocr. Call.* 13, *the award of the umpires*). *Ἀστύοχος τὴν χώραν καταδρομαῖς λείαν ἐποιεῖτο* (*Thuc.* 8, 41).

Some verbs govern, besides the object itself, the accusative of a § 24.
substantive or adjective, which, as apposition or predicate-noun to (227)
the object, serves to complete the notion of the verb. In the passive, these verbs usually take a predicate-noun in the nominative by § 20. Such verbs are:

a) Those which denote: *to make* (to be) something (elect, nominate, appoint); *to have* (take, give) as something; *to show* and *exhibit* somewhat in a certain way, as something. Δαρεῖος Κῦρον σατράπην ἐποίησε καὶ στρατηγὸν ἀπέδειξε πάντων, ὅσοι εἰς Καστώλου πεδίον ἀθροίζονται (*Xen. An.* 1, 1, 2). Θρασύβουλος ὑμᾶς μὲν πενεστέρους ἀπέδειξε, τοὺς δὲ κόλακας τοὺς αὐτοῦ πλουσιωτάτους τῶν πολιτῶν ἐποίησεν (*Lys.* 28, 4). Οἱ στρατιῶται Ἀλκιβιάδην στρατηγὸν εἵλοντο (*Thuc.* 8, 82). Ἀριαῖον ἠθέλομεν βασιλέα καθιστάναι (*Xen. An.* 3, 2, 5). Τῷ Ἀλκιβιάδῃ Περικλῆς ἐπέστησε παιδαγωγὸν τῶν οἰκετῶν τὸν ἀχρειότατον ὑπὸ γήρως (*Pl. Alc. P.* 122). Τὰ περιττὰ χρήματα πράγματα ἔχουσιν (*Xen. Cyr.* 8, 2, 21). Λύσανδρος στεφάνους παρὰ τῶν πόλεων ἐλάμβανε δῶρα (*Xen. Hell.* 3, 3, 8. See § 19). Τὸν ἰδιώτην χρὴ ἑαυτὸν παρέχειν εὐπειθῆ τοῖς ἄρχουσιν (*Xen. Cyr.* 2, 1, 22). Λῆρον ἀποδεικνύασιν Ἐνδυμίωνα (*Pl. Phæd.* 72; *they make Endymion a farce; surpass him so much that he becomes mere child's-play in comparison*). Οὐδεὶς ἕξει ψευδῆ ἀποφῆναι, ἃ εἰρήκαμεν (*Pl.*).

Rem. The Greeks even say [*proleptically*], αὐξάνειν τινὰ μέγαν, αἴρειν τι μέγα, and the like; where the notion expressed in the apposition is already involved in the verb, and διδάσκεσθαί τινα σκυτέα, *to set a person to learn to be a shoemaker*.

b) The verbs which denote *to name, call* (λέγω, καλῶ, ἀποκαλῶ, ὀνομάζω, προσαγορεύω, προσεῖπον); and *to regard* (*hold, account, declare*) *as something* (νομίζω, ἡγοῦμαι, κρίνω). Οἱ Ἕλληνες τοὺς ἄλλους πάντας βαρβάρους ὠνόμαζον. Φίλον σε ἡγοῦμαι (*Pl. Gorg.* 473). Ἀθλιωτάτην ταύτην τῶν πόλεων κρίνω (*Pl. Rep.* 9, 578).

Rem. 1. Instead of the name, title, or denomination itself, a pronoun may stand in the neuter: Τί σε καλῶμεν; Τοῦτο καλοῦμαι. Ἀντὶ φίλων καὶ ξένων, ἃ τότε ὠνομάζοντο, νῦν κόλακες ἀκούουσιν (*Dem.* 18, 46). Also, καλεῖν τινα ὄνομά τι. Ἀνακαλοῦσι ταῦτα τὰ ὀνόματα ἑαυτούς, ἀδελφούς, πατέρας, υἱεῖς (*Pl. Rep.* 5, 471). Καλεῖν, τίθεσθαι, προσειπεῖν τινι ὄνομά τι, *to give a person a name*; τίθεσθαί τινι ὄνομα Σωσίαν (*Dem.* 43, 74). (Ἐπωνυμίαν ἔχω τύραννος.)

Rem. 2. ἡγοῦμαι, νομίζω, κρίνω, often take an accusative with infinitive (εἶναι), sometimes even ὀνομάζω: Σοφιστὴν ὀνομάζουσι τὸν ἄνδρα εἶναι (*Pl. Prot.* 311).

c) The verbs which denote, *to distribute into* (to make into somewhat by parting, διαιρῶ, διανέμω, κατανέμω): Ὁ Κῦρος τὸ στράτευμα κατένειμε δώδεκα μέρη (*Xen. Cyr.* 7, 5, 13). (In the passive: Ἡ γῆ τὰ αὐτὰ μέρη διανέμεται, *Pl. Legg.* 5, 737.) Also Περσῶν δώδεκα φυλὰς διαιρεῖν (*Xen. Cyr.* 1, 2, 5).

A double accusative, to express a nearer and a more remote object § 25.

[§ 25.] (the former a person, or something conceived as person) is taken by verbs which denote, *to demand* (αἰτῶ, ἀπαιτῶ, πράττομαι, more rarely πράττω, εἰςπράττω), *to deprive, bereave, make to lose* (ἀφαιροῦμαι, ἀποστερῶ, also συλῶ), *clothe* and *strip, invest* and *divest* (ἐνδύω, ἐκδύω, ἀμφιέννυμι [1]), *teach* (διδάσκω, διδάσκομαι, *set to learn, have a person taught to be somewhat*), *admonish, make to remember* (ἀναμιμνήσκω, ὑπομιμνήσκω), *conceal* (κρύπτω, ἀποκρύπτω). In the passive construction, the nearer object becomes the nominative, while the accusative of the more remote object remains: Πολλοί με σῖτον αἰτοῦσι, πολλοὶ δὲ ἱμάτια (*Xen. Cyr.* 8, 3, 41). Σωκράτης οὐδένα τῆς συνουσίας ἀργύριον ἐπράττετο (*Xen. Mem.* 1, 6, 11). Μεσσήνην ὑμᾶς οἱ Θηβαῖοι ἐπιχειροῦσιν ἀποστερεῖν (*Isocr. Arch.* 16). Ὁ μέγας παῖς τὸν μικρὸν παῖδα τὸν ἑαυτοῦ χιτῶνα ἠμφίεσεν (*Xen. Cyr.* 1, 3, 17). Πόθεν Διονυσόδωρος ἤρξατό σε διδάσκειν τὴν στρατηγίαν; (*Xen. Mem.* 3, 1, 5). Ἀναμνήσω ὑμᾶς καὶ τοὺς τῶν προγόνων κινδύνους (*Xen. An.* 3, 2, 11). Διογείτων τὴν θυγατέρα ἔκρυπτε τὸν θάνατον τοῦ ἀνδρός (*Lys.* 32, 7). — Τισσαφέρνης ὑπὸ βασιλέως ἐτύγχανε πεπραγμένος τοὺς ἐκ τῆς ἑαυτοῦ ἀρχῆς φόρους (*Thuc.* 8, 5). Ὅσοι τε τῶν πολεμίων ὅπλα ἀφῄρηνται, ταχὺ ἄλλα ποιήσονται, ὅσοι τε ἵππους ἀπεστέρηνται, ταχὺ πάλιν ἄλλους κτήσονται (*Xen. Cyr.* 6, 1, 12). Ἡρακλῆς τὰς βοῦς ὑπὸ Νηλέως καὶ τῶν παίδων ἐσυλήθη (*Isocr. Arch.* 19). Ἀδύνατοί εἰσί τινες ταύτην τὴν ἐπιμέλειαν διδαχθῆναι (*Xen. Œc.* 12, 12).

Rem. 1. Some of these verbs also admit a different construction, especially ἀποστερεῖν, viz., τινά τινος, *to deprive a person of a thing*: ἀποστερεῖν τινα τῶν πατρῴων (*Dem.* 29, 3), ἀποστερεῖσθαι μεγάλων (*Pl. Rep.* 1, 329). (Ἀφαιρεῖσθαί τί τινος, *to take something from some one*; and so παραιρεῖσθαι: Τὰ ὅπλα τοῦ πλήθους παρῃροῦντο, *Xen. Hell.* 2, 3, 41. Ἀφαιρεῖν in the active has τινί τι, *to take something from some one.* Αἰτεῖν τι παρά τινος. Ἀναμιμνήσκειν τινά τινος, e. g. Γοργίου.)

Rem. 2. Now and then, such a substantive accusative of the remoter object is found with some other verbs, which otherwise have instead of it a preposition, e. g. in προκαλοῦμαι and ἐρωτῶ: Λακεδαιμόνιοι ὑμᾶς τὴν εἰρήνην προκαλοῦνται (*Arist. Ach.* 652. Usually it is: προκαλεῖσθαί τινα εἰς εἰρήνην. Ταῦτά σε προκαλοῦμαι, with the pronoun in the neuter by § 27). Κῦρος ἠρώτα τοὺς αὐτομόλους τὰ ἐκ τῶν πολεμίων (*Xen. Cyr.* 3, 3, 48). Ἐρωτᾶσθαι τὸ ὄνομα (*Pl. Legg.* 10, 895. Usually περί τινος). With others (ἀναγκάζω, ἀποκωλύω) we find, as accusative of the *thing*, only a neuter adjective or pronoun (see § 27): Τοῦτο μὴ ἀνάγκαζέ με (*Pl. Rep.* 5, 473). Ἀπέρχομαι πρὶν ὑπὸ σοῦ τι μεῖζον ἀναγκασθῆναι (*Pl. Phæd.* 242).

Rem. 3. The verbs, *to make* (ποιῶ, ἀντιποιῶ, δρῶ, ἐργάζομαι, poetically, ἔρδω), and *say, speak* (λέγω, εἶπον, ἀγορεύω) in the sense, to *speak to*, or address a person in a certain manner (especially in an evil manner), sometimes also *to make*

[1] ἐνδύομαι, ἐνέδυν, ἐκδύομαι, ἐξέδυν, ἀμφιέννυμαι χιτῶνα, *put on, put off.*

mention of, take the accusative of the person with another accusative, mostly a neuter adjective or pronoun, denoting that which is done to or said of or to the person: Ἐκ τούτων τῶν ἀνδρῶν καὶ οἱ τὰ μέγιστα κακὰ ἐργαζόμενοι τὰς πόλεις γίγνονται καὶ οἱ ἀγαθά· σμικρὰ δὲ φύσις οὐδὲν μέγα οὐδέποτε οὐδένα δρᾷ (*Pl. Rep.* 6, 495). Οἱ ὑποκριταὶ ἐν ταῖς τραγῳδίαις ἀλλήλους τὰ ἔσχατα λέγουσιν (*Xen. Mem.* 2. 2. 9). Instead of the second accusative we may also have merely the adverbs εὖ and κακῶς: Κακῶς λέγουσιν οἱ ἀγαθοὶ τοὺς κακούς (*Pl. Euthyd.* 284)[1]. [§ 25.]

a) Verbs in themselves incapable of an object-accusative have nevertheless not unfrequently the accusative of a substantive derived from the same root or of corresponding meaning, usually connected with an adjective or pronoun or similar adjunct serving to define and characterize the action more closely. (In English, we usually employ a verb of general signification, which can take the substantive as its regular object, in place of the special and intransitive verb in the Greek.) Ἥδομαι τὰς μεγίστας ἡδονάς (*Pl. Phil.* 21; *I feel, experience, enjoy*). Χαιρεφῶν ξυνέφυγε τὴν φυγὴν ταύτην (*Pl. Apol.* 21; *took part in; shared*). Οἱ Θρᾶκες, ἐπεὶ εὐτύχησαν τοῦτο τὸ εὐτύχημα, συνελέγοντο τῆς νυκτός (*Xen. An.* 6, 1, 6). Λακεδαιμόνιοι μετὰ ταῦτα τὸν ἱερὸν καλούμενον πόλεμον ἐστράτευσαν (*Thuc.* 1, 112). Ἀπήραμεν τὴν προτέραν πρεσβείαν (*Dem.* 19, 163; *we set out on the first embassy*). Νικᾶν νίκην καλλίστην. Λακεδαιμονίους φασὶν ἐν Πλαταιαῖς πρῶτον μὲν φεύγειν, ἔπειτα δὲ ἀναστρεφομένους ὥσπερ ἱππέας μάχεσθαι καὶ οὕτω νικῆσαι τὴν ἐκεῖ μάχην (*Pl. Lach.* 191). Τὰς μὲν νενικήκατε ναυμαχίας, τὴν δ' ἐκ τοῦ εἰκότος νῦν νικήσετε (*Thuc.* 7, 66)[2]. Πάσας νόσους κάμνω (*Pl. Rep.* 3, 408). Νόσον νοσοῦμεν τὴν ἐναντίαν (*Arist. Ares*, 31). Ἤδη ἠσθένει ταύτην τὴν νόσον (*Isæ.* 1, 14). Πρὸς τὸ αὑτοῖς συμφέρον καὶ τοὺς νόμους τίθενται καὶ τοὺς ἐπαίνους ἐπαινοῦσι καὶ τοὺς ψόγους ψέγουσιν (*Pl. Gorg.* 483; *praise, when they praise, and blame, when they blame*). Hence sometimes a passive is formed: Ὁ βεβιωμένος σοι βίος (*Dem.* 19, 200, *the life you have led* [so *we: the life you have lived*]). Οἱ πόλεμοι οἱ ἐπὶ Θησέως πολεμηθέντες (*Xen. Mem.* 3, 5, 10). § 26. (223, R. 4)

Rem. 1. The poets employ even bolder constructions, e.g. Τίς δῆτ' ἂν εἴη τήνδ' ὁ προσθακῶν ἕδραν; (*Soph. Œd. C.* 1166, *that sits here in this sort?*).

Rem. 2. In the same manner, some phrases are formed of a verb with a substantive, related in signification, but more special, without adjective or pronoun: νικᾶν Ἴσθμια (*to gain an Isthmian victory* = νικᾶν τοὺς στεφανίτας ἀγῶνας), θύειν εὐαγγέλια, θύειν τὰ Λύκαια, ἑστιᾶν γάμους. (Ἑστιᾶν θεσμοφόρια τὰς γυναῖκας, *Isæ.* 3, 10, see *b*.)

---

[1] Ἔξεστιν ὑμῖν ἄνευ δαπάνης τὰ δίκαια ποιῆσαι τοῖς εὐεργέταις (*Dem.* 20, 12).

[2] Νικᾶν, κρατεῖν τῇ μάχῃ, *to conquer in the fight* (ἣ ἐς τοὺς Λακεδαιμονίους δόξα, ἣν διὰ τὸ αἰσχρὸν δὴ βοηθήσειν ὑμῖν πιστεύετε αὐτούς. *Thuc.* 5, 105, *the confidence you have in the Lacedæmonians, that they of very shame*, etc.).

[§ 26.] Rem. 3. This accusative may also stand with verbs which govern a genitive or dative: Δημοσθένης δέησίν τινα ἰσχυρὰν ἐμοῦ ἐδεήθη μὴ παραλιπεῖν τοῦτο (*Æsch.* 2, 43). (Δεινὰ ἔπη κατηγορεῖν τινος, *Soph. Œd. R.* 513.)

b) Such an accusative of the notion contained in the verb, or of one nearly related to it, together with a defining and characterizing adjunct, may also stand with a verb which governs a proper object-accusative: Θρασύβουλος καὶ Θράσυλλος ὥρκωσαν πάντας τοὺς στρατιώτας τοὺς μεγίστους ὅρκους, ἦ μὴν δημοκρατήσεσθαι καὶ ὁμονοήσειν (*Thuc.* 8, 75). Τοὺς πολίτας μεταδιδόναι ἀλλήλοις χρὴ τῆς ὠφελείας, ἣν ἂν ἕκαστοι τὸ κοινὸν δυνατοὶ ὦσιν ὠφελεῖν (*Pl. Rep.* 7, 519). Μιλτιάδης ὁ τὴν ἐν Μαραθῶνι μάχην τοὺς βαρβάρους νικήσας (*Æsch.* 3, 181)[1]. Αἰσχίνης Κτησιφῶντα γραφὴν ἱερῶν χρημάτων ἐδίωκεν (*Dem.* 19, 293). Τιμωρία ὑμῖν ἥξει εὐθὺς μετὰ τὸν ἐμὸν θάνατον πολὺ χαλεπωτέρα ἢ οἵαν ἐμὲ ἀπεκτόνατε (*Pl. Apol.* 39). This accusative may remain, when the proposition is expressed passively, and consequently the proper object becomes subject: Τοιοῦτον τμῆμα τέμνεται τὸ τεμνόμενον, οἷον τὸ τέμνον τέμνει (*Pl. Gorg.* 476; *is cut with such a cut*). Οὐδὲν ὄρνεον ᾄδει, ὅταν πεινῇ ἢ ῥιγοῖ ἤ τινα ἄλλην λύπην λυπῆται (*Pl. Phæd.* 85). Τὰς ἄλλας μάχας, ὅσας Πέρσαι ἡττήθησαν, ἐῶ (*Isocr. Paneg.* 145). Θρασύβουλος ἐδέθη καὶ ἐκρίθη ἀμφοτέρας τὰς κρίσεις ἐν τῷ δήμῳ (*Dem.* 24, 134). Τύπτεσθαι τῇ δημοσίᾳ μάστιγι πεντήκοντα πληγάς (*Æsch.* 1, 139).

§ 27. (229) *a*) Verbs which in themselves cannot govern an object-accusative, may take the neuter accusative of a pronoun or of a numeral adjective, to denote the *contents* and *compass* of the action; and in like manner sometimes another description of adjective which serves to characterize the *measure* and *extent* of the action. (The pronoun or adjective belongs, properly speaking, to the substantive notion involved in the verb.) Ἕν σοι (τοῦτο, πολλὰ) οὐχ ὁμολογῶ. Τί διαφέρει ταῦτα; Κῦρος Λυσάνδρῳ ἄλλα τ' ἐφιλοφρονεῖτο καὶ τὸν ἐν Σάρδεσι παράδεισον ἐπέδειξε (*Xen. Œc.* 24). Σμικρόν τι ἀπορῶ (*Pl. Theæt.* 145). Ταὐτὰ λυποῦμαι καὶ ταὐτὰ χαίρω τοῖς πολλοῖς (*Dem.* 18, 292). Ὁ ὀργισθεὶς οὐκ ἐλάσσω πταίει ἢ ὁ εὐοργήτως τοῖς πράγμασιν ὁμιλήσας (*Thuc.* 1, 122). Δέομαι μέτρια καὶ δίκαια ὑμῶν (*Dem.* 37, 3; *my request does not exceed the bounds of moderation and justice*). Δέομαι ὑμῶν, ὦ ἄνδρες δικασταί, βοηθῆσαι ἡμῖν τὰ δίκαια (*Dem.* 27, 68). Τέχνῃ ἔσθ' ὅ,τι προςδεῖταί τινος ἀρετῆς; (*Pl. Rep.* 1, 342; *is there any respect in which Art requires any additional virtue?*).—Ὅσα διαγωνίζονται πολλάκις ἥλικες πρὸς ἀλλήλους (*Xen. Cyr.* 1, 4, 4; *what they contend*, i. e.

---

[1] Usually νικᾶν τινα μάχῃ μεγάλῃ.

the contests they make). Οὐκ ἀξίως ἐκείνων ὧν (for ἅ by attraction, see ch. 9) ἐναυμαχήσαμεν (*Arist. Aves*, 677; *what we fought*, i. e. *the way we fought in the naval engagement*). Hence sometimes the passive is formed, especially in the participle: Τά σοι πεπρεσβευμένα (*Dem.* 19, 240; *your acts as ambassador* = ἃ σὺ πεπρέσβευκας). Τὰ ἐν ὅπλοις καὶ κατὰ τὴν στρατηγίαν ἀτυχηθέντα (*Dem.* 18, 212; *the mishaps sustained*). [§ 27.]

REM. 1. Especially we must remark the use of a pronoun in the accusative neuter with χρῶμαι (χρῶμαί τινί τι, *make a certain use of an object, use it for* [*a certain purpose*]): Τί βούλεται Κῦρος ἡμῖν χρῆσθαι; (*Xen. An.* 1, 3, 28). Ὑμεῖς νυκτί, ὥσπερ οἱ ἄλλοι ἡμέρᾳ, δύνασθε χρῆσθαι (*Xen. Cyr.* 1, 5, 12). Πολλὰ χρῆσθαί τινι (*Pl. Theæt.* 157). Οὐκ ἔχω, ὅ,τι χρήσομαι τούτῳ τῷ ἀνθρώπῳ (*Pl. Symp.* 216; *what I shall do with him: what to do with him*). (Χρῆσθαί τινι ἐπὶ πρᾶγμά τι, χρῆσθαί τοῖς νεύροις εἰς τὰς σφενδόνας).

REM. 2. Sometimes an adjective thus accompanying the verb acquires almost the force of an adverb; see *Adjectives*, ch. 8. Τί (*somewhat, in a certain degree*) and (σμικρόν τι) and οὐδέν are used as complete adverbs even with adjectives (οἱ ἀρετῆς τι μεταποιούμενοι. *Thuc.* 2, 51, οὐδὲν ὅμοιος, σμικρόν τι ὅμοιος), and with adverbs (σχεδόν τι, πάνυ τι). Ταῦτα acquires sometimes the sense *for this reason, therefore*: Αὐτὰ ταῦτα καὶ νῦν ἥκω παρὰ σέ (*Pl. Prot.* 310, *this is the very reason of my now coming*). Ταῦτ' ἄρα καὶ ἐνεώρας μοι; (*Xen. Cyr.* 1, 4, 27). (In the poets also τάδε, τοιαῦτα = οὕτως.)

b) Such an accusative may also stand with a transitive verb which governs an object-accusative (the adjectives almost always in the plural): Ἐὰν ἐμὲ ἀποκτείνητε, οὐκ ἐμὲ μείζω βλάψετε ἢ ὑμᾶς αὐτούς (*Pl. Apol.* 30; *will bring greater hurts*, = *will harm more*). Ταῦτα καὶ ἄλλα τοιαῦτα ἐγκωμιάζουσι τὴν δικαιοσύνην (*Pl. Rep.* 2, 363). Λακεδαιμόνιοι πολλὰ τὴν πόλιν ἡμῶν ἠδικήκασι καὶ μεγάλα (*Dem.* 18, 98). This accusative may remain with the passive: Πολλὰ καὶ δεινὰ ἠδικήθην (*Isæ.* 8, 4). Οὐ βλάψονται ἄξια λόγου (*Thuc.* 6, 64; *they will suffer no loss worth mentioning*). (Θαυμάζεσθαι τὰ εἰκότα, *Thuc.* 1, 38, *to enjoy becoming honours*. Τοιαῦτ' ἔπη κλύων, ἃ νῦν σὺ τήνδ' ἀτιμάζεις πόλιν, *Soph. Œd. R.* 340, = ταῦτα, ἃ—, *the affront thou puttest upon the city*.)

a) The accusative stands with the prepositions ἀνά, *up along something, along through something* (of space and time), *up to* (ἀνὰ τὸ ὄρος), and εἰς, *to, into something*, together with ὡς, *to*, and with ἀμφί, διά, ἐπί, κατά, μετά, παρά, περί, πρός, ὑπέρ, ὑπό, in certain significations (those which start from the conception of a motion *to something*, a spreading *round* or *over something*. § 28. (230)

REM. 1. Εἰς (agreeably with its signification *into*) is never (in Attic, rarely in Ionic writers) applied to individual persons (πρός, ὡς). To persons in the plural it is applied, when these persons denote an assembly (εἰς τοὺς δικαστάς, εἰς ὑμᾶς, *into the assembly of the people*), a definite place (εἰς τοὺς πολεμίους, εἰς τοὺς ὑστάτους

[§ 28.] ἐμβάλλειν), or an extension (*land and people*) and expansion: (Ἐπορεύθησαν εἰς Ταόχους, *Xen. An.* 4, 7, 1. Πέλοψ ἐκ τῆς Ἀσίας χρήματα ἔχων ἦλθεν εἰς ἀνθρώπους ἀπόρους, *Thuc.* 1, 9. Παρὰ βασιλέα καὶ ἄλλοσε ἐς τοὺς βαρβάρους, *Thuc.* 1, 9. Διαβέβληνται εἰς τοὺς ἄλλους, *Pl. Rep.* 7, 539, *in the minds of.* Τῆς πόλεως ἡ δύναμις εἰς ἅπαντας ἀνθρώπους διαφανὴς ἐγένετο, *Pl. Tim.* 25). In speaking of disposition and behaviour towards any one, εἰς is also applied to individuals (εὔνοια εἴς τινα, ὑβρίζειν εἴς τινα, λέγειν τι εἴς τινα, *of and against him*). Ὡς is used only of *persons*[1].

REM. 2. The poets use with verbs of motion an accusative without εἰς or πρός: Δόμους στείχω ἐμούς (*Soph. Œd. C.* 643). Πάρειμι (= ἥκω) Δίρκης νάματ' Ἰσμηνοῦ θ' ὕδωρ (*Eur. Bacch.* 5). In prose we find instead of εἰς, only some names of cities in the form δε (ζε, cf. the *Accidence*): ἐξελθεῖν Ἐλευσίναδε, Ὀλυμπίαζε.

REM. 3. Transitive verbs compounded with the prepositions διά and ὑπέρ, in their proper local signification, sometimes take besides their object-accusative, the accusative of the name of the place through or over which the motion takes place: Ὑπερήνεγκαν τὸν Λευκαδίων ἰσθμὸν τὰς ναῦς (*Thuc.* 3, 81). (In Herodotus also τεῖχος περιβάλλεσθαι τὴν πόλιν, *Hdt.* 1, 163.)

b) Likewise with the particle μά in asseverations: Ναὶ μὰ τὸν Δία. Οὐ μὰ Δία. (In the poets sometimes οὐ without μά: Οὔ, τὸν πάντων θεῶν θεὸν πρόμον Ἅλιον. *Soph. Œd. C.* 666.)

§ 29. (234) Verbs denoting an extension, motion, or distance, take the name of the measure in the accusative, so γέγονα, *am—old*, the specification of the age. Κῦρος ἐξελαύνει διὰ τῆς Λυδίας σταθμοὺς τρεῖς, παρασάγγας εἴκοσι καὶ δύο (*Xen. An.* 1, 2, 5). Βασιλεύς τε καὶ οἱ Ἕλληνες διέσχον ἀλλήλων ὡς τριάκοντα στάδια (*Xen. An.* 1, 2, 4). (Πολλῶν ἡμερῶν ὁδὸν ἀπέχειν.) Θρασύβουλος ἔθετο τὰ ὅπλα ὅσον τρία στάδια ἀπὸ τῶν φρουρῶν (*Xen. Hell.* 2, 4, 5; *took up a position at a distance of—*). Οὔπω εἴκοσιν ἔτη γεγονώς (*Xen. Mem.* 3, 6, 1).

REM. In adjectives denoting an extent (*long*, &c.) the accusative of the measure is not usual in Greek. It says: μῆκος ἔχων τριῶν ποδῶν (τρεῖς πόδας), τάφρος τριῶν ποδῶν τὸ μῆκος.

§ 30. (235) In statements of duration and extent of time (*how long*), the measure of time is put in the accusative: Ἐνταῦθα Κῦρος ἔμεινεν ἡμέρας πέντε (ταύτην τὴν ἡμέραν) (*Xen. An.* 1, 2, 6). Οἱ τῶν Περσῶν ἔφηβοι δέκα ἔτη, ἀφ' οὗ ἂν ἐκ παίδων ἐξέλθωσι, κοιμῶνται περὶ τὰ ἀρχεῖα (*Xen. Cyr.* 1, 2, 9). Γένεσθέ μοι μικρὸν χρόνον τὴν διάνοιαν (*in imagination*, see § 31) ἐν τῷ θεάτρῳ (*Æsch.* 3, 153). Πολλοῖς καὶ μεγάλοις κακοῖς καὶ πράγμασι τὴν ἀποδημίαν πᾶσαν συνειχόμην (*Dem.* 19, 177. Also παρὰ πᾶσαν τὴν ἀποδ., *during the whole journey*. Διὰ παντὸς τοῦ χρόνου, *Lys.* 7, 8; *throughout the whole time*). Σπουδὴ ὁμοίως καὶ νύκτα καὶ ἡμέραν ἔσται τῆς ὁδοῦ (*Thuc.* 7, 77; *through the night*

[1] Ἀνά in Epic and lyric poetry with the dative, *on*, *upon*, not implying motion.

and the day: night and day alike. Νυκτὸς καὶ ἡμέρας, *by night and by day*, § 66[1]). [§ 30.]

Rem. The accusative of a denomination of time with an ordinal number denotes *how long ago* (properly, *what time it is now, since the thing happened*: Ἡ θυγατὴρ αὐτῷ ἑβδόμην ἡμέραν ἐτετελευτήκει (*Æsch.* 3, 77). Τρίτην ἡμέραν Ἀστυόχου ἥκοντος, αἱ Ἀττικαὶ νῆες ἔπλεον ἐς Λέσβον (*Thuc.* 8, 23, (on) *the third day after A. was come*). Τὴν μητέρα τρέφων πέπαυμαι τρίτον ἔτος τοῦτο (*Lys.* 24, 6. *now* (is it) *the third year* (*that*) —). (More rarely: Ἀλκίας τέθνηκε ταῦτα τρία ἔτη, *Lys.* 7, 10, with the cardinal number.)

a) Where a quality or state is mentioned, expressed either by a § 31. (237 and 253) passive or intransitive verb, or by an attributive adjective, or by a predicate-noun, the accusative is often added, to denote to what part of the subject, or to what side of it, or to what general conception (e. g. size, number, name, &c.) any thing predicated of the subject refers (in, in respect of): Τὰ σώματα πρὸς ὥραν καὶ τὰς ψυχὰς πρὸς ἀρετὴν εὖ πεφυκότες (*Xen. Mem.* 4, 1, 2). Οἱ στρατιῶται εὖ μὲν εἶχον τὰ σώματα πρὸς τὸ δύνασθαι στρατιωτικοὺς πόνους φέρειν, εὖ δὲ τὰς ψυχὰς πρὸς τὸ καταφρονεῖν τῶν πολεμίων (*Xen. Cyr.* 3, 3, 9). Ἀλγεῖν τὸν δάκτυλον, τὰ ὄμματα, κάμνειν τοὺς πόδας. Γένεσθέ μοι μικρὸν χρόνον τὴν διάνοιαν μὴ ἐν τῷ δικαστηρίῳ, ἀλλ' ἐν τῷ θεάτρῳ (*Æsch.* 3, 153). Ἡ πενία τοῦ πλούτου βελτίονας ἄνδρας παρέχει καὶ τὴν γνώμην καὶ τὴν ἰδέαν (*Arist. Pl.* 558). Τὸ νόσημα τοιοῦτον ἦν ἐπὶ πᾶν (*in its general nature*) τὴν ἰδέαν (*Thuc.* 2, 51). Πάντας χρὴ καὶ τοὺς εὐφυεστέρους καὶ τοὺς ἀμβλυτέρους τὴν φύσιν, ἐν οἷς ἂν ἀξιόλογοι βούλωνται γενέσθαι, ταῦτα καὶ μανθάνειν καὶ μελετᾶν (*Xen. Mem.* 3, 9, 3). Δίκαιος τὸν τρόπον (*Dem.* 56, 2). Δισχίλιοι, ἄπειροι τὸ πλῆθος. Ἑξακόσιοι τὸν ἀριθμόν (*Arist. Aves*, 1251). Ξένον ἄγομεν, τὸ μὲν γένος ἐξ Ἐλέας, ἑταῖρον δὲ τῶν ἀμφὶ Παρμενίδην καὶ Ζήνωνα (*Pl. Soph.* 216). Σκύθης τὸ γένος. Διὰ μέσης τῆς πόλεως ῥεῖ ποταμὸς Κύδνος ὄνομα, εὖρος δύο πλέθρων (*Xen. An.* 1, 2, 23). Λύσανδρος προσέβαλε πόλει τῶν Ἀθηναίων ξυμμάχῳ ὄνομα Κεδρείαις (*Xen. Hell.* 2, 1, 15). Εὖ ἔχω τὰ κατὰ τὸ σῶμα, *as far as the body is concerned.*

Rem. 1. Sometimes κατά is used to denote the part of the subject: Καθαρὸς καὶ κατὰ τὸ σῶμα καὶ κατὰ τὴν ψυχήν (*Pl. Crat.* 405). In certain connexions we have the dative (*by*), e. g. φύσει, γένει. See § 40.

Rem. 2. The poets add to the object-accusative of a person the accusative of a part of the body (also φρένας), to which the exercise of the action refers: Μέθες με, πρὸς θεῶν, χεῖρα, φίλτατον τέκνον (*Soph. Phil.* 1301).

---

[1] Οὐκ ἀηδὲς κατὰ τὸ ὑδάτιον ἰέναι ἄλλως τε καὶ τήνδε τὴν ὥραν τοῦ ἔτους τε καὶ τῆς ἡμέρας (*Pl. Phædr.* 229). Herodotus uses τοῦτον τὸν χρόνον quite in place of ἐν τούτῳ τῷ χρόνῳ, κατὰ τοῦτον τὸν χρόνον, and νύκτα (τὰς νύκτας), instead of νυκτός.

[§ 31.] *b*) Adjectives denoting *cleverness*, *skilfulness*, or *knowledge* often take an accusative of the object in which the knowledge or skill is ascribed to a person, but for the most part only a neuter adjective (in the plural) or a pronoun (also τέχνην, ἀρετήν). Ὁ πάντα σοφὸς ποιητής (*Pl. Theæt.* 194). Ἀνὴρ ἀγαθὸς (δεινὸς) τὰ πολιτικά. Ἐάν τις φῇ ἀγαθὸς αὐλητὴς εἶναι ἢ ἄλλην ἥντινοῦν τέχνην, ἣν μή ἐστιν, καταγελῶσιν (*Pl. Prot.* 323). Οἱ στρατιῶται ἐπιστήμονες ἦσαν τὰ προσήκοντα τῇ ἑαυτῶν ἕκαστος ὁπλίσει (*Xen. Cyr.* 3, 3, 9[1]). (Also, Ὅσα μοι χρήσιμοί ἐστε, οἶδα, *Xen. An.* 2, 5, 23.)

REM. Κακὸς πᾶσαν κακίαν (*Pl. Rep.* 6, 490), with a substantive of the same origin; as in verbs, § 26.

c) In certain cases an accusative is used to denote something external to the subject (a certain extent, range, sphere) to which the predicate refers (*as regards*). In this manner are used the substantive μέρος (τὸ ἐμὸν μέρος, τὸ σὸν μ., etc.); some adjectives with the article in the neuter, which then for the most part have quite the signification of adverbs of extent and time; and the neuter article with a preposition or an adverb (in like manner forming adverbial expressions). Οἱ παῖδες, τὸ σὸν μέρος, ὅ τι ἂν τύχωσι, τοῦτο πράξουσι (*Pl. Criton.* 45). Τὸ Αἰτωλικὸν πάθος διὰ τὴν ὕλην μέρος τι ἐγένετο (*Thuc.* 4, 30; *the defeat in Æt.*). Οὐ μόνον τὰ μεγάλα, ἀλλὰ καὶ τὰ μικρὰ πειρῶμαι ἀεὶ ἀπὸ θεῶν ἄρχεσθαι (*Xen. Cyr.* 1, 5, 14). Τὰ μὲν παρελθόντα (*hitherto*) ὑμεῖς μὲν Κῦρον ηὐξήσατε, Κῦρος δ' εὐκλεεῖς ὑμᾶς ἐποίησεν (*Xen. Cyr.* 8, 5, 23). Τὸ λοιπόν, τὸ ξύμπαν, etc. (see *The Article*, § 14 a. Rem. 2). Τὸ κατ' ἐμὲ οὐδὲν ἐλλείψει (*on my part*). Τὸ πρίν, etc. (see *ib.* § 14 b. Rem. 2). Ἡ πόλις εἰρήνην ἄγει τὰ περὶ τὴν χώραν (*Isocr. Areop.* 1). Οἱ στρατηγοὶ σπονδὰς ἐποιήσαντο τὰ περὶ Πύλον (*Thuc.* 4, 15; *on account of P., as regarded matters at P.*).

d) The accusative τρόπον is put adverbially, and so likewise ὁδόν, in certain expressions (as '*manner*,' '*way*,' in English). Τοῦτον τὸν τρόπον πράξας ὅλου τοῦ πράγματος ἀπαλλάξομαι (*Dem.* 30, 22). (Πάντα τρόπον, ἕτερον τρόπον, ὃν τρόπον, etc. Also τίνι τρόπῳ, τούτῳ τῷ τρόπῳ. See *Dative*, § 41.) Κῦρος τὴν Κίλισσαν εἰς Κιλικίαν ἀποπέμπει τὴν ταχίστην ὁδόν (*Xen. An.* 1, 2, 20).

REM. In this manner several adverbial expressions are formed elliptically by omission of ὁδόν, e. g. τὴν ταχίστην, τὴν πρώτην. The accusative of some particular substantives is used adverbially without an adjective or pronoun annexed: ἀρχήν, τὴν ἀρχήν, *at all*, τέλος, τὸ τέλος, πέρας, *at last*, πρόφασιν, *in pretence*, προῖκα, *gratis*; δίκην, *after the manner of*, and χάριν, *for the sake of*, have the force

[1] Φροντιστὴς τὰ μετέωρα (*Pl. Apol.* 18), as adjective.

of a preposition with the genitive, thus: ἀγγείου δίκην πεπληρῶσθαι (*Pl. Phæd.* [§ 31.]
235), Τίνος χάριν; τοῦ λόγου χάριν (*Pl.*), the latter also accompanied by a possessive pronoun: ἐμὴν χάριν, σὴν χάριν. In the same way ὅσον, ὅσα (ὅσον γε, ὅσα γε) are used as adverbs.

c) Of the accusative absolute of a participle (ἐξόν) to denote a circumstance, see under *Participles*, § 182. § 32.

The accusative is put elliptically in the phrase μή μοι —, *come not to me with —, don't talk to me of —*: μή μοι πρόφασιν (*Arist. Ach.* 345; *no shuffling*), and in calling a person: Οὗτος, ὦ σέ τοι (*Arist. Aves* 274; *hark ye, there! you there!*).

Rem. 1. In later writers, we sometimes find the article followed by an accusative in the sense, *he with, he that has*, e.g. Ὁ τὴν πορφυρίδα (*Lucian*). In Herodotus sometimes the name of a part of the object is put with a participle as apposition to the object: Τοὺς βοῦς κατορύσσουσι ἐν τοῖς προαστείοις, τὸ κέρας τὸ ἕτερον ἢ καὶ ἀμφότερα ὑπερέχοντα, 2, 41, *the one horn projecting*, i.e. *so that —*, or, *with —*.

Rem. 2. On the particular use of the accusative with the gerundive, see § 85: on the accusative of a relative changed into the dative or genitive, see *Relative*, § 103: on the subject of a dependent proposition drawn into the primary proposition as accusative, § 191.

CHAPTER IV.

Dative.

The *Dative* in Greek denotes generally the relation of a person or thing *to* and *in* a state or action, in which however it is not the passive object, and indicates, first, that person or thing *for* which something has *interest*, and *to* which it refers; secondly, that which, as an appurtenance or circumstance, belongs to and forms part of the predicate[1]. § 33. (241, 252)

Under the first of these heads the dative marks the person, or the thing conceived of as person, *for* which something takes place, or has the predicated quality: Σόλων Ἀθηναίοις νόμους ἔθηκεν. Αἱ βάλανοι τοῖς δεσπόταις ἀπόκεινται (*Xen. An.* 2, 3, 15; *are reserved for the masters*). Οὐ τῷ πατρὶ καὶ τῇ μητρὶ μόνον γεγενήμεθα, ἀλλὰ καὶ τῇ πατρίδι (*Dem.* 18, 205). Ἀνάγκη μοι ἀπιέναι. Φθόνος μέγιστον κακὸν τοῖς ἔχουσιν αὐτόν (*Isocr. Euag.* 6). Μέθη φύλαξιν ἀπρεπέστατον (*Pl. Rep.* 3, 398). Σωκράτης ἄξιος θανάτου ἐστὶ τῇ πόλει (*Xen. Mem.* 1, 1, 1; *has deserved death from the city, owes death as his deserts to the city*). Οἷα ἕκαστα ἐμοὶ φαίνεται, τοιαῦτα καὶ ἔστιν ἐμοί § 34. (241)

[1] The Greek dative, therefore, corresponds not only with the Latin dative, but also, to a great extent, with the Latin ablative.

[§ 34.] (*Pl. Theæt.* 152). Ἄφοβος τὰς εἰσφορὰς ἐμοὶ λογίζεται (*Dem.* 27, 46; *debits the taxes to me as expenditure*). (Dat. commodi et incommodi.)

Rem. 1. Sometimes the dative has directly the meaning *in honour of, to the advantage of*: στεφανοῦσθαι τῷ θεῷ (*Xen. Ages.* 2, 15), λαγχάνειν τοῦ κλήρου (*to claim the inheritance*) τῇ γυναικί (*Isæ.* 3, 32, = ὑπὲρ τῆς γυναικός, *in behalf of*; *for*; ib. 30).

Rem. 2. Such a dative is sometimes, in speaking of something that one has, or needs, or must bring about, immediately attached to a substantive, to denote for whom it is had or wanted, etc.: Χρημάτων Ἀριστοφάνει προσέδει πρὸς τὸν μισθὸν τοῖς πελτασταῖς (*Lys.* 19, 22). Ἐσπάνιζον τροφῆς τοῖς πολλοῖς (*Thuc.* 4, 6). Πείσανδρος ἠρώτα ἕνα ἕκαστον, ἥντινα ἐλπίδα ἔχει σωτηρίας τῇ πόλει (*Thuc.* 8, 53).

§ 35. (242) *a*) The dative stands with transitive verbs, which either usually (like δίδωμι), or in certain phrases (e. g. πόλεμον ἀναιρεῖσθαι, *to declare war*), denote an action in reference to another person or thing besides the proper object, as object of reference (both with the active and with the passive), e. g. μισθὸν διδόναι (ὑπισχνεῖσθαι, τάττειν) τοῖς στρατιώταις, διανέμειν χρήματα τοῖς πολίταις, ἀσφάλειαν παρέχειν τοῖς φίλοις, ἐπιτρέπειν τὰ πράγματα τοῖς ἐμπειροτάτοις, χρήματα πολλοῖς ὀφείλειν, βοήθειαν πέμπειν τινί, λέγειν (διηγεῖσθαι, ἀγγέλλειν) τινὶ τὰ πεπραγμένα, ὀνειδίζειν τινὶ δειλίαν, διαλλάττειν τινά τινι (*to reconcile a person with, to, some one*), δίκην λαγχάνειν τινί (*to commence a law-suit against a person*), χεῖρας ἀνέχειν θεῷ. Βοήθεια ἐπέμφθη Βοιωτοῖς. Ἡ γεγενημένη μάχη τῷ βασιλεῖ ἀγγέλλεται.

(243) *b*) Such a reference to something else besides the proper object is often denoted by the composition of the verb with one of the prepositions ἀντί, ἐν, ἐπί, περί, πρός, σύν, ὑπό. For example, ἀντιτάττειν τοὺς ἱππέας τοῖς πολεμίοις, ἐμβάλλειν τινὶ ἔρωτα, ἐμποιεῖν (ἐνεργάζεσθαι, ἐμφύειν) ἐπιθυμίαν τῇ ψυχῇ, ἐγχειρίζειν τινὶ τὰ πράγματα, (ἐντρέφειν, ἐντραφεὶς τῇ βασιλείᾳ), ἐνορᾶν κακόνοιάν τινά τινι, ἐπάγειν αἰτίαν ψευδῆ τινι, τέλος ἐπιθεῖναι πράγματι, ἐπιφέρειν ὅπλα ἀλλήλοις, ἐπιστέλλειν τινί τι, ἐπιτάττειν φόρον τοῖς συμμάχοις, περιάπτειν τῇ πόλει αἰσχύνην (τιμήν, ὄνειδος, δόξαν αἰσχράν), περιτιθέναι τινὶ στέφανον (ἀτιμίαν), περιβάλλεσθαι ταῖς πόλεσιν ἐρύματα[1]), προστιθέναι τι τῷ νόμῳ, προσέχειν τὸν νοῦν τῷ λόγῳ, προστάττειν τοῖς δούλοις ἔργα, προσφέρειν τῷ σώματι τροφήν, συνιστάναι τινὰ διδασκάλῳ, ὑποβάλλειν τινὶ λόγον, ὑποτάττεσθαί τινι. The reference, however, is denoted by a repetition of the preposition, whenever the conception of place or of a motion is prominent: Περιθεῖναι πιλίδια περὶ τὴν κεφαλήν (*Pl. Rep.* 3, 406). Τὸ ἐν Μιλήτῳ ἐνῳκοδομημένον φρούριον

---

[1] But also περιβάλλεσθαι τὴν νῆσον τείχει, *with a wall.*

(*Thuc.* 8, 4). (In some cases the usage of the language somewhat varies: this [§ 35.]
must be learnt from the Lexicon.)

Rem. 1. Transitive compounds with παρά are fond of repeating the preposition. (Also παραβάλλειν τι πρός τι.) (Παραμιγνύναι τί τινι, *to mix something with a thing;* also simply μιγνύναι τί τινι.)

Rem. 2. An object of reference in the dative may also stand with verbs which govern the genitive, e. g. ἀμφισβητεῖν τινι τοῦ σίτου, ἀντιποιεῖσθαι τῷ βασιλεῖ τῆς ἀρχῆς, μεταδιδόναι τινὶ τῶν ἀγαθῶν, μετέχειν τινὶ τῶν κακῶν, ξυλλαμβάνειν τινὶ τοῦ πόνου.

Rem. 3. With an inaccuracy, peculiar to themselves, some such verbs in the passive, instead of being predicated of the proper (accusative) object, take for their subject the object of reference, e. g. those which denote *transferring* and *giving in charge.* The proper object then remains in the accusative, as in the verbs which have a double accusative in the active (§ 25): Οἱ ἐπιτετραμμένοι τὴν φυλακήν (*Thuc.* 1, 126). Ἄλλο τι μεῖζον ἐπιταχθήσεσθε *Thuc.* 1, 140, = ὑμῖν ἐπιταχθήσεται). So in the passive: ἀποτέμνεσθαι τὴν κεφαλήν, ἐκκαίεσθαι or ἐκκόπτεσθαι τὠφθαλμώ of the person to whom this is done. (Οἱ ἀποσεσηπότες τοὺς δακτύλους τῶν ποδῶν, *Xen. An.* 4, 5, 12, = ἐκεῖνοι, ὧν ἀποσεσήπασιν οἱ δάκτυλοι.)

a) The dative stands as object of reference with intransitive verbs § 36.
which denote an action, disposition of mind, or situation in reference (204)
to a person or thing, but, in the view of the Greeks, do not imply a passive attitude on the part of the object, e. g. πείθεσθαι τοῖς ἄρχουσιν, πολεμεῖν Λακεδαιμονίοις, εὔχεσθαι τοῖς θεοῖς, ὁμιλεῖν τοῖς ἀγαθοῖς, ἀπαντᾶν τοῖς ἀπιοῦσιν. Ἔοικας παιδί. So likewise in phrases which have the signification of such a verb, e. g. Ἀθηναίοις διὰ πολέμου ἰέναι, ὁμόσε χωρεῖν τινι.

Of such verbs the most important are: those which denote an unfavourable *state of mind, blame, threatening, resistance, strife,* together with those which denote *obedience* and *compliance:* ὀργίζομαι, θυμοῦμαι, χαλεπαίνω, ἀπεχθάνομαι, φθονῶ, λοιδοροῦμαι[1], ἐπιτιμῶ, ἐπιπλήττω, ἐγκαλῶ, ἀπειλῶ, ἐναντιοῦμαι, πολεμῶ, παρατάττομαι, ἐρίζω, στασιάζω, ἀμφισβητῶ, πείθομαι, ἀπειθῶ, πειθαρχῶ, ὑπηρετῶ, ὑπουργῶ, δουλεύω, λατρεύω, εἴκω, ὑπείκω, ὑποχωρῶ, χαρίζομαι, συγγιγνώσκω: further, those which denote *help* and *assistance, counsel, cheering,* and *confidence:* βοηθῶ, ἀμύνω, ἐπικουρῶ, τιμωρῶ (poet. ἀρήγω), συμβουλεύω, παραινῶ, ὑποτίθεμαι, παρακελεύομαι, πιστεύω, ἀπιστῶ: and those which denote *meeting, approaching, following,* and *communing* or *companionship:* ἀπαντῶ, ἐντυγχάνω, πλησιάζω[2], ἀκολουθῶ, ἕπομαι, ὁμιλῶ, κοινωνῶ: lastly, some which do not belong to the foregoing classes, viz. ἔοικα (*am like*), διαλέγομαι (*converse with;* ἐς λόγους ἔρχομαι), εὔχομαι, λυσιτελῶ, and the impersonals δοκεῖ, συμφέρει, πρέπει, προσήκει, μέλει[3].

Rem. 1. As in some verbs the mode of viewing the relation wavers between the notion of a mere reference, and that of a transitive working upon the object,

[1] λοιδορῶ in the active with the accusative.

[2] The poetical words πελάζομαι, ἐμπελάζομαι, προσπελάζομαι have also the genitive. Active: πελάζειν τινά τινι.

[3] Δεῖ μοι (τινός, *I have need of, something is needful to me,* Dat. commodi), poetically also δεῖ μέ (and χρή μέ) τινος. Δεῖ με, χρή με ποιεῖν (rarely δεῖ μοι ποιεῖν, *I must do*).

[§ 36.] they occur both with the dative and with the accusative, especially ἀρέσκω, *please*, ἀπαρέσκω, *displease* (λυμαίνομαι, φιλοφρονοῦμαι, ἐνοχλῶ), sometimes with a somewhat altered meaning, thus μέμφομαι, *blame*, with the accusative, μέμφομαί τινί τι, *cast up something* to a person as a reproach. (Ὑπακούειν τινί and τινός.)

Rem. 2. In some of these verbs, the reference may also be expressed by a preposition, e. g. διαλέγεσθαι πρός τινα, πολεμεῖν, μάχεσθαι πρός τινα, ἕπεσθαι μετά τινος, σύν τινι, ἀκολουθεῖν μετά τινος.

Rem. 3. Some of these verbs may also have an object-accusative, either merely of a neuter pronoun or adjective, e. g. χαρίζομαι, or also of substantives, e. g. πιστεύω, *entrust*.

Rem. 4. Occasionally the passive of a verb of this sort also is (less accurately) predicated of an object of reference as its subject, e. g. Οἱ Κερκυραῖοι οὐκ εἰκότως πολεμοῦνται ὑπὸ Κορινθίων (*Thuc.* 1, 37, *are warred upon*). Ξύμπαντες οἱ τῆς Σικελίας ἔνοικοι ἐπιβουλευόμεθα (*Thuc.* 4, 61), especially in the participle or infinitive, for the sake of conciseness: Παλαμήδης διὰ σοφίαν φθονηθεὶς ὑπὸ τοῦ Ὀδυσσέως ἀπόλλυται (*Xen. Mem.* 4, 2, 33). Κρεῖττόν ἐστι πιστεύεσθαι ὑπὸ τῆς πατρίδος ἢ ἀπιστεῖσθαι (*Xen. Symp.* 4, 29). (In Thucydides, even verbs in which the construction with the dative rests on the composition (*b*): Αἱ εἴκοσι νῆες τῶν Πελοποννησίων, ἐφορμούμεναι ἴσῳ ἀριθμῷ ὑπὸ Ἀθηναίων, ἐπέκπλουν ἐποιήσαντο, 8, 20.)

(245) *b*) The dative is often put in this manner with intransitive verbs, which by composition with one of the prepositions ἀντί, ἐν, ἐπί, παρά, περί, πρός, σύν, ὑπό, or with the particle ὁμοῦ, come to denote a reference to something else, especially in a figurative sense, e. g. ἀντέχειν (*to hold out against*), ἀντιβλέπειν τοῖς πολεμίοις, ἐμμένειν ταῖς συνθήκαις (τοῖς ὅρκοις, τοῖς δεδογμένοις), ἐπιέναι τοῖς ὁπλίταις, ἐπικεῖσθαι τοῖς φεύγουσιν, ἐφορμεῖν τῷ λιμένι, ἐφήδεσθαι, ἐπεγγελᾶν τινι (τοῖς κακοῖς τινος), ἐπιστρατεύειν (ἐπιστρατεύεσθαι) τοῖς Ἕλλησιν, παραμένειν τοῖς συμμάχοις, παρακαθῆσθαι Σωκράτει, περιπίπτειν συμφορᾷ (φυγῇ), περιτυγχάνειν κριτῇ ἀγνώμονι, προσοικεῖν ποταμοῖς καὶ θαλάσσῃ, προσήκειν τινί (*to be related to a person*), συνεῖναι, συζῆν τινι (συνεῖναι, συνέχεσθαι, συζεύγνυσθαι, συστῆναι κακοῖς, νόσῳ, πόνῳ), συνεργεῖν τινι, συνοικεῖν γυναικί (συγχαίρειν τοῖς εὐτυχοῦσιν), ὑποκεῖσθαι τῷ ἄρχοντι, ὁμολογεῖν, ὁμογνωμονεῖν, ὁμονοεῖν τινι. Πόλλ' ἔνεστι τῷ γήρᾳ κακά (*Arist. Sph.* 411). Ἔρως φιλοσοφίας ἐμπίπτει τοῖς ἀνδράσιν (*Pl. Rep.* 6, 499). Ἐπέρχεταί (ἔπεισί) μοι λέγειν. Τῇ βίᾳ πρόσεισιν ἔχθραι (*Xen. Mem.* 1, 2, 10). Τὰ ἔργα τοῖς λόγοις οὐ συμφωνεῖ. Ἑκάστῳ τῶν ὀνομάτων τούτων ὑπόκειταί τις ἴδιος οὐσία (*Pl. Prot.* 349). When the literal signification, and, in general, the notion of space and motion, is prominent, the preposition is usually repeated: ἐμμένειν ἐν τῇ τάξει, ἐμπίπτειν εἰς φρέαρ, εἰς ἀνάγκην. Ἄλφιτ' οὐκ ἔνεστιν ἐν τῷ θυλάκῳ (*Arist. Pl.* 763). In this point, however, the individual verbs somewhat vary [1].

Rem. 1. The compounds of verbs of motion with παρά, περί, ὑπό are transitive,

[1] The compounds of ἧμαι and κεῖμαι, even in their literal signification, have, for the most part, the dative without prepositions; on the other hand, προσφέρεσθαι πρός τινα μετὰ πρᾳότητος, *to deal with, bear oneself* towards, a person.

and have the accusative (§ 23). (More rarely, and chiefly in poetry, certain others: ἐπιστρατεύειν τινά, προσπαίζειν τινά: in Thucydid. προσοικεῖν, προσκαθέζεσθαι πόλιν instead of πόλει.) [§ 36.]

Rem. 2. In some compounds with σύν, the dative denotes another subject who takes part in the action, e.g. συγκαταγηράσκειν τινί. Οἱ συναναβάντες τῷ Κύρῳ (also σὺν τῷ Κύρῳ).

§ 37. (247 b) Besides the usage assigned to the dat. in § 34 of denoting the person *for whom* something has a certain quality, the dative stands as object of reference (*a*) with the adjectives which denote *likeness* (*correspondency*) and *unlikeness, friendly* and *hostile disposition*, as also (*b*) with the adjectives which, by composition with ἐν, σύν, or ὁμοῦ, denote a reference to something, and a *community* or *companionship*, or which (*c*) are derived from verbs governing the dative, and express the action of the verb, (*d*) also with the adverbs derived from these adjectives, and with the verbs which signify, *to make like*, e.g. Ὅμοιος Φιλίππῳ, ἀνόμοιος τοῖς ἀδελφοῖς. Γυναῖκα κοινωνὸν ἀγαθὴν οἴκου οὖσαν ἀντίῤῥοπον εἶναι τῷ ἀνδρὶ νομίζω (*Xen. Œc.* 3, 15). Τάχος καὶ ὀργὴ εὐβουλίᾳ ἐναντία (*Thuc.* 3, 42). Εὔνους Ἀθηναίοις, ἐχθρὸς Λακεδαιμονίοις. Συγγενής, σύντροφός τινι. Ἀσύμφωνον ἑαυτῷ. Ἔνοχος ταῖς μεγίσταις αἰτίαις. Ὅμοροι τοῖς Ἀρμενίοις. Ὁμώνυμος ἐμοί. Κύνες ἐπιθετικαὶ τοῖς θηρίοις (*Xen. Mem.* 4, 1, 3). — Ἀκολούθως τοῖς εἰρημένοις. Εὐνοϊκῶς ἔχειν τινί. Συμφερόντως ἑαυτοῖς. — Ὁμοιοῦσθαι τῷ θεῷ.

Rem. 1. The adjectives which denote a correspondency, even when they are compounded with σύν or ὁμοῦ (e.g. ἀκόλουθος, ἀντίστροφος, ἰσόῤῥοπος, ὁμώνυμος, σύμφωνος), together with ἐναντίος, often also take the genitive, e.g. συμμαχία τούτων ἀντίῤῥοπος (*Dem.* 1. 10, *evenly balancing, counterpoising, this*). Τεῦκρος Σαλαμῖνα κατῴκισεν ἐν Κύπρῳ, ὁμώνυμον ποιήσας τῆς πρότερον αὐτῷ πατρίδος οὔσης (*Isocr. Evag.* 18). Τὰ ἐναντία τῶν συμφερόντων συμβουλεύειν. (Rarely ὅμοιος.) Φίλος, ἐχθρός, πολέμιος, ὅμορος, as substantives are used with the genitive (even in the superlative: οἱ ἐκείνου ἔχθιστοι, *Xen. An.* 3, 2, 5).

Rem. 2. When it is denoted by ὅμοιος, ἴσος, παραπλήσιος, or the adverbs formed from them, that two subjects (or objects) have something equally or similarly, that something in them is equal or alike, the regular construction is, that the subjects are coupled by καί (Ὁμοίαν γνώμην ἔχω καὶ σύ), or by a relative word (ἴσος ὅσοσπερ, παραπλήσιος οἷόσπερ); but by a less exact way of putting it, the Greeks often have the second subject (or object) in the dative, as governed by the adjective (or adverb): Ὁμοίαν γνώμην σοι ἔχω. Τοὺς κακοὺς εὖ ποιῶν ὅμοια πείσει τοῖς τὰς ἀλλοτρίας κύνας σιτίζουσιν (*Isocr. Dem.* 29). Οὐ καὶ σὺ τύπτει τὰς ἴσας πληγὰς ἐμοί; (*Arist. Ran.* 636. On the accusative, see § 26, b.). Ἐπιθυμῶ παραπλησίως σοι (*Pl. Phæd.* 255). Μέθην καὶ ὕπνον ὁμοίως ἐνέδρᾳ φυλάττομαι (*Xen. Hier.* 6, 3, = ὁμοίως καὶ ἐνέδραν). In the same manner, ὁ αὐτός, *the same*, is constructed: Τὰ αὐτὰ φρονῶ Δημοσθένει (*Dem.* 18, 304, = ἃ Δημοσθένης). Τὸν δοῦλον τοῖς αὐτοῖς χαίρειν καὶ ἄχθεσθαι τῷ δεσπότῃ χρή (*Pl. Gorg.* 510, = οἷς ὁ δεσπότης χαίρει). Ἐν τῷ αὐτῷ κινδύνῳ τοῖς φαυλοτάτοις αἰωροῦμαι (*Thuc.* 7, 77).

[§ 37.] (Sometimes even where the same verb cannot be repeated: Ἀπέθανε Σιτάλκης ὑπὸ τὰς αὐτὰς ἡμέρας τοῖς ἐπὶ Δηλίῳ, *Thuc.* 4, 101, = αἷς ἐγένετο τὰ ἐπὶ Δ.)

Rem. 3. (To § 34—37.) Sometimes the dative is used even with a substantive, when it is derived from a verb or adjective which has an object of reference in the dative: Μὴ ἐξαμάρτητε περὶ τὴν τοῦ θεοῦ δόσιν ὑμῖν (*Pl. Apol.* 30). Ξύμμαχοι ἐγενόμεθα οὐκ ἐπὶ καταδουλώσει τῶν Ἑλλήνων τοῖς Ἀθηναίοις (*Thuc.* 3, 10). Τὴν αὐτοῖς ὁμοιότητα τῆς διαγωγῆς ἀεὶ ἕξουσιν (*Pl. Theæt.* 177). Ὁ τούτους τοὺς νόμους λύων τοὺς τῷ γήρᾳ βοηθοὺς λυμαίνεται (*Dem.* 24, 107, usually τοῦ γήρως).

§ 38. The dative of reference serves in Greek, in some special cases, to denote a certain particular way and manner, and a certain sense, in which the thing predicated takes place for, and in reference to, some person or some thing.

(246) *a*) The dative with εἰμί, ὑπάρχω, γίγνομαι denotes the person for whom something is or comes to be, i. e. who *has it* or *comes to have* it: Νῆες οὐκ εἰσὶν ἡμῖν. Τοιαῦτα ἡμῖν εἰς φιλίαν ὑπάρχει (*Xen.*). (Παρύσατις ἡ μήτηρ ὑπῆρχε τῷ Κύρῳ, φιλοῦσα αὐτὸν μᾶλλον ἢ Ἀρταξέρξην (*Xen. An.* 1, 1, 4, *was devotedly attached to*). Ἐκ τῶν δούλων δώδεκα μναῖ ἑκάστου τοῦ ἐνιαυτοῦ τῷ πατρὶ ἐγίγνοντο (*Dem.* 27, 24). Πόθεν αἱ διαβολαί σοι αὗται γεγόνασιν; (*Pl. Apol.* 20.) (Οὐδὲν ἐμοὶ καὶ Φιλίππῳ, *I and Ph. have nothing to do with each other.* Τί ἐμοὶ καὶ σοί;)

b) The dative stands in statements of the time that has elapsed since a person has been in a certain state, or since a certain action: Ἡμέρα ἦν πέμπτη ἐπιπλέουσιν Ἀθηναίοις (*Xen. Hell.* 2, 1, 27, *it was the fifth day on which the Athenians; the Athenians had been five days* —). Ἡμέραι μάλιστα ἦσαν τῇ Μιτυλήνῃ ἑαλωκυίᾳ ἑπτά, ὅτ' ἐς τὸ Ἔμβατον οἱ Λακεδαιμόνιοι κατέπλευσαν (*Thuc.* 3, 29). (Rarely without a participle subjoined: Ἔτη ταύτῃ τῇ ναυμαχίᾳ ἑξήκοντα καὶ διακόσιά ἐστι μεχρὶ τῆς τελευτῆς τοῦδε τοῦ πολέμου, *Thuc.* 1, 13.)

c) The dative of a participle is used to denote when, or in what situation, something shows itself (especially when a relation of place is assigned): Τὸ μὲν ἔξωθεν ἁπτομένῳ σῶμα οὐκ ἄγαν θερμὸν ἦν, τὰ δ' ἐντὸς ἐκαίετο (*Thuc.* 2, 49). (Ἡ διαβάντι τὸν ποταμὸν πρὸς ἑσπέραν ὁδὸς ἐπὶ Λυδίαν φέρει, *Xen. An.* 3, 5, 15, *the road to the west, when you have crossed the river.*) Πρὸς εὐδοξίαν καὶ ὠφέλειαν σκοπουμένῳ ὁ μὲν ἐπαινέτης τοῦ δικαίου ἀληθεύει, ὁ δὲ ψέκτης οὐδὲν ὑγιὲς λέγει, *Pl. Rep.* 9, 589. Hence συνελόντι (συντέμνοντι) εἰπεῖν, *to speak it briefly*, and simply συνελόντι, without the infinitive, *in brief; in short*. (On εἰπεῖν, see § 151, R. 1.)

(246, R. 2) *d*) The dative of a noun with a participle is used with ἐστίν, to denote a person's state of mind upon something (especially of *inclination* or *aversion*, βουλομένῳ): Τῷ πλήθει τῶν Πλαταιέων οὐ βουλομένῳ ἦν τῶν Ἀθηναίων ἀφίστασθαι (*Thuc.* 2, 3). Ἐπανέλθωμεν, ὅθεν ἀπελίπομεν, εἴ σοι ἡδομένῳ ἐστίν (*Pl. Phæd.* 78).

e) Often a dative of reference denotes the person in whom, and *in whose affairs*, and, at the same time, in whose interest, something takes place; so that, instead of the dative referred to the predicate, we might have, with only a slight modification of the way of conceiving the relation, a genitive referred to the subject: *Οἱ Ἀθηναῖοι ἀντεῖχον, μέχρι οἱ τοξόται εἶχόν τε τὰ βέλη αὐτοῖς καὶ οἷοί τε ἦσαν χρῆσθαι* (*Thuc.* 3, 98). *Οἱ Περσῶν νόμοι δοκοῦσιν ἄρχεσθαι τοῦ κοινοῦ ἀγαθοῦ ἐπιμελούμενοι* (*begin with the care for the common good*) *οὐκ ἔνθεν ταῖς πλείσταις πόλεσιν ἄρχονται* (*Xen. Cyr.* 1, 2, 2; *those of most states, in most states*). (*Ὁ αὐτοέντης ἡμῖν πατρός, Soph. Pl.* 272, *he that slew our father.*) With a participle added, approximating now and then to the signification of a double genitive: *Ξενοφῶντι διὰ τῆς μεσογαίας πορευομένῳ οἱ ἱππεῖς προκαταθέοντες ἐντυγχάνουσι πρεσβύταις πορευομένοις ποι* (*Xen. An.* 6, 3 (1) 10; *on Xenophon's march, his horsemen fall in with* —). *Εἰργομένοις οὖν αὐτοῖς (τοῖς Χίοις) τῆς θαλάσσης καὶ κατὰ γῆν πορθουμένοις ἐνεχείρησάν τινες πρὸς Ἀθηναίους ἀγαγεῖν τὴν πόλιν* (*Thuc.* 8, 24). [§ 38.]

f) The dative of the personal pronouns, especially of the first person, is added in expressions of *surprise* and of *blame*, in *demands, expostulations*, and the like, to denote a certain participation, and an interest in the person speaking, spoken to, or spoken of: *Σωφροσύνης ἄρα οὐ δεήσει ἡμῖν τοῖς νεανίαις;* (*Pl. Rep.* 3, 389.) *Τούτῳ πάνυ μοι προσέχετε τὸν νοῦν* (*Dem.* 18, 178). [This dat. is called the *Dativus Ethicus*.] (248)

g) Sometimes the dative of the agent stands with passive verbs instead of *ὑπό* with the genitive; but in prose, for the most part, only with the perfect and pluperfect (to denote what one has complete and ready): *Ἃ ὑπισχνοῦ ποιήσειν ἀγαθὰ ἡμᾶς, ἀποτετέλεσταί σοι ἤδη* (*Xen. Cyr.* 3, 2, 16). *Τὰ σοὶ πεπραγμένα* (*Dem.* 19, 291). (*Τίνες ἂν ὑμῶν δικαιότερον πᾶσι τοῖς Ἕλλησι μισοῖντο;* *Thuc.* 3, 64.) (250)

§ 39. (252, 254)

As the case which denotes circumstance and appurtenance (Lat. ablative), the dative stands, partly by itself, used in different ways, partly with the prepositions *ἐν* and *σύν*, together with *ἅμα* (which in prose is used, for the most part, only in definitions of time, *ἅμα τῇ ἕῳ, ἅμα τῷ σίτῳ ἀκμάζοντι*), and with other prepositions (*ἀμφί, ἐπί* [*μετά*], *παρά, περί, πρός, ὑπό*) in certain significations which arise out of the signification *on, at, by*: *Βάλλειν τινὰ λίθοις, ξίφει, ὠθεῖν τινα ταῖς χερσίν* (*ἐν χειρί, διὰ χειρῶν ἔχειν τι*), *φαρμάκῳ ἀποθνήσκειν, γιγνώσκειν τινὰ τῇ σκευῇ* (*Thuc.* 1, 8), *πολέμῳ χώραν προσκτᾶσθαι, καταπλήττειν τοὺς ἄλλους τῷ ἀξιώματι, ἐκπεπλῆχθαι ταῖς συμφοραῖς, τιμᾶν* (*κοσμεῖν*) *τινα στεφάνοις, ζημιοῦν τινα θανάτῳ, φυγῇ, χρήμασιν* (*in money*), *ἀνηκέστῳ πονηρίᾳ νοσεῖν* (*Xen. Mem.* 3, 5, 18, *of, with*), *οἰκίαι κατεσκευασμέναι χαλκώμασι παμπόλλοις* (*provided with*), *κέρδει καὶ πλούτῳ κρίνειν τι* (*Pl. Rep.* 9, 582, *judge by, according to*). *Δέχεσθαί τινα πόλει, in the city* (usually *εἰς πόλιν, into the city*).

Rem. *Διά* with the genitive denotes the more remote means, *by means of*: CHAP. IV.]

[§ 39.] Ποτέρα ὀρθοτέρα ἀπόκρισις, ᾧ ὁρῶμεν, τοῦτ' εἶναι ὀφθαλμούς, ἢ δι' οὗ ὁρῶμεν; (*Pl. Theæt.* 184.) In certain connexions ἀπό is used of origin, beginning, starting-point (Οὐκ ἀπὸ τύχης ἐγένετο, *Lys.* 21, 10, ἀπὸ τῶν αὐτῶν λόγων ἀποτρέπειν τὸν δῆμον, *Thuc.* 6, 19, ἀπὸ τῶν ἔργων κρίνειν, ἀπὸ σημείου ἑνός, adverbially: ἀπὸ στόματος), especially of resources (of money, and the like, *from, by, with, by means of*, ζῆν ἀπὸ λείας, ἀπὸ τῶν χρημάτων στράτευμα συλλέγειν, *Xen. An.* 2, 6, 5, τὸ ναυτικὸν τρέφειν ἀπὸ προσόδων τινῶν, *Thuc.* 1, 81, ἀπὸ διακοσίων νεῶν καὶ χιλίων ταλάντων καταπολεμεῖν τινα, *Isocr. Antid.* 111); in other connexions ἐξ, of the occasion, source, etc. (ἐκ τοιᾶσδε προφάσεως, ἐξ ἁπάντων τούτων ἄχθεσθαι, *Pl. Rep.* 8, 549, ἐξ εὐεργεσιῶν εὐμενῶς διατίθεσθαί τινι, *Isocr. Paneg.* 28). In certain connexions sometimes ἐν, *in*, i. e. *by*, of the *distinctive mark by which* any thing is recognized: Ὅτι οἱ θεοί σε εὐμενῶς πέμπουσι, καὶ ἐν ἱεροῖς δῆλον καὶ ἐν οὐρανίοις σημείοις (*Xen. Cyr.* 1, 6, 2). (Ὁρᾶν ἐν ὀφθαλμοῖς, *to see before one's eyes*, etc.)

§ 40. (253) The dative denotes the side, aspect, regard or property, *on* and *in* which the predicate shows itself, the notion to which it refers: Γένει Ἕλλην, φύσει κακός, ἡλικίᾳ νέος, ὑπερβάλλειν (προέχειν, διαφέρειν) ἀρετῇ, φρονήσει, πλήθει, μεγέθει, πλεονεκτεῖν τινος τιμαῖς καὶ χρήμασιν (*Xen. An.* 3, 1, 37). Ἔργῳ, τῷ ὄντι, λόγῳ, τῇ ἀληθείᾳ, *in deed, in reality, in word, in truth.* Τὸ πράττειν τοῦ λέγειν ὕστερον ὂν τῇ τάξει, πρότερον τῇ δυνάμει ἐστίν (*Dem.* 3, 15). Ναυσὶ καὶ πεζῷ νικᾶσθαι. Σώμασιν ἰσχύειν. Βλάπτεσθαι τῷ βελτίστῳ τοῦ ὁπλιτικοῦ (*Thuc.* 4, 73; *to suffer loss in the best part, the flower, of* —).

REM. To denote a part of the subject itself, the accusative is used, § 31. In certain general notions to which a term predicated of the subject refers, both cases are used, partly without any distinction, e. g. πόλις μεγάλη, Θάψακος ὀνόματι and ὄνομα Θ., γένει Ἕλλην and τὸ γένος Ἕ. (with the article; but also Κορίνθιος γένος, *Thuc.* 1, 24), partly with a slight distinction, e. g. δισχίλιοι τὸ πλῆθος, but διαφέρειν (ὑπερβάλλειν, etc.) πλήθει, φύσει ἀγαθός, *by nature, naturally*, ἀμβλύτερος τὴν φύσιν, *duller in natural gifts; of duller nature* or *capacity*.

§ 41. (255) The dative denotes the efficient cause *from* or *through which* any thing is done: Ἀγνοίᾳ ἁμαρτάνειν, φόβῳ (εὐνοίᾳ) τὰ προστεταγμένα ποιεῖν. Μέλητος τὴν γραφὴν ταύτην ὕβρει τινὶ καὶ ἀκολασίᾳ καὶ νεότητι γράψασθαι δοκεῖ (*Pl. Apol.* 26).

REM. The moving cause, or that on account of which any thing is done, is denoted by διά with the accusative; sometimes, however, the dative approximates to this signification: Δημοσθένης τοῖς πεπραγμένοις ἐφοβεῖτο τοὺς Ἀθηναίους (*Thuc.* 3, 98). (Ὑφ' ἡδονῆς, *for pleasure, for joy*, e. g. γελᾶν.)

§ 42. (257) The dative is sometimes used to denote the manner and the accompanying circumstance (with): Παντὶ τρόπῳ πειρᾶσθαι (also πάντα τρόπον, § 30, d), οὐδενὶ κόσμῳ εἰσπίπτειν (*Thuc.* 7, 84), βίᾳ εσιέναι, κραυγῇ πολλῇ ἐπιέναι (*Xen. An.* 1, 7, 4). (Οἱ Ἀθηναῖοι ἀτέλει τῇ νίκῃ ἀπὸ Μιλήτου ἀνέστησαν, *Thuc.* 8, 27; *with the victory incomplete.*)

REM. 1. Usually, however, it is only of some particular substantives that the simple dative is thus used, adverbially, e. g. δρόμῳ, *at a run, at full speed*, κύκλῳ,

round about, ὀργῇ διώκειν, θυμῷ φέρειν τι, σιγῇ ἀκούειν, (σπουδῇ). Otherwise σύν or [§ 42.]
μετά is used, e.g. σὺν δίκῃ, μετὰ δίκης, and with addition of an adjective, μετὰ πολλῆς ἀκριβείας (ἀκριβῶς). (*With joy, joyfully*, ἡδέως, ἀσμένως, etc.)

Rem. 2. To this use of the dative belong also the datives of feminine adjectives and pronouns, with a substantive notion understood (such as ὁδῷ, or the like), used as adverbs of manner, e. g. δημοσίᾳ, ἰδίᾳ, πεζῇ, ταύτῃ, ἐκείνῃ, ᾗ, πῇ, etc.

Rem. 3. The military or naval force with which a movement or enterprise is conducted, is often put in the dative without a preposition: Ἀφικνεῖσθαι εἴκοσι ναυσί, πολλῷ στόλῳ, χειρὶ πολλῇ. Ἀθηναῖοι δισχιλίοις ὁπλίταις ἑαυτῶν καὶ ἱππεῦσι διακοσίοις ἐστράτευσαν ἐπὶ Χαλκιδέας (*Thuc.* 2, 79). Μνάσιππος κατεστρατοπεδεύσατο τῷ πεζῷ ἐπὶ λόφῳ ἀπέχοντι τῆς πόλεως ὡς πέντε στάδια (*Xen. Hell.* 6, 2, 7). But σύν may be prefixed: Βασιλεὺς σὺν στρατεύματι πολλῷ προσέρχεται (*Xen. An.* 1, 8, 1). (Σύν is also omitted from the dative with αὐτός in the sense, *with — self and all; together with*: Οἱ Ἀθηναῖοι πέντε ναῦς ἔλαβον καὶ μίαν τούτων αὐτοῖς ἀνδράσιν, *Thuc.* 4, 14; *men and all*, i. e. *with its crew*.)

With comparatives, and with πρό and μετά, the measure *by how* § 43.
much something is greater or less, earlier or later, is put in the (270)
dative: Τέτταρσι μναῖς ἔλαττον. Πολλαῖς γενεαῖς ὕστερα τῶν Τρωικῶν. Δέκα ἔτεσι πρὸ τῆς ἐν Σαλαμῖνι ναυμαχίας. (Πολλῷ, μακρῷ, ὀλίγῳ, βραχεῖ, μικρῷ μείζων, ὀλίγῳ τινὶ ἐλάττων. Τῷ παντὶ κρείττων, *infinitely better*. Τοσούτῳ κρείττων, ὅσῳ πρεσβύτερος.) (Μακρῷ ἄριστος, with the superlative. Πολλῷ προὔλαβον, *Thuc.* 7, 80, *had greatly the advantage*.)

Rem. But we also find πολὺ and ὀλίγον (πολὺ μείζων), and always (when no substantive is added) τί and οὐδέν (μᾶλλόν τι, οὐδὲν μᾶλλον). (Τοσούτῳ δεινότερος, ὅσῳ καὶ ψεύδεσθαι τολμᾷ, without comparative in the second member: *so much worse, as* —.)

a) Verbs which denote an affection of the mind, *at* and *because of* § 44.
something, take this object in the dative: thus ἥδομαι, χαίρω, ἄχθο- (264)
μαι, ἀθυμῶ, ἀγάλλομαι, ἐπαίρομαι: Ἄχθομαι τοῖς παροῦσιν, τοῖς γεγενημένοις. Ἐπαιρόμενος ἢ πλούτῳ ἢ ἰσχύϊ ἢ ἄλλῳ τῷ τοιούτῳ (*Pl. Rep.* 4, 434). But ἐπί is also added: Ἐπὶ τῇ τῶν Ἀρκαδίων τύχῃ οὐχ ἧττον τῶν Λακεδαιμονίων ἤσθησαν οἱ Θηβαῖοι (*Xen. Hell.* 7, 1, 32).

Rem. Some verbs most frequently take ἐπί (χαίρω), with others it is rare (ἐπαίρομαι). The dative is also found with ἀγαπᾶν and στέργειν, e.g. στέργειν τῇ ἑαυτοῦ τύχῃ (*Pl. Hipp. Maj.* 295); but usually the accusative, e. g. στέργειν τὰ παρόντα. We also find βαρέως (χαλεπῶς) φέρειν τί, ἐπί τινι.

b) The verb χρῶμαι, *use*, and νομίζω, when it has the same mean- (265)
ing, govern the dative: Σωματοφύλαξι χρῶνται βαρβάροις. Χρῶμαί τινι φίλῳ. Οἱ Ἀθηναῖοι ἀγῶσι καὶ θυσίαις διετησίοις ἐνόμιζον (*Thuc.* 2, 38).

a) The dative serves to mark the time at which (*when*) a thing § 45.
takes place, when a definite point of time (day, night, month, year), (276)
or a festival is assigned (and with ὥρᾳ, e. g. χειμῶνος ὥρᾳ): Τῇ αὐτῇ

[§ 45.] ἡμέρᾳ (ταύτῃ τῇ νυκτὶ) ἀπέθανεν. Τῷ τρίτῳ ἔτει οἴκαδε ἀπέπλευσα. Τῇ ὑστεραίᾳ ὁ Κῦρος τὸ στράτευμα ἀνέπαυεν (*Xen. Cyr.* 3, 3, 29). Τοῖς Παναθηναίοις, τοῖς Διονυσίοις, *at [the festival of] the Panathenæa, the Dionysia.* (Τῇ νουμηνίᾳ, ταῖς πομπαῖς.) With other words ἐν is added: Ἐν τούτῳ τῷ χρόνῳ, ἐν ἐκείνῳ τῷ καιρῷ. ἐν τῷ παρόντι, ἐν τῷ τότε, sometimes also with the words above named: ἐν τῇδε τῇ ἡμέρᾳ, ἐν τῷ Θαργηλιῶνι μηνί (*Dem.* 49, 60). (The omission of ἐν is very rare with words which in themselves do not denote a point of time but an event, e. g. Ἐς τὸ πεδίον Ἀρχίδαμος ἐκείνῃ τῇ ἐσβολῇ οὐ κατέβη, *in that invasion. Thuc.* 2, 20.)

REM. On the genitive in notes of time, see § 66.

b) To denote the place *where* a thing takes place, the poets sometimes use the dative without ἐν, e. g. ἀγροῖς τυγχάνειν (*Soph. Pl.* 313). Ἐτέοκλος πλείστας τιμὰς ἔσχεν Ἀργείᾳ χθονί (*Eur. Suppl.* 874), especially of names of cities, e. g. Δωδῶνι, Μυκήναις. In prose the name of the city is thus put: Μαραθῶνι (Μαραθῶνι καὶ Σαλαμῖνι καὶ Πλαταιαῖς, *Pl. Menex.* 245), and besides, the adverbial forms derived from the ancient dative plural, in the sense *at the place*, e. g. Ἀθήνησι, Πλαταιᾶσιν; see the *Accidence.* (Ὀλυμπίασι καὶ Δελφοῖς, *Thuc.* 1, 143.) (So too Σφηττοῖ, Ἰσθμοῖ, Πυθοῖ.)

REM. (To § 39 seqq.) A dative, denoting circumstance or appurtenance, may sometimes be attached to an individual substantive, instead of to the predicate, e. g. ὁ γόνῳ πατήρ (*Lys.* 13, 91); sometimes even without the article: Ἱπποθάλης λέγει περὶ τῶν προγόνων Λύσιδος πλούτους τε καὶ ἱπποτροφίας καὶ νίκας Πυθοῖ καὶ Ἰσθμοῖ τεθρίπποις τε καὶ κέλησιν (*Pl. Lys.* 205).

CHAPTER V.

Genitive.

§ 46. (279) THE genitive in Greek denotes, in general, a connexion of dependence between the person or thing which is named in the genitive, and some other person or thing which is referred to it. The connexion is either immediate, between two substantives, one of which is defined by the other; or it appears in this, that something is referred to some other thing through an action or quality which goes to, is directed at, and exerted towards, or enters into, that other; or in this, that something is ranged under some other thing as the whole, of which it is the part. Further, the genitive denotes a *parting from*, and a *going out from* something, because this supposes a previously existing connexion [1].

[1] This latter sense is not possessed by the Latin genitive, where the ablative is used in this way with prepositions, adjectives, and verbs. The use of the genitive to denote a connexion or hanging together, as the result of an action which aims at

In the genitive is put with a substantive the name of the person § 47.
or thing which possesses what the substantive denotes; the person (280)
or thing to which it belongs, and by which therefore it can be denominated and designated (genitive of connexion and possession): Υἱὸς Δαρείου. Κῆποι Ἐπικούρου. Οἰκέτης Δημοσθένους. Φύλαξ πόλεως. Σύγγραμμα Πλάτωνος. Ἔργον Πραξιτέλους. Ἡ τῶν πολεμίων τροπή. Τὸ γένος τῶν ἀνθρώπων. Μισθὸς τεττάρων μηνῶν. Ἀριθμὸς πεντακισχιλίων ἐτῶν (*Pl. Tim.* 23; *an amount of* —). Κλήρωσις ἀρχῶν. Αἱ τῶν νεῶν τιμαί (*honours which the young enjoy, or which they show*). Αἱ τῶν κακῶν συνουσίαι (*bad men's society, intercourse with bad men*). (Ὁ τῆς ἡσυχίας βίοτος, *Eur. Bacch.* 388, poetical.) Ἑκάστου [τούτων τῶν μαθημάτων] ὄργανόν τι ψυχῆς ἐκκαθαίρεται (*Pl. Rep.* 7, 527. *In the case of each*). Εἶναί τινος, γίγνεσθαί τινος. Ὁ (289)
λόγος Δημοσθένους ἐστίν (*is D.s's, νομίζεται, is ascribed to D.*). Εἰμὶ τῆς πόλεως καὶ τῶν τὰ βέλτιστα λεγόντων (*Isocr. de Pac.* 129. *I belong to* —). Εἶναι τῶν ἐπιτιθεμένων (*Pl. Pol.* 307, *to be the prey of* —, *at the mercy of* —). Οἱ Πέρσαι τὴν Ἀσίαν ἑαυτῶν ποιοῦνται (*Xen. Ages.* 1, 33). (Οἱ Πελοποννήσιοι δύο καὶ εἴκοσι ναῦς τῶν Ἀθηναίων ἔλαβον, *Thuc.* 8, 95, *two and twenty ships of the Athenians, Athenian ships.*)

Rem. 1. The usual way of describing the *son* of such a man, is to put the *father's* name in the genitive without υἱός: Λέαρχος Καλλιμάχου and Λ. ὁ Καλλιμάχου. (See the *Article*, § 13, a. R.) (Τὴν Σμικυθίωνος οὐχ ὁρᾷς Μελιστίχην; *Arist. Eccl.* 46, *M. the wife of Sm.*)

Rem. 2. The prepositions ἐν and ἐς (sometimes ἐξ) in the language of common life, and in imitations of it, often stand before a genitive with omission of the governing substantive οἰκία (also ἱερόν): Περικλῆς Κλεινίαν καταθέμενος ἐν Ἀρίφρονος ἐπαίδευεν (*Pl. Prot.* 320, *placed him in A.'s house*). Μανθάνειν ἐν κιθαριστοῦ (*Pl. Theæt.* 206, *at a cithara player's*). Πότερον τὸ παρὰ σοὶ ὕδωρ θερμότερον πιεῖν ἐστιν ἢ τὸ ἐν Ἀσκληπιοῦ; (*Xen. Mem.* 3, 13, 3.) Ἐν Ἅιδου. Σωκράτης ἔφη ἰέναι ἐπὶ δεῖπνον εἰς Ἀγάθωνος (*Pl. Symp.* 174). Φοιτᾶν ἐς διδασκάλου (διδασκάλων), *to attend such a master;* πέμπειν εἰς διδασκάλων (*Pl. Prot.* 325). Εἰσῆλθον οἴκαδε ἐς ἐμαυτοῦ (*Pl. Hipp. Maj.* 304). Ἐς Ἅιδου. (Ἐκ διδασκάλων ἀπαλλάττεσθαι, *Pl. Prot.* 326, *to leave school.*)

Rem. 3. On the genitive under the government of the article, see § 14, c. (Ἃ εἶχον ἀλλήλων, *Thuc.* 5, 39, *what they had of one another's, belonging to one another;* ὁπόσα ἀλλήλων εἶχον, *Thuc.* 5, 80.)

The genitive is put, as objective genitive, to transitive substantives, § 48.
i. e. such as are derived from transitive verbs, or from verbs or (281)
adjectives which govern the genitive, and such as denote a capacity,

---

something and enters into it, is in Latin much more circumscribed, especially in verbs, so that in this regard also the Greek genitive is much more comprehensive than the Latin.

[§ 48.] an opportunity, an influence, for and upon something: Ἔρως (Ἁράσπᾳ ἐνέπεσε) τῆς γυναικός. Φόβος τῶν πολεμίων, *fear of* (i. e. the being afraid of) *the enemies; ὁ τῶν πολεμίων φόβος, the enemy's fear* (of something), *or* (*some one's*) *fear of the enemy*. Πόθος τοῦ ἀποθανόντος. Διὰ Παυσανίου μῖσος (*Thuc.* 1, 96; *out of hatred towards P.*). Διδάσκαλος λόγων (= ὁ λόγους διδάσκων). Ἐπιθυμία χρημάτων. Ἐπιμέλεια τῶν πραγμάτων. Ἀμέλεια γονέων. Ἡγεμονία τῆς Ἑλλάδος. Γραφὴ φόνου (γράφεσθαι φόνου). Ἐμπειρία τῶν πολεμικῶν. Ἐγκράτεια ἡδονῆς καὶ λύπης. Εἰρήνη καὶ ἐλευθερία τῶν τοιούτων (*Pl. Rep.* 1, 329; *freedom from* —). Ἀγγείων ἀπορίᾳ (*Thuc.* 4, 4. *from lack of vessels*). Ἀφορμὴν (ἄδειαν) διδόναι τινὶ τοῦ λοιδορεῖσθαι. Ἀφορμὴ ἔργων (*Xen. Mem.* 2, 7, 11, *as a means of setting about a work*).

Rem. Sometimes an objective genitive is even used with substantives derived from verbs or adjectives which take a dative or a preposition (especially πρός, εἰς, *towards*): but if any obscurity might result from the use of the genitive, a preposition is used: Ἐμμονὴ τοῦ κακοῦ (*Pl. Gorg.* 479, from ἐμμένειν τῷ κακῷ). Πρόβλημα χειμόνων (*Pl. Tim.* 74, *a protection against*). Ἐπικούρημα τῆς χιόνος (*Xen. An.* 4, 5, 13, also πρός). Οὐ λόγων τοὺς ἀγῶνας προτίθεμεν ἀλλ' ἔργων (*Thuc.* 3, 67). Δῆλον ἐγένετο, ὅτι οὐ τῆς τῶν Ἑλλήνων εὐνοίας ἕνεκα ὁ ἡγεμὼν ἔλθοι (*Xen. An.* 4, 7, 20). Δημοσθένους φιλίᾳ καὶ Ἀθηναίων εὐνοίᾳ (*Thuc.* 7, 57; *out of friendship for D., and goodwill towards the A.*). Ἡσυχία ἐχθρῶν (*Pl. Rep.* 8, 566, *repose from* —). Sometimes the genitive is used even more harshly, instead of περί or a preposition of place: Τὸ τῶν Μεγαρέων ψήφισμα (*Thuc.* 1, 140). Ἡ τοῦ πηλοῦ ἐρώτησις (*Pl. Theaet.* 147). Μετὰ τὴν τῆς Αἰτωλίας ξυμφοράν (*Thuc.* 3, 114, = τὴν ἐν τῇ Αἰτωλίᾳ). Ἀπόστασις τῶν Ἀθηναίων (*Thuc.* 8, 5, = ἀπὸ τῶν Ἀθ.).

§ 49. (282) *a*) In the genitive (*g. definitivus*) is sometimes added that in which the generic notion expressed by the governing word is in a special manner contained and denominated (but usually only the genitive of an infinitive): Ἡ τοῦ χαίρειν διάθεσις (*Pl. Phil.* 11, *the affection, or mood, of rejoicing*), ἡ τοῦ πείθειν τέχνη (*Pl. Phil.* 58). Ἀμαθία αὕτη ἡ ἐπονείδιστος ἡ τοῦ οἴεσθαι εἰδέναι, ἃ οὐκ οἶδεν (*Pl. Apol.* 29, *that of conceiting oneself to know* —) [1].

(283) *b*) The genitive with words signifying a measure, number, or quantity, denotes the kind, the thing measured or numbered (g. generis): Πλῆθος ἀνθρώπων οὐ σμικρόν, βοῶν ἀγέλη, οἴνου δέκα ἀμφορεῖς, μέδιμνος σίτου, ἅμαξαι σίτου (*Xen. Cyr.* 2, 4, 18, *wagon-loads of corn*), τριάκοντα μυριάδες στρατιᾶς (*Xen. An.* 1, 4, 5), τριακόσια τάλαντα φόρου (*Thuc.* 2, 13, *in taxes*). Ἦν τι στασιασμοῦ ἐν τῇ πόλει (*Thuc.* 4, 130). (Rarely with a neuter adjective as substantive: Ἀμήχανον

[1] Τὸ ὄνομα ὁ Μακάρτατος, *the name M.* (*Dem.* 43, 77). Τὸ τοῦ πατρὸς ἐμοῦ ὄνομα Σωσίαν τῷ υἱῷ ἐθέμην (*Dem.* 43, 74). (In apposition, not in the genitive. Very rarely τῷ ὄρει τῆς Ἰστώνης, *Thuc.* 4, 46, instead of τῷ ὄρει τῇ Ἰστώνῃ, see in § 13, R. Ἰλίου πτολίεθρον, poetic.)

εὐδαιμονίας, Pl. Apol. 41; *something inconceivably great in the way of blessedness; inconceivable happiness.* [§ 49.] Ἀθηναῖοι ἐπὶ μέγα ἐχώρησαν δυνάμεως, *Thuc.* 1, 118. Ἐπὶ πλεῖστον ἀνθρώπων, *Thuc.* 1, 1.) (Ἅλις τούτων.)

Rem. 1. Especially we may remark the expression ἐν παντὶ κακοῦ (ἀθυμίας, etc.) εἶναι (ἐς πᾶν κακοῦ ἀφικνεῖσθαι).

Rem. 2. In like manner, a genitive is appended to adverbs (especially πῶς, ὡς, and ὅπως. ὡσαύτως. εὖ, καλῶς, κακῶς, ἱκανῶς) with the verb ἔχω, in the sense *am qualified, disposed, provided, in regard of—, find myself in point of—, have a certain measure of—:* Πῶς ἔχεις δόξης τοῦ τοιοῦδε πέρι; (*Pl. Rep.* 5, 456.) Πελοποννήσιοι ἔπλεον, ὡς εἶχε τάχους ἕκαστος (*Thuc.* 2, 90). Ἆρ' οὖν οὗτος ἱκανῶς ἐπιστήμης ἕξει; (*Pl. Phil.* 62.) Συμμέτρως λεπτότητος ἔχειν καὶ πάχους (*Pl. Tim.* 85). (Ὡς ποδῶν εἶχον, *as fast as my legs would carry me*, τάχιστα. *Hdt.* 6, 116.) (Ἡ Κέρκυρα τῆς Ἰταλίας καὶ Σικελίας καλῶς παράπλου κεῖται, *Thuc.* 1, 36; *lies exceedingly well for the voyage to S.*) In Hdt. and the poets also, Πῶς ἀγῶνος ἥκομεν; εὖ ἥκειν χρημάτων, etc. (always without article.)

a) The genitive stands with words which denote a *part* of some- § 50.
thing, in order to assign the whole (*g. partitivus*). In this manner (284)
the genitive is governed by substantives and words used substantively, (pronouns, numerals, adjectives, and participles with the article, the article with an adverb or with a preposition and its case), by superlatives and by verbs involving the signification of the superlative: Μέρος τι (τὰ δύο μέρη) τῆς στρατιᾶς. Τῶν γερόντων τις. Ἐν ἐνίαις τῶν πόλεων. Τῶν πολιτῶν οἱ μὲν ἀπώλοντο, οἱ δὲ ἔφυγον. Δέκα (πολλοὶ) τῶν στρατιωτῶν. Ὁ τέταρτος τῶν παίδων. Οἱ δεινότατοι τῶν ῥητόρων. Τὰ καλὰ τῶν ζώων, οἱ σπουδαῖοι τῶν γονέων (*Isocr. Dem.* 11). Οἱ χρηστοὶ τῶν ἀνθρώπων (*Arist. Pl.* 490). Ἐπὶ πολὺ τῆς χώρας (*Thuc.* 4, 3, *over a great part of the land*). Ἀθηναίων ὁ βουλόμενος. Ὅ,τι περ ὄφελος ἦν τοῦ στρατεύματος (*Xen. Hell.* 5, 3, 6). Τὸ καταντικρὺ αὐτῶν τοῦ σπηλαίου (*Pl. Rep.* 7, 515, *the part of the cavern facing them*). Οἱ πολλοὶ χαίρουσι καὶ τῶν ἐδεσμάτων καὶ τῶν ἐπιτηδευμάτων τοῖς καὶ τὸ σῶμα καὶ τὴν ψυχὴν βλάπτουσιν (*Isocr. Pac.* 109). Σύμβουλος ἀγαθὸς χρησιμώτατον ἁπάντων τῶν κτημάτων ἐστίν (*Isocr. Nicocl.* 53). Μόνος πάντων φρονεῖς. Ὀρθότατα ἀνθρώπων λέγεις (*Pl. Theæt.* 195). Ἡ ναῦς ἄριστα ἔπλει παντὸς τοῦ στρατοπέδου (*Lys.* 21, 6). Οἱ παλαιότατοι τῶν Ἀθηναίων πρόγονοι τῶν καθ' ἑαυτοὺς ἀνθρώπων ἠρίστευσαν (*Xen. Mem.* 3, 5, 10).—Τῷ ὁρῶμεν ἡμῶν αὐτῶν τὰ ὁρώμενα; (*Pl. Rep.* 6, 507; *with what part of ourselves —?*) Ἐν τοιούτῳ τῆς οἰκίας, ὅπου πλειστάκις ὁ δεσπότης ὄψεται (*Xen. Hipp.* 4, 1; *in such a part of the house —*). Οἱ Ἀθηναῖοι ἐν τούτῳ παρασκευῆς ἦσαν (*Thuc.* 2, 17).—Εἰς τοῦτό τινες ἀνοίας ἐληλύθασιν (*Isocr. Pac.* 31). Εἰς τοσοῦτο ἀμαθίας ἥκω (*Pl. Apol.* 25).

[§ 50.] Rem. 1. We must note the different positions of the words, when the partitive genitive is governed by a participle with the article which has with it other definitions (case, adverbs, etc.): Οἱ Ἀρκάδων ἡμέτεροι ὄντες ξύμμαχοι (*Thuc.* 5, 64, *those of the Arc. who* —). Αἱ ἄριστα τῶν νεῶν πλέουσαι (*Thuc.* 1, 48). Οἱ ξυμπροθυμηθέντες τῶν ῥητόρων τὸν ἔκπλουν (*Thuc.* 8, 1).

Rem. 2. With numbers or words of number (μόνος, ὀλίγοι) now and then ἀπό. ἐξ are added, especially to denote that which is drawn off from, or remains: Ἄγνων ἀπὸ τετρακισχιλίων ὁπλιτῶν χιλίους καὶ πεντήκοντα τῇ νόσῳ ἀπώλεσεν (*Thuc.* 2, 58). Ἐκ τριῶν ἕν ἂν εἱλόμην (*Soph. Tr.* 734, *I should have chosen one of three*).

Rem. 3. Instead of the neuter singular of an adjective denoting magnitude (πολύς, etc.), or a certain part (e. g. ἥμισυς, λοιπός) with a partitive genitive, in Greek the adjective often takes the gender of the genitive: Ὁ ἥμισυς, ὁ λοιπὸς τοῦ χρόνου. Εὐκτήμων ἐβίω ἔτη ἓξ καὶ ἐνενήκοντα, τούτου δὲ τοῦ χρόνου τὸν πλεῖστον ἐδόκει εὐδαίμων εἶναι (*Isæ.* 6, 18). Κῦρος κατενόει πολλὴν τῆς χώρας τοῖς Ἀρμενίοις ἔρημον καὶ ἀργὸν οὖσαν διὰ τὸν πόλεμον (*Xen. Cyr.* 3, 2, 2). (Rarely with other adjectives: Τῆς γῆς ἡ ἀρίστη, *Thuc.* 1, 2.)

Rem. 4. Sometimes a general subject (or object) is put first, and then instead of the partitive genitive, we have, by way of apposition, a partition with pronouns or words of number (e. g. οἱ μὲν — οἱ δέ, etc.) or a limitation (οἱ πολλοί, *partly* —, *partly* —, *for the most part*): Οἱ τῇ φιλοσοφίᾳ μεμφόμενοι λέγουσι, ὅτι οἱ ξυνόντες αὐτῇ οἱ μὲν οὐδενὸς ἄξιοι, οἱ δὲ πολλοὶ πολλῶν κακῶν ἄξιοί εἰσιν (*Pl. Rep.* 6, 495). Οἶδα ἀδελφούς, οἳ τὰ ἴσα λαχόντες ὁ μὲν αὐτῶν τἀρκοῦντα ἔχει, ὁ δὲ τοῦ παντὸς ἐνδεῖται (*Xen. Conv.* 4, 35). Πελοποννήσιοι καὶ οἱ ξύμμαχοι, τὰ δύο μέρη, ἐνέβαλον ἐς τὴν Ἀττικήν (*Thuc.* 2, 47). Οἱ ἐναντίοι τοῖς Λακεδαιμονίοις δεξιὸν μὲν κέρας οἱ Μαντινεῖς εἶχον, παρὰ δ' αὐτοῖς οἱ ξύμμαχοι Ἀρκάδων ἦσαν, ἔπειτα Ἀργείων οἱ χίλιοι λογάδες (*Thuc.* 5, 67). Cf. § 5, ἕκαστος and ἄλλος ἄλλο.

b) A partitive genitive is also governed by an adverb of place or time, denoting a point in and of the whole: Ἐξάγγελλε τοῖς πολεμίοις, ἡμᾶς παρασκευάζεσθαι ἐμβαλεῖν που τῆς ἐκείνων χώρας (*Xen. Cyr.* 6, 1, 42). Οὐκ οἶσθα, ὅπου γῆς εἶ (*Pl. Rep.* 3, 403). Πανταχοῦ τῆς γῆς, οὐδαμοῦ γῆς. (Οὐ βλέπεις, ἵν' εἶ κακοῦ. *Soph. (Ed. R.* 413.) Ἄλλοι ἄλλῃ τῆς πόλεως ἀπώλλυντο (*Thuc.* 2, 4). Οἱ ἄλλοι, ὅσοι ἐνταῦθα ἦλθον ἡλικίας (*Pl. Rep.* 1, 329). Οἱ ἄνω τοῦ γένους (*Pl. Legg.* 9, 378, *those higher up in the race*, i. e. *the ancestors*), ἐγγύτατα γένους (*Isæ.* 3, 64). Πόρρω σοφίας ἐλαύνειν (*Pl. Euthyphr.* 4, *a long way into* —). Πόρρω τῶν νυκτῶν, πρωῒ τῆς ἡμέρας, ὀψὲ τῆς ὥρας. Πηνίκα τῆς ἡμέρας; (*Arist. Ares* 1498; *at what time of day?*)

§ 51. (284, R. 1) A partitive genitive not unfrequently stands in Greek without an expressly governing word, in the following cases:

a) When to an indefinite substantive (without article) there is added the mention of a special sort, by an adjective or participle: Ἔρχεται ὀρχηστρὶς τῶν τὰ θαύματα δυναμένων ποιεῖν (*Xen. Symp.* 2, 1, *a dancing-girl, of those who* —). Παταγύας, ἀνὴρ Πέρσης τῶν ἀμφὶ Κῦρον πιστῶν (*Xen. An.* 1, 8, 1. Similarly: Ἀνὴρ τῶν ῥητόρων, *Arist. Eq.* 423. Ἄνδρες τῶν φυλάκων, *Thuc.* 6, 43. Ἀνήρ almost merely = τίς).

b) When to the whole expressed in the genitive there is immediately annexed the special name of the individual (not a general class-notion): Τῆς Ἰταλίας Λοκροὶ μὲν [§ 51.] Συρακουσίων ἦσαν, Ῥηγῖνοι δέ, κατὰ τὸ ξυγγενές, Λεοντίνων (*Thuc.* 3, 86, *of Italy, in It., of the Italian cities*). Οἱ Δωριῆς ἡμῶν (*Thuc.* 4, 61, = οἱ Δωριῆς ὄντες ἡμῶν). Λακεδαιμόνιοι τῶν περιοίκων (*Thuc.* 4, 53, *Lac. of the class of the Periœci*). Especially in this manner is used the genitive of a country (a place) with the name of a single point in it: Παραλαβόντες Βοιωτοὺς καὶ Φωκέας Ἀθηναῖοι ἐστράτευσαν τῆς Θεσσαλίας ἐπὶ Φάρσαλον (*Thuc.* 1, 111, *to Ph. in Th.*). Οἱ Ἀθηναῖοι ὡρμίσαντο τῆς Χερρονήσου ἐν Ἐλεοῦντι (*Xen. Hell.* 2, 1, 10). (The genitive here has always the article, the governing word never, the place in itself less known being referred to the well-known country.)

c) With the verbs *εἶναι, γίγνεσθαι, to be, become, one of* — (i. e. *to belong to* —), and after all verbs denoting the being in one or another way received into a class, counting or being counted with a class. But with *εἶναι, γίγνεσθαι*, and sometimes with other verbs, *εἷς* may be prefixed to the genitive, e. g. Κριτίας τῶν τριάκοντα ἦν (*Xen. Mem.* 1, 2, 31, *one of the thirty tyrants*). Τῶν Ἀλκμαιονιδῶν εἶναι (*Dem.* 21, 144). Ἐξῆν Εὐκράτει τῶν τριάκοντα γενέσθαι (*Lys.* 18, 5). Ἔστι τῶν αἰσχρῶν, μᾶλλον δὲ τῶν αἰσχίστων τοὺς ξυμμάχους φαίνεσθαι προδιδόντα (*Dem.* 2, 2. So ἔστι τῶν λυσιτελούντων, τῶν ἀδίκων, τῶν καλῶν, nearly = *αἰσχρόν, ἄδικον*, etc.). But also Ἔστιν ἓν τῶν αἰσχρῶν, *Isocr. Arch.* 97; ἔστι τῶν φαύλων τι, *Pl. Rep.* 10, 603; ἔν τι τῶν αἰσχρῶν ἐστιν, *Dem.* 20, 135. Τῶν εἰς τὴν πόλιν ἀνηλωκότων τὴν οὐσίαν εἷς ἐγὼ φανήσομαι γεγενημένος (*Isocr. Call.* 62). Ὁ Θράσυλος τῶν ἐν Σικελίᾳ κατελέγη τριηράρχων (*Isæ.* 7, 5). Σόλων τῶν ἑπτὰ σοφιστῶν ἐκλήθη (*Isocr. Antid.* 235). Γράφε με τῶν ἱππεύειν ἐπιθυμούντων (*Xen. Cyr.* 4, 3, 21). Καὶ ἐμὲ θὲς τῶν πεπεισμένων (*Pl. Rep.* 4, 424). Οὐδαμοῦ πώποτε Μειδίας τῶν συγχαιρόντων ἐξητάσθη τῷ δήμῳ (*Dem.* 21, 202). Also: Αἰσχίνης τῶν ἐχθρῶν τῶν σῶν εἷς ἐξητάζετο (*Dem.* 19, 291). Μειδίας εὔχετο μὴ λαχεῖν τῶν ἐξιόντων (*Dem.* 21, 133, = στρατευσομένων).

d) With verbs which otherwise govern the accusative (especially in the sense *give* or *take*), when a certain indefinite portion (*somewhat, some*) of a whole is denoted as their object (as in English: *to eat of* this or that): Πολὺ μᾶλλον ὑμῖν προσήκει τῶν ὑμετέρων ἐμοὶ διδόναι ἢ τῶν ἐμῶν ἐμοὶ ἀμφισβητῆσαι (*Lys.* 21, 15). Ὁ Κυαξάρης λαβὼν τῶν ἐρρωμένων ἵππων τε καὶ ἀνδρῶν προσελαύνει (*Xen. Cyr.* 1, 4, 20). Ὁ Κῦρος ἔταξε Γλοῦν καὶ Πίγρητα, λαβόντας τοῦ βαρβαρικοῦ στρατοῦ, συνεκβιβάζειν τὰς ἁμάξας (*Xen. An.* 1, 5, 7). Ὅσοι ἔφαγον τῶν κηρίων, πάντες ἄφρονες ἐγίγνοντο (*Xen. An.* 4, 8, 20, *ate of the honeycombs*). Οἱ Συρακούσιοι ἐς τὸ Ὀλυμπιεῖον παρέπεμψαν φυλακήν, δείσαντες, μὴ οἱ Ἀθηναῖοι τῶν χρημάτων, ἃ ἦν αὐτόθι, κινήσωσιν (*Thuc.* 6, 70, *take of the money*). Ἀθηναῖοι ἀφίκοντο ἐς Πρασιὰς καὶ τῆς τε γῆς ἔτεμον (ἐδῄωσαν) καὶ αὐτὸ τὸ πόλισμα εἷλον (*Thuc.* 2, 56, *laid waste a part of the land.* Ibid. ἔτεμον τὴν Τροιζηνίδα γῆν and ἔτεμον τῆς γῆς τὴν πολλήν). Βρασίδας διελὼν τοῦ παλαιοῦ τείχους μίαν ἐποίησε πόλιν ἐκ δυοῖν (*Thuc.* 5, 2,
CHAP. V.]

[§ 51.] a. E; *B. made a breach in* —). Ἀνιέναι ὀργῆς, *to abate of* (*lay aside*) *his anger, Arist. Ran.* 700, and τῆς ἐφόδου, *to relax in their attack, Thuc.* 7, 43 [1].

REM. In like manner (with the notion of part and piece), it is said, ἰέναι τοῦ πρόσω (*Xen. An.* 1, 3, 1, *to go forward*), ἐπιταχύνειν τῆς ὁδοῦ τοὺς σχολαίτερον προσιόντας (*Thuc.* 4, 47, *to hasten them on their way*), προκόπτειν τινὶ τῆς ἀρχῆς (*Thuc.* 4, 60, *to further a person's progress to dominion; to pave the way to his dominion*). Κατέαγα (μέγα) τῆς κεφαλῆς (*Pl. Arist.*), *I have got a* (*great*) *hole in my head* (*somewhere in my head*), συνετρίβην τῆς κεφαλῆς (also συντρίβεσθαι τὴν κεφαλήν, *Lys.* 3, 18, by § 31).

§ 52. Two genitives may stand in different senses with the same substantive: Οἱ ἄνθρωποι διὰ τὸ αὐτῶν δέος τοῦ θανάτου καὶ τῶν κύκνων καταψεύδονται (*Pl. Phæd.* 85).
(286) Ἵππου δρόμος ἡμέρας (*Dem.* 19, 273, *a day's running of a horse*). Διὰ τὴν τοῦ ἀνέμου ἄπωσιν τῶν ναυαγίων ἐς τὸ πέλαγος (*Thuc.* 7, 34, *by the wind's drifting the wrecks out to sea*). (One genitive is governed by another: μετὰ τῆς συμμαχίας τῆς αἰτήσεως, *Thuc.* 1, 32, *together with their desire of*, or *application for, an alliance.*)

§ 53. Instead of a substantive for the governing word, a possessive genitive (§ 47) may be governed by a neuter pronoun, or by the word ἕν in the sense of something *in* or *on the part of* some person, so that the pronoun is often explained by a sentence with ὅτι annexed, or a dependent interrogative proposition: Τοῦτό μοι ἔδοξε τῶν κατηγόρων ἀναισχυντότατον εἶναι (*Pl. Apol.* 17). Μάλιστα τῶν κατηγόρων ἓν ἐθαύμασα τῶν πολλῶν, ὧν ἐψεύσαντο, τοῦτο, ἐν ᾧ ἔλεγον, ὡς χρῆν ὑμᾶς εὐλαβεῖσθαι, μὴ ὑπ' ἐμοῦ ἐξαπατηθῆτε (*Pl. Apol.* 17, *at one thing among many in them*). Ἄλλα τέ σου πολλὰ ἄγαμαι καὶ ὅτι νῦν ἅμα χαριζόμενος Καλλίᾳ καὶ παιδεύεις αὐτόν (*Xen. Conv.* 8, 12). Τὸ βραδύ, ὃ μέμφονται μάλιστα ἡμῶν, μὴ αἰσχύνεσθε (*Thuc.* 1, 84). Ἃ διώκει Αἰσχίνης τοῦ ψηφίσματος, ταῦτ' ἐστίν (*Dem.* 18, 56). With verbs denoting *to perceive* and *remark*, when such a sentence is added, the pronoun is often omitted; so that the genitive is proximately governed by the following sentence: Ἐγὼ οὔποτε ἐπαυόμην βασιλέα καὶ τοὺς σὺν αὐτῷ μακαρίζων, διαθεώμενος αὐτῶν, ὅσην μὲν χώραν καὶ οἵαν ἔχοιεν, ὡς δ' ἄφθονα τὰ ἐπιτήδεια (*Xen. An.* 3, 1, 19). Ἀγνοοῦμεν ἀλλήλων ὅ,τι λέγομεν (*Pl. Gorg.* 517, *each other's speech and meaning*). Ἐγὼ μάλιστα ἐθαύμασα Σωκράτους πρῶτον μὲν τοῦτο, ὡς εὐμενῶς τῶν νεανίσκων τὸν λόγον ἀπεδέξατο, ἔπειτα ἡμῶν ὡς ὀξέως ᾔσθετο, ὃ πεπόνθειμεν ὑπὸ τῶν λόγων (*Pl. Phæd.* 89). Καὶ πρῶτον μὲν Σωκράτης αὐτῶν (τῶν τὰ μετέωρα ἐρευνώντων) ἐσκόπει, πότερά ποτε νομίσαντες ἱκανῶς ἤδη τἀνθρώπεια εἰδέναι ἔρχονται ἐπὶ τὸ περὶ τῶν τοιούτων φροντίζειν, ἢ τἀνθρώπεια παρέντες τὰ δαιμόνια σκοποῦσιν (*Xen. Mem.* 1, 1, 12, *the first thing that he considered in them was, whether* —).

REM. From this usage of the language, or from some such way of taking the relation, it results that the poets use the genitive with the verbs *say* and *hear* in the sense *of, about*: (Τῆς μητρὸς ἥκω τῆς ἐμῆς φράσων ἐν οἷς νῦν ἔστιν, *Soph. Trach.* 1122, in what condition she is, *the state of my mother*:) and also, that in passing to a new matter, a genitive is put at the head of a sentence unconnected with the following construction, in the sense, *as touching* —: Τί δὲ ἵππων οἴει ἢ τῶν ἄλλων

---

[1] Ἐπιμίγνυσθαι ἔφασαν οἱ Πέρσαι σφῶν τε πρὸς Καρδούχους καὶ ἐκείνων πρὸς αὐτούς (*Xen. An.* 3, 5, 16. The elliptic genitive as subject). Κατεσκάφη τῶν τειχῶν τῶν μακρῶν ἐπὶ δέκα στάδια ἑκατέρου (*Lys.* 13, 8; as if it were, *of the long walls there was thrown down to the extent of ten stadia*).

ζώων; ἢ ἄλλῃ πῃ ἔχειν; (*Pl. Rep.* 5, 459.) Τί δὲ γῆς τε τμήσεως τῆς Ἑλληνικῆς καὶ οἰκιῶν ἐμπρήσεως, ποῖόν τί σοι δράσουσιν οἱ στρατιῶται πρὸς τοὺς πολεμίους (ibid. 470).

a) The genitive with *εἰμί* sometimes denotes the person or thing to § 54.
which something *belongs* and is *appropriate, becoming, suitable, competent* [is his *part, duty*, &c.]: Ἔστιν ἄρα δικαίου ἀνδρὸς βλάπτειν καὶ ὁντινοῦν ἄνθρωπον; (*Pl. Rep.* 1, 335.) Οἰκονόμου ἀγαθοῦ ἐστιν εὖ οἰκεῖν τὸν ἑαυτοῦ οἶκον (*Xen. Œc.* 1, 2). Οὐ παντὸς ἀνδρός ἐστιν ἐκλέξασθαι, ποῖα ἀγαθὰ τῶν ἡδέων ἐστὶ καὶ ὁποῖα κακά (*Pl. Gorg.* 500). Ἀπόστασις τῶν βίαιόν τι πασχόντων ἐστίν (*Thuc.* 3, 39; *takes place only in the case of those who suffer harsh treatment; is for those who* —). (Νομίσατε εἶναι τοῦ καλῶς πολεμεῖν τὸ αἰσχύνεσθαι καὶ τοῖς ἄρχουσι πείθεσθαι, *Thuc.* 5, 9. *that to the right conduct of war it is essential.*) (Εἶναι πρός τινος, see under the prep. πρός.) (290)

b) A genitive of a substantive with an adjective (pronoun or nume- (285)
ral) is either referred by *εἰμί* to a subject, or even immediately connected with a substantive, to denote its demands and consequence (what it calls for, and brings with it), its *magnitude, value*, also *age* (*descriptive genitive*): Ὡς μὲν ἐγὼ οὐκ ἀδικῶ κατὰ τὴν Μελήτου γραφήν, οὐ πολλῆς μοι δοκεῖ εἶναι ἀπολογίας (*Pl. Apol.* 28). Ταῦτα καὶ δαπάνης μεγάλης καὶ πόνων πολλῶν καὶ πραγματείας εἶναι δοκεῖ (*Dem.* 8, 48). Οὐσία τεττάρων καὶ δέκα ταλάντων (*Dem.* 27, 4). Χωρίον δέκα μνῶν (*Isæ.* 2, 35). Ἐπὶ τὸν Εὐφράτην ποταμόν, ὄντα τὸ εὖρος τεττάρων πλέθρων (*Xen. An.* 1, 4, 11. Here also without adjective, as the substantive πλέθρον in itself expresses a definite magnitude: Ποταμὸς Κέρσος ὄνομα, εὖρος πλέθρου, *Xen. An.* 1, 4, 4). Τὸ τίμημα τῆς χώρας ἑξακισχιλίων ταλάντων ἐστίν (*Dem.* 14, 19, *comes to*). Τοῦ Μαρσύου ποταμοῦ τὸ εὖρός ἐστιν εἴκοσι καὶ πέντε ποδῶν (*Xen. An.* 1, 2, 8 [1]). Μανία ἦν ἐτῶν πλέον ἢ τετταράκοντα (*Xen. Hell.* 3, 1, 14).

REM. 1. But the descriptive genitive in Greek is not used of *properties* and make or nature in general, except in one or two idioms with εἰμί. (Τούτου τοῦ τρόπου εἰμί, *Arist. Pl.* 246. Τῆς αὐτῆς γνώμης εἶναι, *Thuc.* 5, 46, τῶν αὐτῶν λόγων, *Pl. Gorg.* 482, *to keep to the same tale.*)

REM. 2. Beside πρόσοδος δυοῖν μναῖν (*Xen. Vectig.* 3, 10), we find also δύο μναῖ προσόδου by § 49, b. Likewise apposition is used: τριάκοντα μνᾶς πρόσοδον ἔχειν or τὴν πρόσοδον (*Dem.* 27, 9), by § 19, R. 2.

c) The genitive with εἰμί and γίγνεσθαι denotes the *extraction* and *birth-place*, also the *material*: Βούσιρις πατρὸς μὲν ἦν Ποσειδῶνος, μητρὸς δὲ Λιβύης (*Isocr. Bus.* 10). Πατρὸς λέγεται Κῦρος γενέσθαι Καμβύσου, μητρὸς δὲ ὁμολογεῖται Μανδάνης γενέσθαι (*Xen. Cyr.* 1, 2, 1 [2]).

---

[1] But also: Ὁ φόρος ἦν τετρακόσια τάλαντα καὶ ἑξήκοντα (*Thuc.* 1, 96). Τοῦ τείχους ἦν τὸ εὖρος πέντε καὶ εἴκοσι πόδες (*Xen. An.* 3, 4, 7).

[2] Often γίγνεσθαι ἔκ τινος. (Ἀπό τινος γίγν., *to be descended from some one.*) Poetically φῦναι, βλαστεῖν τινος.

CHAP. V.]

[§ 54.] Ἱπποκράτης ὅδε ἐστὶν Ἀπολλοδώρου υἱός, οἰκίας μεγάλης τε καὶ εὐδαίμονος (*Pl. Prot.* 316). Τίμαιος ὅδε εὐνομωτάτης ἐστὶ πόλεως τῆς ἐν Ἰταλίᾳ Λοκρίδος, οὐσίᾳ καὶ γένει οὐδενὸς ὕστερος τῶν ἐκεῖ (*Pl. Tim.* 20). Ἡ κρηπὶς (*the foundation*) ἦν λίθου ξεστοῦ κογχυλιάτου (*Xen. An.* 3, 4, 10). (Also without εἶναι and with ποιεῖν: Θεμέλιοι παντοίων λίθων, *Thuc.* 1, 93. Φοίνικος αἱ θύραι πεποιημέναι ἦσαν, *Xen. Cyr.* 7, 5, 22[1].)

§ 55. The genitive stands with the prepositions ἄνευ, ἀντί, ἀπό, ἕνεκα, ἐξ, πρό always, and with the prepositions διά, ἐπί, κατά, μετά, παρά, περί, πρός, ὑπέρ, and ὑπό in certain significations (those which spring from the conception of a *hanging together with*, and *a going forth from*; see chap. 6); also with all the adverbs which, as prepositions, serve to denote a relation to something in regard of place and space (sometimes also of time [2]); also with πλήν, *except*, λάθρᾳ (κρύφα), *privily from* (λάθρᾳ τῶν στρατιωτῶν), ἐμποδών, *in the way of* (obstructive: πολλῶν ἀγαθῶν ἀλλήλοις ἐμποδὼν γίγνεσθαι, *Xen. Cyr.* 8, 5, 24), lastly with expressions which are compounded with prepositions to denote *on a certain side of*: ἐπὶ τάδε Φασήλιδος (*Isocr. Areop.* 80), τοῦ Ἡρακλείου ἐπέκεινα (*Xen. Hell.* 5, 1, 10), τὰ πρὸς ἕω τῆς Θηβαίων πόλεως (*Xen. Hell.* 5, 4, 49; *the country to the east of Thebes*). (On χάριν, δίκην with the gen., see § 31, d. R.)

Rem. 1. With ἄγχι, ἐγγύς, and πλησίον, the poets sometimes use the dative, for the most part so that it can refer to the verb (ἐγγὺς εἶναί τινι). (Ἐγγύτερον τῷ θανάτῳ, *Xen. Cyr.* 8, 7, 21, of a similarity.) Ἑξῆς and ἐφεξῆς have also the dative, especially in connexion with εἶναι or κεῖσθαι (ἐφεξῆς κεῖσθαί τινι, *to follow immediately upon something*).

Rem. 2. How *from, out of*, is denoted by the genitive without preposition, see § 60.

§ 56. (291-293 & 259-262) The genitive stands as object with a multitude of verbs, which in their original signification, involve more or less nearly the conception of a connexion or coherence with, or a coming out (a being parted) from the same; either as principal object (sometimes with an object of reference in the dative), or as accessory definition (more remote object) along with a passive object in the accusative; e. g. Τυγχάνειν

---

[1] In Herodot. πεποιημένος ἔκ τινος and ἀπό τινος.

[2] Such adverbs are: ἄγχι, ἀγχοῦ (with its degrees of comparison, mostly poetical), ἐγγύς (with its degrees of comparison: τοῦ καιροῦ ἐγγυτέρω τοῦ τείχους διώξαντες, (*Xen. Hell.* 5, 3, 5, with the genitive of comparison, by § 64 and § 90, R. 4), πλησίον (*the same*), πόῤῥω, (poet. σχεδόν, ἑκάς, τῆλε, τηλοῦ, τηλόθε,) χωρίς, (δίχα poet.,) εἴσω, ἔξω, ἐντός, ἐκτός (with ἔξωθεν, etc.), μεταξύ, πρόσθεν, ὄπισθεν, ἐπίπροσθεν, ὕπερθεν, ἔνερθεν (poet.), ἔνθεν καὶ ἔνθεν, ἀμφοτέρωθεν, ἑκατέρωθεν, πέρα, πέραν (καταντιπέρας), ἐναντίον (ἄντα, ἀντίον poet. [ἐνώπιον]), καταντικρύ (ἀντικρύ), εὐθύ (ἰθύς), ἄχρις, μέχρις (in later writers ἕως), ἑξῆς, ἐφεξῆς.

τοῦ σκοποῦ, ἅπτεσθαι τῆς χειρός, τοῦ πράγματος, ἐπιθυμεῖν εἰρήνης, ἐρᾶν φρονήσεως, μετέχειν τῶν ἀγαθῶν, μεταδιδόναι τοῖς ἄλλοις τῶν ἀγαθῶν, ἐπιμελεῖσθαι τῶν πραγμάτων, ἄρχειν τῶν Ἑλλήνων, παύειν τινὰ ὕβρεως, αἰτιᾶσθαί τινα τῶν ἐν τῷ πολέμῳ πραχθέντων, καταγιγνώσκειν φυγήν τινος (*to condemn a man to exile*). [§ 56.]

Rem. 1. In some such verbs the construction is somewhat variable in consequence of a different view of the meaning; for particular instances of this, the Lexicon must be consulted. Some verbs have the genitive in some one special sense, but otherwise have different constructions.

Rem. 2. Although the genitive does not denote an object passively recipient of the action, yet verbs which govern a genitive (as principal object, not as secondary definition along with an accusative) are sometimes predicated in the passive of a subject which, in the active, would stand in the genitive: Νικήρατος ἐρῶν τῆς γυναικὸς ἀντερᾶται (*Xen. Conv.* 8, 3). Ἀσκεῖται ἀεὶ τὸ τιμώμενον, ἀμελεῖται δὲ τὸ ἀτιμαζόμενον (*Pl. Rep.* 8, 551. Ἀμελεῖν τινος). Ὅστις ἄρχεται ὑπὸ τῶν διὰ τοῦ σώματος ἡδονῶν, οὐκ ἐλεύθερός ἐστιν (*Xen. Mem.* 4, 5, 3. Ἄρχειν τινός); especially those compounded with κατά (§ 59), as κατακρίνεσθαι, καταφρονεῖσθαι, καταγελᾶσθαι, e. g. Ἐπειδάν τις ἐγγὺς ᾖ τοῦ οἴεσθαι τελευτήσειν, οἱ λεγόμενοι μῦθοι περὶ τῶν ἐν Ἅιδου, καταγελώμενοι τέως, τότε δὴ στρέφουσιν αὐτοῦ τὴν ψυχήν, μὴ ἀληθεῖς ὦσιν (*Pl. Rep.* 1, 330). Ἰσμηνίας κατεψηφίσθη καὶ ἀποθνήσκει (*Xen. Hell.* 5, 2, 36, from καταψηφίζομαι, deponent middle).

a) The genitive is governed by the verbs which involve the conception of attaching to, and adherence to a thing; viz. such as mean *to seize* or *lay hold by* or *upon*, *to hold to*, *catch at*, *get to* (hit), *aim at*, and *be studious of*, *crave*, *be in need of*, *lay claim to*, *be* or *make partaker of*, *fill with*, *be full of* and *rich in*, *make a beginning of*: thus, λαμβάνομαι (in the middle), ἐπιλαμβάνομαι, ἀντιλαμβάνομαι, συλλαμβάνομαι, ἔχομαι, ἀντέχομαι (also figuratively, e. g. ἐπιλαμβάνομαι τοῦ νόμου, *lay hold upon and find fault with*, τὰ τούτων ἐχόμενα, *what hangs together with these and borders thereon*)[1], ἅπτομαι, καθάπτομαι, ψαύω, θιγγάνω, — ὀρέγομαι, στοχάζομαι, τυγχάνω (*hit* — *attain*, *get*), ἐφικνοῦμαι, ἐξικνοῦμαι (κυρῶ). — ἐπιθυμῶ, ἐρῶ[2], ἐφίεμαι, γλίχομαι, (διψῶ, *thirst after*, ἐλευθερίας), — δεῖ (μοι, *I need*), δέομαι (τινός, of a person: *I beg of some one*), προσδέομαι (χρῄζω)[3], ἐλλείπει (μοι, *I have lack of*). — ἀντιποιοῦμαι (τῆς ἀρχῆς τινι, *contest the government with some one*), μεταποιοῦμαι, ἀμφισβητῶ (τινός τινι), προσήκει (μοι τῆς ἀρχῆς, *I have a right to*, *have to do with* —), μετέχω, μεταλαγχάνω, μεταλαμβάνω, μέτεστι (τινός μοι), μεταδίδωμι[4], κοινωνῶ (τινός τινι), συναίρομαι (τινὶ τοῦ κιν- § 57.

---

[1] The actives λαμβάνω, *take* (not *take by*), ἔχω, *hold*, *have*, govern the accusative.

[2] But φιλῶ τινα, as it does not express desire.

[3] Πολλοῦ δέω, ὀλίγου δέω, *I am far from* —, *within a little of* —, ὀλίγου δεῖ, *it wants little of*, or *but that* —. Τριακοστὸν ἔτος ἑνὸς δέον, not δέοντος, i. e. *the twenty-ninth year*; δυοῖν δέοντες πεντήκοντα ἄνδρες, *forty-eight men*. (Ὀκτὼ ἀποδέοντες τριακόσιοι, *Thuc.* 4, 38; ὀκτώ as genitive.) (Ὀλίγου, μικροῦ without δεῖ, adverbially: *within a little*, *almost*, *nearly*.)

[4] Μετέχω, μεταλαμβάνω μέρος, μέτεστί μοι μέρος, as the genitive denotes the whole, of which the person has part. Λαγχάνω τι, *obtain by lot*; in the poets also τινός.

[§ 57.] δύνου)[1], κληρονομῶ (τῆς οὐσίας), ἀπολαύω[2], γεύομαι (μέλιτος, μαθήματος, γεύω τοὺς
(259) παῖδας αἵματος), ἐμφοροῦμαι, ὀσφραίνομαι, — πίμπλημι (ἐμπ., ἀναπ.), πληρῶ, πλήθω, γέμω, εὐπορῶ, πλουτῶ, — ἄρχω (ὑπάρχω, κατάρχω), ἄρχομαι[3], and other more special expressions.

(260) Rem. The verbs *to take, to hold*, have also the genitive of the part by which one lays hold: Οἱ παρόντες ἔλαβον τῆς ζώνης τὸν Ὀρόντην (*Xen. An.* 1, 6, 10). Καί μου ἐλάβετο τῆς χειρὸς ὁ Ἀδείμαντος (*Pl. Parm.* 126, *took me by the hand*). So ἕλκειν τινὰ ποδῶν (*by the feet*), and the like.

b) Further, the verbs which convey the notion of removal from and depriving of: viz. such as *to give up* (*one's claim to*), *forego, miss of, be* and *make far from, shut out of, hinder of, deprive of, begrudge, free from, lack, refrain from* (*spare*), *desist from, make an end of*, together with *be different from*; thus, ἀφίεμαι, μεθίεμαι (τινός)[4].—ἀποτυγχάνω, ἁμαρτάνω, σφάλλομαι, ψεύδομαι (ἀπολείπομαι τῶν καιρῶν). — ἀπέχω, διέχω, χωρίζω, ἀφίστημι (Ὀρχομενίους Θηβαίων, *move them to revolt from the Th.*, ἀφίστασθαι Θηβαίων),— εἴργω (τινὰ τῆς διόδου), ἴσχω, κωλύω (ἐναντιοῦμαί τινί τινος), στερῶ, ἀποστερῶ (τινά τινος)[5], φθονῶ (γυμνῶ, μονῶ, *strip, make deserted*, i. e. *bereave of*; καταλύω τινὰ τῆς ἀρχῆς), ἐλευθερῶ, ἀπαλλάττω (τινὰ κακῶν, ἀπαλλάττομαι πόνων), ἀφίημι, ἀπολύω (τινὰ τῆς αἰτίας). — ἀπέχομαι, φείδομαι, — εἴκω, ὑπείκω, παραχωρῶ (τινί τινος), ὑποχωρῶ, ἐξίσταμαι (τῆς οὐσίας, τοῦ φρονεῖν), (ἐξανίσταμαι, ὑπανίσταμαί τινι ἕδρας), — παύω (τινὰ τῆς ἐπιθυμίας, παύομαι τῆς ἐπ.), ἐπέχω (τοῦ λόγου, ὑφίεμαι τοῦ μέγα φρονεῖν), — διαφέρω, διέστηκα, and other more special phrases (e. g. λωφῶ ὀδύνης, *feel myself relieved of*), or such as are used in a more free sense by the poets (e. g. ἀτιμάζειν τινὰ ὧν δεῖται, *Soph. Œd. Col.* 49, *to refuse a person something, and count him unworthy of it*, πεφευγέναι νόσου, *Soph. Phil.* 1011).

Rem. In different verbs the sense which requires the genitive, results from their composition with ἀπό, or ἐξ, thus (besides the verbs above given) in ἀπελαύνω, ἀποτρέπω (τινὰ τῆς ἀλαζονείας), ἀποπηδῶ (Σωκράτους, *Xen. Mem.* 1, 2, 16, *desert him suddenly*), ἐκβαίνω (τῆς ἐμαυτοῦ ἰδέας), ἐκβάλλω (τινὰ τιμῆς), ἐκδιαιτῶμαι (τῶν καθεστώτων νομίμων, *Thuc.* 1, 132), ἐξίστημι (τινὰ τοῦ φρονεῖν, ἐξίσταμαι τῆς ἀρχῆς), ἐκλύω (τινὰ ἀπορίας). Where the local notion *from, out*, is prominent, we have (both in these compounds, and in other verbs) ἀπό or ἐξ, e. g. Ἡ ψυχὴ ἀπὸ τοῦ σώματος χωρίζεται. Αἱ ὄχθαι τρία πλέθρα ἀπὸ τοῦ ποταμοῦ ἀπεῖχον (*Xen. An.* 4, 35). Ἀπαλλάττειν τινὰ ἐκ πόνων. (Ἐλευθεροῦν, ἀπαλλάττειν τινὰ ἀπὸ Μήδων, of persons.)

§ 58 *a*) Further, the genitive is governed by the verbs which denote
(291) *being careful* or *neglectful of, mindful* or *forgetful of* (the conception being, that the mind is directed to something), as ἐπιμελοῦμαι, μέλει μοι, μεταμέλει μοι (*it repents me of*), φροντίζω, κήδομαι, ἐντρέπομαι (*have a care of, regard for*), προνοῶ, προορῶ, ἀμελῶ, ὀλιγωρῶ, — μέμνημαι, ἐπιμέμνημαι, λανθάνομαι, ἐπιλανθάνομαι, ἀναμιμνήσκω (τινά τινος), sometimes ἐνθυμοῦμαι (usually with the accusative), and the verb πειρῶμαι (πειρῶ), *attempt*.

---

[1] Also συναίρομαι τὸν κίνδυνον, *share the danger*.
[2] Also ἀπολαύω ἀγαθόν (φλαῦρόν) τί τινος.
[3] Ἄρχομαι ἀπό τινος, *begin with, at something*.
[4] But ἀφίημι, μεθίημί τινα, *let a person go, set him at liberty*.
[5] Also ἀποστερῶ τινά τι, § 25.

Rem. 1. The constructions μέλει μοι, φροντίζω περί τινος also occur. (Μέλει μοι ταῦτα, personally. Ἑορταὶ καὶ χοροὶ πᾶσι μέλουσιν, *Pl. Legg.* 8, 835.) [§ 58.]

Rem. 2. Μέμνημαι has also the accusative (*bear in mind and know*: τοὺς ἀδικοῦντας); ἀναμιμνήσκω two accusatives (§ 25). Μνημονεύω has usually the accusative.

Rem. 3. After the same analogy, the genitive is sometimes found also with αἰσθάνομαι, have a perception of (by the senses, e. g. κραυγῆς), and ἀκούω, *hear to* (e. g. τῶν Σειρήνων), different from ἀκούω τινός, *hear from a person*, § 60. Ἀκούω τινὸς διαλεγομένου, *I hear some one speaking.*

b) Likewise the verbs which signify *to be leader* and *ruler of*, as ἄρχω, ἡγοῦμαι, κρατῶ, βασιλεύω, δεσπόζω, προστατῶ, τυραννεύω, στρατηγῶ, ἡγεμονεύω, and the verb ἀκούω (κλύω) in the signification *obey* (and ἀνηκουστῶ)[1].

Rem. Ἡγοῦμαί τινι, *am leader to a person, show him the way*, κρατῶ τινα, *overcome a person* (μάχῃ). In the poets, the verbs of *ruling* have also the dative. As ἀκούω, so ὑπακούω occurs with the genitive (usually with the dative).

a) The genitive stands with various verbs which are compounded with a preposition governing the genitive, as the object of the relation denoted by the preposition, either alone, or with an object-accusative; especially (besides the verbs with ἀπό and ἐξ, § 57 b, R.) those compounds with κατά which denote an action *directed to*, or *against a person*, e. g. καταγελῶ, καταφρονῶ, καταβοῶ (τῶν στρατηγῶν, *cry out against the generals, in accusation or complaint*), καταντλῶ (γελωτά τινος), καταχέω, καταπροίξομαι, καταψεύδομαι, καθυβρίζω. In those which denote accusation and condemnation (κατηγορῶ, καταγιγνώσκω, καταδικάζω, κατακρίνω, καταψηφίζομαι), the offence or the punishment stands as object in the accusative: κατηγορεῖν ἀδικίαν, μωρίαν τινός (literally, *to charge injustice against a person*), so that the Greek construction is often the converse of the English. Ὅταν του καταγνῶτε ἱεροσυλίαν ἢ κλοπήν, οὐ πρὸς τὸ μέγεθος ὧν ἂν λάβωσι, τὴν τιμωρίαν ποιεῖσθε, ἀλλ' ὁμοίως ἁπάντων θάνατον κατακρίνετε (*Isocr. in Loch.* 6). (Καταψηφίζεσθαι δειλίαν, θάνατόν τινος.) In the passive: Τά μου ψευδῆ κατηγορημένα (*Pl. Apol.* 18). Ὁ κατεψηφισμένος ἡμῶν θάνατος. (Πολλὴν δυστυχίαν καταγιγνώσκειν τινός, *to pronounce a person to be very unfortunate.*) § 59.

b) Further, in some verbs compounded with πρό and ὑπέρ (partly in their proper signification, partly with the sense of a preference or advantage), e. g. προτιθέναι προοίμιον τοῦ λόγου (*Pl. Legg.* 4, 723, *prefix*), προτιμᾶν σωτηρίαν κέρδους (*Ant.* 2, β. 5), προέχειν τινός τινι (*to surpass a person in something*), ὑπερέχειν σκιάδειόν τινος (*Arist. Aves*, 1508), ὑπερφρονεῖν τινος (*to look down upon*), ὑπερέχειν πάντων κάλλει καὶ μεγέθει.

---

[1] In Herodotus also πείθομαί τινος.

[§ 59.] Rem. Ὑπερορῶ, *I overlook, look down upon*, and ὑπεραίρω, ὑπερβάλλω, *surpass*, have the accusative. In the proper signification, the preposition is usually repeated.

c) With ἐπιβαίνω, *set foot upon*, e.g. τῆς Λακωνικῆς. (Ἐπιβαίνω ἐπὶ τὴν ναῦν, *go on board the ship*.)

§ 60. *a*) With the verbs *to hear, learn, ask*, the name of the person *from whom* the thing is heard, &c., is sometimes put in the genitive: Ὑμεῖς ἐμοῦ ἀκούσεσθε πᾶσαν τὴν ἀλήθειαν (*Pl. Apol.* 17). Ἄγγελος οὐδεὶς πάρεστιν, ὅτου πευσόμεθα τἀκεῖ πράγματα (*Arist. Aves* 1120). It is more usual, however (except with πυνθάνομαι), to add παρά (πρός, ἐξ).

Rem. 1. Ἀποδέχομαί τινος, properly *accept from some one and approve of*, e.g. Μὴ ταῦτα ἀποδέχεσθε Ἀγοράτου (*Lys.* 13, 83). Οὐκ ἀποδέξομαί σου, ἐὰν τοιαῦτα φλυαρῇς (*Pl. Rep.* 1, 337), then usually with participle annexed (ἀποδέχομαί τινος λέγοντος): *accept willingly, approve that* (prop. *while, if*) *a person does so and so* [1].

Rem. 2. Ὄζω μύρου, *smell of perfume* (with the accompanying notion of fulness). Τῆς κεφαλῆς ὄζω μύρου (*Arist. Eccl.* 524), *in the head* (*from the head*).

Rem. 3. The poets put passive verbs with the genitive, in the sense *of, from* (Ἂν ᾖ θέλουσα, πάντ' ἐμοῦ κομίζεται, *Soph. Œd. R.* 580, *what she will*), especially participles, denoting extraction or origin, e.g. φύς, τραφείς τινος. (Cf. § 54, c.)

(269) (275, R. 3) Rem. 4. The poets sometimes use with verbs which in general denote a motion, the genitive of the place from which the motion commences: Δόμων ὁρῶ Χρυσόθεμιν ἐντάφια χεροῖν φέρουσαν (*Soph. El.* 324). Παῖδας γῆς ἐλᾶν Κορινθίας (*Eur. Med.* 70, *out of*—). The more ancient language had for this sense the particular termination θεν, which has remained in local adverbs (cf. the *Accidence*). (Also ἐξ οὐρανόθεν.)

§ 61. (293) *a*) A genitive stands with verbs and phrases, denoting crimination and impeachment of a person, or conviction and condemnation, to denote the matter of the crimination (charge, &c.), e.g. Γράφομαι Φίλιππον φόνου, as with αἰτιῶμαι (also αἰτιῶμαι τοὺς θεοὺς τῶν ἀγαθῶν), ἐπαιτιῶμαι, διώκω, εἰσάγω, ὑπάγω, γράφομαι, αἱρῶ (τινὰ φόνου, κλοπῆς), ἐπέξειμι (τινὶ φόνου), δίκην λαγχάνω (or simply λαγχάνω), δικάζομαι (τινὶ κλήρου, *go to law with a person because of an inheritance*), φεύγω, ἁλίσκομαι, ὀφλισκάνω (ἀσεβείας). (Ἀπολύω, ἀφίημί τινα τῆς αἰτίας, § 57, b [2].)

Rem. 1. With some of these verbs the name of the *punishment* also stands in the genitive: Ὑπάγω τινὰ θανάτου. Κρίνομαι θανάτου (*am upon my trial for life and death*, but also περὶ θανάτου, *Xen. Hell.* 5, 5, 25). (Τιμῶ τινι τῶν ἐσχάτων. Τιμᾶταί μοι ὁ κατήγορος θανάτου, *lays the punishment at, demands that death be the punishment*.)

---

[1] In like manner ἀνέχομαί τινος ποιοῦντός τι, *put up with, tolerate that* (prop. when) *a person does so and so*. Hence with gen. alone, ἀνέχομαί τινος.

[2] The conception on which the genitive rests, seems to be either that of a bringing under a certain notion (on account of, under the head of), or, of a direction to something (that to which the charge comes).

REM. 2. On the verbs compounded with *κατά*, see § 59, a. *'Οφλισκάνω* stands [§ 61.] also with the accusative of the things one is accounted guilty of, and of the punishment: *'Ωφλήκασι μοχθηρίαν καὶ ἀδικίαν* (*Pl. Apol.* 39), *ὀφλεῖν χιλίας δραχμάς*, *ὀφλεῖν γέλωτα*. (*'Εγκαλεῖν τινι ἀδικίαν*.)

b) With some verbs and phrases denoting to *praise* or *count happy*, to *compassionate* or *take revenge for*, the object on account of which one is praised or pitied, or revenge is taken, stands in the genitive: Εὐδαιμονίζω σε τοῦ τρόπου (*Pl. Crit.* 43). Νῦν ἔξεστι Λακεδαιμονίους πάντων, ὧν πεποιήκασιν ἡμᾶς, τιμωρήσασθαι (*Xen. Hell.* 6, 4, 19); so with *ἄγαμαι, εὐδαιμονίζω, μακαρίζω, ζηλῶ, οἰκτείρω, ἀμύνομαι, τιμωροῦμαι.* (With an adjective: *Εὐδαίμων μοι ἀνὴρ ἐφαίνετο τοῦ τρόπου*, *Pl. Phæd.* 58.)

REM. 1. Occasionally some other verbs of kindred meaning are thus used, e. g. *συγγιγνώσκω τινὶ τῆς ἐπιθυμίας* (*Pl. Euthyd.* 306; as *τιμωροῦμαι*, otherwise *συγγιγνώσκειν τῇ ἐπιθυμίᾳ τινός*). *Λακεδαιμόνιοι ὠργίζοντο Θηβαίοις τῆς ἀντιλήψεως τῆς τοῦ 'Απόλλωνος δεκάτης* (*Xen. Hell.* 3, 5, 5). The poets use this genitive with all verbs which denote praise, blame, or anger at something, e. g. *πατρὶ μηνίσας φόνου* (*Soph. Ant.* 1177). Verbs of *wondering* are also found with a single genitive of the person wondered at: *Θαυμάζω τῶν ὑπὲρ τῆς ἰδίας δόξης ἀποθνήσκειν ἐθελόντων, ὑπὲρ δὲ τῆς κοινῆς μὴ τὴν αὐτὴν γνώμην ἐχόντων* (*Isocr. Archid.* 93).

REM. 2. In the same manner the genitive is used in crying out at something, with an adjective, an interjection, or alone: *Σχετλία τόλμης* (*Eur. Alc.* 741). *Φεῦ τοῦ ἀνδρός* (*Xen. Cyr.* 2, 1, 39). *Τῆς τύχης, τὸ ἐμὲ νῦν δεῦρο κληθέντα τυχεῖν* (*Xen. Cyr.* 2, 2, 3, *what a misfortune, that I* —).

The genitive stands (as possessive) with the adjectives which denote *belonging to*, or the contrary, viz. *οἰκεῖος, ἴδιος, ἱερός* (*consecrated to a god*), *κοινός, ἀλλότριος*. Τὰ τῶν τὴν πόλιν οἰκούντων οἰκεῖα τῶν καλῶς βασιλευόντων ἐστίν (*Isocr. ad Nic.* 21). 'Η πόλις ἁπάντων τῶν πολιτευομένων κοινή ἐστιν (*Andoc.* 2, 1). 'Ιερὸς ὁ χῶρος τῆς 'Αρτέμιδος (*Xen. An.* 5, 3, 13). § 62. (288 f.)

REM. *Οἰκεῖος*, in the sense *inclined* and *appropriate to*, and *ἀλλότριος*, *unfavourable to, alienated from*, have the dative: *'Η Θάσος τότε Λακεδαιμονίοις μὲν οἰκεία, ἡμῖν δ' ἀλλοτρία ἦν* (*Dem.* 20, 61). *Κοινός* has more frequently the dative (*κοινὸν πᾶσιν, κοινὸς ὁ ἀγὼν ἐμοί τε καὶ σοί*).

The genitive stands, as objective genitive, with adjectives denoting a property which refers to a certain object (transitive adjectives), viz.: § 63.

a) With the adjectives denoting *full of, deficient in, needy, unparticipant of, void*, or *free from* (cf. § 57, the genitive with the corresponding verbs), e. g. Τὰ κοῖλα τῆς γῆς ὕδατος ἔμπλεά ἐστιν (*Pl. Phæd.* 110). Πόλις μεστὴ ἐμπόρων καὶ ξένων (*Isocr. Pac.* 21). Ἔρημοι συμμάχων ἐσμέν. Πῶς ἂν θεὸς εἴη ὁ τῶν καλῶν καὶ ἀγαθῶν ἄμοιρος; (*Pl. Conv.* 202.) Καθαρὸς φόνου (*Pl. Legg.* 9, 864). Such adjectives are *πλήρης, πλέως, ἔμπλεως, σύμπλεως, μεστός, πλούσιος*, — *ἐνδεής, ἐπιδεής, κενός, ἔρημος, πένης, μέτοχος, ἄμοιρος* (*ἀκέραιος, ἀκέραστος*), *καθαρός, ἐλεύθερος*, and some in which the signification is more special, e. g. *ὀρφανός* (*παίδων*), *γυμνός* (*ψυχὴ γυμνὴ σώματος*). (268, 288 d. e)

CHAP. V.]

[§ 63.] REM. 1. To an adjective formed from a substantive with ἀ *privativum*, and expressing a notion complete in itself without the addition of an object, the Greeks sometimes annex for more exact definition the genitive of a kindred substantive, so that the adjective expresses no more than the general notion *bereft of, free from*, e. g. ἄπαις ἀῤῥένων παίδων (*Xen. Cyr.* 4, 6, 2), ἄτιμος πάσης τιμῆς (*Pl. Legg.* 6, 774, also τούτων ἄτιμοι, *Andoc.* 1, 75, *deprived of this honour*), ἀδωρότατος χρημάτων (*Thuc.* 2, 65, *uncorrupted by*), ἀθῷος τῆς Φιλίππου δυναστείας (*Dem.* 18, 270, *free from, unhurt by*). But especially in the poets, e. g. ἀνήνεμος πάντων χειμώνων (*Soph. Œd. C.* 677), ἄπεπλος φαρέων (*Eur. Phœn.* 324), ἄφωνος τῆσδε τῆς ἀρᾶς (*Soph. Œd. C.* 685, *without uttering this curse*), ἄλυπος γήρως (*Soph. Œd. C.* 1519, *untouched by*).

REM. 2. The poets form numerous compound adjectives with the sense of fulness or abundance of a certain special kind, and give them a genitive, e. g. πολυστεφὴς δάφνης (*Soph. Œd. R.* 83), πολυκτήμων βίου (*Eur. Ion*, 581).

(287 b, 288 c) *b*) With the adjectives which denote *knowledge, experience, carefulness, capacity, power*, or *being guilty* (or *the cause*) of something, e. g. Ἐπιστήμων τῆς θαλάττης (*Thuc.* 1, 142), ἐγκρατὴς ὕπνου, γαστρός. Such adjectives are ἔμπειρος, ἄπειρος, ἐπιστήμων, ἀνεπιστήμων, ἀήθης (τοῦ κακῶς ἀκούειν), ἐπιμελής, ἀμελής, ἀμνήμων, ἐγκρατής, ἀκρατής, κύριος, αἴτιος, with others of more special signification, e. g. φιλομαθής, ἀμαθής (ὡραία γάμου, *ripe for marriage*).

(287 a) *c*) With adjectives derived from verbs which govern the accusative or genitive, and denoting either the action, or (especially with the ending ικός) the *capacity* for it, or (with ἀ *privativum*) the forbearance of the action, e. g. Κακοῦργος τῶν ἄλλων, κατήκοος Μήδων, φειδωλὸς χρημάτων, ἀνατρεπτικὸς πόλεως, ἐξεργαστικώτατοι ὧν ἂν (= τούτων, ἃ ἂν) ἐγχειρῶσιν (*Xen. Mem.* 4, 1, 4), ἄγευστος ἐλευθερίας (*Pl. Rep.* 9, 576), ἀπαθὴς κακῶν (*Pl. Phæd.* 250), ἄπρακτοι ὧν ἐφίενται (*Thuc.* 6, 33), ἀνήκοος τοῦ πάντων ἡδίστου ἀκούσματος (*Xen. Mem.* 2, 1, 31). Φιλόδωρος (*fond of giving*) εὐμενείας, ἄδωρος δυσμενείας (*Pl. Conv.* 197).

REM. 1. Κατήκοος and ὑπήκοος have also the dative, like the corresponding verbs.

REM. 2. A genitive is also used with adverbs formed from the adjectives described under *b* and *c*, especially with ἔχω (instead of εἶναι with the adjective): ἐρωτικῶς, ἐμπείρως, ἀνακῶς, ἀμελῶς ἔχειν τινός. (Ἀπεχώρουν μάλα ὑπεροπτικῶς τῶν ἐναντίων, *Xen. Hell.* 7, 1, 18.) Likewise with διαφερόντως (τῶν ἄλλων), from διαφέρων (τινός).

d) With some which are compounded with a substantive capable of governing the genitive, and contain its notion, e. g. ὑπεύθυνος (τῆς ἀρχῆς, *he who has to give an account of an office administered by him*), ὑποτελὴς φόρου (*Thuc.* 7, 57), ὑπόδικος φόνου, ἀσεβείας.

REM. The poets sometimes construct compound adjectives in a harsh manner with a genitive governed by the substantive contained in the adjective, e. g. δωμάτων ὑπόστεγος (*Soph. El.* 1386, *who is under the roof of the house*). Χρόνος ἡμερῶν ἀνήριθμος (*Soph. Trach.* 247, *a time consisting of days of which there is no number*).

e) With ἄξιος, ἀνάξιος, ἀντάξιος, together with the corresponding

adverbs, and the verb *ἀξιῶ*, *account worthy*, e. g. *Ἄξιος ἐπαίνου*, [§ 63.]
κολάζειν τινὰ ἀξίως τῶν ἀδικημάτων, ἀξιοῦσθαι τῶν ἴσων.

REM. 1. *Ἄξιον* with the dative denotes *it is worth some one's while*, e. g. *Ἄξιόν σοι καὶ τῶν εἰς τὸν μέλλοντα χρόνον τοῦ βίου φροντίζειν* (*Xen. Mem.* 2, 1, 34).

REM. 2. Of the genitive with adjectives which denote something corresponding with a thing, see the dative, § 37, R. 1.

The genitive stands with the comparative of adjectives and adverbs, to § 64.
denote the second member of the comparison (*καλλίων Ἀλκιβιάδου, ἀμεῖ-* (271)
νον ζῆν τῶν ἄλλων), in the same signification with the adjectives which denote *double of*, *twice as great*, and the like (— *πλάσιος*, — *πλοῦς*), and sometimes with *ἄλλος* (see comparative, § 91); further, with some verbs derived from a comparative and expressing a comparison, together with one or two others, which, without being so derived, have a similar signification, as *πλεονεκτῶ* (*τῶν ἐχθρῶν*), *μειονεκτῶ*, *ἡσσῶμαι*. (*τῶν ἐπιθυμιῶν*), *ἐλασσοῦμαι*, *ὑστερῶ* and *ὑστερίζω* (*τῆς μάχης*), — *περιγίγνομαι*, *περίειμι* (*τινὸς πλήθει, σοφίᾳ*) *λείπομαι* (*πλήθει ὑμῶν*), *ἀπολείπομαι* (*am left behind*, *fall short of*, *τῆς ἀληθείας*).

a) The genitive serves to denote the *price* at which a thing is § 65.
bought, sold, exchanged, given in pledge, for which it is done, or at (258)
which it is set: *Πολλῶν χρημάτων* (*πολλοῦ*) *ὠνεῖσθαί τι* (*πρίασθαι, κτᾶσθαι, πωλεῖν, ἀποδίδοσθαι*). *Δόξα χρημάτων οὐκ ὠνητή* (*Isocr. ad Nic.* 32). *Καὶ τῆς ψυχῆς ἂν τοῦτο πριαίμην. Οὐδεμιᾶς χάριτος οὐδ' ὠφελείας ἀνταλλάξαισθε ἂν τὴν εἰς τοὺς Ἕλληνας εὔνοιαν* (*Dem.* 6, 10). *Ὑποτιθέναι* (*ὑποκεῖσθαι*) *πέντε μνῶν. Πόσου Εὔηνος διδάσκει;* (*Pl. Apol.* 20.) *Μισθοῦ* (*for pay*) *Τιμοκράτης νόμους εἰσφέρει* (*Dem.* 24, 66). *Χρημάτων ἐπικουρεῖν* (*Pl. Rep.* 9, 575, *for money*). *Οἱ τῆς παρ' ἡμέραν χάριτος τὰ μέγιστα τῆς πόλεως ἀπολωλεκότες* (*Dem.* 8, 70). *Τὰ τῶν εὖ καὶ κακῶς ποιεῖν δυναμένων δῶρα μείζονος τιμῶνται οἱ λαμβάνοντες ἢ τῶν ἄλλων* (*Xen. Cyr.* 2, 11, 13). *Πλοῖα χρημάτων τετιμημένα* (*Thuc.* 4, 26).

REM. *Ποιοῦμαί τι* (*τινά*) *περὶ πολλοῦ* (*πλείονος, ὀλίγου*). With *ἀλλάττομαι*, *ἀνταλλάττομαι* the preposition *ἀντί* is also added.

b) In the genitive is also set that for which pay is demanded or given: *Σωκράτης οὐδένα τῆς συνουσίας ἀργύριον ἐπράττετο* (*Xen. Mem.* 1, 6, 11).

a) The genitive serves to denote the *time* within which, or at a § 66.
certain point of which, something takes place (with partitive concep- (276)
tion), therefore partly in specifying a natural undefined time, or a time often recurring (as e. g. *νυκτός*, *at* or *by night*, *τῆς ἡμέρας*, *by day* = *per diem*); partly in specifying the definite period of time *in the course of which* something takes place (e. g. *τοῦ αὐτοῦ θέρους*, *in the*

[§ 66.] *same summer*, τῆς ἐπιούσης ἡμέρας, *in the course of the following day*) ; partly in specifying the time *within which* something takes place, or in the course of which something has not taken place (does not take place) : Δείλης ἀφίκοντο οἱ Ἕλληνες εἰς τὰς κώμας (*Xen. An.* 3, 3, 11). Ἔτι βαθέος ὄρθρου (*Pl.*). Σωκράτης τὸ αὐτὸ ἱμάτιον ἠμφίεστο θέρους τε καὶ χειμῶνος (*Xen. Mem.* 1, 6, 2). (More rarely ἐν θέρει, in the poets also simply θέρει.) Δαρεικὸν ἕκαστος οἴσει τοῦ μηνὸς ὑμῶν (*Xen. An.* 7, 6, 7 ; also τοῦ μηνὸς ἑκάστου). — Τοῦ αὐτοῦ θέρους Ἅγνων καὶ Κλεόπομπος ἐστράτευσαν ἐπὶ Χαλκιδέας τοὺς ἐπὶ Θρᾴκης (*Thuc.* 2, 58). Ἐπράχθη ταῦτα Ἐλαφηβολιῶνος μηνὸς ἐπὶ Θεοφίλου ἄρχοντος (*Dem.* 37. 6). Δήλια (*the Delos festival*) ἦν ἐκείνου τοῦ μηνός (*Xen. Mem.* 4, 8, 2). Οἱ ἡμέτεροι πρόγονοι τῆς αὐτῆς ἡμέρας ἐπύθοντό τε τὴν ἀπόβασιν τὴν τῶν βαρβάρων καὶ ἐβοήθησαν ἐπὶ τοὺς ὅρους τῆς χώρας καὶ μάχῃ νικήσαντες τρόπαιον ἔστησαν τῶν πολεμίων (*Isocr. Paneg.* 87). — Γύλιππος ἔλεγεν. εἰ βούλονται ἐξιέναι οἱ Ἀθηναῖοι ἐκ τῆς Σικελίας πέντε ἡμερῶν, ἕτοιμος εἶναι σπένδεσθαι (*Thuc.* 7, 3). Προσετάχθη Νικομάχῳ τεττάρων μηνῶν ἀναγράψαι τοὺς νόμους τοὺς Σόλωνος (*Lys.* 30, 2). Πολλῶν ἐτῶν Ἀγάθων ἐνθάδε οὐκ ἐπιδεδήμηκεν (*Pl. Conv.* 172). Οὔπω δὴ πολλοῦ χρόνου τούτου ἡδίονι οἴνῳ ἐπέτυχον (*Xen. An.* 1, 9, 25).

REM. 1. Τῆς αὐτῆς ἡμέρας, *in the course of the same day, yet on the same day, on one and the same day*, τῇ αὐτῇ ἡμέρᾳ (§ 45), *the same day*, often with small difference. Τοῦ αὐτοῦ θέρους, ἐν τῷ αὐτῷ θέρει (*Thuc.* 4, 133). Τοῦ λοιποῦ, *in future* (οὐ βλάψομεν τοῦ λοιποῦ ἑκόντες τὸ ἱερόν, *Thuc.* 4, 98) and τὸ λοιπόν.

REM. 2. *The time in the progress of which* is also denoted by the dative with ἐν: Ἐν τεσσαράκοντα μάλιστα ἡμέραις Ἅγνων χιλίους καὶ πεντήκοντα ὁπλίτας τῇ νόσῳ ἀπώλεσεν (*Thuc.* 2, 58). Ἐν τρισὶν ἡμέραις καὶ τοσαύταις νυξὶ διακόσια καὶ χίλια στάδια οἱ Λακεδαιμόνιοι διῆλθον (*Isocr. Paneg.* 187)[1].

(277) *b*) The genitive of a substantive (or word used substantively) and a participle serves to denote the time (and the circumstance), and indicates that something goes on while the subject is doing the thing, or is in the situation. denoted by the participle : Κύρου βασιλεύοντος, στρατηγοῦντος, *in the reign, under the command, of Cyrus.* See *Participles*, § 181.

§ 67. *a*) The general (possessive) genitive relation may be denoted in Greek alike by the possessive pronouns and by the genitive of the personal pronouns : τὰ ἡμέτερα ὅπλα, τὰ ὅπλα ἡμῶν. A possessive pronoun may have a genitive standing in apposition to it, especially that of αὐτός : Ἐμὸς αὐτοῦ (αὐτῆς), ἡμέτερος αὐτῶν, *my own, our own.*

---

[1] Λακεδαιμονίων βασιλεὺς ἐντὸς τριῶν ἐτῶν ἀφείλετο τὴν ἀρχήν (*Isocr. Euag.* 64, *in less than* —).

Εἶδον τὴν σὴν ἀνδρίαν καὶ μεγαλοφροσύνην, ἀναβαίνοντος ἐπὶ τὸν ὀκρί- [§ 67.]
βαντα (*on the stage*) μετὰ τῶν ὑποκριτῶν (*Pl. Conv.* 194).

b) The objective genitive relation is sometimes denoted by a possessive pronoun: Εὐνοίᾳ ἐρῶ τῇ σῇ (*Pl. Gorg.* 486). Οἱ Λακεδαιμόνιοι φόβῳ τῷ ὑμετέρῳ πολεμησείουσιν (*Thuc.* 1, 33)[1].

CHAPTER VI.

Appendix to the doctrine of Cases: Of the Prepositions, especially such as govern several cases.

§ 68. The prepositions which govern more than one case, are partial to the *accusative* (a case in itself not conveying the notion of any particular relation), when they denote a motion to, along, or over any thing; or when they have a figurative meaning derived from this (of a relation which is neither local nor corporeal); sometimes even (e. g. διά and κατά), when the thought of a local relation altogether disappears in the figurative meaning. The *dative* they take in the signification *on, at, by:* the *genitive,* when they call forth the notion either of a going out *from,* or of a connexion *with,* or of an entering *into* (e. g. μετά, διά), or of a part (a point) of the whole (e. g. ἐπί, *upon*).

Rem. The different construction, and the difference of meaning therewith connected, results—apart from the consideration of the way in which it is influenced by the notion of *rest* or of *motion* involved in the relation—from the circumstance, that some prepositions in themselves originally denote an undefined relation capable of being put in various ways; which relation is specifically determined by the verb and the governing word, e. g. ἐπί, *by* and *upon*, but especially παρά and πρός of a relation *beside*, and *in the direction from* something. In the figurative usage of the prepositions, the original signification, from which that usage is derived, is in many instances not so easy to discover. The particulars of these figurative senses in the several constructions must be learnt from the Lexicon; here, only the primary distinctions are assigned, together with some examples of the manner in which the more special and less proper applications are

---

[1] Of the vocative, we have only to remark, that in prose it has ὦ before it, with very rare exceptions where there is a forcible brevity in the expression: Ἄνδρες, διαπλεῖν μέν, ἔνθα βουλόμεθα, Ἀρίσταρχος ὅδε τριήρεις ἔχων κωλύει (*Xen. An.* 7, 3, 3); in the poets ὦ is very often omitted. An adjective is put between ὦ and the substantive, when it is emphatic (ὦ καλὲ παῖ); otherwise it is put after it (ὦ Πρώταρχε φίλε, *Pl. Phil.* 53), and always in customary forms of address, as ὦ ἄνδρες Ἀθηναῖοι. Instead of the vocative the poets sometimes put the nominative (δύστηνος, ἀντὶ τοῦ; *Soph. Œ. R.* 1155.) In prose only with οὗτος, *this person here*, which is also used in the sense *ho, there! you there!* An adjective or participle may be annexed as apposition in the nominative with the article: Σὺ δέ, ὁ ἄρχων τῶν ἐπὶ ταῖς καμήλοις ἀνδρῶν (*Xen. Cyr.* 6, 3, 33). (Ὦ Ὑστάσπα καὶ οἱ ἄλλοι οἱ παρόντες, *Xen. Cyr.* 8, 4, 17.)

[§ 68.] deduced from the primary senses. In some instances, the senses of two constructions border closely upon one another, and the construction varies in different authors. From the Lexicon and by practice it must also be learnt, how, even in prepositions governing only one case, the Greeks apprehended this or that operation or condition under a different view of the relation in space from that which lies at the foundation of *our* constructions: e.g. μάχεσθαι, θηρεύειν ἀφ' ἵππου, *from a horse*, i.e. *on horse-back*.

§ 69. Διά. 1. With the accusative: *by reason of* (*through*, of the cause and the author): διὰ ταύτην τὴν αἰτίαν (διὰ τοῦτο). Διὰ τὸ κάλλος καὶ τὴν ἀρετὴν φιλεῖσθαι. Διὰ τοὺς ἐπανορθοῦντας ἀεί τι τῶν μὴ καλῶς ἐχόντων αἱ ἐπιδόσεις γίγνονται ταῖς πόλεσιν (*Isocr. Evag.* 7). Δικαιοσύνη αὐτὴ δι' ἑαυτὴν τὸν ἔχοντα ὀνίνησιν (*Pl. Rep.* 2, 367). (In the poets, but rarely in the Attic poets, *through, along*: διὰ πόντου βαίνειν, *Pind.*, διὰ στόμα ἱεὶς λιγνὺν μέλαιναν, *Æschyl.*, διὰ στόμα ἔχειν, *Arist.*)

2. With the genitive: a) *through* (local): διὰ Συρίας πορεύεσθαι, διὰ τῆς ἀγορᾶς ἕλκειν τινά. (Διὰ χειρὸς ἔχειν τι, διὰ στόματος ἔχειν τινά, διὰ φόβου εἶναι, διὰ φιλίας ἰέναι τινί—δι' ὀλίγου, *within a little of, at a short distance from*, διὰ δεκάτου ἔτους, *with an interval of ten years*, διὰ δέκα ἐπάλξεων, *Thuc.* 3, 21, *at every tenth battlement.*) b) *by means of, through* (of the means): δι' ἀγγέλων διαπράττεσθαί τι, δι' ἑρμηνέως διαλέγεσθαί τινι, διὰ γραμμάτων χρηματίζειν τινί. Δι' ὧν ἐκ χρηστῶν φαῦλα τὰ πράγματα τῆς πόλεως γέγονε, διὰ τούτων ἐλπίζετε τῶν αὐτῶν πράξεων ἐκ φαύλων αὐτὰ χρηστὰ γενήσεσθαι; (*Dem.* 2, 26.)

§ 70. Κατά. 1. With the accusative: a) *over* along something (of diffusion or expansion over, or of abiding somewhere in), *in, upon, at, over against*: Μέγα πένθος ἦν κατὰ τὸ Λακωνικὸν στράτευμα (*Xen. Hell.* 4, 5, 10). Οὐκ ἦν κατὰ πόλιν (*Pl. Theæt.* 142; *in town*). Κατὰ Μαλέαν, *directly over against*. Οἱ κατὰ ταῦτα οἰκοῦντες (*Xen. An.* 7, 5, 13; *here-abouts, in these parts*). Κατὰ γῆν, κατὰ θάλασσαν. Of time: Κατὰ τοὺς Ἡρακλείδας, οἱ καθ' ἡμᾶς, κατ' εἰρήνην, *in time of peace*. b) *according to, agreeably with, after—in proportion* or *relation to*, and *concerning* (of that which belongs to something and points to it),—*after the manner of, answering to,—wise* (of the sort or manner denoted by the substantive, especially in distribution, where a certain number recurs continually): Κατὰ τοὺς νόμους ζῆν (*Pl. Prot.* 326). Κατὰ νοῦν ἐμοὶ τὰ πράγματα γέγονεν. Κατὰ Θουκυδίδην, κατὰ τὸν σὸν λόγον. Πλείω ἢ κατὰ τὸ ἡμέτερον πλῆθος. Κατὰ τὴν χρείαν καλὰ ταῦτα λέγω (*Pl. Gorg.* 474.) Τὰ κατὰ Παυσανίαν (*the affair of P., the account concerning him*). Κατὰ τὸ σῶμα, *as to* or *in the body*. Οὐ κατὰ τούτους ῥήτωρ εἰμί (*Pl. Apol.* 17, *in their manner, after their measure*).—Κατὰ πόλεις, *city-wise, city by city, each city by itself*, καθ' ἕνα (καθ' ἕνα τῶν Ἑλλήνων, *Dem., the Greeks, man by man*), κατ' ὀλίγους. c) *on account of, for* (of cause and purpose): Οἱ πρόγονοι ἡμῶν τὴν προξενίαν ὑμῶν κατά τι ἔγκλημα ἀπεῖπον (*Thuc.* 6, 89). Ἀφιγμένοι κατὰ χρημάτων πόρον (*Xen. Hell.* 5, 1, 7, *with intent to get,—for*). Ἀναβαίνειν κατὰ θέαν τοῦ χωρίου (*Thuc.* 5, 7, *to get a view of —; for a view of—*). [§ 70.]

2. With the genitive: a) *down upon* or *over*, also *under*: κατὰ τῆς πέτρας, κατὰ τῆς κεφαλῆς, μυρίας κατὰ γῆς ὀργυίας γενέσθαι (*Xen. An.* 7, 1, 30). b) *against, upon, of* (in expressions denoting a complaint against or a sentence upon, or generally something said of a person). Μηνύειν κατά τινος (*Thuc.* 6, 60). Λέγω οὐ καθ' ἁπάντων, ἀλλὰ κατὰ τῶν ἐνόχων τοῖς εἰρημένοις ὄντων (*Isocr. ad Nic.* 47). Μέγιστον ἐγκώμιον κατὰ τῶν Ἀθηναίων. Ὥσπερ λέγεται κατὰ τῶν μεμυνημένων (*Pl. Phæd.* 81, *in the case of*).

Ὑπέρ. 1. With the accusative: *over, above* (of exceeding and surpassing): ὑπὲρ τριάκοντα ἔτη, μεγέθει καὶ ῥώμῃ ὑπὲρ τοὺς ἐν τῇ νηὶ πάντας εἶναι (*Pl. Rep.* 6, 488), ὑπὲρ ἄνθρωπον φρονεῖν. (Rarely *beyond*, to denote distance: πεζῇ βαδίζειν ὑπὲρ τὰς Πύλας καὶ Φωκέας (*Dem.* 6, 36; *to beyond*). Poetically and in Herodotus, *over*, so that the goal lies on the farther side: ῥιπτεῖν τι ὑπὲρ τὸν δόμον, *over the house, to the other side of it*. § 71.

2. With the genitive: a) *over, above* (denoting the *where*): Ὁ ὑπὲρ τῆς κώμης γήλοφος. Ἥλιος ὑπὲρ ἡμῶν καὶ τῶν στεγῶν πορεύεται (*Xen. Mem.* 3, 8, 9). Οἱ ὑπὲρ Χεῤῥονήσου Θρᾷκες (*Xen. An.* 2, 6, 2). b) *for* (*in defence of, for the good of*): Λέγειν, μάχεσθαι ὑπέρ τινος, *for, instead of*. Ἐγὼ ὑπὲρ σοῦ ἀποκρινοῦμαι.

Ἀμφί. 1. With the accusative: a) *about*, of motion, tarrying and surrounding; mostly poetical; in prose οἱ ἀμφί τινα, *those about, the train* or *suit of, a person* (οἱ ἀμφὶ Κῦρον), *the person himself with his companions* or *those like him* (οἱ ἀμφὶ Ἄνυτον); ἀμφί τι ἔχειν (εἶναι), *to be busied about a thing*. b) *about, towards* (of time, or magnitude): ἀμφὶ δείλην, ἀμφὶ τὰ ἑκκαίδεκα ἔτη γεγονώς. § 72.

2. With the dative: a) *on, with*, or *in* a thing *about* me (ἀμφὶ κλάδοις ἕζεσθαι, *with boughs about me*), merely poetical. b) *about, for, of*: φοβεῖσθαι ἀμφὶ γυναικί, poetical, and in Herodotus.

3. With the genitive: *about, around* (rare), *of*, poetical. (Ἡ δίκη ἡ ἀμφὶ τοῦ πατρός, *Xen. Cyr.* iii. 1, 8.)

Ἐπί. 1. With the accusative: a) *upon* (Lat. *in* with accusative): ἀναβαίνειν ἀνὰ ἵππον. b) *to* (towards, to fetch something), *against* (persons): ἰέναι ἐπὶ τὰς τῶν πλουσίων θύρας, καταφεύγειν ἐπὶ λόφον (ἐπὶ δεξιὰ κεῖσθαι), καλεῖσθαι ἐπὶ δεῖπνον, ἄγειν τινὰ ἐπὶ τὰ καλὰ κἀγαθά, ἰέναι ἐπὶ πῦρ, ἐφ' ὕδωρ, ἐπὶ ξύλα τὰς ναῦς πέμπειν ποι, συνίστασθαι ἐπὶ τοὺς ἄρχειν ἐπιχειροῦντας (*Xen. Cyr.* 1, 1, 2). Θρασύμαχος § 73.

[§ 73.] ἧκεν ἐφ' ἡμᾶς ὡς διαρπασόμενος (*Pl. Rep.* 1, 336). Μηχανᾶσθαί τι ἐπί τινα. (Πεφυκέναι ἐπί τι, *to be made for something.*) c) *over* (of expansion in space and time): ἐπὶ τεσσαράκοντα στάδια διήκειν, ἐπὶ πᾶσαν Εὐρώπην καὶ Ἀσίαν ἐλλόγιμος. Οἱ Ἀθηναῖοι ἐδῄουν τὴν γῆν ἐπὶ δύο ἡμέρας, *Thuc.* 2, 25, *for two days, for the space of.* (Ἐπὶ δέκα ἔτη ἀπομισθοῦν τι, *Thuc.* 3, 68, *to let for ten years.*) (Ἐπὶ πλέον, ἐπὶ μεῖζον, adverbially, *in greater extent;* ἐπὶ πᾶν, *Thuc.* 5, 68, *on the whole, on the average.*)

2. With the dative: a) *on, by, beside* (of place and of things): οἰκεῖν ἐπὶ τῇ θαλάττῃ, εἶναι ἐπὶ ταῖς πύλαις, μένειν ἐπὶ τῷ ἀληθεῖ, οἱ ἐπὶ ταῖς μηχαναῖς (*Xen. Cyr.* 6, 3, 28, *the people with the engines*). b) (more rarely in prose) *on* (Lat. *in* with abl.): κείμενος ἐπὶ τῇ πυρᾷ (*Pl. Rep.* 10, 614), ἀλωπεκίδας ἐπὶ ταῖς κεφαλαῖς φορεῖν (*Xen. An.* 7, 4, 4). c) *at, against:* τόξα τιταίνειν ἐπί τινι, poetically and Ionic. d) *besides, in addition to, after* (of accompaniment and immediate sequence): ἐπὶ τῷ σίτῳ ὄψον ἐσθίειν, ἀργύριον ἔχειν ἐπὶ τῇ γυναικί (*Isæ.* 3, 28, *to get money with his wife, his wife and money besides*). Ἀνέστη ἐπ' αὐτῷ Φεραύλας (*Xen. Cyr.* 2, 3, 7). Ἡ ἐπὶ τῇ νυκτί, ᾗ ἐξῆλθον, ἡμέρα (*Xen. Hell.* 4, 4, 9). Οἱ ἐπὶ πᾶσι, *the last.* e) *upon, on account of, for* (the occasion): θαυμάζεσθαι ἐπὶ ζωγραφίᾳ, φθονεῖν τινι ἐπί τινι, λέγειν ἐπί τινι (*to speak upon a person, over his grave*). Ἐπὶ μὲν τοῖς τῶν φίλων ἀγαθοῖς φαιδροί, ἐπὶ δὲ τοῖς κακοῖς σκυθρωποὶ γιγνόμεθα (*Xen. Mem.* 3, 10, 4). f) *for, with a view to* (the condition on account of which something is done, with a view to obtain it): ἐπὶ μισθῷ, *for pay.* Ἐπὶ πόσῳ ἂν ἐθέλοις τὴν γυναῖκά σου ἀκοῦσαι, ὅτι σκευοφορεῖς; (*Xen. Cyr.* 3, 1, 43.) Ἐπὶ τούτῳ πέφυκεν (παρεσκεύασται) ἡ τέχνη. Ἄγειν τὴν βασιλέως θυγατέρα ἐπὶ γάμῳ (*Xen. An.* 2, 4, 8). Ἐπὶ τῷ ἡμετέρῳ ἀγαθῷ Ἀράσπας ἐκινδύνευσεν (*Xen. Cyr.* 6, 3, 16). Δέομαι ἄγειν σχολὴν ἐπὶ τῇ ὑμετέρᾳ παρακελεύσει (*Pl. Apol.* 36, *in order to exhorting you.*) g) *in the power, at the command* (of a person): Ὁπόταν βούλῃ εἰσιέναι ὡς ἐμέ, ἐπὶ σοὶ ἔσται (*Xen. Cyr.* 1, 3, 14). Τὰ ἐφ' ἡμῖν, *what we have in our own power, what rests with us.*

3. With the genitive: a) *upon* (in answer to the question *where?*): καθῆσθαι ἐπὶ δίφρου, ὀχεῖσθαι ἐφ' ἁμάξης, περιάγειν τινὰ ἐφ' ἵππου, ἐπὶ τοῦ αἰγιαλοῦ αὐλίζεσθαι, ἐπ' ἀγκύρας ὁρμεῖν, ἐπὶ τεττάρων τετάχθαι (*by fours,* i. e. *four men deep*). Hence b) (close) *beside:* μένειν ἐπὶ τοῦ ποταμοῦ (*Xen. An.* 4, 3, 28). Τὰ ἐπὶ Θρᾴκης. c) *before, by* (in presence of): ἐπὶ τῶν στρατηγῶν, ἐπὶ μαρτύρων (ἐφ' ἑαυτοῦ, *by themselves alone*). d) *by, upon* (i. e. in the case, or, in the matter of): ὅπερ ἐπὶ τῶν δούλων λέγομεν. Ἃ ἐπὶ τῶν ἄλλων ὁρᾶτε, ἐφ' ὑμῶν αὐτῶν ἀγνοεῖτε (*Isocr.*). Ταῦτα τοιαῦτα ὄντα ἐπ' αὐτῆς τῆς ἀληθείας δείκνυται (*Dem.* 18,

22, *in truth itself*). e) *with* (so that one has and uses something): [§ 73.]
Ἐπ' ἐξουσίας, ὁπόσης ἠβούλοντο, ἔπραττον, ὅπως ἡ πόλις ληφθήσεται (*Dem.* 9, 61). Ἐπὶ τοῦ ὀνόματος τούτου πάντα τὸν χρόνον ἦν (*Dem.* 39, 21, *have always gone by this name*). (Ἐπὶ τῆς τοιαύτης γίγνεσθαι γνώμης, *Dem.* 4, 6, *to keep to this opinion.*) f) *in the time of*: ἐπὶ τῶν ἡμετέρων προγόνων (*Xen. Cyr.* 1, 6, 31). Ἐπὶ τοῦ Δεκελεικοῦ πολέμου (*Dem.* 22, 15). Οἱ ἐφ' ἡμῶν.—g) (set) *over* (of office and business): οἱ ἐπὶ τῶν πραγμάτων (*Dem.* 18, 247).—h) *towards* (in the direction of): ἀποπλεῖν ἐπ' Αἰγύπτου, ἐπὶ Σαρδέων φεύγειν, ἀποχωρεῖν ἐπ' οἴκου (*homewards*).

Μετά. 1. With the accusative: a) *after* (of time and order): μετὰ ταῦτα, *thereupon*; μετὰ τοὺς θεούς, *next to the gods*. b) *after* (to go after a thing and fetch it): πλεῖν μετὰ χαλκόν, poetical, whence μετέρχομαι, μεταπέμπομαι. c) Μεθ' ἡμέραν, *by day*; μετὰ χεῖρας ἔχειν, *to have in hand*. § 74.

2. With the dative: *among, amid*, poetical: μετ' Ἀργείοις, μετὰ φρεσίν.

3. With the genitive: *with* (following and connected with): ἰέναι μετά τινος, καθῆσθαι μετὰ τῶν ἄλλων, οἰκεῖν μετὰ θεῶν (*among*), μετὰ τοῦ δικαίου (μετ' ἀδικίας) κτᾶσθαί τι, μετὰ πόνων καὶ κινδύνων ἐλευθεροῦν τὴν πατρίδα. (Σύν has partly the same signification; but σύν expresses rather a union, μετά participation and companionship, e. g. in compounds, συνέχω, *hold together*, μετέχω, *share in*.)

Παρά. 1. With the accusative: a) *along*, (past) *by, beside, in course of* (*during*, of time): παρὰ τὴν θάλατταν ἰέναι (*Xen. An.* 5, 10, 18). Κῶμαι πολλαὶ ἦσαν παρὰ τὸν ποταμόν (*Xen. An.* 3, 5, 1). Παρὰ τὰς ναῦς ἀριστοποιεῖσθαι (*Thuc.* 7, 39). Παρὰ τὴν ὁδὸν κρήνη ἦν (*Xen. An.* 1, 2, 13). Μεθύοντα ἄνδρα παρὰ νηφόντων λόγους παραβάλλειν (*Pl. Conv.* 214; *to place them side by side with*, for comparison). (Seldom precisely *with*, εἶναι παρά τινα.) Παρὰ τὸν νεὼν ποταμὸς παραῤῥεῖ. Παρὰ τὴν Βαβυλῶνα παριέναι. Παρὰ τὸν πότον, παρὰ πάντα τὸν βίον. παρ' ἑκάστην ἡμέραν, παρὰ τὴν ἀρχήν τινος. (Παρ' αὐτὰ τὰ ἀδικήματα, *Dem.* 37, 2, *immediately upon, after.*) b) *to* (mostly of persons): ἡ παρ' ἐμὲ εἴςοδος (*Xen. Cyr.* 1, 3, 14), ἀπιέναι παρὰ τὸν θεόν (*Pl. Phæd.* 85). c) *In comparison with* (in preference to): Ἀχιλλεὺς τοῦ κινδύνου κατεφρόνησε παρὰ τὸ αἰσχρόν τι ὑπομεῖναι (*Pl. Apol.* 28). Διάδηλος ἦν παρὰ τοὺς ἄλλους εὐτακτῶν (*Xen. Mem.* 4, 4, 2). d) *beside, except*: ἄλλο τι παρὰ ταῦτα (*Pl. Apol.* 6, 406). e) *against* (not in accordance with: otherwise than): παρὰ φύσιν, παρὰ δόξαν (γνώμην), παρὰ τοὺς νόμους, παρὰ τὰ σημαινόμενα (*contrary to the orders*). f) *by, with the distinction of* (of the thing which turns the scale, of the magnitude or amount of the difference, properly, *past* so much): παρὰ μικρόν, παρ' ὀλίγον ἀποφεύγειν (*barely to escape*, with but a little between that and de- § 75.

CHAP. VI.]

[§ 75.] struction), παρὰ πολὺ νικᾶν. Οὐκ ᾤμην οὕτω παρ' ὀλίγον ἔσεσθαι, ἀλλὰ παρὰ πολύ (*Pl. Apol.* 36). Παρ' ὀλίγας ψήφους Φίλιππον ἠτιμώσατε (*Dem.* 24, 138; *by a small majority*). Παρὰ μικρὸν ἦλθον ἀποθανεῖν (*Isocr. Æg.* 22; *was within a little of* —). g) *through, by means of* (of that which turns the scale, and on which the result critically depends): Οὐ παρ' ἓν οὐδὲ δύο εἰς τοῦτο τὰ πράγματα ἀφῖκται (*Dem.* 9, 2). Ὑπὸ πάντων ὁμολογεῖται, παρὰ τοῦτον γενέσθαι τὴν σωτηρίαν τοῖς πολιορκουμένοις (*Isocr. Archid.* 52). Ἕκαστος οὐ παρὰ τὴν ἑαυτοῦ ἀμέλειαν οἴεται βλάψειν, μέλειν δέ τινι καὶ ἄλλῳ ὑπὲρ ἑαυτοῦ τι προϊδεῖν (*Thuc.* 1, 141; *for him, instead of his taking care for himself*). h) παρ' οὐδὲν ποιεῖσθαι, παρ' οὐδὲν εἶναι, *to make of no account, to go for nothing.*

2. With the dative: *with* (in answer to the question *where?* usually of persons): παρὰ τῷ βασιλεῖ τιμῆς τυγχάνειν, σιτεῖσθαι παρὰ τῇ μητρί. Παρὰ θεοῖς καὶ παρ' ἀνθρώποις τοῖς νοῦν ἔχουσι δικαιοσύνη διαφερόντως τετίμηται (*Pl. Alc.* ii. 150).

3. With the genitive: *from, of* (a person, or a thing conceived of as a person), *from beside*: Ἄγγελοι ἦλθον παρὰ τοῦ βασιλέως. Παρὰ Κύρου οὐδεὶς λέγεται αὐτομολῆσαι πρὸς βασιλέα, παρὰ δὲ βασιλέως πολλαὶ μυριάδες πρὸς Κῦρον (*Xen. Œcon.* 4, 18). Οἱ παρὰ Νικίου. Παρ' ἑαυτοῦ διδόναι. Εὔνοια παρὰ θεῶν. Ὁμολογεῖται παρὰ πάντων. Ὀφείλεται παρὰ τοῦ ἐχθροῦ τῷ ἐχθρῷ κακόν (*Pl. Rep.* 1, 332). Μανθάνειν τι παρά τινος.

§ 76. Περί. 1. With the accusative: a) *round, about* (somewhere *among, in*): Τὸν ἥλιον ἐνόμιζον ἰέναι περὶ τὴν γῆν. Οἱ περὶ Κῦρον. (Cf. ἀμφί.) Ὤικουν Φοίνικες περὶ πᾶσαν τὴν Σικελίαν (*Thuc.* 6, 2). Εἶναι περὶ Ἑλλήσποντον. Ταύτας τὰς πολιτείας εὕροι ἄν τις οὐκ ἐλάττους περὶ τοὺς βαρβάρους ἢ περὶ τοὺς Ἕλληνας (*Pl. Rep.* 8, 544). Περὶ τούτους τοὺς χρόνους, περὶ μέσας νύκτας. Περὶ τρισχιλίους (somewhere about, more or less). b) *about*, i. e. with regard to, *towards* (of that which one is occupied about, or bearing towards): εἶναι περὶ τὴν θήραν, διατρίβειν περὶ τὴν γεωμετρίαν, σπουδάζειν περί τι, εὐσεβεῖν, σωφρονεῖν περὶ θεούς, ἄδικος, πονηρός, ἀνὴρ ἀγαθὸς περί τινα, περὶ τὴν πόλιν. Αἱ νομοθεσίαι περὶ τὸ μέλλον εἰσίν. Τὰ περὶ τὴν δίκην (*what belongs to the cause*), τὰ περί τινα (but τὰ περὶ τῆς δίκης πυνθάνεσθαι, *Pl. Phæd.* 58, as in 3).

2. With the dative: a) *about, on* (a part of the body): Οἱ Θρᾷκες χίτωνας φοροῦσιν οὐ μόνον περὶ τοῖς στέρνοις, ἀλλὰ καὶ περὶ τοῖς μηροῖς (*Xen. An.* 7, 4, 4). b) *about, for* (of a care): φοβεῖσθαι περί τινι, θαῤῥεῖν περί τινι. (Poetically also of *fighting for, in defence of*: μάχεσθαι περὶ τοῖς σκύμνοις.)

3. With the genitive: a) *about, of* (something as matter of discourse, knowledge, treatment, endeavour): *διαλέγεσθαι, βουλεύεσθαι, πυνθάνεσθαι, πρέσβεις πέμπειν, μάχεσθαι περί τινος, κινδυνεύειν περὶ τῶν ἐσχάτων. Περὶ τούτων οὕτως ἔδοξεν. Περὶ μὲν δὴ βρώσεως καὶ πόσεως οὕτω Σωκράτης παρεσκευασμένος ἦν* (*Xen. Mem.* 1, 3, 15; *as regards, when one comes to speak of*—). *Τί οἴει ποιήσειν αὐτὸν πρὸς τοὺς νόμους τιμῆς τε πέρι καὶ πειθαρχίας;* (*Pl. Rep.* 7, 538; *in point of*—.) (Sometimes instead of with the accusative in sense *b*: *τὰ περὶ τῆς ἀρετῆς*, especially with reference to the added verb, e. g. *Τὰ περὶ Εὔφρονος εἴρηται, Xen. Hell.* 7, 4, 1 [which may be said to be compounded of *τὰ περὶ Εὔφρονα*, and *εἴρηται περὶ Εὔφρονος*].) b) *Περὶ πολλοῦ, παντὸς, ὀλίγου, οὐδενὸς ποιεῖσθαι, to value much*, &c. (literally, *to make to oneself a question about something great*), *to account of much importance.* (Poetical: *about* (round. *περὶ σπείους γλαφυροῖο, Od.* 5, 68); *before*, of pre-eminence, *περὶ πάντων ἔμμεναι ἄλλων, Il.* 1, 287.) [§ 76.]

Πρός. 1. With the accusative: a) *to, towards* (of persons and things): *ἀπελθεῖν πρός τινα, προσάγειν πρὸς τὸ τεῖχος, ἀποβλέπειν πρὸς τὸν θεόν, παροξύνειν πρὸς τὰ καλά, σκοπεῖν πρός τι. Πρὸς ἕω, east-ward, τὰ πρὸς βορέαν.* (*Πρὸς ἕω* also *towards morning.*) b) *to, against, with*, of an action in relation to some person who, from the other side, takes part in the action; of a state of mind towards a person or thing: *διηγεῖσθαί τι πρός τινας, διαγωνίζεσθαι πρὸς τοὺς πολεμίους, μάχη Περσῶν πρὸς Ἀθηναίους, στασιάζειν πρὸς τὸν ἄρχοντα, σπονδὰς ποιεῖσθαι πρὸς τοὺς στρατηγοὺς τῶν Ἀθηναίων, αἱ πρὸς τοὺς τυράννους ὁμιλίαι* (*Dem.* 6, 21), *ἀγυμνάστως ἔχειν πρὸς θάλπη καὶ ψύχη* (*Xen. Mem.* 2, 1, 6), *ἀθυμεῖν πρὸς τὴν ἔξοδον* (*Xen. An.* 7, 1, 9), *λόγος πρὸς Λεπτίνην* (*against*; of an impeachment: *κατὰ Λεπτίνου*). (*Οὐδὲν πρὸς ἐμέ, it is nothing to me.*) c) *in relation to; for: καλὸς πρὸς δρόμον, οὐδενὸς ἄξιος πρὸς σοφίαν. Λέγειν πρὸς τὸ βέλτιστον. Βουλεύεσθαι πρὸς τὸ παρόν. Τείχη καὶ τάφροι ταῖς πόλεσι πρὸς φυλακὴν καὶ σωτηρίαν εὑρημέναι εἰσίν* (*Dem.* 6, 23). *Upon* (of the occasion): *Πρὸς τὴν τῶν Ἀθηναίων μεγάλην κακοπραγίαν εὐθὺς οἱ Ἕλληνες πάντες ἐπηρμένοι ἦσαν, Thuc.* 8, 2. *Πρὸς τοῦτο, πρὸς ταῦτα, consequently.* d) *in comparison with: Φαῦλοι πρὸς ἡμᾶς. Ἀστύοχος πάντα ὕστερα ἐνόμισε πρὸς τὸ ναῦς τοσαύτας ξυμπαρακομίσαι* (*Thuc.* 8, 41). *Παρορᾶν τι πρὸς τὰ δίκαια.* e) *Πρὸς βίαν, πρὸς φιλίαν, πρὸς ὀργήν, πρὸς χάριν*, adverbially, *violently*, &c. § 77.

2. With the dative: a) *by, at: Πρὸς Βαβυλῶνι ἦν ὁ Κῦρος* (*Xen. Cyr.* 7, 5, 1). *Πρὸς τοῖς κριταῖς* (more usually *ἐπὶ τῶν κριτῶν, παρὰ τοῖς κ.*). *Εἶναι πρός τινι, to be at* (occupied about) *something*, to have one's mind directed *to something*. b) *besides*, in addition to: *Πρὸς*

[§ 77.] τοῖς ἄλλοις πᾶσιν καὶ πανοῦργός ἐστιν. Πρὸς τούτοις. (Πρὸς δέ, *and besides.*)

3. With the genitive: a) *from*, and *from the side of* a person or thing (of that which comes from it, is viewed in reference to it): Τὰ πρὸς νότου. Τὰ ὑποζύγια ἔχειν πρὸς τοῦ ποταμοῦ (*Xen. An.* 2, 2, 4, *on the side turned towards the river*). Πρὸς πατρός, πρὸς μητρός, *on the father's, mother's side.* Πρὸς μὲν θεῶν ἀσεβές, πρὸς δὲ ἀνθρώπων αἰσχρόν (*Xen. An.* 2, 5, 20). b) *in favour of, on the side of a person, in accordance with:* ἡ ἐν στενῷ ναυμαχία πρὸς Λακεδαιμονίων ἐστίν (*Thuc.* 2, 86). Ὁ θεὸς πρὸς ἡμῶν ἔσται (*Thuc.* 4, 92). Τὰ ὅπλα (τὴν ψῆφον) τίθεσθαι πρός τινος. Οὐκ ἦν πρὸς τοῦ Κύρου τρόπου, ἔχοντα μὴ ἀποδιδόναι (*Xen. An.* 1, 2, 11). Ἄτοπα λέγεις καὶ οὐδαμῶς πρὸς σοῦ (*Xen. Mem.* 2, 3, 15). c) *from* (of that which proceeds from a person through an action; poet. and in Herodot.): Κακόν τι πρὸς θεῶν ἢ ἀνθρώπων λαβεῖν (*Hdt.*), μανθάνειν τι πρός τινος (*Soph.*, usually παρά). Πρὸς τοῦ διδαχθείς; (*Soph.* = ὑπό.) Ἀδικεῖσθαι πρός τινος (*Eur.* = ὑπό), τιμᾶσθαι πρός τινος (*Hdt.*). d) *by*, in prayer and adjuration by something (on behalf of it): Πρὸς παίδων καὶ γυναικῶν ἱκετεύω καὶ ἀντιβολῶ (*Lys.* 4, 20). Μή, πρὸς θεῶν, ποιήσῃς. (With the accusative σέ elliptically: Μή, πρὸς σὲ γονάτων τῆς τε νεογάμου κόρης, *Eur. Med.* 324.)

§ 78. Ὑπό. 1. With the accusative: a) *under*, in answer to the question *whither?* ἰέναι ὑπὸ γῆν, ὑπ' αὐτὰ τὰ τείχη ἄγειν τὸ στράτευμα, ὑπὸ τειχίον ἀποστῆναι (*Pl.* 6, 496), and figuratively, of a higher power: ὑπάγειν τινὰ ὑπὸ τοὺς νόμους, ὑπὸ τὴν ψῆφον ἔρχεσθαι. Αἴγυπτος ὑπὸ βασιλέα ἐγένετο (*Thuc.* 1, 110). Τάδε πάντα Ἀθηναῖοι πειράσονται ὑπὸ σφᾶς ποιεῖσθαι (*Thuc.* 4, 60). Also ποιεῖσθαι ὑφ' ἑαυτῷ). b) *towards, about*, of time: ὑπὸ τὴν νύκτα, ὑπὸ τὴν ἕω. Οἱ Αἰγινῆται Λακεδαιμονίων εὐεργέται ἦσαν ὑπὸ τὸν σεισμὸν καὶ τῶν Εἱλώτων τὴν ἐπανάστασιν (*Thuc.* 2, 27). c) sometimes *under*, in answer to the question *where?* αἱ ὑπὸ τὸ ὄρος κῶμαι (*Xen. An.* 7, 4, 5), οἱ ὑπὸ βασιλέα βάρβαροι (*Xen. Cyr.* 6, 2, 11).

2. With the dative: *under* (of the place and situation): ὑπὸ τῇ Αἴτνῃ οἰκεῖν, ὑπὸ τῇ ἀκροπόλει, ἔχειν τι ὑπὸ τῷ ἱματίῳ, πολλὰς πόλεις ἔχειν ὑφ' ἑαυτῷ (ποιεῖσθαι ὑφ' ἑαυτῷ), τρέφεσθαι ὑπὸ τῷ πατρί. Ἡγοῦμαι τοῦτ' εἶναι τῶν καλῶν ὑπὸ τοιούτοις ἤθεσι τραφῆναι καὶ παιδευθῆναι (*Isocr. de Big.* 28; *under a man of such character*).

3. With the genitive: a) *from under*, sometimes simply *under:* Ἡ πηγὴ χαριεστάτη ὑπὸ τῆς πλατάνου ῥεῖ (*Pl. Phæd.* 230). Τὰ ὑπὸ γῆς δικαιωτήρια (*Pl. Phæd.* 249). b) *by*, of the acting person or efficient cause with passives: Τιτρώσκεσθαι, αἱρεῖσθαι ὑπό τινος, τείχη ἀνάλωτα ὑπὸ πολεμίων. Also with neuters, and with phrases in which the

subject is passive to the action, and which therefore have a significa- [§ 78.] tion similar to the passive: *εἶναι ἐν μεγάλῳ ἀξιώματι ὑπὸ τῶν ἀστῶν* (*Thuc.* 1. 130), *δίκην διδόναι ὑπὸ θεῶν, συμφορᾷ περιπίπτειν, πληγὰς λαμβάνειν ὑπό τινος, ἐκπίπτειν* (*to be driven into exile*) *ὑπὸ τῶν τυράννων.* *Ὅ,τι ὑμεῖς, ὦ ἄνδρες Ἀθηναῖοι, πεπόνθατε ὑπὸ τῶν ἐμῶν κατηγόρων, οὐκ οἶδα· ἐγὼ δ' οὖν καὶ αὐτὸς ὑπ' αὐτῶν ὀλίγου ἐμαυτοῦ ἐπελαθόμην* (*Pl. Apol.* 17). With verbal substantives: *Τὰ τοῦ Κρόνου ἔργα καὶ παθήματα ὑπὸ τοῦ υἱέος* (*Pl. Rep.* 2, 378). c) *from, in consequence of*, of cause and occasion: *Καμβύσης μαινόμενος ὑπὸ μέθης τὴν ἀρχὴν ἀπώλεσεν ὑπὸ Μήδων* (*Pl. Legg.* 3, 695). *Δημοσθένης ἡσύχαζεν ὑπ ἀπλοίας* (*Thuc.* 4, 4). *Οὐχ οἷόν τε ἦν ἀποχωρεῖν ὑπὸ τῶν ἱππέων* (*Thuc.* 7, 78). d) *under, to*, of an accompaniment (*to the sound of*), cheering, quickening, or compulsion: *ὑπὸ σάλπιγγος πίνειν, χωρεῖν ὑπ' αὐλητῶν, ὑπὸ μαστίγων τοξεύειν* (*under the lash*, compelled by it). (In later writers with the dative.)

Rem. The acting person with a passive verb is sometimes denoted by *παρά*, when the action is to be conceived as coming *from*, from the side of, the person: *Οἶμαί με παρὰ σοῦ πολλῆς καὶ καλῆς σοφίας πληρωθήσεσθαι* (*Pl. Conv.* 175). in the poets and Herodotus also by *πρός* (see *πρός*, genitive, *c*) and by *ἐξ*: *Τὰ γενόμενα ἐξ ἀνθρώπων* (*Hdt.* 1, 1), *πεισθῆναι ἔκ τινος* (*Soph. El.* 409). (*Δημαράτῳ αὕτη ἡ χώρα δῶρον ἐκ βασιλέως ἐδόθη*, *Xen. Hell.* 3, 1, 6, *on the part of the king.*) *Ἀπό* also is occasionally used by some (Thucydid.) in the sense of proceeding from a person, with the passive of certain verbs, e. g. *do, say*: *Οἱ τύραννοι δι' ἀσφαλείας ὅσον ἐδύναντο μάλιστα τὰς πόλεις ᾤκουν, ἐπράχθη τε ἀπ' αὐτῶν οὐδὲν ἔργον ἀξιόλογον* (*Thuc.* 1, 17).

a) Sometimes a verb, not in itself denoting any motion, is so conceived as to § 79. include the notion of an antecedent or accompanying motion, on which accordingly depends the preposition or a local adverb, especially *πάρειμι*: *παρεῖναι ἐς ἄστυ. Ἐνταυθοῖ πάρεισιν* (*Pl. Apol.* 33). (*Καθέζεσθαι ἐς τὸ Ἡραῖον, ἐπὶ τὴν ἑστίαν, ἄλλοσέ ποι*, *to seat*, betake, *oneself thither.*) Conversely, prepositions and adverbs denoting rest and continuance, stand with verbs which in themselves denote the antecedent motion, e. g. *ἐκ τῆς πόλεως, οὗ κατέφυγεν*, *Xen. Cyr.* 5, 4, 15. *Ἀνέβην ἐνθάδε*, *Xen. Hell.* 1, 7, 16. *Ἐνταῦθα ἦα*, *Pl. Apol.* 36.

b) The prepositions *ἀπό* and *ἐξ*, together with *παρά*, are sometimes (as also occasionally in English) annexed adjectively with the article to a substantive, where one should rather expect *ἐν* or *παρά* with the dative (denoting residence in or at a place, or with some one), viz. when a motion of the person or thing to another place, or a residence at another place is denoted: *Κλέανδρος, ὁ ἐκ Βυζαντίου ἁρμοστής, μέλλει ἥξειν* (*Xen. An.* 6, 4, 18; *the governor from Byzantium*). *Οἱ ἀπὸ θαλάσσης Ἀκαρνᾶνες ἀδύνατοι ἦσαν ξυμβοηθεῖν* (*Thuc.* 2, 80). *Ὅστις ἀφικνεῖτο τῶν παρὰ βασιλέως πρὸς Κῦρον, πάντας οὕτως διετίθη ὥσθ' ἑαυτῷ μᾶλλον φίλους εἶναι ἢ βασιλεῖ* (*Xen. An.* 1, 1, 15). (*Δημοσθένης ἔτι ἐτύγχανεν ὢν μετὰ τὰ ἐκ τῆς Αἰτωλίας περὶ Ναύπακτον*, *Thuc.* 3, 102, *was still, after the events in Ætolia, about N.*) So likewise *ἐνθένδε, ἐκεῖθεν*. *Ἄγγελοι τῶν ἔνδοθεν* (*Thuc.* 7, 73).

a) Between a preposition and its case, besides the definitions belonging to this § 80. case (e. g. *ἐκ τῶν ἔργων τῆς ἐπιμελείας*, *Thuc.* 3, 46, for *ἐκ τῆς ἐπ. τ. ἔργων*, *ἐπὶ πολλὰς ναῦς κεκτημένους*, *Xen. Hell.* 5, 1, 19, *against people possessed of many ships*), there

[§ 80.] may stand a particle of transition or connexion (as τέ, γέ, μέν, δέ, γάρ, αὖ, οὖν, ἄρα), sometimes several of these, and enclitic cases of the pronouns, e. g. ἐν αὖ τοῖς δημοσίοις κινδύνοις (*Pl. Rep.* 9, 577). Πρὸς μὲν ἄρα σοι τὸν πατέρα (*Pl. Crit.* 50). (Ἐξ, οἶμαι, τῆς ἀκροτάτης ἐλευθερίας, *Pl. Rep.* 8, 564.)

REM. An adjective or participle, as apposition to the governed word, stands sometimes between this and the preposition: ἐν μόνῃ τῶν πασῶν πόλεων τῇ ὑμετέρᾳ (*Dem.* 8, 61). Διὰ φιλίας τῆς Θρᾴκης πορεύομαι (*Xen. Hell.* 3, 2, 9).

b) Prepositions are often put after their case by the poets (ἀναστροφή), but in prose only περί is thus put (when the substantive has the emphasis, e. g. Εὐβοίας μὲν πέρι, sometimes after several words: ὧν ἐγὼ οὐδὲν οὔτε μέγα οὔτε σμικρὸν πέρι ἐπαΐω, *Pl. Apol.* 19), and most frequently ἕνεκα. (Ὧν ἄνευ in Xenophon.)

c) The position between the adjective and its substantive is rare in prose (chiefly with pronouns: τοιᾷδε ἐν τάξει), in the poets frequent.

d) The preposition may stand between an adjective and an adverb of degree belonging to the adjective: πολὺ ἐν δεινοτέροις, ὡς διὰ βραχυτάτων.

REM. Whether the preposition with connected substantives shall be repeated with each, depends upon the consideration, whether the connected words coalesce into one notion, or whether they are separated (as with ἀλλά, οὔτε, ἤ); sometimes, however, the preposition is omitted, where we should have expected it to be repeated, e. g. with ἤ[1]. If to the governed substantive there is annexed a comparison by ὡς (ὥσπερ), in Greek the comparison is often put first, and usually is immediately followed by the preposition without repeating this with the principal substantive: Ὡς περὶ μητρὸς καὶ τροφοῦ τῆς χώρας, ἐν ᾗ τεθράμμεθα, βουλεύεσθαι δεῖ (*Pl. Rep.* 3, 414 = περὶ τῆς χ. ὡς περὶ μητρός). Ὡς πρὸς εὖ βουλευομένους τοὺς ἐναντίους παρασκευάζεσθαι χρή (*Thuc.* 1, 84).

§ 81. Εἰς, *until*, *for*, is connected with adverbs of time: εἰς ἀεί, εἰς αὖθις, ἐς αὔριον, ἐς ἔπειτα, ἐς ὁπότ' ἔσται (*Æsch.* 3, 99), μέχρι with adverbs of place: μέχρι ἐνταῦθα, μέχρι δεῦρο, βουλεύεσθαι, μέχρι ὅποι τὴν σοφίαν ἀσκητέον ἐστίν (*Pl. Gorg.* 487). (Also μέχρι ὀψέ, *Thuc.*)

CHAPTER VII.

The Verb and its kinds, and the Gerundive[2].

§ 82. IN point of syntax, it is indifferent, whether the active (transitive or intransitive) signification is attached to a verb of active form, or to the middle of an otherwise active verb, or to a deponent, whether it be only in the middle (form), or have the passive tenses in an active signification. Which form is the usual one, must be learnt from the Lexicon. If of an active verb the middle is also used (not only in the forms which coincide with the passive, but also in those in which middle

[1] Poetically, Δελφῶν κἀπὸ Δαυλίας for ἀπὸ Δ. καὶ ἀπὸ Δ.
[2] § 82 and 83, strictly speaking, do not belong to syntax.

and passive are distinct, and with difference of meaning), then concerning the signification we must remark : [§ 82.]

a) Most commonly, the middle voice denotes the same transitive action as the verb in the active does, but as undertaken in reference to the subject itself, and in its interest, or as performed upon something belonging to or concerning the subject, e. g. αἱροῦμαι, *I take me, choose myself a* — (ἡγεμόνα), παρασκευάζομαι, *procure myself* (παρασκευάζω, *prepare*), δουλοῦμαί τινα, *make a person my slave* (δουλῶ τινα τῷ βασιλεῖ), πορίζομαι, *get me* (πορίζω, *bring about*), αἰτοῦμαι, *ask for myself*, τίθεμαι νόμον, *make a law* (at the same time also for myself), διαμετροῦμαι σῖτον, *mete out grain to myself, have it meted to me* (διαμετρῶ, *mete out*), προβάλλομαι τὰ ὅπλα, *hold out before me, couch, lay in rest*, ἀμφιβάλλομαι ἱμάτια, ἀποσείομαι τὸ γῆρας, *shake off old age from me*, περιῤῥήγνυμαι τὸν χιτῶνα, *tear off my coat*, ἐσπασάμην τὸ ξίφος, *drew my sword*. Πλαταιῆς παῖδας καὶ γυναῖκας ἐκκεκομισμένοι ἦσαν ἐς Ἀθήνας (*Thuc.* 2, 78, *had conveyed away their wives and children*). Οἱ στρατιῶται ἠκονῶντο καὶ λόγχας καὶ μαχαίρας καὶ ἐλαμπρύνοντο τὰς ἀσπίδας (*Xen. Hell.* 7, 5, 20; *their spears and swords* —).

Rem. 1. Some verbs which, when they are simple, have active forms, by composition take the form of a middle deponent, with such a signification, e. g. μεταπέμπομαι, *send after, for* (Thucydides also μεταπέμπω), ἐφέλκομαι, *drag with me*. Sometimes ἑαυτῷ (ἐμαυτῷ, σαυτῷ) is added to the middle in this sense, to mark it more strongly, e. g. ἑαυτῷ δύναμιν περιποιεῖσθαι. Sometimes the active and the middle are used with little difference, because the reference to the subject itself is not necessary to be expressed, e. g. πράττω, *exact, call in*, and πράττομαι (*for myself*), φέρομαι μισθόν, but also simply φέρω, ἀποπέμπω, *send away*, ἀποπέμπομαι, *send away from me*.

Rem. 2. Ποιοῦμαι ὅπλα, *make myself arms*, i. e. *have them made for me*, διδάσκομαι, ἐδιδαξάμην τὸν υἱόν, *I had my son instructed* (but ἀποκτείνω, *cause to be killed*, without such a reference, &c.).

b) Sometimes the middle denotes an action upon and in the subject itself; this however is not the case, when the subject is at the same time plainly conceived as special object of the action, and consequently an express reflexive relation takes place, but where the action is rather taken as a merely intransitive one, without a definite external object (in the accusative), e. g. λούομαι (ἐλουσάμην), ἀλείφομαι (ἠλειψάμην), ἐπιδείκνυμαι (ἐπεδειξάμην), *show oneself* (my art and skill), τρέπομαι (ἐτραπόμην), *turn oneself to, attend to*, a thing, ἔχομαι (ἐσχόμην), *keep* (myself) *close* (τινός, *to something*), ἀπέχομαι, *abstain from*, λαμβάνομαι, *lay hold upon* (τινός, *something*). With expressly reflexive signification, the active stands with ἑαυτόν, e. g. σώζειν, ἀποκτείνειν ἑαυτόν, ἀναλαμβάνειν ἑαυτόν, παρέχω ἐμαυτὸν τέμνειν (*to cut*), (rarely ἐπισφάττεσθαι ἑαυτόν τινι,) and where the

[§ 82.] notion of a condition in which the subject is, or into which it is brought, or of something that goes on in it, is more strongly prominent, there the passive form (middle with passive aorist) is very frequent, where the English sometimes, and much oftener the German, has the reflexive form, e. g. φέρομαι (ἠνέχθην), κινοῦμαι (ἐκινήθην, *put myself in motion, get in motion, am set in motion*), ἀθροίζομαι (ἠθροίσθην, but ἠθροισάμην δύναμιν, *gathered me a force*, as in *a*), διεσπάρην, ἐπεραιώθην, ὡρμήθην. ἐπλανήθην, ἀπηλλάγην, συνεθίσθην, διηνέχθην, ἐμαλθακίσθην, sometimes where the passive view does not seem very obvious, e. g. in φαίνομαι (ἐφάνην). (Ἐπαυσάμην, *I ceased*, ἐπαύσθην, *was made to cease.*)

Rem. 1. A similar view lies at the foundation of the form of several verbs as deponent with middle or passive aorist, e. g. νεανιεύομαι, *behave myself like a young man*, ἐνεανιευσάμην, but ὀργίζομαι, *become wroth* (am wroth), ὠργίσθεν (ὀργίζω, *move to wrath*, rare), μαίνομαι, *become mad*, ἐμάνην. Where the view wavered between the two, the result was a deponent with alternating form of middle and passive; cf. the *Accidence*.

Rem. 2. Sometimes a verb lays aside the transitive signification, and yet keeps the active form. Originally, this is apt to take place in consequence of an ellipse, some object, more general or special, being understood, and the verb thereby acquiring a specific meaning, although in process of time the ellipse quite disappears from the signification, e. g. ἄγω (viz. τὸ στράτευμα), *lead on* (in war), ἐλαύνω, *ride* (τὸν ἵππον). βάλλω λίθοις, *pelt with stones*, ἐσβάλλω, *make an attack, charge*, μεταβάλλω, *change myself* (*undergo a change*), ἔχω εἰς Σκιώνην, *steer* (τὴν ναῦν), ἐπέχω, *hold up, stay, pause*, ἀνίημι, *leave off, cease*, στρέφω, ὑποστρέφω, *turn round*, φυλάσσω, *keep guard*. Sometimes both the active and passive are used in the same signification, e. g. ὑποφαίνει ἡ ἡμέρα and ὑποφαίνεται.

Rem. 3. In some particular transitive verbs, certain forms have intransitive signification, especially the perfect, plusquamperfect, and aor. 2, in δύω, φύω, and ἵστημι, then the perf. 2, and its pluperf. in certain verbs, e. g. ὄλωλα (cf. the *Accidence*).

c) Sometimes the middle assumes a somewhat different and more special active signification, in which there lies concealed an original relation to the subject, e. g. φυλάττω, *guard*, φυλάττομαι, *am on my guard against* (τί or τινά), ἀποδίδωμι, *give back, pay*, ἀποδίδομαι, *give back from me*, i. e. *sell*, γράφω, *write*, γράφομαι, *indite, lay a charge against*, ἐπαγγέλλω, *announce, pass the order for something*, ἐπαγγέλλομαι (*announce myself*), *promise, make profession of*, ἀμύνω, *ward off*, ἀμύνομαι, *ward off from myself, defend myself against*. (Τιμωρῶ τινι, *help*, intransitively, τιμωροῦμαί τινα, *avenge myself upon some one.*)

Rem. 1. Sometimes the middle is used, without any strongly marked difference, but still in certain particular constructions of the verb, e. g. ποιῶ, *make, bring forth*, but ποιοῦμαι λόγον, θήραν, *hold* (in periphrases); ποιοῦμαι περὶ πολλοῦ, ἐν ὀργῇ ποιοῦμαί τινα, ποιοῦμαι τὸν ποταμὸν ὄπισθεν, *get the river in my rear*.

Rem. 2. Sometimes out of the purely passive conception (with the passive forms) there developes itself a new active signification, as a deponent passive, e. g. φοβῶ, *I make afraid*, φοβοῦμαι, ἐφοβήθην τοὺς πολεμίους, *I fear*, καταπλήττω, *beat down, dismay*, κατεπλάγην τὴν δύναμιν αὐτῶν, *was dismayed at*, αἰσχύνω, *put to shame*, αἰσχύνομαι, ᾐσχύνθην (τινά or τί), *to be ashamed of; to feel shame at*. (Πείθω, *persuade*, πείθομαι, *obey*, ἐπείσθην, but with the dative.) [§ 82.]

d) In some instances the distinction almost entirely disappears, so that active and middle of the same verb are used in the same signification; e. g. this is often the case with παρέχω and παρέχομαι, *afford, supply, exhibit*, προτρέπω and προτρέπομαι, *put forward, instigate*, ἀποκρύπτω and ἀποκρύπτομαι, *conceal* (ἀποκρύπτομαι ἐμαυτόν, *Pl. Rep.* 3, 393, but usually ἀποκρύπτομαί τινά τι, *hide a thing from*). (Compare the use of the fut. middle with the other tenses active, on which see *Accidence*.)

Rem. 1. Λοιδορῶ τινα, λοιδοροῦμαί τινι, with change of construction.

Rem. 2. There are also intransitive verbs which have both an active and a middle with different signification, the middle denoting the action more as referred to the subject alone, the active in relation to others; e. g. ἄρχω, *begin*, i. e. *am the first among several* (*take the lead*), ἄρχομαι, *begin*, i. e. *take the first step* (of my own actions), βουλεύω, *am counsellor*, βουλεύομαι, *deliberate, take counsel*, συμβουλεύω τινί, *give counsel*, συμβουλεύομαί τινι, *take counsel with some one* (on my own concerns). Some other intransitive verbs have active and middle used with no perceptible difference of meaning; but usually the one form is more frequent than the other, e. g. πειρῶμαι more frequent than πειρῶ. (Ἐτρεψάμην, *put to flight*, ἐτραπόμην, *turned myself*.)

Of the use of the several forms in middle and passive it is to be remarked: § 83.

a) The future middle, like the tenses which coincide for act. and pass., is often used in a purely passive sense, e. g. θρέψομαι = τραφήσομαι, βλάψομαι, ὠφελήσομαι = βλαβήσομαι, ὠφεληθήσομαι (rarely the future of the *verba liquida*, φανοῦμαι = φανήσομαι), but not of those verbs which to the present active take the future in the middle (cf. the *Accidence*), e. g. λήψομαι, γνώσομαι, γελάσομαι. (But aor. 2 middle, in a passive sense, is very rare and limited to a few verbs; thus κατασχόμενος.)

b) Of transitive deponents the perfect middle is used in the passive beside the active sense, e. g. εἴργασμαι, κεκτημένος (κατακέχρηται, *is used up*, *Isocr. Paneg.* 74, although the verb governs the dative); so from transitive medial deponents sometimes the passive aor. and fut. are formed and used as such, e. g. εἰργάσθην (middle εἰργασάμην), ἐκτήθην (ἐκτησάμην), αἰτιαθείς (ᾐτιασάμην), ἐργασθήσομαι. The other tenses of a transitive deponent in the middle are rarely used passively, e. g. ὠνούμενα καὶ πιπρασκόμενα (*Pl. Phæd.* 69).

c) That in Greek there are passives of sundry verbs which are not transitive, or do not take a proper object-accusative, was noted in § 26, § 27, § 35 b. R. 3, § 36 a. R. 4, and § 56, R. 2.

a) The gerundive of transitive verbs (active or middle) is an adjective with the signification *fit* or *necessary*, and is predicated of the § 84. (420)

[§ 84.] subject with *εἰμί*. (The *εἰμί* is often omitted in the indicative, sometimes also in the infinitive.) Ὠφελητέα σοι ἡ πόλις ἐστίν (*Xen. Mem.* 3, 6, 3). Νικίας ἔλεγεν, ὁπλιταγωγοὺς (ναῦς) ἐκ τῶν ξυμμάχων μεταπεμπτέας εἶναι (*Thuc.* 6, 25). Ποιητέα ἃ λέγεις.

(421 a) *b*) Of intransitive verbs the gerundive is formed only in the neuter, and is used with *ἐστίν* as an impersonal predicate, which is construed with the dative or genitive when the verb governs these cases. Ἰτέον ἐστίν (ἰτητέα ἐστίν, § 1 b, R. 4). Ἐπιχειρητέον τῷ ἔργῳ. Ἀπτέον τοῦ πολέμου (from ἅπτομαι in middle). Ἐπιμελητέον τῶν βοσκημάτων.

(421 b) *c*) As from intransitive, so, by analogy, from transitive verbs also, the gerundive is used impersonally with *ἐστίν*, and governs the accusative: Θεραπευτέον τοὺς θεούς (*Xen. Mem.* 2, 1, 28). Ἀσκητέον τὴν σοφίαν. Τοὺς παῖδας εἰς τὸν πόλεμον ἀκτέον καὶ γευστέον αἵματος (*Pl. Rep.* 7, 537, from γεύειν τινὰ αἵματος, *to give one a taste of blood*).

REM. From verbs which are used both in active and middle in different senses, the gerundive may be used impersonally in both significations, e. g. γυμναστέον τὸ σῶμα (γυμνάζω) and γυμναστέον ἐστίν, *one must exercise* (γυμνάζομαι), πειστέον, *one must obey* (πείθομαι).

§ 85. The name of the person who has to perform the action, is taken by the gerundive in the dative (of relation, by § 34): Ὠφελητέα ἡμῖν ἡ πόλις. Ἰτητέον σοι. But with the impersonally used gerundive the name of the acting person also stands in the accusative: Οὐ δουλευτέον τοὺς νοῦν ἔχοντας τοῖς οὕτω κακῶς φρονοῦσιν (*Isocr. Euag.* 7). Τὸν βουλόμενον εὐδαίμονα εἶναι σωφροσύνην διωκτέον καὶ ἀσκητέον (*Pl. Gorg.* 507). Οὐ δίκαις καὶ λόγοις διακριτέα ἐστίν, μὴ λόγῳ καὶ αὐτοὺς βλαπτομένους (*Thuc.* 1, 86; *we must not seek to decide by law and words, not being ourselves injured in words only*).

REM. The acting person was conceived in general, without the special relation denoted by the dative, and yet not as actual grammatical subject (nominative).

CHAPTER VIII.

The relations of Adjectives (and Adverbs), especially the degrees of Comparison.

§ 86. *a*) THE adjectives which express *order* and *sequence*, as also those
(300) which denote *inclination, contentment* with an action, or a *multitude* and *vehemence*, together with some others (e.g. μόνος), stand in Greek as apposition to the subject, sometimes also to the object, where we use an adverb to denote the situation and relation of the

subject (or object) during the action: Οἱ Ἀθηναῖοι πρότεροι ἐπῄεσαν. [§ 86.] Ἡρόδοτος πρῶτος τὰ Περσικὰ συνέγραψεν (but πρῶτον τὰ Περσικά, *first the Persian war*, then something else). Ὕστατος ἥκω. Ὁ δῆμος Μιλτιάδῃ συνεχώρησε πρώτῳ γραφῆναι παρακαλοῦντι τοὺς στρατιώτας (*Æsch.* 3, 186). Ὁ ἐπιβὰς πρῶτος τοῦ τείχους. Τρεψαμένων τῶν Ἀθηναίων τοὺς Χίους πρώτους, νικᾶται καὶ τὸ ἄλλο στράτευμα (*Thuc.* 8, 55. Here more usually πρῶτον τοὺς Χ.).—Ἑκόντες ἁμαρτάνετε. (Οἱ ἄκοντες ἁμαρτόντες, *Dem.* 24, 49.) Λύσανδρος τὰς πόλεις ἑκούσας παρελάμβανεν. Ἄσμενος (and ἀσμένως) ὑμᾶς εἶδον.—Ὁ ἄνεμος ἐκπνεῖ μέγας (*Thuc.* 6, 104). Κρήνη ἄφθονος ῥέουσα (*Xen. An.* 6, 2, 4).—Οἱ Ἀθηναῖοι ὑποσπόνδους τοὺς νεκροὺς ἀπέδοσαν τοῖς Συρακουσίοις. Μόνοις τοῖς καλῶς τεθραμμένοις σωφροσύνη ἐγγίγνεται (*Isocr. Panath.* 198). (Ἄπρακτος ἀποχωρῶ, &c. [= *re infecta*.])

REM. In particular, note the use of the adjectives in αῖος formed from the numerals, in apposition to the subject, to denote the day on which the thing took place: Διεφθείροντο οἱ πλεῖστοι ἐναταῖοι καὶ ἑβδομαῖοι (*Thuc.* 2, 49). Τεταρταῖοι ἐπὶ τοῖς ὁρίοις ἐγένοντο (*Xen. Cyr.* 5, 3, 8). (Σκοταῖος, *Xen.*, ὄρθριος, *Pl.*) In the poets some other adjectives of place and time are also used instead of adverbs: Χρόνιος ἐφάνην (*Soph.*). Θυραῖος οἰχνῶ (*Soph.*). Ταχὺς ὁρμῶμαι (*Soph.*).

b) Often where we should put the adjective as attributive to an indefinite substantive (subject, object, or preposition with its case), the adjective stands as apposition to the substantive with the definite article prefixed, the substantive notion being put as something given, and previously known or presupposed, and the adjective being put as its predicate; the principal point being to describe the nature, condition, or circumstances of that thing (see § 12, with the examples): Τοὺς στρατηγοὺς ὀλίγους χρὴ ἑλέσθαι (*Thuc.* 6, 72, *it behoves to choose few generals: the generals to be chosen should be few*). Τοὺς ἀκουσομένους ἑτέρους τοιούτους ἔχουσιν (*Pl. Phæd.* 58; *they have other such hearers*). Διαχειμάζειν ἐν ἀφθόνοις τοῖς ἐπιτηδείοις (*Xen. An.* 7, 6, 31). (Cf. § 100 a).

§ 87. (301) *a*) Adjectives with the article in the masculine, whether singular or plural, are used as substantives to denote a certain class of persons: Συμφέρει τοῖς πολίταις, τὸν ἀσθενῆ παρὰ τοῦ πλουσίου δίκην, ἣν ἀδικῆται, δύνασθαι λαβεῖν (*Dem.* 45, 67). In the neuter, the singular denotes a certain notion in general, something as a whole; the plural, on the other hand, denotes the several individuals of a certain kind: Τὸ ἀγαθόν, τὸ δίκαιον, τὸ μέσον (*the mean*), τὸ ὑπήκοον τῶν ξυμμάχων (*the obedient portion of the allies*),—τὰ ἀγαθά, τὰ καλά, τὰ πολιτικά (*affairs of the state*). The neuter of adjectives in ικός denotes the collective body of persons of a certain kind: τὸ Ἑλλη-

[§ 87.] νικόν (*the Grecian race, the Grecian portion of a certain population*), τὸ βαρβαρικόν, τὸ ξυμμαχικόν, τὸ πελταστικόν. (Τὸ ναυτικόν. *the naval force.*) It is more rare, especially in prose, for a masculine adjective without the article to be used of indefinite persons of a certain kind: Ἀγαθῷ οὐδεὶς οὐδέποτε ἐγγίγνεται φθόνος (*Pl. Tim.* 29). (Usually ἀνὴρ ἀγαθός. On the other hand, in the neuter: Δεινὰ λέγεις. Ἐν δεινοτέροις νῦν ἐσμεν ἢ τότε. Even in the singular: Ἄτοπον λέγεις, *Pl. Conv.* 175, = ἄτοπόν τι. Οὐκ ἔχουσι τούτου βέλτιον λέγειν, *Pl. Soph.* 247, *any thing better.*)

Rem. 1. The poets and some prose writers (Thucydides) use a neuter adjective with the article instead of the corresponding abstract substantive: ἐκ τοῦ περιχαροῦς τῆς νίκης (*Thuc.* 7, 73, *from the exceeding joy of victory*), διὰ τὸ ἀνθρώπειον κομπῶδες (*Thuc.* 5, 68, *from the natural boastfulness of man*).

Rem. 2. From prepositions and adjectives are formed adverbial expressions, e. g. διὰ βραχέων, *briefly*, ἐκ τοῦ φανεροῦ, *openly*.

b) Certain adjectives are used quite as substantives (with or without the article, with a genitive or possessive pronoun) to denote persons or things; thus, ἐχθρός, φίλος (οἱ ἐμοὶ δυσμενεῖς, εὖνοι, *Pl.*), ἀγαθόν, κακόν, *a good, an evil.* With some, especially in the feminine, a particular substantive was originally understood, e. g. ἡ πατρίς, *the father-land, country* (πόλις, γῆ), δεξιά, ἀριστερά (χείρ), ἡ μουσική, ἡ γραμματική (τέχνη).

Rem. 1. Especially, there is in some expressions an omission of the following substantives: γῆ (ἡ ὑμετέρα, ἡ οἰκουμένη, ἡ βασιλέως), ὁδός (τὴν ἐπὶ Βαβυλῶνος ἰέναι, see § 17, and in adverbial expressions, § 31 d, Rem., μακρὰν ἀπεῖναι), ἡμέρα (ἡ ἐπιοῦσα, ἡ ὑστεραία, ἡ αὔριον, Ἐλαφηβολιῶνος ἕκτῃ ἱσταμένου), μοῖρα (ἡ εἱμαρμένη, ἐπ' ἴσῃ καὶ ὁμοίᾳ), and others in particular constructions and phrases, e. g. ἡ ἐμὴ νικᾷ (γνώμη), τὴν ἐναντίαν τίθεσθαι (ψῆφον), χιλίας λαμβάνειν (δραχμάς), or in technical terms, e. g. ἡ ὀρθή, ἡ γενική (πτῶσις), ὁ μέλλων (χρόνος) in Grammar.

Rem. 2. Names of nations are used adjectively of persons: οἱ Μακεδόνες ἱππεῖς. The words ἀνήρ and ἄνθρωπος have another substantive joined to them as if this were an adjective to them: ἀνὴρ μάντις, ἄνθρωπος δούλη, ἄνθρωποι πολῖται, especially ἄνδρες in addresses: ὦ ἄνδρες δικασταί. (Poetically, τύχη τις σωτήρ, for σωτηρία, *Soph. Œd. R.* 80.)

§ 88. *a*) Adjectives in the neuter plural, are sometimes used in the
(302) manner indicated under *Accusative*, § 27, *a*, to characterize the substantive notion implied in the verb (where the action admits of a plural conception, i. e. a number of individual acts of the kind), so that the adjective is almost used as an adverb: Ἥλλοντο ὑψηλά (*Xen. An.* 4, 9, 5, *made high leaps*). Θαυμαστὰ ἐκπλήττονται φιλίᾳ τε καὶ οἰκειότητι καὶ ἔρωτι (*Pl. Conv.* 192, *are put in wondrous* (sorts of) *motion*). Τὸ παλαιὸν Ἑλληνικὸν (*the ancient Greeks*) ὁμοιότροπα τῷ

νῦν βαρβαρικῷ ἐδιαιτᾶτο (*Thuc.* 1, 6). Πολλά (*πολλὰ χρῆσθαί τινι*) and *πυκνά*, *frequently*, are used quite as adverbs. [§ 88.]

Rem. The poets also use other adjectives in the neuter plural quite as adverbs, e. g. *ἄλεκτρα γηράσκειν ἀνυμέναιά τε* (*Soph. El.* 962). (*Φονικὸς ὅμοια τοῖς μάλιστα τοῦ βαρβαρικοῦ*, *Thuc.* 7, 29.)

b) Some adjectives are used adverbially in the neuter singular with certain intransitive verbs, to denote the sensible quality of the action: *μέγα φθέγγεσθαι, βοᾶν, λέγειν, ἡδὺ* (*κακὸν*) *ὄζειν, ὀξὺ ὁρᾶν.* (Also *μέγα φρονεῖν.*)

Rem. Of certain adjectives with the article used as adverbs, see § 14, a. Rem. 3.

§ 89. (303) To the comparative of an adjective or adverb, the second member of the comparison is joined by *ἤ*, *than*, in the same case as the first, when the same verb or the same governing term also belongs to the second member, and might be repeated with it: *Μείζων εἶ καὶ πλείω ἔχεις ἢ ἐγώ. Τίνι ἂν μᾶλλον πιστεύσαιμι ἢ σοί;* If this is not the case, then, properly speaking, a new sentence should be formed with *εἰμί*, or some other verb, to be taken from the first member; usually, however, the verb is dropt, so that the nominative stands alone: *Ἀνδρὸς πολὺ δυνατωτέρου, ἢ ἐγώ, υἱὸν ὁ Ἀρμενίων βασιλεὺς πίνοντα παρ᾽ ἑαυτῷ συνέλαβεν* (*Xen. Cyr.* 5, 2, 28). *Τοῖς νεωτέροις καὶ μᾶλλον ἀκμάζουσιν ἢ ἐγώ, παραινῶ ταῦτα ποιεῖν* (*Isocr. Pac.* 145). *Τῶν ἄλλων οἰκετῶν οὐκ ἤθελεν Ἄφοβος παραλαμβάνειν οὐδένα τῶν ταῦτ᾽ εἰδότων μᾶλλον ἢ Μιλύας* (*Dem.* 29, 56, viz. *οἶδεν*). But when it would be necessary to understand *εἰμί*, the Greeks not unfrequently retain, by an attraction, the preceding case: *Πλουσιωτέρῳ ἄν, εἰ ἐσωφρόνεις, ἢ ἐμοί, τὸν ἵππον ἐδίδους* (*Xen. Cyr.* 8, 3, 32, = *ἢ ἐγώ εἰμι*). *Ἤδη τινὲς καὶ ἐκ δεινοτέρων ἢ τοιῶνδε ἐσώθησαν* (*Thuc.* 7, 77).

Rem. 1. Occasionally a comparative is followed by the preposition *πρό*, *before*, or *παρά* (*ἀντί*).

Rem. 2. For *μᾶλλον ἤ* (*rather than*), the Greeks are fond of saying, *μᾶλλον ἢ οὐ*, when the principal proposition is negative, or interrogative in the negative sense, or expressive of censure (so that what is said in the last member, is considered as the thing which holds, or must be done, &c., to the exclusion of the other): *Οὐ περὶ τῶν ἐμῶν ἰδίων μᾶλλον τιμωρήσεσθε Πολυκλέα ἢ οὐχ ὑπὲρ ὑμῶν αὐτῶν* (*Dem.* 50, 66). *Τί οὖν δεῖ ἐκεῖνον τὸν χρόνον ἀναμένειν, ἕως ἂν ὑπὸ πλήθους κακῶν ἀπείπωμεν, μᾶλλον ἢ οὐχ ὡς τάχιστα τὴν εἰρήνην ποιήσασθαι;* (*Xen. Hell.* 6, 3, 15.) *Ὠμὸν τὸ βούλευμα πόλιν ὅλην διαφθεῖραι μᾶλλον ἢ οὐ τοὺς αἰτίους* (*Thuc.* 3, 36).

§ 90. (304) When the first member of the comparison is a nominative or an accusative, *ἤ* may be omitted, and the second member put in the genitive (see § 64). This is also done, not unfrequently, where the first member is a dative: *Μείζων ἐμοῦ εἶ. Οἰκίαν τῆς ἡμετέρας πολὺ μείζω κέκτησαι. Λυσιτελεῖν οἴεται πᾶς ἀνὴρ πολὺ μᾶλλον ἰδίᾳ τὴν*

[§ 90.] *ἀδικίαν τῆς δικαιοσύνης* (*Pl. Rep.* 2, 360). *Ὑμῖν αἴσχιον τῶν ἄλλων ἐστὶ τὸ δοκεῖν ἐξηπατηκέναι τοὺς ἀγαθόν τι ποιήσαντας* (*Dem.* 20, 135, = *ἢ τοῖς ἄλλοις*). *Τοῦτο καὶ ἡμῖν, τοῖς ἥττοσιν ἐκείνου, ξυμφέρον* (*Pl. Rep.* 1, 338, = *ἢ ἐκεῖνός ἐστιν*). *Ἔξεστιν ἡμῖν μᾶλλον ἑτέρων καθ' ἡσυχίαν βουλεύειν* (*Thuc.* 1, 85, = *ἢ ἑτέροις*)[1].

REM. 1. Strictly considered, the comparative should take after it the genitive only where a substantive (or substantively conceived word) is directly compared with the first member as the subject of the comparative, or of an adjective or verb to which an adverb in the comparative is attached: thus, *οἰκία μείζων τῆς ὑμετέρας* = *ἢ ἡ ὑμετέρα, οἰκίαν μείζω ἢ τὴν ὑμετέραν* or *ἢ ἡ ὑμετέρα ἐστίν. σὺ μᾶλλον ἐμοῦ* = *ἢ ἐγώ*: but by a less exact way of putting the comparison, and from a desire of brevity, the Greeks also put with the comparative the genitive of a substantive which is compared with another in reference to the degree of a third object [*comparatio compendiaria*]: (*ἐγὼ μείζω οἰκίαν ἔχω σοῦ* = *ἢ σύ*): *Ἔδοξε τῷ ἀνδρὶ ἄλλος μεῖζον ἑαυτοῦ λαβεῖν*, *Xen. Cyr.* 2, 2, 4, = *ἢ αὐτὸς λάβοι*. *Χώραν ἔχετε οὐδὲν ἧττον ἡμῶν ἔντιμον* (*Xen. Cyr.* 3, 3, 41, = *ἢ ἡμεῖς*). *Οἱ Πελοποννήσιοι πλείοσι ναυσὶ τῶν Ἀθηναίων παρῆσαν* (*Thuc.* 8, 52, = *ἢ οἱ Ἀθ.*). (With even less exactness the genitive in some other places is put with the comparative, e.g. *Ἀθλιώτερόν ἐστι μὴ ὑγιοῦς σώματος μὴ ὑγιεῖ ψυχῇ συνοικεῖν*, *Pl. Gorg.* 479, = *ἢ μὴ ὑγιεῖ σώματι συνοικεῖν*.)

304, 2. 1) REM. 2. Pleonastically, the comparative takes first the genitive of a pronoun, and then, with *ἤ*, a more particular statement: *Ποιήσετε τοὺς πολλοὺς ἐν ἁπάσαις ταῖς πόλεσι τοῦτο ποιεῖσθαι σύμβολον τῆς αὑτῶν σωτηρίας, ἐὰν ὑμῖν ὦσι φίλοι, οὗ μεῖζον οὐδὲν ἂν ὑμῖν γένοιτο ἀγαθὸν ἢ παρὰ πάντων ἑκόντων ἀνυπόπτου τυχεῖν εὐνοίας* (*Dem.* 15, 4). *Τίς ἂν αἰσχίων εἴη ταύτης δόξα ἢ δοκεῖν χρήματα περὶ πλείονος ποιεῖσθαι ἢ φίλους;* (*Pl. Crit.* 44.)

REM. 3. By attaching to a comparative with *αὐτός* the genitive of a reflexive pronoun, or personal pronoun used reflexively, it is expressed, that the subject has for a certain time or for a certain case a higher degree than usual of the quality denoted by the adjective: *Πάντα ἄνδρα καὶ θαρραλεώτερον καὶ ἀνδρειότερον ἂν ποιήσειεν αὐτὸν αὑτοῦ οὐκ ὀλίγῳ ἡ τῆς ὁπλομαχίας ἐπιστήμη* (*Pl. Lach.* 182). *Θαρραλεώτεροί εἰσιν αὐτοὶ ἑαυτῶν, ἐπειδὰν μάθωσιν, ἢ πρὶν μαθεῖν* (*Pl. Prot.* 350, where *ἤ* annexes a more particular statement).

REM. 4. (*a*) To express that something surpasses hope, description, &c., the comparative is used with one of the genitives *ἐλπίδος* (*μείζων ἐλπίδος*), *λόγου* (*κρείττων λόγου*, *better than can be told*), *καιροῦ* (*πορρωτέρω τοῦ καιροῦ*), *γνώμης, τοῦ δέοντος*, and the like. (*Ἐρυθρότερος τοῦ ὄντος*, *than in reality*.) (*b*) *Too great for* (in proportion to) is expressed by the comparative with *ἢ κατά*: *Μείζους ἐπιθυμίαι ἢ κατὰ τὴν ὑπάρχουσαν οὐσίαν* (*Thuc.* 6, 15). (Also *μεῖζον παρά* —, *μεῖζον ἢ πρός* —.) (*c*) *Too great to* —, *μείζων ἢ* (*ὥστε*) with the infinitive, see § 150, c (*μέγας ὥστε*, ibid. b).

91. Like comparatives are constructed *ἄλλος* (*ἄλλα ἢ τὰ γιγνόμενα*, and with the genitive, *ἄλλα τῶν δικαίων*, *different from* —), the adjectives in *πλάσιος* denoting (many)*fold greater*, &c. *than*, together with *προτεραῖος, ὑστεραῖος*. *Πολλαπλάσια*

---

[1] Even *μετὰ τῶν πρεσβυτέρων ἡμῶν* (*Pl. Prot.* 314), instead of *ἢ ἡμῶν*, by § 89.

ἀπέδωκα τῶν ληφθέντων (ἢ ὅσα εἴληφα). Διπλάσια Ἀλκιβιάδῃ ἠξίουν αἱ πόλεις διδόναι [§ 91.] ἢ ἄλλῳ τινὶ τῶν στρατηγῶν (*Lys.* 19, 52). Τῇ προτεραίᾳ τῆς μάχης [1].

Rem. 1. Η is also used after words denoting an opposition, and after διαφέρω: τοὐναντίον ἢ τὸ προσδοκώμενον (*Pl. Legg.* 12, 966). Τὸ τῶν ἀνδρῶν γένος διαφερόντως ἔχει ἢ τὸ τῶν γυναικῶν (*Pl. Rep.* 5. 455). (Δίκαιόν ἐστι ποιεῖν τοὐναντίον ἢ ὃ σὺ λέγεις, *Pl. Rep.* 1, 339, and αὐτὸ τοὐναντίον ἐροῦμεν ἢ τὸν Σιμωνίδην ἔφαμεν λέγειν, *Pl. Rep.* 1, 334, without pronoun. Οἱ Πλαταιῆς προσέβαλλον τῷ τείχει τῶν Πελοποννησίων ἐκ τοὔμπαλιν ἢ οἱ ἄνδρες αὐτῶν ὑπερέβαινον, *Thuc.* 322, or ᾗ ἤ. Also τῇ ὑστεραίᾳ ᾗ, τῇ ὑστεραίᾳ ὅτε for ᾗ ἤ, or ᾗ ὅτε.)

Rem. 2. With ἄλλος note the expression οὐδεὶς ἄλλος πλήν (αὐτός, *none other but only himself*), and the adverbial expression ἄλλ' ἤ (*further than, save only*), after a negation or in a question equivalent to a negation: Ἐὰν σωφρονῆτε, τοῖς μαθηταῖς συμβουλεύσετε, μηδέποτε μηδενὶ ἀνθρώπων διαλέγεσθαι ἄλλ' ἢ ὑμῖν τε καὶ αὐτοῖς (*Pl. Euthyd.* 304). Ἄνδρες οὐδαμῇ φυλάττοντες ἡμᾶς φανεροί εἰσιν ἄλλ' ἢ κατὰ ταύτην τὴν ὁδόν (*Xen. An.* 4, 6. 11); also with ἄλλος preceding: Τίς ἂν εἰς ἄλλο τι ἀποβλέψας ἢ δειλὴν ἢ ἀνδρείαν πόλιν εἴποι ἄλλ' ἢ εἰς τοῦτο τὸ μέρος, ὃ προπολεμεῖ τε καὶ στρατεύεται ὑπὲρ αὐτῆς; (*Pl. Rep.* 4, 429.) Often incorrectly written ἀλλ' ἤ, as if from ἀλλά.)

When a magnitude expressed in numbers is increased by πλέον § 92.
(πλεῖον, πλεῖν), or diminished by ἔλαττον (μεῖον), these words, with (305)
or without ἤ, are attached to the denomination of the magnitude, without influencing its case. Πλέον ἢ τριάκοντα πλέθρα γῆς κτήσασθαι (*Lys.* 19, 29). Οὐσία πλέον ἢ πέντε ταλάντων (*Lys.* 19, 42). Ἐν πλέον ἢ διακοσίοις ἔτεσιν (*Thuc.*).—Ἡ λεία ἐπράθη ταλάντων οὐκ ἔλαττον πέντε καὶ εἴκοσιν (*Thuc.* 6, 95). Οἱ ἱππεῖς ἀποκτείνουσι τῶν ἀνδρῶν οὐ μεῖον πεντακοσίους (*Xen. An.* 6, 2, 24). Πέμψω ὄρνις ἐπ' αὐτὸν πλεῖν ἑξακοσίους τὸν ἀριθμόν (*Arist. Aves*, 1251). When the case is nominative or accusative, πλέον and ἔλαττον themselves may stand in the nominative or accusative, and govern the name of the magnitude in the genitive: Εἰσενήνεκται ὑπὲρ Ἀριστοφάνους καὶ τοῦ πατρὸς οὐκ ἔλαττον μνῶν τετταράκοντα (*Lys.* 19, 43). Πολύστρατος οὐ πλέον ὀκτὼ ἡμερῶν ἦλθεν εἰς τὸ βουλευτήριον (*Lys.* 20, 14).

Rem. Also frequently πλείους (μείους, ἐλάσσους) ἢ χίλιοι and πλείους χιλίων, e. g. Οὐ μεθεκτέον τῶν πραγμάτων πλείοσιν ἢ πεντακισχιλίοις (*Thuc.* 8, 65). Πλευστέα τριήρεσι μὲν οὐκ ἔλασσον ἢ ἑκατόν, ὁπλίταις δὲ τοῖς ξύμπασι πεντακισχιλίων οὐκ ἐλάσσοσιν (*Thuc.* 6, 25). Ξενοκλῆς συνοικεῖ τῇ γυναικὶ πλείω ἢ ὀκτὼ ἔτη ἤδη (*Isæ.* 3, 31). (Ὀλίγῳ ἐλάσσους πεντήκοντα, *Thuc.* 4, 44; πεντήκοντα as genitive [2].)

a) A comparison of two properties of the same subject is expressed § 93.
by two comparatives: Φιλόμηλον οἱ πολλοὶ βελτίονα ἡγοῦνται εἶναι ἢ (307)

---

[1] Περιττὰ τῶν ἀρκούντων, *Xen. Cyr.* 8, 2, 22.

[2] Νεώτερος τριάκοντα ἐτῶν (*Xen. Mem.* 1, 2, 35), = γεγονὼς ἔτη ἔλαττον (ἢ) τριάκοντα.

CHAP. VIII.]

§ 93.] πλουσιώτερον (*Lys.* 19, 15). (Ἀγαθὸς μᾶλλον ἢ πλούσιος, *rather good* —.)

308) *b*) The comparative sometimes denotes, without any definite comparison, a *somewhat* (tolerably) high degree, e. g. αὐθαδέστερόν τι ἀποκρίνεσθαι (*Thuc.* 8, 84). Ἐνθυμοῦμαι, μὴ ἀγροικότερον ᾖ λέγειν (*Pl. Gorg.* 462). Of some particular adjectives (*good, bad, beautiful*) the comparative is sometimes applied in the neuter to an action or procedure merely to denote a reference to the opposite procedure: Ἐθυόμην (*sacrificed in order to consult the god*), εἰ βέλτιον εἴη ὑμῖν τε ἐμοὶ ἐπιτρέψαι ταύτην τὴν ἀρχὴν καὶ ἐμοὶ ὑποστῆναι (*Xen. An.* 5, 9, 31). Μαλακώτεροι ἢ ὡς κάλλιον αὐτοῖς (*Pl. Rep.* 3, 410); especially in negation (οὐ κρεῖττον, βέλτιον, κάλλιον, χεῖρον, κάκιον): Πάλιν ἀναμιμνήσκου· οὐ γὰρ χεῖρον πολλάκις ἀκούειν (*Pl. Phæd.* 105, *it does no harm, one is none the worse for* —). Πρὸς τὸ φυλάττειν οὐ κάκιόν ἐστι φοβερὰν εἶναι τὴν ψυχήν (*Xen. Œcon.* 7, 25). (Νεώτερος and καινότερος with the accessory meaning of an alteration of what previously existed.)

308, R. 2) *c*) By an irregularity, the comparative takes after it a superfluous μᾶλλον, e. g. αἰσχυντηρότερος μᾶλλον τοῦ δέοντος (*Pl. Gorg.* 487). Αἱρετώτερόν ἐστι μαχομένους ἀποθανεῖν μᾶλλον ἢ φεύγοντας σώζεσθαι (*Xen. Cyr.* 3, 3, 51). Conversely, in verbs denoting a wish or choice, μᾶλλον is now and then omitted before ἤ (Ἀγησίλαος ᾑρεῖτο σὺν τῷ γενναίῳ μειονεκτεῖν ἢ σὺν τῷ ἀδίκῳ πλέον ἔχειν, *Xen. Ag.* 4, 5). (Οὐδὲν ἤ instead of οὐδὲν ἄλλο ἤ.)

§ 94. (309) The comparative is used to denote the highest degree, in speaking of two persons (also of two sets of persons): Ὁ πρεσβύτερος τῶν παίδων παρὼν ἐτύγχανεν (*Xen. An.* 1, 1, 1). Πότεροι μᾶλλον χαίρουσι καὶ λυποῦνται, οἱ φρόνιμοι ἢ οἱ ἄφρονες; (*Pl. Gorg.* 498.)

§ 95. (310) The superlative often denotes merely a very high degree [*superlative of eminence*]: Κάλλιστα λέγεις. Κῦρος φιλομαθέστατος ἦν. (Without the article, § 8, Rem. 3.) The exclusive sense is gathered from the context, or from a partitive genitive annexed.

Rem. 1. A superlative belonging to the predicate, sometimes governs a partitive genitive, which refers to the subject of the proposition, or to some other word of which the predicate holds in the highest degree: Οἱ Ἀθηναῖοι πάντων ἀνθρώπων πλείστῳ σίτῳ χρῶνται ἐπεισάκτῳ (*Dem.* 18, 87). Φιλοσοφία ἐστὶ παλαιοτάτη τε καὶ πλείστη τῶν Ἑλλήνων ἐν Κρήτῃ καὶ ἐν Λακεδαίμονι (*Pl. Prot.* 342). Ἀθήναζε ἀφῖξαι, οὗ τῆς Ἑλλάδος πλείστη ἐστὶν ἐξουσία τοῦ λέγειν (*Pl. Gorg.* 461). A genitive with the superlative of an adverb in the predicate, may refer, not only to the subject, but also to the object or another case: Σωκράτης προετρέπετο πάντων μάλιστα τοὺς συνόντας πρὸς ἐγκράτειαν (*Xen. Mem.* 4, 5, 1, *above all else to self-command*).

Rem. 2. The superlative with the genitive of a reflexive pronoun, or personal pronoun used reflexively, denotes the highest degree to which the property attains in one and the same subject at a certain time: Εἴθε σοι, ὦ Περίκλεις, τότε συνεγενόμην, ὅτε δεινότατος σαυτοῦ ἦσθα (*Xen. Mem.* 1, 2, 46).

§ 96. For additional force, the superlative takes before it the words

(denoting the excess or distance from others) πολλῷ, μακρῷ (παρὰ [§ 96.]
πολύ, poet. πολύ), e. g. μακρῷ εὐνούστατος (*Arist. Pac.* 673). (Ὅσῳ μέγιστον τὸ τῶν φυλάκων ἔργον, τοσούτῳ ἂν εἴη τέχνης τε καὶ ἐπιστήμης μεγίστης δεόμενον, *Pl. Rep.* 2, 374; *in the same degree, as*—.) The highest possible degree is denoted by additions such as ὡς (ὅπως) δυνατόν, ὡς, ὅπως (ᾗ) δύναμαι, *as—as possible* (e. g. ναῦς ὡς δύνανται πλείστας πληροῦσιν, *Thuc.* 7, 21, ὡς δύναμαι μάλιστα and ὡς μάλιστα δύναμαι), ὅσος, ὁπόσος with δύναμαι or οἷός τ' εἰμί (e. g. ὁπόσον δύνανται πλεῖστον σῖτον λαμβάνουσιν, *Xen. Œcon.* 20, 28, δύναμιν ὅσην οἷός τε ἦν πλείστην συμπαρασκευασάμενος, *Isocr. Phil.* 101), — or also by simply putting before the superlative ὡς or ὅτι (ὅ,τι), with adverbs also ὅπως (ᾗ), e. g. ὡς βέλτιστος, ὡς ἄριστα, ὅτι μάλιστα, ὅτι πλεῖστον χρόνον, ὅπως ἄριστα (ᾗ ῥᾷστα). [Cf. Lat. *quam* (*quantum, ut*) *maxime*; alone, or combined with *possum*, &c.]

REM. 1. Expressions such as οἱ μάλιστα ἀνοητότατοι (*Pl. Tim.* 92) (πλεῖστον ἔχθιστος, *Soph. Phil.* 631), are rare. Especially we may note the superlative with οἷος: χωρίον οἷον χαλεπώτατον (*Xen. An.* 4, 8, 2), literally, *a place such as the most difficult is* (with ἐστίν omitted); but by attraction οἷος and the superlative are treated as one word: ὄντος πάγου οἵου δεινοτάτου (*Pl. Conv.* 220).

REM. 2. A special way of adding force to the superlative, in some writers, is the prefixing of ἐν τοῖς (without regard to the gender of the superlative), e. g. ἐν τοῖς πρῶτοι (*Thuc.* 1, 6, *first of all*), ἐν τοῖς πλεῖσται νῆες (*Thuc.* 3, 17), ἐν τοῖς μάλιστα (*Pl. Crit.* 52, *most of all*), which perhaps originated in an ellipsis, the original expression being ἐν τοῖς μάλιστα, with the participle of the verb understood (ἐν τοῖς μάλιστα ὁμολογῶ, = ἐν τοῖς μάλιστα ὁμολογοῦσιν ὁμολογῶ), whence ἐν τοῖς came to be used as an adverb.

REM. 3. Sometimes the superlative may be said to take the place of the comparative, by taking (as also does μόνος) to the partitive genitive the word ἄλλων (or ἄλλων by itself, as the partitive genitive), which, in strictness, is suitable only to the comparative, e. g. Μάλιστα τῶν ἄλλων ἀνθρώπων. Ἡ μόνοι ἢ κάλλιστα τῶν ἄλλων (*Pl. Rep.* 1, 353). Μόνοι τῶν ἄλλων Ἑλλήνων (*Æsch.* 2, 37, *alone among, or of all, the Greeks*)[1].

CHAPTER IX.

Peculiarities in the Adjective construction of the Demonstrative and Relative Pronouns, and in their relations in the sentence.

a) THE demonstrative and relative pronouns take their gender and § 97.
number in accordance with the substantive words to which they (312)
refer, or which the speaker has in his thoughts (e. g. ἥδε, *this woman*).

[1] Μεγίστη στρατεία τῶν πρὸ αὐτῆς (*Thuc.* 1, 10), = μεγίστη πασῶν μέχρι ἐκείνου τοῦ χρόνου καὶ μείζων τῶν πρὸ αὐτῆς.

CHAP. IX.]

§ 97.] When the pronoun refers to several connected substantives of different genders, the rule § 2, *b* and *d*, is followed: *ἀδελφοὶ καὶ ἀδελφαί, οὓς εἶχον.* *Ἐκκλησιάζομεν περὶ πολέμου καὶ εἰρήνης, ἃ μεγίστην ἔχει δύναμιν ἐν τῷ βίῳ τῷ τῶν ἀνθρώπων* (*Isocr. Pac.* 2). Likewise a relative in the neuter may refer to a number of inanimate antecedents, even when they are all masculine or feminine: *Ταῦτα εἶπον οὐ πρὸς τὴν εὐσέβειαν οὐδὲ πρὸς τὴν δικαιοσύνην οὐδὲ πρὸς τὴν φρόνησιν ἀποβλέψας, ἃ σὺ διῆλθες* (*Isocr. Panath.* 217).

REM. The relative to an antecedent in the dual, may stand in the plural: *τὼ χεῖρε, ἃς ὁ θεὸς ἐπὶ τὸ συλλαμβάνειν ἀλλήλαιν ἐποίησεν* (*Xen. Mem.* 2, 3, 18).

b) When a demonstrative or relative pronoun, not referring to a particular substantive, denotes something comprising a number of units or individuals, it stands in the neuter plural: *Ταῦτα οὔπω ἠκηκόειν.* *Ἐρῶ σοι, ἃ οἶδα.* (*Ταῦτα γὰρ καὶ καλὰ καὶ δίκαια, μὴ περιορᾶν πόλεις ἀρχαίας ἐξανεστώσας*, *Dem.* 16, 25, where the pronoun is conceived in a general way: *this procedure*[1].)

§ 98. *a*) A demonstrative pronoun to which a substantive is attached as
313) predicate-noun by *εἰμί*, or by a verb denoting *to call*, *consider as*, &c., is apt to assume the gender and number of the substantive (attraction): *Οὗτος ὅρος ἐστὶ δικαιοσύνης ἀληθῆ τε λέγειν καὶ ἃ ἂν λάβῃ τις, ἀποδιδόναι* (*Pl. Rep.* 1, 331). *Κίνησις αὕτη μεγίστη τοῖς Ἕλλησιν ἐγένετο* (*Thuc.* 1, 1; different from *αὕτη ἡ κίνησις*, § 11, R. 1). *Αὕτη πενία ἐστὶ σαφής, τὸ δεόμενόν τινος μὴ ἔχειν χρῆσθαι* (*Xen. Œcon.* 8, 2). *Καὶ ψυχῆς ἄρα καθ' ὅσον ἂν εὑρίσκωμεν κακίας ἀφαιρεσίν τινα, καθαρμὸν αὐτὸν λέγοντες ἐν μέλει φθεγξόμεθα* (*Pl. Soph.* 227).

REM. The pronoun however stands in the neuter, when the general reference of the demonstrative is purposely retained, and with a stress upon it: *Εὐδαιμονίαν τοῦτο νομίζω, τὸ πολλὰ ἔχοντα πολλὰ καὶ δαπανᾶν* (*Xen.*). *Τοῦτο πῶς οὐκ ἀμαθία ἐστίν;* (*Pl. Apol.* 29)[2]. *Οὐ λόγων κόμπος τάδε μᾶλλον ἢ ἔργων ἐστὶν ἀλήθεια* (*Thuc.*). *Ἔγωγέ φημι ταῦτα φλυαρίας εἶναι* (*Xen. An.* 1, 3, 18). (*Τούτῳ τροφῇ χρῶνται*, *Xen. Mem.* 3, 11, 6.)

315) *b*) A relative pronoun, having an antecedent and also followed by another substantive as predicate-noun, may conform itself to either: the latter, when the relative clause merely adds a remark as apposi-

---

[1] In questions the singular *τί* is applied to such a subject of the neuter plural: *Τί ταῦτά ἐστιν;* (*Xen. An.* 2, 1, 22.) *Σκεψώμεθα, τί ποτ' ἐστὶν ἃ σὺ ἐμοὶ ὀνειδίζεις* (*Pl. Gorg.* 508). *Σκεπτέον, τί τὰ συμβαίνοντα* (*Pl. ibid.*).

[2] *Ἀπόλλων τάδ' ἦν* (*Soph. Œd. R.* 1329, *it was A.*). *Οὐκ Ἴωνες τάδε εἰσὶν οὐδὲ Ἑλλησπόντιοι* (*Thuc.* 6, 77, *these are not Ionians, here are no Ionians*). *Τοῦτο ἀνάγκη* (*Pl. Gorg.* 475) = *ἀναγκαῖον*.

tion to a notion in itself known or defined, so that even without the [§ 98.]
relative clause the sense would be complete: Ἡ πόλις τοῦ μεγίστου νοσήματος οὐ μεθέξει, ὃ στάσις καλεῖται (*Pl. Legg.* 5, 744, where the relative clause is essential to the completeness of the notion, "the disease called faction").—Φίλον, ὃ μέγιστον ἀγαθὸν εἶναί φασιν, οἱ πολλοὶ ὅπως κτήσονται, οὐ φροντίζουσιν (*Xen. Mem.* 2, 4, 2, where the relative clause might be omitted, without making the notion incomplete). Ἡ τοῦ ῥεύματος ἐκείνου πηγή, ὃν ἵμερον Ζεὺς ὠνόμασεν (*Pl. Phædr.* 255). When the antecedent is the predicate of the principal proposition, or the purport of the entire proposition, the relative may also, if a predicate-noun be attached, either be put in the neuter, or, which is more frequent, conform itself to the predicate-noun: Οἱ αὐτοὶ πολέμιοι ἡμῖν ἦσαν, ὅπερ σαφεστάτη πίστις (*Thuc.* 1, 35). Οὐδὲν ἄδικον διαγεγένημαι ποιῶν, ἥνπερ νομίζω μελέτην εἶναι καλλίστην ἀπολογίας (*Xen. Apol.* 3).

Sometimes the reference of a pronoun to its antecedent is less exact, the sense of § 99.
the antecedent being considered rather than its grammatical form. (316)

a) A masc. or fem. antecedent may be followed by a pronoun in the neuter, which puts the notion as a thing in a general way: Ἐπειδὴ τοίνυν ἡ αὐτὴ ἀρετὴ πάντων ἐστί, πειρῶ εἰπεῖν καὶ ἀναμνησθῆναι, τί αὐτό φησι Γοργίας εἶναι (*Pl. Meno*, 73, *that it*, the thing in question, *is*). Ὡμολογοῦμεν ἐπιστήμης μηδὲν εἶναι κρεῖττον, ἀλλὰ τοῦτο ἀεὶ κρατεῖν, ὅπου ἂν ἐνῇ, καὶ ἡδονῆς καὶ τῶν ἄλλων ἁπάντων (*Pl. Prot.* 357).

b) A pronoun refers to an antecedent contained in, and to be extracted from, a previous word, e. g. a relative to the personal pronoun involved in a possessive pronoun: Καὶ οἰκία γε πολὺ μείζων ἡ ὑμετέρα τῆς ἐμῆς, οἵ γε οἰκίᾳ χρῆσθε γῇ τε καὶ οὐρανῷ (*Xen. Cyr.* 5, 2, 15) [1]. Especially after a collective term, or the name of a city or country, the pronoun refers to the individuals composing the class, or inhabiting the place: Συνεφείπετο δὲ τοῖς πελτασταῖς καὶ τὸ Ἀρκαδικὸν ὁπλιτικόν, ὧν ἦρχε Κλεάνωρ (*Xen. An.* 4, 8, 18). Μελέτω σοι τοῦ πλήθους καὶ περὶ παντὸς ποιοῦ κεχαρισμένως αὐτοῖς ἄρχειν (*Isocr. ad Nic.* 15). Θεμιστοκλῆς φεύγει ἐκ Πελοποννήσου ἐς Κέρκυραν, ὢν αὐτῶν εὐεργέτης (*Thuc.* 1, 136). Καὶ ἀπὸ Πελοποννήσου παρέσται ὠφέλεια (= βοήθεια), οἳ τῶνδε κρείσσους εἰσὶ τὸ παρὰ πᾶν τὰ πολέμια (*Thuc.* 6, 80).

c) A substantive in the singular is followed by a relative pronoun in the plural, the thought passing on to more of the same kind, and to the whole genus: Αὐχμηρός τις καὶ ἀπὸ παντὸς περιουσίαν ποιούμενος, θησαυροποιὸς ἀνήρ, οὓς δὴ καὶ ἐπαινεῖ τὸ πλῆθος (*Pl. Rep.* 8, 554).

d) A preceding εἴ τις (ἤν τις) has sometimes a demonstrative referred to it in the plural, and in like manner a plural term may be the antecedent of the indefinite relative ὅστις, ὃς ἄν: Εἴς γε μὴν δικαιοσύνην εἴ τις Κύρῳ φανερὸς γένοιτο ἐπιδείκνυσθαι βουλόμενος, περὶ παντὸς ἐποιεῖτο τούτους πλουσιωτέρους ποιεῖν τῶν ἐκ τοῦ ἀδίκου φιλοκερδούντων (*Xen. An.* 1, 9, 16). Ἢν παρὰ ταῦτα ἀδικεῖν τις ἐπιχειρῇ, τούτοις Κῦρος

---

[1] Ἔρχεται πόλιν τὴν Εὐρυτείαν· τόνδε γὰρ (viz. Εὔρυτον) μεταίτιον μόνον βροτῶν ἔφασκε τοῦδ' εἶναι πάθους (*Soph. Trach.* 260).

[§ 99.] τε καὶ ἡμεῖς πολέμιοι ἐσόμεθα (*Xen. Cyr.* 7, 4, 5). Αἱ γυναῖκες ἱκέτευον πάντας, ὅτῳ ἐντυγχάνοιεν, μὴ φεύγειν καταλιπόντας αὐτάς (*Xen. Cyr.* 3, 3, 67). Αἱ πόλεις προαγορεύουσι τοῖς πολίταις τὴν κατάστασιν τῆς πόλεως μὴ κινεῖν, ὡς ἀποθανουμένους, ὃς ἂν τοῦτο δρᾷ (*Pl. Rep.* 426).

c) Where the antecedent is a neuter term denoting persons, the relative pronoun sometimes (especially in figurative expressions) resumes the natural gender: τὰ τοιαῦτα κινάδη, οἳ πεποιήκασιν οὐδὲν οὐδὲ πράξουσιν ἀγαθὸν ὑπὲρ τῆς πόλεως (*Dein.* 1, 40). (Τέκνον τόδε, ὃν οὐδὲν αἴτιον μέλλουσι σὺν ἐμοὶ τῇ ταλαιπώρῳ κτενεῖν, *Eur. Androm.* 570.)

§ 100. On the construction of the demonstrative pronoun it is to be further remarked:

a) A demonstrative pronoun is put as object, so that it is characterized by an adjective, or by an indefinite substantive with an adjective, attached by way of apposition, in which case the demonstrative, by an attraction (as § 98, a), conforms itself to the attached substantive. (In English we use either a demonstrative adverb, as *herein* or the like, or a circumlocution with relative and verb substantive): Ταῦτ' ἀληθῆ λέγω (*Pl. Prot.* 342, *herein I speak truth*, or, *this that I say, is true*). Λέγε μοι, εἴ τί σοι δοκῶ τοῦτο χαλεπὸν ποιῆσαι, ὅτι ᾔτησά σε δοῦναί μοι τὸν βουλόμενον τῶν Μήδων μοι ἕπεσθαι (*Xen. Cyr.* 5, 5, 21). Τούτους ἔλεγον οἱ στρατιῶται βαρβαρωτάτους διελθεῖν (*Xen. An.* 5, 4, 34, *these, the soldier said, were the most barbarous that* —). Καλὴν ἐκείνην δωρεὰν αὐτῷ δεδώκατε (*Lys.*). Οὐκέτι τοῦτο φαῦλον οὐδ' ἁπλοῦν ἔργον ἐρωτᾷς (*Xen. Cyr.* 1, 6, 27, *what thou here askest, is* —). (Ἔθος τι τοῦτο Σωκράτης ἔχει, *Pl. Conv.* 175. Τί οὖν δὴ τοῦτο λέγεις; *Pl. Gorg.* 452, *what then meanest thou by this?*)

b) A demonstrative is attached, as apposition, to an interrogative pronoun (τίς οὗτος, τίς ὅδε), to mark that the thing asked about is something that has been already intimated, or that is at the same time referred to: Ἀγγελίαν φέρω χαλεπὴν καὶ βαρεῖαν. Τίνα ταύτην; (*Pl. Crit.* 43, *what, pray?*) (Τίνας ἕδρας τάσδε θοάζετε; *Soph. Œd. R.* 2.) Ἐνδοῦνται αἱ ψυχαὶ εἰς τοιαῦτα ἤθη ὁποῖ' ἄττ' ἂν καὶ μεμελετηκυῖαι τύχωσιν ἐν τῷ βίῳ. Τὰ ποῖα δὴ ταῦτα λέγεις, ὦ Σώκρατες; (*Pl. Phæd.* 81, *what meanest thou by these? what are these, that you speak of?*)

c) Οὗτος and ὅδε are added by way of apposition, in the sense of the adverb *here:* Καὶ ἐγὼ ἠρόμην, ὅπου Πολέμαρχος εἴη. Οὗτος, ἔφη, ὄπισθεν προσέρχεται (*Pl. Rep.* 1, 327).

d) A demonstrative pronoun, when not particularly emphatic, is regularly omitted in the accusative, and often even in the dative: Εἰσῄεσαν παρὰ Κῦρον τῶν στρατιωτῶν τινες, ἀξιοῦντες εἰδέναι, τί σφισιν ἔσται, ἐὰν κρατήσωσιν· ὁ δὲ ἐμπιπλὰς ἁπάντων τὴν γνώμην ἀπέπεμπεν (*Xen. An.* 1. 7, 8). Γύλιππος μέρος τι πέμψας πρὸς τὸ φρούριον αἱρεῖ (*Thuc.* 7, 3). Ἐπαγγειλαμένου τοῦ Ἀγησιλάου τὴν στρατείαν, διδόασιν οἱ Λακεδαιμόνιοι ὥσπερ ᾔτησεν (*Xen. Hell.* 3, 4, 3). (Πρεσβυτέρῳ νεωτέρων πάντων ἄρχειν τε καὶ κολάζειν προστέτακται, *Pl. Rep.* 5, 465, without a pronoun to κολάζειν, although it governs a different case from ἄρχειν.)

e) Sometimes a demonstrative pronoun is put superfluously to enforce some substantive notion preceding in the same sentence; especially οὗτος after substantives which are separated by a parenthetic clause from the rest of the sentence: Κλέαρχος Τολμίδην Ἠλεῖον, ὃν ἐτύγχανεν ἔχων παρ' ἑαυτῷ, κήρυκα ἄριστον τῶν τότε, τοῦτον ἀνειπεῖν ἐκέλευσε, κτλ. (*Xen. An.* 2, 2, 20). Τοῖς ἀγαθοῖς κακῶς χρῶνται καὶ τοῖς ὠφελεῖν δυναμένοις τούτοις βλάπτειν τοὺς συμπολιτευομένους ἐπιχειροῦσιν (*Isocr. Nic.* 4).

More rarely and without emphasis *αὐτός*: Ἦ καί, ὥσπερ τῶν ἄλλων τεχνῶν ἔχοιμεν ἂν εἰπεῖν ὅ,τι ἔργον ἑκάστης, οὕτω καὶ τῆς οἰκονομίας δυναίμεθ' ἂν εἰπεῖν ὅ,τι ἔργον αὐτῆς ἐστιν; (*Xen. Œc.* 1, 2.) In comparisons ἐκεῖνος: Ὁ θεὸς δέδωκεν αὐτοῖς (τοῖς Λακεδαιμονίοις), ὥσπερ ὑμῖν κατὰ θάλατταν εὐτυχεῖν, οὕτως ἐκείνοις κατὰ γῆν (*Xen. Hell.* 7, 1, 9). [§ 100.]

REM. Adverbially ταῦτα, *therefore* (§ 27. a. R. 2), καὶ ταῦτα, *and that, and that too* (Μένωνα οὐκ ἐζήτει ὁ ἄνθρωπος, καὶ ταῦτα παρ' Ἀριαίου ὢν τοῦ Μένωνος ξένου, *Xen. An.* 2, 4, 15), τάδε in the expression τὰ νῦν τάδε (§ 14, b. R. 2).

§ 101. (322) In the structure of the relative proposition there are various peculiarities, of which we must note the following.

a) The substantive defined by the relative clause, is often drawn [*attracted*] into it, in prose most commonly so that the relative clause precedes the demonstrative: *Πολλοὶ τὰ χρήματα καταναλώσαντες, ὧν πρόσθεν ἀπείχοντο κερδῶν, αἰσχρὰ νομίζοντες, τούτων οὐκ ἀπέχονται* (*Xen. Mem.* 1, 2, 22). *Κῦρος, εἴ τινα ὁρῴη κατασκευάζοντα, ἧς ἄρχοι χώρας, καὶ προσόδους ποιοῦντα, οὐδένα ἂν πώποτε ἀφείλετο, ἀλλ' ἀεὶ πλείω προσεδίδου* (*Xen. An.* 1, 9, 19). (With *ὅςτις*: *Πᾶν, ὅ,τι πάσχων τις πάθος ἄνοιαν ἴσχει, νόσον προσρητέον.* *Pl. Tim.* 86.)

REM. Sometimes the substantive, when separated by the relative clause from the remainder of the sentence, takes its case from the relative, but without being drawn into the relative clause: Νικήρατος ἀργύριον μὲν ἢ χρυσίον οὐδ' αὐτὸς ἔφη καταλιπεῖν οὐδέν, ἀλλὰ τὴν ἄλλην οὐσίαν, ἣν κατέλιπε τῷ υἱεῖ, οὐ πλείονος ἀξία ἐστὶν ἢ τεττάρων καὶ δέκα ταλάντων (*Lys.* 19, 47). Ἐν πόλει ᾗ ἥκιστα πρόθυμοι ἄρχειν οἱ μέλλοντες ἄρξειν, ταύτην ἄριστα καὶ ἀστασιαστότατα ἀνάγκη οἰκεῖσθαι (*Pl. Rep.* 7, 520). This however is an irregularity (*anacoluthon*) and occurs most frequently in poets. (Τὸν ἄνδρα τοῦτον, ὃν πάλαι ζητεῖς, οὗτός ἐστιν ἐνθάδε, *Soph. Œd. C.* 449.)

b) Especially the substantive is drawn into the relative clause, when it is a new term annexed to the preceding: *ὁ πατήρ, ὃν μόνον εἴχομεν βοηθόν, ἀπῆν, = ὁ μόνος βοηθὸς ὃν εἴχομεν.* An adjective or genitive belonging to the antecedent is also often drawn into the relative clause: Λόγους ἄκουσον, οὓς σοι δυστυχεῖς ἥκω φέρων (*Eur. Or.* 854). Περὶ ὧν μεγίστων καὶ καλλίστων ἐπιχειρεῖ λέγειν Ὅμηρος, πολέμων τε καὶ στρατηγιῶν καὶ διοικήσεων πόλεων, δίκαιόν που ἐρωτᾶν αὐτόν (*Pl. Rep.* 10, 599). Οἱ Λακεδαιμόνιοι τοὺς ἐμπόρους, οὓς ἔλαβον Ἀθηναίων καὶ τῶν ξυμμάχων, ἐν ὁλκάσι πλέοντας, ἀπέκτειναν (*Thuc.* 2, 67). Οἱ Ἀθηναῖοι τοὺς ὀχετοὺς τῶν Συρακουσίων, οἳ ἐς τὴν πόλιν ὑπονομηδὸν ποτοῦ ὕδατος ἠγμένοι ἦσαν, διέφθειραν (*Thuc.* 6, 100).

§ 102. (324) *a*) A demonstrative pronoun standing alone as antecedent to a relative, is often omitted, especially in the nominative or accusative: *Οἷς μάλιστα τὰ παρόντα ἀρκεῖ, ἥκιστα τῶν ἀλλοτρίων ὀρέγονται* (*Xen. Conv.* 4, 42). *Τίς μισεῖν δύναιτο ἄν, ὑφ' οὗ εἰδείη καλός τε καὶ ἀγαθὸς νομιζόμενος;* (*Xen.*) Sometimes even in other cases: *Οὐδεμία πάρεστιν, ἃς ἥκειν ἐχρῆν* (*Arist. Eccl.* 19). *Ἀναγκαῖον αὐτοῖς ἐστι διαλέ-*

[§ 102.] γεσθαι παρ' ὧν ἂν λάβωσι τὸν μισθόν (*Xen. Mem.* 1, 2, 6). Οὐ περὶ ὀνόματος ἡ ἀμφισβήτησις, οἷς τοσούτων πέρι σκέψις πρόκειται (*Pl. Rep.* 7, 533). Ὅσα πώποθ' ἅπαντες ὑμεῖς ἠβουλήθητε, οὐδὲν πώποθ' ὑμᾶς ἐξέφυγεν (*Dem.* 14, 15). Ἀναλίσκουσιν οὐκ εἰς ἃ δεῖ (*Xen. Œc.* 3, 5; = εἰς ταῦτα, εἰς ἅ, omission of the demonstrative and of the preposition which should be repeated before the relative).

Rem. The demonstrative in all cases is frequently omitted, when its place is supplied by the attraction; see § 103. Before relative adverbs of place demonstrative adverbs are omitted: Κατατίθημι πάλιν ὅθεν ἂν ἕκαστα λαμβάνω (*Xen.*).

(324, R. 3) *b*) The indefinite pronoun which is the subject to the verb and the antecedent to the relative in ἔστιν ὅς, εἰσὶν οἵ, &c., is usually omitted: Οἱ μὲν πολλοὶ κατέμενον, ἦσαν δέ, οἳ ὑπεχώρουν σὺν τῷ βασιλεῖ (*Xen. Cyr.* 3, 1, 3). Τῶν συμμάχων ὑμῖν εἰσιν, οἳ διαλέγονται περὶ φιλίας τοῖς πολεμίοις (*Xen. Hell.* 6, 4, 24).

Rem. 1. As ἔστιν ὅς. ἔστιν ἅ, so, without change of the verb, ἔστιν οἵ (οὕς, ὧν, οἷς, sometimes even οἵτινες), and this ἔστιν οἵ, thus declined through all the cases, is sometimes treated as a single word, in the sense of *some, certain*, like the word ἔνιοι thence formed: Ἐνταῦθα ἔβαλλον ταῖς βώλοις καὶ ἔστιν οἳ ἐτύγχανον καὶ θωράκων καὶ γέρρων (*Xen. Cyr.* 2, 3, 18). Εἰπέ μοι· Ἔστιν οὕστινας ἀνθρώπων τεθαύμακας ἐπὶ σοφίᾳ; (*Xen. Mem.* 1, 4, 2.) (With the negation: Προγόνων καλὰ ἔργα οὐκ ἔστιν οἷς μείζω καὶ πλείω ὑπάρχει ἢ Ἀθηναίοις. *Xen. Mem.* 3, 5, 3.) Ἦλθε Γύλιππος στρατιὰν ἔχων ἐκ Πελοποννήσου καὶ ἀπὸ τῶν ἐν Σικελίᾳ πόλεων ἔστιν ὧν (*Thuc.* 7, 11). Οἱ Λακεδαιμόνιοι τῶν ἄλλων Ἑλλήνων τὸν βουλόμενον ἐκέλευον ἕπεσθαι πλὴν Ἰώνων καὶ Ἀχαιῶν καὶ ἔστιν ὧν ἄλλων ἐθνῶν (*Thuc.* 3, 92; ἔστιν ἐν οἷς, *Thuc.* 5, 25, *in some things*). (But also εἰσὶν οἵ, *Thuc.* 6, 10.) But the imperfect ἦν οἵ for ἦσαν οἵ is rare, e.g. Ἦν τούτων τῶν σταθμῶν, οὓς πάνυ μακροὺς ἤλαυνεν (*Xen. An.* 1, 5, 7).

Rem. 2. In the same manner an indefinite pronoun, a pronominal adverb, and the substantive designation of a place, or of a kind and manner, is omitted before relative adverbs of place or manner, especially with ἔστιν: Οἱ ἡγεμόνες τοὺς Ἕλληνας ἄξουσιν, ἔνθεν ἕξουσι τὰ ἐπιτήδεια (*Xen. An.* 2, 3, 6). Ἀγορὰν οὐδεὶς ἡμῖν παρέξει οὐδ' ὁπόθεν ἐπισιτιούμεθα (*Xen. An.* 2, 4, 5). Ἔστιν ἔνθα ἰσχυρῶς ὠφελοῦσι σφενδονῆται παρόντες (*Xen. Cyr.* 7, 4, 15). Ὁ κόσμιος καὶ μὴ φιλοχρήματος μηδ' ἀνελεύθερος ἔσθ' ὅπη ἂν δυςξύμβολος ἢ ἄδικος γένοιτο; (*Pl. Rep.* 6, 486.) Οὐκ ἔστιν ὅπως οὐκ ἐπιθήσεται ἡμῖν βασιλεύς (*Xen. An.* 2, 4, 3, *it is not to be thought that the king will not* —, i. e. *he undoubtedly will* —). (Ἔστιν ὅπου, ᾗ. Οὐκ ἔσθ' ὅπου.) Also ἔστιν ὅτε, *sometimes.*

§ 103. When the relative in its own clause should be an accusative of the *object*, but the antecedent is a substantive or a demonstrative in the dative or genitive, the relative often assumes this case by attraction (τῶν δώρων, ὧν —, τούτοις, οἷς, instead of ἅ). This may even take place, when the demonstrative follows the relative clause (οἷς —, τούτοις, instead of ἃ —, τούτοις), or so, that the substantive to which the relative refers, is put in the relative clause (§ 101, a: αἷς ἔλαβον ναυσίν, *περὶ ὧν ἔλαβον νεῶν*, for *ταῖς ναυσίν, ἃς—, περὶ τῶν νεῶν, ἃς —*). A [§ 103.] demonstrative, not emphatic and merely introducing the relative clause (§ 102), is usually omitted, and its place supplied by the relative's assuming its case (*περὶ ὧν* = *περὶ ἐκείνων, οὓς, ἃς* or *ἃ —, οἷς* = *ἐκείνοις, οὓς, ἃς* or *ἃ*). *Τούτων, ὧν νῦν ὑμῖν παρακελεύομαι, οὐδὲν τοῖς δούλοις προστάττω* (*Xen. Cyr.* 8, 6, 13). *Εἴ τινος ἄλλου δεῖ πρὸς τούτοις, οἷς εἶπε Ξενοφῶν, καὶ αὐτίκα ἐξέσται ποιεῖν* (*Xen. An.* 3, 2, 33). *Τίς ἡ ὠφέλεια τοῖς θεοῖς τυγχάνει οὖσα ἀπὸ τῶν δώρων, ὧν παρ' ἡμῶν λαμβάνουσιν;* (*Pl. Euthyph.* 14.) *Ἀπεστέλλετ' αὖθις αὖ τὸ τρίτον πρέσβεις ὡς τὸν Φίλιππον ἐπὶ ταῖς καλαῖς καὶ μεγάλαις ἐλπίσι ταύταις, αἷς Αἰσχίνης ὑπέσχητο* (*Dem.* 19, 121). *Οἷς ἂν οἱ ἄλλοι ἐργάζωνται, τούτοις σὺ χρήσῃ* (*Xen. Mem.* 2, 1, 25). *Ὧν Χαρίδημος κακῶς ὑμᾶς ποιεῖν ἐπιχειρεῖ, τούτων αὐτῷ ὀργίζεσθαι ὑμᾶς προσήκει* (*Dem.* 23, 184). *Συρακούσιοι μὲν τῆς ναυμαχίας τροπαῖον ἔστησαν, Ἀθηναῖοι δέ, ἧς οἱ Τυρσηνοὶ τροπῆς ἐποιήσαντο τῶν πεζῶν ἐς τὴν λίμνην* (*Thuc.* 7, 54). *Τοὺς μὲν ἄλλους νόμους ἐάσω, περὶ δ' οὗ πρότερόν ποτ' αὐτὸς Τιμοκράτης ἔθηκε νόμου, διέξειμι* (*Dem.* 24, 61). *Καλλικρατίδας πρὸς αἷς παρὰ Λυσάνδρου ἔλαβε ναυσί, προσεπλήρωσεν ἐκ Χίου καὶ Ῥόδου πεντήκοντα ναῦς* (*Xen. Hell.* 1, 6, 3). *Ἡ πόλις ἡμῶν, ὧν ἔλαβε, πᾶσιν μετέδωκεν* (*Isocr. Paneg.* 29). *Ἀμελῶ ὧν με δεῖ πράττειν* (*Xen. Cyr.* 5, 1, 8). *Ναυμαχία παλαιτάτη ὧν ἴσμεν* (*Thuc.* 1, 13). *Τοῦτον τὸν οἶνον Κῦρος δεῖταί σου ἐκπιεῖν σὺν οἷς μάλιστα φιλεῖς* (*Xen. An.* 1, 9, 25). *Οἱ Θηβαῖοι οἷς εὐτυχήκεσαν ἐν Λεύκτροις, οὐ μετρίως ἐκέχρηντο* (*Dem.* 18, 18. Because the phrase is, *ἃ εὐτύχηκα*, *the good fortune I have had*).

Rem. 1. This attraction, however, can only take place when the relative clause really serves to assign and define the matter in hand, i. e. is essential to complete the sense; never, when it is only added in continuation or as a remark. e. g. *Πάντων, ὧν εἶχον, ἀγαθῶν σοι μετέδωκα, ἃ* (not *ὧν*) *σὺ τότε μὲν λόγῳ ἐμεγάλυνες, νῦν δὲ φαυλίζεις.* The attraction is also not unfrequently forborne where it might have place, both after substantives and after demonstratives standing alone: *Οἱ Κορίνθιοι τὰ σκάφη μὲν οὐχ εἷλκον ἀναδούμενοι τῶν νεῶν, ἃς καταδύσειαν, πρὸς δὲ τοὺς ἀνθρώπους ἐτράποντο* (*Thuc.* 1, 50). *Μέμνησθε τοῦ νόμου καὶ τοῦ ὅρκου, ὃν ὀμωμόκατε* (*Isæ.* 2, 47; but *Lys.* 10, 32: *Βοηθήσατε τοῖς νόμοις καὶ τοῖς ὅρκοις οἷς ὀμωμόκατε*). *Ἔνεστιν ἡμῖν τυχεῖν παρὰ τῶν Ἑλλήνων τῆς τιμῆς ταύτης, ἥνπερ οἱ ἐν Λακεδαίμονι βασιλεῖς παρὰ τῶν πολιτῶν ἔχουσιν* (*Isocr. de Pac.* 144). *Οὐ συμφέροντα ἐκείνοις, οὓς ἐγκωμιάζουσι, ποιοῦσιν* (*Dem.* 14, 1). *Τοιαύτης τινὸς ἡμῖν ἐπιστήμης δεῖ, ἣ ἐπίσταται χρῆσθαι τούτῳ, ὃ ἂν ποιῇ* (*Pl. Euthyd.* 289). It is very unusual for the attraction to be omitted where the relative corresponds with an omitted demonstrative (*Ὄμνυμι ἐμμενεῖν ἃ σοῦ κλύω*, *Eur. Med.* 753).

Rem. 2. It sometimes happens, that a neuter relative which ought to stand in the *nominative* (coincident in form with the accusative), passes by attraction into the dative or genitive: *Εἴ σοι δοκεῖ ἐμμένειν οἷς ἄρτι ἔδοξεν ἡμῖν, ἕπου* (*Pl. Prot.* 353). *Βλαβήσονται αἱ τῶν πολεμίων νῆες ἀφ' ὧν ἡμῖν παρεσκεύασται* (*Thuc.* 7, 67). (*Ἀναλίσκουσιν οὐκ εἰς ἃ δεῖ μόνον, ἀλλὰ καὶ εἰς ἃ βλάβην φέρει*, *Xen. Œc.* 3, 5. = *εἰς ταῦτα, ἃ —*.) Likewise the dative of a relative now and then passes by attrac-

[§ 103.] tion into the genitive: *Παρ' ὧν βοηθεῖς, οὐκ ἀπολήψῃ χάριν* (*Æsch.* 2, 117, = *παρὰ τούτων, οἷς* —)[1].

Rem. 3. Sometimes the accusative of the neuter relative which is changed by attraction, stands, not as object in the proper sense, but to denote the whole extent of the predicate (by § 27), especially in the plural: *Ἐξ ὧν τὰ σαυτοῦ ἐπαινεῖς, τίνι δικαίῳ λόγῳ τοῦ μηχανοποιοῦ καταφρονεῖς;* (*Pl. Gorg.* 512, *from what thou sayest in praise of thine own.*) *Δίκην ἐβούλοντο λαβεῖν ὧν ἐπὶ τῶν ἄλλων ἐτεθέαντο Μειδίαν θρασὺν ὄντα καὶ βδελυρόν* (*Dem.* 21, 3). By this means, an attracted relative in the neuter plural sometimes approximates to the signification of a demonstrative with *ὅτι*. (*Ἀνθ' ὧν*, *in requital for that* —, i. e. *because, forasmuch as*: *Οἱ Ἕλληνες τὰ τείχη ἡμῶν καθεῖλον ἀνθ' ὧν ἡμεῖς τἀκείνων ἐκωλύσαμεν πεσεῖν.* *Pl. Menex.* 244; mostly poetical.) From an attraction, and a coalition of a demonstrative and a relative adverb, result the expressions, used as conjunctions, *ἀφ' οὗ* (= *ἀπ' ἐκείνου, ὅτε* —, *ἀπ' ἐκείνου τοῦ χρόνου, ὅτε* —), *ἐξ οὗ*, *ἐν ᾧ*, *μέχρι οὗ* (*μέχρις οὗ*, but also simply *μέχρι*, *μέχρι ἄν*, without *οὗ*), *ἄχρι οὗ* (in Herod. *ἐς ὅ*), together with *ἐφ' ᾧ* or *ἐφ' ᾧ τε* (= *ἐπὶ τοῖσδε, ὥστε*, *on condition of* —).

Rem. 4. When the relative ought to have before it the same preposition as its antecedent, this preposition is usually dropt, especially when the verb in both clauses is the same: *Τὸν πλοῦν ἐποιησάμην ἐκ τῆς Μιτυλήνης ἐν τῷ πλοίῳ, ᾧ Ἡρώδης οὗτος* (*Ant.* 5, 20). *Ἐγὼ ἐν τῷ χρόνῳ, ᾧ ὑμῶν ἀκούω ἀπορούντων, τί τὸ δίκαιον, ἐν τούτῳ δικαιοτέρους τοὺς ἀνθρώπους ποιῶ* (*Xen. Conv.* 4, 1).

§ 104. (32.) *a*) When in two connected relative clauses, both referring to the same antecedent, the relative would stand first in the accusative, dative, or genitive, and then in the nominative or accusative, the relative is often omitted in the latter clause, and left to be supplied from the former: *Τούτοις ἅπασιν ἐκεῖνοι, οἷς τι μέλει τῆς ἑαυτῶν ψυχῆς ἀλλὰ μὴ σώματα πλάττοντες ζῶσι, χαίρειν λέγουσιν* (*Pl. Phæd.* 82). *Τῶν παρόντων τοῖς ἀνθρώποις ἀγαθῶν, ὅσα μὴ παρὰ θεῶν ἔχομεν, ἀλλὰ δι' ἀλλήλους ἡμῖν γέγονεν, οὐδὲν ἄνευ τῆς πόλεως τῆς ἡμετέρας γεγένηται* (*Isocr. Paneg.* 38). *Περὶ ὧν δικαστήριον ἔγνωκε καὶ τέλος ἔσχηκε, πῶς οὐ δεινὰ ποιεῖ Τιμοκράτης νόμον εἰσφέρων, δι' οὗ ταῦτα λυθήσεται;* (*Dem.* 24, 73, = *καὶ ἃ τέλος ἔσχηκεν.*)

b) Sometimes, especially when the relative should stand first in the nominative, and then in a different case, a demonstrative or personal pronoun is put the second time instead of the relative: *Ποῦ δὴ ἐκεῖνός ἐστιν ὁ ἀνήρ, ὃς συνεθήρα ἡμῖν καὶ σύ μοι*

---

[1] Other more rare and anomalous instances of attraction in the relative: *a*) *Ὁ ἀντειπὼν οἷς ἐκεῖνοι ἐβούλοντο πραχθῆναι* (*Lys.* 12, 27: the subject-accusative of the infinitive attracted. *Μὴ ὄντων τῶν ὑπηρετῶν, οἵων δεῖ*, *Xen. Cyr.* 8, 1, 12, = *οἵους δεῖ εἶναι*). *b*) *Δεῖ τοὺς μέλλοντας διοίσειν περί τι πρῶτον πρὸς τοῦτο πεφυκέναι καλῶς, πρὸς ὃ ἂν προῃρημένοι τυγχάνωσιν* (*Isocr. Antid.* 187: the preposition of the demonstrative repeated with the infinitive, to which it does not belong). *c*) *Ἀφ' ἧς ὠμόσατε ἡμέρας* (*Dem.* 18, 26, = *ἀπὸ τῆς ἡμέρας, ἐν ᾗ ὠμόσατε*); *ἡμέρᾳ πέμπτῃ, ἀφ' ἧς ἐσέβαλεν Ἀγησίλαος* (*Xen. Hell.* 4, 6, 6: the relative attracted by the preposition of the omitted demonstrative or of the substantive, even when it ought not to have been governed by it). *d*) *Ἡ Μιλησία ἐκφεύγει πρὸς τῶν Ἑλλήνων οἳ ἔτυχον ἐν τοῖς σκευοφόροις ὅπλα ἔχοντες* (*Xen. An.* 1, 10, 3, = *πρὸς ἐκείνους τῶν Ἑλλήνων, οἵ*: the demonstrative with a partitive genitive, after a preposition, omitted before a relative in the nominative). *e*) *Διεκομίζοντο εὐθὺς, ὅθεν ὑπεξέθεντο, παῖδας καὶ γυναῖκας* (*Thuc.* 1, 89, = *ἐκεῖθεν, ὅποι*: attraction in relative adverbs of place). *f*) *Τούτων ὃς βούλει ἕκαστος* (*Pl. Gorg.* 517, for *ὅντινα*, *quivis*; *ὅστις βούλει*, *Pl. Crat.* 432).

μάλα ἐδύκεις θαυμάζειν αὐτόν; (*Xen. Cyr.* 3, 1, 38). Ἆρ' οὖν ταῦτα ἡγεῖ σὰ εἶναι, ὧν ἂν ἄρξῃς καὶ ἐξῇ σοι αὐτοῖς χρῆσθαι ὅ,τι ἂν βούλῃ; (*Pl. Euthyd.* 301.) Ὅσοι τὸν δῆμον πολλὰ καὶ ἀγαθὰ εἰργασμένοι εἰσὶν ὀφείλεται δ' αὐτοῖς χάριν κομίσασθαι παρ' ὑμῶν μᾶλλον ἢ δίκην δοῦναι τῶν πεπραγμένων, οὐκ ἄξιον κατὰ τούτων ὑποδέχεσθαι διαβολάς (*Lys.* 25, 11). [§ 104.]

The indefinite relative ὅστις (in which no attraction of case takes place) is used in some connexions as a simple relative, viz.: § 105.

a) In denoting a *person* or *thing which can* or *shall be something, which serves for something*, both after an indefinite substantive and after an indefinite pronoun, which is usually omitted (§ 102, a): Ἡγεμόνα αἰτήσομεν Κῦρον, ὅστις ἡμᾶς ἀπάξει (*Xen. An.* 1, 3, 14). Αἰσχίνης συνεβούλευεν ὑμῖν πέμπειν τινὰς εἰς Ἀρκαδίαν, οἵτινες κατηγορήσουσι τῶν τὰ Φιλίππου πραττόντων (*Dem.* 19, 306). Οὐκ ἔχομεν, ὅτου σῖτον ὠνησόμεθα (*Xen. An.* 3, 1, 20). Οὐκ ἔστιν, ὅτῳ ἐγὼ καταλείψω τὸν ἐμὸν οἶκον (*Xen. Cyr.* 5, 4. 30). Οὐδὲν προσδεόμεθα οὔτε Ὁμήρου ἐπαινέτου οὔτε ὅστις ἔπεσι τὸ αὐτίκα τέρψει (*Thuc.* 2, 41).

b) After ἔστιν (without indefinite pronoun, § 102, b. Rem. 1), but mostly after a negative, or in a question equivalent to a negation: Οἱ Ἕλληνες ἐπεὶ προΐδοιεν τὰ ἅρματα φερόμενα, διίσταντο· ἔστι δὲ ὅστις καὶ κατελήφθη, ὥσπερ ἐν ἱπποδρόμῳ, ἐκπλαγείς (*Xen. An.* 1, 8, 20). Εἰπέ μοι· ἔστιν οὕστινας ἀνθρώπων τεθαύμακας ἐπὶ σοφίᾳ; (*Xen. An.* 1, 4, 2; with unchanged ἔστιν, as in ἔστιν οἵ.) Ἔστιν ὅτῳ ἄλλῳ πλείω ἐπιτρέπεις ἢ τῇ γυναικί; (*Xen. Œcon.* 3, 12.)

Rem. Especially note the expression οὐδεὶς ὅστις οὐ (οὐδὲν ὅ,τι οὐ), with omitted ἔστιν, in the sense *every, all*: Καὶ πεζὸς καὶ νῆες καὶ οὐδὲν ὅ,τι οὐκ ἀπώλετο (*Thuc.* 7, 87). The origin of the phrase being forgotten, it is treated as one word, and οὐδείς conforms itself in case to the following ὅστις: Ἀπολλόδωρος κλαίων καὶ ἀγανακτῶν οὐδένα ὅντινα οὐ κατέκλασε τῶν παρόντων (*Pl. Phæd.* 117). Οὐδενὸς ὅτου οὐ πάντων ἂν ὑμῶν καθ' ἡλικίαν πατὴρ εἴην (*Pl. Prot.* 317). Σωκράτης παρέχει ἑαυτὸν ἐρωτᾶν τῶν Ἑλλήνων τῷ βουλομένῳ καὶ οὐδενὶ ὅτῳ οὐκ ἀποκρίνεται (*Pl. Menon.* 70)[1].

c) After οὕτως in negations, or questions equivalent to such: Τίς οὕτω μαίνεται, ὅστις οὐ βούλεται σοὶ φίλος εἶναι; (*Xen. An.* 2, 5, 12.) (Also ὅς: Οὐδεὶς ἂν γένοιτο οὕτως ἀδαμάντινος, ὃς ἂν μείνειεν ἐν τῇ δικαιοσύνῃ, *Pl. Rep.* 2, 360.)

d) In relative sentences which single out, in a definite subject, a particular quality, or a particular circumstance, as the ground or explanation of what precedes (*quippe qui, a person who —, one who —*): Πῶς οὐ κάκιστος ἁπάντων ἀνθρώπων δικαίως ἂν νομίζοιο, ὅστις, ὦ κατάρατε, περὶ πλείονος φαίνῃ τοὺς κακούργους ποιούμενος τῆς πατρίδος; (*Dem.* 24, 107.) Οὔκουν δικαίως (ἔπνιγόν σε καὶ ἐπέτριβον), ὅστις οὐκ Εὐριπίδην ἐπαινεῖς; (*Arist. Nub.* 1377.) (In the same sense often ὅς, ὅς γε, *Xen. Mem.* 3, 5, 15; *Pl. Phæd.* 96, &c.)

Rem. Otherwise ὅστις for ὅς is found only in single, in part uncertain, passages of the poets and Herodotus. Yet ἐξ ὅτου is used as ἐξ οὗ (§ 103, R. 3) with attraction (*Xen. An.* 7, 8, 4).

The relative adjectives οἷος, ὅσος, ἡλίκος in the accusative are attracted into the dative or genitive in the same manner as ὅς: Μήδων, ὅσων ἑώρακα, πολὺ οὗτος ὁ ἐμὸς πάππος κάλλιστος (*Xen. Cyr.* 1, 3, 2). Τοιαύτας ἐπιδόσεις αἱ πόλεις οὐ λαμβάνουσιν, ἣν μή τις αὐτὰς διοικῇ § 106.

[1] Οὐδαμῶς ὅπως (ὡς) οὐ φήσω (*Pl. Rep.* 2, 376; *Pol.* 308).

[§ 106.] τοιούτοις ἤθεσιν, οἵοις Εὐαγόρας εἶχεν (*Isocr. Euag.* 48). (Yet also: Τοσαύτης οὐσίας καταλειφθείσης, ὅσην ἐξ ἀρχῆς ἠκούσατε, *Dem.* 27, 60.)

REM. 1. The preposition already given with the demonstrative correlative may be omitted for the relative (§ 103, R. 4): Οὐ περὶ ὀνόματος ἡ ἀμφισβήτησις, οἷς τοσούτων πέρι σκέψις ὅσων ἡμῖν πρόκειται (*Pl. Rep.* 7, 533).

REM. 2. In οἷος (ἡλίκος) note the peculiar attraction of the relative and the following subject into the case preceding, with omission of the verb substantive: Πολλῷ ἥδιόν ἐστι χαρίζεσθαι οἵῳ σοὶ ἀνδρὶ ἢ ἀπεχθέσθαι (*Xen. Mem.* 1, 9, 3, = ἀνδρὶ οἷος σὺ εἶ, which complete expression is more rare). Τοῖς οἵοις ἡμῖν τε καὶ ὑμῖν χαλεπὴ πολιτεία ἐστὶ δημοκρατία (*Xen. Hell.* 2, 3, 25). Ἐκεῖνο δεινὸν τοῖσιν ἡλίκοισιν νῷν (*Arist. Eccl.* 465). (Yet also: Σόλων ἐμίσει τοὺς οἷος οὗτος ἀνθρώπους, *Dem.* 19, 254.)[1]

REM. 3. In ὅσος note the elliptical expressions ὅσαι ἡμέραι (viz. εἰσίν), used as adverb in the form ὁσημέραι (*daily*), and ὅσοι μῆνες, *monthly*, ὅσα ἔτη.

---

§ 106, b. *Note on Reflexive and Reciprocal Pronouns*[2].]

1. *a*) Οὗ is a *secondary* or *indirect* reflexive: i.e. is used with (*acc. c.*) *infin.* with *participles*, and in such *secondary* sentences as relate the thoughts, &c., of the *subject* of the principal sentence (e. g. in *object-sentences* introduced by ὅτι, ὡς, *that*, or by interrogative pronouns or particles; in sentences denoting *purpose*: ἵνα, ὅπως, *that*; μή, *lest*). Λέγεται Ἀπόλλων ἐκδεῖραι τὸν Μαρσύαν ἐρίζοντά οἱ περὶ σοφίας (*Xen.*). Κελεύει δέ οἱ συμπέμψαι ἄνδρας (*Xen.*). Εἶπεν ὅτι ἐπιδημεῖν οἱ παρηγγελμένον εἴη (*Xen.*). Ἐγκλήματα ἐποιοῦντο, ὅπως σφίσιν . . . πρόφασις εἴη (*Th.*).—*b*) Also in *explanatory* clauses introduced by γάρ: Βραχέα ἀπελογήσαντο, οὐ γὰρ προὐτέθη σφίσι λόγος κατὰ τὸν νόμον (*Xen.*).—*c*) The dative *usually* occurs only as enclitic.

Οὗ, ἕ are not found in Attic prose, except in two or three passages (some of them *poetical*) of Plato. Even οἱ is *rare* in the orators.

2. Sometimes, however, ἑαυτοῦ is used as a *secondary* reflexive, and even αὐτοῦ, &c., the speaker making the statement *his own*. Νομίζει τοὺς πολίτας ὑπηρετεῖν ἑαυτῷ (*sibi*. *Xen.*). Ὁ Κῦρος τοῦ Σάκα ἐδεῖτο πάντως σημαίνειν αὐτῷ (*to let him* [Cyrus] *know*), ὁπότε κτλ. (*Xen.*).

3. Now and then, even σφίσιν αὐτοῖς, σφᾶς αὐτούς, are found as (emphatic) *secondary reflexives*. Ἐπισκήπτουσι τιμωρῆσαι σφίσιν αὐτοῖς ἠδικημένοις (*Ant.*).

4. *a*) In Thuc. and in some late writers οὗ relates to the subject of *its own* verb, and (*b*) sometimes, even in Attic writers, is used for the simple pron. αὐτοῦ: (1) Τοῖς λίθοις χρώμενος, οὓς οἱ Ἀθηναῖοι προπαρεβάλοντο σφίσιν (*Th.*).—2) Συνέφασάν οἱ, καὶ κτλ. (*Xen.*).

5. Ἑαυτοῦ (αὑτοῦ) sometimes refer to the *first* or *second* person. Οὕτω παιδεύεις τοὺς ἑαυτῆς φίλους (*amicos tuos*, *Xen.*). Μηδὲν ἐπιδεικνὺς τῶν ἑαυτοῦ (*rerum mearum*: *Isocr.*).

6. When it is sufficiently understood from the context that the *action* is *mutual*, the cases of the *reflexive* pronouns (ἑαυτοῦ, &c.) are used for those of the *reciprocal* ἀλλήλων (especially when the opposed notion is *others*). Φθονοῦσιν ἑαυτοῖς μᾶλλον ἢ τοῖς ἄλλοις ἀνθρώποις (*Xen.*).

---

[1] Τοιοῦτοί εἰσιν οἱ ποταμοί, δι' οἵας ἂν καὶ τῆς γῆς ῥέωσιν (*Pl. Phæd.* 112, i. e. *as the land through which*).

[2] Principally from Krüger.

PART II.

THE RELATIONS OF PROPOSITIONS ONE TO ANOTHER, ESPECIALLY THE WAY OF DENOTING THE MODE OR MANNER OF PREDICATION, AND THE TIME OF THE THING PREDICATED.

CHAPTER I.

The Moods in general, and especially the Indicative and its Tenses: the Indicative with ἄν.

To denote the relations of propositions, the Greeks have four personal §
and definite *moods:* the indicative, the subjunctive (conjunctive), the 107.
optative, and the imperative, of which the subjunctive and optative are related in point of conception; and besides these, the infinitive and the participle.

Both to the indicative (in certain tenses) and to the optative, as also to the infinitive and the participle, may be annexed the particle *ἄν* (Ionic and Epic *κέ* and *κέν*), to denote what is predicated upon the assumption of something being so and so, which is not actually so and so. The same particle, moreover, attaches itself to relative words (*ὃς ἄν, ὅταν,* &c.), and takes the subjunctive to denote an indefinite contingency.

The *Indicative* is the mood in which a thing is predicated abso- §
lutely, without any accessory modifications, or in which a thing is 108.
enquired about in the same way. It therefore stands in all both (331,
principal and accessory propositions, where no special rules, to be 332)
presently described, demand a different mood. *Ὁ πατὴρ τέθνηκεν. Πόθεν ἥκεις; Λέγουσιν, ὅτι ἡ πόλις ᾕρηται ὑπὸ τῶν πολεμίων. Ποιητέα ταῦτα, ἐπεὶ ὑμῖν δοκεῖ. Τούτου ἕνεκα οὐκ ἦλθον, ὅτι ᾔδειν τὰ γενησόμενα. Εἰ θεοὶ εἰσίν, ἔστι καὶ ἔργα θεῶν. Εἰ μὲν θεοῦ υἱὸς ἦν Ἀσκλη-*

[§ 108.] πιός, οὐκ ἦν αἰσχροκερδής, εἰ δὲ αἰσχροκερδής, οὐκ ἦν θεοῦ (*Pl. Rep.* 3, 408. A simply conditional proposition, without any accompanying regard to the condition as actually obtaining or not). Ὀλοίμην, εἰ τοῦτο πεποίηκα. Εἰ μηδὲν ἐπεποιήκεις, τί ἐφόβου;

REM. In some kinds of dependent propositions, which, especially in Latin, are expressed in the subjunctive, the indicative is retained in Greek: on this see at end of Chapter III.

§ 109. The principal *times*, together with imperfect, plusquamperfect, and future perf. passive, are expressed in Greek by the simple tenses of the verbs, and only in some passive forms by corresponding composite forms. To denote other relations of time, there are periphrastic combinations of the perf. participle with the tenses of εἰμί, or of μέλλω, *am about*, with the infinitive.

§ 110. *a*) The *Present Tense* is used of that which is, or is conceived to be, now present: Ὁμολογεῖ τούτοις Ὅμηρος.

(334) (234, R.) REM. 1. The present is often used of that which has been for some time, and still is, going on, especially with πάλαι [where we use our *progressive* form for the perf. *have been —ing*]: Πάλαι τοῦτο σκοπῶ. Οὐ πάλαι σοι λέγω, ὅτι ταὐτόν φημι εἶναι τὸ βέλτιον καὶ τὸ κρεῖττον; (*Pl. Gorg.* 489). Πολλὰ ἤδη ἔτη ἐν Ἀθήναις οἰκεῖτε.

REM. 2. The present of certain verbs denotes, by an idiom of the language, either generally or in certain special senses, the past action as still going on, or still continued in its result; e. g. ἥκω, *am come*, φεύγω, *am in exile*, οἴχομαι, *am gone*: Οἶδα, ὅπῃ οἴχονται (*Xen. An.* 1, 4, 8). (So sometimes: ἀδικῶ, *am in the wrong in what I have done*, ἀποστερῶ, *am keeping a person out of possession of —*, νικῶ, *am conqueror, have conquered*: Ἀπαγγέλλετε Ἀριαίῳ, ὅτι ἡμεῖς γε νικῶμεν βασιλέα καὶ οὐδεὶς ἔτι ἡμῖν μάχεται, *Xen. An.* 2, 1, 4.)

REM. 3. Sometimes the present is put for the future, in speaking of being about to do something immediately: Εἴ φησι τοιοῦτόν τι εἶναι, δειξάτω καὶ παρασχέσθω, κἀγὼ καταβαίνω (*Dem.* 19, 32). (Εἶμι, ἰέναι, ἰών, present and future.)

(336) *b*) In lively connected narrative the *presens historicum* is often used: Ἐπειδὴ δὲ ἐτελεύτησε Δαρεῖος καὶ κατέστη εἰς τὴν βασιλείαν Ἀρταξέρξης, Τισσαφέρνης διαβάλλει τὸν Κῦρον πρὸς τὸν ἀδελφόν, ὡς ἐπιβουλεύοι αὐτῷ· ὁ δὲ πείθεταί τε καὶ συλλαμβάνει Κῦρον ὡς ἀποκτενῶν (*Xen. An.* 1, 1, 3).

(336. R. 1) REM. More rarely in the protasis with ἐπειδή: Ἐπειδὴ δὲ Δικαιογένης οὐκέτι ὑμᾶς δύναται ἐξαπατᾶν, πείθει Μενέξενον ἡμᾶς προδοῦναι (*Isæ.* 5, 13), or in stating an individual fact: Δαρείου καὶ Παρυσάτιδος γίγνονται παῖδες δύο (*Xen. An.* 1, 1, 1, *there were born to D. and P. —; D. and P. had two sons*). But the poets often put the present for the aorist even in speaking of a single fact: Τίς μ' ἐκφύει βροτῶν; (*Soph. Œd. R.* 437.) Διόνυσος, ὃν τίκτει ποθ' ἡ Κάδμου κόρη (*Eur. Bacch.* 2).

In the past the Greek distinguishes two states: the narrative, denoted by the aorist, and the absolute (in English, *have, am*), denoted by the perfect[1]. § 111.

The *Aorist* is used in accounts and narratives of past occurrences, in historical connexion, or in stating a past occurrence, without relation to the present and a present result: (335. a) *Παυσανίας ὁ Κλεομβρότου ἐκ Λακεδαίμονος στρατηγὸς ὑπὸ Ἑλλήνων ἐξεπέμφθη μετὰ εἴκοσι νεῶν ἀπὸ Πελοποννήσου· ξυνέπλεον δὲ καὶ Ἀθηναῖοι τριάκοντα ναυσὶ καὶ ἐστράτευσαν ἐς Κύπρον καὶ αὐτῆς τὰ πολλὰ κατεστρέψαντο* (*Thuc.* 1, 49. Of *ξυνέπλεον*, see § 113). *Ὡς ἠθροίσθη Κύρῳ τὸ Ἑλληνικόν* (*the Grecian troops*), *ὅτε ἐπὶ τὸν ἀδελφὸν Ἀρταξέρξην ἐστρατεύετο, καὶ ὅσα ἐν τῇ ἀνόδῳ ἐπράχθη καὶ ὡς ἡ μάχη ἐγένετο καὶ ὡς ὁ Κῦρος ἐτελεύτησεν, ἐν τῷ ἔμπροσθεν λόγῳ δεδήλωται* (*Xen. An.* 2, 1, 1. On *δεδήλωται*, see § 112). *Οὑμὸς πατὴρ Κέφαλος ἐπείσθη μὲν ὑπὸ Περικλέους ἐς ταύτην τὴν γῆν ἀφικέσθαι, ἔτη δὲ τριάκοντα ᾤκησεν* (*Lys.* 12, 1). *Ὡς (ἐπεὶ) εἶδον τὸν πατέρα, ἠσπασάμην.* (See *Plusquamperf.*, § 114 c.) *Πολλοὶ πόλεις ἔπεισαν πόλεμον ἄρασθαι πρὸς τούτους. ὑφ' ὧν οἱ πεισθέντες ἀπώλοντο* (*Xen. Cyr.* 1, 6, 45; of that which has sometimes happened: *Many a time* (ere now) *have states let themselves be persuaded*—). *Ἤδη δὲ καί τινα οὐκ ἐθέλοντα ἀνίστασθαι ἀλλὰ προϊέμενον αὑτὸν τοῖς πολεμίοις καὶ ἔπαισα καὶ ἐβιασάμην πορεύεσθαι* (*Xen. An.* 5, 8, 14. *It has happened now and then that I*—).

Rem. The Aorist is sometimes used in a somewhat peculiar manner:

a) The Aorist is used of that which has often happened, and consequently (in cases singly occurring) is *wont* to happen; in which sense it may then be found coupled with the present (which expresses the general relation absolutely): (335. R. 3) *Τὰς τῶν φαύλων συνουσίας ὀλίγος χρόνος διέλυσε, τὰς δὲ τῶν σπουδαίων φιλίας οὐδ' ἂν ὁ πᾶς αἰὼν ἐξαλείψειεν* (*Isocr. Dem.* 1). *Ὁ τύραννος ταῖς μὲν πρώταις ἡμέραις προσγελᾷ τε καὶ ἀσπάζεται πάντας ὑπισχνεῖταί τε πολλὰ καὶ ἰδίᾳ καὶ δημοσίᾳ, χρεῶν τε ἠλευθέρωσε καὶ γῆν διένειμε δήμῳ τε καὶ τοῖς περὶ ἑαυτὸν καὶ πᾶσιν ἵλεώς τε καὶ πρᾶος εἶναι προσποιεῖται* (*Pl. Rep.* 8, 566). *Ὅταν πᾶσι ταὐτὰ συμφέρῃ τοῖς μετέχουσι τοῦ πολέμου, καὶ συμπονεῖν καὶ φέρειν τὰς συμφορὰς καὶ μένειν ἐθέλουσιν οἱ ἄνθρωποι· ὅταν δ' ἐκ πλεονεξίας καὶ πονηρίας τις ὥσπερ Φίλιππος ἰσχύσῃ, ἡ πρώτη πρόφασις καὶ μικρὸν πταῖσμα ἅπαντα ἀνεχαίτισε καὶ διέλυσεν* (*Dem.* 2, 9).

b) The first person of the aorist is sometimes applied to the expression of one's state of mind by words or gestures, occurring at the moment of speaking (the past tense referring to the preceding emotion which is in the speaker's thoughts): *Ὦ 'γαθέ, καὶ αὐτὸς ἐμαυτοῦ νῦν δὴ κατεγέλασα* (*Pl. Legg.* 3, 686, *I felt*

---

[1] The Aorist bears the signification of past time only in the indicative and participle, and in some sorts of [subjunctive] optative and infinitive propositions; of the Aorist in the other moods, see under these in ch. 2, 3, 4, and 5.

[§ 111.] *myself forced to laugh*). (So ἐγέλασα, ᾔνεσα, ἐπῄνεσα, ἥσθην, ἐδεξάμην, ἀπέπτυσα, &c. in the dramatic poets.)

c) Of the Aorist in negative questions which stand in place of a demand or summons (τί οὐκ), see *Imperative*, § 141, R. 3.

d) *Aor. of first attainment: = came to —*] Verbs signifying to have a public dignity, office, or power, are often used in the aorist in the sense of attaining to the same: Ἐπειδὴ Θησεὺς ἐβασίλευσεν, εἰς τὴν νῦν πόλιν οὖσαν ξυνῴκισε πάντας τοὺς ἐν τῇ Ἀττικῇ (*Thuc.* 2, 15, *became king*; βασιλεύω, *am king*). (So ἦρξα, *came to the government, became Archon*, ἴσχυσα, ἡγησάμην, ἐταμίευσα, ἐτυράννευσα, ἐβούλευσα, *became a councillor*, &c. So in the participle: Βουλεύσας ποτὲ Σωκράτης, ἐπιθυμήσαντος τοῦ δήμου παρὰ τοὺς νόμους ἐννέα στρατηγοὺς μιᾷ ψήφῳ ἀποκτεῖναι πάντας, οὐκ ἠθέλησεν ἐπιψηφίσαι, *Xen. Mem.* 1, 1, 8.)

§ 112. (335, b) The *Perfect* is used to denote an action as done and finished, not now going on, but now complete, or subsisting in its consequences: Ὁ πατήρ μου τέθνηκεν (*is dead*: but τοῦ αὐτοῦ ἐνιαυτοῦ ἀπέθανεν, *died in the same year*). Ἐξηπατήμεθα αἴσχιστα ὑπὸ τῶν ῥητορῶν. Πολλὰ καὶ μεγάλα οἱ θεοὶ τοὺς ἀνθρώπους εὐηργετήκασιν. Εὑρήκαμεν ὃ πάλαι ἐζητοῦμεν. Ὅμηρος πεποίηκε (*has composed*) σχεδὸν περὶ πάντων τῶν ἀνθρωπίνων. Ὁ πόλεμος ἁπάντων ἡμᾶς τῶν εἰρημένων ἀπεστέρηκε· καὶ γὰρ πενεστέρους πεποίηκε καὶ πολλοὺς κινδύνους ὑπομένειν ἠνάγκασε (*compelled us while it lasted*), καὶ πρὸς τοὺς Ἕλληνας διαβέβληκε καὶ πάντας τρόπους τεταλαιπώρηκεν (*Isocr. de Pac.* 19). Ὁ δῆμος τῇ βουλῇ πολλάκις τὴν πολιτείαν ἐγκεχείρικεν (*Dein.* 1, 9).

Rem. 1. Sometimes it makes little difference, whether a thing is denoted as a result, in reference to the present (perfect), or whether it is simply represented as an action and occurrence of the past (aorist). Φανήσομαι οὐδένα μὲν πώποτε ἀδικήσας, πλείους δὲ καὶ τῶν πολιτῶν καὶ τῶν ἄλλων Ἑλλήνων εὖ πεποιηκὼς ἢ σύμπαντες οἱ πρὸ ἐμοῦ βασιλεύσαντες (*Isocr. Nic.* 35).

Rem. 2. In some verbs, the perfect is used with the accessory signification of the present, in consequence of a peculiar way of taking its meaning, the present condition being denoted as produced by a preceding action, and as the result of the same. Such perfects are δέδοικα (δέδια), ἐγρήγορα, εἴωθα, ἔοικα, ἕστηκα, κέκτημαι (*possess*, κτῶμαι, *acquire*), κέκλημαι (*am called*), οἶδα, πέφυκα (πεφόβημαι in some writers = φοβοῦμαι). The plusquamperf. has then the signification of the imperfect: ὥσπερ εἰώθεσαν, *as they used*; ᾔδειν, *I knew*.

§ 113. (337) The *Imperfect* is used of the condition at a certain time, or of actions which at a certain time were going on (still current, and not finished), or of that which was a custom at a certain time, the current or customary view, &c. of a certain person, or often repeating itself: Ἐπὶ Κέκροπος καὶ τῶν πρώτων βασιλέων ἡ Ἀττικὴ κατὰ πόλεις ᾠκεῖτο καὶ αὐτοὶ ἕκαστοι ἐπολιτεύοντο καὶ ἐβουλεύοντο. Ἐπειδὴ δὲ Θησεὺς ἐβασίλευσεν, ἐς τὴν νῦν πόλιν οὖσαν ξυνῴκισε πάντας (*Thuc.* 2, 15). Ὅςτις ἀφικνεῖτο τῶν παρὰ βασιλέως πρὸς Κῦρον, πάντας οὕτω διατιθεὶς ἀπεπέμπετο ὥςθ' ἑαυτῷ μᾶλλον φίλους εἶναι ἢ βασιλεῖ. Καὶ τῶν παρ' ἑαυτῷ βαρβάρων ἐπεμελεῖτο, ὡς πολεμεῖν ἱκανοὶ εἴησαν. Τὴν δὲ Ἑλληνικὴν δύναμιν ἤθροιζεν ὡς μάλιστα ἐδύνατο ἐπικρυπτόμενος, κ.τ.λ. (*Xen. An.* 1, 1, 5; in the description of Cyrus's preparations for the war with Artaxerxes). [§ 113.] Κλέαρχος Λακεδαιμόνιος φυγὰς ἦν. Τούτῳ συγγενόμενος ὁ Κῦρος ἠγάσθη τε καὶ δίδωσιν αὐτῷ μυρίους Δαρεικούς· ὁ δὲ λαβὼν τὸ χρυσίον στράτευμα συνέλεξεν ἀπὸ τῶν χρημάτων καὶ ἐ π ο λ έ μ ε ι ἐκ Πελοποννήσου ὁρμώμενος τοῖς Θρᾳξὶ καὶ ὠ φ έ λ ε ι τοὺς Ἕλληνας (*Xen. An.* 1, 1, 9; *was still carrying on the war*, at the time in question). Κριτίας καὶ Ἀλκιβιάδης οὐκ ἀρέσκοντος αὐτοῖς Σωκράτους (= οὐχ ὅτι ἤρεσκεν αὐτοῖς Σωκράτης) ὡμιλησάτην, ὃν χρόνον ὡμιλείτην αὐτῷ (*Xen. Mem.* 1, 2, 39). Σωκράτης τοὺς ἑαυτοῦ ἐπιθυμοῦντας οὐκ ἐπράττετο χρήματα (*Xen. Mem.* 1, 2, 5, but Σ. οὐδένα πώποτε μισθὸν τῆς συνουσίας ἐπράξατο, *Xen. Mem.* 1, 2, 60; *never once demanded*). Κορίνθιοι οὐδὲν τούτων ὑπήκουον (*Thuc.* 1, 29; said of their state of mind as a whole, not of a single determination).

Rem. 1. Sometimes the imperfect denotes something about to be done, what a person was going or *proposing* to do: Ἡγέστρατος καταβὰς τῆς νυκτὸς εἰς κοίλην ναῦν διέκοπτε τοῦ πλοίου τὸ ἔδαφος (*Dem.* 32, 5, *was beginning to cut through —*: he was hindered from doing it). Φίλιππος Ἀλόννησον ἐδίδου, Δημοσθένης δὲ ἀπηγόρευε μὴ λαμβάνειν (*Æsch.*, 3, 83, *was for giving, offered to give.*—And so ἐδίδουν is frequently used). (Ἔπειθον, *I sought to persuade*, ἔπεισα, *I persuaded.*) Ἦν ἄξιος ὁ ἀγών, ὅτι οὐχὶ Ἀθηναίων μόνον οἱ Συρακούσιοι περιεγίγνοντο ἀλλὰ καὶ τῶν ἄλλων ξυμμάχων (*Thuc.* 7, 56, *had the prospect of conquering —*). Διὰ ταῦτα οἱ Λακεδαιμόνιοι ἐποιήσαντο τὴν ξυμμαχίαν καὶ τὸ Πάνακτον εὐθὺς καθῃρεῖτο (*Thuc.* 5, 39, *and they immediately were beginning to pull down —, proceeded* to pull down).

Rem. 2. Sometimes (especially by Herodot. and Thucyd.) in continued narrative, an imperfect is used with but little difference from the aorist, the action being denoted as the beginning of one or more undertakings, or as a proceeding of longer duration: Τοῦτο ποιήσαντες οἱ Πλαταιεῖς ἔς τε τὰς Ἀθήνας ἄγγελον ἔ π ε μ π ο ν (*set about sending*) καὶ τοὺς νεκροὺς ὑποσπόνδους ἀ π έ δ ο σ α ν τοῖς Θηβαίοις τά τ' ἐν τῇ πόλει καθίσταντο πρὸς τὰ παρόντα, ᾗ ἐδόκει αὐτοῖς (*Thuc.* 2, 6). Παρελθόντες οἱ Ἀθηναῖοι ἔλεγον τοιάδε (*Thuc.* 1, 72; but ch. 67, Παρελθόντες δὲ οἱ Κορίνθιοι εἶπον τοιάδε). Τοιαῦτα δὴ ἀφίκοντο διαλεγόμενοι μέχρι τῶν ὁρίων τῆς Περσίδος· ἐπεὶ δὲ αὐτοῖς ἀετὸς δεξιὸς φανεὶς προηγεῖτο, προσευξάμενοι θεοῖς καὶ ἥρωσι τοῖς Περσίδα γῆν κατέχουσιν οὕτω δ ι έ β α ι ν ο ν τὰ ὅρια (*set about crossing —; proceeded to cross*). Ἐπειδὴ δὲ διέβησαν, π ρ ο σ ε ύ χ ο ν τ ο αὖθις θεοῖς τοῖς Μηδίαν γῆν κατέχουσιν (*Xen. Cyr.* 2, 1, 1). [So especially verbs *jubendi et mittendi*: πέμπειν, ἀποστέλλειν, κελεύειν, βοηθεῖν, &c., *Schmidt.*] The imperfects ᾔειν (ᾖα), ἧκον, and ἔφην (*inquam*) are used at the same time in the aorist sense.

Rem. 3. The imperfect ἦν is sometimes found where we might expect the present, in reference to an earlier condition, or an earlier appearance: Εἰ ἄρα τὰ ὀφειλόμενα ἑκάστῳ ἀποδιδόναι φησί τις δίκαιον εἶναι, τοῦτο δὲ δὴ νοεῖ αὐτῷ (*has for him the meaning*), τοῖς μὲν ἐχθροῖς βλάβην ὀφείλεσθαι παρὰ τοῦ δικαίου ἀνδρός, τοῖς δὲ φίλοις ὠφέλειαν, οὐκ ἦν σοφὸς ὁ τοῦτο εἰπών (*Pl. Rep.* 1, 335; viz. as he before seemed to us to be). Πολλοὶ ἄνθρωποι ἀποθνήσκουσι πρότερον πρὶν δῆλοι γενέσθαι, οἷοι ἦσαν (*Xen. Cyr.* 5, 2, 9).

a) The *Plusquamperfectum* is used of that which at a certain past § 114.

[§ 114.] time had already taken place: Ἡ Οἰνόη, οὖσα ἐν μεθορίοις τῆς Ἀττικῆς καὶ Βοιωτίας, ἐτετείχιστο καὶ αὐτῷ φρουρίῳ οἱ Ἀθηναῖοι ἐχρῶντο (*Thuc.* 2, 18).

b) Instead of the simple plusquamperf. in the active, we have sometimes a periphrastic expression by the participle perf. with ἦν: Οὔπω δύο ἢ τρεῖς δρόμους περιεληλυθότε ἤστην ὁ Εὐθύδημος καὶ ὁ Διονυσόδωρος, καὶ εἰσέρχεται Κλεινίας (*Pl. Euthyd.* 273).

c) When by means of the conjunctions ἐπεί, ἐπειδή (Ionic ἐπεί τε), *after that*, or ὡς, *when* (ὡς τάχιστα), it is denoted that one action followed upon another, usually not the plusquamperf. is employed but the aorist, or, if a state and continued relation be denoted, the imperfect: Ἐπειδὴ ἐτελεύτησε Δαρεῖος καὶ κατέστη εἰς τὴν βασιλείαν Ἀρταξέρξης, Τισσαφέρνης διαβάλλει τὸν Κῦρον πρὸς τὸν ἀδελφόν (*Xen. An.* 1, 1, 3). Ἐπεὶ Κῦρος κατεπέμφθη σατράπης Λυδίας καὶ Φρυγίας, πρῶτον ἐπέδειξεν αὐτόν, ὅτι περὶ πλείστου ποιοῖτο, εἴ τῳ ὑπόσχοιτό τι, μηδὲν ψεύδεσθαι (*Xen. An.* 1, 9, 7). Οἱ πολέμιοι ὡς εἶδον τοὺς Ἕλληνας, ἀντιπορεύονται (*Xen. An.* 4, 8, 17).—Ἐπεὶ ἠσθένει Δαρεῖος καὶ ὑπώπτευε τὴν τελευτὴν τοῦ βίου, ἐβούλετό οἱ τὼ παῖδε ἀμφοτέρω παρεῖναι (*Xen. An.* 1, 1, 1). Οἱ τῶν Ἀθηναίων στρατηγοί, ὡς αὐτοὺς οἱ Καταναῖοι οὐκ ἐδέχοντο, ἐκομίσθησαν ἐπὶ τὸν Τηρίαν ποταμόν (*Thuc.* 6, 50, *when the Cat. were not for receiving them*).—Ἀλκιβιάδης λόγους ποιησάμενος πρὸς τοὺς Μεσσηνίους, ὡς οὐκ ἔπειθεν, ἀλλ' ἀπεκρίναντο, πόλει μὲν ἂν οὐ δέξασθαι, ἀγορὰν δ' ἔξω παρέξειν, ἀπέπλει ἐς τὸ Ῥήγιον. (Ibid., *when he could not persuade them, when they were not for letting themselves be persuaded*; ἀπεκρίναντο single fact.) The plusquamperf., however, may be used with ἐπειδή, where the thing denoted is the complete ending of the preceding action, or the complete production of the state: Πυθόμενος ὁ Κρατῖνος τὰς τούτων ἐπιβουλὰς τὸν μὲν ἄλλον χρόνον ἡσυχίαν ἦγεν, ἐπειδὴ δὲ ὁ κηδεστὴς μὲν ἦν ὁ Καλλιμάχου κατηγορηκὼς αὐτοῦ (τοῦ Κρατίνου), Καλλίμακος δὲ μεμαρτυρηκώς, ἦ μὴν τεθνάναι τὴν ἄνθρωπον, ἐλθόντες εἰς τὴν οἰκίαν, ἵνα ἦν κεκρυμμένη, ἀγαγόντες ἐπὶ τὸ δικαστήριον ζῶσαν ἅπασιν τοῖς παροῦσιν ἐπέδειξαν (*Isocr. Call.* 54). Ἐπειδὴ δὲ ἐξηπάτησθε μὲν ὑμεῖς ὑπὸ τοῦ Φιλίππου, ἐξηπάτηντο δὲ οἱ ταλαίπωροι Φωκεῖς καὶ ἀνῄρηντο αἱ πόλεις αὐτῶν, τί ἐγένετο; (*Dem.* 18, 42.)

(338, R. 5) REM. 1. In the same way, the aorist, not the plusquamperf., is used after ἕως (ἕως περ), ἔστε, μέχρι, πρίν (οὐ — πρίν): Εὔδικος καὶ Σῖμος οἱ Λαρισσαῖοι μέχρι τούτου φίλοι ὠνομάζοντο Φιλίππου, ἕως Θετταλίαν ὑπὸ Φιλίππῳ ἐποίησαν (*Dem.* 18, 48). Οἱ βάρβαροι οὐ πρόσθεν ἐξενεγκεῖν ἐτόλμησαν πρὸς ἡμᾶς πόλεμον πρὶν τοὺς στρατηγοὺς ἡμῶν συνελάβον (*Xen. An.* 3, 2, 29). Ἐχρῆν τοὺς ῥήτορας μὴ πρότερον περὶ τῶν ὁμολογουμένων συμβουλεύειν πρὶν περὶ τῶν ἀμφισβητουμένων ἐδίδαξαν (*Isocr. Paneg.* 19).

REM. 2. Now and then, the special relation of time which should be denoted by the plusquamperf. is not expressed, but the action is simply set in the past by the aorist: Οἱ Πελοποννήσιοι ὀλίγον μὲν χρόνον ὑπέμειναν, ἔπειτα δὲ ἐτράποντο ἐς τὸν Πάνορμον, ὅθενπερ ἀνηγάγοντο (*Thuc.* 2, 92; *had put to sea*).

[PART II.

REM. 3. Of the aorist and perfect (not plusquamperf.) of the indicative in propositions dependent upon a governing proposition in a præteritum [in an '*historical tense*'], see *Optative*, § 130, b. R. 2. [§ 114.]

a) The *Future* denotes simply a future action or a future state or condition: *Εἰ τοῦτο ποιήσομεν, ῥᾳδίως τὰ ἐπιτήδεια ἕξομεν. ὅσον χρόνον ἐν τῇ πολεμίᾳ ἐσόμεθα.* § 115.

REM. Especially note the use of the future indicative in relative clauses denoting the being intended for, or calculated to serve, a *purpose* (*one who*, or, *a thing which*, *may* or *shall*, &c.; *whom* or *which*, *one may*, &c.): Οὐχ ὅ,τι τις κατηγορήσει τούτων. χαλεπὸν εὑρεῖν (*Dem.* 15, 34). Εἰ οἴει ὁντινοῦν ἀνθρώπων παραδώσειν τέχνην τινὰ τοιαύτην, ἥτις σε ποιήσει μέγα δύνασθαι ἐν τῇ πόλει τῇδε ἀνόμοιον ὄντα τῇ πολιτείᾳ, οὐκ ὀρθῶς βουλεύῃ (*Pl. Gorg.* 513). Other examples in § 105, a.

b) The *Futurum exactum* (in the active, *πεποιηκὼς ἔσομαι*: in the deponent, *εἰργασμένος ἔσομαι*; and in the passive, *διεφθαρμένος ἔσομαι*, *πεπράξομαι*) expresses, that at a certain future instant something will be finished, and will show itself as finished. Thus it denotes (1) that which, as the immediate consequence of another action, will therewith ensue and be ready; (2) that which will be soon accomplished and done; (3) the future result of a preceding action (it corresponds, therefore, more to the English than to the Latin *futurum exactum*): *Ἐὰν καταψηφισάμενοι τούτων θανάτου τιμήσετε, τῇ αὐτῇ ψήφῳ τούς τε ἄλλους κοσμιωτέρους ποιήσετε ἢ νῦν εἰσι, καὶ παρὰ τούτων δίκην εἰληφότες ἔσεσθε* (*Lys.* 27, 7). *Εἰ παρελθὼν εἷς, ὁστισοῦν δύναιτο διδάξαι, τίς παρασκευὴ χρήσιμος ἔσται τῇ πόλει, πᾶς ὁ παρὼν φόβος λελύσεται* (*Dem.* 14, 2). *Τί γὰρ ποιήσει (ὁ θεός); Φράζε, καὶ πεπράξεται* (*Arist. Pl.* 1027). *Μάτην μοι κεκλαύσεται* (*Arist. Nub.* 1436; *in vain shall I have wept*). (Τῆς δυνάμεως ἡμῶν εἰς ἀΐδιον τοῖς ἐπιγιγνομένοις μνήμη καταλελείψεται, *Thuc.* 2, 64; of a future action conceived of as an *abiding result*.)[1] (340)

REM. In those verbs in which the perfect middle has the signification of the present (§ 112, R. 2), the fut. exact. has the signification of the simple future: μεμνήσομαι, κεκτήσομαι (*shall possess*, different from κτήσομαι, *shall acquire*), κεκλήσομαι (*shall have the name*). Likewise two others (εἰρήσομαι, δεδήσομαι).

The verb *μέλλω* with the infinitive of the future or present, rarely of the aorist, forms a peculiar mode of denoting the future as something which one has at this present time in hand, and is about to do (*futurum in præsenti*), which notation by means of the imperfect (*ἤμελλον*) is applied to the past (*futurum in præterito*): *Μέλλω ὑμᾶς διδάξειν, ὅθεν μοι ἡ διαβολὴ γέγονεν* (*Pl. Apol.* 21). *Ἐνεθυμοῦντο οἱ Ἕλληνες, ὅτι ἀγορὰν οὐδεὶς ἔτι παρέξειν ἤμελλεν* (*Xen. An.* 3, 1, 2). § 116. (341, 342)

---

[1] *Si fecero, ἐὰν ποιήσω*, see *Subjunctive*.

[§ 116.] Ἀκούω τινὰ διαβάλλειν, ὡς ἐγὼ ἄρα ἐξαπατήσας ὑμᾶς μέλλω ἄγειν εἰς Φᾶσιν (*Xen. An.* 5, 7, 5)[1].

Rem. 1. Especially frequent εἰ μέλλω, *if I am to* —, and ὁ μέλλων, *he that would*, in denoting that which must be done in order to secure some object: Δεῖ στρατιάν, εἰ μέλλει πράξειν τὰ δέοντα, μηδέποτε παύεσθαι τοῖς πολεμίοις κακὰ πορσύνουσαν (*Xen. Cyr.* 1, 6, 17). Τὸν μέλλοντα εὖ γεωργήσειν δεῖ τοὺς ἐργάτας καὶ προθύμους παρασκευάζειν καὶ πείθεσθαι θέλοντας (*Xen. Œcon.* 5, 15). But also Ἀνδρεῖον δεῖ εἶναι τὸν εὐγενῆ νεάνισκον, εἴπερ εὖ μαχεῖται (*Pl. Rep.* 2, 375).

Rem. 2. Of the simple indicative future (not *fut. in præterito*) instead of the optative in propositions dependent on a verb in the preterite, see *Optative*, § 130, b. R. 2.

§ 117. (347) *a*) With the addition of ἄν the imperfect, aorist, and sometimes plusquamperf. of the indicative is used to predicate something which, under the supposition of a certain condition, would find (or have found) place, but which does not do so, because the condition does not exist. The condition is expressed in the indicative with εἰ. Of that which, *as it is*, does not find place, but would do so, and of a condition assumed in opposition to the actual present state of the case, the imperfect is used (εἰ ἐδυνάμην, ἐποίουν ἄν); if the condition and conditional result, under the same supposition, belong to the past, both of them stand in the aorist (εἰ ἐκέλευσας, ἐποίησα ἄν, εἰ μὴ ἐκέλευσας, οὐκ ἂν ἐποίησα). The plusquamperf. with ἄν in conditional propositions, is used only when an action (then or now) completed, and a state which has (then or now) ended, is meant to be denoted. (A plusquamperf. having the sense of the imperf. is used as imperf., e. g. εἰ ᾔδειν, ἔλεγον ἄν.) The time in the conditional, and that in the principal, proposition, may differ according to the sense. (There can rarely be occasion to use the plusquamperf. in both clauses.) Εἴ τι ἐμοῦ ἐκήδου, οὐδενὸς ἂν οὕτως μ' ἀποστερεῖν ἐφυλάττου, ὡς ἀξιώματος καὶ τιμῆς (*Xen. Cyr.* 5, 5, 34). Οὐχ οὕτως ἂν προθύμως ἐπὶ τὸν πόλεμον ὑμᾶς παρεκάλουν, εἰ μὴ τὴν εἰρήνην ἑώρων ἐκ τοῦ πολέμου καλὴν καὶ βεβαίαν γενησομένην (*Isocr. Arch.* 87).—Εἰ ὁ Φίλιππος τότε ταύτην ἔσχε τὴν γνώμην, ὡς χαλεπὸν πολεμεῖν ἐστιν Ἀθηναίοις, οὐδὲν ἄν, ὧν νυνὶ πεποίηκεν, ἔπραξεν (*Dem.* 4, 5). Ἴσως ἂν ἀπέθανον, εἰ μὴ ἡ τῶν τριάκοντα ἀρχὴ διὰ ταχέων κατελύθη (*Pl. Apol.* 32). — Εἰ μὴ ὑμεῖς ἤλθετε, ἐπορευόμεθα ἂν ἐπὶ βασιλέα (*Xen. An.* 2, 1, 4; *had ye not come, we should now* —). Εἰ ἐγὼ ἐτόλμων τοῦτο ποιεῖν, ἐπέτρεψας ἄν, ὦ Δημόσθενες, καὶ οὐκ ἐνέπλησας βοῆς καὶ κραυγῆς τὴν ἀγοράν; (*Æsch.* 2, 86; *had I dared it, wouldst thou have suffered it?*) — Εἰ, ὅ σε

[1] Ἤδη ἤμελλον ἀλλήλους ἀπολιπεῖν (*Thuc.* 6, 31). (Ἠμέλλησα ἰέναι.)

ἠρώτων, ἀπεκρίνω, ἱκανῶς ἂν ἤδη παρὰ σοῦ τὴν ὁσιότητα ἐμεμαθήκειν (*Pl. Euthyph.* 14; *I should already have finished my task of learning* —). Λοιπὸν ἂν ἦν ἡμῖν περὶ τῆς πόλεως διαλεχθῆναι τῆς ἡμετέρας, εἰ μὴ προτέρα τῶν ἄλλων εὖ φρονήσασα τὴν εἰρήνην ἐπεποίητο (*Isocr. Phil.* 56; *were it not the case that it had already concluded a peace*). Εἰ ἐγὼ πάλαι ἐπεχείρησα πράττειν τὰ πολιτικὰ πράγματα, πάλαι ἂν ἀπολώλειν καὶ οὔτ' ἂν ὑμᾶς ὠφελήκειν οὐδὲν οὔτ' ἂν ἐμαυτόν (*Pl. Apol.* 31; *I should long ago have perished, without benefiting either you or myself*, from ἀπόλωλα)[1]. [§ 117.]

Rem. 1. Sometimes, either in both clauses or in only one of them, the imperfect is used instead of the aorist, of relations belonging to the past; mostly (yet not always, especially in the poets) to denote an abiding state or a continued series of actions: Σωκράτης οὔτ' ἠλίθιος οὔτ' ἀλαζὼν φαίνεσθαι τοῖς συνοῦσιν ἐβούλετο· ἐδόκει δ' ἂν ἀμφότερα ταῦτα, εἰ προαγορεύων ὡς ἀπὸ θεοῦ φαινόμενα ψευδόμενος ἐφαίνετο. Δῆλον οὖν, ὅτι οὐκ ἂν προέλεγεν, εἰ μὴ ἐπίστευεν ἀληθεύσειν (*Xen. Mem.* 1, 1, 5). Ἐγὼ ἐχθές, εἰ μὴ πολλοῖς διεπύκτευσα, οὐκ ἂν ἐδυνάμην σοι προσελθεῖν (*Xen. Cyr.* 7, 5, 53). Λιπόντες τὰς τάξεις προθέοντες ἁρπάζειν ἤθελον καὶ ἡμῶν πλεονεκτεῖν· εἰ δὲ τοῦτο πάντες ἐποιοῦμεν, ἅπαντες ἂν ἀπωλόμεθα (*Xen. An.* 5, 8, 13). The aorist is put instead of the imperfect in the principal proposition only when, with less accuracy, the relation is referred to the past or to a different time: Εἰ μὲν τὸ σῶμα ἐπιτρέπειν σε ἔδει τῳ, διακινδυνεύοντα ἢ χρηστὸν αὐτὸ γενέσθαι ἢ πονηρόν, πολλὰ ἂν περιεσκέψω, εἴτ' ἐπιτρεπτέον εἴτε οὔ, καὶ εἰς συμβουλὴν τούς τε φίλους ἂν παρεκάλεις καὶ τοὺς οἰκείους, σκοπούμενος ἡμέρας συχνάς, ὃ δὲ περὶ πλείονος τοῦ σώματος ἡγεῖ, τὴν ψυχήν, περὶ δὲ τούτου οὔτε τῷ πατρὶ οὔτε τῷ ἀδελφῷ ἐπεκοινώσω, εἴτ' ἐπιτρεπτέον εἴτε καὶ οὐ τῷ ἀφικομένῳ τούτῳ ξένῳ τὴν σὴν ψυχήν (*Pl. Prot.* 313). (347, R. 2)

Rem. 2. Relative and conjunctional clauses which come to be enclosed in such a conditional or conditionated proposition, are expressed in the indicative. Εἰ ξένος ἐτύγχανον ὤν, ξυνεγιγνώσκετε δήπου ἄν μοι, εἰ ἐν ἐκείνῃ τῇ φωνῇ τε καὶ τῷ τρόπῳ ἔλεγον, ἐν οἷσπερ ἐτεθράμμην (*Pl. Apol.* 17). Εἰ πλούτῳ καὶ κέρδει ἄριστα ἐκρίνετο τὰ κρινόμενα, ἃ ἐπῄνει ὁ φιλοκερδὴς καὶ ἔψεγεν, ἀνάγκη ἂν ταῦτα ἀληθέστατα εἶναι (*Pl. Rep.* 9, 382). Ἡδέως ἂν Καλλικλεῖ ἔτι διελεγόμην, ἕως αὐτῷ τὴν τοῦ Ἀμφίονος ἀπέδωκα ῥῆσιν ἀντὶ τῆς τοῦ Ζήθου (*Pl. Gorg.* 506). Ἐχρῆν τοὺς ῥήτορας μὴ πρότερον περὶ τῶν ὁμολογουμένων συμβουλεύειν, πρὶν περὶ τῶν ἀμφισβητουμένων ἡμᾶς ἐδίδαξαν (*Isocr. Paneg.* 19).

b) The condition which does not obtain, is not always expressed in a proposition of its own, but may be given in a different turn of expression, or be implied in the context of the passage as a whole: Βοὸς ἔχοντες σῶμα, ἀνθρώπου δὲ γνώμην, οὐκ ἂν ἠδυνάμεθα ποιεῖν ἃ ἐβουλόμεθα (*Xen. Mem.* 1, 4, 14). Ὥστε ἀπελάσαι Χαλδαίους ἀπὸ τούτων τῶν ἄκρων (*in order to expel*), πολλαπλάσια ἂν ἔδωκα χρήματα ὧν σὺ νῦν ἔχεις παρ' ἐμοῦ (*Xen. Cyr.* 3, 2, 16; *I would have given*). Ξένος οὐδεὶς ἀφῖκται χρόνου συχνοῦ ἐξ Ἀθηνῶν, ὅστις ἂν ἡμῖν σαφές τι ἀγγεῖλαι οἷός τε ἦν περὶ τούτων (*Pl. Phæd.* 57; *who would have*

---

[1] Ὁπότερον τούτων ἐποίησε Διογείτων, οὐδενὸς ἂν ἧττον Ἀθηναίων πλούσιος ἦν (*Lys.* 32, 23).

[§ 117.] *been in a condition —*). Ἑάλωκα οὐ λόγων ἀπορίᾳ ἀλλ' ἀναισχυντίας καὶ τοῦ ἐθέλειν λέγειν πρὸς ὑμᾶς τοιαῦτα, οἷ' ἂν ὑμῖν ἥδιστα ἦν ἀκούειν, θρηνοῦντός τέ μου καὶ ὀλοφυρομένου (*Pl. Apol.* 38; *as would have been to you —*). Especially note ἄν with the indicative, where in English we use *otherwise* with the conditional mood, to denote a relation different from the actual one: Ἐπιστευόμην ὑπὸ Λακεδαιμονίων· οὐ γὰρ ἄν με ἔπεμπον πάλιν πρὸς ὑμᾶς (*Xen. An.* 6, 6, 33). (Ἤλπιζόν σε παρέσεσθαι· ἢ οὐκ ἂν ἦλθον.)

Rem. 1. The hypothetical proposition with ἄν may have an object-proposition (with ὅτι or ὡς, or as dependent question) subordinated to it, or an inference (ὥστε), sometimes also in a different way: Ἡδέως ἂν πυθοίμην, τίν' ἄν ποτε γνώμην περὶ ἐμοῦ εἴχετε, εἰ μὴ ἐτριηράρχησα (*Dem.* 50, 67). Οὕτω σαφῶς ὁ πατὴρ ἐμὸς τοὺς κατηγόρους ψευδομένους ἐπέδειξεν, ὥστε ἡδέως ἂν ὁ δῆμος δίκην παρ' αὐτῶν ἔλαβεν (*Isocr. de Big.* 7; *would have been delighted to take —*). Ἔστιν οὖν ὅπως ταῦτ' ἄν, ἐκεῖνα προειρηκώς, ὁ αὐτὸς ἀνὴρ μὴ διαφθαρεὶς ἐτόλμησεν εἰπεῖν; (*Dem.* 19, 308.) Such a proposition may even itself be made the condition: Εἰ τοίνυν ἂν ἐμοὶ τότε ὠργίζεσθε, ὅτι οὐκ ἐτριηράρχησα, πῶς οὐχὶ νῦν προσήκει ὑμᾶς εἰσπρᾶξαί μοι τὰ ἀναλώματα; (*Dem.* 50, 67; *if then the case be so, that ye would have been angry with me —*.)

Rem. 2. Sometimes the aorist (rarely the imperfect) with ἄν denotes what would have happened at a past time, if the attempt had been made, and therefore what *might, could,* or *should have taken place:* Καὶ αὐτοὶ ἂν ἐπορεύθησαν, ᾗπερ οἱ ἄλλοι, τὰ δὲ ὑποζύγια οὐκ ἦν ἄλλῃ ἢ ταύτῃ ἐκβῆναι (*Xen. An.* 4, 2, 10). Ἐκ τίνος ἂν φιλίας ποτ' ἐδάνεισεν ὁ πατὴρ ὁ ἐμὸς τῷ ναυάρχῳ τὰς χιλίας δραχμάς, ὃν οὐκ ἐγίγνωσκεν; (*Dem.* 49, 50; *could* (or *should*) *my father have lent —!*) Οἱ Πέρσαι θᾶττον, ἢ ὥς τις ἂν ᾤετο, μετεώρους ἐξεκόμισαν τὰς ἁμάξας (*Xen. An.* 1, 5, 8). Οὐ γὰρ ἦν, ὅ,τι ἂν ἐποιεῖτε μόνοι (*Dem.* 18, 43; *there was nothing that you could have done alone*). Especially note ἠβουλόμην ἄν, *I should* (under other circumstances) *have wished, I could have wished* (said of wishes that are not to be fulfilled, *vellem*): Ἠβουλόμην ἄν, ὥσπερ πρόχειρόν ἐστιν ἐπαινέσαι τὴν ἀρετήν, οὕτω ῥᾴδιον εἶναι τοὺς ἀκούοντας πεῖσαι ἀσκεῖν αὐτήν (*Isocr. de Pac.* 36).

Rem. 3. Sometimes the imperfect or aorist with ἄν is used to denote what in time past might, upon a given occasion, take place, i. e. what was wont to, and now and then did, take place. (The imperfect more of the recurrence of a state, or of an operation lasting some time; the aorist, of the repetition and recurrence of several actions.) Κῦρος, μεταξὺ τῶν ἁρμάτων καὶ τῶν θωρακοφόρων διαπορευόμενος, ὁπότε προσβλέψειέ τινας τῶν ἐν ταῖς τάξεσι, τοτὲ μὲν εἶπεν ἄν· (*would say*) Ὦ ἄνδρες, ὡς ἡδὺ ὑμῶν τὰ πρόσωπα θεάσασθαι· τοτὲ δ' αὖ ἐν ἄλλοις ἔλεξεν· Ἆρα ἐννοεῖτε, ἄνδρες, κ.τ.λ. (*Xen. Cyr.* 7, 1, 10.) Ἀναλαμβάνων οὖν τῶν τραγῳδοποιῶν καὶ τῶν διθυραμβοποιῶν τὰ ποιήματα, ἅ μοι ἐδόκει μάλιστα πεπραγματεῦσθαι, διηρώτων ἂν αὐτούς, τί λέγοιεν (*Pl. Apol.* 22).

§ 118. In some cases, however, the apodosis has the imperfect without ἄν, although depending on a condition which is intimated as not existing.

(348) *a*) In speaking of what in a certain case in the past or present would be right, suitable, allowable, &c., but was not done, or is not done, the imperfects ἐχρῆν, προσῆκεν, ἔδει, ἥρμοττεν (καλῶς εἶχεν), ἐξῆν (ἦν, ὑπῆρχεν), and adjectives (also

gerundives) with ἦν (κάλλιον, δίκαιον, κρεῖττον), are put without ἄν, in order to denote the duty or proper conduct unconditionally. [§ 118.] *Εἰ ἅπαντες ὡμολογοῦμεν Φίλιππον τὴν εἰρήνην παραβαίνειν, οὐδὲν ἄλλο ἔδει τὸν παριόντα* (*an orator, who rose to speak*) *λέγειν καὶ συμβουλεύειν ἢ ὅπως ἀσφαλέστατα αὐτὸν ἀμυνούμεθα* (*Dem.* 9, 6). Καλὸν *ἦν τοῖσδε, εἰ καὶ ἡμαρτάνομεν, εἶξαι τῇ ἡμετέρᾳ ὀργῇ* (*Thuc.* 1, 38). *Εἰ αἰσχρόν τι αἱ γυναῖκες ἔμελλον ἐργάσεσθαι, θάνατον ἀντ' αὐτοῦ προαιρετέον ἦν* (*Xen. Mem.* 2, 7, 10). (Εἰ δ' *ἦν ἀναγκαῖον ῥηθῆναι, οὐ Δημοσθένους ἦν ὁ λόγος, Æsch.* 3, 229; *it was not for D. to say it.*) Τῶν *ἐμοὶ συγγεγονότων τινὰ ἐχρῆν Μέλητον παρασχέσθαι μάρτυρα* (*Pl. Apol.* 34). But also ἔδει ἄν: Εἰ *ἐγὼ ἔτι ἐν δυνάμει ἦν τοῦ ῥᾳδίως πορεύεσθαι πρὸς τὸ ἄστυ, οὐδὲν ἄν σε ἔδει δεῦρο ἰέναι* (*Pl. Rep.* 1, 328; *thou hadst no need, there would be no occasion, &c.*)[1].

b) By a rhetorical mode of expression, the imperfect without ἄν is used to denote what would be (or have been) an immediate and easily-foreseen consequence of any thing (instead of the aorist with ἄν.—The consequence or prospective result denoted as already in the act of taking place). Ὡρμημένων τῶν ἐν Σάμῳ Ἀθηναίων *πλεῖν ἐπὶ σφᾶς αὐτούς* (*against their countrymen at home*), *ἐν ᾧ σαφέστατα Ἰωνίαν καὶ Ἑλλήσποντον εὐθὺς εἶχον οἱ πολέμιοι, κωλυτὴς Ἀλκιβιάδης ἐγένετο* (*Thuc.* 8, 86). Οὔτε ὡς ἀποκτείναιεν οἱ θεοὶ τὸ τῶν ἀνθρώπων γένος, *εἶχον — αἱ τιμαὶ γὰρ αὐτοῖς καὶ τὰ ἱερὰ τὰ παρὰ τῶν ἀνθρώπων ἠφανίζετο — οὔθ' ὅπως ἐῷεν ἀσελγαίνειν* (*Pl. Conv.* 190). Ταῦτα πράξας (*had I done this—, by such actions*), ἃ οὗτός μου κατηγορεῖ, ἐκέρδαινον μὲν οὐδέν, ἐμαυτὸν δ' εἰς κίνδυνον καθίστην (*Lys.* 7, 32). (Ἦν is also now and then put, without this meaning, for ἦν ἄν (*would have been*), the hypothetical being rhetorically represented as actual: Μετὰ τὴν μάχην εὐθὺς ὁ δῆμος, ἐν αὐτοῖς τοῖς δεινοῖς ἐμβεβηκώς, ἡνίκ' οὐδ' ἀγνωμονῆσαί τι θαυμαστὸν ἦν τοὺς πολλοὺς πρὸς ἐμέ, περὶ σωτηρίας τῆς πόλεως τὰς ἐμὰς γνώμας ἐχειροτόνει, *Dem.* 18, 218. Other omissions of ἄν are very questionable[2].)

Rem. 1. Of ἵν' εἶχον (*that I might have*) without ἄν (hypothetical *final sentence*) see *Optative*. § 131 b. R. 3.

Rem. 2. The aorist with ὀλίγου, *within a little, almost*, always without ἄν: Ὀλίγου ἐξηπάτησάς με (*Pl. Meno*, 80).

Rem. 3. The present and perfect indicative never take ἄν. In the older poetical language (Homer, Pindar, Choral Odes) occasionally ἄν (κέν) occurs with the future indicative by a mixture of a simple mode of assertion with a dubitative (Pres. or Aor. Optat. with ἄν). In Attic writers (except in Choral Odes) this usage is very questionable.

Rem. 4. On the place of ἄν, its repetition, &c., see *Optative with ἄν*, § 139.

---

[1] Ἠβουλόμην now and then for ἠβουλόμην ἄν (e.g. *Arist. Ran.* 866).

[2] Ἡ πόλις ἐκινδύνευσε πᾶσα διαφθαρῆναι, εἰ ἄνεμος ἐπεγένετο τῇ φλογί. *Thuc.* 3, 74. Ἐκινδύνευσε stands unconditionally (*—and would have been ruined, if —*). Οὐ γὰρ δή που σοῦ γε οὐδὲν τῶν ἄλλων περιττότερον πραγματευομένου ἔπειτα τοσαύτη φήμη τε καὶ λόγος γέγονεν, εἰ μή τι ἔπραττες ἀλλοῖον ἢ οἱ ἄλλοι (*Pl. Apol.* 20. A mixture of an unconditional expression: *has not arisen without thy doing —*, and a conditional, *if thou didst not —*).

CHAPTER II.

The Subjunctive (Conjunctive) and its Tenses.

§ 119. (346) Both in the Subjunctive and in the Optative an action or state is put as a conception presented to the speaker's mind, without his at the same time enunciating it as real: but the subjunctive denotes the thing as said in reference to present or future time, and to reality, as something demanded, or as something purposed and aimed at, or as a case of possible occurrence; whereas the optative denotes it either in reference to the past, as something that was once purposed and aimed at, or a case conceived as having occurred in the past, or also as a quite indefinite possibility (as a wish, or dubitatively with *ἄν*). The Greeks, however, in certain kinds of dependent propositions, not unfrequently omit to intimate the reference to the past, so that the subjunctive is put for the optative (but never conversely). In other kinds of dependent propositions, where the optative should stand, it not unfrequently happens, that the relation is left unmarked and the indicative is used.

Rem. The subjunctive and optative are far from being constantly used in all sorts of dependent propositions which denote something merely conceived and thought; they are employed only where a need had been felt for denoting this, while in others the speaker, not caring to denote this, uses the indicative (see after *Optative*, at the end of chapter 3). In certain kinds of subordinate propositions, e.g. in object-sentences with *ὅτι* and *ὡς*, or in dependent interrogative sentences, the modification is not denoted, when they belong to a governing sentence in the present or future (they stand therefore in the indicative, not in the subjunctive); but is denoted, when the tense used in the governing sentence is a *præteritum* (then they stand in the optative). With less exact accuracy, and by reason of a certain liveliness in the expression, it sometimes happens, that something which is part of a conception belonging to the past, is put as part of a conception belonging to the present, and so the optative passes into the subjunctive, or (where this is not used) into the indicative, without in any remarkable way affecting the thought.

§ 120. (352 a, b) *a*) The *Subjunctive* in the first person (in the singular not usually without a preceding *φέρε* or *ἄγε*) is used in exhortation and demand, affirmatively, or with the negation *μή*. *Ἴωμεν. Μὴ φοβώμεθα. Φέρε δή, τὰς μαρτυρίας ὑμῖν ἀναγνῶ* (*Dem.* 18, 267). *Φέρε δὴ καὶ ὅσους αὐτὸς ἐλυσάμην τῶν αἰχμαλώτων, εἴπω πρὸς ὑμᾶς* (*Dem.* 19, 169).

b) In the second and third person, the aorist of the subjunctive stands with *μή* in prohibitions: *Μὴ ποιήσῃς τοῦτο.* See *Imperative*, § 142.

REM. Rarely, and poetically, *μή* is used with the first person, in praying that something may not befall the speaker: Ἀλλά μ' ἐκ τῆσδε γῆς πόρθμευσον ὡς τάχιστα μηδ' αὐτοῦ θανῶ (*Soph. Trach.* 801).

Subj. dubitativus.] The subjunctive is used in simple interrogations or in doubting questions (expressive of disapprobation, displeasure, denial), of that which *shall* come to pass, *is to be* done (what one is challenged to do, what one is required to do by the will of another, what can and shall be done), both when they are direct, and when they are dependent on a leading verb in the present or future[1]: Τί φῶ; τί δρῶ; Πῶς οὖν δὴ περὶ αὐτῶν τούτων λέγωμεν καὶ πῶς ποιῶμεν; (*Pl. Phil.* 63.) Δοκεῖ χρῆναι, ὦ Ἐρυξίμαχε; ἐπιθῶμαι τῷ ἀνδρὶ καὶ τιμωρήσωμαι ὑμῶν ἐναντίον; (*Pl. Conv.* 214.) Δέξεσθε ἡμᾶς ἢ ἀπίωμεν; (*Pl. Conv.* 212. *Will ye receive us, or are we to go away?*) Ἵνα οὖν τριάκοντα ἄνθρωποι λειτουργήσωσιν ἡμῖν, τοὺς ἅπαντας ἀπίστως πρὸς ἡμᾶς αὐτοὺς διαθῶμεν; (*Dem.* 20, 22.) Ἆρα, ἔφη ὁ Σωκράτης, μὴ αἰσχυνθῶμεν τὸν Περσῶν βασιλέα μιμήσασθαι; (*Xen. Œcon.* 4, 4.) Πόθεν οὖν τις ἄρξηται, πολλῆς οὔσης περὶ τὰ ἀμφισβητούμενα μάχης; (*Pl. Phil.* 15.) Τίνος ἕνεκα ἐφ' ἡμῶν πρῶτον καταδειχθῇ τοιοῦτον ἔργον; (*Dem.* 20, 117; *why is such a deed to be done for the first time in our days?*) — Ἀπορῶ, τήν τ' ἀδελφὴν ὅπως ἐκδῶ καὶ τἆλλ' ὁπόθεν διοικῶ (*Dem.* 27, 66). Βουλεύομαι, πῶς σε ἀποδρῶ (*Xen. Cyr.* 1, 4, 13). Οὐκ ἔχω, ὅπως σοι εἴπω ἃ νοῶ (*Pl. Euthyph.* 11). Οἱ κάπηλοι φροντίζουσιν, ὅ,τι ἐλάττονος πριάμενοι πλείονος ἀποδῶνται (*Xen. Mem.* 3, 7, 6). Τὰ ἐκπώματα οὐκ οἶδ' εἰ Χρυσάντᾳ τούτῳ δῶ, ἐπεὶ καὶ τὴν ἕδραν σου ὑφήρπασεν (*Xen. Cyr.* 8, 4, 16). (Ἔχω and οὐκ ἔχω ὅ, τι (ὅ) with the subjunctive often occur in the sense, *have something* (*nothing*) *to* —: Οὐδὲν Σωκράτει διοίσει, ἐὰν μόνον ἔχῃ, ὅτῳ διαλέγηται (*Pl. Conv.* 194; *somebody to converse with*). Ἑκάτεροι ἔχουσιν ἐφ' οἷς φιλοτιμηθῶσιν. *Isocr. Paneg.* 44.) § 121. (351)

REM. 1. When the speaker is less concerned to mark the notion of requirement (the *is to be*), it is not unfrequently omitted, and such a question, whether direct or indirect, is put in the indicative future (as a question what will happen): Τί οὖν ποιήσομεν; πότερον εἰς τὴν πόλιν πάντας τούτους παραδεξόμεθα ἢ τοὺς μέν, τοὺς δ' οὔ; (*Pl. Rep.* 3, 397.) Ἆρ' οὖν θησόμεθα νόμον διὰ ταῦτα μηδὲ τὸ λοιπὸν ἐξεῖναι τῇ βουλῇ μηδὲ τῷ δήμῳ μήτε προβουλεύειν μήτε χειροτονεῖν μηδέν; (*Dem.* 20, 4; *shall we make a law?*) Οὐκ ἔχετε, οἶμαι, ὅ, τι ποιήσετε (*Dem.* 8, 32). Hence the phrase is either οὐκ ἔχω, ὅ,τι χρήσωμαι τῷ ἀνθρώπῳ, τῷ ἀργυρίῳ (*what to do with* —), or, sometimes χρήσομαι. (Εἴπωμεν ἢ σιγῶμεν, ἢ τί δράσομεν; *Eur. Ion*, 758. Ἁμιλλῶνται, ὁπότεροι φθήσονται τὴν πόλιν ἀγαθόν τι ποιήσαντες, *Isocr. Paneg.* 79.)

REM. 2. In deliberating with oneself or others what to do (say, think) now immediately, the question is sometimes put in the first person of the present

---

[1] Viz. regularly; of the subjunctive instead of the optative after a leading verb in a præteritum (§ 119, R.), see *Optative*, § 130 b, and also the following §§.

[§ 121.] indicative: Πῶς οὖν, ὦ Ἀλκιβιάδη, ποιοῦμεν; οὕτως οὔτε τι λέγομεν ἐπὶ τῇ κύλικι οὔτ' ἐπᾴδομεν, ἀλλ' ἀτεχνῶς ὥσπερ οἱ διψῶντες πιόμεθα; (*Pl. Conv.* 214. *What do we then, Alcibiades!* Directly afterwards we have Ἀλλὰ τί ποιῶμεν;)

REM. 3. Of the dubitative question in the optative with ἄν, see *Optative*, § 136.

§ 122. (355) The subjunctive stands in propositions of intention (*final sentences*) with the conjunctions *ἵνα, ὡς* (poet. *ὄφρα*), *ὅπως*, *in order that* (*ἵνα μή, ὡς μή, ὅπως μή*, sometimes simply *μή*, *that—not; lest*) after a governing verb in the present or future. Ὡς and ὅπως in this sense sometimes take *ἄν*, never *ἵνα* or the simple *μή*[1]. Ὅπως (without *ἄν*) and *ὅπως μή*, however, sometimes take, instead of the aor. 1 of the subjunctive, the future indicative, whereby the thing intended, is brought out more independently, as a thing that will occur. (See note at end of following §.) *Βασιλεὺς αἱρεῖται, οὐχ ἵνα ἑαυτοῦ καλῶς ἐπιμελῆται, ἀλλ' ἵνα καὶ οἱ ἑλόμενοι δι' αὐτὸν εὖ πράττωσιν* (*Xen. Mem.* 3, 2, 3). *Δοκεῖ μοι κατακαῦσαι τὰς ἁμάξας, ἃς ἔχομεν, ἵνα μὴ τὰ ζεύγη ἡμῶν στρατηγῇ, ἀλλὰ τραπώμεθα, ὅπῃ ἂν τῇ στρατιᾷ συμφέρῃ* (*Xen. An.* 3, 2, 27). *Τισσαφέρνης διανοεῖται τὴν γέφυραν λῦσαι τῆς νυκτός, ὡς μὴ διαβῆτε, ἀλλ' ἐν μέσῳ ἀποληφθῆτε τοῦ ποταμοῦ καὶ τῆς διώρυχος* (*Xen. An.* 2, 4, 17). *Εἰς καιρὸν ἥκεις, ὅπως τῆς δίκης ἀκούσῃς παρὼν τῆς ἀμφὶ τοῦ πατρός* (*Xen. Cyr.* 3, 1, 8). *Ἐάν τίς σοι κάμνῃ τῶν οἰκετῶν, παρακαλεῖς ἰατρούς, ὅπως μὴ ἀποθάνῃ* (*Xen. Mem.* 2, 10, 2). *Ταῦτα γίγνεται, οὐχ ὅπως τοὺς αὐτοὺς αὐλητὰς ἐπαινῶσιν οἱ πολῖται οὐδ' ὅπως τοὺς αὐτοὺς ποιητὰς αἱρῶνται, οὐδ' ἵνα τοῖς αὐτοῖς ἥδωνται, ἀλλ' ἵνα τοῖς νόμοις πείθωνται* (*Xen. Mem.* 4, 4, 16). *Σύ, ὦ παῖ, ἂν σωφρονῇς, τοὺς θεοὺς παραιτήσῃ συγγνώμονάς σοι εἶναι, εἴ τι παρημέληκας τῆς μητρός, μή σε καὶ οὗτοι νομίσαντες ἀχάριστον εἶναι οὐκ ἐθέλωσιν εὖ ποιεῖν* (*Xen. Mem.* 2, 2, 14). — *Τουτὶ λαβών μου τὸ σκιάδειον ὑπέρεχε ἄνωθεν, ὡς ἂν μή*[2] *μ' ὁρῶσιν οἱ θεοί* (*Arist. Aves* 1509). *Ὁ τύραννος πολέμους τινὰς ἀεὶ κινεῖ, ἵν' ἐν χρείᾳ ἡγεμόνος ὁ δῆμος ᾖ καί, ἐάν τινας ὑποπτεύῃ ἐλεύθερα φρονήματα ἔχοντας μὴ ἐπιτρέψειν αὐτῷ ἄρχειν, ὅπως ἂν τούτους μετὰ προφάσεως ἀπολλύῃ, ἐνδοὺς τοῖς πολεμίοις* (*Pl. Rep.* 8, 567). — *Οἱ σύμμαχοι οὐδὲ δι' ἓν ἄλλο τρέφονται ἢ ὅπως μαχοῦνται ὑπὲρ τῶν τρεφόντων* (*Xen. Cyr.* 2, 1, 21). *Χρὴ ἀναβιβάζειν ἐπὶ τὸν τροχὸν τοὺς*

---

[1] Where ἵνα ἄν occurs, ἵνα means *where*. With ὡς and ὅπως, ἄν effects no perceptible change of meaning. [But Hermann, ὡς, or ὅπως, ἂν ἔλθω, *ut veniam si forte venias; that, if so be, may come*. T. K. A.—Rather (comp. *Particles*, § 302), the ἄν denotes that the thing intended will ensue—ὅπως ἔλθω, *that I may come*, such being the intention whether realized or not; but ὅπως ἂν ἔλθω, THAT *I may come, as, in the case supposed, I shall*: almost = *so shall I come*. So in the place cited, Aristoph. Av. 1509, ὡς ἂν μή μ' ὁρῶσιν οἱ θεοί, *so shall the gods not see me*. II. B.]

[2] ὡς ἂν μή μ' ὁρῶσιν οἱ θεοί, *that, as far as this goes, the gods see me not—so shall the gods not see me*; without ἄν, *merely to the intent that they*, &c.

ἀναγραφέντας (*to put the persons denounced upon the rack*), *ὅπως μὴ πρότερον νὺξ ἔσται πρὶν πυθέσθαι τοὺς ἄνδρας ἅπαντας* (*Andoc.* 1, 43).

§ 123. (354, 372)

The subjunctive stands in object-sentences annexed by *ὅπως* or *ὅπως μή* to the present or future of verbs or phrases denoting, *to endeavour* (*to take care, to work upon others*) that something may, or may not, be done (as *ἐπιμελεῖσθαι, σπουδάζειν, παρασκευάζειν, πράττειν, μηχανᾶσθαι, παραγγέλλειν, πρόνοιαν ἔχειν, περὶ πολλοῦ ποιεῖσθαι, πρὸς τοῦτο τὸν νοῦν ἔχειν*, &c.). But the future indicative is also used, in order to mark the object prominently as something that will occur, or as a state that continues in the future, and this is the most usual form; somewhat less frequent the subjunctive of the present and aor. 2, while that of the aor. 1 active and middle is even very rare in object-sentences with *ὅπως*. Now and then *ἄν* is added to *ὅπως*, and then always the subjunctive: *Ἄλλου του ἄρα ἐπιμελήσει ἡμῖν ἐλθὼν ἐπὶ τὰ τῆς πόλεως πράγματα ἢ ὅπως ὅτι βέλτιστοι οἱ πολῖται ὦμεν;* (*Pl. Gorg.* 515.) *Σεύθης κελεύει Ξενοφῶντα προθυμεῖσθαι, ὅπως διαβῇ τὸ στράτευμα* (*Xen. An.* 7, 1, 5). *Εἴ τίς σοι τῶν γνωρίμων κινδυνεύει δι' ἔνδειαν ἀπολέσθαι, οὐκ οἴει σοι ἄξιον εἶναι ἐπιμεληθῆναι, ὅπως διασωθῇ;* (*Xen. Mem.* 2, 10, 2.) *Φίλιππος ὠνεῖται παρὰ τῶν πρέσβεων, ὅπως μὴ ἀπίωμεν ἐκ Μακεδονίας* (*Dem.* 18, 32).—*Ὥσπερ τὸν ποιμένα δεῖ ἐπιμελεῖσθαι, ὅπως σῶαί τε ἔσονται αἱ οἶες καὶ τὰ ἐπιτήδεια ἕξουσιν, οὕτω καὶ τὸν στρατηγὸν ἐπιμελεῖσθαι δεῖ, ὅπως σῶοί τε οἱ στρατιῶται ἔσονται καὶ τὰ ἐπιτήδεια ἕξουσιν* (*Xen. Mem.* 3, 2, 1). *Καλὸν παρασκευάζειν, ὅπως ὡς βέλτισται ἔσονται τῶν πολιτῶν αἱ ψυχαί* (*Pl. Gorg.* 503). *Οὐ μικρὰν πρόνοιαν ἔχειν δεῖ, ὅπως κύριος ἔσται ὁ νόμος καὶ μήτε συγχυθήσεται μήτ' αὖ μεταποιηθήσεται* (*Dem.* 23, 62). *Τί μάλιστα ἐν ἅπασι διεσπούδασται τοῖς νόμοις; Ὅπως μὴ γενήσονται οἱ περὶ ἀλλήλους φόνοι* (*Dem.* 20, 157)[1].—*Οἱ ναῦται τῷ ναυκλήρῳ περικέχυνται δεόμενοι καὶ πάντα ποιοῦντες, ὅπως ἂν σφισι τὸ πηδάλιον ἐπιτρέψῃ* (*Pl. Rep.* 6, 488). (*Εἰ τὸν ἐχθρὸν κακῶς ποιητέον ἐστίν, κακὸν δὲ μέγιστον αὐτῇ ἡ ἀδικία ἐστὶν ἐν τῇ ψυχῇ ἐνοῦσα μηδὲ τιμωρίᾳ ἐκκαθαιρομένη, ἐάν τινα ἀδικῇ ὁ ἐχθρός, παντὶ τρόπῳ παρασκευαστέον, ὅπως μηδὲ ἔλθῃ παρὰ τὸν δικαστήν· ἐὰν δὲ ἔλθῃ, μηχανητέον, ὅπως ἂν διαφύγῃ καὶ μὴ δῷ δίκην, ἀλλ', ἐάν τε χρυσίον ἡρπακὼς ᾖ πολύ, μὴ ἀποδιδῷ τοῦτο ἀλλ' ἔχων ἀναλίσκῃ ἀδίκως καὶ ἀθέως, ἐάν τε αὖ θανάτου ἄξια ἠδικηκὼς ᾖ, ὅπως μὴ ἀποθανεῖται, μάλιστα μὲν μηδέποτε ἀλλ' ἀθάνατος ἔσται πονηρὸς ὤν, εἰ δὲ μή, ὅπως ὡς πλεῖστον χρόνον βιώσεται*, *Pl. Gorg.* 480.)

Rem. 1. Ὅπως is originally an interrogative particle (*how*), in which signification it is frequently used. Verbs like σκοπεῖν, βουλεύεσθαι, &c., denote therefore, in the first instance: to consider *how* a thing *may* be done (as intention), in which sense the fut. indic. is exclusively used (*Ἀνάγκη σκοπεῖν, ὅπως τὰ πράγματα*

---

[1] *Σινωπεῖς Τιμασίωνα κελεύουσι προστατεῦσαι, ὅπως ἐκπλεύσῃ ἡ στρατιά* (*Xen. An.* 5, 6, 21).

[§ 123.] *σωθήσεται, Dem.* 9. 63. Τιμοκράτης τοῖς πονηροῖς, ὅπως μὴ δώσουσι δίκην, ὁδὸν δείκνυσιν, *Dem.* 24. 106); consequently, at the same time, to take measures *that* it may be done, in which sense the subjunctive may also be used. (Οὐ μόνον ψηφίζεσθαι τὴν εἰρήνην δεῖ, ἀλλὰ καὶ βουλεύεσθαι, ὅπως ἄξομεν αὐτὴν καὶ μὴ πάλιν εἰς τὰς αὐτὰς καταστησόμεθα ταραχάς, *Isocr. de Pac.* 25. Τοῦτό μοι δοκεῖ σκεπτέον εἶναι, ὅπως ὡς ἐλάχιστα μὲν τραύματα λάβωμεν, ὡς ἐλάχιστα δὲ σώματα ἀνδρῶν ἀποβάλωμεν, *Xen. An.* 4, 6, 10. Σκοπεῖ, ὅπως μὴ ἔξαρνος ἔσει ἃ νῦν λέγεις, *Pl. Euthyd.* 283.)[1] Then it comes to be used with all verbs which denote an *endeavouring* and an *acting in order to a purpose*, with loss of the interrogative sense, and consequently with mixed construction, rarely with aor. 1, which so much resembles the future. Lastly, it also denotes merely the *intention* (§ 122), in which sense the subjunctive predominates, and the fut. indic. is more rare.

Rem. 2. This construction of ὅπως must be kept quite distinct from the relative ὅπως in the expression οὐκ ἔστιν ὅπως, *there is no way in which —, it is not possible that* (§ 102, b. R. 2), which never has the subjunctive.

Rem. 3. After verbs like σκοπῶ, βουλεύομαι, &c., there may also be attached by ὅπως a dependent interrogative sentence with (potential) optative and ἄν (see § 137), of that which may probably take place: Σκοπῶ, ὅπως ἂν ὁ μὲν παῖς ὅδε ὁ σὸς καὶ ἡ παῖς ἥδε ὡς ῥᾷστα διάγοιεν, ἡμεῖς δ' ἂν μάλιστα εὐφραινοίμεθα θεώμενοι αὐτούς (*Xen. Conv.* 2).

Rem. 4. Elliptically ὅπως, ὅπως μή, μηδείς, &c. stand often with the second, more rarely with the third or first person of the fut. indic. to denote a command, a prohibition, instead of the imperative (*see to it, that*): Ὅπως οὖν ἔσεσθε ἄνδρες ἄξιοι τῆς ἐλευθερίας, ἣν κέκτησθε (*Xen. An.* 1, 7, 3). Ὅπως ἐπέξει τῷ μιαρῷ καὶ μὴ διαλύσῃ (*Dem.* 21, 216. *Prosecute the rascal, and make no terms*[2]). Ὅπως τοίνυν περὶ τοῦ πολέμου μηδὲν ἐρεῖς· οὐδεὶς γὰρ οὐδὲν αἰτιᾶται περὶ αὐτοῦ σε (*Dem.* 19, 92). (Τούτοις ἐγὼ ἀποκρινοῦμαι καθ' ἕκαστον ἀκριβῶς· καὶ ὅπως, ὥσπερ ἐρωτῶσι προθύμως, οὕτω καὶ ποιεῖν ἐθελήσουσιν. *Dem.* 8, 38. Ὅπως δὲ τὸ σύμβολον λαβόντες ἔπειτα πλησίον καθεδούμεθα, *Arist. Eccl.* 297.) (The aorist subjunctive only in uncertain passages.) (Of another elliptic use of ὅπως μή, see § 124, b. R. 1.)

Rem. 5. After βούλει, βούλεσθε (mostly interrogative) the aorist subjunctive is used with ὅπως omitted (never the fut. indic.): Βούλεσθ' οὖν ὑμῖν αὐτοὺς παρασχῶμαι μάρτυρας τουτουσί, ὅτι πάντα τἀναντία ἐμοὶ καὶ τούτοις πέπρακται; (*Dem.* 19. 205.)

Rem. 6. Rarely ὡς for ὅπως in object-sentences: Οἱ μὲν τούτου ἐπιμελοῦνται, ὡς ἔχῃ οὕτως, οἱ δὲ οὐκ ἐπιμελοῦνται (*Xen. Œcon.* 20, 8).

§ 124. (354, 376) *a*) The subjunctive stands in propositions with μή after verbs and phrases denoting fear and apprehension (**δέδοικα, φοβοῦμαι, ὀκνῶ, φροντίζω, οὐδὲν δεινόν**, *there is no danger of*, &c.), or taking heed and precautions against (**φυλάττομαι, εὐλαβοῦμαι, ὁρῶ, σκοπῶ**), to denote

---

[1] Cf. Σκοποῦσιν, ἐξ ὅτου τρόπου οἱ Μεγαλοπολῖται φίλοι ὑμῖν μὴ γενήσονται (*Dem.* 16, 19; *shall be hindered that they may not become —*). Ἀριστεὺς ἔπρασσε, ὅπῃ ὠφέλειά τις γενήσεται (*Thuc.* 1, 65; *negotiated how succour should come*).

[2] The present of εἶμι is treated as future.

that of which one is afraid, or against which one is on his guard (*ne*; *μὴ οὐ*, *ne non*): ὁρῶ and σκοπῶ, μή often merely denotes a suspicion [§ 124]
or surmise (*see whether—not*). Of a fear, in reference to the past, μή is mostly used with the perfect indicative: Δέδοικα, μὴ ἐπιλαθώμεθα τῆς οἴκαδε ὁδοῦ (*Xen. An.* 3, 2, 25). Φροντίζω, μὴ κράτιστον ᾖ μοι σιγᾶν· κινδυνεύω γὰρ ἁπλῶς οὐδὲν εἰδέναι (*Xen. Mem.* 4, 2, 39). Τὰ περὶ τῆς ψυχῆς πολλὴν ἀπιστίαν (*mistrust and fear*) παρέχει τοῖς ἀνθρώποις, μή, ἐπειδὰν ἀπαλλαγῇ τοῦ σώματος, οὐδαμοῦ ἔτι ᾖ ἀλλ' ἐκείνῃ τῇ ἡμέρᾳ διαφθείρηται καὶ ἀπολλύηται, ᾗ ἂν ἄνθρωπος ἀποθάνῃ (*Pl. Phæd.* 70). Τῶν φυλάκων ἐν ἑαυτοῖς μὴ στασιαζόντων, οὐδὲν δέος, μήποτε ἡ ἄλλη πόλις πρὸς τούτους διχοστατήσῃ (*Pl. Phæd.* 465). Εὐθύδημος φυλάττεται, μὴ δόξῃ τὸν Σωκράτην θαυμάζειν ἐπὶ σοφίᾳ (*Xen. Mem.* 4, 2, 3). Ὅρα οὖν, μή τι καὶ νῦν Ἀλκιβιάδης ἐργάσηται (*Pl. Conv.* 213).—Φοβούμεθα, μὴ ἀμφοτέρων ἡμαρτήκαμεν (*Thuc.* 3, 53).

Rem. 1. Now and then μή with the future indicative stands after verbs denoting a fear, to express rather a mere *suspicion* of what will happen, and to give prominence to the notion of futurity: Φοβοῦμαι, μή τινας ἡδονὰς ἡδοναῖς εὑρήσομεν ἐναντίας (*Pl. Phil.* 13). Εἰ μαθήσονται οἱ πολέμιοι, χωρὶς γενόμενοι οἱ μὲν κατὰ πρόσωπον ἡμῖν, ὥσπερ νῦν, ἐναντιοῦσθαι, αἱ δ' ἐκ πλαγίου, αἱ δὲ καὶ ὄπισθεν, ὅρα, μὴ πολλῶν ἑκάστῳ ἡμῶν καὶ ὀφθαλμῶν καὶ χειρῶν δεήσει (*Xen. Cyr.* 4, 1, 18). Also μή after ὁρῶ stands with the pres. indic. as a merely interrogative particle (*whether*): Ὁρῶμεν, μὴ Νικίας οἴεταί τι λέγειν καὶ οὐ λόγου ἕνεκα ταῦτα λέγει (*Pl. Lach.* 196).

Rem. 2. Μή stands elliptically with the pres. subjunctive to express a fear, or usually merely a suspicion (*if only—not*; *I fear that*): Μὴ ἀγροικότερον ᾖ τὸ ἀληθὲς εἰπεῖν· ὀκνῶ γὰρ Γοργίου ἕνεκα λέγειν (*Pl. Gorg.* 462). Ἀλλὰ μὴ οὐ τοῦτ' ᾖ χαλεπόν, θάνατον ἐκφυγεῖν, ἀλλὰ πολὺ χαλεπώτερον, πονηρίαν· θᾶττον γὰρ θανάτου θεῖ (*Pl. Apol.* 39. *I fear the difficulty is not* —). Ἀλλὰ μὴ οὐχ οὕτως ἔχῃ, ὦ Σώκρατες, ἀλλ' ἀναγκαῖον ᾖ εἰδότα τίθεσθαι τὸν τιθέμενον τὰ ὀνόματα (*Pl. Crat.* 436; *that he who gave the names must have given them after knowledge* of the things). See b. Rem.

Rem. 3. From putting οὐκ (οὐδείς, οὐκέτι, οὔκουν) before the elliptic μή (μήποτε) with the subjunctive, there results the denial of a fear (*I am not afraid that* = οὐδὲν δεινόν, μή, *there is no danger*, *no fear*, *that* —, or, *of* —), which is frequently used merely as a strong denial of the thing itself; *a future with strong negation.* Instead of the aor. subjunct. sometimes (cf. R. 1) the fut. indic. is used without perceptible difference of meaning: Ἐπὶ τούτου τοῦ ἵππου καὶ διώκων, ὃν ἂν θέλῃς, αἱρήσεις καὶ ἀποχωρῶν οὐ μὴ δείσῃς τὸν πολέμιον (*Xen. An.* 7, 3, 26). Σωκράτης, ὁπόσον ἂν κελεύῃ τις, ἐκπιὼν οὐδὲν μᾶλλον μήποτε μεθυσθῇ (*Pl. Conv.* 214). Ἐὰν ἀπογνῶτε τὴν γραφὴν ταύτην, ἅπαντές εἰσιν ἀπηλλαγμένοι καὶ δίκην οὐδεὶς οὐδεμίαν μὴ δῷ (*Dem.* 22, 39).—Τοιούτου ἐστέρημαι ἐπιτηδείου, οἷον οὐδένα μήποτε εὑρήσω (*Pl. Crit.* 44). Καλλικρατίδας εἶπεν, ὅτι ἡ Σπάρτη οὐδὲν μὴ κάκιον οἰκεῖται αὐτοῦ ἀποθανόντος, φεύγειν δ' αἰσχρὸν εἶναι ἔφη (*Xen. Hell.* 1, 6, 32).

Rem. 4. From the use of οὐ μή, explained in the preceding remark, we must carefully distinguish the use of οὐ μή, with the second person of the fut. indic. (never the subjunctive) in questions expressive of a peremptory and vehement prohibition, the μή with the verb forming a negative notion (*will thou not give over doing it —? will thou not not-do it?*). A positive command, in the shape of a question, may

[§ 124.] precede with simple οὐ, or follow with ἀλλά: Οὐ μὴ ληρήσεις; (*Arist. Nub.* 367.) Οὔκουν καλεῖς αὐτὸν καὶ μὴ ἀφήσεις; (*Pl. Conv.* 175. *Wilt thou not call him, and not let him go! = call him, do, and don't let him go!*) Οὐ μὴ λαλήσεις ἀλλ' ἀκολουθήσεις ἐμοὶ ἀνύσας τι δευρὶ θᾶττον; (*Arist. Nub.* 505.)

b) Instead of μή, verbs denoting *to fear, be apprehensive, beware, take care*, take also ὅπως μή with the subjunct. or indic. fut. by § 123. Likewise ὅπως μή is put after verbs denoting a prohibition (ἀπαγορεύω). Οὐ φοβεῖ, δικαζόμενος τῷ πατρί, ὅπως μὴ ἀνόσιον πρᾶγμα τυγχάνῃς πράττων; (*Pl. Euthyph.* 4.) Φυλάττου, ὅπως μὴ τοῦ εὐδοξεῖν ἐπιθυμῶν εἰς τοὐναντίον ἔλθῃς (*Xen. Mem.* 3, 6, 16). Δέδοικα, ὅπως μὴ πάνθ' ἅμα, ὅσα οὐ βουλόμεθα, ποιεῖν ἡμῖν ἀνάγκη γενήσεται (*Dem.* 9, 75). Εὐλαβεῖσθε, ὅπως μὴ ἐγὼ ὑπὸ προθυμίας ἅμα ἐμαυτόν τε καὶ ὑμᾶς ἐξαπατήσας οἰχήσομαι (*Pl. Phæd.* 91). Ἀπείρηταί μοι, ὅπως μηδὲν ἐρῶ ὧν ἡγοῦμαι (*Pl. Rep.* 1, 337).

Rem. 1. Ὅπως μή is often put elliptically (see a. R. 2) with the fut. indic. (hardly the subjunctive) in the sense, *see to it that — not*: Εἰ τῶν διωκόντων καὶ κατακαινόντων τοὺς ἡμετέρους πολεμίους δόξομεν ἀμελεῖν, ὅπως μὴ αἰσχροὶ μὲν φανούμεθα, ἀσθενεῖς δ' ἐσόμεθα, συμμάχων ἀποροῦντες (*Xen. Cyr.* 4, 2, 39; *it is to be feared we shall —*). Ὅπως μὴ ἀπολεῖ μαστιγούμενος, ἐπειδὰν οἴκοι ᾖς (*Xen. Cyr.* 1, 3, 18). Οἴμοι τάλας, ὁ Ζεὺς ὅπως μή μ' ὄψεται (*Arist. Aves* 1494). With the indic. of a preterite by *a*: Ἀλλ' ὅπως μὴ 'ν τοῖς τρίβωσιν ἐγκάθηνται οἱ λίθοι (*Arist. Ach.* 343).

Rem. 2. Verbs denoting a fear rarely take ὡς (with the indic., as after the verbs denoting *to think, be of opinion*): Μὴ δείσητε ὡς οὐχ ἡδέως καθευδήσετε (*Xen. Cyr.* 6, 2, 30).

Rem. 3. (To § 123 and 124.) On the mood in object-sentences after a præteritum, see *Optative*, § 131.

§ 125. The subjunctive is used in conditional sentences with ἐάν (ἤν, ἄν, from εἰ ἄν), which are only used of that which is possible now or at a future time: Ἅπας λόγος, ἂν ἀπῇ τὰ πράγματα, μάταιόν τι φαίνεται καὶ κενόν (*Dem.* 2, 12). Ἤν τις ἀνθιστῆται, πειρασόμεθα χειροῦσθαι (*Xen. An.* 7, 3, 11).

Rem. 1. Ἐάν carries with it in a more marked way than εἰ, the notion that the supposition is an indefinite, single case, of (merely) possible occurrence [1]: *if = should it turn out to be the fact that*; but the difference is sometimes scarcely perceptible: Ἐὰν μὲν οὖν (ὁ Ἄφοβος) ἀργὸν φῇ γενέσθαι τὸ ἐργαστήριον, λόγον αὐτὸς ἀπενήνοχεν ἀναλωμάτων εἰς ἔργα· εἰ δ' αὖ γενέσθαι ἐργασίαν φήσει, τῶν δ' ἔργων ἀπρασίαν εἶναι, δεῖ δήπου τά γ' ἔργα αὐτὸν ἀποδεδωκότα φαίνεσθαι (*Dem.* 27, 20).

Rem. 2. In the Ionic and Doric poets the subjunctive sometimes follows εἰ without ἄν (κέν): in the Attic poets (except in the Choral Odes), or in prose (except in the archaic phraseology of law) there are no sure examples of this.

---

[1] [According to Buttmann, ἐάν puts the case as *uncertain*, but possible, and to be determined by subsequent experience.—T. K. A.]

The subjunctive stands with relative words (pronouns, adjectives, adverbs) which take ἄν (ὃς ἄν, ὅστις ἄν, οἷος ἄν, ὅσος ἄν, ὡς ἄν, ὅπου ἄν, &c.). Hereby, in reference to the present or future, an individual contingency among several that are possible, is put more prominently than by the simple relative (*whoever, whosoever; such . . . as*). Συμμαχεῖν τούτοις ἐθέλουσιν ἅπαντες, οὓς ἂν ὁρῶσι παρεσκευασμένους καὶ πράττειν ἐθέλοντας ἃ χρή (*Dem.* 4, 6). Οἱ ἄνθρωποι, ἐν ᾧ ἂν (*so long as*) πολεμῶσι, τὸν παρόντα πόλεμον ἀεὶ μέγιστον κρίνουσιν (*Thuc.* 1, 21). Ἅττ' ἄν σοι λογιζομένῳ φαίνηται βέλτιστα, ταῦτα τοῖς ἔργοις ἐπιτέλει (*Isocr. de Nic.* 38). Ὅσῳ ἂν ἀκριβέστερον τὰ πεπραγμένα μάθητε, τοσούτῳ δικαιοτέραν θήσεσθε τὴν ψῆφον (*Dem.* 29, 4). Ἕπεσθε ὅπῃ ἄν τις ἡγῆται, κόσμον καὶ φυλακὴν περὶ παντὸς ποιούμενοι (*Thuc.* 2, 11). § 126.

Rem. 1. Often the difference between ὅς and ὃς ἄν is very small: Αἰτία ἐστίν, ὅταν τις ψιλῷ χρησάμενος λόγῳ μὴ παράσχηται πίστιν, ὧν λέγει, ἔλεγχος δέ, ὅταν, ὧν ἂν εἴπῃ τις, καὶ τἀληθὲς ὁμοῦ δείξῃ (*Dem.* 22, 22).

Rem. 2. In the poets this subjunctive is found with the relative put indefinitely, even without ἄν; e. g. Γέροντα δ' ὀρθοῦν φλαῦρον, ὃς νέος πέσῃ (*Soph. Œd. C.* 395; *to raise up when old one who fell when young*).

Rem. 3. Quite distinct from this use of the subjunctive after the relative with ἄν (belonging to the relative) is the potential optative with ἄν (§ 137), or the hypothetical indicative with ἄν (§ 117, b) in a relative sentence: Ἄρξομαι ἐντεῦθεν, ὅθεν καὶ ὑμεῖς ῥᾷστ' ἂν μάθοιτε κἀγὼ τάχιστ' ἂν διδάξαιμι (*Dem.* 29, 5; *from the point, from which you may most easily apprehend, and I most speedily unfold the matter*).

The subjunctive stands with all conjunctions of *time* to which ἄν is annexed (ὅταν, ὁπόταν, ἐπειδάν, ἐπάν, ἡνίκ' ἄν, ἕως ἄν, ἔστ' ἄν, μέχρις ἄν, μέχρι οὗ ἄν, πρὶν ἄν); they serve to denote the indefinite point of time, and contingency in the present or future: Τοῦτο καὶ νῦν ποιοῦσιν οἱ βάρβαροι βασιλεῖς, ὁπόταν (*whenever; when*) στρατοπεδεύωνται· τάφρον περιβάλλονται εὐπετῶς διὰ τὴν πολυχειρίαν (*Xen. Cyr.* 3, 3, 26). Ἕως ἂν (*so long as*) σώζηται τὸ σκάφος, τότε χρὴ καὶ ναύτην καὶ κυβερνήτην καὶ πάντ' ἄνδρα ἑξῆς προθύμους εἶναι· ἐπειδὰν δὲ ἡ θάλαττα ὑπέρσχῃ, μάταιος ἡ σπουδή (*Dem.* 9, 69). Νῦν μὲν ἄπειμι ὡς βασιλέα· ἐπειδὰν δὲ διαπράξωμαι, ἃ δέομαι, ἥξω ἀπάξων ὑμᾶς εἰς τὴν Ἑλλάδα (*Xen. An.* 2, 3, 29). Οὐκ ἀναμένομεν, ἕως ἂν (*till*) ἡ ἡμετέρα χώρα κακῶται, ἀλλὰ φθάνοντες ἤδη δῃοῦμεν τὴν τῶν πολεμίων γῆν (*Xen. Cyr.* 3, 3, 18). Σπονδαὶ ἔσονται, μέχρις ἂν βασιλεῖ τὰ παρ' ὑμῶν διαγγελθῇ (*Xen. An.* 2, 3, 7). Ἐὰν φαίνωμαι ἀδικεῖν, οὐ χρή μ' ἐνθένδε ἀπελθεῖν, πρὶν ἂν δῶ δίκην (*Xen. An.* 5, 7, 5). § 127.

Rem. 1. Without ἄν these conjunctions stand with the indicative, partly to denote the definite present time (Ἕως ἔτι νέος εἰμί, τὴν ψυχὴν γυμνάζω. Ἐν μὲν τῷ στρα-

[§ 127.] *τοπέδῳ οἱ ἄρχοντες περιεώρων Ἀλκιβιάδην ὑπὸ πάντων προπηλακιζόμενον, ἐπειδὴ δὲ ὑμᾶς δεῖ παρ' αὐτοῦ δίκην λαμβάνειν, χαριζόμενοι αὐτῷ ψευδομαρτυροῦσιν*, *Lys.* 15, 6; also *ἐπεί, ἐπειδή, ὅτε, ὁπότε*, in causal signification: *since, whereas*); partly to denote a past time. Of *πρίν* with the infinitive, and its difference from (*οὐ* —) *πρὶν ἄν*, see *Infinitive*, § 167.

REM. 2. *Πρίν, μέχρι, ἕως, ἔστε* sometimes in the poets take the subjunctive without *ἄν* (*Μὴ στέναζε, πρὶν μάθῃς*, *Soph. Phil.* 917): *πρίν* and *μέχρι* (*μέχρι οὗ*) also in some individual passages of prose writers; e. g. *Οὐ πρότερον αὐτὸν ἀποκτιννύναι δεῖ, πρὶν ἀνάγκην τινὰ ὁ θεὸς ἐπιπέμψῃ* (*Pl. Phæd.* 62). (*Ὅτε* and *ἐπεί* only in Ionic poets; *ἐπεί τε* in Hdt.)

REM. 3 (to § 125—127). On the mood, in sentences of the kind here spoken of in the *oratio obliqua*, after a præteritum, see *Optative*, § 132.

§ 128. (The Tenses of the Subjunctive.) *a*) The subjunctive has no narrative tense, and no tense of the relative past, because it never denotes an action in reference to the past. The subjunctive has also no separate future, as the reference to the future results from the construction of the sentence itself, and in some instances is made prominent by the transition to the future indicative (see § 123 and 124). The subjunctive of the aorist, as it does not at all express the past[1], comes very near in point of signification to the present, and the difference is only this, that the aorist denotes the action as single and transient, or as taking place at one definite instant distinct from the actual present, while the present denotes more in general the action and the state as going on, or at least not as occurring singly and with limitation to a point of time. Hence the aorist, both in object-sentences and in final sentences (of intention), contains a reference to the future (*φοβοῦμαι, μὴ γένωμαι*, *I fear I shall become*, *μὴ γίγνωμαι*, *lest I become*), and denotes, especially in sentences with *ἐάν*, or with relatives or temporal conjunctions with *ἄν*, a single and separate future action (like the Lat. *futurum exactum* in temporal and conditional propositions: *ὅταν ὁρῶ*, *quum, quoties video*, *ὅταν ἴδω*, *quum videro*). This reference, however, is not always made prominent, so that the present stands where the aorist might have stood, to mark the action as less transient; and conversely the aorist is used of a present action, to denote it as transient and single. Sometimes the difference almost entirely disappears. *Φέρε, ἴωμεν.* *Ἀπορῶ, τὴν ἀδελφὴν ὅπως ἐκδῶ* (once for all) *καὶ τἄλλ' ὁπόθεν διοικῶ* (with continuance, and generally; *Dem.* 27, 66). *Ἐάν τις κάμνῃ τῶν οἰκετῶν* (*is sick*; *κάμῃ*, *should become sick*; *should fall sick*), *παρακαλεῖς ἰατρούς, ὅπως μὴ ἀποθάνῃ* (*Xen. Œcon.* 11, 9). *Τοῦτον ἡμεῖς φοβώμεθα*; (*Dem.* 14, 36; *are we to fear?* *φοβηθώμεθα*, *are we to take alarm at?*) *Ἐπισκόπει τοὺς*

[1] [Of course, when = *fut. exactum*, it denotes a future action as *completed*.—T. K. A.]

λόγους ἀεὶ τοὺς σαυτοῦ καὶ τὰς πράξεις, ἵν' ὡς ἐλαχίστοις ἁμαρτήμασι περιπίπτῃς (*Isocr. de Nic.* 33). Ὑποδήματα ὑποδοῦνται, ὅπως μὴ διὰ τὰ λυποῦντα τοὺς πόδας κωλύωνται πορεύεσθαι (*Xen. Mem.* 1, 6, 6). (Examples with ὁπόταν and ἕως ἂν with the present, see § 127; with ἐάν § 125, with ὃς ἄν, &c. § 126.)—Σοῦ ἀκούσωμεν; (*Arist. Ach.* 295, single, transient act.) Πολλοὶ ἀποθνήσκειν ἐθέλουσιν, ἵνα τελευτήσαντες ἐπαινεθῶσιν (*Isocr. de Nic.* 36). Σεύθης κελεύει Ξενοφῶντα προθυμεῖσθαι, ὅπως διαβῇ τὸ στράτευμα (*Xen. An.* 7, 1, 5). Εὐθύδημος φυλάττεται, μὴ δόξῃ τὸν Σωκράτην θαυμάζειν ἐπὶ σοφίᾳ (*Xen. Mem.* 4, 2, 3; *not to get the appearance as though he* —). (So usually after φυλάττομαι, εὐλαβοῦμαι, cf. on οὐ μή, § 124, a. R. 3.) Ἐπειδὰν διαπράξωμαι, ἃ δέομαι, ἥξω ἀπάξων ὑμᾶς εἰς τὴν Ἑλλάδα (*Xen. An.* 2, 3, 29). Εἰκὸς, τοὺς Ἀθηναίους, ὅταν γνῶσιν ἡμᾶς τετρυχωμένους, πειράσεσθαι ὑπὸ σφᾶς ποιεῖσθαι (*Thuc.* 4, 60).—Ἐπειδὰν σὺ βούλῃ διαλέγεσθαι, ὡς ἐγὼ δύναμαι ἕπεσθαι, τότε σοι διαλέξομαι (*Pl. Prot.* 335, of the *being willing*, as a continued state). Ἤν τις ἀνθιστῆται, πειρασόμεθα χειροῦσθαι (*Xen. An.* 7, 3, 11). Οὐκ ἀναμένομεν ἕως ἂν ἡ ἡμετέρα χώρα κακῶται, ἀλλὰ φθάνοντες ἤδη δῃοῦμεν τὴν ἐκείνων γῆν (*Xen. Cyr.* 3, 3, 18).—Οἱ μὴ καλῶς βεβουλευμένοι, ἐὰν καὶ κατορθώσωσι (as single act) περί τινας τῶν πράξεων, μικρὸν διαλιπόντες εἰς τὰς αὐτὰς ἀπορίας κατέστησαν (*Isocr. Areop.* 11). Ἐπειδὰν αἱ ἐπιθυμίαι παύσωνται κατατείνουσαι καὶ χαλάσωσι, παντάπασι τὸ τοῦ Σοφοκλέους γίγνεται· δεσποτῶν πάνυ πολλῶν ἔστι καὶ μαινομένων ἀπηλλάχθαι (*Pl. Rep.* 1, 329, said of something that happens to the man at a certain particular point to which it is confined, *have come to cease*).—Ἤν τι σ' ἐγὼ φ α ν ῶ κακὸν πεποιηκώς, ὁμολογῶ ἀδικεῖν· ἂν μέντοι μηδὲν φαίνωμαι κακὸν πεποιηκὼς μηδὲ βουληθείς, οὐ καὶ σὺ αὖ ὁμολογήσεις μηδὲν ὑπ' ἐμοῦ ἀδικεῖσθαι; (*Xen. Cyr.* 5, 5, 13.) (In εἰμί, εἶμι, and other verbs which want the aorist, the distinction falls away.)

b) The subjunctive of the perfect serves to denote the action as past and completed, in opposition to the present, after ἐάν and relatives or temporal conjunctions with ἄν. In verbs whose perfect has the signification of the present, the perfect subjunctive is also used as present: Ὁ κύων, ὃν ἂν γνώριμον ἴδῃ, ἀσπάζεται, κἂν μηδὲν πώποτε ὑπ' αὐτοῦ ἀγαθὸν πεπόνθῃ (*Pl. Rep.* 2, 376). Ὅταν οἱ δεσπόται ἐσπουδάκωσι, κλαύμαθ' ἡμῖν (τοῖς δούλοις) γίγνεται (*Arist. Ran.* 813).—Τοσούτῳ πλείω οἱ Θηβαῖοι ποιήσονται θεραπείαν ὑμῶν (*will show you so much the more attention and regard*), ὅσωπερ ἂν μᾶλλον περὶ σφῶν αὐτῶν δεδίωσιν (*Isocr. Plat.* 36). Ἀπέχεσθε τῶν ἀλλοτρίων, ἵν' ἀσφαλέστερον τοὺς οἴκους τοὺς ὑμετέρους αὐτῶν κεκτῆσθε (*Isocr. Nic.* 49, from κέκτημαι, *possess*).

[§ 128.] Rem. Now and then the perf. subjunctive denotes as purpose the complete finishing of the act: Χρὴ ἀκοῦσαι, ἃ τόν τε δίκαιον καὶ τὸν ἄδικον τελευτήσαντα περιμένει, ἵνα τελέως ἑκάτερος αὐτῶν ἀπειλήφῃ τὰ ὑπὸ τοῦ λόγου ὀφειλόμενα (*Pl. Rep.* 10, 614, *may have received*).

CHAPTER III.

The Optative and its Tenses: the Optative with ἄν.

§ 129. The Optative (on the meaning of which see § 119) in independent propositions serves only to denote a wish that something may happen, or not happen, now or in the future: often with prefixed εἰ, εἰ γάρ *if but —!*), εἴθε (*oh that —!*) — (in Homer αἰ γάρ, αἴθε). Ἐπειδὴ πάντως ὁρῶ ὑμᾶς, Ἀθηναῖοι, ὡρμημένους στρατεύειν, ξυνενέγκοι ταῦτα (*Thuc.* 6, 20). Τούτων ἐγὼ εἴην (*Eur. Were I but one of these!*). Σὺ αὐτὸς ἅπαντα ἐπιστήσει, ἂν ἐγὼ βούλωμαι. Ἀλλὰ βουληθείης (*Pl. Euthyd.* 296. *Would that thou mightest will it!*). Μήτε Θηβαῖοί ποτε παύσαιντο, εἰ ἄρ' εὔξασθαι δεῖ, τοὺς ἑαυτοὺς ἀγαθόν τι ποιοῦντας ἀτιμάζοντες, μήθ' ὑμεῖς, τὰ ἐναντία τούτοις, τοὺς εὐεργέτας τιμῶντες (*Dem.* 20, 109). Εἴθ', ὦ λῷστε, σὺ τοιοῦτος ὢν φίλος ἡμῖν γένοιο (*Xen. Hell.* 4, 1, 38). Οὕτως ὄναισθε τῶν ὄντων ἀγαθῶν ἡμῖν, μὴ περιίδητέ με ἀπολλύμενον (*Dem.* 28, 20; *so may you enjoy —, as you do not suffer me to —*).

Rem. 1. Different from the simple wish is a question about possibility in the optative with ἄν: Ὦ Ζεῦ, πῶς ἂν τὸν αἱμυλώτατον ὀλέσσας τέλος θάνοιμι καὐτός; (*Soph. Aj.* 388. *How may I find a way to destroy that most crafty man, and then at last myself to die?* i.e. *Might I but —.*) Πῶς ἂν ὀλοίμην; (*Eur. Med.* 97.)[1]

Rem. 2. A wish relating to the past which can no longer be fulfilled, is expressed by εἴθε with the indicative: Εἴθε σοι τότε συνεγενόμην, ὅτε δεινότατος σαυτοῦ ἦσθα (*Xen. Mem.* 1, 2, 46). By ὤφελον (*debebam*), εἴθε (εἰ γὰρ) ὤφελον (*might I*): negatively, μὴ ὤφελον, with the infinitive, is expressed a wish that cannot be fulfilled, whether relating to the present or to the past. Εἰ γὰρ ὤφελον οἷοί τε εἶναι οἱ πολλοὶ τὰ μέγιστα κακὰ ἐξεργάζεσθαι, ἵνα οἷοί τε ἦσαν αὖ καὶ ἀγαθὰ τὰ μέγιστα (viz. ἐξεργάζεσθαι, *Pl. Crit.* 44). (Εἰ γὰρ ὤφελον. *O, if that could but be! I wish I might; Pl. Rep.* 4, 432, with infinitive understood.) Μήποτ' ὤφελον λιπεῖν τὴν Σκῦρον (*Soph. Phil.* 969; *oh that I had only never —*).

§ 130. *a*) The optative (by § 119 with Rem.) is used in dependent sentences which put something merely as a thought, and belong to a principal sentence in the past (aor., imperf., plusquamp., or historical present); in this manner it is put first in object-sentences with ὅτι,

[1] In the editions often erroneously without the note of interrogation.

ὡς after verbs denoting an expression, opinion or knowledge (*verba declarandi et sentiendi*), and in dependent questions both about what *is*, and what *shall be*. (After the present and the future, the indicative is used; in questions of that which shall be, the subjunctive or the indic. future by § 121.) Περικλῆς προηγόρευε τοῖς Ἀθηναίοις ἐν τῇ ἐκκλησίᾳ, ὅτι Ἀρχίδαμος μέν οἱ ξένος εἴη, οὐ μέντοι ἐπὶ κακῷ γε τῆς πόλεως γένοιτο (*Thuc.* 2, 13). Προαγορεύω, ὅτι — ἐστὶν — ἐγένετο. Κῦρος μεταπεμψάμενος τοὺς στρατηγοὺς τῶν Ἑλλήνων ἔλεγεν, ὅτι ἡ ὁδὸς ἔσοιτο πρὸς βασιλέα μέγαν εἰς Βαβυλῶνα (*Xen. An.* 1, 4, 11). Ἐπεὶ ταῦτα ἐκηρύχθη, ἔγνωσαν οἱ στρατιῶται, ὅτι κενὸς ὁ φόβος εἴη (*Xen. An.* 2, 3, 21). Ἐπεὶ ἀφίκοντο οἱ πρέσβεις οἴκαδε, τὸν Τιμαγόραν ἀπέκτειναν οἱ Ἀθηναῖοι, κατηγοροῦντος τοῦ Λέοντος, ὅτι μετὰ Πελοπίδου πάντα βουλεύοιτο (*Xen. Hell.* 7, 1, 38 = ἐβουλεύετο in the *oratio recta*). Οἱ Ἰνδοὶ ἔλεξαν, ὅτι πέμψειε σφᾶς ὁ Ἰνδῶν βασιλεὺς καὶ κελεύσειεν ἐρωτᾶν, ἐξ ὅτου ὁ πόλεμος εἴη Μήδοις τε καὶ Ἀσσυρίοις (*Xen. Cyr.* 2, 4, 7). Τότε ἐγνώσθη, ὅτι οἱ βάρβαροι τὸν ἄνθρωπον ὑποπέμψαιεν (*Xen. An.* 2, 4, 22). Τῇ ὑστεραίᾳ ἧκεν ἄγγελος λέγων, ὅτι Συέννεσις λελοιπὼς εἴη τὰ ἄκρα (*Xen. An.* 1, 2, 21). Τισσαφέρνης διαβάλλει τὸν Κῦρον πρὸς τὸν ἀδελφόν, ὡς ἐπιβουλεύοι αὐτῷ (*Xen. An.* 1, 1, 3).—Ἠρώτων Πολυκλέα, εἰ ἀναπλεύσειεν (*he had put to sea*) ἔχων ἀργύριον (*Dem.* 50, 55). Ἔδοξεν αὐτοῖς πειρᾶσαι, εἰ δύναιντο ἐπιφλέξαι τὴν πόλιν (*Thuc.* 2, 77). Οἱ Ἐπιδάμνιοι πέμψαντες ἐς Δελφοὺς τὸν θεὸν ἐπήροντο, εἰ παραδοῖεν Κορινθίοις τὴν πόλιν (*Thuc.* 1, 25; *whether they should deliver*). Ἀλκιβιάδης ἀπορῶν, ὅ,τι χρήσαιτο τοῖς παροῦσι κακοῖς, τελευτῶν ἐπὶ Λακεδαιμονίους ἠναγκάσθη καταφυγεῖν (*Isocr. de Big.* 9).

Rem. As the perfect denotes the past in reference to the present (as a still existing result), a dependent sentence after the perf. does not take the optative: Ὡς ἠθροίσθη Κύρῳ τὸ Ἑλληνικόν, ὅτε ἐπὶ Ἀρταξέρξην ἐστρατεύετο, καὶ ὅσα ἐν τῇ ἀνόδῳ ἐπράχθη, καὶ ὡς ἡ μάχη ἐγένετο, ἐν τῷ ἔμπροσθεν λόγῳ δεδήλωται (*Xen. An.* 2, 1, 1). The historical present, in reference to the dependent sentence, may be treated as present or as a præteritum. An infinitive with a participle or a præteritum itself acquires the force of a præteritum.

b) Often, however, the speaker, instead of denoting the relation of the dependent sentence, puts this in a livelier way immediately in the mood and tense which it would have in the *oratio recta*; consequently in the indicative (in questions of what *shall be*, *is to be*, in the subjunctive or future indicative): εἶπον, ὅτι ἐλεύθερος εἴην and ὅτι ἐλεύθερός εἰμι. Where in the *oratio recta* the present indicative would stand, sometimes the imperfect is put (of that which coincides in time with the principal sentence), so that the mood, but not the tense, is retained from the *oratio recta*: ᾔδειν, ὅτι ἐψεύδου. Ἔλεγον οἱ ἐπιτή-

[§ 130.] δειοί μου, ὡς ἐλπίζουσι τὴν πόλιν ἕξειν μοι χάριν ὑπὲρ τῶν εἰρημένων (*Isocr. Phil.* 23). Πολλάκις ἐθαύμασα, τίσι ποτὲ λόγοις Ἀθηναίους ἔπεισαν οἱ γραψάμενοι Σωκράτην, ὡς ἄξιος εἴη θανάτου (*Xen. Mem.* 1, 1, 1). Ἔγνω Ἀρχίδαμος, ὅτι οἱ Ἀθηναῖοι οὐδὲν ἐνδώσουσιν (*Thuc.* 2, 12). Ἤιδει Ἄφοβος σαφῶς, ὅτι ἐξελεγχθήσεται (*Dem.* 29, 9). Ἧκεν ἀγγέλλων τις πρὸς τοὺς πρυτάνεις, ὡς Ἐλάτεια κατείληπται (*Dem.* 18, 169). Ἀνδροτίων ἐτόλμα λέγειν, ὡς ὑπὲρ ὑμῶν καὶ δι' ὑμᾶς ἐχθροὺς ἐφ' ἑαυτὸν εἵλκυσε καὶ νῦν ἐν τοῖς ἐσχάτοις ἐστὶ κινδύνοις (*Dem.* 22, 59). Ἠτιάσατό με Ἀνδροτίων, ἃ καὶ λέγειν ὀκνήσειέ τις, τὸν πατέρα ὡς ἀπέκτονα ἐγὼ τὸν ἐμαυτοῦ (*Dem.* 22, 2). Πολὺν χρόνον ἠπόρουν, τί ποτε λέγει ὁ θεός (*Pl. Apol.* 21). Περιουσίαν χρημάτων οἱ παλαιοὶ οὐκ εἶχον οὐδὲ γῆν ἐφύτευον, ἄδηλον ὄν, ὁπότε τις ἐπελθὼν ἄλλος ἀφαιρήσεται (*Thuc.* 1, 2; *since they could not tell when* . . .). Σιμμίου λέγοντος πάνυ ἐθαύμαζον, εἴ τι ἕξει τις χρήσασθαι τῷ λόγῳ αὐτοῦ (*Pl. Phæd.* 95). Ἠρόμην Ἄφοβον, εἴ τινες παρῆσαν, ὅτε παρελάμβανε τὴν προῖκα (*Dem.* 30, 19, = Ἆρα παρῆσάν τινες — ;). Πελοπίδας εἶχε λέγειν, ὅτι μόνοι τῶν Ἑλλήνων βασιλεῖ συνεμάχοντο ἐν Πλαταιαῖς (*Xen. Hell.* 7, 1, 34). —Ἔγραφον ἂν διαῤῥήδην ἥλικα ὑμᾶς εὖ ποιήσω, εἰ εὖ ᾔδειν καὶ τὴν συμμαχίαν μοι γενησομένην (*Dem.* 19, 40) [1]. — Οἱ Πλαταιῆς ἐβουλεύοντο, εἴτε κατακαύσωσιν [in *or. rect.* κατακαύσωμεν; *subj. dubitat.*] τοὺς Θηβαίους, ὥσπερ ἔχουσιν, ἐμπρήσαντες τὸ οἴκημα, εἴτε τι ἄλλο χρήσωνται (*Thuc.* 2, 4). — Κατανοῶν ὁ Κῦρος, ὡς εὖ μὲν αὐτῷ εἶχον τὰ σώματα οἱ στρατιῶται πρὸς τὸ δύνασθαι πόνους φέρειν, εὖ δὲ τὰς ψυχὰς πρὸς τὸ καταφρονεῖν τῶν πολεμίων, ἐπεθύμει τι ἤδη πρὸς τοὺς πολεμίους πράττειν (*Xen. Cyr.* 3, 3, 9, = εὖ ἔχουσιν).

Rem. 1. Now and then the indicative and optative alternate, and are coupled together: Προκλῆς καὶ Γλοῦς ἔλεγον, ὅτι Κῦρος μὲν τέθνηκεν, Ἀριαῖος δὲ πεφευγὼς ἐν τῷ σταθμῷ εἴη μετὰ τῶν ἄλλων βαρβάρων (*Xen. An.* 2, 1, 3). Περὶ τῶν σκευῶν (*concerning the tackling*) ἠρώτων Πολυκλῆ, πότερον παραλήψεται παρ' ἐμοῦ ἢ ἴδια σκεύη ἔχων ἥκοι ἐπὶ τὴν ναῦν (*Dem.* 50, 33). Ἔγνω Φρύνιχος, ὅτι ἔσοιτο περὶ τῆς τοῦ Ἀλκιβιάδου καθόδου λόγος καὶ ὅτι Ἀθηναῖοι ἐνδέξονται αὐτήν (*Thuc.* 8, 50) [2].

Rem. 2. In this use of the indicative, the special notation of the *præsens*, *præteritum*, or *futurum in præterito* consequently falls away, except where the imperfect is put for the present of the *oratio recta*. The beginner must especially notice how the aor. is retained from the *oratio recta* where we expect the plusquamperf.: Ἔγνων, ὅτι Πρωταγόρας οὐκ ἤρεσεν αὐτὸς αὑτῷ ταῖς ἀποκρίσεσι ταῖς ἔμπροσθεν (*Pl. Prot.* 335). Ἐπήρου με, εἴ τί μοι ὁ διδάσκαλος ὑγιείας πέρι ἔλεξεν καὶ ῥώμης (*Xen. Cyr.* 1, 6, 12).

---

[1] So always after a hypothetical imperfect or aorist (with ἄν, or in the sentence with εἰ).

[2] Τότε δῆλον ἐγένετο, οὗ ἕνεκα οἱ Θρᾷκες τὰς ἀλωπεκίδας ἐπὶ ταῖς κεφαλαῖς φοροῦσιν (*Xen. An.* 7, 4, 4. Statement in the præteritum of a relation existing in the present time).

REM. 3. A hypothetical indicative with ἄν (or an imperf. without ἄν, put hypothetically) never passes into the optative when the verb of the principal sentence becomes a præteritum, because this would obscure the sense: Θεμιστοκλῆς ἀπεκρίνατο, ὅτι οὔτ' ἂν αὐτὸς Σερίφιος ὢν ὀνομαστὸς ἐγένετο οὔτ' ἐκεῖνος, 'Αθηναῖος (viz. ὤν. *Pl. Rep.* 1, 330). Διονύσιος ἔλεγεν, ὅτι δυστυχεστάτην ἐκείνην εἴημεν στρατείαν ἐστρατευμένοι, κρεῖττον δ' ἦν (*would have been*) αὐτῷ τότε (viz. ἐν τῷ πολέμῳ) ἀποθανεῖν ἢ οἴκαδ' ἐλθόντι τοιαύτῃ τύχῃ χρῆσθαι (*Lys.* 10, 25). [§ 130.]

REM. 4. To an object-sentence with ὅτι or ὡς in the optative, or in the indicative instead of the optative, a continuation may be added in the optative by οὖν, or ὥστε (*so that* —, with indic. in *oratio recta*; see *Infinitive*, § 166): 'Αποκρίνεται Ποσείδιππος ὁ κυβερνήτης, ὅτι τριήραρχός τε ἐγὼ τῆς νεὼς εἴην καὶ τὸν μισθὸν παρ' ἐμοῦ λαμβάνοι· πλεύσοιτο οὖν, οἷ ἐγὼ κελεύω, εἰς Θάσον (*Dem.* 50, 50). 'Αφικνοῦνταί τινες ἀπαγγέλλοντες, ὅτι ὁ πατήρ μου ἀφεῖται (*was set at liberty*) καὶ Σατύρῳ οὕτως μεταμέλει τῶν πεπραγμένων, ὥστε πίστεις τὰς μεγίστας δεδωκὼς εἴη (*Isocr. Trap.* 11). A continuation of the reported speech or opinion, with γάρ, also stands after an optative in the optative, after an indicative either in the optative or in the indicative: Ἤκουον ἔγωγε, ὦ Σώκρατες, ἑκάστοτε Γοργίου πολλάκις, ὡς ἡ τοῦ πείθειν (τέχνη) πολὺ διαφέροι πασῶν τεχνῶν· πάντα γὰρ ὑφ' αὑτῇ δοῦλα δι' ἑκόντων (*with people's consent*) ἀλλ' οὐ διὰ βίας ποιοῖτο (*Pl. Phil.* 58). Ἤιδειν, ὅτι Πολυκλῆς παραλαβὼν τὴν ναῦν κακῶς ἤμελλε τριηραρχήσειν· οὔτε γὰρ τοῖς ἐπιβάταις οὔτε τῇ ὑπηρεσίᾳ χρήσοιτο· οὐδεὶς γὰρ αὐτῷ παραμενεῖ (*Dem.* 50, 44).

a) The optative stands in sentences of intention (*final* sentences) with ἵνα, ὡς, ὅπως (poet. ὄφρα), and in object-sentences with ὅπως and μή after § 131.
a principal verb of past time (in aorist, imperf., plusquamperf., or historical present). (After a present or future, the subjunctive is put, or in certain cases the indic. fut., § 122, 123.) Μένων ὁ Θετταλὸς δῆλος ἦν ἐπιθυμῶν μὲν πλουτεῖν ἰσχυρῶς, ἐπιθυμῶν δ' ἄρχειν, ὅπως πλείω λαμβάνοι, ἐπιθυμῶν δὲ τιμᾶσθαι, ἵνα πλείω κερδαίνοι· φίλος τ' ἐβούλετο εἶναι τοῖς μέγιστα δυναμένοις, ἵνα ἀδικῶν μὴ διδοίη δίκην (*Xen. An.* 2, 6, 21). Κῦρος φίλων ᾤετο δεῖσθαι, ὡς συνεργοὺς ἔχοι (*Xen. An.* 1, 9, 21).—Ἐπεμελεῖτο Κῦρος, ὅπως μήποτε ἀνίδρωτοι οἱ στρατιῶται ἐπὶ τὸ ἄριστον καὶ τὸ δεῖπνον εἰσίοιεν (*Xen. Cyr.* 2, 1, 29). Κλέαρχος ἀπεκρίνατο Κύρῳ, ὅτι αὐτῷ μέλοι, ὅπως καλῶς ἔχοι (*Xen. An.* 1, 8, 13). Ἔδεισαν οἱ Ἕλληνες, μὴ οἱ Πέρσαι προσαγάγοιεν πρὸς τὸ κέρας (*Xen. An.* 1, 10, 9). Φίλιππος ἐν φόβῳ καὶ πολλῇ ἀγωνίᾳ ἦν, μὴ ἐκφύγοι τὰ πράγματα αὐτόν (*Dem.* 18, 33). Ἔδεισαν οἱ Κερασούντιοι, μὴ λύσσα τις ὥσπερ κυσὶν ἡμῖν ἐμπεπτώκοι (*Xen. An.* 5, 7, 26. Δέδοικα, μὴ— ἐμπέπτωκε, § 124). Εἰ μὴ ᾔδησθα σαφῶς τό τε ὅσιον καὶ τὸ ἀνόσιον, τοὺς θεοὺς ἂν ἔδεισας παρακινδυνεύειν, μὴ οὐκ ὀρθῶς ποιήσοις ὑπὲρ ἀνδρὸς θητὸς ἄνδρα πρεσβύτην πατέρα διωκάθων φόνου (*Pl. Euthyphr.* 15). (After a wish in the optative: Θυμὸν γένοιτο χειρὶ πληρῶσαί ποτε, ἵν' αἱ Μυκῆναι γνοῖεν, ὅτι χἠ Σκῦρος ἀνδρῶν ἀλκίμων μήτηρ ἔφυ, *Soph. Phil.* 324.)

REM. Ὅπως with the optative in a sentence of intention or an object-sentence rarely retains the ἄν (oftenest so in Herodot.): Προεθυμέετο Λοξίας ὅκως ἂν κατὰ

[§ 131.]

τοὺς παῖδας τοῦ Κροίσου γένοιτο τὸ Σαρδίων πάθος (*Hdt.* 1, 91). Οἱ Συρακούσιοι τὰς πρῴρας κατεβύρσωσαν, ὅπως ἂν ἀπολισθάνοι ἡ χεὶρ ἐπιβαλλομένη (*Thuc.* 7, 65).

b) Often, however, after a præteritum, the sentence of intention or an object-sentence with ὅπως or *μή*, is put in the subjunctive (indic. fut.) as after a present, the sentence being so put as not to mark that it forms part of a representation belonging to the past (cf. § 130, b): Ἐπίτηδές σε οὐκ ἤγειρον, ἵνα ὡς ἥδιστα διάγῃς (*Pl. Crit.* 43). Ἀριστεύς, ἀποτειχισθείσης Ποτιδαίας, ξυνεβούλευε πλὴν πεντακοσίων τοῖς ἄλλοις (*with the rest of the soldiers*) ἐκπλεῦσαι, ὅπως ἐπὶ πλέον ὁ σῖτος ἀντίσχῃ (*Thuc.* 1, 65). Ἀβροκόμας τὰ πλοῖα κατέκαυσεν, ἵνα μὴ Κῦρος διαβῇ (*Xen. An.* 1, 4, 18).—Περδίκκας ἔπρασσεν, ὅπως πόλεμος γένηται Ἀθηναίοις πρὸς Πελοποννησίους (*Thuc.* 1, 57). Αἰσχίνης τὸ καθ' αὐτόν, ὅπως ἐπὶ τοῖς ἐχθροῖς ἡ πόλις ἔσται, παρεσκεύασεν (*Dem.* 19, 250). Οἱ Ἀθηναῖοι τοὺς ξυμμάχους ἐδεδίεσαν σφῶν, μὴ ἀποστῶσιν (*Thuc.* 5, 14). Κῦρος δῆλος ἦν πᾶσιν ὅτι ὑπερεφοβεῖτο, μή οἱ ὁ πάππος ἀποθάνῃ (*Xen. Cyr.* 1, 4, 2). Εἰ μὴ ξυνῄδειν Σωκράτει τε καὶ Ἀγάθωνι δεινοῖς οὖσι περὶ τὰ ἐρωτικά, πάνυ ἂν ἐφοβούμην, μὴ ἀπορήσωσι λόγων διὰ τὸ πολλὰ ἤδη εἰρῆσθαι (*Pl. Conv.* 193) [1].

Rem. 1. Occasionally the optative and subjunctive alternate and are coupled together: Τιμόθεος δανείζεται (*hist. præs.*) χιλίας δραχμὰς παρ' Ἀντιφάνους, ἵνα διαδιδοίη τοῖς Βοιωτίοις τριηράρχοις καὶ παραμένωσιν ἕως ἂν αὐτῷ ἡ κρίσις γένηται (*Dem.* 49, 14). Παρανίσχον (*likewise lifted up*) καὶ οἱ ἐκ τῆς πόλεως Πλαταιῆς ἀπὸ τοῦ τείχους φρυκτοὺς πολλοὺς πρότερον παρεσκευασμένους (plusquamperf.) ἐπ' αὐτὸ τοῦτο, ὅπως ἀσαφῆ τὰ σημεῖα τῆς φρυκτωρίας τοῖς πολεμίοις ᾖ καὶ μὴ βοηθοῖεν (*Thuc.* 3, 22).

Rem. 2. Some writers, as Thucyd., use the subjunctive (indic. fut.) oftener than others.

Rem. 3. In stating why something that has *not* happened, ought to have taken place, or was to be wished, ἵνα (ὡς, ὅπως) with the indic. imperfect or aorist is put after a præteritum: Εἰ γὰρ ὤφελον οἷοί τε εἶναί οἱ πολλοὶ τὰ μέγιστα κακὰ ἐξεργάζεσθαι, ἵνα οἷοί τ' ἦσαν αὖ καὶ τὰ ἀγαθὰ τὰ μέγιστα (ἐξεργάζεσθαι, *Pl. Crit.* 44). Καὶ μὴν ἄξιόν γ' ἦν ἀκοῦσαι. Τί δέ; ἦν δ' ἐγώ. (*How so!*) Ἵν' ἤκουσας (= *that you might have heard* [2]) ἀνδρῶν διαλεγομένων, οἳ νῦν σοφώτατοί εἰσι τῶν περὶ τοὺς τοιούτους λόγους (*Pl. Euthyd.* 304; *of those who have to do with —; who occupy themselves with —*).

Rem. 4 (to § 130 and 131). When to an object-sentence or sentence of intention dependent on a præteritum, another such sentence is attached and made dependent on it, the latter, as a general rule, also takes the optative, but may also take the indicative or subjunctive: Κῦρος προσκαλῶν τοὺς φίλους ἐσπουδαιολογεῖτο, ὡς δηλοίη, οὓς τιμᾷ (*Xen. An.* 1, 9, 28). Τὸν σοφιστὴν εἴπομεν, ὅτι ἀποροῖμεν, εἰς ὁπότερον τοῖν δυοῖν εἰδοῖν θήσομεν (*Pl. Soph.* 264; *we should put*); but when the first passes into the indic. or subjunctive, the latter is also treated as after a present: Οὐ

---

[1] So for the most part after a hypothetical imperfect or aorist.

[2] [Properly (*where =*) *in which case you heard* (for conditional, *would have heard*).]

[PART II.

τούτου ἕνεκα ἠρχόμεθα διαλεγόμενοι, ἵνα εὕρωμεν, τί ποτ' οὐκ ἔστ' ἐπιστήμη, ἀλλὰ τί ἔστιν (*Pl. Theæt.* 186):

a) In dependent sentences with relatives or conjunctions which are accessory to an object-sentence, or sentence of intention, or infinitive clause, or single infinitive, and are put as forming part of the object (the thing said to be spoken, thought, perceived, &c.), or of the thing intended, and which in the *oratio recta* would stand in the indicative of the present, future, or perfect, or in the subjunctive (with ἄν after the relative or conjunction), the optative is used (without ἄν), when the principal verb on which the ὅτι, ὅπως, &c., depends is a preteritum, and so the following verb would regularly be in the optative by § 130 and § 131[1]: Ἤιδει Κῦρος, ὅτι, εἴ τι μάχης δεήσοι, ἐκ τῶν φίλων αὐτῷ καὶ παραστάτας καὶ ἐπιστάτας ληπτέον εἴη (*Xen. Cyr.* 8, 1, 10 = Εἴ τι μ. δεήσει, λήψομαι). Θηραμένης εἶπεν, ὅτι οὐδὲν αὐτῷ μέλοι τοῦ ὑμετέρου θορύβου, ἐπειδὴ πολλοὺς μὲν Ἀθηναίων εἰδείη τοὺς τὰ ὅμοια πράττοντας αὐτῷ, δοκοῦντα δὲ Λυσάνδρῳ καὶ Λακεδαιμονίοις λέγοι (*Lys.* 12, 74 = Οὐδέν μοι μέλει —, ἐπειδὴ — οἶδα — δοκοῦντα δὲ — λέγω). Ἀναξίβιος ἀπεκρίνατο, ὅτι βουλεύσοιτο περὶ τῶν στρατιωτῶν, ὅ,τι δύναιτο ἀγαθόν (*Xen. An.* 7, 1, 35 = βουλεύσομαι, ὅ,τι ἂν δύνωμαι ἀγαθόν).

---

[1] [These rules have been defended by Madvig in a separate publication, where he lays them down thus: *a*) *In the* oratio obliqua, *clauses dependent on an historical tense pass into the optative; but not, if in the* oratio recta *they would have the* imperfect *or* aorist *of the indicative; for then these forms of the verb are retained: b*) *except in clauses with* ὅτι (= because; therein that —, in that [he &c.]), *in which even these* tenses *pass into the optative.*

a) Thus whilst the sentences δώσω ἃ δυνήσομαι or ἃ ἂν εὕρω, δίδωμ' ἃ ἔχω, πέμψω ὅταν δυνηθῶ become regularly ἔλεγεν ὅτι δώσοι (ἔφη δώσειν) ἃ δυνήσοιτο, ἃ εὕροι· ἔφη διδόναι ἃ ἔχοι, πέμψειν ὅτε δυνηθείη, but may *also*, from the freedom of Greek construction, be expressed thus: ἔλεγεν ὅτι δώσει ἃ δυνήσεται, ἃ ἂν εὕρῃ· ἔφη πέμψειν, ὅταν δυνηθῇ· on the other hand the sentence ἔδωκα ἃ εἶχον can appear in *no other form* than ἔλεγεν, ὅτι δοίη (ἔδωκεν) ἃ εἶχεν: and so, ὅτε ἔπεμψα τὸν ἄγγελον, οὔπω ταῦτα ᾔδειν, becomes ἔλεγεν, ὅτι ταῦτα οὔπω ᾔδη (εἰδείη), ὅτ' ἔπεμψε τὸν ἄγγελον: or, ἔφη, ὅτ' ἔπεμψε τὸν ἄγγελον, οὔπω ταῦτα εἰδέναι.

b) He has convinced himself, he says, of the *limitation* expressed in *b*, since the publication of his Syntax, from a comparison of the two following passages, to which at present he cannot add a third. *Xen. Hell.* vii. 1, 34: εἶχε γὰρ λέγειν (Πελοπίδας) ὡς Λακεδαιμόνιοι διὰ τοῦτο πολεμήσειαν αὐτοῖς (τοῖς Θηβαίοις), ὅτι οὐκ ἐθελήσαιεν μετ' Ἀγησιλάου ἐλθεῖν ἐπ' αὐτὸν (τὸν βασιλέα) οὐδὲ θῦσαι ἐάσειεν αὐτὸν ἐν Αὐλίδι τῇ Ἀρτέμιδι. The other passage is *Herod.* ii. 121, 5: ἀπηγήσασθαι αὐτόν (φασιν), ὡς ἀνοσιώτατον μὲν εἴη εἰργασμένος, ὅτι [in our edd. ὅτε, which would be *against* the rule, but Madvig '*has no hesitation*' in reading ὅτι] τοῦ ἀδελφεοῦ . . . ἀποτάμοι (= *in* [*having cut*] *cutting off* —) τὴν κεφαλήν, σοφώτατον δέ, ὅτι τοὺς φυλάκους καταμεθύσας καταλύσειε τοῦ ἀδελφεοῦ κρεμάμενον τὸν νέκυν.]

[§ 132.] Κλέανδρος εἶπεν, ὅτι Δέξιππον οὐκ ἐπαινοίη, εἰ ταῦτα πεποιηκὼς εἴη (*Xen. An.* 6, 4, 25. Οὐκ ἐπαινῶ, εἰ — πεποίηκεν). Ἐσκόπει Μενεκλῆς, ὅπως μὴ ἔσοιτο ἄπαις ἀλλ' ἔσοιτο αὐτῷ ὅςτις ζῶντά τε γηροτροφήσοι καὶ τελευτήσαντα θάψοι (*Isæ.* 2, 10. Σκοπῶ, ὅπως ἔσται ὅςτις — γηροτροφήσει — θάψει). Οἱ Ἀθηναῖοι ἐςβάντες ἐς τὴν ὁδὸν τὴν Ἑλωρινὴν ἐπορεύοντο, ὅπως, ἐπειδὴ γένοιντο παρὰ τῷ ποταμῷ τῷ Κακυπάρει, παρὰ τὸν ποταμὸν ἴοιεν ἄνω διὰ μεσογείας (*Thuc.* 7, 80 = ὅπως, ἐπειδὰν — γενώμεθα, ἴωμεν). Οἱ Πλαταιῆς ἀσαφῆ τὰ σημεῖα τοῖς πολεμίοις ποιεῖν ἐμηχανῶντο, ὅπως μὴ βοηθοῖεν, πρὶν σφῶν οἱ ἄνδρες οἱ ἐξιόντες διαφύγοιεν (*Thuc.* 3, 22 = μηχανώμεθα, ὅπως μὴ — βοηθῶσι, πρὶν ἂν — διαφύγωσιν). Γεωμετρίαν Σωκράτης μέχρι τούτου ἔφη δεῖν μανθάνειν, ἕως ἱκανός τις γένοιτο, εἴποτε δεήσειε, γῆν μέτρῳ ὀρθῶς ἢ παραλαβεῖν ἢ παραδοῦναι ἢ διανεῖμαι (*Xen. Mem.* 4, 7, 2; = δεῖ, ἕως ἂν — γένηται, εἴποτε δεήσει. —). Τισσαφέρνης ὤμοσεν Ἀγησιλάῳ, εἰ σπείσαιτο, ἕως ἔλθοιεν, οὓς πέμψειε πρὸς βασιλέα ἀγγέλους, διαπράξεσθαι αὐτῷ, ἀφεθῆναι αὐτονόμους τὰς ἐν Ἀσίᾳ πόλεις Ἑλληνίδας (*Xen. Ages.* 1, 10. Ἐὰν σπείσῃ, ἕως ἂν ἔλθωσιν, οὓς πέμψω —, διαπράξομαι).

Rem. 1. If, on the other hand, the accessory sentence in the *oratio recta* would stand in the aor. or imperf. indic., this is retained in the *oratio obliqua*, because the optative would not express the proper relation of time. We even find, not unfrequently, the aorist indicative, where the *oratio recta* would have the perfect indicative (and where, consequently, the optative might stand in the *oratio obliqua*); cf. § 112, R. 1. Οἱ Λακεδαιμόνιοι ἔλεγον, μὴ ἐπηγγέλθαι πω ἐς Λακεδαίμονα τὰς σπονδάς, ὅτε ἐσέπεμψαν τοὺς ὁπλίτας ἐς Λέπρεον (*Thuc.* 5, 49). Ἠρόμην, εἴ τινες εἶεν μάρτυρες, ὧν ἐναντίον ἀπέδοσαν (*Dem.* 30, 19. Ἆρά τινες μάρτυρές εἰσιν, — ἀπέδοτε;). Ἤκουσα, ὅτι Περικλῆς πολλὰς ἐπίσταιτο ἐπῳδάς, ἃς ἐπᾴδων τῇ πόλει ἐποίει αὐτὴν φιλεῖν αὐτόν (*Xen. Mem.* 4, 7, 2). Λέγουσί τινες Θεμιστοκλέα ἑκούσιον φαρμάκῳ ἀποθανεῖν, ἀδύνατον νομίσαντα εἶναι ἐπιτελέσαι βασιλεῖ ἃ ὑπέσχετο (*Thuc.* 1, 138. Ἀδύνατόν ἐστιν ἐπ. ἃ ὑπέσχημαι).

Rem. 2. Sometimes the optative stands even in a sentence dependent on an *object-sentence* or sentence *of intention* (one with ὅτι, ὅπως, &c.), which has itself not taken the optative: Ἐδήλωσε Κῦρος, ὅτι ἕτοιμός ἐστι μάχεσθαι, εἴ τις ἐξέρχοιτο (*Xen. Cyr.* 4, 1, 1). Ἐφοβεῖτο Θεμιστοκλῆς, μὴ οἱ Λακεδαιμόνιοι σφᾶς, ὁπότε σαφῶς ἀκούσειαν τὰ περὶ τὸ τεῖχος, οὐκέτι ἀφῶσιν (*Thuc.* 1, 91). Usually, however, in this case the indicative or subjunctive is used.

b) Often in such sentences the same form is retained as they would have in *oratio recta* (cf. § 130, b, and § 131, b). But instead of the indic. present sometimes the imperfect is put (in the same tense with the governing verb; cf. § 130, b): Προὔλεγον, ὦ Σώκρατες, ὅτι πάντα μᾶλλον ποιήσοις ἢ ἀποκρινοῖο, εἴ τίς τί σε ἐρωτᾷ (*Pl. Rep.* 1, 337). Ἔλεγον οἱ ἄγγελοι, ὅτι ἥκοιεν ἡγεμόνας ἔχοντες, οἳ αὐτούς, ἐὰν αἱ σπονδαὶ γένωνται, ἄξουσιν, ἔνθεν ἕξουσι τὰ ἐπιτήδεια (*Xen. An.* 2, 3, 6. Regularly, οἳ, εἰ — γένοιντο, ἄξοιεν, ἔνθεν ἕξοιεν —). Κῦρος ἐπηρώτα τὸν Τιγράνην, ποῖα εἴη τῶν ὀρέων, ὁπόθεν οἱ Χαλδαῖοι καταθέοντες λῄζονται (*Xen. Cyr.* 3, 2, 1). Ποτιδαιᾶται ἦλθον ἐς Λακεδαίμονα μετὰ Κορινθίων, ὅπως ἑτοιμάσαιντο τιμωρίαν (= βοήθειαν), ἣν δέῃ (*Thuc.* 1, 58 = εἰ δεήσοι). Οἱ στρατιῶται κατασχίσειν τὰς πύλας ἔφασαν, εἰ μὴ ἑκόντες οἱ ἔνδον ἀνοίξουσιν (*Xen. An.* 7, 1, 16). Οἱ Πλαταιῆς τοῖς Θηβαίοις ἔλεγον τὰ ἔξω τῆς πόλεως μὴ ἀδικεῖν· εἰ δὲ μή, καὶ αὐτοὶ ἔφασαν αὐτῶν τοὺς ἄνδρας ἀποκτενεῖν, οὓς ἔχουσι ζῶντας (*Thuc.* 2, 5). Παρήγγειλαν οἱ στρατηγοί, ἐπειδὴ δειπνήσειαν, συσκευασαμένους πάντας ἀναπαύεσθαι καὶ ἕπεσθαι, ἡνίκ' ἄν τις παραγγείλῃ (*Xen. An.* 3, 5, 18; observe the alteration of the two forms). Οἱ στρατιῶται οὐκ ἔφασαν ἰέναι, ἐὰν μή τις χρήματα διδῷ. Ὁ δὲ Κῦρος ὑπέσχετο ἀνδρὶ ἑκάστῳ δώσειν πέντε ἀργυρίου μνᾶς, ἐπὰν εἰς Βαβυλῶνα ἥκωσιν (*Xen. An.* 1, 4, 12 and 13). Κλέαρχος ἔφη χρῆναι, οἳ ἂν ἐξελεγχθῶσι διαβάλλοντες (*those who should be convicted of circulating calumnious reports*), ὡς προδότας ὄντας τιμωρηθῆναι (*Xen. An.* 2, 5, 27). Φίλιππος, εἰ τοῦτο τῶν παρ' ἑαυτοῦ πεμπομένων ἱερομνημόνων εἰσηγοῖτό τις, ὑπόψεσθαι τὸ πρᾶγμα ἐνόμιζε καὶ τοὺς Θηβαίους καὶ τοὺς Θετταλούς, ἣν δ' Ἀθηναῖος ᾖ ὁ τοῦτο ποιῶν, εὐπόρως λήσειν (*Dem.* 18, 148). — Κῦρος ὑπέσχετο τοῖς Μιλησίοις φυγάσιν, εἰ καλῶς καταπράξειεν, ἐφ' ἃ ἐστρατεύετο, μὴ πρόσθεν παύσεσθαι, πρὶν αὐτοὺς καταγάγοι οἴκαδε (*Xen. An.* 1, 2, 2 = ἢν καταπράξω, ἐφ' ἃ στρατεύομαι, οὐ — παύσομαι, πρὶν ἂν καταγάγω). Μέγα τὸ δέος ἐγένετο, μὴ οἱ Πελοποννήσιοι, εἰ καὶ μὴ διενοοῦντο μένειν, πορθῶσιν ἅμα προσπίπτοντες τὰς πόλεις (*Thuc.* 3, 33).

Rem. It is a rare anomaly, when an accessory sentence passes into the optative, and yet ἄν with the relative or conjunction is retained: Οὐδεὶς ὅστις οὐχ ἡγεῖτο δίκην με λήψεσθαι παρὰ τῶν ἐπιτρόπων, ἐπειδὰν τάχιστα ἀνὴρ εἶναι δοκιμασθείην (*Dem.* 30, 6 = ἐπειδὰν δοκιμασθῶ or ἐπειδὴ δοκιμασθείην). (*Soph. Trach.* 687.)

c) The same rule and exception hold for accessory sentences dependent on a participle which has the force of an object-sentence (see *Participles*, § 177, b. 178): Ἡ αἰτία πρόδηλος ἦν ἐπ' ἐκείνους ἥξουσα, εἴ τι πάθοι Χαρίδημος (*Dem.* 23, 12 = πρόδηλον ἦν, ὅτι — ἥξοι).— Τοῦτο πρόδηλον ἦν ἐσόμενον, εἰ μὴ ὑμεῖς κωλύσετε (*Æsch.* 3, 90).

d) Likewise the optative stands in dependent sentences which are so immediately attached to a leading sentence whose verb is a præteritum, that they form part of the thought of the person mentioned in the leading sentence (of something then present, or future, or so *past* as to be still *present* in its results—the perfect), especially with εἰ, with ὅτι (*because, for that*[1]), with ἕως, μέχρι οὗ (*until* —

[[1] "This mode of expression is usually met with only with reference to what is

could), and with relatives: Οἱ μὲν εὔχοντο, Ξενίαν καὶ Πασίωνα ὡς δολίους ὄντας ληφθῆναι, οἱ δὲ ᾤκτειρον, εἰ ἁλώσοιντο (*Xen. An.* 1, 4, 7; *felt compassion at the thought* —). Οὐκ ἦν τοῦ πρὸς ὑμᾶς πολέμου πέρας οὐδ' ἀπαλλαγὴ Φιλίππῳ, εἰ μὴ Θηβαίους καὶ Θετταλοὺς ἐχθροὺς ποιήσειε τῇ πόλει (*Dem.* 18, 145; *Philip had*, saw *no means of ending* —). Οἱ Ἀθηναῖοι Περικλέα ἐκάκιζον, ὅτι, στρατηγὸς ὤν, οὐκ ἐπεξάγοι ἐπὶ τοὺς πολεμίους (*Thuc.* 2, 21). Δερκυλλίδας καὶ Τισσαφέρνης σπονδὰς ἀλλήλοις ἐποιήσαντο, ἕως ἀπαγγελθείη τὰ λεχθέντα ἐς Λακεδαίμονα καὶ ἐπὶ βασιλέα (*Xen. Hell.* 3, 2, 20). Ἄνδρα οὐδέν' ἔντοπον ἑώρων, ὅστις ἀρκέσειεν (*Soph. Phil.* 280; *from whom I could expect help*). Ἱπποκράτης, ὁπότε καιρὸς εἴη, ἔμελλε στρατεύειν ἐς τοὺς Βοιωτούς (*Thuc.* 1, 77; *intended, when it should be the fit time*). But sometimes here also, especially with εἰ and in relative sentences, that form (present, future, or perfect indicative) is retained, in which the person mentioned would himself express the thought: Ἐμακάρισα τὸν Εὔηνον, εἰ ὡς ἀληθῶς ἔχει ταύτην τὴν τέχνην (*Pl. Apol.* 20). Τῷ μηδὲν ἑαυτῷ συνειδότι δεινὸν εἰσῄει (*it seemed hard*), εἰ πονηρῶν ἔργων δόξει κοινωνεῖν τῷ σιωπῆσαι (*Dem.* 19, 33). — (For the indicative present sometimes the imperfect is found: Ἐμαυτὸν ἀπωλοφυράμην, ὅστις τοῦτο μὲν (*on the one hand*), ἐν ᾧ ἐδόκει ὁ δῆμος κακοῦσθαι, ἐγὼ ἀντὶ τούτου (*therefore*) κακὰ εἶχον, τοῦτο δέ, ἐπειδὴ ἐφαίνετο εὖ ὑπ' ἐμοῦ πεπονθώς, πάλιν αὖ καὶ διὰ τοῦτ' ἐγὼ ἀπολοίμην, *Andoc.* 2, 16.)

Rem. 1. On dependent sentences with a hypothetical imperfect or aorist indicative, see § 117 a. R. 2.

Rem. 2. If the leading sentence contains a wish in the optative, a sentence dependent on this also takes the optative: Ὄλοιο μήπω, πρὶν μάθοιμ', εἰ καὶ πάλιν γνώμην μετοίσεις (*Soph. Phil.* 961).[1]

---

present or *future*, as compared with the time of the principal action, except in two cases. (1) One of these is again (cf. note on p. 113) that of clauses introduced by ὅτι. And since here no change or ambiguity is possible, I assert, without hesitation, though I have not any example at hand, that as Thucyd. 2, 21 says Περικλέα ἐκάκιζον, ὅτι, οὐκ ἐπεξάγοι ἐπὶ τοὺς πολεμίους, so he might have said ὅτι οὐκ ἐξαγάγοι, in the sense of *because he* had *not* led *them out*."

"(2) Then an additional thought, referred to *the person spoken of*, may be attached, by means of a relative pronoun, to a single definite notion; and in this added thought, that which would have stood in the *aorist of the indicative*, if there were no intimation of its being the thought of *another*, may be expressed by the *aorist of the optative*, because here, in the case of a principal verb in the present, no ὃς ἄν with *aorist of the subjunctive* is conceivable, and therefore no confounding with an aorist of the optative, as representing an ὃς ἄν *c. aor. subj.*, can take place. The only instance I can at present produce is *Soph. Œd. Tyr.* 1246: μνήμην παλαιῶν σπερμάτων ἔχουσ', ὑφ' ὧν θάνοι μὲν αὐτός· τὴν δὲ τίκτουσαν λίποι τοῖς οἷσιν αὐτοῦ δύστεκνον παιδουργίαν." Madvig, p. 17.]

[1] Occasionally the optative is put, irregularly, in sentences dependent on an infinitive in general reflexions: Τοῦ αὐτὸν λέγειν, ἃ μὴ σαφῶς εἰδείη, φείδεσθαι δεῖ

The optative (present or aorist) stands after conjunctions of time (without ἄν), relative words (without ἄν), and εἰ (*if*, i. e. *as often as*), in connexion with a leading sentence whose verb is a præteritum, when the thing denoted is, not what took place in a certain individual case, or with a certain individual person or thing, but what recurred and was repeated so often as a case befell, or a person or thing of a certain kind occurred [opt. of *indefinite frequency*]. (Ὁπότε ἀφίκοιτο, *when he came*, if he did come, *whenever he came*; ὅτε ἀφίκετο, *when he came*, ὅταν ἀφίκηται, *when he comes*: Ὅσους εἶδον, *so many as I saw* on the whole; ὅσους ἴδοιμι, *so many as I saw from time to time, so often as I saw any*.) Κῦρος, παρελαύνων τὸν ἵππον εἰς τὸ πρόσθεν ἥσυχος, κατεθεᾶτο τὰς τάξεις· καὶ οὓς μὲν ἴδοι εὐτάκτως καὶ σιωπῇ ἰόντας, προσελαύνων αὐτοῖς, τίνες τε εἶεν, ἤρετο καί, ἐπεὶ πύθοιτο, ἐπῄνει· εἰ δέ τινας θορυβουμένους αἴσθοιτο, τὸ αἴτιον τούτου σκοπῶν κατασβεννύναι τὴν ταραχὴν ἐπειρᾶτο (*Xen. Cyr.* 5, 3, 55). Σόλων ἐν ἅπασιν, οἷς ἐτίθει, νόμοις περὶ τῆς πολιτείας μᾶλλον ἐσπούδαζεν ἢ περὶ τοῦ πράγματος αὐτοῦ, οὗ τιθείη τὸν νόμον (*Dem.* 22, 30; *about which*, whatever it was —). Οἱ ὄνοι, ἐπεί τις διώκοι, προδραμόντες ἂν εἱστήκεσαν· καὶ πάλιν, ἐπεὶ πλησιάζοι ὁ ἵππος, ταὐτὸν ἐποίουν (*Xen. An.* 1, 5, 2. Of ἄν, see § 117 b, R. 3; εἱστήκεσαν counts as an imperfect). Περιεμένομεν ἑκάστοτε, ἕως ἀνοιχθείη τὸ δεσμωτήριον (*Pl. Phæd.* 59). (Ὁπότε ἔλθοιεν, οὐ αὐλίζεσθαι δέοι, φύλακας καθίστασαν, with the relative sentence necessary to the completion of the notion likewise in the optative.)

(The Tenses of the Optative.) *a*) In object-sentences with ὅτι and ὡς, and in dependent interrogative sentences, which in their independent form would have the indicative, the tenses of the optative correspond entirely with the same tenses of the indicative (so that the aorist is a præteritum), yet so that the present at the same time comprises the imperfect, and the perfect the pluperfect. In connexion, therefore, with the same leading verb in the præteritum on which the optative sentence depends, the present acquires the sense of the *præsens* or *imperfectum in præterito*, the aorist and the imperfect that of the *præteritum in præterito* (but with the same distinction which appears in the *oratio recta* between the aorist and the perfect), and the future that of the *futurum in præterito*. See the examples in § 130, a. (But in a dependent question which in the *oratio recta* or after a present might have the subjunctive, the aorist has not the signification of a præteritum: Οἱ Ἐπιδάμνιοι τὸν ἐν Δελφοῖς θεὸν ἐπήροντο, εἰ παραδοῖεν Κορινθίοις τὴν πόλιν. *Thuc.* 1, 25 = παραδῶμεν or παραδώσομεν.) *Xen. An.* 7, 4, 10. *Mem.* 4, 2, 10 (σκοπῶν ὅ,τι ἀποκρίναιτο) and Herod. 5, 67, ἐχρηστηριάζετο εἰ ἐκβάλοι (where even Dobree, with *Werfer*) would read ἐκβάλλῃ.

(*Xen. Cyr.* 1. 6, 19; *what one does not himself know*). Εἰκῇ κράτιστον ζῆν, ὅπως δύναιτό τις (*Soph. Œd. R.* 979).

CHAP. III.]

[§ 134.] Rem. As in the indicative the aorist stands now and then where we should expect the perfect (§ 112, R. 1), so also in the optative: *Οἱ Πλαταιῆς κήρυκα ἐξέπεμψαν παρὰ τοὺς Θηβαίους, ὅτι τὰ πεποιημένα οὐχ ὁσίως δράσειαν* (*Thuc.* 2, 5; almost = *δεδράκατε*).

b) In the sentences treated of in § 133 (optative of the thing repeated [*indefinite frequency*]), the present optative corresponds with the imperfect indicative, and denotes the action in the dependent sentence to be contemporaneous with that in the leading sentence; the aorist with the aorist indicative after conjunctions of time (§ 114, c), and therefore denotes the action of the protasis as a single act recurring each time before the action of the apodosis; often, however, the difference is very slight: *Ὁπότε οἱ τότε βασιλεύοντες αὐτὸν μὲν Εὐαγόραν ὁ ρ ῷ ε ν, ἐξεπλήττοντο καὶ ἐφοβοῦντο περὶ τῆς ἀρχῆς, ὁπότε δὲ εἰς τοὺς τρόπους ἀ π ο β λ έ ψ α ι ε ν, σφόδρα ἐπίστευον* (*Isocr. Evag.* 21).

c) In all other sentences the present and perfect of the optative answer to the present or perfect of the indicative or subjunctive, the future optative to the future indicative (therefore never in sentences of intention after *ἵνα* or *ὡς*). The aorist answers to the aorist subjunctive, therefore loses the sense of a præteritum, and differs from the present only as giving prominence to the consideration of the action as transient and occupying a single point of time, usually with more express reference to the future. (Cf. § 128.) *Μένων ἐπεθύμει ἄρχειν, ὅπως πλείω λαμβάνοι* (*Xen. An.* 2, 6, 21; *to get more*, in general or for ever). *Ἔδεισαν οἱ Ἕλληνες, μὴ οἱ Πέρσαι προςαγάγοιεν πρὸς τὸ κέρας* (*Xen. An.* 1, 10, 9). *Ἤιδει Κῦρος, ὅτι, εἴ τι μάχης ποτὲ δεήσοι, ἐκ τῶν φίλων αὐτῷ καὶ παραστάτας καὶ ἐπιστάτας ληπτέον εἴη* (*Xen. Cyr.* 8, 1, 10). *Ἔδεισαν οἱ Κερασούντιοι, μὴ λύσσα τις ὥςπερ κυσὶν ἡμῖν ἐμπεπτώκοι* (*Xen. An.* 5, 7, 26). See further examples in § 131 and 132.

Rem. 1. As in certain sorts of sentences the distinction between future indic. and aor. subjunctive is but small (with *ὅπως* in an object-sentence, *εἰ δώσω* and *ἐὰν δῶ*), so in the same sorts of sentences the distinction is also but small in the optative between the future and the aorist. It should be remarked, however, that in object-sentences in the optative with *ὅπως*, the aor. is much more frequent than the future. (Both tenses in connexion: *Τὸν ἔμπροσθεν χρόνον ἔζων ὑπὸ πολλῆς ἐπιμελείας ὅπως ὡς ἐλάχιστα μὲν ὀ ψ ο ί μ η ν, ἐλάχιστα δ' ἀ κ ο υ σ ο ί μ η ν, ἐλάχιστα δ' ἐ ρ ο ί μ η ν*, *Xen. Œcon.* 7, 5.) Even more rare than in such sentences is the optat. future in sentences of intention with *ὅπως* or *μή*. (*Ἀγαμέμνων ἠγρίαινεν ἐντελλόμενος Χρύσῃ νῦν τε ἀπιέναι καὶ αὖθις μὴ ἐλθεῖν, μὴ αὐτῷ τὰ τοῦ θεοῦ στέμματα οὐκ ἐπαρκέσοι*, *Pl. Rep.* 3, 393.) In conditional sentences in the *oratio obliqua* after a præteritum, *εἰ* with the aorist rather denotes the action as a condition going before (*εἰ δοίην*, *si dedissem* = *ἐὰν δῶ*, *si dedero*), the future, on the contrary, denotes it merely as going on at the same time (*εἰ δώσοιμι*, *si darem* = *εἰ δώσω*, *si dabo*); sometimes, however, the future (occasionally even the present) is put where the aorist might stand: *Ἐνόμιζε Πασίων εἰ μὲν ἐν Ἀθήναις μένειν ἐ π ι χ ε ι ρ ο ί η ν* (*immediately, where I already was*), *ἐκδοθήσεσθαί μ' ὑπὸ τῆς πόλεως Σατύρῳ, εἰ δ' ἄλλοσέ ποι τ ρ α π ο ί μ η ν, οὐδὲν* μελήσειν αὐτῷ (τῷ Πασίωνι) τῶν ἐμῶν λόγων, εἰ δ' εἰσπλευσοίμην εἰς τὸν Πόντον, ἀποθανεῖσθαί με μετὰ τοῦ πατρὸς ὑπὸ Σατύρου (*Isocr. Trap.* 9). Ὁ ἡγεμὼν ἔφη εἶναι ἄκρον, ὃ εἰ μή τις (*one*) προκαταλήψοιτο, ἀδύνατον ἔσεσθαι παρελθεῖν (*Xen. An.* 4, 1, 25). In relative sentences ὃς δώσοι and ὃς δοίη differ, as ὃς δώσει and ὃς ἂν δῷ. Therefore, Ἔλεγεν ἄξειν αὐτούς, ἔνθα λήψοιντο τὰ ἐπιτήδεια, and εἰπόν τινες, ὅτι εἴη Παγκλέωνι ἀδελφός, ὅστις ἐξαιρήσοιτο αὐτὸν εἰς ἐλευθερίαν (*Lys.* 23, 9), because representing ἄξω, ἔνθα λήψεσθε, and ἔστιν ἀδελφός, ὅστις ἐξαιρήσεται. But ἔφη παραμενεῖν, ἕως ἔλθοιεν οὓς πέμψειεν = οὓς ἂν πέμψῃς (§ 132, a, last example).

[Rem. 2. "In fact the *future of the optative* is formed and used for the *sole purpose* (to which it is most strictly confined) of representing the *future indicative* in the *oratio obliqua* after a *præteritum*.—Hence it appears (1) in clauses with ὅτι, ὡς, and in *dependent questions*: (2) in *conjunctional* and *relative* accessory sentences of the *oratio obliqua* after a *præteritum*; and also in such accessory clauses as are immediately attached to a principal sentence (*in præterito*) of the *oratio recta*[1], whilst they themselves, as *orat. obliqua*, form a *member of the thought* attributed to the person spoken of: οἱ μὲν (κ.τ.λ.) . . . οἱ δὲ ᾤκτειρον, εἰ ἁλώσοιντο = *felt compassion for them at the thought* —).—(3) in sentences with ὅπως (= *how, that* — [not after ὅπως, as *final particle*, = *ut*, cf. (5)], inasmuch as here the *future of the indicative* may follow a present. Here, however, it does not occur *often* (usually the aorist): τούτους, ὅπως ὡς βέλτιστοι ἔσοιντο, αὐτὸς ἐσκόπει (*Xen.*).—(4) *Very seldom* with μή (without ὅπως) after *verba timendi*. I have only remarked *Pl. Euthyphr.* 15, D; and *Xen. Hellen.* vi. 4. 27.—(5) In *final* sentences after ὅπως (ὅπως μή), the fut. of the optative must be looked upon as *doubtful*." (Madvig.)]

(Optative with ἄν, and in conditional sentences in the *oratio recta*[2].) *a*) With ἄν the present and the aorist stand in the optative (now and then also the perfect as denoting the now existing result, besides the perfects which are present in signification) to express a possible contingency, which will be actual under a certain condition, which it is admitted does not at present hold, but is easy to be conceived as occurring, and which for the moment one chooses to assume and presuppose. The condition is expressed by εἰ, with the optative of the present or aorist. The apodosis here approximates sometimes to a simply conditional apodosis in the indic. future, sometimes to a hypothetical apodosis in the imperf. indic. with ἄν, so that the thing put as contingent is more opposed to the actual state of the case, yet with a certain reference to what is still possible or probable; sometimes this form is merely a more delicate mode of expression instead of the imperf. with ἄν. The aorist differs from the present only in the way explained above (§ 134, c): Ὅσον αἱ μοναρχίαι πρὸς τὸ πρᾶξαί τι τῶν δεόντων διαφέρουσι τῶν ὀλιγαρχιῶν καὶ τῶν δημοκρατιῶν, οὕτως ἂν

---

[1] Printed *obliqua* in Schneidewin.

[2] Not to be confounded with the optative after εἰ in *oratio obliqua* after a præteritum (§ 131, 132) and the optat. of recurring acts (§ 133).

[§ 135.] κάλλιστα θεωρήσαιμεν, εἰ- τὰς μεγίστας τῶν πράξεων παρ' ἀλλήλας τιθέντες ἐξετάζειν ἐπιχειρήσαιμεν (*Isocr. Nic.* 17; *we might perhaps best see, if —; and therefore we will do so*). Εἰ ἀμελῆσαι δόξαιμεν Γαδάτα, τοῦ τοσαῦτα ἡμᾶς ὠφεληκότος, ποίοις λόγοις ἄλλους πείθοιμεν ἂν χαρίζεσθαί τι ἡμῖν; (*Xen. Cyr.* 5, 3, 33. *And therefore we will avoid this appearance*). Χρὴ ὑμᾶς, ὦ Ἀθηναῖοι, τοιαῦτα φρονεῖν περὶ τῶν ἀτυχούντων δήμων, οἷάπερ ἂν τοὺς ἄλλους ἀξιώσαιτε φρονεῖν περὶ ὑμῶν, εἴ ποθ', ὃ μὴ γένοιτο, τοιοῦτό τι συμβαίη (*Dem.* 15, 21; *as you might look for from them, if we imagine that* —). Ἐπιλήσμων ἂν εἴην, ὦ Ἀγάθων, εἰ, ἰδὼν τὴν σὴν ἀνδρείαν, βλέψαντος ἐναντία τοσούτῳ θεάτρῳ νῦν οἰηθείην σε θορυβήσεσθαι ἕνεκα ἡμῶν, ὀλίγων ἀνθρώπων (*Pl. Conv.* 194. *I must be forgetful, if I were to think* —). Εἰ, ἐπὶ πῦρ ἐλθόντος σου καὶ μὴ ὄντος παρ' ἐμοί, ἄλλοσε ἡγησάμην, ὁπόθεν σοι εἴη λαβεῖν, οὐκ ἂν ἐμέμφου μοι. Καὶ εἰ, βουλομένου μουσικὴν μαθεῖν σου παρ' ἐμοῦ, δείξαιμί σοι πολὺ δεινοτέρους ἐμοῦ περὶ μουσικὴν καί σοι χάριν ἂν εἰδότας, εἰ ἐθέλοις παρ' αὐτῶν μανθάνειν, τί ἂν ἔτι μοι μέμφοιο; Οὕτως οὖν καὶ περὶ τῆς οἰκονομικῆς ποιήσω (*Xen. Oecon.* 2, 15).

b) The condition, instead of being expressed in a sentence of its own, may be intimated by a single word, or by the context: Ἐκ τῶν ἐμπορίων τῆς Χεῤῥονήσου, ἃ τότ' ἂν κλεισθείη (*which* then, *i.e. in case Kersobleptes should conquer the Chersonese*), πλέον ἢ τριακόσια τάλαντά ἐσθ' ἡ πρόσοδος (*Dem.* 23, 110).

c) The protasis retains its form, when the apodosis passes into the infinitive or the participle: Ἐλπίζω, εἰ τὴν πρὸς ἐμὲ ὁδὸν τράποιο, σφόδρ' ἄν σε τῶν καλῶν καὶ σεμνῶν ἐργάτην ἀγαθὸν γενέσθαι (*Xen. Mem.* 2, 1, 27 = σφόδρ' ἂν ἀγαθὸς ἐργάτης γένοιο). See *Infinitive* and *Participle with* ἄν.

Rem. 1. As this form of hypothetical declaration differs but little from a simply conditional statement which refers to the future, it sometimes happens that both forms are combined:

a) The condition is expressed absolutely in the present or fut. indicative, or in the subjunctive with ἐάν, but the apodosis nevertheless stands in the optative with ἄν as something possible and conceivable: Οὐ δεινὰ ἂν ἐγὼ πάθοιμι, εἰ μὴ ἐξέσται μοι ἀπιέναι καὶ μὴ ἀκούειν σου; (*Pl. Gorg.* 461.) Πολλὴ ἄν τις εὐδαιμονία εἴη περὶ τοὺς νέους, εἰ εἷς μὲν μόνος αὐτοὺς διαφθείρει, οἱ δ' ἄλλοι ὠφελοῦσιν (*Pl. Apol.* 25). Ἢν φθάσωμεν, πρὶν τοὺς πολεμίους συλλεγῆναι, ἀναβάντες, ἀμαχεὶ λάβοιμεν ἂν τὸ ἄκρον (*Xen. Cyr.* 3, 2, 5). The apodosis sometimes expresses, not a direct consequence of the condition, but something which *even then* is only *possible*, so that the optative with ἄν is purely potential, as in the following §: Εἰ θέλετε σκέψασθαι παρ' ὑμῖν αὐτοῖς, τί δοῦλον ἢ ἐλεύθερον εἶναι διαφέρει, τοῦτο μέγιστον ἂν εὕροιτε, ὅτι τοῖς μὲν δούλοις τὸ σῶμα τῶν ἀδικημάτων πάντων ὑπεύθυνόν ἐστι (*is answerable for, must atone for*, § 63, d), τοῖς δ' ἐλευθέροις ὕστατον τοῦτο προσήκει κολάζειν (*Dem.* 24, 167).

b) The apodosis is put in the indicative, as simply conditional, while the protasis is marked by the optative as an assumed possibility. Often the former is, properly considered, an unconditional and general assertion, and the optative with εἰ only assigns a possible case in which the assertion will apply: Τίνα εὑρήσομεν τῶν τοῖς Τρωικοῖς χρόνοις γενομένων, εἰ τοὺς μύθους ἀφέντες τὴν ἀλήθειαν σκοποῖμεν, τοιαῦτα διαπεπραγμένον οἷα Εὐαγόραν; (*Isocr. Evag.* 66.) Εἰ ἐθέλοις τρεῖς τοιούτους ἀνθρώπους ἐν μέρει ἀνερωτᾶν, τίς τούτων τῶν βίων ἥδιστος, τὸν ἑαυτοῦ ἕκαστος μάλιστα ἐγκωμιάσεται (*Pl. Rep.* 9, 581).—Ἐπισκοπῶ, ὦ ξένε, εἴ τι συμβαίνοι γίγνεσθαι, πῶς κεῖται τὰ ἐν τῇ νηί (*Xen. Œcon.* 8, 15; *if any thing; in case of any thing happening*). Ἔστιν οἰκονομίαν ἐπισταμένῳ, καὶ εἰ μὴ αὐτὸς τύχοι χρήματα ἔχων, τὸν ἄλλου οἶκον οἰκονομοῦντα μισθοφορεῖν (*Xen. Œcon.* 1, 4; *even if he himself should possess no property*). (So likewise where the apodosis becomes infinitive: Ἡγοῦμαι, εἰ καὶ μηδενὸς ἄλλου μνησθείην ἀλλ' ἐνταῦθα καταλείποιμι τὸν λόγον, ῥᾴδιον ἐκ τούτων εἶναι γνῶναι τὴν ἀρετὴν τοῦ Εὐαγόρου, *Isocr. Evag.* 33. *I take it to be easy, even if I should mention nothing more* —.)[1] [§ 135.]

REM. 2. Other quite occasional and isolated deviations from the regular form of hypothetical statements rest upon an inaccuracy in the expression. On εἰ with *one* indicative and *one* optative, when a judgment is pronounced on the connexion between a past fact and a possible action which has not yet occurred (Δεινὰ ἂν εἴην εἰργασμένος, εἰ τότε μὲν ἔμενον, νῦν δὲ τὴν τάξιν λίποιμι), see *Connexion of Sentences with* μὲν — δέ, § 189, a.

REM. 3. Εἰ with the optative, is used in sentences of comparison, which denote something merely thought, but yet possible: Οἱ τοιοῦτοι ὅμοιον ἐμοὶ δοκοῦσι πεπονθέναι, οἷον εἴ τις εὖ σπείρων καὶ εὖ φυτεύων, ὁπότε καρποῦσθαι ταῦτα δέοι, ἐῴη τὸν καρπὸν ἀσυγκόμιστον εἰς τὴν γῆν πάλιν καταρρεῖν (*Xen. Cyr.* 1, 5, 10). (A direct opposition to reality is expressed by the imperf. indicative: Οὐδέν τι διάφορον πάσχει ἢ εἰ μόνος ἐστρατεύετο, *Xen. Cyr.* 5, 4. 29.)

Without any definite condition either expressed or implied in the context, the optative with ἄν (present, aorist, sometimes perfect) is very frequently used to denote something as what is conceivable, and, under certain circumstances, could and might easily occur, or to which some person might be inclined; in general, as the form of a modest expression of opinion on the present or the future. (*Optativus potentialis, dubitativus.* The aorist, of that which is single and transient.) Ὥρα ἂν ἡμῖν συσκευάζεσθαι εἴη (*Xen. Cyr.* 3, 1, 41). Ἴσως ἂν οὖν τις ἐπιτιμήσειεν τοῖς εἰρημένοις, ὅτι τὰς μὲν πράξεις ἐπαινῶ, τὰς δ' αἰτίας οὐ φράζω (*Isocr. Areop.* 36). Ταῦθ' ὡς οὐ παρὰ τὸν νόμον ἐστίν, οὔτ' ἂν Ἀνδροτίων ἔχοι λέγειν οὔθ' ὑμεῖς πεισθείητε ἄν (*Dem.* 22, 17). Ἡδέως ἂν ἔγωγ' ἐροίμην Λεπτίνην, τίς αὕτη ἡ ἀτέλειά (*exemption from taxes*) ἐστιν (*Dem.* 20, 129). (Βουλοίμην ἄν, *velim.*) Ἆρ' οὖν ἐθελήσαις ἄν, ὦ Γοργία, ὥσπερ νῦν διαλεγόμεθα, διατελέσαι τὸ μὲν ἐρωτῶν, τὸ δ' ἀποκρινόμενος; (*Pl. Gorg.* 449. *Should you feel* § 136.

[1] Οἱ ἵπποι τοῖς Πέρσαις νυκτὸς ὡς ἐπὶ τὸ πολὺ πεποδισμένοι εἰσί, τοῦ μὴ φεύγειν ἕνεκα, εἰ λυθείησαν (*Xen. An.* 3, 4, 35; *that they might not run away, if by chance they should get loose*).

[§ 136.] *inclined? should you mind* (doing it)? modest request.) Ἆρα ἐθελήσειεν ἂν Γοργίας ἡμῖν διαλεχθῆναι; (*Pl. Gorg.* 447.) Ποῖ οὖν, ἔφην ἐγώ, τραποίμεθ' ἂν ἔτι; (*Pl. Euthyd.* 290. *Whither then should we* [*can we, are we to*] *turn ourselves?* cf. § 121.) Πῶς ἂν ὀλοίμην; (*Eur. Med.* 97, expressing, virtually, a wish.) Χωροῖς ἂν εἴσω (*Soph. Phil.* 674. *Thou mightest go in;* [*you may go in*] approximating to the imperative). Λέληθέ σε, ὅτι καὶ οἱ ῥαψῳδοὶ πάντες ἐπίστανται τὰ Ὁμήρου ἔπη; Καὶ πῶς ἄν, ἔφη, λελήθοι, ἀκροώμενόν γε αὐτῶν ὀλίγου ἀν' ἑκάστην ἡμέραν; (*Xen. Conv.* 3, 6.)

§ 137. The potential optative with *ἄν* stands, not only in principal sentences but also in accessory sentences, which admit of such a conception and mode of expression, especially in declarative object-sentences with ὅτι or ὡς, in dependent interrogative sentences which would have the same form in the *oratio recta* (without reference to the time of the principal verb), and in relative sentences (with pronoun or relative particles): Ἀπεκρίνατο Κλεάνωρ, ὅτι πρόσθεν ἂν ἀποθάνοιεν ἢ τὰ ὅπλα παραδοῖεν (*Xen. An.* 2, 1, 10 = Πρόσθεν ἂν ἀποθάνοιμεν ἢ — παραδοῖμεν). Ἐννοεῖτε (imperat.), ὅτι ἧττον ἂν — στάσις εἴη ἑνὸς ἄρχοντος (*Xen. An.* 5, 9, 29). Ἐσκόπουν, τίν' ἂν τρόπον ἡσυχίαν ἔχειν Ἀθηνόδωρος ἀναγκασθείη (*Dem.* 23, 11). Ἠρώτων οἱ πρέσβεις τοὺς στρατηγούς, εἰ δοῖεν ἂν τούτων τὰ πιστά (*Xen. An.* 4, 8, 7 = Ἆρ' ἂν δοίητε —;). Οὐκ οἶδ', ὅ,τι ἄν τις χρήσαιτο στρατιώταις οὕτως ἀθύμως ἔχουσιν (*Xen. An.* 3, 1, 40). Χρὴ τοὺς μέγα φρονοῦντας μὴ τοῖς τοιούτοις ἐπιχειρεῖν, ἃ καὶ τῶν τυχόντων ἄν τις καταπράξειεν (*Isocr. Phil.* 41). Εἴπατέ μοι, εἴ τινα ἐγὼ νῦν τῶν ἐμῶν ἀποστέλλοιμι πρὸς τὸν Ἰνδόν, συμπέμψαιτε ἄν μοι τῶν ὑμετέρων οἵτινες αὐτῷ τὴν ὁδὸν ἡγοῖντο ἄν; (*Xen. Cyr.* 3, 2, 28; *who could show him the way.*) Ἄφοβος τὴν οὐσίαν μοι οὕτως διῴκηκεν ὡς οὐδ' ἂν οἱ ἔχθιστοι διοικήσειαν (*Dem.* 27, 48). Μανία τὸν Μειδίαν ἠσπάζετο, ὥσπερ ἂν γυνὴ γάμβρον ἀσπάζοιτο (*Xen. Hell.* 3, 1, 14). Ὁ Ἀρμένιος τὰ βασίλεια οἰκοδομεῖν ἤρχετο ὡς ἂν ἱκανὰ ἀπομάχεσθαι εἴη (*Xen. Cyr.* 3, 1, 1; *in such wise as they might be;* i. e. *so that* —). Ὑμεῖς, ὦ Ἀθηναῖοι, ὡς μὲν ἂν εἴποιτε δικαίους λόγους, ἄμεινον Φιλίππου παρεσκεύασθε, ὡς δὲ κωλύσαιτ' ἂν ἐκεῖνον πράττειν, ἃ βούλεται, παντελῶς ἀργῶς ἔχετε (*Dem.* 6, 4. *You are prepared for this, how you might be able;* i. e. *to be able.* So ὡς frequently with the potential optative, and an accessory signification of a purpose or aim). Διάφορόν τι ποιεῖς, εἰ τοὺς τοῖς νόμοις πειθομένους φαυλίζεις, ὅτι καταλυθεῖεν ἂν οἱ νόμοι, ἢ εἰ . . ψέγοις (*Xen. Mem.* 4, 4, 14; *because the laws might possibly be annulled*). (Potential optative in a conditional sentence: Ἀλλὰ μήν, εἴ γε μηδὲ δοῦλον ἀκρατῆ δεξαίμεθ' ἄν, πῶς οὐκ ἄξιον αὐτόν γε φυλάξασθαι τοιοῦτον γενέσθαι; *Xen. Mem.* 1, 5, 3: *if we should not even receive.* Cf. § 117 b. R. 1.)[1]

---

[1] Εἰ δοκοίην, ὅπου δυναίμην, ἄκυρον ποιεῖν τὸ Λακεδαιμονίων ἀξίωμα, ἐννοῶ, μὴ λίαν ἂν ταχὺ σωφρονισθείην (*Xen. An.* 5, 9, 28; *I fear I should but too soon be brought to*

§ 138. Relative and conjunctional sentences which are appended to a sentence in the optative with ἄν, or to a conditional sentence in the optative, to define the hypothetical statement more accurately, without being predicated for themselves as actual, and which belong to present or future time, are themselves (as denoting something assumed or possible) put in the optative (as in *oratio obliqua* after a præteritum, § 132). On the other hand, declarative object-sentences and dependent interrogative sentences stand in the indicative, as after a present or future indicative (from which the optative with ἄν in a principal sentence, deviates only in form). In object-sentences with ὅπως, and in sentences of intention, the subjunctive is also usually put, but also the optative: (a) Πῶς ἄν τις, ἅ γε μὴ ἐπίσταιτο, ταῦτα σοφὸς εἴη; (*Xen. Mem.* 4, 6, 7.) Χρημάτων ὁ τοιοῦτος ἀνὴρ νέος μὲν ὢν καταφρονοῖ ἄν, ὅσῳ δὲ πρεσβύτερος γένοιτο, μᾶλλον ἀεὶ ἀσπάζοιτο ἄν (*Pl. Rep.* 8, 549). Οὕτω γιγνομένων (*if such becomes the state of the case*) σαφῶς οἶδα, ὅτι ὁ φρούραρχος δέοιτο ἂν Γαδάτα μένειν, ἕως σὺ ἀπέλθοις (*Xen. Cyr.* 5, 3, 13). Εἰ ἀποθνήσκοι μὲν πάντα, ὅσα τοῦ ζῆν μεταλάβοι, ἐπειδὴ δὲ ἀποθάνοι, μένοι ἐν τούτῳ τῷ σχήματι καὶ μὴ πάλιν ἀναβιώσκοιτο, ἆρ' οὐ πολλὴ ἀνάγκη, τελευτῶντα πάντα τεθνάναι καὶ μηδὲν ζῆν; (*Pl. Phæd.* 72.)[1]—(b) Οὐδ' ἂν εἷς ἀντείποι, ὡς οὐ συμφέρει τῇ πόλει, καὶ Λακεδαιμονίους ἀσθενεῖς εἶναι καὶ Θηβαίους (*Dem.* 16, 4). Εἴ τις λέγοι ἄνθρωπον ἑστηκότα, κινοῦντα δὲ τὰς χεῖράς τε καὶ τὴν κεφαλήν, ὅτι ὁ αὐτὸς ἕστηκέ τε καὶ κινεῖται, οὐκ ἂν ἀξιοῖμεν οὕτω λέγειν δεῖν, ἀλλ' ὅτι τὸ μέν τι αὐτοῦ ἕστηκε, τὸ δέ τι κινεῖται (*Pl. Rep.* 4, 436). Ὁ πρωρεὺς τῆς νεὼς οὕτως ἐπίσταται ἑκάστων τῶν ἐν τῷ πλοίῳ τὴν χώραν, ὥστε καὶ ἀπὼν ἂν εἴποι, ὅπου ἕκαστα κεῖται καὶ ὁπόσα ἐστίν (*Xen. Œcon.* 8, 14). Οὐκ ἂν ἔχοιμί γ' εἰπεῖν, ὅτι οὐ προσεῖχον τὸν νοῦν Εὐθυδήμῳ καὶ Διονυσοδώρῳ (*Pl. Euthyd.* 272).—(c) Μέγα ἂν ὀνήσαιτε τὸ στράτευμα, εἰ ἐπιμεληθείητε, ὅπως ἀντὶ τῶν ἀπολωλότων ὡς τάχιστα στρατηγοὶ κατασταθῶσιν (*Xen. An.* 3, 1, 38). Ὀκνοίην ἂν εἰς τὰ πλοῖα ἐμβαίνειν, ἃ Κῦρος ἡμῖν δοίη, μὴ ἡμᾶς αὐταῖς ταῖς τριήρεσι καταδύσῃ (*Xen. An.* 1, 3, 17).—Ἡ ἐμὴ φυλακὴ τῶν ἔνδον, ἔφη ἡ γυνή, γελοία τις ἂν φαίνοιτο, εἰ μὴ σύ γε ἐπιμελοῖο, ὅπως ἔξωθέν τι εἰσφέροιτο (*Xen. Œcon.* 7, 39). Αὐτὸς ἂν ἔχων τὴν ἄλλην δύναμιν πειρῴμην μὴ πρόσω ὑμῶν εἶναι, ἵνα, εἴ που καιρὸς εἴη, ἐπιφανείην (*Xen. Cyr.* 2, 4, 17).

---

my senses, for Indic. Fut., § 124 a. R. 1; ἐννοῶ μή being inserted without influencing the hypothetical form of the sentence).

[1] Dependent sentences containing a statement of the past in the indicative (§ 132 a. R. 1): Τίς οὐκ ἂν μισήσειεν Φίλιππον, εἰ φαίνοιτο τούτοις ἐπιβουλεύων, ὑπὲρ ὧν ὁ πρόγονος αὐτοῦ προείλετο κινδυνεύειν; (*Isocr. Phil.* 77.)

[§ 138.] REM. 1. Now and then, however, a relative or conjunctional sentence has the subjunctive with *ἄν*, as after a condition put simply in the indicative: *Μάλιστα ἂν αἰσθοίμεθα, ὃ ζητοῦμεν, εἰ τοιόνδε ποιήσαιμεν τῇ διανοίᾳ· δόντες ἐξουσίαν ἑκατέρῳ ποιεῖν ὅ,τι ἂν βούληται, τῷ τε δικαίῳ καὶ τῷ ἀδίκῳ, εἶτ' ἐπακολουθήσαιμεν θεώμενοι, ποῖ ἡ ἐπιθυμία ἑκάτερον ἄξει* (*Pl. Rep.* 2, 359). A dependent sentence which states something independently as matter of fact, has the indicative: *Τίνι ἂν θεῷ εὐχόμενος κάλλιστ' ἂν ἔλθοιμι τὴν ὁδόν, ἣν ἐπινοῶ;* and consequently in the *oratio obliqua* after a præteritum: *Ξενοφῶν ἐπήρετο τὸν Ἀπόλλω, τίνι ἂν θεῷ εὐχόμενος κάλλιστ' ἂν ἔλθοι τὴν ὁδόν, ἣν ἐπινοεῖ* (*Xen. An.* 3, 1, 6) or *ἐπινοοῖ* by § 132, a *and* b.

REM. 2. (to § 135—138.) Whether *ἄν* with the potential optative is sometimes omitted by Attic poets, is uncertain: in prose this is never the case. *Ἄν* with the fut. of the opt. is found only in doubtful readings.

§ 139. On the use of *ἄν* in general, and with the indicative and optative, remark further:

a) In the copulative, disjunctive, or adversative connexion of two verbs, *ἄν* is commonly put only once (with the first), except where the addition of special definitions to each verb, or the emphasis of the passage, causes the two notions to stand more apart, and gives more prominence to the hypothetical character of each severally: *Εἰ ὁ Φίλιππος ὑμᾶς ἐξελθεῖν ἐβουλήθη, οὐκ ἄν ποτε τοὺς χρόνους ἀνελών, ἐν οἷς ἠδυνήθητ' ἂν ἐξελθεῖν, τηνικαῦτ' ἐκάλει, οὐδ' ἂν ἐμέ, ἡνίκα δεῦρο ἀποπλεῖν ἐβουλόμην, κατεκώλυεν, οὐδὲ τοιαῦτα λέγειν Αἰσχίνῃ προσέταττεν, ἐξ ὧν ἥκισθ' ὑμεῖς ἠμέλλετ' ἐξιέναι* (*Dem.* 19, 51). (It is never repeated, where two predicates are put comparatively: *Ἥδιον ἂν ἀποθάνοιμι ἢ τὰ ὅπλα παραδοίην.*) Sometimes *ἄν* is left to be understood from a preceding clause, rhetorically corresponding with the latter: *Τί ἐποίησεν ἄν; ἢ δῆλον, ὅτι ὤμοσεν;* (*Dem.* 31, 9.) *Τί οὖν τῷ θεῷ τὸ ψεῦδος χρήσιμον; πότερον διὰ τὸ μὴ εἰδέναι τὰ παλαιὰ ψεύδοιτο ἄν; Γελοῖον μέντ' ἄν, ἔφη. Ἀλλὰ δεδιὼς τοὺς ἐχθροὺς ψεύδοιτο; Πολλοῦ γε δεῖ* (*Pl. Rep.* 2, 382).

b) Usually *ἄν* is put before the verb, when the emphasis lies on some definition of the verb that stands before it (the verb) in the sentence; otherwise directly after it. In this way, *ἄν* often comes to stand at some considerable distance before the verb, being attached to an interrogative word, a negation, or some other emphatic word in the opening of the sentence: *Εἰ μὲν ἐπαινῶ Σεύθην, δικαίως ἄν με καὶ αἰτιῷσθε καὶ μισοῖτε· εἰ δέ, πρόσθεν αὐτῷ πάντων μάλιστα φίλος ὤν, νῦν πάντων διαφορώτατός εἰμι, πῶς ἂν* (or *οὐκ ἂν*) *ἔτι δικαίως, ὑμᾶς αἱρούμενος ἀντὶ Σεύθου, ὑφ' ὑμῶν αἰτίαν ἔχοιμι;* (*Xen. An.* 7, 6, 15.) *Οὕτω γὰρ καὶ ἑπόμενοι ἂν φίλοι τῷ Κύρῳ καὶ πρόθυμοι ἑποίμεθα καὶ ἀπιόντες ἀσφαλῶς ἂν ἀπίοιμεν* (*Xen. An.* 1, 3, 19. The *ἄν* of the principal verb is often put in this way, where a participle precedes the verb). When *ἄν* is thus removed to a distance from its verb, it is sometimes repeated in immediate connexion with the verb: *Ὥσπερ ἄν, εἰ τῷ ὄντι ξένος ἐτύγχανον ὤν, ξυνεγιγνώσκετε δήπου ἄν μοι, εἰ ἐν ἐκείνῃ τῇ φωνῇ τε καὶ τῷ τρόπῳ ἔλεγον, ἐν οἷσπερ ἐτεθράμμην, καὶ δὴ καὶ νῦν ὑμῶν δέομαι τὸν μὲν τρόπον τῆς λέξεως ἐᾶν, τούτῳ δὲ τὸν νοῦν προσέχειν, εἰ δίκαια λέγω* (*Pl. Apol.* 17). *Ξενοφῶν ἐπήρετο τὸν Ἀπόλλω, τίνι ἂν θεῶν θύων καὶ εὐχόμενος κάλλιστ' ἂν ἔλθοι τὴν ὁδόν, ἣν ἐπινοεῖ* (*Xen. An.* 3, 1, 6). *Οἶδα ὑμᾶς ταῦτα ἐμοὶ ἐπισταμένους, ὥστε κἂν ἄλλους εἰκότως ἂν διδάσκοιτε* (*Xen. Cyr.* 3, 3, 35).[1]

---

[1] *Ἂν* repeated where the same verb is put with two single and several definitions (*οὔτε — οὔτε, μὲν — δέ*): *Εἰ ἐγὼ πάλαι ἐπεχείρησα πράττειν τὰ πολιτικά, πάλαι ἂν ἀπολώλειν καὶ οὔτ' ἂν ὑμᾶς ὠφελήκειν οὐδὲν οὔτ' ἂν ἐμαυτόν* (*Pl. Apol.* 31). *Δίκαιος μὲν ἂν εἴης, σοφὸς δ' οὐκ ἄν* (*Xen. Mem.* 1, 6, 12).

REM. An inversion of the place of ἄν is seen in the expression οὐκ οἶδ' ἂν εἰ, or οὐκ ἂν οἶδ' εἰ, for οὐκ οἶδα, εἰ — ἄν, e.g. Ἐγὼ ἃ χθὲς ἤκουσα, οὐκ ἂν οἶδα εἰ δυναίμην ἅπαντα ἐν μνήμῃ πάλιν λαβεῖν (*Pl. Tim.* 26). Οὐκ οἶδ' ἂν εἰ πείσαιμι, πειρᾶσθαι δὲ χρή (*Eur. Med.* 941). We may also notice the connexion of the ἄν belonging to the verb with the concessive καί, so that εἰ after κἄν follows with the indicative or optative according to the usual rules (κἂν εἰ = ἄν — καὶ εἰ): Νῦν μοι δοκεῖ κἂν ἀσέβειαν εἰ καταγιγνώσκοι τις Μειδίου, τὰ προσήκοντα ποιεῖν (*Dem.* 21, 51, = καὶ εἰ — καταγιγνώσκοι, τὰ πρ. ἂν ποιεῖν). Hence sometimes κἂν εἰ merely for καὶ εἰ in an appended concession: *even if.* (Different from κἄν = καὶ ἐάν.) [§ 139.]

c) Ἄν sometimes stands elliptically, so that a verb immediately preceding is understood in the hypothetical indicative or optative: Οὐδεμία ἐστὶν οὕτω καλὴ παραίνεσις, ἥτις τοὺς μὴ ὄντας ἀγαθοὺς αὐθήμερον ἀκούσαντας ἀγαθοὺς ποιήσει· οὐκ ἂν οὖν τοξότας γε (*Xen. Cyr.* 3, 3, 50; viz. ποιήσειεν: *good archers, at any rate, it would not make them*). Πάλαι γ' ἀλεκτρυόνος ἤκουσ' ἐγώ· οἱ δ' οἰκέται ῥέγκουσιν· ἀλλ' οὐκ ἂν πρὸ τοῦ (*Arist. Nub.* 5; viz. ἔρεγκον: *they would not have done that in time past*). Ἐπ' οὐδενὶ βρώματι οὐδὲ πώματι ἀνὴρ Πέρσης οὕτως ἐκπλαγείη ἂν ὥστε μὴ οὐ προνοεῖν, ἅπερ ἂν καὶ μὴ ἐπὶ σίτῳ ὢν (*Xen. Cyr.* 5, 2, 17; viz. προνοοίη). Especially note the elliptical ὥσπερ ἂν εἰ (ὅσον περ ἂν εἰ), *as though* (strictly speaking: *as one might, or would, have done, if*—): Εἰ ὁ συμβὰς σκηπτὸς (*sudden burst of calamity*) μὴ μόνον ἡμῶν ἀλλὰ πάντων τῶν ἄλλων Ἑλλήνων μείζων γέγονε, τί χρὴ ποιεῖν; ὥσπερ ἂν εἴ τις ναύκληρον πάντ' ἐπὶ σωτηρίᾳ πράξαντα εἶτα, συντριβέντων αὐτῷ τῶν σκευῶν, τῆς ναυαγίας αἰτιῷτο (*Dem.* 18, 194).[1]

(Concluding Remarks to Chap. 1. 2, 3.) With respect to the cases in which the Greeks do not mark by the mood of the verb, that the thing said is not absolutely asserted as actual, though there might be occasion so to mark it, but, deviating from the Latin, and, in some cases, from the English idiom, retain the indicative without ἄν (besides those cases which have been named as exceptions in the preceding rules on the optative and subjunctive), the following require to be specially noted: *a*) declarative object-sentences (with ὅτι and ὡς) and dependent interrogative sentences after a present or future (after a præteritum in the optative, see § 130); *b*) relative sentences denoting an intention and definition, after a present or future; cf. § 115 a. R. (after a præteritum in the optative, see § 132 d); likewise those which express the consequence of a quality (Lat. Gr. § 364, *qui* = *talis ut*, &c.), or a cause (Lat. Gr. § 366, *qui* = *quum is*), or which belong to a negative statement: Οὐχ ἕξουσι δεῖξαι νόμον, καθ' ὃν ἐξῆν αὐτοῖς ταῦτα πρᾶξαι (*Isæ.* 10, 11). *c*) Accessory sentences which belong to a hypothetical sentence in the indicative with ἄν, or to a condition in the indicative put as not existing; see § 117 a. R. 2. *d*) Relative or conjunctional sentences which, as members of a dependent statement, are necessary to complete the sense of object-sentences, or sentences of intention, or infinitive sentences (or statements expressed by a single infinitive), where the principal sentences have the verb in the present or future: Σκεπτέον, μὴ πρότερον τούσδε γενέσθαι μεγάλους ἐάσωμεν ἢ ἐκεῖνοι μικροὶ γενήσονται (*Dem.* 16, 5: except in the cases where the relative or conjunction is used with ἄν and the subjunctive). (For inferential (or *consecutive*) sentences with ὥστε in the indic. or infin., see *Infinitive*, § 166.) § 140.

---

[1] Ὥσπερ ἂν εἰ παῖς, *as if one were a child* = *like a child* (*Pl. Gorg.* 479).

CHAP. III.]

CHAPTER IV.

The Imperative.

§ 141. THE Imperative expresses an entreaty, a command, an instruction or exhortation, together with a concession and permission; in the present tense quite generally, or when the action is continued and recurring; in the aorist, when it is single and transient. Sometimes the distinction between the present and the aorist is small, and it falls away, where only the one or the other form is in use. The imperative of the perfect middle with passive signification is used where the entreaty, command, &c. relates to a completed action. Where the perfect indicative has the signification of a present, the perfect imperative (active and middle) is used in the same signification. Θάῤῥει. Τοὺς μὲν θεοὺς φοβοῦ, τοὺς δὲ γονεῖς τίμα, τοὺς δὲ φίλους αἰσχύνου, τοῖς δὲ νόμοις πείθου (*Isocr. Demon.* 16). Βοώντων (*Arist. Ach.* 186. *Let them cry!*).—Εἰπέ μοι (*tell me;* but λέγε, *speak!*). Ἐπίσχες (*hold a moment!*). Λαβὲ τὰς μαρτυρίας καὶ ἀνάγνωθι (*Dem.* 27, 17, *et passim*, but also λαβέ μοι τὰς μ. καὶ ἀναγίγνωσκε, *Id.* 27, 26, because the reading, in comparison with the momentary act of taking, forms a continued action). Σκοπῶμεν κοινῇ, καὶ εἴ πῃ ἔχεις ἀντιλέγειν ἐμοῦ λέγοντος, ἀντίλεγε (*frequently and at greater length*) καί σοι πείσομαι· εἰ δὲ μή, παῦσαι ἤδη (*cease at once, and have done with it*) πολλάκις μοι λέγων τὸν αὐτὸν λόγον (*Pl. Crito*, 48). Ἐὰν δοῦλος ἐλεύθερον ἀποκτείνῃ θυμῷ, παραδιδόντων οἱ δεσπόται τὸν δοῦλον τοῖς προσήκουσι τοῦ τελευτήσαντος (*Pl. Legg.* 9, 868; but *Ibid.* 879, παραδότω τὸν δοῦλον ὁ κεκτημένος). Ὃς ἂν ἱεροσυλῶν ληφθῇ, ἐκτὸς τῶν ὅρων τῆς χώρας γυμνὸς ἐκβληθήτω (*Pl. Legg.* 9, 854). Περὶ τῶν ἰδίων ταῦτά μοι προειρήσθω (*Isocr. Paneg.* 14; *let thus much be said by way of preface*). Μέμνησο τῶν λόγων. Κεκράγετε. Ἴσθι θνητὸς ὤν.

REM. 1. Especially note the blending of interrogation and command in the expression οἶσθ' ὃ (ὡς) δρᾶσον; (*knowest thou what thou must do?* lit. *knowest thou what?* (*how?*)—*do it*) with command following. (Poetical. In Plato: Τί οὖν; τετάχθω ἡμῖν κατὰ δημοκρατίαν τοιοῦτος ἀνήρ, ὡς δημοκρατικὸς ὀρθῶς ἂν προσαγορευόμενος; Τετάχθω, ἔφη. *Rep.* 8, 562.)

REM. 2. Instead of the imperative in the second and sometimes in the third person, the older language used also the infinitive, and after this example sometimes the Attic poets (but only for the second person), and occasionally Plato and Thucydides (so that the action is presented in quite a general way): Καὶ ταῦτ' ἰὼν Εἴσω λογίζου, κἂν λάβῃς μ' ἐψευσμένον, Φάσκειν ἔμ' ἤδη μαντικῇ μηδὲν φρονεῖν (*Soph. Œd. R.* 462). Ἐγὼ ἔχων τοὺς μετ' ἐμαυτοῦ, προσπεσοῦμαι δρόμῳ κατὰ μέσον τὸ στρατόπεδον· σὺ δέ, Κλεαρίδα, ὕστερον, ὅταν ἐμὲ ὁρᾷς ἤδη προσκείμενον, τοὺς μετὰ σαυτοῦ καὶ τοὺς ξυμμάχους ἄγων αἰφνιδίως τὰς πύλας ἀνοίξας ἐπεκθεῖν (*Thuc.* 5, 9). [§ 141.] (On the accus. with inf. see § 168 a. 1.)

Rem. 3. Instead of the imperative in commands and invitations, we have also ὅπως (in prohibitions ὅπως μή) with the future indicative; see § 123, R. 4. (Πρὸς ταῦτα πράξεις, οἷον ἂν θέλῃς, *Soph. Œd. C.* 956, *thou mayest do* — [as *we* could say: '*you* will do *as you please*']. An eager and vehement command is expressed in the form of a negative question in the future indicative: Παῖδες, οὐ σκέψεσθε; (*Pl. Conv.* 212. *Look after it immediately, slaves!*) Οὐκ ἀποδιώξεις σαυτὸν ἀπὸ τῆς οἰκίας; (*Arist. Nub.* 1296. *Be off this moment!*) Invitation or summons is also expressed by a negative question with Τί οὐ in the present, or (more commonly) the aorist: Τί οὖν οὐ σκοποῦμεν, πῶς ἂν τῶν καλῶν καὶ ἀγαθῶν ἀνδρῶν μὴ διαμαρτάνοιμεν; (*Xen. Mem.* 3, 1, 10.) Τί οὖν οὐ διηγήσω μοι τὴν συνουσίαν σοῦ καὶ Πρωταγόρου, εἰ μή τί σε κωλύει; (*Pl. Prot.* 310.) (Λέγοις ἄν, *thou mightest say*; nearly = *say*; see § 136.)

A prohibition is expressed by *μή* (*μηδείς*) with the imperative of § 142. the present, or where, agreeably with the distinction assigned in the preceding paragraphs, the aorist is required, with the subjunctive of the aorist. Μὴ φοβοῦ! Μηδένα φίλον ποιοῦ πρὶν ἂν ἐξετάσῃς, πῶς κέχρηται τοῖς πρότερον φίλοις (*Isocr. Dem.* 24).—Μηδενὶ συμφορὰν ὀνειδίσῃς, κοινὴ γὰρ ἡ τύχη καὶ τὸ μέλλον ἀόρατον (*Isocr. Dem.* 29). Μηδεὶς ὑπολάβῃ με βούλεσθαι λαθεῖν, ὅτι τούτων ἔνια πέφρακα τὸν αὐτὸν τρόπον ὅνπερ πρότερον (*Isocr. Phil.* 93). Μὴ ἀποῦσι μὲν τοῖς τριάκοντα ἐπιβουλεύετε, παρόντας δ' ἀφῆτε (*Lys.* 12, 80). Μὴ θῆσθε νόμον μηδένα, ἀλλὰ τοὺς εἰς τὸ παρὸν βλάπτοντας ὑμᾶς λύσατε (*Dem.* 3, 10).

Rem. 1. Μή with the imperative of the aorist in the second person is not usual in Attic writers; with the third person, it does now and then occur: Οὐ κεκοσμημένους λόγους ἀλλ' ἀκούσεσθε εἰκῇ λεγόμενα τοῖς ἐπιτυχοῦσιν ὀνόμασι· καὶ μηδεὶς ὑμῶν προσδοκησάτω ἄλλως (*Pl. Apol.* 17).

Rem. 2. A stern prohibition is also expressed by a question with οὐ μή (§ 124 a. R. 4).

CHAPTER V.

The Infinitive and its Tenses.

The Infinitive expresses the notion of the verb in general in its § different tenses. By prefixing the article to the infinitive, the notion 143. of the verb is brought out as definite, and having a substantive exist- (387) ence. By this means, the infinitive is at the same time enabled to enter into relations with the other members of the sentence in the manner of a substantive in the different cases.

[§ 143.] Rem. The infinitive in Greek (as partly in English) is sometimes annexed, in a somewhat lax connexion, to a predicate for the purpose of defining it more nearly, so that it is difficult to assign the limits of the relation, and sometimes the same combination may be taken in a different sense in different connexions, e. g. δυνατὸς ποιεῖν (see § 149, 150; *able to do*, and *in one's power to do* = *possible to be done*). In some constructions, instead of the mere infinitive (more or less rarely) with little or no difference of meaning, the infinitive is used with ὥστε, which particle in general denotes an effect or an intention (*so that, in order that*), though sometimes the definite meaning of the particle almost entirely disappears.

§ 144. (388) The infinitive may stand, either as subject or as predicate-noun, when an action is characterized in general (e. g. Τοῦτο μανθάνειν καλεῖται). The infinitive as subject has the article, when it stands out as the given and first term of the sentence, of which something is to be predicated; but it is without the article, where the predicate-noun with ἐστίν coalesces, so to say, into an impersonal expression which stands forward as the principal term, and is completed by the infinitive (in English: IT *is good*, IT *is a sin, to* —), or where the predicate consists of a single verb which may be taken in the same way: Τὸ δίκην διδόναι πότερον πάσχειν τί ἐστιν ἢ ποιεῖν; (*Pl. Gorg.* 476.) Οὐχ οὕτως ἡδύ ἐστι τὸ ἔχειν χρήματα ὡς ἀνιαρὸν τὸ ἀποβάλλειν (*Xen. Cyr.* 8, 3, 42). Πολλὰ συμβάλλεται εἰς τὰς πράξεις τὸ εὔνους ἔχειν τοὺς ὑπηρέτας. Μεγίστην ἡγοῦμαι συμμαχίαν εἶναι τὸ τὰ δίκαια πράττειν (*Isocr. Archid.* 59). Τοῦτό ἐστι τὸ ἀδικεῖν, τὸ πλέον τῶν ἄλλων ζητεῖν ἔχειν (*Pl. Gorg.* 483. So almost always with an infinitive, which is first intimated by a pronoun). — Οὐχ ἡδὺ πολλοὺς ἐχθροὺς ἔχειν (*Dem.* 19, 221). Οἰκονόμου ἀγαθοῦ ἐστιν εὖ οἰκεῖν τὸν ἑαυτοῦ οἶκον (*Xen. Œcon.* 1, 2). Ὥσπερ ἐν ἵπποις, οὕτω καὶ ἐν ἀνθρώποις τισὶν ἐγγίγνεται, ὅσῳ ἂν ἔκπλεω τὰ δέοντα ἔχωσι, τοσούτῳ ὑβριστοτέροις εἶναι (*Xen. Hier.* 10, 1; *it lies in the nature of some men to be;* but τὸ αἰδεῖσθαι ἐν τοῖς τοιούτοις οὐκ ἔνεστιν). Νομίσατε ἀσέβημα μηδὲν ἔλαττον εἶναι τῶν μηδὲν ἠδικηκότων καταγνῶναι ἢ τοὺς ἠσεβηκότας μὴ τιμωρεῖσθαι (*Andoc.* 1, 32). (Ἡλίκα ἐστὶ τὰ διάφορα ἐνθάδε ἢ ἐκεῖ πολεμεῖν, οὐδὲ λόγου προσδεῖ. *Dem.* 1, 27; *how great the difference is — to make war.*)

Rem. 1. Ὥστε before the infinitive, in this impersonal mode of expression, is very rare: Ἀδύνατον ὑμῖν ὥστε Πρωταγόρου τοῦδε σοφώτερόν τινα ἑλέσθαι βραβευτὴν τῶν λόγων (*Pl. Prot.* 338).

Rem. 2. To an infinitive predicated generally (without a definite subject), a dependent sentence in the third person may be annexed without an expressly assigned subject, this being the same as the subject mentally supplied to the infinitive (*one, a person*); (but more commonly τίς is added.) Τὸ θάνατον δεδιέναι οὐδὲν ἄλλο ἐστὶν ἢ δοκεῖν σοφὸν εἶναι μὴ ὄντα· δοκεῖν γὰρ εἰδέναι ἐστίν, ἃ οὐκ οἶδεν (*Pl. Apol.* 29). Οὔτ' ἀνταδικεῖν δεῖ οὔτε κακῶς ποιεῖν οὐδένα ἀνθρώπων, οὐδ' ἂν ὁτιοῦν πάσχῃ ὑπ' αὐτῶν (*Pl. Crito*, 49). Likewise αὐτός, ἑαυτοῦ may be referred to the subject implied in the infinitive: Οὐκ ἄρα τοῦτ' ἐστὶ τὸ μέγα δύνασθαι, τὸ ποιεῖν, ἃ δοκεῖ αὐτῷ (*Pl. Gorg.* 469).

§ 145. (389) The infinitive stands (without article) with verbs, the meaning of which refers directly to a certain action of the same subject, and its accomplishment, to indicate that action; likewise with impersonal verbs which express a similar relation between a subject and an action (e. g. possibility or duty), and with many phrases which have the signification of such a personal or impersonal verb. Ἐπιθυμῶ αὐτοκράτωρ γίγνεσθαι ἄρχων (*Xen. An.* 5, 9, 21). Ἔγνων (*I resolved*) τὸν ποταμὸν διαβῆναι. Ἡ πόλις ἐκινδύνευσε πᾶσα διαφθαρῆναι (*Thuc.* 3, 74). Οὐ πέφυκας δουλεύειν. Αἰσχύνομαι πτωχεύειν. Ὀκνῶ λέγειν. Φοβοῦμαι διελέγχειν σε.—Δέδοκται ἡμῖν (ἔδοξεν) ἀπιέναι. Ἐξῆν μένειν. Συνέβη μοι πεσεῖν. Ὦ Ζεῦ, λαβεῖν μοι γένοιτο τοὺς πολεμίους ὡς ἐγὼ βούλομαι (*Xen. Cyr.* 6, 3, 11). Ἐκ τοῦ ταῦθ' οὕτως ἔχειν ὑπάρχει ὑμῖν ἀσφαλῶς οἰκεῖν (*Dem.* 23, 102).—Ἐν νῷ ἔχω ἐκπλεῖν. Οὐχ ὥρα καθεύδειν. Ἃ τυγχάνω ἀκηκοώς, οὐδεὶς φθόνος λέγειν (*Pl. Phæd.* 61; *I am quite ready to* —). [§ 145.]

Rem. 1. Besides the verbs which in general denote a being willing (a requirement or demand, ἀξιῶ), an ability (πέφυκα, *am naturally qualified to, it is my nature to*), a duty, habit, inclination (φιλῶ), disinclination (οὐ φθονῶ διδάσκειν ὑμᾶς), fear (αἰσχύνομαι[1], εὐλαβοῦμαι), a beginning, lingering, forgetting; in some writers verbs, which in themselves have no such meaning, are occasionally used in a particular connexion with the infinitive; e. g. ξυμβαίνω τινὶ παραδιδόναι ἐμαυτόν (*Thuc.* 2, 4; *agree with a person to surrender myself*), πιστεύω παρακατατίθεσθαί τινι χρήματα ἢ υἱοὺς ἢ θυγατέρας (*Xen. Mem.* 4, 4, 17 = τολμῶ), &c. (Poetically: ἐνίκησε δεῦρο μολεῖν, *Soph. Ant.* 233, *the opinion prevailed* = ἔδοξεν. Μένει σε πυθέσθαι παιδὸς δύσφορον ἄταν, *Soph. Ajax*, 641, *it awaits thee.*) In particular, many phrases which govern the infinitive, are formed with a substantive denoting a state of mind, or circumstances in reference to an action, and by itself capable of taking an objective genitive, either with ἐστίν, γίγνεται (e. g. φόβος, ὄκνος ἐστὶ τοῖς Ἕλλησι στρατεύειν ἐπὶ τὸν μέγαν βασιλέα, ἀνάγκη γίγνεταί μοι ἀπιέναι, or merely ἀνάγκη ἀπιέναι, οὐδεὶς κίνδυνός μοι πάσχειν τι), or with another verb (Δέδοικα, μὴ ἃ νῦν οὐ βουλόμεθα, ὕστερον εἰς ἀνάγκην ἔλθωμεν ποιεῖν, *Dem.* 1, 15. Ἀνάγκη τίς μοι ἐκ τύχης παραβάλλει ἐπιμεληθῆναι τῆς πόλεως, *Pl. Rep.* 6, 499. Τῶν ζώων τινὰ φύσιν ἔχει τιθασεύεσθαι, *Pl. Pol.* 264, = πέφυκεν. Ἐν ἀπόρῳ εἴχοντο οἱ Ἐπιδάμνιοι θέσθαι τὸ παρόν, *Thuc.* 1. 25. Τοῖς στρατιώταις ὁρμὴ ἐνέπεσεν ἐκτειχίσαι τὸ χωρίον, *Thuc.* 4, 4). Cf. *Genitive of Infinitive*, § 156, R. 1. Πολλοῦ. μικροῦ δέω ποιεῖν τι. Σμικροῦ τινος ἐνδεὴς εἰμι πάντ' ἔχειν (*Pl. Prot.* 329). Βραχὺ ἀπολείπομεν διακόσιοι εἶναι (*Thuc.* 7, 70). Παρὰ μικρὸν ἦλθον ἀποθανεῖν (*Isocr. Ægin.* 22).

Rem. 2. Some verbs denoting a meditating and endeavouring (μηχανῶμαι, φροντίζω), are usually followed by ὅπως (§ 122, 123) or an interrogative sentence (εἴ πως, ὡς ἄν).

Rem. 3. With some of these verbs and phrases ὥστε is now and then prefixed to the infin., the governing verb being conceived more by and for itself. Οἱ Κορίνθιοι εὐθὺς πρῶτοι ἐψηφίσαντο ὥστε πάσῃ προθυμίᾳ ἀμύνειν τοῖς Συρακουσίοις (*Thuc.* 6, 88;

---

[1] Αἰσχύνομαι θεοὺς Κῦρον προδοῦναι (*Xen. An.* 2, 3, 22; *I am ashamed in the presence of the gods, to betray Cyrus*).

[§ 145.] *immediately made a decree, the object of which was —*). Πάνυ μοι ἐμέλησεν ὥστε εἰδέναι, ὁπόσον οἱ πολέμιοι κατεῖχον χωρίον (*Xen. Cyr.* 6, 3, 19; *I have taken much pains in the direction towards*, i. e. *in order to* —). Εἰς ἀνάγκην καθέσταμεν ὥστε κινδυνεύειν (*Isocr. Archid.* 51). (On the insertion of the article, see § 154 b. Rem.)

§ 146. (390) (372) The infinitive stands after the verbs which denote a working upon others in order to move them to an action (such as, *to pray, persuade, instigate, seduce, accustom, command, permit, constrain, counsel, teach*, &c.), or a *forbidding, dissuading, hindering*, to denote the action to which the influence refers; likewise after phrases which have the signification of such a verb: *Οἱ νόμοι οὐκ εἴων ἄλλως ποιεῖν* (*οὐκ εἴων ἡμᾶς ἄλλως ποιεῖν*). *Ἐκέλευσα τὸν κήρυκα περιμεῖναί με. Δέομαι ὑμῶν συγγνώμην μοι ἔχειν. Παραινοῦμέν σοι πείθεσθαι τοῖς βελτίοσιν. Ἐπήρθην* (*felt myself impelled*) *πάλιν γράφειν περὶ ταύτης τῆς ὑποθέσεως* (*Isocr. Phil.* 10). *Εἷς τῶν στρατιωτῶν εἶπε* (*proposed*) *στρατηγοὺς ἑλέσθαι ἄλλους ὡς τάχιστα* (*Xen. An.* 1, 3, 14). *Οἱ Ἕλληνες ἐβόων ἀλλήλοις μὴ θεῖν δρόμῳ, ἀλλ' ἐν τάξει ἕπεσθαι* (*Xen. An.* 1, 8, 19; *called one to another not to* —). *Οἱ ἰατροὶ πάντες ἀπαγορεύουσι τοῖς ἀσθενοῦσι μὴ χρῆσθαι ἐλαίῳ* (*Pl. Prot.* 334. Of *μή*, see *Negations*, § 210). *Τί Φίλιππον κωλύσει βαδίζειν ὅποι βούλεται;* (*Dem.* 1, 12.)—*Περδίκκας προσέφερε λόγους τοῖς ἐπὶ Θρᾴκης Χαλκιδεῦσι ξυναποστῆναι* (*Thuc.* 1, 57; *made overtures to the Ch.*—). *Ψήφισμα εἶπεν ἐν ὑμῖν Ἀριστοφῶν ἑλέσθαι ζητητάς* (*Dem.* 24, 11). *Ἡ πόλις ἐν τῷ παρόντι τοῖς πονηροῖς ἐξουσίαν δίδωσι καὶ λέγειν καὶ ποιεῖν ὅ,τι ἂν βουληθῶσιν* (*Isocr. Antid.* 164). *Οὐκ ἐνδώσομεν πρόφασιν οὐδενὶ κακῷ γενέσθαι* (*Thuc.* 2, 87).

Rem. 1. Besides the verbs which in general have such a signification (among them λέγω, εἶπον, *I tell a person to*), some are more rarely, or in a special and derived signification, thus used, e. g. δίδωμι, ἀποδίδωμι, *allow*, ἐξάγω, *seduce* (ἐπεκλάσθην τῇ γνώμῃ τὰ ὅπλα παραδοῦναι, *Thuc.* 4, 37, *let myself be swayed, was induced* —), ἀγγέλλω τινὶ παρεῖναι (*send a person word to be forthcoming*, συγκαλέσας τοὺς στρατηγοὺς παρεῖναι, *Thuc.* 2, 10), τῷ ναυτικῷ περιαγγέλλω πλεῖν (*send round orders to the fleet to sail*, *Thuc.* 2, 80), παιδεύω τινὰ στρατηγεῖν (*to be commander*), ἐναντιοῦμαί τινι μὴ ποιεῖν τι (*oppose a person's doing something*), &c. On phrases with a substantive in itself capable of governing a genitive, see *Genitive of Infinitive*, § 156, R. 1. On the verbs denoting to *hold back from*, &c., see § 156, R. 3.

Rem. 2. Some of these verbs, especially those denoting a *giving orders* (παραγγέλλω, διακελεύομαι), or a prohibition (ἀπαγορεύω), also take after them a sentence with ὅπως (ὅπως μή): Διακελεύονται τῷ νέῳ, ὅπως, ἐπειδὰν ἀνὴρ γένηται τιμωρήσεται τοὺς ἀδικήσαντας (*Pl. Rep.* 8, 549). Some verbs denoting *instance* (e.g. πείθω, δέομαι) occasionally (Thucyd.) take the infinitive with ὥστε: Οἱ Ἀμπρακιῶται ἐλθόντες πρὸς Εὐρύλοχον πείθουσιν ὥστε μετὰ σφῶν Ἄργει τῷ Ἀμφιλοχικῷ ἐπιχειρῆσαι (*Thuc.* 3, 102). Ἀφίκετο ἐπιστολὴ πρὸς Ἀστύοχον ἐκ Λακεδαίμονος ὥστε ἀποκτεῖναι Ἀλκιβιάδην (*Thuc.* 8, 35; *a letter to*, or, *that he should* —).

The infinitive stands with verbs denoting an opinion or utterance (*v. sentiendi et declarandi*), when this concerns an action or state of the same subject (φημὶ εἶναι, ὑπισχνοῦμαι ἐλεύσεσθαι), and likewise with verbs denoting *to effect* (*v. faciendi*), when the thing effected is an action of the same subject (Γύγης διεπράξατο τῶν ἀγγέλων γενέσθαι τῶν παρὰ βασιλέα, *Pl. Rep.* 2, 360). See the more particular rules under *Accusative with Infinitive*, § 160 and 164. § 147.

The infinitive is added in different ways to some verbs to denote the *intent* of the action: § 148.

a) To the verbs signifying *to elect* or *appoint* a person to do or be something; sometimes even to those which denote *to bring* or *convey to a place* (send, leave behind), or (more rarely), *give*, in order to be or to do something, so that the object-accusative (in the passive the subject-nominative) of the leading verb is the *subject* of the infinitive. (But with the latter verbs, a participle as apposition is more usual, which may also be used with the former sort; see *Participles*.) Οἱ πρόγονοι τὴν ἐξ Ἀρείου πάγου βουλὴν ἐπέστησαν ἐπιμελεῖσθαι τῆς εὐκοσμίας (*Isocr. Areop.* 37). Δῆλον, ὅτι κυβερνᾶν κατασταθεὶς ὁ μὴ ἐπιστάμενος ἀπολέσειεν ἂν οὓς ἥκιστα βούλοιτο (*Xen. Mem.* 1, 7, 3). Καὶ γυναῖκες ἄρα αἱ τοιαῦται τοῖς τοιούτοις ἀνδράσιν ἐκλεκτέαι συνοικεῖν (*Pl. Rep.* 5, 456 = αἵτινες συνοικήσουσιν). Ξενοφῶν τὸ ἥμισυ τοῦ στρατεύματος κατέλιπε φυλάττειν τὸ στρατόπεδον (*Xen. An.* 5, 2, 1). Οἱ Ἀθηναῖοι δέκα τῶν νεῶν προὔπεμψαν ἐς τὸν μέγαν λιμένα (τῶν Συρακουσίων) πλεῦσαί τε καὶ κατασκέψασθαι, εἴ τι ναυτικόν ἐστι καθειλκυσμένον (*Thuc.* 6, 50. More usually πλευσουμένας καὶ κατασκεψομένας). Βοιωτοὶ τοὺς ἱππέας παρείχοντο τοῖς Πελοποννησίοις ξυστρατεύειν (*Thuc.* 2, 12. Usually ξυστρατεύσοντας). (411, R. 2)

Rem. In the poets also with εἶμι, ἥκω, βαίνω, and with εἰμί (*am here to* —): Μανθάνειν ἥκομεν ξένοι πρὸς ἀστῶν (*Soph. Œd. C.* 12). Ποῦ δῆτ' ἀμύνειν οἱ κατὰ στέγας Φρύγες; (*Eur. Orest.* 1473.)

b) To the verbs which denote *to give* (sacrifice, offer), and *take*, in order to do something with or to the object given, &c., so that the object of the governing verb is also the object of the infinitive: Παρέχω ἐμαυτὸν τέμνειν καὶ καίειν (*Pl. Gorg.* 480). Οἱ Φλιάσιοι τὴν πόλιν φυλάττειν τοῖς Λακεδαιμονίοις παρέδωκαν (*Xen. Hell.* 4, 4, 15). Ὅσοι περιῆσαν τῶν Θηβαίων, παρέδοσαν σφᾶς αὐτοὺς τοῖς Πλαταιεῦσι χρήσασθαι ὅ,τι ἂν βούλωνται (*Thuc.* 2, 4; *to do with them as they pleased*). Εἰ βουλοίμεθά τῳ ἐπιτρέψαι παῖδας παιδεῦσαι, ἆρ' ἀξιόπιστον εἰς ταῦτα ἡγησαίμεθ' ἂν τὸν ἀκρατῆ; (*Xen. Mem.* 1, 5, 2.) Ὅταν οἱ τύραννοι τοὺς κοσμίους καὶ δικαίους διὰ τὸν φόβον (422) ὑπεξαιρῶνται, τίνες ἄλλοι αὐτοῖς καταλείπονται χρῆσθαι (*for use*) ἀλλ' ἢ οἱ ἄδικοι καὶ ἀκρατεῖς; (*Xen. Hier.* 5, 2.) (Αἰτῶ πιεῖν, *ask to drink*; αἱ γυναῖκες πιεῖν ἔφερον τοῖς ἀνδράσιν, *Xen. Hell.* 7. 2, 9.)

REM. 1. This infinitive rarely stands in the passive, so that the object of the governing verb is taken as the subject of the infinitive: Μηδείς σε πείσῃ τῷ φαρμάκῳ τούτῳ τὴν αὑτοῦ κεφαλὴν θεραπεύειν, ὃς ἂν μὴ τὴν ψυχὴν πρῶτον παράσχῃ τῇ ἐπῳδῇ ὑπὸ σοῦ θεραπευθῆναι (*Pl. Charm.* 157).

REM. 2. Poetical; Στέφεα δίδοτε, φέρετε· πλόκαμος ὅδε καταστέφειν (*Eur. Iph. Aul.* 1478, viz. ἐστίν: *here is my hair to crown, to be crowned*).

REM. 3. Now and then an infinitive stands with the verbs *give, have, am here*, in the sense *to do something with* (as instrument, means), *do something on*, or *in*, &c.: Οἱ στρατιῶται οὐκ εἶχον ἀργύριον ἐπισιτίζεσθαι (*Xen. An.* 7, 1, 7). Ἀριστάρχῳ ἔδοτε ἡμέραν ἀπολογήσασθαι (*Xen. Hell.* 1, 7. 28). Ἐκεῖ σκιά τ' ἐστὶ καὶ πόα καθίζεσθαι ἤ, ἐὰν βουλώμεθα, κατακλιθῆναι (*Pl. Phæd.* 229). Especially the infinitive of an intransitive verb compounded with ἐν is often thus used, to denote that something is given up (is there, &c.) in order that something may be done *thereon* (as object), *therein* (as place): Οὐ πάνυ δέδοκται ἐμαυτόν σοι ἐμμελετᾶν παρέχειν (*Pl. Phæd.* 228). Τὰ τῶν Ἑλλήνων ἀτυχήματα Αἰσχίνῃ ἐνευδοκιμεῖν ἀπέκειτο (*Dem.* 18, 198).

The infinitive stands with adjectives denoting ability, cleverness, and capacity, or forwardness and readiness *for* something, excellence *in* something, or the contrary, and with ἄξιος and ἀνάξιος, to define the adjective more nearly (as with the verbs enumerated § 145, so that the subject of the adjective is also that of the infinitive): Θεμιστοκλῆς ἱκανώτατος ἦν εἰπεῖν καὶ γνῶναι καὶ πρᾶξαι (*Lys.* 2, 48). Τούτου μεῖζον ἀγαθὸν σωφροσύνη οὐ δυνατὴ πορίσαι ἀνθρώπῳ (*Pl. Phæd.* 256). Ἆρα δυνατὴ αὕτη ἡ πολιτεία γενέσθαι; (*Pl. Rep.* 5, 471.) Ὁ δῆμος τὸν Εὔφραιον ἐπιτήδειον εἶναι ταῦτα παθεῖν ἔφη (*Dem.* 9, 61; *was fit to be so treated*, i. e. *deserved*—). Ταπεινὴ ὑμῶν ἡ διάνοια ἐγκαρτερεῖν, ἃ ἔγνωτε (*Thuc.* 2, 61). Μαλακὸς καρτερεῖν πρὸς ἡδονάς τε καὶ λύπας (*Pl. Rep.* 8, 556). Τὴν βουλὴν κυρίαν ἐποίησαν τῆς εὐταξίας ἐπιμελεῖσθαι (*Isocr. Areop.* 39).—Ἑτοῖμοι ἦσαν πάντα κίνδῡνον ὑπομένειν. Οὐ πρόθῡμός με εἶ διδάξαι (*Pl. Euthyph.* 14).—Ἀνὴρ δεινὸς λέγειν. Αἱ εὐπραξίαι δειναὶ συγκρύψαι τὰ τοιαῦτα ὀνείδη (*Dem.* 2, 20). Πιθανώτατος λέγειν (*Pl. Gorg.* 479).—Ἄξιός εἰμι πληγὰς λαβεῖν (*Arist. Eccl.* 324). Ἡ πόλις ἀξία ἐστὶ θαυμάζεσθαι (*Thuc.* 2, 40). Ἀνάξιος τιμᾶσθαι.

REM. With the adjectives which denote, not absolutely a capacity but a quality which comes into consideration on occasion of the action, we have also ὥστε, *so as to* e. g. Πότερα παῖδές εἰσι φρονιμώτεροι ὥστε μαθεῖν τὰ φραζόμενα καὶ δεικνύμενα ἢ ἄνδρες; (*Xen. Cyr.* 4, 3, 11.) Ὀλίγοι ἐσμὲν ἀμύνειν (*Thuc.* 1, 50), and ὀλίγοι ἐσμὲν ὥστε ἐγκρατεῖς εἶναι τῶν ἀγαθῶν (*Xen. Cyr.* 4. 5, 15). Also sometimes ἱκανός is followed by ὥστε. Ἄξιος has also an active infinitive in the same sense as the passive, by § 150 a: Ἄξιος θαυμάσαι (*Thuc.* 1, 138). (Ἀνάξια ἡ βουλὴ πεποίηκε τοῦ στεφανωθῆναι, *Dem.* 22, 36, by § 156.)

a) An infinitive (active in form or signification) stands with adjectives, to denote that the quality is ascribed to its subject in reference § 150. (412)
to a certain action conceived as performed upon (and taking place, or going on in) the subject (so that the subject of the adjective is conceived as the object of the infinitive, or as the dative with those verbs which govern this case): Χρῆσθαι τοῖς ῥᾴστοις ἐντυγχάνειν (*Xen. Mem.* 1, 6, 9; *what is easiest to meet with*). Ἀνὴρ χαλεπὸς συζῆν (*Pl. Pol.* 302). Λόγοι ἐμοὶ μὲν ἀναγκαιότατοι προειπεῖν, ὑμῖν δὲ χρησιμώτατοι ἀκοῦσαι (*Dem.* 21, 24). Καλὸς (αἰσχρὸς) ὁρᾶν, ἰδεῖν (*to behold*). Λόγος δυνατὸς κατανοῆσαι (*Pl. Phæd.* 90). Οἰκία ἡδίστη ἐνδιαιτᾶσθαι (*Xen. Mem.* 3, 3, 8; *to live in.* So very often the infinitive of verbs compounded with ἐν).

Rem. 1. A passive infinitive is rarely used here (so that the subject of the adj. would also be taken as the subject of the infinitive): Κύνες ἄμορφοι καὶ αἰσχραὶ ὁρᾶσθαι (*Xen. Cyneg.* 3, 3).

Rem. 2. In the same manner an infinitive (especially ἀκούειν, ἀκοῦσαι, ὁρᾶν, ἰδεῖν) is sometimes added to intransitive verbs and phrases denoting a quality: Ἀκοῦσαι οὑτωσὶ παγκάλως ἔχει τὸ ψήφισμα (*Dem.* 19, 47). Οὐδὲν οὗτοι διαφέρουσιν ἰδεῖν χαλκέως φαλακροῦ καὶ σμικροῦ (*Pl. Rep.* 6, 495). (Πράγματα οἱ ἵπποι παρέξουσιν ἐπιμέλεσθαι, *Xen. Cyr.* 4, 5, 46, *will give trouble*, i. e. *will be troublesome, to attend to.* Ἡ στρατιά, πολλὴ οὖσα, οὐ πάσης ἔσται πόλεως ὑποδέξασθαι, *not one for every city to receive. Thuc.* 6, 22.)

b) Sometimes the infinitive with the adjective denotes a reference to the action of a different subject, which action is conceived as going on, not upon the subject of the adj. as its object, but *in*, *with*, or *at* the same (as *place, instrument, material*, &c.), especially with adjectives denoting *qualified, adapted*, or *sufficient*, or when the *degree* of the quality is mentioned in reference to the action: Ὁ χρόνος βραχὺς ἀξίως διηγήσασθαι τὰ πραχθέντα (*Pl. Menex.* 239). Ἡ ὁδὸς ἡ εἰς ἄστυ ἐπιτηδεία πορευομένοις καὶ λέγειν καὶ ἀκούειν (*Pl. Conv.* 173). Πότερον λούσασθαι ψυχρότερον τὸ παρὰ σοὶ ὕδωρ ἢ τὸ ἐν Ἀμφιαράου; (*Xen. Mem.* 3, 13, 3; *to bathe in*[1].) (Also: Ψυχρὸν τὸ ὕδωρ ὥστε λούσασθαι, *Xen.* ibid.) (Ὁ αὐτὸς χρόνος ἀρκεῖ ἑνί τε μέρει καὶ πᾶσι πεποιῆσθαι τὰ ἐπιτήδεια, *Xen. Cyr.* 8, 5, 5, *for the provisions to be prepared.*)

c) After a comparative with ἤ, the infinitive stands in the sense *too* (*great*, &c.) *to.*—The infinitive may not only be referred, either actively or passively, to the subject of the adjective (as in English

[1] But ibid.: πότερον τὸ παρὰ σοὶ ὕδωρ θερμότερον πιεῖν ἢ τὸ ἐν Ἀσκληπίου; (*to drink*; by *a*.)

[§ 150.] *too weak to go*, i. e. than that he could go; *too heavy to bear*, i. e. than that it could be borne), but also (by *b*) so that the subject of the adj. is neither subject nor direct object of the infinitive: Ἡ ἀνθρωπίνη φύσις ἀσθενεστέρα ἐστὶν ἢ λαβεῖν τέχνην ὧν ἂν ᾖ ἄπειρος (*Pl. Theæt.* 149). Τὸ νόσημα μεῖζον ἢ φέρειν (*Soph. Œd. R.* 1293). The infinitive may take ὥςτε: Οἱ Λακεδαιμόνιοι ᾔσθοντο Ἔκδικον ἐλάττω δύναμιν ἔχοντα ἢ ὥςτε τοὺς φίλους ὠφελεῖν (*Xen. Hell.* 4, 8, 23). Φοβοῦμαι, μή τι μεῖζον ἢ ὥςτε φέρειν δύνασθαι κακὸν τῇ πόλει συμβῇ (*Xen. Mem.* 3, 5, 17). (Also ὡς, § 166 c. R. 2.)

§ 151. An active infinitive with ὡς (more strongly ὥς γε) is prefixed to an infinitive for limitation, to denote the reference to a certain manner of treating the thing, or a certain intention; in general, a certain measure in relation to which the predicate is spoken (*if we confine ourselves to this —, if the question be about this*, &c.). It is not required, that the infinitive itself should have the given subject as its subj. or obj., but this may happen: Οἱ πολέμιοι ἄοπλοί εἰσιν ὡς ἐκ χειρὸς μάχεσθαι (*Xen. Cyr.* 6, 4, 16). Οὗτοι οἱ ἄνθρωποι ἀτοπώτατοί τινές εἰσιν, ὥς γ' ἐν φιλοσόφοις τιθέναι (*Pl. Rep.* 5, 475; *when one speaks of reckoning them among the philosophers*). Εὖ λέγει ὁ ἀνὴρ ὥς γε οὑτωσὶ ἀκοῦσαι (*Pl. Euthyph.* 3, *to listen to in this way*). Ταῦτ' οὖν, ὡς ὑπομνῆσαι, νῦν ἱκανῶς εἴρηται (*Dem.* 6. 37). (Ὡς ἐπὶ πᾶν εἰπεῖν, *Pl. Euthyd.* 279, *to speak generally*, ὡς πρὸς ὑμᾶς εἰρῆσθαι, *Pl. Rep.* 10, 595, *to be spoken merely to you*, i. e. *speaking between ourselves*; ὡς ἔπος εἰπεῖν, also simply ὡς εἰπεῖν, *so to say*, ὡς ἁπλῶς εἰπεῖν, ὡς συνελόντι εἰπεῖν, cf. § 38 c, *to speak it briefly*.) Οὐδ' ἐγὼ ψέγω τούτους τοὺς ἄνδρας, ὥς γε διακόνους εἶναι πόλεως (*Pl. Gorg.* 517, *when the question relates to their being servants of a state; considered as servants of —*).

Rem. 1. With ἀκούειν and especially εἰπεῖν in certain current expressions ὡς may be dropt, more rarely with other infinitives: Ἐς τὸ ἀκριβὲς εἰπεῖν (ἀκριβῶς εἰπεῖν), οὐδὲ ἀδίκως κατεστρεψάμεθα τοὺς Ἴωνας (*Thuc.* 6, 82; *strictly speaking*). (Σὺν θεῷ εἰπεῖν, *in God's name*; σχεδὸν εἰπεῖν, *so to say, almost*.) (Cf. § 168 b.)

Rem. 2. The infinitive εἶναι stands in a restrictive sense with the adj. ἑκών in negative sentences (*to be willing*, i.e. *at least willingly*), rarely in affirmative sentences (= *and that willingly*): Οὐκ ᾤμην ὑπὸ σοῦ ἑκόντος εἶναι ἐξαπατηθήσεσθαι (*Pl. Gorg.* 499). In the same manner εἶναι stands with certain constructions of a preposition with a case, or of the article with an adverb, which are used in a limiting and restrictive sense; thus, κατὰ δύναμιν (εἰς δύναμιν) εἶναι, *according to one's ability*, τὸ κατὰ τοῦτον εἶναι, *as far as concerns him, as far as depends on him*, τὸ ἐπ' ἐκείνοις εἶναι, *so far as is in their power*, τὸ νῦν εἶναι, τὸ τήμερον εἶναι, *for to-day*. (Ὠμόσαμεν εὖ ποιεῖν ἀλλήλους ἐκ τοῦ ἐπιλοίπου χρόνου, κατὰ δύναμιν εἶναι, καὶ λόγῳ καὶ ἔργῳ, *Isæ.* 2, 32.)

§ 152. The infinitive is used with ὥςτε (οὕτως ὥςτε, *so that*), to denote the way and manner (degree) and consequence of the principal sentence, and with ἐφ' ᾧτε (*on condition that*, or *to —*). See *Accus. with Infinitive*,

§ 166, and ibid. of the infinitive with *οἷος* for *τοιοῦτος ὥστε*. Likewise the infinitive stands with *πρίν, before*; see *Accus. with Inf.* § 167.

Now and then an infinitive may be said to stand *extra structuram*, the object which should be governed by the infinitive, being immediately attached to the verb or phrase on which the infinitive should depend, while yet the infin., for the sake of clearness and precision, is brought in immediately afterwards, in order to assign the action (upon the object) more nearly (suppletory infinitive): Οὐδ' ἐπιθυμία σε ἄλλης πόλεως οὐδ' ἄλλων νόμων ἔλαβεν εἰδέναι (*Pl. Criton* 52 = Οὐδ' ἐπ. σ' ἔλαβεν ἄλλην πόλιν εἰδέναι). Οἱ Ἀθηναῖοι τῆς θαλάσσης εἶργον μὴ χρῆσθαι τοὺς Μιτυληναίους (*Thuc.* 3, 3 = εἶργον τοὺς Μιτ. μὴ χρ. τῇ θαλάσσῃ). Ἀριστείδης κύριος τῶν φόρων ἐγένετο τάξαι (*Dem.* 23, 209). Εὐθὺς ἀρχόμενοι τῆς πόλεως οἰκίζειν κατὰ θεόν τινα εἰς τύπον τινὰ τῆς δικαιοσύνης κινδυνεύομεν ἐμβεβηκέναι (*Pl. Rep.* 4, 443, *when we began with our city, to construct it* = ἀρχόμενοι οἰκίζειν τὴν πόλιν).[1]

Rem. On the infinitive instead of the imperative, see § 141, R. 2.

a) *With the article*, the infinitive (apart from its nominative, of which see § 144) stands also as a substantive member of the sentence, and so that the action thereby denoted is to be conceived as predicate in reference to the subject or object of the sentence, or to a subject implied in the context. Such a substantive infinitive cannot, however, agreeably with the nature of its notion and the Greek idiom, enter into all the relations in which the cases of an actual substantive can be used.

Rem. The accessory terms belonging to an inf. with the article are inserted between the article and the infinitive (τὸ τοὺς εὐηργετηκότας ἀεὶ καὶ παντὶ τρόπῳ ἀντευεργετεῖν) or follow after the infinitive (τὸ ζῆν ἡδέως).

b) The *accusative of the infinitive* occurs (besides where it stands as the subject in the *accus. c. infin.*) sometimes as the object of transitive verbs (where a corresponding verbal substantive is either wanting, or the notion of the action, as taking place singly and by itself, is not so clearly expressed, or does not so well suit the form of the sentence in other respects): Τὸ τελευτῆσαι πάντων ἡ πεπρωμένη κατέκρινεν, τὸ δὲ καλῶς ἀποθανεῖν ἴδιον τοῖς σπουδαίοις ἡ φύσις ἀπένειμεν (*Isocr. Dem.* 43). Πειρῶ κατεργάσασθαι ὡς μάλιστα τὸ εἰδέναι, ἃ βούλει πράττειν (*Xen. Mem.* 3, 6, 18). Εἰ τὸ κωλῦσαι τὴν τῶν Ἑλλήνων κοινωνίαν ἐπεπράκειν ἐγὼ Φιλίππῳ, σοὶ τὸ μὴ σιγῆσαι λοιπὸν ἦν, ἀλλὰ δηλοῦν τῷ δήμῳ (*Dem.* 18, 23).

Rem. Now and then the article is found with the inf. after the verbs and adjectives with *εἰμί* described in §§ 145, 146, 147, and 149, in order to give special prominence to the notion as opposed to others, or as already mentioned; often so that the infinitive is emphatically put foremost in the sentence (almost as if it

---

[1] Even more harshly: Ἀθηναῖοι μαχούμενοι ἐχώρουν περί τε τῆς ἀλλοτρίας, οἰκείαν σχεῖν, καὶ τὴν οἰκείαν μὴ βλάψαι ἡσσώμενοι (*Thuc.* 6, 69 = περί τε τοῦ τὴν ἀλλοτρίαν οἰκείαν σχεῖν καὶ τὴν οἰκείαν μὴ βλάψαι ἡσσώμενοι. Literally: *both for the foreign land, to win it for themselves, as also not, by sustaining a defeat, to injure their own*).

[§ 154.] were, *as regards the*): Τὸ δ' αὖ ξυνοικεῖν τῇδ' ὁμοῦ τίς ἂν γυνὴ δύναιτο; (*Soph. Trach.* 545.) Καὶ πῶς δή, ἔφη ὁ Σωκράτης, τὸ ἀρχικοὺς εἶναι ἀνθρώπων παιδεύεις αὐτούς; (*Xen. Œcon.* 13, 4; the notion has already occurred in the context.) Τὸ προσταλαιπωρεῖν τῷ δόξαντι καλῷ οὐδεὶς πρόθυμος ἦν (*Thuc.* 2, 53).

c) Further, the accusative of the infinitive stands with the prepositions, διά, *by means of*, ἐπί and πρός, *to* (of goal and object), εἰς and κατά, *in reference to*, παρά, *in comparison with*: Διὰ τὸ ξένος εἶναι οὐκ ἂν οἴει ἀδικηθῆναι; (*Xen. Mem.* 2, 1, 15.) Πρὸς τὸ μετρίων δεῖσθαι καλῶς πεπαίδευμαι (*Xen. Mem.* 1, 2, 1). Κῦρος πάντων τῶν ἡλίκων διαφέρων ἐφαίνετο εἰς τὸ ταχὺ μανθάνειν ἃ δέοι (*Xen. Cyr.* 1, 3, 1).

REM. On the infinitive preceded by τὸ μή in certain verbs and phrases, see § 156, R. 4.

§ 155. (415, 416) The *dative of the infinitive* may be governed by certain verbs and adjectives (as πιστεύω, ἔοικα, ὅμοιος, ἐναντίος) and by the prepositions ἐν, ἐπί, and πρός (*besides, in addition to*); often it stands also as dative of the means, the cause, or the relation (*by means of, in consequence of, for*): Πιστεύω τῷ κοσμίως ζῆν (*Isocr. Antid.* 24). Ἐν τῷ πολίτην ποιεῖσθαι Χαρίδημον ταῦτ' ἀμφότερα ἐνῆν (*Dem.* 23, 188; *each of these was involved*). Σωκράτης ἐθαυμάζετο ἐπὶ τῷ εὐθύμως ζῆν (*Xen. Mem.* 4, 8, 2). Οἱ ἐν τοῖς ὅπλοις μάχεσθαι διδάσκοντες τὴν τέχνην παραδιδόασι ἐπὶ τῷ δικαίως χρῆσθαι αὐτῇ πρὸς τοὺς πολεμίους (*Pl. Gorg.* 456; *thereunto that they should* —, = *upon condition*, or, *on the understanding that* —): Πρὸς τῷ μηδὲν ἐκ τῆς πρεσβείας λαβεῖν τοὺς αἰχμαλώτους ἐκ τῶν ἰδίων ἐλυσάμην (*Dem.* 19, 229). Σωκράτης τῷ φανερὸς εἶναι καλὸς καὶ ἀγαθὸς ὢν ἐλπίζειν ἐποίει τοὺς συνδιατρίβοντας ἑαυτῷ, μιμουμένους ἐκεῖνον τοιούςδε γενήσεσθαι (*Xen. Mem.* 1, 2, 3). Αἱ καλῶς πολιτευόμεναι δημοκρατίαι προέχουσι τῷ δικαιότεραι εἶναι (*Dem.*).

§ 156. (417) The *genitive of the infinitive* stands as an *objective* genitive with substantives, verbs, adjectives, and adverbs, and with the prepositions ἄνευ, ἀντί, διά, ἐξ, ἕνεκα, ὑπέρ, μετά, περί, πρό, and with several of the adverbs which are used as prepositions (ἐμποδών, ἔξω, μέχρι, πλήν, πόῤῥω, χωρίς), lastly, as definitive genitive (§ 49 a): Οἱ Ἀθηναῖοι ἠπείγοντο πρὸς τὸν ποταμὸν τοῦ πιεῖν ἐπιθυμίᾳ (*Thuc.* 7, 84). Τὸ εὖ πράττειν παρὰ τὴν ἀξίαν ἀφορμὴ τοῦ κακῶς φρονεῖν τοῖς ἀνοήτοις γίγνεται (*Dem.* 1, 23). Πόνους τοῦ ζῆν ἡδέως ἡγεμόνας νομίζετε (*Xen. Cyr.* 1, 5, 12). Ἀήθης τοῦ κατακούειν τινός (*Dem.* 1, 23). Ἐπιμελοῦμαι τοῦ ὡς φρονιμώτατος εἶναι (*Xen. Mem.* 1, 2, 55). Ἐπέσχομεν τοῦ δακρύειν (*Pl. Phæd.* 117, *stopped from* —). Οἱ ἔμποροι τὰ πελάγη διαπερῶσιν ἕνεκα τοῦ πλείω ποιῆσαι τὴν ὑπάρχουσαν οὐσίαν (*Isocr. Dem.* 19). (Ἄνευ τοῦ εὐφραίνειν, *besides giving pleasure* —, ἀντὶ τοῦ ἀποκρίνεσθαι, ἐκ τοῦ ταῦτα γνῶναι, *in consequence of knowing this* —, ὑπὲρ τοῦ μὴ ποιεῖν τὸ *προσταττόμενον, for the sake of having no orders to execute* —, *μετὰ τοῦ προσοφλεῖν αἰσχύνην, along with the incurring a disgrace, so that one incurs a disgrace withal* —. [§ 156.] *περὶ τοῦ τιμωρεῖσθαι Φίλιππον ἡ ἀρχὴ τοῦ πολέμου ἦν* —. *Φίλιππος ὅσα προλάβοι πρὸ τοῦ τοὺς ὅρκους ἀποδοῦναι, βεβαίως ἕξειν ἐνόμιζεν, Dem.* 18, 26. — *ἔξω εἶναι τοῦ κακῶς πάσχειν* — &c.)

Rem. 1. When a substantive with a verb (as subject with *ἐστίν, γίγνεται*, or as object with a transitive verb, or as case to a preposition with an intransitive or passive verb) forms a phrase which corresponds with, or in point of signification approximates to, one or other of the verbs mentioned in §§ 145, 146, it is followed, as a general rule, by a simple infinitive, see § 145, R. 1; moreover, *σχολὴν διδόναι* or *ἀσχολίαν παρέχειν τινὶ ποιεῖν τι, ἄδειαν, ἐξουσίαν διδόναι, ἀσφάλειαν ποιεῖν, πρόφασιν παρέχειν τινὶ ποιεῖν τι*, &c.), and but rarely the genitive (*παράδειγμα ἔσται τοῦ μὴ ὑμᾶς ἀδικεῖν, Lys.* 27, 5, but shortly afterwards (§ 6) *παράδειγμα ποιήσετε τοῖς ἄλλοις δικαίοις εἶναι*). The poets go still further in the use of the simple infinitive instead of the genitive: *Φόβῳ δ', ἃ μὴ χρῆν, εἰσορᾶν καθήμεθα σιγῇ* (*Eur. Iph. T.* 1342, *from fear of seeing*). (417, R. 2)

Rem. 2. In some few verbs the usage is undecided between the simple infinitive by § 145 and the genitive of the infinitive, e. g. *ἀμελῶ* (*ἠμέλησεν ἐρωτᾶν τὸν θεόν* and *ἠμέλησα τοῦ ὀργίζεσθαί σοι*). But with the rest of the verbs which in point of signification come under § 145 (*ἐπιθυμῶ, μέμνημαι, ἐπιλανθάνομαι, πολλοῦ, μικροῦ δέω*), the simple genitive is almost exclusively used. (Ἐπιμελοῦμαι τοῦ εἶναι and ὅπως ὦ, § 123.)

Rem. 3. Especially note the interchangeable idiom with verbs denoting *to restrain, exclude, withdraw, deliver*, and sometimes *escape from* (*ἐκφεύγειν*), and with some kindred phrases (e. g. *ἐν ἀδείᾳ, ἐν ἀσφαλεῖ εἶναι*, especially *ἐμποδὼν εἶναι*). These take either the simple infinitive (by § 146) or its genitive; both, either in the affirmative form, or with *μή* prefixed, the idiom of the language being such, that the negative notion of the verb (e. g. *restrain* = *not* allow) is repeated with the infinitive; see *Negations*, § 210, with R. 1. *a*) *Ἄλλως πως πορίζεσθαι τὰ ἐπιτήδεια ἢ ὠνουμένους ὅρκοι ἤδη κατέχουσιν ἡμᾶς* (*Xen. An.* 3, 1, 20). Οὐδενὶ *ἐμποδὼν γενήσομαι λαβεῖν τὸ διδόμενον ὑπὸ τῆς πόλεως* (*Isocr. Antid.* 152). — *b*) Αἰδὼς *τοὺς νεωτέρους τῶν πρεσβυτέρων μὴ ἅπτεσθαι εἴρξει* (*Pl. Rep.* 5, 465). Ὁ Ἀλκιβιάδης *ἐμποδὼν ἦν αὐτοῖς μὴ τοῦ δήμου βεβαίως προεστάναι* (*Thuc.* 6, 28). — *c*) Τοῦ *δραπετεύειν δεσμοῖς οἱ δεσπόται τοὺς οἰκέτας εἴργουσιν* (*Xen. An.* 2, 1, 16). Τὸ *ψευδόμενον φαίνεσθαι τοῦ συγγνώμης τινὸς τυγχάνειν ἐμποδὼν μάλιστα ἀνθρώποις γίγνεται* (*Xen. Cyr.* 3, 1, 9). — *d*) Ὁ *ἀσκὸς δύο ἄνδρας ἕξει τοῦ μὴ καταδῦναι* (*Xen. An.* 3, 5, 11). Ἐμποδών *τι ἐγένετο τοῦ μὴ εὐθὺς τότε δικάσασθαι* (*Dem.* 33, 25). Ἡ *πόλις μικρὸν ἀπέλιπε τοῦ μὴ ταῖς ἐσχάταις συμφοραῖς περιπεσεῖν* (*Isocr. Antid.* 122). (To the simple infinitive sometimes *ὥστε* is prefixed: Οἱ Ἀθηναῖοι *τὸ πρῶτον ἀπείχοντο ὥστε μὴ ἐμβάλλειν τινί. Thuc.* 1, 49.)[1]

Rem. 4. Verbs of *withholding, restraining*, occasionally in affirmative sentences take the accusative of the infinitive with *μή* (*τὸ μή*), so that the action hindered or forborne may be said to stand loosely in the sentence (almost = *so that — not*): Οἱ Ἀθηναῖοι *ἱππεῖς τὸν πλεῖστον ὅμιλον τῶν ψιλῶν εἶργον τὸ μὴ προεξιόντας τῶν ὅπλων* (= *τοῦ στρατοπέδου*) *τὰ ἐγγὺς τῆς πόλεως κακουργεῖν* (*Thuc.* 3, 1). Such

---

[1] Κωλύω, with its compounds, very rarely takes the genitive of the infin.

[§ 156.] an infinitive with τὸ μή is added even to verbs and phrases in themselves incapable of taking an infinitive, but which denote a *hindering* or *forbearing*, in order to assign an action forborne: Κίμωνα Ἀθηναῖοι παρὰ τρεῖς ἀφεῖσαν ψήφους τὸ μὴ θανάτῳ ζημιῶσαι (*Dem.* 23, 205; *acquitted him by three votes so as not to condemn him*). Lastly, the infinitive with τὸ μή and τὸ μὴ οὐ (to cancel the preceding negation, see *Negations*, § 211), is frequently put after a negation of a leading verb (or phrase) denoting to *withhold, hinder, forbear, omit* or *deny, prove that — not*, to denote the action which is not forborne, &c., even when the verb or the phrase is not capable of taking the infinitive or its accusative: Ἐμπεσόντος ὕστερον λόγου, ὅτι λυσιτελέστερον ἡ ἀδικία τῆς δικαιοσύνης, οὐκ ἀπεσχόμην τὸ μὴ οὐκ ἐπὶ τοῦτο ἐλθεῖν ἀπ' ἐκείνου, ὃ πρότερον ἐσκοποῦμεν (*Pl. Rep.* 1, 354). Οὐδὲν τοὺς γέροντας ἐπιλύεται ἡ ἡλικία τὸ μὴ οὐχὶ ἀγανακτεῖν τῇ παρούσῃ τύχῃ (*Pl. Crito*, 43). Τίς Μήδων ἢ νέος ἢ γέρων σοῦ ἀπελείφθη τὸ μή σοι ἀκολουθεῖν; (*Xen. Cyr.* 5, 1, 25; *so that he did not follow thee?*) Οὐδ' ἄρνησίς ἐστιν αὐτοῖς τὸ μὴ ταῦθ' ὑπὲρ Φιλίππου πράττειν (*Dem.* 19, 163. *They cannot deny but that they act in Philip's interest*). Ὁ Ἰσμηνίας ἀπελογεῖτο μέν, οὐ μέντοι ἔπειθέ γε τὸ μὴ οὐ μεγαλοπράγμων τε καὶ κακοπράγμων εἶναι (*Xen. Hell.* 5, 2, 36).

REM. 5. On the genitive of the infinitive in the sense of ἕνεκα, see § 170 c. R.

§ 157. Sometimes a notion is represented first by a demonstrative pronoun, especially τοῦτο (αὐτὸ τοῦτο, with addition of an adjective, τοῦτο μόνον, sometimes of a substantive, τοῦτο τὸ πάθος), and then more closely defined by an infinitive [*epexegetical infin.*] as apposition to the pronoun, with or without the article, according as the latter would be required or not, if the infinitive were attached immediately to the governing word; the article, therefore, is almost always used where the pronoun is dative or genitive: Δεῖ καὶ τοῦτο προθυμηθῆναι σὴν χάριν, ἀποδεῖξαι, πῇ δυνατὸν ταῦτα γίγνεσθαι (*Pl. Rep.* 5, 472). (Ἐκέλευσα τοῦτο μόνον ὁρᾶν πάντας τοὺς στρατιώτας, τῷ πρόσθεν ἕπεσθαι, *Xen. Cyr.* 2, 2, 8, referred to ἐκέλευσα.) Ὅσοι ἀνδράποδα πολλὰ κέκτηνται, τοῦτό γε προσόμοιον ἔχουσι τοῖς τυράννοις, τὸ πολλῶν ἄρχειν (*Pl. Rep.* 9, 578). Δοκεῖ μοι τούτῳ διαφέρειν ἀνὴρ τῶν ἄλλων ζώων, τῷ τιμῆς ὀρέγεσθαι (*Xen. Hier.* 7, 3). Τί τούτου μακαριώτερον τοῦ γῇ μιχθῆναι; (*Xen. Cyr.* 8, 7, 25.) (But Ἆρα τοῦδε ἐπιθυμεῖτε, ἐν τῷ αὐτῷ γενέσθαι τόπῳ; *Pl. Conv.* 192, after ἐπιθυμῶ γενέσθαι.) In the poets the article is sometimes omitted, contrary to the rule. (Τάδε ποιοῦντες δυοῖν ἀγαθοῖν οὐ στερήσομεν τὴν Σικελίαν, Ἀθηναίων τε ἀπαλλαγῆναι καὶ οἰκείου πολέμου, *Thuc.* 464.)

a) An adjective, participle, or substantive which, as predicate-noun or as apposition belongs to an infinitive with or without the article, stands in the accusative, when the infinitive is not referred by the governing verb (or phrase) to a definite grammatical subject: Κρεῖττόν ἐστι σὺν πολλοῖς οἰκοῦντα ἀσφαλῶς τἀρκοῦντα ἔχειν ἢ μόνον διαιτώμενον ἐπικινδύνως πάντα κεκτῆσθαι (*Xen. Mem.* 2, 3, 2). Τὰ τοιαῦτα ἔξεστιν ἀριθμήσαντας ἢ μετρήσαντας εἰδέναι (*Xen. Mem.* 1, 1, 9. *Such things as these one can get to know by counting or measuring them*).

§ 158. (393) *b*) If, on the other hand, the infinitive is referred to a definite substantive word in the sentence, as its subject, then the predicate-noun or the apposition always conforms itself to the case of that word, if it be nominative or accusative, usually also if it be dative: but in the

[PART II.

last case the accusative also is used, especially of a (predicative) apposition, e. g. a participle (*ἔξεστιν ἡμῖν ἀπιέναι τὰ ὅπλα ἔχοντας*). After a genitive, the predicate with *εἶναι* or *γίγνεσθαι* usually stands in the genitive (after the genitive of a participle of a verb *declarandi* or *sentiendi* always so), but an apposition appended to the infinitive stands in the accusative. 1) (Nominative): *Ἐψηφίσασθε ἐξελθεῖν βοηθήσοντες. Οὐδέν ἐστιν ὄνειδος, ὅτουποῤῥωτέρω ἐστὶν ἡ πόλις ἡμῶν ἢ τοῦ φθονερὰ δοκεῖν εἶναι* (*Dem.* 20, 140). *Ἀντὶ τοῦ ἐπελθεῖν αὐτοὶ ἀμύνεσθαι βούλεσθε μᾶλλον ἐπιόντας* (*Thuc.* 1, 69). *Σκεπτέον, ὅπως μὴ Φίλιππος τὴν τοῦ φίλος τοῖς Ἕλλησιν εἶναι πίστιν λήψεται* (*Dem.* 14, 7). *Τιμόθεος τῷ ἤθει τὴν εὔνοιαν τὴν τῶν ἀνθρώπων προσήγετο, νομίζων τοῦτο μεῖζον στρατήγημα εἶναι ἢ πολλάκις νικῆσαι μαχόμενος* (*Isocr. Antid.* 122. The nominative referred to the leading verb, notwithstanding the intervening *τοῦτο μεῖζον στρατήγημα εἶναι*). — 2) (Dative): *Εὐδαίμοσιν ὑμῖν ἔξεστι γίγνεσθαι* (*Dem.* 3, 23). *Οὐκ ἐνδώσομεν πρόφασιν οὐδενὶ κακῷ γενέσθαι* (*Thuc.* 2, 87). *Κῦρος ἀνεγέλασεν ἐπὶ τῷ κρείττονι τοῦ ἔρωτος φάσκοντι εἶναι* (*Xen. Cyr.* 6, 1, 34). *Συνέβη τῷ Χαβρίᾳ ἐκπλεῖν μίαν ναῦν ἔχοντι* (*Dem.* 23, 171). *Τίμιόν ἐστι πᾶσιν ἀνθρώποις τὸ γενέσθαι πολίταις παρ' ὑμῖν* (*Dem.* 23, 200). (Even without a dative expressly preceding, but with reference to a subject in the dative to be mentally supplied: *Μεγάλων εὐεργεσιῶν οὐκ ἴσως ῥᾴδιον αἰτίῳ γενέσθαι*, *Dem.* 20, 121.) — 3) (Accusative for dative): *Σοί, ὦ Ταναοξάρη, σατράπην εἶναι δίδωμι Μήδων τε καὶ Ἀσσυρίων* (*Xen. Cyr.* 8, 7, 11. Examples of this kind with the predicate to *εἶναι* in the accusative, are rare). *Ἔξεστιν ὑμῖν, εἰ βούλεσθε, λαβόντας ὅπλα, οἷάπερ ἡμεῖς ἔχομεν, εἰς τὸν αὐτὸν ἐμβαίνειν κίνδυνον* (*Xen. Cyr.* 2, 1, 15). *Οὐ προσήκει ὑμῖν τῆς τῶν Θηβαίων πόλεως πλείω ποιήσασθαι λόγον ἢ τῶν συνθηκῶν, ἐνθυμουμένους, ὡς οὐ τοὺς κινδύνους, ἀλλὰ τὰς ἀδοξίας φοβεῖσθαι πάτριον ὑμῖν ἐστιν* (*Isocr. Plat.* 39). (*Ἀνάγκη μοι ἦν δυοῖν θάτερον ἑλέσθαι, ἢ μὴ βουληθέντι κατειπεῖν τοὺς ταῦτα ποιήσαντας καὶ περὶ ἐμοῦ καὶ περὶ τοῦ πατρὸς ὀῤῥωδεῖν, ἢ κατειπόντι τὰ γεγενημένα αὐτὸν μὲν ἀφεθέντα μὴ τεθνάναι, τοῦ δὲ πατρὸς μὴ φονέα γενέσθαι*, *Andoc.* 2, 7.)— 4) (Genitive): *Ἦλθον ἐπί τινα τῶν δοκούντων σοφῶν εἶναι* (*Pl. Apol.* 22; ibid. 41: *τῶν φασκόντων δικαστῶν εἶναι*).[1] *Ἐδέοντο Κύρου ὡς προθυμοτάτου πρὸς τὸν πόλεμον γενέσθαι* (*Xen. Hell.* 1, 5, 2). — 5) (Accusative after genitive): *Ἐδέοντό μου προστάτην γενέσθαι* (*Xen. Cyr.* 7, 2, 23). *Δέομαι ὑμῶν καταψηφίσασθαι Θεομνήστου, ἐνθυμουμένους, ὅσος μοι ὁ ἀγών ἐστιν* (*Lys.* 10, 31).

The *accusative with the infinitive* is used to express a proposition as the object or subject of another proposition. The accus. with inf. stands § 159. (394)

[1] *Τῶν δοκούντων τι εἶναι* (*Pl. Gorg.* 472; *εἶναί τι*, a phrase not admitting of grammatical change, as *ἀνδρὶ οἰομένῳ τι εἶναι*, *Pl. Menex.* 247).

[§ 159.] (primarily) after verbs and phrases denoting an utterance (say, deny, answer, relate, narrate, concede, assert, declare, judge, &c.) or opinion (think, assume, make to believe, hope; *verba declarandi et sentiendi*). The verbs of utterance sometimes take an object-sentence with ὅτι or ὡς, the verbs of opinion sometimes one with ὡς. *Τὸν καλὸν κἀγαθόν ἄνδρα εὐδαίμονα εἶναί φημι* (*Pl. Gorg.* 470). *Ὁμολογῶ σὸν τὸ εὕρημα εἶναι. Ὑπέσχου βοήθειαν μοι ἥξειν. Τί ποτε λέγουσιν οἱ κινεῖσθαι τὰ πάντα ἀποφαινόμενοι;* (*Pl. Theæt.* 168.) *Οἱ ἄνθρωποι ὑπολαμβάνουσι, τοὺς θεοὺς διὰ τῶν ὀρνίθων τὰ συμφέροντα σημαίνειν* (*Xen. Mem.* 1, 1, 3). *Ἀκούω καὶ ἄλλα ἔθνη πολλὰ τοιαῦτα εἶναι* (*Xen. An.* 2, 5, 13). *Πέπεισθε ἀδικίαν δικαιοσύνης ἄμεινον εἶναι* (*Pl. Rep.* 2, 368). *Ἐλπὶς πάντα καλῶς ἕξειν.*

REM. 1. Of the verbs *to know, perceive, see, show, remember*, which take a participle or a sentence with ὅτι or ὡς, and of the verbs *to hear, learn*, which take a participle, an accus. with inf. or ὅτι, see *Participles*, § 178, a. with R. 6.

REM. 2. Μετατίθεμαι, εὐδαιμονεστέρους εἶναι τοὺς κοσμίους τῶν ἀκολάστων (*Pl. Gorg.* 493), *I change my opinion*, AND ASSUME. Ἐλέγχω, *refute*, AND PROVE. So the acc. with inf. often to a sense indirectly contained in the verb. (Κατεφρόνουν οἱ Λακεδαιμόνιοι, διὰ τὰς ἔμπροσθεν τύχας, μηδένʼ ἂν ἐπιχειρῆσαί σφισιν, *Xen. Hell.* 4, 5, 12; *despised the enemy*, AND THOUGHT *that nobody would* —.)

REM. 3. Whether, in any given case, the acc. with inf. shall be used, or a sentence with ὅτι, or one with ὡς, is, for the most part, optional with the writer, and depends on his view of what is required for perspicuity and suitableness in reference to the structure of the dependent sentence as a whole, and of the period. It may be remarked, however, with respect to the difference of these three constructions, that affirmative *verba declarandi* (put simply, without secondary meaning) almost always take the acc. with inf. or ὅτι: but that ὡς is put, when the thing said is marked as an uncertain or untrue assertion, pretext, or evasion, therefore also after a negatived verb (οὐ λέγω, ὡς —, or, if the thing uttered itself is negative, οὐ λέγω, ὡς οὐ). After *verba sentiendi* only ὡς, not ὅτι, is used, and in this also there is apt to be involved the secondary notion of a false opinion (πείθω, ὡς —, *seek to persuade that* —). Παρέξονται νόμον οὐδὲν προσέχοντα τῇδε τῇ γραφῇ καὶ λέξουσιν, ὡς εἰσὶ τῇ πόλει δύο νόμοι κείμενοι περὶ τῶν κηρυγμάτων (*Æsch.* 3, 35. Often τοῦτο ἐρεῖ, ἐκεῖνον ἐρεῖ τὸν λόγον, ὡς —). Τισσαφέρνης διαβάλλει τὸν Κῦρον πρὸς τὸν ἀδελφόν, ὡς ἐπιβουλεύοι αὐτῷ (*Xen. An.* 1, 1, 3). Οὐ μὲν δὴ οὐδὲ τοῦτʼ ἄν τις εἴποι, ὡς τοὺς κακούργους καὶ ἀδίκους Κῦρος εἴα καταγελᾶν (*Xen. An.* 1, 9, 13). Οὐ τοῦτο λέγω, ὡς οὐ δεῖ ἰέναι ἐπὶ τοὺς πολεμίους (*Xen. Cyr.* 5, 4, 20). Ἔχομέν τι παρὰ ταῦτα λέγειν, ὡς οὐχ οὕτως ἔχει; (*Pl. Phæd.* 80.) — Νομίζουσιν οἱ ἐκείνῃ ἄνθρωποι, ὡς Ἥφαιστος χαλκεύει (*Thuc.* 3, 88). Οἱ σοφισταὶ πειρῶνται πείθειν τοὺς νεωτέρους, ὡς, ἢν αὐτοῖς πλησιάζωσιν, ἃ πρακτέον ἐστίν, εἴσονται (*Isocr. Sophist.* 3). (Ἔγνωσαν οἱ Μαντινεῖς ὡς, εἰ μὴ ἀποκρούσονται τοὺς μισθοφόρους, ὅτι πολλοὶ σφῶν κατακοντισθήσονται, *Xen. Hell.* 6, 5, 13.) For ὡς after a negatived verb of utterance or opinion ὅπως is sometimes used: Οὐδέ γε, ὅπως ἄφρων ἔσται ἡ ψυχή, ἐπειδὰν τοῦ ἄφρονος σώματος δίχα γένηται, οὐδὲ τοῦτο πέπεισμαι (*Xen. Cyr.* 8, 7, 20). Ὅπως οὐ πάντων τούτων ἐπιμελητέον, ὦ Ἱέρων, οὐ λέγω (*Xen. Hier.* 9. 1). Διότι for ὅτι, *that*, is rare in the older writers (usually, *because*), in later writers not infrequent. (The poetical οὕνεκα, ὁθούνεκα, *because*, sometimes also for ὅτι, *that*.) [§ 159.]

Rem. 4. Sometimes a report of a view or speech, begun with ὅτι or ὡς, is continued in the accusative (nominative) with the infinitive, or *vice versa*: Οἱ Λακεδαιμόνιοι εἶπον, ὅτι σφίσι μὲν δοκοῖεν ἀδικεῖν οἱ Ἀθηναῖοι, βούλεσθαι δὲ καὶ τοὺς πάντας ξυμμάχους παρακαλέσαντες ψῆφον ἐπαγαγεῖν (*Thuc.* 1, 87). Ἄνυτος ἔλεγεν, ὅτι οὐχ οὕτω διακέοιντο (*were not in such a condition*) ὥστε τιμωρεῖσθαί τινας τῶν ἐχθρῶν, ἀλλὰ νῦν μὲν δεῖν αὐτοὺς ἡσυχίαν ἔχειν, εἰ δὲ οἴκαδε κατέλθοιεν, τότε καὶ τιμωρήσοιντο τοὺς ἀδικοῦντας (*Lys.* 13, 78). By a negligence (anacoluthia) it may even happen, that one and the same sentence begins with ὅτι or ὡς, and then, commonly after a parenthetic sentence, is continued in the acc. with inf.: Λέγεις σύ, ὦ πάτερ, ὡς ἐμοὶ δοκεῖ, ὅτι, ὥσπερ οὐδὲ γεωργοῦ ἀργοῦ οὐδὲν ὄφελος, οὕτως οὐδὲ στρατηγοῦ ἀργοῦ οὐδὲν ὄφελος εἶναι (*Xen. Cyr.* 1, 6, 18). (Conversely, a sentence begun in acc. with inf. passes into a dependent interrogation: Τοὺς μέντοι Ἕλληνας τοὺς ἐν τῇ Ἀσίᾳ οἰκοῦντας, οὐδέν πω σαφῶς λέγεται, εἰ ἕπονται. *Xen. Cyr.* 2, 1, 5.)

If the subject in the infinitive clause is the same as that of the governing verb, as a general rule only a simple infinitive follows, referred to the leading subject (nominative with infinitive, cf. § 147); but the accusative with infinitive also occurs, sometimes with a view to give prominence to the subject of the infinitive as opposed to others: Ὁμολογῶ ἀδικεῖν. Νομίζω οὐδὲν χείρων εἶναι τῶν ἄλλων. Ἔξαρνός ἐστιν ὁ ἄνθρωπος μηδ' ἰδεῖν με πώποτε (*Arist. Pl.* 241 = ἀρνεῖται). Πιστεύω διαλύσειν τὴν διαβολήν (*Thuc.* 1, 101). Σωκράτης, ἔφη ὁ κατήγορος, τοὺς πατέρας προπηλακίζειν διδάσκει, πείθων τοὺς συνόντας αὑτῷ σοφωτέρους ποιεῖν τῶν πατέρων (*Xen. Mem.* 1, 2, 49; *persuading them that he makes them* —). Τιμόθεος τὰς χιλίας δραχμὰς ἰδίᾳ ἔφη δανεῖσαι τὸν πατέρα Ἀντιμάχῳ καὶ οὐκ αὐτὸς λαβεῖν (*Dem.* 49, 44). Κλέων οὐκ ἔφη αὐτὸς ἀλλ' ἐκεῖνον (Νικίαν) στρατηγεῖν (*Thuc.* 4, 28). — Οἶμαι ἐμὲ παρὰ σοῦ πολλῆς καὶ καλῆς σοφίας πληρωθήσεσθαι (*Pl. Conv.* 175). (Αἰτίαν ἔχω μισόδημος εἶναι, *Pl. Rep.* 8, 566. Ὑποψίαν παρέξουσι μὴ ἡμέτεροι εἶναι πατέρες, *Pl. Menex.* 247. Ὕποπτος εἶ φυγεῖν.) § 160. (401, R. 2)

Rem. When φημί, ἡγοῦμαι, οἶμαι ought to be followed by χρῆναι, δεῖν (δίκαιον εἶναι), and an accus. with inf. with the subject of the leading verb, sometimes the ἡγοῦμαι, χρῆναι, &c. is considered as one verb followed by a simple infinitive (nominative), especially οἶμαι δεῖν, *I think I must, think it is necessary for me, to be*, &c.: Ἀλκιβιάδης ὑβριστὴς ᾤετο δεῖν εἶναι (*Dem.* 21, 143).[1]

When a verb of utterance or opinion should be put impersonally in the passive, and followed by an accusative with infinitive, the personal expression in the nominative with infinitive is frequently used [as often in English]; but the impersonal form also occurs: Φῦναι ὁ § 161. (400)

---

[1] Γύλιππος κήρυκα προπέμπει τοῖς Ἀθηναίοις λέγνοτα (= λέγειν κελεύων), εἰ βούλονται ἐξιέναι ἐκ τῆς Σικελίας πέντε ἡμερῶν, ἕτοιμος εἶναι σπένδεσθαι (*Thuc.* 5, 3).

[§ 161.] Κῦρος λέγεται καὶ ᾄδεται ἔτι καὶ νῦν ὑπὸ τῶν βαρβάρων εἶδος μὲν κάλλιστος, ψυχὴν δὲ φιλανθρωπότατος (*Xen. Cyr.* 1, 2, 1). Ὡμολόγηται ὁ ἰατρὸς σωμάτων εἶναι ἄρχων (*Pl. Rep.* 1, 342; *it is confessed that* —, or, *a physician is confessed to be*—). Ἀχιλλεὺς Ὁμήρῳ πεποίηται (*Achilles is represented by Homer to have* —) Πατρόκλῳ ἀποθανόντι ἐκπρεπέστατα τιμωρῆσαι (*Xen. Conv.* 8, 31). Τοῦ ὑπὸ σοῦ κριθέντος χαλεπώτατα ζῆν χαλεπώτερον ἔτι ζῇ ὁ τύραννος (*Pl. Rep.* 9, 579).—Λέγεται, Ἀλκιβιάδην, πρὶν εἴκοσιν ἐτῶν εἶναι, Περικλεῖ τοιάδε διαλεχθῆναι περὶ νόμων (*Xen. Mem.* 1, 2, 40). Ὁμολογεῖται, τοὺς ἀπὸ Διὸς εὐγενεστάτους τῶν ἡμιθέων εἶναι (*Isocr. Evag.* 13). (Ἤγγελται ἡ μάχη ἰσχυρὰ γεγονέναι καὶ ἐν αὐτῇ πολλοὺς τεθνάναι, *Pl. Charm.* 153.)

Rem. The verb δοκῶ (*videor*) is usually put personally, of the person or thing of which something is supposed: εὖ λέγειν μοι δοκεῖτε (even ἀπέπλευσαν, ὡς τοῖς πλείστοις ἐδόκουν, ὀργισθέντες, *Xen. An.* 1, 4, 7, = ὡς τ. π. ἐδόκει); δοκῶ μοι and simply δοκῶ, *I seem to myself to* —, *it seems to me that I* —, *I think that I* —, e.g. ἔδοξα ἀκοῦσαι ὄνομα αὐτῷ εἶναι Ἀγάθωνα (*Pl. Prot.* 315); with the infinitive of the future (of the aorist with ἄν), *I believe I shall — I will*; δοκῶ μοι κατακείσεσθαι. Δοκεῖ μοι (τινι) impersonally with an *accus. c. infin.* is unusual, except in a clause subsequently annexed: Ἐδόκει Ξενοφῶντι, βροντῆς γενομένης, σκηπτὸς πεσεῖν εἰς τὴν πατρῴαν οἰκίαν, καὶ ἐκ τούτου λάμπεσθαι πᾶσαν (*Xen. An.* 3, 1, 11). (Different from this is δοκεῖ, *it is decreed* that something shall be, § 164.) Δοκῶ is also used in the sense *I believe, I think*. Δοκεῖς ἂν ἢ λῃστὰς ἢ κλέπτας πρᾶξαι ἄν τι δύνασθαι, εἰ ἀδικοῖεν ἀλλήλους; (*Pl. Rep.* 1, 351.) Τῷ πατρί, δοκῶ, Πυριλάμπης ὄνομα ἦν (*Pl. Parm.* 126). (Καὶ τούτους τί δοκεῖτε; *Xen. An.* 5, 7, 26. *Quid hos putatis?* Lat. Gr. § 395, R. 7, fin.)

§ 162. When the word which is the subject of the infinitive is itself governed, as dative or genitive, by the verb of utterance or opinion, the infin. attaches itself immediately to this case (without a separate subject in the accusative): Πιστεύω σοι ποιήσειν, *I trust thee that thou wilt do* (and thence οὔ σοι πάνυ πιστεύω ἱκανῷ εἶναι, *Pl. Euthyd.* 296, as πιστεύω τάδε ἀληθῆ εἶναι). Οὐδενὶ ἀνθρώπων ὑφείμην ἂν ἥδιον ἐμοῦ βεβιωκέναι (*Xen. Mem.* 4, 8, 6). Κτησικλέους ὁ δῆμος ἅπας κατεχειροτόνησεν ἀδικεῖν (*Dem.* 21, 180). Κατέγνωκα ἐμαυτοῦ μή ποτ' ἂν δυνατὸς γενέσθαι τοὺς ἄνδρας ἱκανῶς ἐγκωμιάσαι (*Pl. Tim.* 19. Δυνατός to the subject of the principal verb, § 158 b). (Passively, by § 56, R. 2: Κατεγνώσθην ἀδικεῖν, *Xen. Hell.* 1, 7, 20.) (Αἰτιῶμαί τινα κλέπτην εἶναι. Ἠτιάθη Ἀδείμαντος προδοῦναι τὰς ναῦς, *Xen. Hell.* 2, 1, 32.)

§ 163. (403) *a*) Besides the accus. (or nom.) with inf. immediately dependent on a leading verb, the continuation of the utterance or opinion may be carried on in the same form, so that the verb is to be supposed repeated: Δυοῖν χρησίμοιν οὐ διαμαρτήσεσθαι τὴν πόλιν ἡγούμην πλευσάντων ἡμῶν (τῶν πρεσβέων πρὸς Φίλιππον)· ἢ γὰρ Φίλιππον, ἃ μὲν εἰλήφει τῆς πόλεως, ἀποδώσειν, τῶν δὲ λοιπῶν ἀφέξεσθαι, ἤ, μὴ ποιοῦντος ταῦτα, ἀπαγγελεῖν ἡμᾶς εὐθέως δεῦρο, ὥσθ' ἐν ἐκείνους τοῖς πόῤῥω τὴν ἀπιστίαν ἰδόντας ὑμᾶς περὶ τῶνδε τῶν ἐγγὺς οὐ προήσεσθαι· μὴ προλαβόντος δὲ ἐκείνου ταῦτα μηδ' ὑμῶν ἐξαπατηθέντων, ἐν ἀσφαλεῖ τὰ πράγμαθ' ὑμῖν ἔσεσθαι (*Dem.* 19, 151). Ἐμοὶ δοκοῦσιν οἱ ἄνθρωποι παντάπασι τὴν τοῦ ἔρωτος δύναμιν οὐκ ᾐσθῆσθαι· ἐπεὶ αἰσθανόμενοί γε μέγιστ' ἂν αὐτοῦ ἱερὰ κατασκευάσαι καὶ βωμοὺς καὶ θυσίας ἂν ποιεῖν μεγίστας (*Pl. Conv.* 189). (For a longer narration continued in this way, see Xen. Cyr. 1, 3, 4 ff. Plato de Rep. x. p. 614 B. ff.; a speech and argument, Thucyd. vi. 49.)

REM. It is not usual, however, in Greek, in the same degree as in Latin, to report an entire speech (except it be pure narrative) in such a continued acc. with inf. Often εἶπεν, ἔφη, ἤρετο, &c. is repeated, or there is a sudden transition to the *oratio recta* in the proper person of the speaker. See *Connexion of Sentences*, § 192 b. [§ 163.]

b) An acc. (nom.) with inf. sometimes stands without an express verb of utterance or opinion, when this is intimated in some other way: Ἆγις τοὺς πρέσβεις ἐς Λακεδαίμονα ἐκέλευσεν ἰέναι· οὐ γὰρ εἶναι κύριος αὐτός (*Xen. Hell.* 2, 2, 12). Σωκράτης ἐθαύμαζεν, εἰ μὴ φανερὸν τοῖς φιλοσόφοις ἐστίν, ὅτι τὰ μετέωρα οὐ δυνατόν ἐστιν ἀνθρώποις εὑρεῖν· ἐπεὶ καὶ τοὺς μέγιστον φρονοῦντας ἐπὶ τῷ περὶ τούτων λέγειν οὐ ταὐτὰ δοξάζειν ἀλλήλοις (*Xen. Mem.* 1, 1, 13). Ὁ Ἆγις παρῃτεῖτο (τοὺς Λακεδαιμονίους) μὴ ζημιῶσαι αὐτόν· ἔργῳ γὰρ ἀγαθῷ ῥύσεσθαι τὰς αἰτίας στρατευσάμενος (*Thuc.* 5, 63).

Further: the acc. with inf. is put a) with verbs and phrases denoting a *will* (command, prayer, wish, resolve, agreement, taking measures for) that something *shall* (may) take place (which *shall* is not expressed, but is involved in the construction), or a *permission* and a *prohibition* that something should, or should not, take place (verbs of willing); b) with verbs and phrases denoting to *effect* and *cause* that something be, or be not, done (verbs of effecting) (e. g. διαπράττομαι, κατεργάζομαι, ποιῶ, also διαμάχομαι, *contend for it, that*; κατασκευάζω, σπουδάζω, *earnestly endeavour that*; more specially ὠνοῦμαι, *purchase to myself that*, αἴτιός εἰμι, &c.), and to *wait for*; c) with συμβαίνει, συμπίπτει, *it happens*. When with these verbs of will and of effect the leading verb and the infinitive have the same subject, a simple infinitive is put (§ 145 and 147): Πάντας ταῦτα εἰδέναι βούλομαι. Εὔχοντο Ξενίαν καὶ Πασίωνα ὡς δολίους ὄντας ληφθῆναι (*Xen. An.* 1, 4, 7). Ἔδοξε, πλεῖν[1] τὸν Ἀλκιβιάδην (*Thuc.* 6, 29). Ἔγραψα (*I moved that* —, also εἶπον, γνώμην εἶπον, ψήφισμα ἐγένετο, &c.), ἀποπλεῖν[1] τὴν ταχίστην τοὺς πρέσβεις (*Dem.* 18, 25). Οἱ ἄρχοντες οἱ ἐν τῇ Κεφαλληνίᾳ ἔγνωσαν Ἀθήναζε τὴν ναῦν καταπλεῖν (*Dem.* 32, 9; *settled for the ship to sail* —). Ἐκ τούτου ἀνιστάμενοι πάντες ἔλεγον, τοὺς ἀνομίας ἄρξαντας δοῦναι δίκην (*Xen. An.* 5, 7, 34). Ξύγκειται κρατεῖν βασιλέα τῶν πόλεων, ὧν ποτε οἱ πρόγονοι ἦρχον (*Thuc.* 8, 52; *it is settled that* —). Νόμον θησόμεθα, μηδενὶ ἐξεῖναι ἄρχειν, ὃς ἂν μὴ στρατεύσηται. Ἀστυάγης ἀπηγόρευε μηδένα βάλλειν, πρὶν Κῦρος ἐμπλησθείη θηρῶν (*Xen. Cyr.* 1, 4, 14). Ἐγίγνοντο σπονδαὶ τοιαίδε· Λακεδαιμονίους μὲν τὰς ναῦς τὰς ἐν τῇ Λακωνικῇ πάσας, ὅσαι ἦσαν μακραί, παραδοῦναι κομίσαντας ἐς Πύλον Ἀθηναίοις καὶ ὅπλα μὴ ἐπιφέρειν τῷ τειχίσματι· Ἀθηναίους δὲ τοῖς ἐν τῇ νήσῳ ἀνδράσι σῖτον ἐᾶν τοὺς ἐν τῇ ἠπείρῳ Λακεδαιμονίους ἐκπέμπειν τακτόν κ.τ.λ. (*Thuc.* 4, 16.)[2]— Εἴ τινα τῶν γνωρίμων βούλοιο κατεργάζεσθαι καλεῖν σε ἐπὶ δεῖπνον, τί ἂν ποιοίης; (*Xen. Mem.* 2, 3, 11.) Τισσαφέρνης ἔλεγεν, ὅτι διαπεπραγμένος ἥκοι παρὰ βασιλέως, δοθῆναι αὐτῷ σώζειν τοὺς Ἕλληνας § 164.

[[1] The *infin. present* is common, as in Lat., after verbs of *ordering, decreeing*, &c. —T. K. A.]

[2] Δοκοῦντος τοῦ Θίμβρωνος οὐδὲν ποιεῖν, πέμπουσιν οἱ ἔφοροι, ἀπολιπόντα Λάρισσαν στρατεύεσθαι ἐπὶ Καρίαν (*Xen. Hell.* 3, 1, 8, *send him orders to* —).

CHAP. V.]

[§ 164.] (*Xen. An.* 2, 3, 25). Ὠνοῦνται αἱ πόλεις, μὴ ἀδικεῖσθαι τοὺς παρ' αὐτῶν ἐκπλέοντας ἐμπόρους (*Dem.* 8, 25). Ἐγὼ αἴτιος, μὴ καλῶς σε ἀποκρίνασθαι, ὅτι οὐ καλῶς ἠρόμην (*Pl. Lach.* 191). Φορμίων φυλακὴν εἶχε (ἐφύλαττε), μήτ' ἐκπλεῖν ἐκ Κορίνθου μηδένα μήτ' εἰσπλεῖν (*Thuc.* 2, 69). Οὐ περιμενοῦμεν (ἀναμενοῦμεν) ἄλλους ἡμᾶς διολέσαι (*Pl. Rep.* 2, 375). Συνέβη τοὺς Ἀθηναίους θορυβηθῆναι (*Thuc.* 5, 10). (Rarely, and for the sake of an antithesis, the acc. with inf. instead of the simple infinitive: Βουλοίμην ἂν ἐμέ τε τυχεῖν ὧν βούλομαι, τοῦτόν τε παθεῖν ὧν ἄξιός ἐστιν, *Dem.* 24, 8.)

Rem. 1. After the verbs under *b* and *c*, the acc. with inf. sometimes takes ὥστε (*so to arrange that* —), rarely those under *a* (cf. § 145, R. 3). Πειράσομαι ποιῆσαι, ὥστε σε νομίζειν καλῶς βεβουλεῦσθαι (*Xen. Cyr.* 3, 2, 29). Ἐγὼ κἂν τῆς ψυχῆς πριαίμην ὥστε μήποτε λατρεῦσαι τὴν γυναῖκα (*Xen. Cyr.* 3, 1, 36). Ἦ οἴει ψηφίσασθαι ἂν τὸ πλῆθος συνελθὸν ὥστε τοὺς κρατίστους καὶ τιμαῖς καὶ δώροις πλεονεκτεῖν; (*Xen. Cyr.* 2, 2, 20.) Ξυνέβη εὐθὺς μετὰ τὴν ἐν Ἀμφιπόλει μάχην ὥστε πολέμου μηδὲν ἔτι ἅψασθαι μηδετέρους (*Thuc.* 5, 14). (Διαπράττομαι ὥστε μὴ κολάζεσθαι, *Pl. Gorg.* 478.)

Rem. 2. The verbs which denote *endeavour* (to effect), take an object-sentence with ὅπως, e. g. κατασκευάζω, διασπουδάζω (§ 123). With ἐπιμελεῖσθαι, μηχανᾶσθαι the acc. with inf. is rare.

Rem. 3. Sometimes the subject-matter of an agreement, resolution, stipulation, &c. is expressed by the simple infinitive, as the subject is easily seen from the context: Ἦσαν αἱ συγγραφαί, ὥσπερ εἰώθασιν ἅπασαι, σωθείσης τῆς νεὼς ἀποδοῦναι τὰ χρήματα (*Dem.* 32, 5; *were to this effect, that one should pay*). In some cases the construction may be either acc. with inf., or a dative with simple inf. by § 146. Προστάττω τινὶ ποιεῖν (*order a person to do*) and τινὰ ποιεῖν (*that some one should do*). Χαίρειν λέγω τινί and τινά. Ἄνυτος Ἀγοράτῳ αἴτιος ἐγένετο μὴ ἀποθανεῖν (*Lys.* 13, 82). Τοῦ μὴ λαβεῖν Ἀμφίπολιν πάντων οὗτος αἰτιώτατός ἐστιν (*Dem.* 23, 152; viz. ὑμῖν). (Also αἴτιος τοῦ τι γίγνεσθαι, § 170 c.) Οἱ περὶ τὸν Χάροπον, συνθέμενοι τοῖς Ἀρκάσιν ἐπιβοηθεῖν, καταλαμβάνουσι τὴν ἀκρόπολιν (*Xen. Hell.* 7, 4, 15; *having agreed with the Arcadians that these should come and help them*).

§ 165. *a*) The accusative with infinitive stands as the object of a mental judgment expressed impersonally (καλόν ἐστι, χρή, &c.). Καλὸν ἀδελφοὺς ἀλλήλοις ἐπικουρεῖν. Περὶ πολλοῦ ποιητέον, μηδεμίαν πρόφασιν δοθῆναι τοῖς διαβάλλουσιν. Σωτηρία ἄλλη οὐδεμία ἦν, ἢ πυθέσθαι Ἀθηναίους πάντα τὰ πραχθέντα (*Andoc.* 1, 58). (Τίς μηχανὴ μὴ οὐχὶ πάντα καταναλωθῆναι εἰς τὸ τεθνάναι; *Pl. Phæd.* 72 = ἀδύνατον.) Προσήκει μοι ποιεῖν and ἐμέ π. Rarely ἔξεστί με ποιεῖν.

Rem. The adjective δίκαιος is usually (instead of the impersonal form δίκαιόν ἐστι followed by acc. with inf.) put personally, of the person who is bound (entitled) to do something, with infinitive added: Καὶ σὺ ἡμῖν δίκαιος (δικαιότατος) εἶ ἀντιχαρίζεσθαι (*Xen. Cyr.* 4, 1, 20). Πολλῷ μειζόνων ἔτι δωρεῶν δίκαιός εἰμι τυγχάνειν (*Dem.* 18, 53). (Similarly: Ἦν συνιδεῖν τῷ προσέχοντι τὸν νοῦν ἡ βασιλέως ἀρχὴ τοῖς μήκεσι τῶν ὁδῶν καὶ τῷ διεσπάσθαι τὰς δυνάμεις ἀσθενὴς οὖσα, *Xen. An.* 1, 5, 9 = Ἦν συνιδεῖν τὴν ἀρχὴν — οὖσαν.) So sometimes a participle expressing something that is becoming, befitting, or a duty, stands personally with the infinitive, instead of impersonally: Λόγος προσήκων ῥηθῆναι (*Pl. Pol.* 283) = ὃν προσήκει ῥ. Τὰ ἡμῖν ἐξ ἀρχῆς παραγγελθέντα (προσταχθέντα) διελθεῖν (*Pl. Tim.* 90) = ἃ ἡμῖν παρηγγέλθη δ. [§ 165.]

b) An acc. with inf. is sometimes put as an apposition to a demonstrative pronoun (τοῦτο, τόδε, sometimes to a pronoun with a substantive), to denote a conceived relation of which something is predicated: Τὸ δίκαιον τοῦτ' ἐστί, πλέον ἔχειν τοὺς ἄρχοντας τῶν ἀρχομένων (*Pl. Gorg.* 491). Οὐδενὶ πώποτε δεδώκατε τὴν δωρεὰν ταύτην, ἐξεῖναι τοὺς ἰδίους ἐχθροὺς ὑβρίζειν, ὁπότ' ἂν βούληται (*Dem.* 21, 170).

a) The accusative with infinitive stands with ὥςτε, *so that*, to denote the way and manner (the degree) and the consequence of what is predicated in the principal sentence, when the clause with ὥςτε contains a mere mental representation which is not put by the speaker as actual. (Where the subject remains unchanged, the simple infinitive is used.) If the proposition with ὥςτε *is* put as actual, then partly the indicative (or potential optative) is used, especially almost always with narrative statements in the aorist: partly the infinitive, whereby the sentence coalesces more with the leading sentence, and has less prominence in itself (*as to* c. inf., but often, *so that*). Where ὥςτε expresses merely a consequence or inference (*so that consequently, therefore*), but not the way and manner, or the degree (so that οὕτως or τοσοῦτον could not precede), the infinitive is rarely used: Πολλὰς ἐλπίδας ἔχω ἀρκούντως ἐρεῖν, ὥςτ' ὑμᾶς μὴ ἀπολειφθῆναι τῶν πραγμάτων (*Dem.* 27, 2; *so that you shall not be left in ignorance of the state of affairs*). Οὕπω οἱ καιροὶ παρεληλύθασιν, ὥςτ' ἤδη μάτην εἶναι τὸ μεμνῆσθαι περὶ τούτων (*Isocr.*; *so that it should be in vain* —): Καὶ λόγων καὶ βουλευμάτων κοινωνὸν ἄν σε οἱ πολέμιοι ποιοῖντο διὰ τὸ πιστεύειν, ὥστε μηδὲ ἕν σε λεληθέναι, ὧν βουλόμεθα εἰδέναι (*Xen. Cyr.* 6, 1, 40). Οὕτω ἀτόπους τινὰς ἐν τῇ πόλει καὶ δυςχερεῖς ἀνθρώπους Αἰσχίνης ἔλεγεν εἶναι, ὥςτε οὐκ αἰσχύνεσθαι λοιδορουμένους Φιλίππῳ (*Dem.* 19, 308. In the *oratio recta* it might be οὕτως — εἰσίν, ὥςτε οὐκ αἰσχύνονται, or ὥςτε μὴ αἰσχύνεσθαι[1]). Οἱ Λακεδαιμόνιοι εἰς τοῦτο ἀπληστίας ἦλθον, ὥςτε οὐκ ἐξήρκεσεν αὐτοῖς ἔχειν τὴν κατὰ γῆν ἀρχήν (*Isocr. Panath.* 103). Οὕτως ἡμῖν ταῦτα τἀγαθὰ παντὸς ἄξια εἶναι δοκεῖ, ὥςτε τὸ καταλιπεῖν αὐτὰ πάντων μάλιστα φεύγομεν (*Xen. Mem.* 2, 2, 3). Ξέρξης τῆς πεζῆς στρατιᾶς οὕτως ἄπειρον τὸ πλῆθος ἦγεν, ὥςτε καὶ τὰ ἔθνη τὰ μετ' αὐτοῦ ἀκολουθήσαντα πολὺ ἂν ἔργον εἴη καταλέξαι (*Lys.* 2, 27). Καὶ λήθη καὶ μανία πολλάκις πολλοῖς διὰ τὴν τοῦ σώματος καχεξίαν εἰς τὴν διάνοιαν ἐμπίπτουσιν οὕτως, ὥςτε καὶ τὰς ἐπιστήμας ἐκβάλλειν (*Xen. Mem.* 3, 12, 6). Ἡ τῶν Ἀθηναίων πόλις ἐμπόριον ἐν μέσῳ τῆς Ἑλλάδος τὸν Πειραιᾶ κατεσκευάσατο τοσαύτην ἔχον ὑπερβολήν, ὥςθ', ἃ παρὰ τῶν ἄλλων ἓν παρ' ἑκάστων χαλεπόν ἐστι λαβεῖν, ταῦθ' ἅπαντα παρ' § 166.

[1] [It might be ὥςτε οὐκ αἰσχ. (taken as the *opp.* of αἰσχύνεσθαι) in *orat. rect.* Comp. 305, R. 3.—Ed.]

[§ 166.] αὐτῆς ῥᾴδιον εἶναι πορίσασθαι (*Isocr. Paneg.* 42). Εἰς τὴν ὑστεραίαν οὐχ ἧκεν ὁ Τισσαφέρνης· ὥςθ' οἱ Ἕλληνες ἐφρόντιζον (*Xen. An.* 2, 3, 24). Ὥςτε (*in consequence of the foregoing explanations*) ξὺν τῷ πρώτῳ πολέμῳ τῷ δεκαετεῖ καὶ τῇ μετ' αὐτὸν ὑπόπτῳ ἀνακωχῇ καὶ τῷ ὕστερον ἐξ αὐτῆς πολέμῳ εὑρήσει τις τοσαῦτα ἔτη (*Thuc.* 5, 26). (Συντέτακται καὶ συνακολουθεῖ τοῖς μὲν πλούτοις καὶ δυναστείαις ἄνοια καὶ ἀκολασία, ταῖς δ' ἐνδείαις καὶ ταῖς ταπεινότησι σωφροσύνη καὶ μετριότης· ὥςτε χαλεπὸν εἶναι διαγνῶναι, ποτέραν ἄν τις δέξαιτο τῶν μερίδων τούτων τοῖς παισὶ τοῖς αὑτοῦ καταλιπεῖν, *Isocr. Areop.* 5.)

REM. Even after a condition, or after a question equivalent to a negative (where therefore the consequence is not a fact), ὥςτε may stand with the *modus finitus*, if the condition or the question essentially concerns the proposition with ὥςτε: Οὕτως ἀγνωμόνως ἔχετε, ὦ ἄνδρες Ἀθηναῖοι, ὥςτε, δι' ὧν ἐκ χρηστῶν φαῦλα τὰ πράγματα τῆς πόλεως γέγονε, διὰ τούτων ἐλπίζετε τῶν αὐτῶν πράξεων ἐκ φαύλων αὐτὰ χρηστὰ γενήσεσθαι; (*Dem.* 2, 26[1].)

b) Likewise ὥςτε before the accusative with infinitive, or, if the subject be the same, the simple infinitive, denotes a fixed condition (*so that* something shall happen, *under the condition that*), or the price and reward (*so that in return*), sometimes altogether the object and the means (*so that something may*). Just so the acc. with inf. (or simple inf.) with ἐφ' ᾧ, ἐφ' ᾧ τε, *on condition that*: Οἱ Μιτυληναῖοι ὁμολογίαν ποιοῦνται πρὸς Πάχητα, ὥςτε Ἀθηναίοις μὲν ἐξεῖναι βουλεῦσαι περὶ Μιτυληναίων ὁποῖον ἄν τι βούλωνται, πρεσβείαν δ' ἀποστέλλειν ἐς τὰς Ἀθήνας Μιτυληναίους περὶ ἑαυτῶν (*Thuc.* 3, 28. Also ἐπὶ τοῖςδε ὥςτε, *Thuc.* 3, 114). Πάχης Ἱππίαν προεκαλέσατο ἐς λόγους, ὥςτε, ἢν μηδὲν ἀρέσκον λέγῃ, πάλιν αὐτὸν καταστήσειν εἰς τὸ τεῖχος σῶν καὶ ὑγιᾶ (*Thuc.* 3, 34).—Ἐξῆν τοῖς ὑμετέροις προγόνοις τῶν λοιπῶν ἄρχειν Ἑλλήνων, ὥςτε αὐτοὺς ὑπακούειν βασιλεῖ (*Dem.* 6, 11). Ὥςτε τὴν γυναῖκα ἀπολαβεῖν, πόσα ἄν μοι χρήματα δοίης; (*Xen. Cyr.* 3, 1. 35.) Πᾶν ποιοῦσιν, ὥςτε δίκην μὴ διδόναι (*Pl. Gorg.* 479; *to have no punishment to undergo*). Οἱ τριάκοντα ἐβουλήθησαν Ἐλευσῖνα ἐξιδιώσασθαι, ὥςτε εἶναι σφίσι καταφυγήν, εἰ δεήσειε (*Xen. Hell.* 2, 4, 8)[2].—Τηρίβαζος εἶπεν, ὅτι σπείσασθαι βούλοιτο, ἐφ' ᾧ μήτε αὐτὸς τοὺς Ἕλληνας ἀδικεῖν μήτ' ἐκείνους καίειν τὰς οἰκίας (*Xen. An.* 4, 4, 6)[3]. (The verb *can* or *shall* lies in the construction, and is not separately expressed in the Greek.)

c). For τοιοῦτος ὥςτε we have also τοιοῦτος οἷος, or simply οἷος, so

---

[1] Τὰ πράγματα ὁρῶ εἰς τοῦτο προήκοντα ὥςτε, ὅπως μὴ πεισόμεθα αὐτοὶ πρότερον κακῶς, σκέψασθαι δέον (*Dem.* 3, 1; participle instead of infinitive with ὥςτε after a participle preceding, by a kind of attraction).

[2] Μηχαναὶ πολλαί εἰσιν ἐν ἑκάστοις τοῖς κινδύνοις ὥςτε διαφεύγειν θάνατον (*Pl. Apol.* 39; *so that one can escape, in order to escape.*

[3] Ἐφ' ᾧ (ᾧ τε) with fut. indic. in Herodot. and Thucyd.: Οἱ ἐν Ἰθώμῃ Μεσσήνιοι ξυνέβησαν πρὸς τοὺς Λακεδαιμονίους, ἐφ' ᾧ τε ἐξίασιν ἐκ Πελοποννήσου καὶ μηδέποτε ἐπιβήσονται αὐτῆς· ἢν δέ τις ἁλίσκηται, τοῦ λαβόντος εἶναι δοῦλον (*Thuc.* 1, 103).

that *οἷος* is put in the case of the *τοιοῦτος* preceding (or understood), not only with the simple infinitive where the subject is the same, but sometimes also with acc. with inf. Likewise (*τοσοῦτον*) *ὅσον* (*τοσαῦτα ὅσα*) for *τοσοῦτον ὥστε*. *Οἱ Περσικοὶ νόμοι ἐπιμέλονται ὅπως τὴν ἀρχὴν μὴ τοιοῦτοι ἔσονται οἱ πολῖται οἷοι πονηροῦ τινος ἢ αἰσχροῦ ἔργου ἐφίεσθαι* (*Xen. Cyr.* 1, 2, 3). *Οὐκ ἦν ὥρα οἵα ἄρδειν τὸ πεδίον* (*Xen. An.* 2, 3, 13; *the season to irrigate the plain*). *Αἴσχιστα ἀπαλλάττονται λοιδοροῦντές τε καὶ εἰπόντες καὶ ἀκούσαντες περὶ σφῶν αὐτῶν τοιαῦτα οἷα καὶ τοὺς παρόντας ἄχθεσθαι* (*Pl. Conv.* 211). *Ἐλείπετο τῆς νυκτὸς ὅσον σκοταίους τοὺς Ἕλληνας διελθεῖν τὸ πεδίον* (*Xen. An.* 4, 1, 5). [§ 166.]

Rem. 1. From *οἷος* in the sense *τοιοῦτος ὥστε* arose the frequent use of *οἷός τε* with *εἰμί* and an inf. by § 149, in the sense of, *in a condition to* (*to be able*, &c.): *Οὐχ οἷός τέ εἰμι βοηθῆσαι ἐμαυτῷ* (*I am not able* [i.e. *am not such a one as to do it*]. *Pl. Gorg.* 408). Impersonally: *οὐχ οἷόν τε* (*ἐστίν*), *it is not possible*; *ὡς οἷόν τε.*

Rem. 2. For *ὥστε* in the sense *so that*, Herodotus and the Attic poets, sometimes even Xenophon, have *ὡς*: *Ἡ Ῥοδῶπις οὕτω δή τι κλεινὴ ἐγένετο, ὡς καὶ πάντες οἱ Ἕλληνες Ῥοδώπιος τοὔνομα ἐξέμαθον* (*Herod.* 1, 135). *Ἔνθεν ὄρη ἦν ὑπερύψηλα, ἔνθεν δὲ ὁ ποταμὸς τοιοῦτος τὸ βάθος, ὡς μηδὲ τὰ δόρατα ὑπερέχειν πειρωμένοις τοῦ βάθους* (*Xen. An.* 3, 5, 7). (Also *κώθωνα φέρονται, ὡς ἀρύσασθαι ἐκ τοῦ ποταμοῦ*. *Xen. Cyr.* 1, 2, 8, *in order to*. *Τὰς ἀσπίδας μείζους ἔχουσιν ἢ ὡς ποιεῖν ἢ ὁρᾶν τι.* *Xen. Cyr.* 6, 4, 17.)

An accusative with infinitive, or, for the same subject, a simple infinitive, stands after *πρίν* (*πρότερον πρίν*), when it denotes a simple relation of time to an action which has taken place, or to one merely conceived, which is hindered. If *πρίν* after a negative sentence denotes a condition which has not yet taken place (before the fulfilment of which something will not happen), then *πρὶν ἄν* is used with the subjunctive by § 127, or *πρίν* with the optative by § 132. Of a condition which has already taken place, *πρίν* is used with the indicative, § 114 c. R. 1; likewise where *πρίν* denotes merely a change which has taken place: *until*. *Ἡμεῖς (οἱ Λακεδαιμόνιοι) Μεσσήνην εἵλομεν πρὶν Πέρσας λαβεῖν τὴν βασιλείαν καὶ κρατῆσαι τῆς ἠπείρου καὶ πρὶν οἰκισθῆναί τινας τῶν πόλεων τῶν Ἑλληνίδων* (*Isocr. Archid.* 26). *Οὕτω τινὲς εὐπειθεῖς εἰσιν, ὥστε, πρὶν εἰδέναι τὸ προσταττόμενον, πρότερον πείθονται* (*Xen. Cyr.* 2, 2, 10). *Πρὶν ἔχεσθαι τὰ ἄκρα οὐδὲν ἐδεῖσθε εἰρήνης* (*Xen. Cyr.* 3, 2, 12). *Πολλοὶ ἀποθνήσκουσι πρότερον πρὶν δῆλοι γενέσθαι, οἷοι ἦσαν* (*Xen. Cyr.* 5, 2, 9). *Δοκεῖς μοι οὐδαμῶς μ᾽ ἀφήσειν πρὶν ἂν εἴπω* (*Pl. Phaed.* 228). *Ὁ Κῦρος ὑπέσχετο τοῖς φυγάσι μὴ πρόσθεν παύσεσθαι πρὶν αὐτοὺς καταγάγοι οἴκαδε* (*Xen. An.* 1, 2, 2). *Οὐ πρότερον ἐπαύσαντο πρὶν τὸν Ἀλκιβιάδην ἐκ τοῦ στρατοπέδου μετεπέμψαντο* (*Isocr. de Big.* 8). *Τοῖς Κερκυραίοις οὐχ ἑωρῶντο αἱ νῆες, καὶ ἐθαύμαζον τοὺς Κορινθίους πρύμναν κρουομένους· πρίν τινες ἰδόντες εἶπον, ὅτι νῆες ἐκεῖναι ἐπιπλέουσιν* (*Thuc.* 1, 51; *until at last some saw*). § 167.

[§ 167.] REM. For πρίν, the poets, Herodot., and sometimes Attic prose-writers, use πρὶν ἤ. As with πρίν, the infinitive also occurs, but more rarely with πρότερον ἤ, ὕστερον ἤ: Ἀπαγγελθέντος Ἱππίᾳ, ὅτι Ἵππαρχος ἀπέθανεν, ἐπὶ τοὺς ὁπλίτας πρότερον ἢ αἰσθέσθαι εὐθὺς ἐχώρησεν (*Thuc.* 6, 58. Usually ἢ ᾔσθοντο). (Φθάνω ἤ with acc. with inf. for φθάνω πρίν, *Xen. Cyr.* 1, 6, 40.) The infinitive instead of πρὶν ἄν with the subjunctive is very rare.

§ 168. *a*) The acc. with inf. in some places stands without a governing word, expressing merely the thought present to the mind in the form of an indefinite sentence:

1) In commands (legal language) and communications of orders: Τοὺς Θρᾷκας ἀπιέναι, παρεῖναι δ' εἰς ἔνην (*the day after to-morrow. Arist. Ach.* 172. A herald is the speaker). In laws and treaties containing several regulations, among the direct commands expressed in the imperative are blended accusatives with inf., which may be said to attach themselves dependently to a term of appointment or stipulation, &c. understood: *it is enacted, &c. that —.* (See e. g. *Pl. Legg.* 6, 760. *Thuc.* 5, 18, and 23. *Dem.* 24, 20.)

2) In entreaties and wishes: Ἑρμῆ 'μπολαῖε, τὴν γυναῖκα τὴν ἐμὴν οὕτω μ' ἀποδόσθαι τήν τ' ἐμαυτοῦ μητέρα (*Arist. Ach.* 816; *that I could but so sell!*).

3) In exclamations of wonder at something happening [like *our: to think* of his not having, &c.!]: Τοῦτον δ' ὑβρίζειν; ἀναπνεῖν δέ; ὃν εἴ τις εὖ ζῆν, ἀγαπᾶν ἔδει (*Dem.* 21. 209). More usually with the article prefixed: Τὸ δὲ μηδὲ κυνῆν οἴκοθεν ἐλθεῖν ἐμὲ τὸν κακοδαίμον' ἔχοντα (*Arist. Nub.* 268. *That I should not even —!*). (Also simple infinitive: Τῆς μωρίας, τὸ Δία νομίζειν, ὄντα τηλικουτονί, *Arist. Nub.* 819. *For a man of his years to believe in a Zeus!*)

b) As a simple infinitive, so occasionally an acc. with inf. is added [in a *qualifying* or *restrictive* sense] to a statement with ὡς or ὅσον (*so far as —*; see § 151): Ἦ οὖν ζωγραφικὸς Θεόδωρος; Οὐχ, ὅσον γ' ἐμὲ εἰδέναι (*Pl. Theæt.* 145). Οὐδεμία ἔμοιγε δοκεῖ, ὦ Πῶλε, τέχνη ἡ ῥητορικὴ εἶναι, ὡς πρὸς σὲ τἀληθῆ εἰρῆσθαι (*Pl. Gorg.* 462; *if the truth must be told you, to tell you the truth*). Ἰόλην ἔλεξας, ὥς γ' ἐπεικάζειν ἐμέ (*Soph. Trach.* 1220). (Without ὡς: δοκεῖν ἐμοί, *it seems to me, in my opinion*, Herodot., Thuc. In like manner seems to have originated the expression πολλοῦ δεῖν, μικροῦ δ., ὀλίγου δ., *so that much,* or *little, is wanting;* i. e. *far from it, almost.*)

§ 169. (402) *a*) Sentences accessory to an acc. with inf. retain the usual form of the *oratio finita;* but relative sentences to an acc. with inf. are sometimes themselves put in this form when they rather contain a continuation of the infinitive sentence, or a remark added for definition of some term in it, or when they are periphrastic expressions with εἰμί and a relative. (In longer reports parentheses, such as ὡς δοκεῖ, ὡς φαίνεται, also pass into the infinitive.) Γύγην φασὶν ἰδόντα τὸ χάσμα καὶ θαυμάσαντα καταβῆναι καὶ ἰδεῖν ἄλλα τε θαυμαστὰ καὶ ἵππον χαλκοῦν κοῖλον, θυρίδας ἔχοντα, καθ' ἃς ἐγκύψαντα ἰδεῖν ἐνόντα νεκρόν, ὡς φαίνεσθαι, μείζω ἢ κατ' ἄνθρωπον· τοῦτον δὲ ἄλλο μὲν ἔχειν οὐδέν, περὶ δὲ τῇ χειρὶ χρυσοῦν δακτύλιον, ὃν περιελόμενον ἐκβῆναι (*Pl. Rep.* 2. 359). Καλλίας διελογίζετο, ὅσον ἑκάστους ἔδει συντελεῖν, Ἀχαιοὺς μὲν πάντας καὶ Μεγαρέας ἑξήκοντα τάλαντα, τὰς δ' ἐν Εὐβοίᾳ πόλεις ἁπάσας τετταράκοντα· εἶναι δὲ πολλοὺς καὶ ἄλλους τῶν Ἑλλήνων, οὓς βούλεσθαι κοινωνεῖν τῆς συντάξεως (*Æsch.* 3, 96; *to bear their part in the tribute*). (Οὐδέν' ἂν νομίζω τοσαῦτ' ἀγαθὰ ποιῆσαι, δι' ὃν ὑμῖν προσήκειν ἐπιορκῆσαι. *Dem.* 23, 194.)[1]

---

[1] Οἱ Λακεδαιμόνιοι δέκα ἄνδρας Σπαρτιατῶν προσείλοντο τῷ Ἄγιδι ξυμβούλους, ἄνευ

[PART II.

b) It is not altogether a rare construction, especially in a long report of another person's narration or thoughts, for a dependent sentence (protasis) with a conjunction of time (ἐπειδή, ὡς, ὅτε) to be put in the acc. with inf., instead of the *oratio finita* in optative or indicative: Τὸν οὖν Σωκράτη Ἀριστόδημος ἔφη κατὰ τὴν ὁδὸν πορεύεσθαι ὑπολειπόμενον καί, περιμένοντος οὗ, κελεύειν προϊέναι εἰς τὸ πρόσθεν· ἐπειδὴ δὲ γενέσθαι ἐπὶ τῇ οἰκίᾳ τῇ Ἀγάθωνος, ἀνεῳγμένην καταλαμβάνειν τὴν θύραν — —· εὐθὺς δ' οὖν ὡς ἰδεῖν τὸν Ἀγάθωνα, Ὦ, φάναι, Ἀριστόδημε, εἰς καλὸν ἥκεις, ὅπως συνδειπνήσεις (*Pl. Conv.* 174). (Λέγεται καὶ Ἀλκμαίωνι τῷ Ἀμφιάρεω, ὅτε δὴ ἀλᾶσθαι αὐτὸν μετὰ τὸν φόνον τῆς μητρός, τὸν Ἀπόλλω ταύτην τὴν γῆν χρῆσαι οἰκεῖν. *Thuc.* 2, 102.) (In Herodot. and Thucyd. εἰ is likewise so put; in Herodot. also διότι, ἔστε, and ἐς ὅ.) [§ 169.]

Rem. Ἐπεί in the sense *for* with a sentence in acc. with inf. as in § 163 a. does not come under this head.

§ 170. *a*) *An accusative with infinitive* is denoted by *the article* as thereby comprehended into a definite substantive term (*the circumstance that* —). The nominative serves to denote an existing circumstance (*the fact that* —, quod) as subject: Τὸ χρόνον γεγενῆσθαι μετὰ τὴν πρεσβείαν πολύν, δέδοικα, μή τινα λήθην ὑμῖν ἐμπεποιήκῃ (*Dem.* 19, 3). Ἡ εὐεργεσία αὕτη, τὸ δι' ἡμᾶς Πελοποννησίους αὐτοῖς μὴ βοηθῆσαι, παρέσχεν ὑμῖν Σαμίων κόλασιν (*Thuc.* 1, 41). *The accusative* is used to denote a certain relation (conceived or actual) as the object of a verb, or with prepositions, especially διά, εἰς, and πρός: Σκοπῶν τό τε πλῆθος τῶν πολεμίων καὶ τὸ τὰ χωρία πάντα ἀπολωλέναι τῇ πόλει. Διὰ τὸ τοὺς πολεμίους προεισεληλυθέναι. Τὸ εἶναι Φίλιππον πάντων, ἕνα ὄντα, κύριον πρὸς τὸ τὰ τοῦ πολέμου τάχυ καὶ κατὰ καιρὸν πράττεσθαι πολλῷ προέχει (*Dem.* 1, 4). Even with a verb *declarandi vel sentiendi* the acc. with inf. may have the article to denote it as something known and already mentioned, but usually only as an apposition to a pronoun or substantive: Τόδε γέ μοι δοκεῖ εὖ λέγεσθαι, τὸ θεοὺς εἶναι ἡμῶν τοὺς ἐπιμελουμένους καὶ ἡμᾶς τοὺς ἀνθρώπους ἓν τῶν κτημάτων τοῖς θεοῖς εἶναι (*Pl. Phæd.* 62).

Rem. A circumstance or relation which takes place, and of which something is said, is also denoted by a sentence with ὅτι: Αἴτιον ἦν τοῦ ταῦτα τοῖς πολλοῖς ἀρέσκειν, ὅτι μεμαθηκότες ἦσαν ἐργάζεσθαι καὶ φείδεσθαι (*Isocr. Areop.* 24). Εἴρηκε Δημοσθένης πρὸς ὑμᾶς παρὰ τοῦτο διαφθαρῆναι τὰ Κερσοβλέπτου πράγματα, ὅτι τῆς πρεσβείας ὢν ἡγεμὼν ἐγὼ εἰς Θρᾴκην ἰέναι οὐκ ἠθέλησα (*Æsch.* 2, 89. Approximating to the sense, *because*). Τὰ μὲν ἄλλα ὀρθῶς ἤκουσας, ὅτι δὲ καὶ ἐμὲ οἴει εἰπεῖν τοῦτο, παρήκουσας (*Pl. Prot.* 330; *but as to the circumstance that* —, *but if*, thou thinkest —. Lat. Gram. § 398 b. R. 2).

b) The dative of the accusative with infinitive, like that of the simple infinitive, is both used of the means and instrument or cause,

---

ὧν μὴ κύριον εἶναι ἀπάγειν στρατιὰν ἐκ τῆς πόλεως (*Thuc.* 5, 63; *without whom* (it was understood that) *he should have no authority*, —. The acc. with inf. here is dependent on the notion of a decree involved in προσείλοντο).

CHAP. V.]

and also governed by particular adjectives and verbs, or by prepositions: Οὐ πλεονεξίας ἕνεκα ταῦτ' ἔπραξεν Φίλιππος ἀλλὰ τῷ δικαιότερα ἀξιοῦν τοὺς Θηβαίους ἢ ὑμᾶς (*Dem.* 2, 13; *but by reason of the Thebans making a more just demand*). Πάντα ταῦτα οὐκ ἦν ἐμποδὼν τῷ τοὺς Φωκέας σώζεσθαι (*Dem.* 19, 73).

c) The genitive of the accusative with infinitive stands, as objective genitive, with the same words which can take the genitive of the simple infinitive: Οἱ πρόγονοι τὰ πλήθη καὶ τὰς ἀκριβείας τῶν νόμων σημεῖον εἶναι ἐνόμιζον τοῦ κακῶς οἰκεῖσθαι τὴν πόλιν ταύτην (*Isocr. Areop.* 40). Οὐδ' ἐπεμελήθην τοῦ διδάσκαλόν μοί τινα γενέσθαι τῶν ἐπισταμένων (*Xen. Mem.* 4, 2, 4). Αἴτιον ἦν τοῦ ταῦτα τοῖς πολλοῖς ἀρέσκειν, ὅτι μεμαθηκότες ἦσαν ἐργάζεσθαι καὶ φείδεσθαι (*Isocr. Areop.* 24. Cf. § 164 with R. 3). Ἄνευ τοῦ τοῖς πράγμασι μὴ συμφέρειν τὸ ψήφισμα οὐδὲ πρὸς δόξαν συμφέρει τῇ πόλει τοιοῦτον οὐδὲν ἐψηφισμένη φαίνεσθαι (*Dem.* 23, 138). Ὁ ὑπὲρ τοῦ ταῦτα μὴ γενέσθαι ἀγών (*Dem.* 18, 201—*the struggle that this should not take place; the struggle to prevent it*).

Rem. The genitive of an acc. with inf. stands now and then (especially in negation) in the sense *in order that, to the intent that* (otherwise ἕνεκα): Ἐτειχίσθη Ἀταλάντη ὑπ' Ἀθηναίων ἡ ἐπὶ Λοκροῖς τοῖς Ὀπουντίοις νῆσος, τοῦ μὴ λῃστὰς ἐκπλεύντας ἐκ τῆς Λοκρίδος κακουργεῖν τὴν Εὔβοιαν (*Thuc.* 2, 32). Φοβοῦμαι διελέγχειν σε, μή με ὑπολάβῃς οὐ πρὸς τὸ πρᾶγμα φιλονεικοῦντα λέγειν, τοῦ καταφανὲς γενέσθαι, ἀλλὰ πρὸς σέ (*Pl. Gorg.* 457). (Simple infinitive: Ὁ Χαλκιδεὺς καὶ ὁ Ἀλκιβιάδης πλέοντες, ὅσοις ἐπιτύχοιεν, ξυνελάμβανον, τοῦ μὴ ἐξάγγελτοι γενέσθαι, *Thuc.* 8, 14; *that the tidings of their approach might be carried.*) (The genitive, it seems, must be explained from § 65, b.)

(The *Tenses of the Infinitive.*) *a*) The present, imperfect, future, and *futurum exactum* of the infinitive, correspond with the same tenses in the indicative (especially with the same distinction of the perfect and the narrative aorist). Πρὸς τῷ τῆς εἰρήνης αἴτιος γεγενῆσθαι καὶ ἄλλα πολλὰ τὴν πόλιν ἠδίκηκας (*Dem.* 18, 22). Οἶμαι μὲν εἰρηκέναι τι καὶ τοιοῦτον, οὐ μὴν ἀλλ' ἔτι πλείω καὶ σαφέστερον πειράσομαι διαλεχθῆναι (*Isocr. Areop.* 36). Δυοῖν ἢ τριῶν ἡμερῶν ταῦτα πεπράξεσθαί φημι (*Dem.* 19, 74).

Rem. 1. The infinitive of the perfect is sometimes put where the present might have been used, to denote the complete accomplishment of the action, or the state thereby produced, especially after verbs of willing: Βούλομαι ἀγῶνί μοι καὶ δικαστηρίῳ διωρίσθαι παρ' ὑμῖν, ὅτι τἀναντία ἐμοὶ καὶ τούτοις πέπρακται (*Dem.* 19, 223; *I wish it decided and settled* —). Ὁ κάμνων ἀξιοῖ παρὰ τοῦ ἰατροῦ καύσει καὶ τομῇ χρησάμενος ἀπηλλάχθαι τοῦ νοσήματος (*Pl. Rep.* 3, 406). Ἐθέλω ὑμᾶς συντῆξαι καὶ συμφῦσαι εἰς τὸ αὐτό, ὥστε δύ' ὄντας ἕνα γεγονέναι καί, ἕως ἂν ζῆτε, ὡς ἕνα ὄντα κοινῇ ἀμφοτέρους ζῆν (*Pl. Conv.* 192). Εἶπον οἱ ἄνδρες τὴν θύραν κεκλεῖσθαι (*Xen. Hell.* 5, 4, 7; *that the door should be shut*). (Βούλομαι, αἱροῦμαι, δεῖ, μέλλω τεθνάναι for θνήσκειν or θανεῖν.)

[§ 171.

Rem. 2. After the verbs denoting hope and surmise, promise and undertaking, the future is used both in the simple inf. and in the acc. with inf.: Ἐλπίδας ἔχω καὶ σὲ βουλήσεσθαι φίλον ἡμῖν εἶναι (*Xen. An.* 2, 5, 12). Ὑπισχνοῦμαι χρυσῆν εἰκόνα ἀναθήσειν (*Pl. Phæd.* 235). Ὤμοσαν ἦ μὴν βοηθήσειν. Ὁ Νυμφόδωρος τὸν ἐπὶ Θρᾴκης πόλεμον ὑπεδέχετο καταλύσειν (*Thuc.* 2, 29). Occasionally, however, the present is used, where the notion of future time is not meant to be prominent: Ὡμολόγεις (ξυνέθου ἡμῖν) κατὰ τοὺς νόμους πολιτεύεσθαι (*Pl. Crito*, 52). The verbs of hoping and surmising are also followed by the inf. of the aorist with ἄν, see § 173. (Of the aorist without ἄν, see § 172 a. R.)[1]

Rem. 3. Occasionally (especially in Thucydides) the inf. of the future is put instead of the present after the verbs named in § 145, 146 (e. g. δύναμαι, διανοοῦμαι, δέομαι, πείθω, &c.), to mark expressly, that the infinitive action is later and impending: Οἱ Συρακούσιοι τὸ στόμα τοῦ λιμένος διενοοῦντο κλῄσειν (*Thuc.* 7, 56). Οἱ Κορίνθιοι ἐδεήθησαν τῶν Μεγαρέων ναυσὶ σφᾶς ξυμπροπέμψειν (*Thuc.* 1, 27). (That the *shall*, by which in English we denote what is matter of will, condition, endeavour, is not expressed by the inf. of the future, but by the construction, has been already noted, § 164, § 166 b, and § 170 c.)

b) After the præteritum of a verb *declarandi vel sentiendi*, the present, perfect, and future infinitive are put of that which at the time of the principal verb was present, past, or future, consequently as *imperfectum, plusquamperf.*, and *futurum in præterito*: Οὐκ ἔφασαν τὰς ναῦς παρεῖναι. Τοὺς στρατιώτας ἥξειν ἐνόμιζον. Ἁρμόδιος καὶ Ἀριστογείτων ἐνόμισαν μεμηνῦσθαι (*Thuc.* 6, 57). Ἄφοβος ὡμολόγει κεκομίσθαι τὴν προῖκα (*Dem.* 27, 14; *to have received* = *that he had received the dowry*). (Ἡγεῖτο τὴν μεγίστην πίστιν ἔσεσθαι δεδωκώς. *Isocr. Antid.* 125.)

Rem. 1. Sometimes, especially after ἔφην, the inf. present is used even of a more remote past time, where otherwise the aorist is used (see the following §) to denote continuance, state, and recurrence (answering to the imperfect in the *oratio recta*): Μετὰ ταῦτα Ἀριστόδημος ἔφη σφᾶς μὲν δειπνεῖν, τὸν δὲ Σωκράτη οὐκ εἰσιέναι· τὸν οὖν Ἀγάθωνα πολλάκις κελεύειν μεταπέμψασθαι τὸν Σωκράτη, ἓ δὲ οὐκ ἐᾶν (*Pl. Conv.* 175 = ἐδειπνοῦμεν — εἰσῄει — ἐκέλευεν — εἴων). Συντυχεῖν ἔφη Αἰσχίνης Ἀτρεστίδᾳ παρὰ Φιλίππου πορευομένῳ καὶ μετ' αὐτοῦ γύναια καὶ παιδάρια ὡς τριάκοντα βαδίζειν, αὐτὸς δὲ θαυμάσας ἐρέσθαι τινὰ τῶν ἀνθρώπων, τίς ἄνθρωπός ἐστι καὶ τίς ὄχλος ὁ μετ' αὐτοῦ (*Dem.* 19, 305 = συνέτυχον — ἐβάδιζεν — ἠρόμην).

Rem. 2. Even after the present (the future or aorist without preterite signification, also the perfect) of verbs *declarandi vel sentiendi* the inf. present is used (simply and in acc. with inf.) with the sense of past time (instead of the aorist, (see the following §), to denote, like the imperfect, continuance, state, or recurrence: Λακεδαιμονίους φασὶν ἐν Πλαταιαῖς, ἐπειδὴ πρὸς τοῖς γεῤῥοφόροις ἐγένοντο, οὐκ ἐθέλειν μένοντας πρὸς αὐτοὺς μάχεσθαι, ἀλλὰ φεύγειν, ἐπειδὴ δὲ ἐλύθησαν αἱ τάξεις τῶν Περσῶν, ἀναστρεφομένους ὥσπερ ἱππέας μάχεσθαι καὶ οὕτω νικῆσαι τὴν

---

[1] Οὐκ ἔφη πορεύεσθαι (*Xen. An.* 1, 3, 7), because, οὐ πορεύομαι, *I am not going*, may be used as = *I will not go*.

[§ 171.] ἐκεῖ μάχην (*Pl. Lach.* 191 = ἤθελον — ἔφευγον — ἐμάχοντο — ἐνίκησαν). Δόξομεν τὸν παρελθόντα χρόνον ἀλαζονεύεσθαι καὶ τὴν μὲν φύσιν ὅμοιοι τοῖς ἄλλοις εἶναι, ταῖς δὲ σεμνότησιν πεπλασμέναις κεχρῆσθαι (*Isocr. Archid.* 98; *people will say of us*: ἠλαζονεύοντο). Οἶμαι καὶ οἴκοι ἡμᾶς τούτου ἕνεκεν ἀσκεῖν καὶ γαστρὸς κρείττους εἶναι καὶ κερδέων ἀκαίρων, ἵν', εἴ τι δέοι, δυναίμεθα αὐτοῖς συμφόρως χρῆσθαι (*Xen. Cyr.* 4, 2, 45. Not ἀσκοῦμεν, but ἠσκοῦμεν, as ἵνα δυναίμεθα shows). Τί δ' οἱ Θετταλοί; ἆρ' οἴεσθε, ὅτε τοὺς τυράννους Φίλιππος ἐξέβαλλε, προσδοκᾶν τὴν καθεστῶσαν νῦν δεκαδαρχίαν ἔσεσθαι; (*Dem.* 6, 22 = οὐ προσεδόκων.)

§ 172. *a*) The aorist infinitive (without ἄν) has the signification of a præteritum, as in the indicative, when it is governed by a verb *declarandi vel sentiendi*, or by a phrase of the same signification, and likewise in the acc. with inf. when it has the article, except where it serves to denote a purpose: Πατρὸς λέγεται ὁ Κῦρος γενέσθαι Καμβύσου (*Xen. Cyr.* 1, 2, 1). Παλαιότατοι λέγονται ἐν μέρει τινὶ τῆς Σικελίας Κύκλωπες οἰκῆσαι (*Thuc.* 6, 2). Ἀθηναίων τὸ πλῆθος Ἵππαρχον οἴονται ὑφ' Ἁρμοδίου καὶ Ἀριστογείτονος τύραννον ὄντα ἀποθανεῖν (*Thuc.* 1, 20). Ἄφοβος ἐξαρνεῖται μὴ λαβεῖν τὴν προῖκα (*Dem.* 27, 16). Διετεθρύλλητο, ὡς φαίη Σωκράτης, τὸ δαιμόνιον ἑαυτῷ σημαίνειν· ὅθεν δὴ καὶ μάλιστά μοι δοκοῦσιν αὐτὸν αἰτιάσασθαι καινὰ δαιμόνια εἰσφέρειν (*Xen. Mem.* 1, 1, 2; *to have accused him*). Τὸ μηδεμίαν τῶν πόλεων ἁλῶναι πολιορκίᾳ, μέγιστόν ἐστι σημεῖον τοῦ διὰ τούτους πεισθέντας τοὺς Φωκέας ταῦτα παθεῖν (*Dem.* 19, 61)[1]. Therefore, after a præteritum of such a verb, the aorist acquires the signification of a more remote past (as aorist): Ἐπύαξα ἐλέγετο Κύρῳ δοῦναι πολλὰ χρήματα (*Xen. An.* 1, 2, 12; *was said to have given* = *it was said that she had given*; ἐλέγετο, ὅτι ἔδωκεν by § 130 b. R. 2, not ἐδεδώκει). Οἱ Καμαριναῖοι ὕποπτοι τοῖς Συρακουσίοις ἦσαν (*were suspected by the S.*), μὴ προθύμως σφίσι μηδ' ἐπὶ τὴν πρώτην μάχην πέμψαι ἃ ἔπεμψαν (*Thuc.* 6, 75; *the help which they had sent*)[2].

REM. In some passages, ἐλπίζειν, ἐλπίς ἐστιν, ἐν ἐλπίδι εἰμί, ἐλπίδα παρέχω, προσδοκῶ, also δοκῶ, εἰκός (ἐστιν), consequently the expressions which directly denote an expectation, take the inf. aorist (without ἄν) without preterite signification, instead of the future or aorist with ἄν: Ἄσμενοι ἐκεῖσε ἴασι, οἷ ἀφικομένοις ἐλπίς ἐστιν, οὗ διὰ βίου ἤρων, τυχεῖν (*Pl. Phæd.* 57). Βρασίδας ἔλεγεν ἐν ἐλπίδι εἶναι ἀναλαβεῖν Νίσαιαν (*Thuc.* 4, 70). Μῶρος (εἶ), εἰ δοκεῖς με τλῆναι σὴν καθαιμάξαι δέρην (*Eur. Or.* 1527). Οὐκ εἰκός, ἐς νῆσον τοὺς Λακεδαιμονίους ἡμῶν ναυκρατόρων ὄντων περαιωθῆναι (*Thuc.* 5, 109). There are passages here and there in the common editions, where other verbs *declarandi vel sentiendi* are followed by

---

[1] Where the acc. with inf. with the article denotes a purpose (e. g. after ἐπιμελοῦμαι, after ὑπέρ or for ἕνεκα, § 170 c. R.) the aorist is put, without preterite signification: Ὁ ὑπὲρ τοῦ μὴ γενέσθαι ταῦτα ἀγών (*Dem.* 18, 201). Οὐδ' ἐπεμελήθην τοῦ διδάσκαλόν τινά μοι γενέσθαι (*Xen. Mem.* 4, 2, 4).

[2] Ἀντειπεῖν τοῖς πρεσβυτέροις ἢ λοιδορήσασθαι δεινότερον ἐνόμιζον ἢ νῦν περὶ τοὺς γονέας ἐξαμαρτεῖν (*Isocr.*). Here ἀντειπεῖν, &c., are not governed as verbs by ἐνόμιζον, but stand as the subject.

an aorist inf. without *ἄν* in future sense (e. g. *νομίζω κρατῆσαι* for *κρατήσειν* or *κρατῆσαι ἄν*, *ἔφη δέξασθαι*), but these undoubtedly rest upon a false reading, either *ἄν* having been accidentally omitted, or the aorist written by mistake for the future (*δέξασθαι* for *δέξεσθαι*). [§ 172.]

b) In all other connexions, the aorist infinitive is without preterite meaning, and differs from the present only as denoting a single transient action, as in the subjunctive and partly in the optative; and even this secondary distinction in many cases falls away, inasmuch as after the verbs named in § 145, 146, when these as governing verbs are in the aorist, usually (without any kind of secondary distinction) the aorist infinitive is put, rarely the present, viz. where duration, or the notion in its generality is to be expressed (but after present and future both present and aorist): *Αἱρετώτερόν ἐστι καλῶς ἀποθανεῖν ἢ ζῆν αἰσχρῶς* (*Isocr. Paneg.* 95. The dying as momentary, life as duration). *Ἡ γεωργία μαθεῖν τε ῥάστη ἐδόκει εἶναι καὶ ἡδίστη ἐργάζεσθαι* (*Xen. Œcon.* 6, 9. *Μαθεῖν*, transient). *Οἱ Ἐπιδάμνιοι ἐδέοντο τῶν Κερκυραίων μὴ σφᾶς περιορᾶν φθειρομένους ἀλλὰ τούς τε φεύγοντας ξυναλλάξαι σφίσι καὶ τὸν τῶν βαρβάρων πόλεμον καταλῦσαι* (*Thuc.* 1, 24. *Περιορᾶν* generally, *ξυναλλάξαι* and *καταλῦσαι* of single acts). *Παρῆλθε Περικλῆς ὁ Ξανθίππου, ἀνὴρ λέγειν καὶ πράττειν δυνατώτατος* (*Thuc.* 1, 139; generally). *Σωκράτην ἴσως τινὲς νομίζουσι προτρέψασθαι μὲν ἀνθρώπους ἐπ' ἀρετὴν κράτιστον γεγονέναι, προαγαγεῖν δ' ἐπ' αὐτὴν οὐχ ἱκανόν* (*Xen. Mem.* 1, 4, 1. The individual instances are in his thoughts). *Βούλομαι δηλῶσαι καὶ διελθεῖν, ὅσον αὕτη ἡ πολιτεία τῆς τότε διήνεγκεν* (*Isocr. Areop.* 62. Transient object). *Ὅσα ἐπυθόμεθα περὶ Κύρου, πειρασόμεθα δηλῶσαι* (*Xen. Cyr.* 1, 1, 6). *Εὔχοντο Ξενίαν καὶ Πασίωνα ληφθῆναι* (*Xen. An.* 1, 4, 7). *Φθησόμεθα, πρὶν τοὺς πολεμίους συλλεγῆναι, ἀναβάντες εἰς τὰ ὄρη* (*Xen. Cyr.* 3, 2, 4). *Οὕτω σφόδρ' ἠπείχθησαν μετασχεῖν τῶν κινδύνων* (*Isocr. Paneg.* 87). *Αἱ ἐκ τῆς Κορίνθου νῆες ἠναγκάσθησαν ναυμαχῆσαι πρὸς Φορμίωνα* (*Thuc.* 2, 83. Shortly afterwards: *οὕτω δὴ ἀναγκάζονται ναυμαχεῖν κατὰ μέσον τὸν πορθμόν*). *Οὐχ εἱλόμην ῥᾳθυμεῖν* (*Isocr. Paneg.* 3; of the usual manner of life). *Ὀρχεῖσθαι ἔμαθον*, not *ὀρχήσασθαι*, of the art in general. *Δημοσθένης ὡς ἅπαξ ἐταράχθη, οὐδ' ἀναλαβεῖν αὐτὸν ἠδυνήθη, ἀλλὰ καὶ πάλιν ἐπιχειρήσας λέγειν ταὐτὸν ἔπαθεν* (*Æsch.* 2, 35, *to speak*; *εἰπεῖν τι*, *to say something*) [1].

(*Infinitive with ἄν.*) The present and aorist infinitive are used with *ἄν* to denote what rests on a merely assumed condition, in the § 173.
same manner as the indicative and optative, so that the inf. present with *ἄν* answers both to the indic. imperfect and the optat. present

[1] Of the inf. with *μέλλω*, see § 116.

[§ 173.] with *ἄν*, the inf. aorist with *ἄν* both to indic. and optat. of aorist with *ἄν*. The inf. with *ἄν* corresponds likewise with the merely potential and dubitative optative with *ἄν* (§ 136), and the inf. aorist with *ἄν* stands therefore after verbs *declarandi et sentiendi* (*hope, surmise*) frequently as a modest expression, instead of the future (often coupled with a future); sometimes also, especially of something in the future with duration, the present inf. with *ἄν*.—The perfect infinitive with *ἄν* is used in the not frequent cases where the plusquamperf. indic. or perfect optative is put with *ἄν* (§ 117 and 135, 136). *Εἰ ὑμᾶς ἐβουλόμεθα ἀπολέσαι, χωρίων ἐπιτηδείων ὑμῖν ἐπιτίθεσθαι ἀπορεῖν ἄν σοι δοκοῦμεν;* (*Xen. An.* 2, 5, 18 = *ἠπoροῦμεν ἄν;*)—*Ἀθυμῶ, ὅτι μοι δοκεῖ τὰς τῶν θεῶν εὐεργεσίας οὐδ' ἂν εἷς ποτε ἀνθρώπων ἀξίαις χάρισιν ἀμείβεσθαι* (*Xen. Mem.* 4, 3. 15 = *οὐδ' ἂν εἷς ἀμείβοιτο*, potentially).—*Οἴει ἂν τοὺς θεοὺς τοῖς ἀνθρώποις δόξαν ἐμφῦσαι, ὡς ἱκανοί εἰσιν* (*οἱ θεοὶ*) *εὖ καὶ κακῶς ποιεῖν, εἰ μὴ δυνατοὶ ἦσαν, καὶ τοὺς ἀνθρώπους ἐξαπατωμένους τὸν πάντα χρόνον οὐδέποτ' ἂν αἰσθέσθαι;* (*Xen. Mem.* 1, 4, 16 = *Ἐνέφυσαν ἂν — οὐδέποτε ἂν ᾔσθοντο;*)—*Ἆρα μικρὰ ἀναλῶσαι ἂν τοῦ μὴ τὰ δίκαια ποιεῖν οἱ πλούσιοι δοκοῦσιν;* (*Dem.* 18, 107 = *Μικρὰ ἂν ἀνάλωσαν; think ye they would have sacrificed little, not to —?*) *Δοκεῖτέ μοι πολὺ βέλτιον ἂν περὶ τοῦ πολέμου βουλεύσασθαι, εἰ τὸν τόπον τῆς χώρας, πρὸς ἣν πολεμεῖτε, ἐνθυμηθείητε* (*Dem.* 4, 31 = *βουλεύσαισθε ἄν*). *Δοκῶ δεκάκις ἂν κατὰ τῆς γῆς καταδῦναι ἥδιον ἢ ὀφθῆναι οὕτω ταπεινός* (*Xen. Cyr.* 5, 5, 9 = *Ἥδιον ἂν ἀποθάνοιμι ἢ ὀφθείην —*). *Δημοσθένης τὴν τάξιν τοῦ πρῶτος λέγειν οὐκ ἂν ἔφη παραλιπεῖν οὐδ' ἐπιτρέψειν τινὶ προκαταλαβεῖν τὰ τοῦ Φιλίππου ὦτα* (*Æsch.* 2, 108). *Οἱ Ἀκαρνᾶνες ἠξίουν Δημοσθένην ἀποτειχίζειν τοὺς Λευκαδίους, νομίζοντες ῥᾳδίως γ' ἂν ἐκπολιορκῆσαι πόλεώς τε ἀεί σφισι πολεμίας ἀπαλλαγῆναι* (*Thuc.* 3, 94). *Οἱ Λακεδαιμόνιοι οὐ τοσοῦτον ἤλπιζον ἐκπεσεῖν ἂν Περικλέα, ὅσον διαβολὴν οἴσειν αὐτῷ πρὸς τὴν πόλιν* (*Thuc.* 1, 127). *Κορίνθιοι καὶ Ἀργεῖοι, εἰ Τέγεά σφισι προσγένοιτο, ἐνόμιζον ἅπασαν ἂν ἔχειν Πελοπόννησον* (*Thuc.* 5, 32).—*Ἡγοῦμαι, ὦ ἄνδρες Ἀθηναῖοι, οὐδ' εἰ ἀπολογουμένων τούτων μὴ ἐθελήσαντες ἀκοῦσαι καταψηφισάμενοι τῶν ἐσχάτων τιμήσαιτε, οὐκ ἂν ἀκρίτους αὐτοὺς ἀπολωλέναι, ἀλλὰ τὴν προσήκουσαν δίκην δεδωκέναι* (*Lys.* 27, 8. *Οὐκ ἂν ἄκριτοι ἀπολώλεσαν—, it could not have been said that they perished—*). *Τοὺς ταῦτα ἀγνοοῦντας Σωκράτης ἀνδραποδώδεις ἂν δικαίως κεκλῆσθαι ἡγεῖτο* (*Xen. Mem.* 1, 1, 16; from *κέκλημαι*. *I am called*). (With the inf. with article: *Πῶς ἔχεις πρὸς τὸ ἐθέλειν ἂν ἰέναι ἄκλητος ἐπὶ δεῖπνον; Pl. Conv.* 174. *Οὐδεὶς ἀντεῖπε διὰ τὸ μὴ ἀνασχέσθαι ἂν τὴν ἐκκλησίαν, Xen. An.* 1, 4, 20; *because the assembly would not have put up with it.*)

REM. 1. The *ἂν* belonging to the inf. is often detached from it, and placed earlier in the sentence (cf. § 139, b); in this way it comes not unfrequently to stand with the governing verb (*οἴει ἄν, οὐκ ἄν μοι δοκῶ*, &c.): *Ἴσθι ἀνόητος ὤν, εἰ οἴει ἂν τὴν ὑμετέραν ἀρετὴν περιγενέσθαι τῆς βασιλέως δυνάμεως* (*Xen. An.* 2, 1, 13;

cf. above, *Xen. Mem.* 1, 4, 16). Ἐμοὶ μὲν οὐδὲν ἂν δοκεῖ τούτου μεῖζον εὑρεθῆναι τεκμήριον (*Dem.* 31, 5). Then sometimes ἄν is repeated with the inf. itself, and so stands twice: Δοκεῖς ἂν ἢ πόλιν ἢ στρατόπεδον ἢ λῃστὰς ἢ κλέπτας ἢ ἄλλο τι ἔθνος, ὅσα κοινῇ ἐπί τι ἔρχεται ἀδίκως, πρᾶξαι ἄν τι δύνασθαι, εἰ ἀδικοῖεν ἀλλήλους; (*Pl. Rep.* 1, 351. Cf. § 139 b.)[1] [§ 173.]

Rem. 2. Ἄν with the fut. inf. in Attic writers, must be regarded as an error of the editions, the ἄν being either improperly inserted, or the aorist changed by mistake into the future.

CHAPTER VI.

The Participle.

a) A participle in Greek is partly used by way of apposition, to denote the relation of time and other circumstances in the principal sentence, partly in nearer connexion with the principal verb, as part of the predicate; likewise by way of apposition to the subject or object (δείκνυμί τινα ποιοῦντά τι), partly as simple attributive, or, with the article, as a substantive instead of a relative circumlocution. § 174.

b) To denote the relation of *time* in the principal sentence, its *manner* or other circumstances, such as *cause, occasion, means, condition, purpose, opposition* (by the assignment of a simultaneous, preceding, or subsequent action belonging to some substantive term contained in the sentence), the participles in Greek have a wide range, inasmuch as the language has participles for all the principal tenses and for the narrative aorist, both active and passive: Ταῦτα εἰπὼν ἀπῄειν. Ταῦτα λέγοντα αὐτὸν οἱ στρατιῶται καταβαίνειν ἐκέλευον. Ἀπήντησα Φιλίππῳ ἀπιόντι ἤδη. Ἱππίας τρία ἔτη τυραννεύσας ἐξέπεσε τῆς ἀρχῆς. Σωκράτης προείλετο μᾶλλον τοῖς νόμοις ἐμμένων ἀποθανεῖν ἢ παρανομῶν ζῆν (*Xen. Mem.* 4, 4, 4). Κῦρος παραγγέλλει Κλεάρχῳ λαβόντι ἥκειν ὅσον ἦν αὐτῷ στράτευμα (*Xen. An.* 1, 2, 1). Τισσαφέρνης πορεύεται ὡς βασιλέα ἱππέας ἔχων ὡς πεντακοσίους (*Xen. An.* 1, 2, 4. So, frequently, ἔχων, ἄγων, φέρων, where in English we should say *with:* Ὤφθη ξίφος ἔχων). Καλὸς καὶ ἀγαθὸς νομιζόμενος πάντα ῥᾷον διαπράξῃ. Τοῦ κέρδους ἀπεσχόμην, αἰσχρὸν νομίζων. Διὰ τί γιγνώσκων ὁ ἄνθρωπος τὰ κακὰ ὅτι κακά ἐστιν, ὅμως αὐτὰ ποιεῖ; Ἡττώμενος ὑπὸ τῆς ἡδονῆς (*Pl. Prot.* 355). Οἴει σὺ Ἄλκηστιν ὑπὲρ Ἀδμήτου ἀποθανεῖν ἄν, μὴ οἰομένην ἀθάνατον μνήμην ἀρετῆς περὶ ἑαυτῆς ἔσεσθαι; (*Pl. Conv.* 208). Παρελήλυθα συμβουλεύσων (424)

---

[1] Ἄν belonging to an infinitive understood: Ἆρ' ἂν ὀλίγα τοιαῦτα ἐν τῷ ἐνιαυτῷ αὐτὸν διαπράξασθαι προσδοκᾶτε; Ἐγὼ μὲν γὰρ οὐκ ἂν οἶμαι (*Lys.* 27, 7. Cf. § 139 c).

[§ 174.] ὑμῖν (*Isocr. Archid.* 1). Οἱ ξύμμαχοι πρέσβεις ἐς Λακεδαίμονα ἔπεμψαν Λύσανδρον αἰτήσοντας ἐπὶ τὰς ναῦς (*Xen. Hell.* 2, 1, 6). Πείθεσθαι χρὴ τῇ πατρίδι κἂν εἰς πόλεμον ἄγῃ τρωθησόμενον ἢ ἀποθανούμενον (*Pl. Crit.* 51). (Ἀλκιβιάδης ἀποκρινάμενος αὐτοῖς ἀπέπεμψεν, ὅτι τοὺς πεντακισχιλίους οὐ κωλύει ἄρχειν, *Thuc.* 8, 86. Ἀνόητον ἐπὶ τοιούτους ἰέναι, ὧν κρατήσας μὴ κατασχήσει τις, *Thuc.* 6, 11. The common object attached to the participle as the nearest or first verb.)

Rem. The position, relation, or circumstances in which a person (or thing) is during an action, which in English is commonly expressed by *when*, is denoted in Greek by ὤν, or the participle of a special verb (unless the purpose and quality in which the person appears in the action is to be denoted, in which case by § 19, the apposition is used without participle): Ταῦτα ἔμαθον ἔτι παῖς ὤν. Ἀπεδήμουν τριηραρχῶν. Ἐπὶ τοιήνδε οὖσαν Σικελίαν οἱ Ἀθηναῖοι στρατεύειν ὥρμηντο (*Thuc.* 6, 6). Ὤν is also added with explanatory appositions and such as assign the occasion or inducement: Ὁ πατήρ, ὅτ' ἤμελλε τελευτᾶν, τὴν οὐσίαν ἐνεχείρισεν Ἀφόβῳ τε καὶ Δημοφῶντι τῷ Δήμωνος υἱεῖ, ἀδελφιδοῖν ὄντοιν (*Dem.* 27, 4; *being*, or, *they being; who were* —). Οἱ Θηβαῖοι ἠνώχλουν μὲν ταῖς πόλεσι ταῖς ἐν Πελοποννήσῳ, Θετταλίαν δ' ἐτόλμων καταδουλοῦσθαι, Μεγαρεῦσι δέ, ὁμόροις οὖσιν, ἠπείλουν (*Isocr. Phil.* 53).

§ 175. The relation of the participle to the principal action is more exactly denoted by the addition of certain adverbs, partly to the principal verb, partly to the participle itself.

a) By τότε (τότε ἤδη), εἶτα, ἔπειτα (τηνικαῦτα), οὕτως, standing after the participle and before the principal verb, it is marked with emphasis that the principal action takes place only *through*, or not *until after*, the action expressed by the participle (as consequence thereof): ἔπειτα, εἶτα sometimes also denotes an antithesis (*then, for all that*), especially in expressions of censure and surprise: Ὁ Ἀναξίβιος τὸν Ξενοφῶντα ἐκέλευσε συνδιαβάντα τὸν Ἑλλήσποντον ἔπειτα οὕτως ἀπαλλάττεσθαι (*Xen. An.* 7, 1, 4; *to go with him over the H., and then* (*not sooner*) *withdraw*). Δέομαι ὑμῶν ἀκροασαμένους διὰ τέλους τῆς ἀπολογίας τότε ἤδη ψηφίζεσθαι τοῦθ' ὅ, τι ἂν ὑμῖν αὐτοῖς ἄριστον νομίζητε εἶναι (*Andoc.* 1, 9).—Δεινὰ μέντ' ἂν πάθοις, ὦ βέλτιστε, εἰ Ἀθήναζε ἀφικόμενος, οὗ τῆς Ἑλλάδος πλείστη ἐστὶν ἐξουσία τοῦ λέγειν, ἔπειτα σὺ ἐνταῦθα τούτου μόνος ἀτυχήσαις (*Pl. Gorg.* 461). (Κᾆτα for simple εἶτα: Ἐὰν ῥητορικὸς γενόμενός τις κᾆτα ταύτῃ τῇ δυνάμει καὶ τῇ τέχνῃ ἀδικῇ, οὐ τὸν διδάξαντα δεῖ μισεῖν, *Pl. Gorg.* 457.)

b) By ἅμα and μεταξύ it is denoted that the main action goes on *with* and *during* (*in the midst of*) the action of the participle. The adverbs, in point of signification, belong, in the first instance, to the leading verb, but in the Greek idiom they usually attach themselves more closely to the participle (ἅμα ἰών, μεταξὺ ἰών, *going the while, in the midst of his going, as he goes*): Ὁ Κῦρος οὐ μόνον τῷ πορεύεσθαι τὴν ὁδὸν προσεῖχε τὸν νοῦν, ἀλλ' ἅμα προϊὼν ἐπεσκοπεῖτο, εἴ τι δυνατὸν εἴη τοὺς πολεμίους ἀσθενεστέρους ποιεῖν (*Xen. Cyr.* 5, 2, 22; *as he went on, he considered at the same time*). Τὸ τοῦ θεοῦ σημεῖον ἐν ἄλλοις λόγοις πολλαχοῦ μ' ἐπέσχε λέγοντα μεταξύ (*Pl. Apol.* 40; *in the midst of my speaking*). So εὐθὺς γενόμενοι, ἀποβεβηκότες, *directly they were born, immediately after landing.*

c) Ἅτε (ἅτε δή), οἷον, οἷα δή with the participle denote that this assigns the ground or cause (*as being*, &c. = *because*): Ὁ Κῦρος, ἅτε παῖς ὢν καὶ φιλόκαλος καὶ

φιλότιμος, ἥδετο τῇ στολῇ (*Xen. Cyr.* 1, 3, 3). Μάλα χαλεπῶς πορευόμενοι οἱ Λακεδαι- [§
μόνιοι, οἷα δὴ ἐν νυκτί τε καὶ ἐν φόβῳ ἀπιόντες, εἰς Αἰγόσθενα τῆς Μεγαρικῆς ἀφικνοῦν- 175.]
ται (*Xen. Hell.* 6, 4, 26). (In Herodotus also ὥστε.) Sometimes ὤν in an apposition with ἅτε, οἷα δή, ὡς is omitted: Τοὺς τῆς τραγῳδίας ποιητὰς εἰς τὴν πολιτείαν οὐ παραδεξόμεθα ἅτε τυραννίδος ὑμνητάς (*Pl. Rep.* 8, 568). Πάντες οἱ τοῦτο ἐπιτηδεύοντες ἄκοντες ἐπιτηδεύουσιν ὡς ἀναγκαῖον ἀλλ' οὐχ ὡς ἀγαθόν (*Pl. Rep.* 2, 358).

d) Ὡς with the participle denotes the *thought*, *opinion*, *supposition*, *purpose*, *pretext*, in, with, or under which the action is done: Ἀγανακτοῦσιν ὡς μεγάλων τινῶν ἀπεστερημένοι (*Pl. Rep.* 1, 329 = *thinking themselves deprived*). Οἱ Ἀθηναῖοι τὸν Περικλέα ἐν αἰτίᾳ εἶχον ὡς π ε ί σ α ν τ α σφᾶς πολεμεῖν καὶ δι' ἐκεῖνον ταῖς ξυμφοραῖς π ε ρ ι π ε π τ ω κ ό τ ε ς (*Thuc.* 2, 59). Μῦθόν τινα Παρμενίδης φαίνεταί μοι διηγεῖσθαι παισὶν ὡς οὖσιν ἡμῖν (*Pl. Soph.* 242; *to children, as if we were such; to us as if we were children*). Ἀρταξέρξης συλλαμβάνει Κῦρον ὡς ἀποκτενῶν (*Xen. An.* 1, 1, 3). Οἱ Λακεδαιμόνιοι ἐν ὀλιγωρίᾳ ἐποιοῦντο ὡς ῥᾳδίως ληψόμενοι βίᾳ τὸ χωρίον (*Thuc.* 4, 5). (Of the omission of ὤν, see under *c*.)

REM. In denoting the purpose after verbs of motion (εἶμι, ἥκω, ἔρχομαι, πάρειμι, πέμπω, ἄγω, and more special verbs of this kind, such as ἀποπλέω) the simple participle is used. See the examples, § 174. (Ἦια ἐρῶν, *I was going to say.*) (Παρασκευάζομαι ὡς ἀπιών, *Xen. Cyr.* 1, 3, 13, and Ἵππαρχος παρεσκευάζετο προπηλακιῶν τὸν Ἁρμόδιον, *Thuc.* 6, 54. Also with the infinitive: παρεσκευάζετο προσβάλλειν τῇ πόλει (*Xen. Hell.* 3, 1, 17); παρασκευαζόμενος πολιορκήσειν (*Xen. Cyr.* 7, 5, 12).

e) An antithesis is denoted by καίπερ (*although*, *albeit*) or simple καί (*even*) before the participle (poetically πέρ or πὲρ ἔμπης after the participle), with sometimes ὅμως (*nevertheless*) before the principal verb: Κἂν σύ, καίπερ οὕτω σοφὸς ὤν, εἴ τίς σε διδάξειεν, ὃ μὴ τυγχάνεις ἐπιστάμενος, βελτίων ἂν γένοιο (*Pl. Prot.* 318). Sometimes ὅμως in connexion with καί attaches itself more nearly to the participle, although in strictness it belongs to the principal verb (like ἅμα and μεταξύ, see under *b*): Τῇ ὑστεραίᾳ οἱ τετρακόσιοι ἐς τὸ βουλευτήριον ὅμως καὶ τεθορυβημένοι ξυνελέγοντο (*Thuc.* 8, 93). (Ὤν with καίπερ omitted: Γιγνώσκω σαφῶς, καίπερ σκοτεινός, τήν γε σὴν αὐδὴν ὅμως, *Soph. Œd. R.* 1326.)[1]

Of the manner in which a defining circumstance is annexed by means of the participle, it is to be observed further: § 176.

a) A participle denoting the *way* and *manner*, the *ground* or *reason*, &c. may govern, or have with it, a relative or interrogative pronoun (or pronominal adjective or adverb): Ἆρ' οὖν τῇδε τῇ ἡμέρᾳ εἰλήφαμεν, ὃ πάλαι καὶ πολλοὶ ζητοῦντες πρὶν εὑρεῖν κατεγήρασαν; (*Pl. Theæt.* 202.) Τί, ἔφη ὁ Ξενοφῶν, ἰδὼν τὸν Κριτόβουλον ποιοῦντα τοιαῦτα κατέγνωκας αὐτοῦ; (*Xen. Mem.* 1, 3, 10.)

b) The Greeks often use a participle to denote the *manner* in which, the *means*

---

[1] Rarer constructions: *a*) Οὐκ ἄν ποτε ἐξεῦρον ὀρθῶς τὰ μετέωρα πράγματα, εἰ μὴ τὴν φροντίδα λεπτὴν καταμίξας εἰς τὸν ὅμοιον ἀέρα (*Arist. Nub.* 229. The participle to denote a negative condition with εἰ prefixed); *b*) Οἱ Ἀθηναῖοι τῆς γῆς ἐκράτουν, ὅσα μὴ προϊόντες πολὺ ἐκ τῶν ὅπλων (*Thuc.* 1, 111; *so far as not —*, = *yet without advancing far from the camp:* ὅσον μή and ὅσα μή); *c*) Ταῦτά σοι ἕνεκα τοῦδε ἐμήκυνα, ὑποπτεύων, σέ, ὥσπερ καὶ αὐτὸς οἴει, ὠδίνειν τι κύοντα ἔνδον (*Pl. Theæt.* 151; *because I suspected*).

[§ 176.] whereby, or generally the *circumstances* under which something takes place, where in other languages this statement of the manner, means, or circumstance is put as the principal proposition, and that which in Greek is the principal proposition becomes the accessory definition (dependent sentence or expression with a preposition); this happens especially where the statement of the circumstance is interrogative or relative in form: Τί δεδιότες σφόδρα οὕτως ἐπείγεσθε; (*Xen. Hell.* 1, 7, 26.) Τί ἂν εἰπών σέ τις ὀρθῶς προσείποι; (*Dem.* 18, 22.) Οἶδα, ὅποι χρὴ ἐλθόντα λαβεῖν ἕκαστα (*Xen. Œcon.* 8, 22; *whither I must go to take* —). Οἱ λίαν φιλοσοφοῦντες τῶν λόγων ἄπειροι γίγνονται, οἷς χρὴ χρώμενον ὁμιλεῖν τοῖς ἀνθρώποις (*Pl. Gorg.* 484; *which one must use in converse with men*). Ξυνελέγη Δημοσθένει τὸ στράτευμα, ὃ ἔδει ἔχοντα εἰς τὴν Σικελίαν βοηθεῖν (*Thuc.* 7, 26). Οὐ διελογίσασθε, ὑπὲρ οἵα πεποιηκότων ἀνθρώπων κινδυνεύσετε (*Dem.* 18, 98). — Τὸν τοιοῦτον ἔξεστιν ἐπὶ κόρρης τύπτοντα μὴ διδόναι δίκην (*Pl. Gorg.* 486; *one can smite such a man on the cheek without being punished for it*). Οἱ Ἀργεῖοι πολλάκις Ἀθηναίους ἐκέλευον σχόντας μόνον σὺν ὅπλοις ἐς τὴν Λακωνικὴν καὶ τὸ ἐλάχιστον μετὰ σφῶν δῃώσαντας ἀπελθεῖν (*Thuc.* 6, 105).

Rem. Especially we may note the expressions τί (ὅ,τι) παθών and τί μαθών, where, with surprise and disapprobation, one asks (directly or indirectly) why a person did this or that (most commonly παθών, denoting affection by some external circumstance, or impulse generally [*what possessed him to* —], μαθών, some notion which the person has taken into his head [*what induced him to* —]: Λέξον δή μοι, τί παθοῦσαι, εἴπερ νεφέλαι γ' εἰσὶν ἀληθῶς, θνηταῖς εἴξασι (ἐοίκασι) γυναιξίν; *Arist. Nub.* 341, *what has come to them, what ails them, that they* —.) (Dependently, without express question, merely attached to the expression of surprise or vexation implied in the principal sentence: Τί ἄξιός εἰμι παθεῖν ἢ ἀποτῖσαι, ὅ, τι μαθὼν ἐν τῷ βίῳ οὐχ ἡσυχίαν ἦγον; *Pl. Apol.* 36, *what do I deserve to suffer because* (*God knows why* —, or, *for some crotchet or other that I had got into my head* —) *I did not keep quiet.* (Τί δῆτα ἔχων στρέφει; *Pl. Phæd.* 236.)

c) The participle, (put as apposition to the subject of a preceding sentence,) gives the character of an action or expression of some other person, mentioned in that sentence, or asks what was the ground or cause of it: Σοί, ὦ Σώκρατες, ἔφη ὁ Θρασύμαχος, χαρίζομαι. Εὖ γε σὺ ποιῶν (*Pl. Rep.* 1, 351; *it is well done of thee*). Ἀπορῶ, τί χρή ποτε εἰπεῖν ὄντως εἶναι τὸν σοφιστήν. Εἰκότως γε σὺ ἀπορῶν (*Pl. Soph.* 231; *no wonder thou art at a loss*). Ὁ ἐμὸς πατὴρ τὸν ἄνδρα ἀπέκτεινεν. Τί λαβὼν ἀδικοῦντα; (*Xen. Cyr.* 3, 1, 37; *what wrong had he found him doing?*) Ἐρωτῶ, εἰ δοκῶ ἂν ὑμῖν περὶ πλείονος τὴν Φιλίππου φιλίαν τῆς τῶν παίδων σωτηρίας ποιήσασθαι; ποίων κρατηθεὶς ἡδονῶν; ἢ τί πώποτε ἄσχημον ἕνεκα χρημάτων πράξας; (*Æsch.* 2, 152.) The speaker himself interposes a parenthetical εὖ ποιῶν, καλῶς ποιῶν in the sense, *with good reason, happily:* Τοῦτο τοίνυν, εὖ ποιοῦν, οὐ συνέβη (*Dem.* 23, 143). (A remark parenthetically interposed in a report of what some person has said: Παρελθὼν Αἰσχίνης, Ἀγνοεῖτ', ἔφη, ὦ βουλή, τὸ πρᾶγμα; καὶ τὸν αὐτόχειρα ἔχοντες (λέγων τὸν Ἀρίσταρχον) μέλλετε καὶ ζητεῖτε; *Dem.* 21, 116. Apposition to the subject of ἔφη.)

Rem. Certain participles are attached to the subject, to characterize the action in respect of its circumstances or manner, almost with an adverbial signification, especially ἀρχόμενος, *at the beginning* (ὅπερ ἀρχόμενος ἔλεγον, *Pl. Theæt.* 174), ἀρξάμενος in the construction ἀρξάμενοι ἀπό τινος (Σωκράτους), *first S. and then the rest, beginning with S.*, τελευτῶν, *at last.* (Οἱ Ἕλληνες κινηθῆναι οὐκ ἐδύναντο ἐκ τοῦ χωρίου, ἀλλὰ τελευτῶντες καὶ ἀπὸ τοῦ ὕδατος εἶργον αὐτοὺς οἱ Θρᾷκες, *Xen. An.* 6,

1, 8.) (In the language of common life: *ἀνύσας ἄνοιγε, make haste and open!* Φλυαρεῖς ἔχων. See the Lexicon.) [§ 176.]

d) Sometimes several participles stand together, either attached, without connexion among themselves, to the same leading verb in order to define the action on several sides of it (by nearer and more remote circumstances), or so that one participle attaches itself to another as its leading verb, especially participles put according to the rules in § 177 and 178: Ἄδικοι ὄντες κερδανοῦμέν τε καὶ λισσόμενοι (*by praying*) ὑπερβαίνοντες καὶ ἁμαρτάνοντες (*when we transgress and sin*) πείθοντες τοὺς θεοὺς ἀζήμιοι ἀπαλλάξομεν (*Pl. Rep.* 2, 366). Φανήσεται ὁ θεσμοθέτης, πεισθεὶς ὁποσῳδήποτε ἀργυρίῳ, καθυφεὶς τὸν ἀγῶνα (*Dem.* 21, 39; *that he has given up the suit, induced by* —). (In the genitive absolute: Οἱ Θηβαῖοι ὕστερον παρεγένοντο, ἤδη τῶν ἀνδρῶν τῶν μὲν διεφθαρμένων, τῶν δὲ ζώντων ἐχομένων, *Thuc.* 2, 5; *being alive in prison.* Τοῦ ἀπὸ τῶν Ἀθηναίων κήρυκος, οὐδὲν ἐπισταμένου τῶν γεγενημένων, ἐλθόντος οὐ πολὺ ὕστερον αὖθις περὶ τῶν νεκρῶν, ἀπέδοσαν οἱ Βοιωτοί, *Thuc.* 4, 101; *without knowing what had happened.*)

e) Sometimes a participle of circumstance is, less accurately (where one would have rather expected a dependent sentence or a double genitive, § 181) attached in the nominative to the subject of the principal sentence, although this cannot, quite unchanged, be the subject of the participle. Namely, either (1) the passage begins with the participle in the plural referred to a plural term (especially one that has been the subject of discourse so far) or to several individuals, and then is carried on in the principal sentence in reference to a part of the plural term or some of the individuals (sometimes even with an extended reference to a larger plural than the one just mentioned), or also (2) after a general statement concerning a plural, a participle follows with an annexed partitive or less comprehensive subject. (1) Ὡς κραυγὴ καὶ κτύπος ἐγίγνετο, αἰσθόμενοι οἱ ἔνδον τοῦ θορύβου, κελεύσαντος τοῦ βασιλέως σκέψασθαι, τί εἴη τὸ πρᾶγμα, ἐκθέουσί τινες ἀνοίξαντες τὰς πύλας (*Xen. Cyr.* 7, 5, 28). Ἐνθαῦτα μαχόμενοι καὶ βασιλεὺς καὶ Κῦρος καὶ οἱ ἀμφ' αὐτοὺς ὑπὲρ ἑκατέρων, ὁπόσοι μὲν τῶν ἀμφὶ βασιλέα ἀπέθνησκον, Κτησίας λέγει. Κῦρος δὲ αὐτός τε ἀπέθανε καὶ ὀκτὼ οἱ ἄριστοι τῶν περὶ αὐτόν (*Xen. An.* 1, 8, 27). Καὶ πείσαντες [οἱ Ἀθηναῖοι] τοὺς ξυμμάχους εὐθὺς ἐχώρουν ἐπὶ Ὀρχομενὸν τὸν Ἀρκαδικὸν πάντες πλὴν Ἀργείων (*Thuc.* 5, 61; *all*, viz. the allies as well as the Athenians). (2) Πίστεις ἔδοσαν ἀλλήλοις οἱ Ἑλένην μνηστεύοντες, ἦ μὴν βοηθήσειν, εἴ τις ἀποστεροίη τὸν ἀξιωθέντα λαβεῖν αὐτήν, νομίζων ἕκαστος τὴν ἐπικουρίαν ταύτην αὑτῷ παρασκευάζειν (*Isocr. Laud. Hel.* 40)[1].

REM. Sometimes an irregularity in the case results, where the sentence begins with a participle in the nominative, and then the construction is altered so that a different case is required. See *Anacoluthia*, § 216. (Of a different irregularity in the case of the participle, see *ibid.* R. 2.)

a) With sundry verbs, mostly intransitive, a participle is (by way of apposition) so constructed with the subject, that it belongs at the same time to the verb which is predicated of the subject in relation to the action (or state) expressed by the participle; the leading verb § 177.

---

[1] Αἱ Ἀττικαὶ νῆες παραγιγνόμεναι τοῖς Κερκυραίοις, εἴ πῃ πιέζοιντο, φόβον μὲν παρεῖχον τοῖς ἐναντίοις, μάχης δὲ οὐκ ἦρχον, δεδιότες οἱ στρατηγοὶ τὴν πρόῤῥησιν τῶν Ἀθηναίων, *Thuc.* 1, 49 (4, 73).

[§ 177.] being in itself incomplete or undefined, and the participle serving to complete it into an entire and definite predicate, in the same manner as an infinitive is used as complement of the predicate. Such verbs are those which denote *continuance* and *perseverance*, or *weariness* and *cessation*, *satisfaction* or *dissatisfaction* (*shame*), *superiority* or its opposite, the *being early* or *late*, also *being right* or *wrong* (διατελῶ, διάγω, διαγίγνομαι, ἀνέχομαι, καρτερῶ, κάμνω, ἀπείρηκα, παύομαι, ἐκλείπω, λήγω. χαίρω, ἀγαπῶ, ἥδομαι, poet. τέρπομαι, ἀγανακτῶ, αἰσχύνομαι, ἄχθομαι, μεταμέλομαι, χαλεπῶς φέρω, νικῶ, ἡττῶμαι, ἐλλείπομαι, ἄρχω, ὑπάρχω, φθάνω, ἀδικῶ, ἁμαρτάνω. εὖ, καλῶς ποιῶ). Σωκράτης οὐδὲν ἄλλο ποιῶν διαγεγένηται ἢ διασκοπῶν τά τε δίκαια καὶ τὰ ἄδικα (*Xen. Mem.* 4, 8, 4). Ἀπείρηκα τρέχων (*Xen. An.* 5, 1, 2). Οὐδὲν παυόμεθα εἰς τὸ αὐτὸ περιφερόμενοι (*Pl. Gorg.* 517). Τοῖς καλῶς ἐρωτῶσιν ἀποκρινόμενος χαίρω (*Pl. Prot.* 318). Φαρνάβαζος τῆς Αἰολίδος χαλεπῶς ἔφερεν ἀπεστερημένος (*Xen. Hell.* 3, 3, 13). Οὐδὲ τὸν ἀδελφὸν ᾐσχύνετο τὸν ἔτι ζῶντα οὕτως ὀλίγον φροντίζουσα τοῦ τεθνεῶτος (*Isocr. Ægin.* 40). Ἐάν τις ἡμᾶς εὖ ποιῶν ὑπάρχῃ (*first confers benefits upon us*), τούτου εἴς γε δύναμιν οὐχ ἡττησόμεθα εὖ ποιοῦντες (*Xen. An.* 2, 3, 23). Τὰ τῆς πόλεως οὕτως ὑπῆρχεν ἔχοντα (*Dem.* 18, 235; *were in this posture*). Οἱ Ἕλληνες φθάνουσιν ἐπὶ τῷ ἄκρῳ γενόμενοι τοὺς πολεμίους (*Xen. An.* 3, 4, 49). Ὁ πεζὸς στρατὸς τῶν Ἀθηναίων φθάνει ἀναβὰς ἐπὶ τὰς Ἐπιπολὰς πρὶν τοὺς Συρακουσίους παραγενέσθαι (*Thuc.* 6, 97). Ἀδικεῖτε πολέμου ἄρχοντες καὶ σπονδὰς λύοντες (*Thuc.* 1, 53). Ἀθηναῖοι τοὺς ἐκ τῆς νήσου δεσμώτας μετεμέλοντο ἀποδεδωκότες Λακεδαιμονίοις (*Thuc.* 5, 35).

b) In the same manner the participle stands with the verbs and phrases τυγχάνω, λανθάνω (τινά), δῆλός εἰμι, φανερός εἰμι, φαίνομαι (*show myself, am seen to* —), which are used personally of the person who accidentally, privately, or openly does or is something: Ἔτυχον ὁπλῖται ἐν τῇ ἀγορᾷ καθεύδοντες ὡς πεντήκοντα (*Thuc.* 4, 113; *so it was that they were asleep* —). Ἔλαθεν ἀφθέντα πάντα καὶ καταφλεχθέντα (*Thuc.* 4, 133). Λέληθα ἐμαυτὸν φίλτρον τι εἰδώς (*Xen. Mem.* 2, 3, 11; *without being myself aware of it, I have the knowledge of* —). Δῆλος εἶ καταφρονῶν μου (*Pl. Theæt.* 189). Κήδεταί τις μάλιστα τούτου, ὃ τυγχάνει φιλῶν (*Pl. Rep.* 3, 412). Οἱ Θηβαῖοι φανεροὶ πᾶσιν ἦσαν ἀναγκασθησόμενοι καταφεύγειν ἐφ' ὑμᾶς (*Dem.* 18, 19). Ἡ ψυχὴ ἀθάνατος φαίνεται οὖσα (*Pl. Phæd.* 107; *it appears that the soul* —).

Rem. 1. When ὤν with an adjective is the participle, it is sometimes omitted, especially with verbs denoting *continuance*, and with τυγχάνω: Σωκράτης ἀνυπόδητος καὶ ἀχίτων διετέλει (*Xen. Mem.* 1, 6, 2). Γίγνεται πόλις, ἐπειδὴ τυγχάνει ἡμῶν ἕκαστος οὐκ αὐτάρκης ἀλλὰ πολλῶν ἐνδεής (*Pl. Rep.* 2, 369)[1]. (Poetically: ἐν ἄγροις τυγχάνω, with a preposition, or with local dative, ἄγροις, *Soph. El.* 313.) With φαίνομαι, the omission of ὤν is the usual practice. Ψευδὴς φαίνεται ὁ Γωβρύας (*Xen. Cyr.* 5, 2, 4).

---

[1] Ὅ, τι, ὅπου, ὅπῃ, ὁπότε τυγχάνω, τυγχάνεις, &c., *what* (*as it*) *may chance* (with me, thee, &c.): Περιέτρεχον, ὅπῃ τύχοιμι (*Pl. Conv.* 173).

Rem. 2. With λανθάνω, δῆλος, and φανερός εἰμι, sometimes a sentence with ὅτι follows: Οἱ πολέμιοι δῆλοι ἦσαν, ὅτι ἐπικείσονται ἐν τῇ καταβάσει (*Xen. An.* 5, 2, 26). Also λανθάνει (τινά), δῆλόν ἐστι, φανερόν ἐ. are put impersonally with ὅτι: Πᾶσιν ἦν φανερόν, ὅτι μᾶλλον ἡσθήσεσθε τοῖς παρακαλοῦσιν ὑμᾶς ἐπὶ τὸν πόλεμον ἢ τοῖς περὶ εἰρήνης συμβουλεύουσιν (*Isocr. de Pac.* 5 = φανεροὶ ἦτε ἡσθησόμενοι). [§ 177]

Rem. 3. Αἰσχύνομαι λέγων, *I am ashamed of saying it*, (even) *while I say it*, αἰσχύνομαι λέγειν, *I am ashamed to say* (*and therefore forbear to say*). Φαίνομαι has the infinitive in the sense *seem* (*seem to myself*): Ἔγωγέ μοι φαίνομαι δύο καθορᾶν εἴδη τῆς μαντικῆς (*Pl. Soph.* 235). (Ἀποκάμνω ποιεῖν τι, *I give over doing something.*) Ἄρχομαι (middle) has usually the infinitive, rarely the participle. Some other verbs and phrases of kindred meaning occur now and then constructed thus with the participle, e.g. πειρῶμαι βασανίζων τι (*Pl. Phil.* 21; *make an attempt at testing something*), κύριός εἰμι ποιῶν τι (*Thuc.* 5, 34; *have a right to do something*), συμβαίνει τι γιγνόμενον (and, without ὤν, μέγιστον κακὸν συμβαίνει ἡ ἀδικία, *Pl. Gorg.* 479), μεστός εἰμι θυμούμενος (*Soph. Œd. C.* 768 = κάμνω, *am tired out and sated*).

Rem. 4. As δῆλός εἰμι, so, in the poets, and sometimes in prose, ἀρκῶ, ἱκανός, κρείττων, βελτίων εἰμί are used personally with a participle instead of an impersonal expression with acc. with inf. (ἀρκεῖ ἐμέ —): Ἀρκέσω θνήσκουσ' ἐγώ (*Soph. Ant.* 547). Κρείττων ἦν ὁ πατήρ σου μὴ λειτουργήσας ἢ τοσαῦτα τῶν ἑαυτοῦ ἀναλώσας (*Lys.* 26, 4).

Rem. 5. With some impersonal verbs and expressions, which denote the consequence and advantage of an action, sometimes, instead of the infinitive, a participle stands as apposition to the dative, so that the use or advantage during (after) the action is denoted: Ἀθηναῖοι πέμψαντες ἐς Δελφοὺς ἐπηρώτων τὸν θεόν, εἰ πολεμοῦσιν ἄμεινον ἔσται (*Thuc.* 1, 118; also λυσιτελήσει, συνοίσει). Ἡμεῖς ἠγανακτοῦμεν μὲν ἐπὶ τοῖς λεγομένοις, πλέον δ' οὐδὲν ἦν ἀγανακτοῦσιν ἡμῖν (*Dem.* 35, 31). In the same manner: Μεταμέλει μοι οὕτως ποιήσαντι, *to have so acted; of having so acted.*[1]

Rem. 6. The verb φθάνω in negative, dubitative expressions is used of that which, when it takes place, will not take place too soon; and, in the second person, (οὐκ ἂν φθάνοις, φθάνοιτε) expresses a challenge or summons to do something immediately: Οὐκ ἂν φθάνοις λέγων, εἴ τι ᾔσθησαί με φίλτρον ἐπιστάμενον (*Xen. Mem.* 2, 3, 11).[2] (More rarely in the third person, of that which, since it *must* be done, may as well be done at once: Εἰ μὴ τιμωρήσεσθε τούτους, οὐκ ἂν φθάνοι τὸ πλῆθος τούτοις δουλεῦον, *Dem.* 24, 143.)

a) A participle is likewise attached to the *object* of certain verbs, to denote that the proper complete (*logical*) *object* of the verbs is not the *grammatical* object, in itself, but that *state* or *action of it* which the participle expresses; so that the object and participle together have the same meaning as the accusative with the infinitive after *verba declarandi*: Δείκνυμί τινα ποιοῦντά τι. If the subject of the leading verb should also be its object, the participle is put in the nominative and re- § 178.

---

[1] Ἔοικας τὴν εὐδαιμονίαν οἰομένῳ τρυφὴν καὶ πολυτέλειαν εἶναι (*Xen. Mem.* 1, 6, 10; *thou art like one who thinks; thou seemest to think*).

[2] In the editions often incorrectly pointed as a question.

[§ 178.] ferred to the subject: *Δείκνυμι ποιήσας τι* (*that I have done something*). With the passive, or the forms used intransitively, the participle is referred to the subject: *Δειχθήσομαι ποιήσας τι.* Such verbs are those which denote *to see, mark, know, experience, remember, show, prove, find* (*find oneself*), *signify* (verbs of knowledge and experience): (ὁρῶ, αἰσθάνομαι, ἀκούω, πυνθάνομαι, μανθάνω, καταμ., οἶδα, ἐπίσταμαι, γιγνώσκω, μέμνημαι, ἐπιλανθάνομαι, δηλῶ, δείκνυμι, ἐπιδ., ἀποδ., ἀποφαίνω, ἐξελέγχω, ἀγγέλλω, εὑρίσκω.) Ὁρῶ τὸν πόλεμον ὑμῖν πολλῶν κακῶν αἴτιον γεγενημένον (*Isocr. Phil.* 2). Ἐπέδειξα Αἰσχίνην οὐδὲν ἀληθὲς ἀπηγγελκότα ἀλλὰ φενακίσανθ' ὑμᾶς (*Dem.* 19, 177). Οἱ Ἕλληνες οὐκ ᾔδεσαν Κῦρον τεθνηκότα (*Xen. An.* 1, 10, 16). Ἄνθρωποι καλοὶ κἀγαθοὶ ἐπειδὰν γνῶσιν ἀπιστούμενοι, οὐ φιλοῦσι τοὺς ἀπιστοῦντας (*Xen. Cyr.* 7, 2, 17). Φίλιππος πάνθ' ἕνεκα ἑαυτοῦ ποιῶν ἐξελήλεγκται (*Dem.* 2, 8). Οἱ τῶν Ἀθηναίων στρατηγοὶ τοῖς τε ἐπιχειρήμασιν ἑώρων οὐ κατορθοῦντες καὶ τοὺς στρατιώτας ἀχθομένους τῇ μονῇ (*Thuc.* 7, 47). Κλέαρχος ἤκουε Κύρου ἔξω ὄντα τοῦ Ἑλληνικοῦ εὐωνύμου βασιλέα (*Xen. An.* 1, 8, 13).[1] Ἀπεφάνην συμφορᾶς μὲν οὐδεμιᾶς αἴτιος γεγενημένος, πολλὰ δὲ κἀγαθὰ εἰργασμένος τὴν πόλιν (*Lys.* 25, 4). Μέμνημαι ἔγωγε καὶ παῖς ὢν (*even from my childhood*) Κριτίᾳ τῷδε ξυνόντα σε (*Pl. Charm.* 156). Ἴσθι ἀνόητος ὤν (*Xen. An.* 2, 1, 13). Σκοπούμενος εὕρισκον οὐδαμῶς ἂν ἄλλως, ὃ ἠβουλόμην, διαπραξάμενος, πλὴν εἰ γραφείη λόγος ὥσπερ εἰκὼν τῆς ἐμῆς διανοίας (*Isocr. Antid.* 7). Πρῶτος βασιλεῖ Κῦρον ἐπιβουλεύοντα ἤγγειλα (*Xen. An.* 2, 3, 19).

Rem. 1. But instead of the nominative referred to the principal subject, occasionally a reflexive pronoun stands with the participle in the accusative (cf. acc. with inf. for the nominative, § 160): Ἢ δεῖξον οὐ πεποιηκότα ταῦτα σαυτὸν ἢ δίκην ὕπεχε (*Dem.* 22, 29). From αἰσθάνομαι ἐμαυτὸν πεπρακώς comes the construction συνέβη μοι αἰσθέσθαι ἐμαυτὸν πεπρακότι (*Dem.* 18, 46), by § 157, b.

Rem. 2. Instead of an object with participle attached, the participle of an impersonal verb or expression may also stand alone: Ὁρῶ καὶ σοὶ τούτων δεῆσον (*Xen. Mem.* 2, 6, 29). Εἶδον οἱ Λακεδαιμόνιοι ἀδύνατον ὂν τιμωρεῖν τοῖς ἀνδράσιν (*Thuc.* 4, 15). (Τοῖς ξυμμάχοις παράδειγμα σαφὲς καταστήσατε, ὃς ἂν ἀφιστῆται, θανάτῳ ζημιωσόμενον, *Thuc.* 3, 40, = δείξατε.)

Rem. 3. Rarely (for the most part poetically) ὡς is prefixed to this participle: Ὡς μηδὲν εἰδότ' ἴσθι μ' ὧν ἀνιστορεῖς (*Soph. Phil.* 253).

Rem. 4. With these verbs also (cf. § 177, R. 1) the participle ὤν is sometimes omitted, e. g. with ἀποφαίνω, οἶδα: Εἴ τις ἔχει ψευδῆ ἀποφῆναι, ἃ εἰρήκαμεν, λεγέτω (*Pl. Rep.* 2, 366).

---

[1] Ἀκούω τινὰ ἥκοντα, *I hear* (*learn, am told*) *that some one is come*, ἀκούω τινὸς διαλεγομένου, *I hear some one speak* (*hear him speaking*), § 58 a. R. 3. Ἀριαῖος ᾔσθετο Κῦρον πεπτωκότα (*Xen. An.* 1, 9, 31), *A. perceived, became aware, that C. was fallen*; ᾔσθησαι πώποτέ μου συκοφαντοῦντος; (*Xen. Mem.* 4, 4, 11,) *hast thou* (thyself as present) *ever perceived me acting the part of a sycophant* (*practising chicane*)? This distinction, however, in the use of αἰσθάνομαι is not always observed.

Rem. 5. The verbs mentioned have also, some more frequently, e.g. οἶδα' [§
others less frequently, a sentence with ὅτι (or ὡς mostly after a negation, see 178.]
§ 159, R. 3) with no difference in point of meaning, but only as the convenience of the general form of the sentence may require: Τοὺς χειροτέχνας ᾔδη, ὅτι εὑρήσοιμι πολλὰ καὶ καλὰ ἐπισταμένους (*Pl. Apol.* 22). Ἤισθοντο οἱ Ἕλληνες, ὅτι βασιλεὺς σὺν τῷ στρατεύματι ἐν τοῖς σκευοφόροις εἴη (*Xen. An.* 1, 10, 5). Οὐδ' ἐκεῖνο δύναμαι ἰδεῖν, ὡς οὐχὶ πάντες ἄνθρωποι τούτων τυχεῖν ἀξιώσουσιν (*Dem.* 23, 123). Ὡς οὐ πεποίηκε Μειδίας, ἃ κατηγόρηκα, τοῦτο δεικνύτω (*Dem.* 21, 28. A challenge which Demosthenes assumes will not be accepted). Ῥᾳδίως αἰσθήσεσθε τούτους, ὅτι εἰσὶ βίαιοι καὶ ἀσελγεῖς ἄνθρωποι (*Dem.* 43, 23; on τούτους, ὅτι, see § 191). (Blending of two constructions: Γνοὺς δὲ ὁ Κλέων καὶ Δημοσθένης, ὅτι, εἰ καὶ ὁποσονοῦν μᾶλλον ἐνδώσουσιν οἱ Λακεδαιμόνιοι, διαφθαρησομένους αὐτοὺς ὑπὸ τῆς σφετέρας στρατιᾶς, ἔπαυσαν τὴν μάχην. *Thuc.* 4, 37. Cf. § 159, R. 4.)[1]

Rem. 6. The verbs signifying *to remark, learn, hear* (also ἀγγέλλω), have also often the accus. with inf., rarely those signifying *to know*: Ἀκούω καὶ ἄλλα ἔθνη πολλὰ τοιαῦτα εἶναι (*Xen. An.* 2, 5, 13). Πυνθάνομαι μέλλειν Δημοσθένην καταριθμεῖσθαι πρὸς ὑμᾶς, ὅσα πεπολίτευται (*Æsch.* 3, 54). (Εὖ νυν ἐπίστω τῶνδέ μ' αἰσχύνην ἔχειν. *Soph. El.* 616.) Γιγνώσκω has the acc. with inf. (not the participle) in the sense *perceive, assume, consider*. Κῦρος ἀγῶνας κατέστησεν ἁπάντων, ὁπόσα ἐγίγνωσκεν ἀσκεῖσθαι ἀγαθὸν εἶναι ὑπὸ στρατιωτῶν (*Xen. Cyr.* 2, 1, 22). (Γιγνώσκω, *give sentence that something shall be done*,—see § 164.) Ἀποφαίνω, ἀποφαίνομαι, *declare* (that something is; not *to prove*), has the acc. with inf.[2]: ἀπέφηναν τοῦτο δίκαιον τοῖς ἀρχομένοις εἶναι (*Pl. Rep.* 338, E).

Rem. 7. Σύνοιδά τινι ἠδικημένῳ (*Dem.* 21, 2) and (the meaning of σύν almost disappearing) Συνίσασι τοὺς πρὸ αὐτῶν τετυραννευκότας τοὺς μὲν ὑπὸ τῶν γονέων ἀνῃρημένους, τοὺς δὲ ὑπὸ τῶν παίδων, τοὺς δὲ ὑπ' ἀδελφῶν (*Isocr. de Pac.* 113). Σύνοιδα ἐμαυτῷ ἐψευσμένος and ἐψευσμένῳ.

b) So likewise a participle is attached to the object, to complete the predicate, with the verbs παύω, *cause a person to have done with something*, περιορῶ, *overlook* (allow something to be done before one's eyes), and (more for the purpose of merely denoting a circumstance) with εὑρίσκω, καταλαμβάνω, φωρῶ, *find, catch* a person doing something (passive ἁλίσκομαι), ποιῶ, *represent in a poem*, ἐγγράφω, *lay an information*: Τὴν φιλοσοφίαν παῦσον ταῦτα λέγουσαν (*Pl. Gorg.* 482). Ἅμα διψῶν τε πέπαυμαι καὶ ἅμα ἡδόμενος διὰ τοῦ πίνειν (*Pl. Gorg.* 497). Μὴ περιίδωμεν ὑβρισθεῖσαν τὴν Λακεδαίμονα καὶ καταφρονηθεῖσαν (*Isocr. Archid.* 108). (Ὤν with εὑρίσκω omitted: Ἐμὲ εὑρήσετε οὐ κακὸν οὐδ' ἄχρηστον, *Isæ.* 7, 41.) (Περιορῶ τι γίγνεσθαι, τοὺς Μαντινεῖς ἄρχειν τῆς Ἀρκαδίας, *Thuc.* 5, 29, = ἐῶ.)

In a special manner (mostly, however, in the poets) a participle of the aorist is §
joined to the verb ἔχω as apposition to the subject, to denote at once the 179.
preceding action and the present state, almost as a mere periphrasis of the perfect:

---

[1] Μέμνημαι, οἶδα, ὅτε (ἡνίκα) —, *I remember the time when* —.

[2] Μανθάνω ὀρχεῖσθαι, ἐπίσταμαι λέγειν, μέμνησο ἀπιστεῖν, &c., by § 145, do not come under this head.

Σοῦ δ' ἔγωγε θαυμάσας ἔχω τόδε (*Soph. Phil.* 1362). Τὸν λόγον σου πάλαι θαυμάσας ἔχω, ὅσῳ καλλίω τοῦ προτέρου ἀπειργάσω (*Pl. Phæd.* 257).

§ 180. (423, b) *a*) A participle stands, with or without the article, and with or without defining accessories, as attributive to a substantive, with the sense of an adjective or of a relative periphrasis: Πόλις κάλλει διαφέρουσα. Ἀνὴρ καλῶς πεπαιδευμένος. Οἱ πρέσβεις οἱ παρὰ Φιλίππου πεμφθέντες. Ἡ Μυσῶν λεία λεγομένη (*the so-called booty of the Mysians; the proverbial Mysian booty*). Αἱ Αἰόλου νῆσοι καλούμεναι (*Thuc.* 3, 88). Ἐν τῇ Μεσσηνίᾳ ποτὲ οὔσῃ γῇ (*Thuc.* 4, 3; *in the land which was once Messenian*). Αἱ ἄρισται δοκοῦσαι εἶναι φύσεις (*Xen. Mem.* 4, 1, 3). (On the position of the words when the participle, as attributive with the article, has accessory definitions, see § 9, R. 1.)

REM. It should be remarked, however, that the participle perfect in Greek, much more rarely than in Latin (*doctus, eruditus, rectus*), assumes the signification of a pure adjective, merely denoting the property in general without reference to the action by which it was produced. (Ἐρρωμένος.) On the other hand, the participial constructions, instead of the relative periphrases used in Latin, are rendered very frequent by the use of ὤν and δοκῶν.

(425) *b*) A participle with the article (with addition of case and other definitions) can likewise stand substantively instead of a relative periphrasis of a person or thing (cf. § 14): Οἱ κρατοῦντες. Ἦν δὲ ὁ τὴν γνώμην ταύτῃ νείπὼν Πείσανδρος (*Thuc.* 8, 68). Ἔδει τὴν πολιτικὴν σοφοὺς ποιεῖν τοὺς πολίτας καὶ ἐπιστήμης μεταδιδόναι, εἴπερ ἔμελλεν αὕτη εἶναι ἡ ὠφελοῦσά τε καὶ εὐδαίμονας ποιοῦσα (*Pl. Euthyd.* 292). Ἀφεκτέον τῶν τοιούτων τῷ σωφρονεῖν δυνησομένῳ (*Xen. Conv.* 4, 26).[1] Παρὰ τοῖς ἀρίστοις δοκοῦσιν εἶναι (*Xen. Mem.* 4, 2, 6). Τοῖς Ἀρκάδων σφετέροις οὖσι ξυμμάχοις (*Thuc.* 5, 64; *those of the Arcadians who were* —, partitively, see § 50 a). Τοὺς πῶς διακειμένους λάβοιεν ἂν οἱ τοιοῦτοι μαθητάς; (*Isocr. Antid.* 222; see 176 a, and 198 a.)

REM. 1. On the other hand, it is more rare for a participle without the article to be put substantively, to denote indefinitely persons of a certain kind, or who do something (cf. § 87 a): Πλέομεν ἐπὶ πολλὰς ναῦς κεκτημένους (*Xen. Hell.* 5, 1, 19). Νόμος ἐστίν, ὅταν πολεμούντων πόλις ἁλῷ, τῶν ἑλόντων εἶναι τὰ χρήματα τῶν ἐν τῇ πόλει (*Xen. Cyr.* 7, 5, 73). Μετὰ ταῦτα ἀφικνοῦνται ἀγγέλλοντες (*with the intelligence*), ὅτι ὁ πατὴρ ἀφεῖται (*is released; Isocr. Trap.* 11: so frequently, Ἧκουσιν, ἧκον λέγοντες). (Ὅταν τις θεῶν βλάπτῃ, δύναιτ' ἂν οὐδ' ἂν ἰσχύων φυγεῖν, *Soph. El.* 697. Elsewhere almost exclusively in the plural.) To denote a person as one *who can, shall, will* do something, the article is usually put to the participle (of the future, rarely of the present: *persons who do*), both adjectively, and especially

---

[1] Τίνας καλεῖν ἔδει ἑτέρους; τούς, ὅτ' ἐγώ, γεγονυίας ἤδη τῆς εἰρήνης, ἀπὸ τῆς ὑστέρας ἥκων πρεσβείας, αἰσθόμενος φενακιζομένην τὴν πόλιν, προὔλεγον καὶ διεμαρτυρόμην καὶ οὐκ εἴων προέσθαι Πύλας οὐδὲ Φωκέας, λέγοντας, ὡς ἐγὼ δύσκολός εἰμί τις ἄνθρωπος (*Dem.* 6. 29).

substantively: Οὐδὲ τοὺς δούλους ὑβρίζειν οἱ Ἕλληνες ἀξιοῦσιν, ἀλλὰ νόμον δημοσίᾳ τὸν ταῦτα κωλύσοντα τέθεινται (*Dem.* 21, 49). Ἡ χώρα πολλὴ καὶ ἀγαθὴ ἦν καὶ ἐνῆσαν οἱ ἐργασόμενοι (*Xen. An.* 2, 4, 22; *people to till it*). Ὁ ἡγησόμενος οὐδεὶς (οὐκ) ἔσται (*Xen. An.* 2. 4, 5). (Πολλοὺς ἕξομεν τοὺς ἑτοίμως καὶ προθύμως συναγωνιζομένους ἡμῖν. *Isocr. de Pac.* 139.) [§ 180.]

Rem. 2. The poets sometimes make a genitive case depend on a participle with the article, as if it were a substantive, e. g. ὁ ἐκείνου τεκών (*Eur. El.* 335). In prose οἱ προσήκοντες, *relations*, and τὸ συμφέρον, *advantage, interest*, are used quite as substantives (τὸ τῆς νεὼς καὶ τῶν ναυτῶν συμφέρον, *Pl. Pol.* 296; τὰ μικρὰ συμφέροντα τῆς πόλεως, *Dem.* 18, 28). The poets and Thucydides sometimes use a present participle in the neuter, instead of an abstract verbal substantive, e. g. τὸ νοσοῦν = ἡ νόσος. Ἐν τῷ μὴ μελετῶντι ἀξυνετώτεροι ἔσονται (*Thuc.* 1, 142; *by want*, or *omission, of practice*); μετὰ τοῦ δρωμένου (*Thuc.* 5, 102; *with action, when there is doing*). (Otherwise: τὸ δοξάζον τῆς ψυχῆς, *that* (part) *of the mind which represents* (images); τὸ κρατοῦν τῆς πόλεως. Partitive genitive, § 50.)

c) Some few present participles, viz. διαφέρων, ἔχων with an adverb (e. g. κάλλιστ' ἔχων), προσήκων, πρέπων, δέον, ἐξόν, συμφέρον, sometimes occur, as adjective predicate-nouns, with εἰμί or γίγνομαι, occasionally also others in connexion with an actual adjective: Τί ποτ' ἐστὶν οὗτος ὁ βίος ἐκείνου διαφέρων; (*Pl. Gorg.* 500.) Τοὺς Λακεδαιμονίους οὐ διὰ τὴν ἀρετὴν αὐτῶν ἐσώσατε, ἀλλ' ὅτι συμφέρον ἦν τῇ πόλει σῶς εἶναι (*Dem.* 19, 75). Δεῖ πολὺ μὲν τοὺς ἄρχοντας ἐπιμελεστέρους γενέσθαι τοὺς νῦν τῶν πρόσθεν, πολὺ δὲ τοὺς ἀρχομένους εὐτακτοτέρους καὶ πειθομένους μᾶλλον τοῖς ἄρχουσι νῦν ἢ πρόσθεν (*Xen. An.* 2, 2, 30).

d) A participle of the present or aorist with εἰμί, as a periphrasis of the simple tense of the verb (in like manner as the participle perf., under certain circumstances, is joined with εἰμί) is a poetical licence of not very frequent occurrence; in the prose passages where it does occur, there is apt to be a certain emphasis in the several and distinct expression of the action (the participle) and its existence (εἰμί). Ἂν ᾖ θέλουσα (ἡ γυνή), πάντ' ἐμοῦ κομίζεται (*Soph. Œd. R.* 580). Οὐκ εἰς ὄλεθρον; οὐ σιωπήσας ἔσει; (*ibid.* 1146.) Παντάπασι θαυμάσαιμ' ἄν, εἴ τί με τούτων διαπέφευγεν. Ἦν μὲν οὖν μετὰ πολλῆς ἡδονῆς καὶ παιδιᾶς τότε ἀκουόμενα (*Pl. Tim.* 26). Ἦ τοῦτο οὐκ ἔστι γιγνόμενον παρ' ἡμῖν; (*Pl. Phil.* 39; or, *is not this a thing that takes place —!*) Ἦν γὰρ ὁ Θεμιστοκλῆς βεβαιότατα φύσεως ἰσχὺν δηλώσας καὶ διαφερόντως τι ἐς αὐτὸ μᾶλλον ἑτέρου ἄξιος θαυμάσαι (*Thuc.* 1, 138; *a man who, in a pre- minent degree, manifested —*). (With γίγνομαι in command and prohibition: Μή, ὦ ξένε, ἡμῖν τήν γε πρώτην αἰτησάντων χάριν ἀπαρνηθεὶς γένῃ. *Pl. Soph.* 217.)

A subject with a participle, conceived as *one* notion, and put in the genitive (*genitivi consequentiæ, double-genitive* [usually, in English, '*genitive absolute*']) is (in the manner assigned in § 66, b) attached to a sentence, where a simple participle could not be annexed, to denote the relation of time of the principal action, its way and manner, circumstances, ground or cause, &c., as the simple participle would do: Τῶν σωμάτων θηλυνομένων καὶ αἱ ψυχαὶ πολὺ ἀῤῥωστότεραι γίγνονται (*Xen. Œcon.* 4, 2; *if* —). Οὐκ ἂν ἦλθον δεῦρο, ὑμῶν μὴ κελευσάντων. Ὅλης τῆς πόλεως ἐν τοῖς πολεμικοῖς κινδύνοις ἐπιτρεπομένης τῷ στρατηγῷ, μεγάλα τά τ' ἀγαθὰ κατορθοῦντος αὐτοῦ καὶ τὰ κακὰ διαμαρτάνοντος εἰκὸς γί- § 181. (428)

[§ 181.] γνεσθαι (*Xen. Mem.* 3, 1, 3; *where the whole city is made over —, —if he succeeds*, &c.). Οἱ Θηβαῖοι ἠβούλοντο τὴν Πλάταιαν ἔτι ἐν εἰρήνῃ τε καὶ τοῦ πολέμου μήπω φανεροῦ καθεστῶτος (= γεγενημένου) προκαταλαβεῖν (*Thuc.* 2, 2). (Ἀφίκετο δεῦρο τὸ πλοῖον, γνόντων τῶν Κεφαλλήνων, ἀντιπράττοντος Ζηνοθέμιδος, ὅθεν ἐξέπλευσε τὸ πλοῖον, ἐνταῦθα καὶ καταπλεῖν αὐτό. *Dem.* 32, 14; *when the Ceph. had determined, in spite of Z.'s resistance, —.* A double-genitive attached to another. Τί τῶν Φωκέων ἢ ἄλλου τινὸς ἀνθρώπων μετὰ τοὺς παρ' Αἰσχίνου λόγους ἐξαμαρτόντος οὐκ ἀπέβη τὰ ὑπ' αὐτοῦ τότε ῥηθέντα; *Dem.* 19, 75; *for what offence of the Phocians —!* See § 176, a.)

Rem. 1. The learner must observe, that as the Greek has the whole series of active participles, the use of the passive double-genitive (as in Latin) is hereby excluded, when the action spoken of is that of the subject of the principal sentence: Ταῦτα εἰπόντες ἀπῆμεν, not τούτων λεχθέντων, which signifies, *after this was said by others.*

Rem. 2. The relation between the principal sentence and the participial sentence is more specifically marked, as is the case with the simple participle, by certain adverbs: see § 175. Πόθεν, ὦ Σώκρατες, αἱ διαβολαί σοι αὗται γεγόνασιν; οὐ γὰρ δή που, σοῦ γε οὐδὲν τῶν ἄλλων περιττότερον πραγματευομένου, ἔπειτα τοσαύτη φήμη τε καὶ λόγος γέγονεν (*Pl. Apol.* 20). Ψήφισμα ἔγραψα πλεῖν ἐπὶ τοὺς τόπους, ἐν οἷς εἴη Φίλιππος, καὶ τοὺς ὅρκους τὴν ταχίστην ἀπολαμβάνειν, ἵν' ἐχόντων τῶν Θρᾳκῶν τῶν ὑμετέρων συμμάχων τὰ χωρία ταῦτα, τὸ Σέρριον καὶ τὸ Μύρτιον καὶ τὴν Ἐργίσκην, οὕτω γίγνοινθ' οἱ ὅρκοι (*Dem.* 18, 27). Διονυσοδώρου μεταξὺ ταῦτα λέγοντος ὁ Κλεινίας ἔτυχεν ἀποκρινάμενος (*Pl. Euthyd.* 275). Especially frequent is the double-genitive with ὡς, to express the *thought* and *supposition* or *pretext* under which something is spoken or done (*because, as though*): Φυλλίδας καὶ Μέλλων ἐκήρυττον ἐξιέναι πάντας Θηβαίους, ὡς τῶν τυράννων τεθνεώτων (*Xen. Hell.* 5, 4, 9). Οὐχ ὡς τοῖς Ἕλλησι πολεμησόντων ἡμῶν εἶπον, ἃ εἶπον (*Xen. An.* 5, 6, 3). Cf. § 175 d. Especially note the use of the double-genitive with ὡς in connexion with verbs or phrases denoting an opinion or utterance, to assign the purport of the opinion or utterance (*to be of opinion, as though*, i.e. *that something should be done*), usually with the imperative, or at least in speaking of that which is to be thought or spoken (often with emphatic οὕτως before the principal verb, after the genitive): Ὡς ἐμοῦ γε καὶ ἀγωνιουμένου καί, ὁποῖος ἄν τις ᾧ, κατὰ τὴν ἀξίαν τιμᾶσθαι ἀξιώσοντος, οὕτως, ὦ Κῦρε, γίγνωσκε (*Xen. Cyr.* 2, 3, 15). Ὡς ἐμοῦ ἰόντος, ὅπῃ ἂν καὶ ὑμεῖς, οὕτω τὴν γνώμην ἔχετε (*Xen. An.* 1, 3, 6). Ἄλλο τι ὡς οὕτω σου νομίζοντος διανοώμεθα; (*Pl. Gorg.* 472; *are we not to assume that this is your opinion?* On ἄλλο τι, see § 199 c.) Εἴπατε καὶ περὶ τούτου, πότερα μενεῖτε καὶ σπονδαί εἰσιν ἢ ὡς πολέμου ὄντος παρ' ὑμῶν ἀπαγγελῶ (*Xen. An.* 2, 1, 21; or, *whether I shall report —*). (Ὄψεσθε, ὥσπερ δούλων ἀποδιδρασκόντων εὑρημένων, τοὺς μὲν ἱκετεύοντας τῶν πολεμίων, τοὺς δὲ φεύγοντας. *Xen. Cyr.* 4, 2, 21; *just as when —.*)[1]

Rem. 3. Sometimes a double-genitive and a simple participle referred to a case (most frequently the subject) in the principal sentence, are connected by *and*, or by μέν and δέ as co-ordinate definitions (e. g. of time, cause, thought, &c.): Κλέων πάντα διαπραξάμενος ἐν τῇ ἐκκλησίᾳ καὶ ψηφισαμένων Ἀθηναίων αὐτῷ τὸν πλοῦν τῶν τε ἐν

---

[1] Ὁ νόμος οὐκ ἐᾷ περὶ τῶν ἀτίμων λέγειν, ἐὰν μὴ τῆς ἀδείας δοθείσης (*Dem.* 24, 46). See § 175 e, foot-note 1 (*a*).

Πύλῳ στρατηγῶν ἕνα προσελόμενος Δημοσθένην τὴν ἀναγωγὴν διὰ τάχους ἐποιεῖτο [§
(*Thuc.* 4, 29). Οἱ Ἕλληνες στραφέντες παρεσκευάζοντο ὡς ταύτῃ προσιόντος βασιλέως 181.]
καὶ δεξόμενοι (*Xen. An.* 1, 10, 6).

Rem. 4. *a*) The subject-genitive in a double-genitive is sometimes omitted, when it is a pronoun easy to be understood from the context and the preceding mention of the same subject, and with no emphasis on it: Εἵποντο δὲ τοῖς Μοσσυνοίκοις τῶν Ἑλλήνων τινές, οὐ ταχθέντες ὑπὸ τῶν στρατηγῶν ἀλλ' ἁρπαγῆς ἕνεκεν. Οἱ δὲ πολέμιοι, προσιόντων, τέως μὲν ἡσύχαζον, ἐπεὶ δ' ἐγγὺς ἐγένοντο τοῦ χωρίου, ἐκδραμόντες τρέπονται αὐτούς (*Xen. An.* 5, 4, 16). (The pronoun of the first person omitted in an assurance by the speaker himself attached to what goes before: Ἐρῶτα, ἔφη, ὦ Κῦρε, ὡς τἀληθῆ ἐροῦντος, *Xen. Cyr.* 3, 1, 9.)

b) Sometimes the double-genitive is a participle plural with an indefinite subject of the third person understood (*the people; one*) (cf. § 6 b): Οὐκ ἐξαιτούμενος, οὐκ Ἀμφικτυονικὰς δίκας ἐπαγόντων, οὐκ ἀπειλούντων, οὐκ ἐπαγγελλομένων, οὐδαμῶς ἐγὼ προδέδωκα τὴν εἰς ὑμᾶς εὔνοιαν (*Dem.* 18, 322; *not when I was demanded to be given up, not when they were for bringing me to trial before the Amphictyons*).

c) A double-genitive of participle without a subject is formed from impersonal expressions with adjectives in the plural (ἕτοιμά ἐστιν, § 7 b. R. 2), or from a verb put impersonally to which some general notion of *things* can be understood as its subject (e. g. ἔχει, ἐπράχθη), usually in the plural, and from the verbs denoting the state of the weather (§ 7, a 1). (Comp. the double-accusative, § 182): Ἔτι ὄντων ἀκρίτων διαλλαγῶμεν (*Thuc.* 1, 7). Οὕτως ἐχόντων (*under such circumstances, such being the case*, more rarely οὕτως ἔχοντος). εἰκὸς τοῖς μὲν πολεμίοις ἐναντίους εἶναι τοὺς θεούς, ἡμῖν δὲ συμμάχους (*Xen. An.* 3, 2, 10). Τοῦτον τὸν τρόπον πραχθέντων, τῆς πόλεως γίγνεται τὰ χρήματα (*Dem.* 24, 12; *such being the facts of the case*). Ἀλκιβιάδης ἀνηγάγετο ἐπὶ τὴν Κύζικον, ὕοντος πολλοῦ (*Xen. Hell.* 1, 1, 16).

d) A passive participle neuter (usually plural, cf. *c*) of a *verbum declarandi* is (429)
sometimes put in the double-genitive, with a sentence with ὅτι added: Περικλῆς ᾤχετο κατὰ τάχος ἐπὶ Καύνου καὶ Καρίας, ἐσαγγελθέντων, ὅτι Φοίνισσαι νῆες ἐπὶ τοὺς Ἀθηναίους πλέουσιν (*Thuc.* 1, 116; but δηλωθέντος, ὅτι —, 1, 74).

Rem. 5. The omission of the participle ὤν in the double-genitive is very rare: Πᾶν ἐν ἡσύχῳ, πάτερ, ἔξεστι φωνεῖν, ὡς ἐμοῦ μόνης πέλας (*Soph. Œd. C.* 83). (Νικίαν καὶ Δημοσθένην οἱ Συρακούσιοι ἄκοντος Γυλίππου ἀπέσφαξαν, *Thuc.* 7, 86, and ἐμοῦ οὐχ ἑκόντος, *Soph. Aj.* 455, as if ἑκών, ἄκων were participles.)

Rem. 6. The double-genitive is usually put only where the subject of the par- (428,
ticiple does not stand in the principal sentence in some other case to which the R. 5)
participle might attach itself. Sometimes, however, although the subject of the participle does so occur, the double-genitive is nevertheless used, in order to give more prominence to the participial sentence as a special circumstance: Διαβεβηκότος ἤδη Περικλέους στρατιᾷ ἐς Εὔβοιαν, ἠγγέλθη αὐτῷ, ὅτι Μέγαρα ἀφέστηκεν (*Thuc.* 1, 114). Τριῶν θυρῶν οὐσῶν, ἃς ἔδει με διελθεῖν, ἅπασαι ἀνεῳγμέναι ἔτυχον (*Lys.* 12, 16). Σὺ μὲν ὡς φάσκοντος εἰδέναι περὶ ὧν ἐρωτῶ, προσφέρῃ πρὸς ἐμέ (*Pl. Charm.* 165; ἐμοῦ omitted agreeably with the concluding remark in R. 4, a).

Rem. 7. Sometimes a substantive takes a participle as apposition, and then, by means of a preposition, especially ἅμα or σύν, is attached to a sentence as a definition of time: Ἅμα ἡλίῳ ἀνίσχοντι ἦλθε Προκλῆς, ὁ Τευθρανίας ἄρχων (*Xen. An.* 2,

[§ 181.] 1, 3). Ἅμα τῷ ἦρι εὐθὺς ἀρχομένῳ τοῦ ἐπιγιγνομένου θέρους οἱ ἐν τῇ Σικελίᾳ Ἀθηναῖοι ἄραντες ἐκ τῆς Κατάνης παρέπλευσαν ἐπὶ Μεγάρων (*Thuc.* 6, 94). Ἡ ὀργὴ αὕτη ὑπό τε τῶν ἀγαθῶν (*the advantages*) πεπανθήσεται καὶ σὺν τῷ φόβῳ λήγοντι ἄπεισι (*Xen. Cyr.* 4, 5, 21). (Πρὸ ἡλίου δύνοντος, *Æsch.* 1, 12. Ἔτει πέμπτῳ μετὰ Συρακούσας οἰκισθείσας, *Thuc.* 6, 3. Ἐπὶ Κόδρου βασιλεύοντος, *Lyc.* 81. Ἐπὶ χιόνι πεσούσῃ, *Hdt.* 2, 22. *after the falling of snow, after it has snowed.*)

§ 182. Instead of the double-genitive, the accusative (*double-accusative* [*accusative absolute*]) of impersonal verbs is used (e. g. δέον, ἐξόν, προσῆκον, παρέχον, μέλον, μεταμέλον, also δοκοῦν, δόξαν, *as* [*when, since*] *it is, was, decreed*) or of passive verbs used impersonally (with an infinitive added, e. g. προσταχθέν, εἰρημένον, γενόμενον ἐπ' ἐμοί, *as it was in my power*, &c.), or of impersonal expressions of εἰμί and an adjective (e. g. ἀδύνατον ὄν). The double-accusative is also used of impersonal expressions (ἐμὲ ποιήσοντα) after ὡς and ὥσπερ, *in the opinion, supposition, belief that*, or, *as though*: Ὅταν ἀναγκασθῇ τις δυοῖν κακοῖν τὸ ἕτερον αἱρεῖσθαι, οὐδεὶς τὸ μεῖζον αἱρήσεται, ἐξὸν τὸ ἔλαττον (viz. αἱρεῖσθαι. *Pl. Prot.* 358). Οἱ Ἀθηναῖοι μετεμέλοντο, ὅτι μετὰ τὰ ἐν Πύλῳ, καλῶς παρασχόν, οὐ ξυνέβησαν (*Thuc.* 5, 14; *a favourable opportunity having offered*). Ὡς Κῦρος ἐγένετο ἐν Μήδοις, συνδόξαν τῷ πατρὶ καὶ τῇ μητρί, γαμεῖ τὴν Κυαξάρου θυγατέρα (*Xen. Cyr.* 8, 5, 28). Προσταχθέν μοι ὑπὸ τοῦ δήμου Μένωνα τὸν στρατηγὸν ἄγειν εἰς Ἑλλήσποντον, ᾠχόμην ἀναγόμενος διὰ τάχους (*Dem.* 50, 12; *I put to sea with speed*). Οἱ Συρακούσιοι παρεκελεύοντο κραυγῇ οὐκ ὀλίγῃ χρώμενοι, ἀδύνατον ὂν ἐν νυκτὶ ἄλλῳ τῳ σημῆναι (*Thuc.* 7, 44). Κῦρος ἀντιπαρεσκευάζετο ἐῤῥωμένως, ὡς μάχης ἔτι δεῆσον (*Xen. Cyr.* 6, 1, 26). Οἶμαι τὸ πλῆθος ψηφιεῖσθαι, ἃ βουλόμεθα, ἅμα μὲν ὑμῶν συναγορευόντων, ἅμα δὲ καὶ αἰσχρὸν ὂν ἀντιλέγειν (*Xen. Cyr.* 2, 2, 20). Οἱ πατέρες τοὺς υἱεῖς ἀπὸ τῶν πονηρῶν ἀνθρώπων εἴργουσιν, ὡς τὴν μὲν τῶν χρηστῶν ὁμιλίαν ἄσκησιν οὖσαν τῆς ἀρετῆς, τὴν δὲ τῶν πονηρῶν κατάλυσιν (*Xen. Mem.* 1, 2, 20). Ἀπεβλέψατε πρὸς ἀλλήλους ὡς αὐτὸς μὲν ἕκαστος οὐ ποιήσων τὸ δόξαν, τὸν δὲ πλησίον πράξοντα (*Dem.* 14, 15). Ἔνιοι φίλους μὲν κτῶνται ὡς βοηθῶν δεόμενοι, τῶν δ' ἀδελφῶν ἀμελοῦσιν, ὥσπερ ἐκ πολιτῶν μὲν γιγνομένους φίλους, ἐξ ἀδελφῶν δ' οὐ γιγνομένους (*Xen. Mem.* 2, 3, 3).[1]

REM. 1. After verbs that themselves express opinion, the double-accusative with ὡς of personal verbs is very rarely put instead of the double-genitive with ὡς (§ 181, R. 2); but where the notion of thinking is merely implied in the ὡς, the double-accusative is even more usual than the double-genitive.

REM. 2. It is very rare to meet with the double-accusative of a personal expression without ὡς (with ὤν or a participle which is commonly used impersonally, or

[1] Hence τυχόν, properly, *it having chanced, as it happened*, is used quite as an adverb, *perchance, mayhap*.

with the neuter of a pronominal word as subject). e.g. προσῆκον ἐμοὶ τοῦ κλήρου μέρος (*Isæ.* 5, 12). Ἤδη ἀμφοτέροις μὲν δοκοῦν ἀναχωρεῖν, κυρωθὲν δὲ οὐδέν, ὁπηνίκα χρὴ ὁρμᾶσθαι, οἱ Μακεδόνες καταστάντες ἐς αἰφνίδιον φυγὴν ἐχώρουν ἐπ' οἴκου (*Thuc.* 4, 125).[1] [§ 182.]

Rem. 3. Now and then in this construction the participle ὢν is omitted: Ἆρα τὴν δίαιτάν μου φαυλίζεις ὡς ἧττον μὲν ὑγιεινὰ ἐσθίοντος ἐμοῦ ἢ σοῦ, ἧττον δὲ ἰσχὺν παρέχοντα, ἢ ὡς χαλεπώτερα (viz. ὄντα) πορίσασθαι τὰ ἐμὰ διαιτήματα τῶν σῶν διὰ τὸ πολυτελέστερα εἶναι; (*Xen. Mem.* 1, 6, 5.)

The *Tenses of the Participle*, present, perfect, and aorist, correspond with the same tenses of the indicative (so that the aorist is a præteritum): Ἢν μηδὲν φαίνωμαι κακόν σε πεποιηκὼς μηδὲ βουληθείς, οὐ καὶ σὺ αὖ ὁμολογήσεις ὑπ' ἐμοῦ μηδὲν ἀδικεῖσθαι; (*Xen. Cyr.* 5, 5, 13; *that I have done thee no evil, neither wished I to do thee any.*) Usually δείκνυμι πεποιηκώς, δ. τινὰ πεποιηκότα, corresponding with πεποίηκα or πεποίηκεν as judgment on the completed relation. For examples of the tenses generally, see the preceding paragraphs. Hence after a verb of past time (since the participle denotes the time in reference to the principal action) the participle of the present answers to the imperfect, that of the perfect to the plusquamperfect, that of the aorist to a more remote past (as aorist, not as perfect): Ταῦτα εἰπόντες ἀπῆλθον (= ἐπειδὴ ταῦτα εἶπον). Ἐπέδειξα Αἰσχίνην οὐδὲν ἀληθὲς ἀπηγγελκότα ἀλλὰ φενακίσανθ' ὑμᾶς (*Dem.* 19, 177. = Οὐδὲν ἀληθὲς ἀπήγγελκεν ἀλλ' ἐφενάκισεν ὑμᾶς. The former said in general, the latter of a particular matter of fact). (Ὁ τὴν γνώμην ταύτην εἰπὼν Πείσανδρος ἦν, *Thuc.* 8, 68, as a circumlocution = εἶπεν. Τίς ἦν ὁ βοηθήσας τοὺς Βυζαντίους καὶ σώσας αὐτούς; τίς δ' ὁ τῇ πόλει λέγων καὶ γράφων καὶ πράττων; *Dem.* 18, 88 = ἐβοήθησεν — ἔλεγεν — ἔγραφεν — ἔπραττεν.) § 183.

Rem. 1. Sometimes, even after a verb of present time, the participle present has the sense of the imperfect, where an anterior time is either plainly denoted by the context or by the addition of τότε: Πρὸς μὲν τοὺς φίλους τε καὶ πρὸς τοὺς πολίτας ταῦτα ὑμᾶς παῖδας ὄντας ἐδιδάσκομεν· ὅπως δὲ πολεμίους δύναισθε κακῶς ποιεῖν, οὐκ οἶσθα μανθάνοντας ὑμᾶς πολλὰς κακουργίας; (*Xen. Cyr.* 1, 6, 28.) Ἀγανακτοῦσιν ὡς μεγάλων τινῶν ἀπεστερημένοι καὶ τότε μὲν (viz. ὅτε νέοι ἦσαν) εὖ ζῶντες, νῦν δὲ οὐδὲ ζῶντες (*Pl. Rep.* 1, 329). Οἵ τε ἐν τῷ δικαστηρίῳ τότε δικάζοντες καὶ τῶν ἔξωθεν παρόντων πολλοὶ ταῦτα συνίσασιν (*Dem.* 30, 32).[2]

Rem. 2. Sometimes, after a verb in the aorist or historical present, an aorist participle stands as apposition to the subject, not to denote an earlier but a contemporary (single and momentary) action (*in that, by —, and*), so that the past is specially denoted in the action of the participle, just as it would be in a *verbum finitum* with *and*, &c.: Εὖ ἐποίησας ἀναμνήσας με (*Pl. Phæd.* 60; *you did well to remind me;*

---

[1] From δόξαν we have also δόξαν ταῦτα (*Xen. An.* 4, 1, 13) for τούτων δοξάντων (*Xen. Hell.* 5, 2, 24).

[2] Οἱ οἰχόμενοι, *the departed, dead*, from οἴχομαι (see § 110 a, R. 2), ὁ φεύγων, *the banished*. Poetically, οἱ θνήσκοντες, ἡ τίκτουσα, for οἱ θανόντες, ἡ τεκοῦσα.

CHAP. VI.]

[§ 183.] *in that thou didst remind me*). Ἤδη πώποτε ἡ μήτηρ ἢ δακοῦσα κακόν τί σοι ἔδωκεν ἢ λακτίσασα; (*Xen. Mem.* 2, 2, 7.) Κίρων ἐκδίδωσι τὴν θυγατέρα Ναυσιμένει πέντε καὶ εἴκοσι μνᾶς ἐπιδούς (*Isæ.* 8, 8). Ὁ Φρύνιχος πέμπει ὡς τὸν Ἀστύοχον, τῶν Λακεδαιμονίων ναύαρχον, κρύφα ἐπιστείλας, ὅτι Ἀλκιβιάδης αὐτῶν τὰ πράγματα φθείρει (*Thuc.* 8, 50; *and gave him to understand.* Shortly afterwards: Ὁ Ἀλκιβιάδης πέμπει εὐθὺς κατὰ Φρυνίχου γράμματα ἐς τὴν Σάμον ἀξιῶν αὐτὸν ἀποθνήσκειν). Especially note, that with the aorists ἔλαθον and ἔφθην (or λανθάνω and φθάνω as historical present) the participle annexed (by § 177) for a single, transient action, is always put in the aorist, and only where an abiding condition (property) is denoted, stands in the present. This aorist of the participle remains, even where the principal verb is aorist without preterite signification (subjunctive, imperative, optative, or infinitive), and with the future indicative. Also with the aorist of περιορᾶν (§ 178 b) and sometimes of ἐφορᾶν, in all the moods (περιίδω, &c.) the participle stands in the aorist for a transient action: Ἔλαθεν ἀφθέντα πάντα καὶ καταφλεχθέντα (*Thuc.* 4, 133). Σμικρὸν ἔφθης με ἐρόμενος (*Pl. Pol.* 293). Ὁ πεζὸς στρατὸς τῶν Ἀθηναίων φθάνει ἀναβὰς ἐπὶ τὰς Ἐπιπολὰς πρὶν τοὺς Συρακουσίους παραγενέσθαι (*Thuc.* 6, 97). Φοβούμεθα περὶ Κλεινία, μή τις φθῇ ἡμᾶς ἐπ' ἄλλο τι ἐπιτήδευμα τρέψας αὐτοῦ τὴν διάνοιαν (*Pl. Euthyd.* 275). Βουλοίμην ἄν, ἄκοντος ἀπιὼν Κύρου, λαθεῖν αὐτὸν ἀπελθών (*Xen. An.* 1, 3, 17). Εὐλαβεῖσθε, ὅπως μὴ πέρα τοῦ δέοντος σοφώτεροι γενόμενοι λήσετε διαφθαρέντες (*Pl. Gorg.* 487). Τοὺς ἀνθρώπους λήσομεν ἐπιπεσόντες (*Xen. An.* 7, 3, 43). Δέομαι ὑμῶν, ὦ ἄνδρες δικασταί, βοηθεῖν ἡμῖν καὶ μὴ περιιδεῖν ὑπὸ τῶν ἐχθρῶν ἀναιρεθέντας (*Lys.* 19, 64; *not to allow us to be destroyed, ruined*, transient action). —Ἐλάθομεν ἡμᾶς αὐτοὺς παίδων οὐδὲν διαφέροντες (*Pl. Crit.* 49). Οἶμαί σε πολλὰ μεριμνᾶν ὅπως μὴ λάθῃς σαυτὸν ἀγνοῶν τι τῶν εἰς στρατηγίαν ὠφελίμων (*Xen. Mem.* 3, 5, 23). Αἰσχυνοίμην ἄν, εἰ περιίδοιμι τὴν χώραν, ἣν ἡμῖν οἱ πατέρες κατέλιπον, ταύτην τοὺς οἰκέτας τοὺς ἡμετέρους ἔχοντας (*Isocr. Archid.* 8). (After ἔφθην an occasion for the present can rarely happen.)[1]

REM. 3. With the article, the participle of the aorist sometimes approximates to that of the perfect: Οἱ θανόντες. Ὁ τὰ ἔργα παρεσχηκώς, περὶ ὧν εἰσὶν οἱ λόγοι, δικαιότατ' ἂν ταύτην ἔχοι τὴν αἰτίαν, οὐχ ὁ ἐσκεμμένος οὐδ' ὁ μεριμνήσας τὰ δίκαια λέγειν νῦν (*Dem.* 21, 192).

§ 184. (*The Participle with ἄν.*) The participle of the present and aorist with ἄν is used in a hypothetical and potential signification, so that it corresponds partly with the imperfect and aorist of the indicative with ἄν, partly, and that more frequently, with the present and aorist of the optative with ἄν. (The aor. as in the opt. or inf. with the signification of a dubitative future.) In this manner the participle may stand both to denote a circumstance (§ 174), and also after the verbs mentioned in §§ 177, 178, in circumlocutions with the article, and in the double-genitive or double-accusative. (By this means, the Greek has often a brevity and flexibility of expression unattainable by languages in which such a hypothetical statement must necessarily be expressed by a finite verb.) *a*) (Corresponding with indicat. with ἄν): Ἡμεῖς ἐπεὶ ἠκούσαμεν, ὅτι ἐστί τι λοιπὸν ἔργον, ὃ

---

[1] Λελήθαμεν ἀμφοτέρων εἰς τὸ μέσον πεπτωκότες (*Pl. Theæt.* 180). Κατατείνας (συντείνας) λέγω, ἐρῶ (*Pl. Rep.* 2, 358), *as forcibly as I can;* i. e. *with exertion of all my powers* (*after collecting them and bending them to the task*).

δεῖ ἐξεργάσασθαι, συνεσκυθρωπάσαμεν, οὐ φοβούμενοι, ἀλλὰ πεποιῆσθαι ἂν ἤδη καὶ τοῦτο βουλόμενοι (*Xen. Cyr.* 6, 2, 21, = ὅτι ἠβουλόμεθ' ἂν καὶ τ. π.). Φίλιππος Ποτίδαιαν ἑλὼν καὶ δυνηθεὶς ἂν αὐτὸς ἔχειν, εἰ ἐβουλήθη, Ὀλυνθίοις παρέδωκεν (*Dem.* 23, 107, = ἠδυνήθη ἄν). Εὖ ἴσθι μηδὲν ἄν με τούτων ἐπιχειρήσαντά σε πείθειν, εἰ δυναστείαν μόνον καὶ πλοῦτον ἑώρων ἐξ αὐτῶν γενησόμενον (*Isocr. Phil.* 133). — *b*) (Answering to the optative with ἄν): Οἱ Ἡρακλέους παῖδες τὰς μὲν ἄλλας πόλεις ὑπερεώρων ὡς οὐκ ἂν δυναμένας βοηθῆσαι ταῖς ἑαυτῶν συμφοραῖς, τὴν δ' ἡμετέραν ἱκανὴν ἐνόμιζον εἶναι μόνην (*Isocr. Paneg.* 56, = οἰόμενοι οὐκ ἂν δύνασθαι = οὐκ ἂν δύναιντο). Ὁ Ἀρίστιππος ἔρχεται πρὸς τὸν Κῦρον καὶ αἰτεῖ αὐτὸν εἰς δισχιλίους ξένους καὶ τριῶν μηνῶν μισθὸν ὡς οὕτως περιγενόμενος ἂν τῶν ἀντιστασιωτῶν (*Xen. An.* 1, 1, 10). Εὑρίσκω ταύτην μόνην ἂν γενομένην τῶν παρόντων κακῶν ἀπαλλαγήν, ἣν ἐθελήσωμεν ἐκείνην τὴν δημοκρατίαν ἀναλαβεῖν, ἣν Σόλων ἐνομοθέτησεν (*Isocr. Areop.* 16. On ἣν ἐθελήσωμεν in the condition, see § 135, R. 1, a). Διακεκρίμεθα χωρίς τάς τε καθαρὰς ἡδονὰς καὶ τὰς σχεδὸν ἀκαθάρτους ὀρθῶς ἂν λεχθείσας (*Pl. Phil.* 52 = αἱ ἀκάθαρτοι ὀρθῶς ἂν λεχθεῖεν). Ἐγώ εἰμι (*belong to; am one of those*) τῶν ἡδέως μὲν ἂν ἐλεγχθέντων, εἴ τι μὴ ἀληθὲς λέγω, ἡδέως δ' ἂν ἐλεγξάντων, εἴ τίς τι μὴ ἀληθὲς λέγοι, οὐκ ἀηδέστερον μέντ' ἂν ἐλεγχθέντων ἢ ἐλεγξάντων (*Pl. Gorg.* 458). Ξενοφῶν διαβὰς τὴν χαράδραν σὺν τοῖς λοχαγοῖς ἐσκοπεῖτο, πότερον εἴη κρεῖττον ἀπαγαγεῖν καὶ τοὺς διαβεβηκότας ἢ καὶ τοὺς ὁπλίτας διαβιβάζειν, ὡς ἁλόντος ἂν τοῦ χωρίου (*Xen. An.* 5, 2, 8; *in the hope that the place might be taken*). Ἐλπίζω τοὺς Ἀθηναίους καταπλαγέντας τῷ ἀδοκήτῳ καταλῦσαι ἂν τὸν πλοῦν, ἄλλως τε καὶ τοῦ ἐμπειροτάτου τῶν στρατηγῶν ἄκοντος ἡγουμένου καὶ ἀσμένου ἂν πρόφασιν λαβόντος, εἴ τι ἀξιόχρεων ἀφ' ἡμῶν ὀφθείη (*Thuc.* 6, 34; *especially as the most experienced of their generals takes the command against his will, and might, or would, gladly catch at a pretext* —). (Χρώμεθα τῷ νόμῳ τούτῳ εἰδότες καὶ ὑμᾶς ἂν καὶ ἄλλους, ἐν τῇ αὐτῇ δυνάμει ἡμῖν γενομένους, δρῶντας ἂν αὐτό. *Thuc.* 5, 105; double ἄν as with the infinitive, see § 173, R. 1.)[1] [§ 184.]

REM. The participle of the future with ἄν rests (in the Attic style) on passages in which the reading is corrupt (λυπήσων or λυπήσας ἄν, not λυπήσων ἄν)[2].

CHAPTER VII.

Peculiarities in the connexion of Co-ordinate Sentences, and of Principal and Accessory Sentences. Interrogative Sentences.

a) Co-ordinate sentences (in prose) are connected copulatively § 185.

[1] Οὐδὲ ταῦτα Τιμοκράτης ἁπλῶς καὶ ἀδόλως φανήσεται γεγραφώς, ἀλλ' ὡς ἂν μάλιστά τις ὑμᾶς ἐξαπατῆσαι βουλόμενος (*Dem.* 24, 79. Elliptical ἄν, as § 139 c). (Εἶναι τῶν δυνατῶν ἂν κρῖναι, *Pl. Rep.* 9, 577, *one of those who might be able;* ἄν belonging to the omitted ὄντων.)

[[2] Krüger defends this construction.—ED.]

CHAP. VII.]

[§ 185.] by *καί*, *and* (*τέ*, *and*), *τέ — καί*, or, *καί — καί*, *both — and*, and (with negation) by *οὐδέ*, *and also not*, *οὔτε — οὔτε*, *neither — nor*. (*Τέ* after the connected word or the first word of the second clause = *que*.)

Rem. 1. A single *τέ* for *καί*, by which the second member is joined to the first as an addition, is poetical, and very rarely occurs in prose: *Τισίαν δὲ Γοργίαν τε ἐάσομεν εὕδειν* (*Pl. Phæd.* 267). Thucydides uses *τέ* to connect a new sentence which serves to corroborate, continue, or enlarge upon the preceding one (almost in the manner of *καί — δέ*): *Καὶ μεχρί τοῦδε πολλὰ τῆς Ἑλλάδος τῷ παλαιῷ τρόπῳ νέμεται, περί τε Λοκροὺς τοὺς Ὀζόλας καὶ Αἰτωλοὺς καὶ Ἀκαρνᾶνας καὶ τὴν ταύτῃ ἤπειρον. Τό τε σιδηροφορεῖσθαι τούτοις τοῖς ἠπειρώταις ἀπὸ τῆς παλαιᾶς λῃστείας ἐμμεμένηκεν* (*Thuc.* 1, 5). (On *τέ — οὔτε*, *οὔτε — τέ*, see *Negations*.)

Rem. 2. By annexing a *δέ* to *καί* (*καί — δέ*), the new member acquires prominence as a special corroboration and enlargement of the preceding (*and — too*, *and also*): *Τὰ παρατιθέμενα ἀεὶ ἴσα αὐτῷ τε τῷ Κύρῳ καὶ τοῖς καλουμένοις ἐπὶ δεῖπνον ἦν· καὶ τοὺς ἀμφὶ τὸ στράτευμα δὲ ὑπηρέτας ἰσομοίρους πάντων ἀεὶ ἐποίει* (*Xen. Cyr.* 2, 1, 31). *Ἤιδει Κῦρος Ἀρταξέρξην, ὅτι μέσον ἔχοι τοῦ Περσικοῦ στρατεύματος. Καὶ πάντες δ' οἱ τῶν βαρβάρων ἄρχοντες μέσον ἔχοντες ἡγοῦνται* (*Xen. An.* 1, 8, 22).

Rem. 3. By *καί — καί* the two connected members are marked each by itself, as several and co-ordinate members, more strongly than by the usual *τέ — καί*, by which they are rather connected so as to form a whole: *Καὶ ζῶν καὶ τελευτήσας* (*Pl. Rep.* 3, 414). *Καὶ πρῶτον καὶ μάλιστα* (*Pl. Rep.* 3, 415). *Καὶ αὐτοὶ ἐμάχοντο καὶ τοῖς ἄλλοις παρεκελεύοντο* (*Xen. Cyr.* 3, 3, 68). *Κάλλιστόν τε καὶ ἄριστον* (*Xen. An.* 2, 1, 9). *Κεραυνός τε ὅτι μὲν ἄνωθεν ἀφίεται, δῆλον, ὁρᾶται δ' οὔτ' ἐπιὼν οὔτε κατασκήψας οὔτε ἀπιών, καὶ ἄνεμοι αὐτοὶ μὲν οὐχ ὁρῶνται, ἃ δὲ ποιοῦσι, φανερὰ ἡμῖν ἐστιν* (*Xen. Mem.* 4, 3, 14). *Τέ — τέ* (= *καί — καί*) is frequent in the poets, rare in prose: *Ἐλείποντο τῶν στρατιωτῶν οἵ τε διεφθαρμένοι ὑπὸ τῆς χιόνος τοὺς ὀφθαλμοὺς οἵ τε ὑπὸ τοῦ ψύχους τοὺς δακτύλους τῶν ποδῶν ἀποσεσηπότες* (*Xen. An.* 4, 5, 12). *Μετὰ τὰ Τρωϊκὰ ἡ Ἑλλὰς ἔτι μετανίστατό τε καὶ κατῳκίζετο. Βοιωτοί τε γὰρ οἱ νῦν ἑξηκοστῷ ἔτει μετὰ Ἰλίου ἅλωσιν ἐξ Ἄρνης ἀναστάντες ὑπὸ Θεσσαλῶν τὴν Καδμηΐδα γῆν καλουμένην ᾤκισαν, Δωριεῖς τε ὀγδοηκοστῷ ἔτει ξὺν Ἡρακλείδαις Πελοπόννησον ἔσχον* (*Thuc.* 1, 12). *Καί — τέ* (*et — que*) is a poetical licence: *Ἴσθι γὰρ δοκῶν ἐμοὶ καὶ ξυμφυτεῦσαι τοὔργον εἰργάσθαι θ', ὅσον μὴ χερσὶ καίνων* (*Soph. Œd. R.* 347).

Rem. 4. Where *τέ — καί* connects two single notions which have a common article, the *τέ* is sometimes attached to the article instead of following the first of the connected terms: *τούς τε εὐοπλοτάτους ἔχων καὶ εὐειδεστάτους* (*Xen. An.* 2, 3, 3; *having those who were both the best-armed and the best-looking*); and so usually with a common preposition: *ἔν τε τῷ θερμοτέρῳ καὶ ψυχροτέρῳ* (*Pl. Phil.* 24). (*Ἐν τοσαύτῃ τε ἀγρυπνίᾳ καὶ λύπῃ.* *Pl. Crit.* 43.)

Rem. 5. Sometimes *τέ* is followed, not by *καί*, but by *δέ*, alone or with another particle (*ἔπειτα δέ*, *ἅμα δέ*, *ἅμα δὲ καί*, *ἔτι δὲ καί*, *ὡσαύτως δέ*, *πολὺ μᾶλλον δέ*), the copulative connexion being abandoned, and an adversative put instead of it, either because the latter member is intended to be made specially prominent, or because it has become remote from *τέ*: *Ἔπεμψεν ἡμᾶς ἡ τῶν Σινωπέων πόλις ἐπαινέσοντάς τε ὑμᾶς, ὅτι ἐνικᾶτε Ἕλληνες ὄντες βαρβάρους, ἔπειτα δὲ καὶ ξυνησθησομένους, ὅτι διὰ πολλῶν τε καὶ δεινῶν πραγμάτων σεσωσμένοι πάρεστε* (*Xen. An.* 5, 5, 8). *Τιμαῖός τε ὅδε, εὐνομωτάτης ὢν πόλεως τῆς ἐν Ἰταλίᾳ Λοκρίδος, οὐσίᾳ καὶ γένει οὐδενὸς ὕστερος ὧν τῶν ἐκεῖ. τὰς μεγίστας μὲν ἀρχάς τε καὶ τιμὰς ἐν τῇ πόλει μετακεχείρισται, φιλοσοφίας δ' αὖ κατ' ἐμὴν δόξαν ἐπ' ἄκρον ἁπάσης ἐλήλυθε· Κριτίαν δέ που πάντες οἱ τῇδ' ἴσμεν οὐδενὸς ἰδιώτην ὄντα ὧν λέγομεν* (*Pl. Tim.* 20). *Ἔν τε τῇ τῶν ἐπῶν ποιήσει πολλαχοῦ δὲ καὶ ἄλλοθι* (*Pl. Rep.* 3, 394). (On the irregularity where two members denoted by *τέ — καί*, as co-ordinate, are not accurately connected, see *Anacoluthia*, § 216, R. 1.) [§ 185.]

Rem. 6. The copulative particle is omitted in oratorical recital, of several (short) members. (Between two members the omission is rare, and poetical, e. g. *Τοῦ τὸν κρατῆρα πλήσας θῶ; Ὕδατος, μελίσσης· μηδὲ προσφέρειν μέθυ.* *Soph. Œd. C.* 481; in prose, in certain particular set phrases of two contrasted words, e. g. *ἄνω κάτω* = *ἄνω καὶ κάτω*.) *Καί* is omitted before *εἶτα, ἔπειτα*, in the sense *and then*, marking continuation and further consequence (especially in conditional and object-sentences): *Εἰ προησόμεθα, ὦ ἄνδρες Ἀθηναῖοι, καὶ τούτους τοὺς ἀνθρώπους, εἶτ' Ὄλυνθον Φίλιππος καταστρέψεται. φρασάτω τις ἐμοί, τί τὸ κωλῦον ἔτ' αὐτὸν ἔσται βαδίζειν, ὅποι βούλεται;* (*Dem.* 1, 12.) *Φοβοῦμαι, μὴ πάντες περὶ τῶν ἰδίων ἕκαστος ὀργιζόμενος κοινὸν ἐφ' ἡμᾶς ἀγάγωσι τὸν πόλεμον, τὰ τῶν Ἀμφικτυόνων δόγματα προστησάμενοι, εἶτ' ἐπισπασθῶσιν ἕκαστοι πέρα τοῦ συμφέροντος ἑαυτοῖς ἡμῖν πολεμῆσαι* (*Dem.* 5, 19).

b) A copulative connexion with *καί* (sometimes *τέ — καί*) is used in Greek, where in a narration it is stated at what point the matter stood, what had taken place, *when* a change or new event occurred: *Οὕτω δύ' ἢ τρεῖς δρόμους περιεληλυθότε ἤστην* (*Εὐθύδημος καὶ Διονυσόδωρος*) *κ α ὶ εἰσέρχεται Κλεινίας* (*Pl. Euthyd.* 273). *Ἑκταῖος ἥκων ἐτύγχανον καὶ ἡ μήτηρ ἰδοῦσά με καὶ προσείπασα τὴν ψυχὴν ἀφῆκεν* (*Dem.* 50, 60). *Οἱ Λακεδαιμόνιοι οὐκ ἔφθησαν πυθόμενοι τὸν περὶ τὴν Ἀττικὴν πόλεμον καὶ πάντων τῶν ἄλλων ἀμελήσαντες ἧκον ἡμῖν ἀμυνοῦντες* (*Isocr. Paneg.* 86. So often *οὐκ ἔφθην ποιήσας — καί*, *I had not got the start in doing it, when* = *I had not done it, before* —).

c) *Καί* also introduces the second term of a comparison with adjectives and adverbs denoting likeness: *Οἱ ἄλλοι ποιηταὶ οὐχ ὁμοίως πεποιήκασι καὶ Ὅμηρος* (*Pl. Ion*, 531; *have not composed*). *Ὅμοιός γ', ὦ ἄνδρες Ἀθηναῖοι, Σόλων νομοθέτης καὶ Τιμοκράτης* (*Dem.* 24, 106. Ironical exclamation). *Παραπλήσια ἐπεπόνθεσαν οἱ Ἀθηναῖοι ἐν Συρακούσαις, καὶ ἔδρασαν αὐτοὶ ἐν Πύλῳ* (*Thuc.* 7, 71; also *οἷάπερ ἔδρασαν*). Cf. § 37, R. 2.[1]

A disjunctive connexion is denoted by *ἤ*, *or*, *ἤ — ἤ*, *either — or* §
(*ἤτοι — ἤ*). (*Εἴτε — εἴτε*, *be it that — or that*; *εἴτε — εἴτε καί*.) 186.

Rem. *Ἤ*, *or else*, is often used to connect a sentence which assigns what is to be assumed and will be the consequence, in case a certain condition is not realized, or a certain command is transgressed: *Τί γὰρ δήποτε τῷ μὲν Φιλίππῳ πάντα τἄλλα ποιεῖν ἐξουσίαν δώσομεν, ἂν τῆς Ἀττικῆς ἀπέχηται, τῷ Διοπείθει δ' οὐδὲ βοηθεῖν τοῖς Θρᾳξὶν ἐξέσται, ἢ πόλεμον ποιεῖν αὐτὸν φήσομεν;* (*Dem.* 8, 8; *or else we shall say that he is commencing a war.*) When *ἤ* in this manner is attached to an impersonal expression

---

[1] On *καί* in the signification *also, even*, and its various applications, see the Appendix.

[§ 186.] denoting necessity or duty with the infinitive, it is also followed by the infinitive (in English we should use the future indicative: *or else will*), although the same governing term cannot be repeated without alteration: Ξένους προσήκει σοι πολλοὺς δέχεσθαι καὶ τούτους μεγαλοπρεπῶς, ἔπειτα δὲ πολίτας δειπνίζειν καὶ εὖ ποιεῖν, ἢ ἔρημον συμμάχων εἶναι (*Xen. Œcon.* 2, 5).

§ 187. An adversative connexion of two members contradicting each other is denoted by *ἀλλά*, so that either (by way of correction) an affirmative clause is joined to a negative (*οὐχ ἅπαξ, ἀλλὰ πολλάκις, οὐ μόνον —ἀλλὰ καί*, or merely *ἀλλά, οὐχ ὅπως — ἀλλά, μὴ ὅτι — ἀλλά*, see *Negations*), or that which is negatived is joined to the affirmative (in English, *and not, only not*, in questions and irony: *and not rather*): *Πρὸς τὴν τῶν προγόνων ἀρετὴν ἀλλ' οὐ πρὸς τὴν τῶν τριάκοντα πονηρίαν ἁμιλλητέον ἡμῖν ἐστιν* (*Isocr. Areop.* 73). *Ἐκ δὴ πάντων τῶν εἰρημένων τίς μηχανή, ὦ Σώκρατες, δικαιοσύνην τιμᾶν ἐθέλειν, ᾧ τις δύναμις ὑπάρχει ψυχῆς ἢ χρημάτων ἢ σώματος ἢ γένους, ἀλλὰ μὴ γελᾶν ἐπαινουμένης ἀκούοντα;* (*Pl. Rep.* 2, 366; *and not rather laugh when one hears it praised.*)[1] Ἀλλὰ γὰρ ἴσως μετὰ μικρᾶς διαβολῆς ἢ φαύλων κατηγόρων ἐκινδύνευον, ἀλλ' οὐ διὰ τῶν ἐρρωμενεστάτων καὶ λέγειν καὶ πράττειν (*Andoc.* 4, 37).

Rem. 1. Sometimes ἀλλά merely adds something that does not correspond with what goes before, but without setting it aside: Καὶ ὁ Ἀβραδάτας εἶπεν· Ἀλλὰ τὰ μὲν καθ' ἡμᾶς ἔμοιγε δοκεῖ, ὦ Κῦρε, καλῶς ἔχειν· ἀλλὰ τὰ πλάγια λυπεῖ με (*Xen. Cyr.* 7, 1, 16). The use of ἀλλά (alone or with other particles), further than as serving for the grammatical connexion of the sentence, must be learnt from the Lexicon: in part the ἀλλά elliptically intimates a thought not expressed.

Rem. 2. With the adversative conjunctions may be reckoned the exceptive particle πλήν: Πάντες τὴν πόλιν ἐξέλιπον πλὴν οἱ τὰ καπηλεῖα ἔχοντες, *Xen. An.* 1, 2, 24, *except, only not —*; πλὴν εἰ, πλὴν ὅτι, πλὴν ὅσον. (§ 91, R. 2.)

§ 188. By *δέ* is denoted something which is distinguished from what goes before, but does not set it aside nor contradict it: *Ξυμπονήσετε ἐν τῇ πόλει ἕκαστοι ἐν μέρει, τὸν δὲ πολὺν χρόνον μετ' ἀλλήλων οἰκήσετε ἐν τῷ καθαρῷ* (*in freedom and rest, Pl. Rep.* 7, 520). *Δέῃ τι βοηθείας; ἢ μάτην ἐφοβήθης, οἱ δὲ πολέμιοι οὐκ ἔρχονται* (*Xen. Cyr.* 2, 1, 3; *and the enemy are not coming?*).[2] Hence *δέ* serves as a particle of transition (adverb), to annex each successive term of the discourse which is not connected with the preceding by another adverb (e. g. a conclusive, *οὖν*, a causal, *γάρ*), and does not commence a new series of thoughts. Answering to a preceding *μέν*, it forms a partitive con-

---

[1] But sometimes also καὶ οὐ (μή) and simply οὐ (μή), e. g. ἂν δὲ ποιῇ, μὴ λέγῃ (*Dem.* 21, 183).

[2] Occasionally, especially in poets, for ἀλλά: Οὐκ ἔπραξαν, ἃ ἠβούλοντο, ἀπῆλθον δὲ διὰ τάχους (*Thuc.* 6, 79). (But never οὐ μόνον — δέ, or the like.)

nexion, by which two terms or clauses (or, with δέ repeated, several) are made to stand out in opposition to each other. (Ὁ μὲν βασιλεύς —, οἱ δὲ στρατιῶται —. Λέγεις μὲν εὖ, πράττεις δ' οὐδέν. Νῦν μέν — τότε δέ —. Πολλὰ μὲν καὶ ἄλλα δύο δὲ μέγιστα. Εἰ μὲν νικήσεις, — εἰ δὲ οἱ θεοὶ ἄλλως βουλεύονται, —. Opposed or contrasted accessory definitions, denoted in two independent sentences by μέν and δέ, by which particles, at the same time the two sentences are connected, have often a different grammatical form: τῷ μὲν πρώτῳ ἔτει —, ἐπεὶ δέ —. Πρὶν μὲν τὴν μάχην γενέσθαι —, νικήσας δέ —. In English, the relation is denoted sometimes more strongly by *but, however, but then*, sometimes more weakly by *and*, or by the mere position of the words and the accent.) Where μέν and δέ connect principal sentences, they are often separated to a distance from each other by a number of clauses attaching themselves to the first clause, in consequence of which the connexion becomes less apparent. See e. g. *Xen. Anab.* ii. 4, 2—5 (τοῖς μὲν πολλοῖς τῶν Ἑλλήνων οὐκ ἤρεσκον — Κλέαρχος δέ, *Cyr.* viii. 2, 2—7).[1] [§ 188.]

REM. 1. Μέν and δέ are placed after the word in which the opposition lies (which word with δέ is always at the beginning of the sentence), or, where the opposition lies in an entire dependent sentence or a relative periphrasis, after the conjunction or the relative (ἐπεὶ δέ, ἃς μέν, ὡς μέν). With a noun with the article μέν and δέ come after the article, δέ also (more rarely) after the noun: τὰ μὲν ἀνθρώπεια παρέντες, τὰ δαιμόνια δὲ σκοποῦντες (*Xen. Mem.* 1, 1, 12. Usually τὰ δὲ δ.). With prepositions, μέν and δέ are apt to come immediately after the preposition (πρὸς μὲν μεσημβρίαν, also with ὁ μέν — ὁ δέ), e. g. ἐν μὲν ἄρα τοῖς συμφωνοῦμεν, ἐν δὲ τοῖς οὔ. (*Pl. Phæd.* 263.) (In the poets some anomalous positions occur.) (Ἦν δ' ἐγώ, ἦ δ' ὅς, after an entire sentence.)

REM. 2. Especially note the use of μέν and δέ with the article (as demonstrative pronoun ὁ μέν — ὁ δέ, in later writers also ὃς μέν — ὃς δέ) and demonstrative adverbs of time and place (τότε μέν — τότε δέ, ἔνθα μέν — ἔνθα δέ) to denote an indefinite and general antithesis: *the one — the other; this — that* (also ὁ μέν τις — ὁ δέ τις), *now — now, here — there.* (Ὁ μέν — οἱ δ' Ἀθηναῖοι, with definite term in the second member. Ἀλγεῖ, τότε δὲ χαίρει, *Pl. Phil.* 35 = Τότε μὲν ἀλγεῖ, τότε δὲ χαίρει.) In Herodotus, when the opposition with μέν and δέ is between two predicates of the same subject, in the second member an ὁ referred to the subject is inserted and the δέ attached to this: Γέλων ταύτην μὲν τὴν ὁδὸν ἠμέλησε, ὁ δὲ ἄλλης εἴχετο (7, 163, = ἄλλης δ' εἴχετο).

---

[1] Rare constructions are: μεμνημένος, ὁρῶν δ' οὔ (*Pl. Theæt.* 164. The first member put absolutely). (Ὦ παῖ Πηλέως, πατὴρ δ' ἐμός. *Eur. Hec.* 534.) (Καὶ σὲ μέν γ' ἤδη ἐάσω, τὸν δὲ λόγον τὸν περὶ τοῦ Ἔρωτος πειράσομαι ὑμῖν διελθεῖν. *Pl. Conv.* 201; μέν made more prominent by γέ. Εἰ μὲν δὴ δίκαια ποιήσω, οὐκ οἶδα· αἱρήσομαι δ' οὖν ὑμᾶς καὶ σὺν ὑμῖν, ὅ, τι ἂν δέῃ, πείσομαι. *Xen. An.* 1, 3, 5. See likewise the Lexicon for μὲν οὖν, μέντοι, &c.) [They are given in the Appendix of this Translation.]

CHAP. VII.]

[§ 188.] Rem. 3. [*Anaphora.*] Often in the opposition of several members, the term (especially the verb) which is common to all is emphatically repeated with *μέν* and *δέ*, instead of a copulative connexion: Πολλὴ ἀθυμία ἦν τοῖς Ἕλλησιν. ὁρῶσι μὲν τοῦ ποταμοῦ τὴν δυσπορίαν, ὁρῶσι δὲ τοὺς διαβαίνειν κωλύσοντας, ὁρῶσι δὲ τοῖς διαβαίνουσιν ἐπικεισομένους τοὺς Καρδούχους ὄπισθεν (*Xen. An.* 4, 3, 7). Σὺν μὲν σοὶ πᾶσα μὲν ἡμῖν ὁδὸς εὔπορος, πᾶς δὲ ποταμὸς διαβατός, ἄνευ δὲ σοῦ πᾶσα μὲν διὰ σκότους ἡ ὁδός, πᾶς δὲ ποταμὸς δύσπορος, πᾶς δὲ ὄχλος φοβερός (*Xen. An.* 2, 5, 9).[1]

Rem. 4. When the opposition denoted by *μέν* and *δέ* lies in a relative sentence, and to this a demonstrative reference is annexed (*οἵ —, οὗτοι, ὅπου —, ἐνταῦθα*), often *μέν* and *δέ*, or one of them, is put twice, first with the relative, then with the demonstrative: Πρωταγόρας λέγει, ὡς, οἷα μὲν ἕκαστα ἐμοὶ φαίνεται, τοιαῦτα μέν ἐστιν ἐμοί, οἷα δὲ σοί, τοιαῦτα δ' αὖ σοί (*Pl. Theæt.* 152). Οἳ μὲν ἂν τῶν σατραπῶν τὸν ἀριθμὸν τὸν τεταγμένον τῶν μισθοφόρων ἔκπλεων ἔχοντες φαίνωνται καὶ τούτους δοκίμοις ἵπποις καὶ ὅπλοις παρεσκευασμένους παρέχωσι, τούτους μὲν τοὺς ἄρχοντας ὁ βασιλεὺς καὶ τιμαῖς αὔξει καὶ δώροις μεγάλοις καταπλουτίζει, οὓς δ' ἂν εὕρῃ τῶν ἀρχόντων καταμελοῦντας, τούτους χαλεπῶς κολάζει (*Xen. Œcon.* 4, 7; only *μέν* repeated). The same takes place, when to a participle with the nominative a demonstrative is afterwards annexed (by § 100 e). *Isocr. Paneg.* § 60.

Rem. 5. Sometimes *μέν* is put to denote the opposition to something following, without a corresponding *δέ* to follow it, when either (*a*) this is considered superfluous because certain adverbs are used which themselves express an opposition to what goes before (*ἔπειτα, εἶτα* after *πρῶτον μέν, τέως μέν*), or (*b*) the opposition is more strongly marked by *μήν*, *yet* (*γὲ μήν*), or *μέντοι*, *however*, or (*c*) the second member, by a less accurate formation of the sentence, follows in a different construction, and is not expressly drawn out as opposition (anacoluthia), or (*d*) *μέν* refers to an opposition which is understood without being expressly mentioned (*ἴσως μέν, εἰκὸς μέν, οἶμαι μέν, ὡς μὲν λέγουσιν, ἐγὼ μέν*, in opposition to some different view or statement which is possible): (*a*) Ἔγωγε μάλιστα ἐθαύμασα τοῦ Σωκράτους πρῶτον μὲν τοῦτο, ὡς ἡδέως καὶ εὐμενῶς τῶν νεανίσκων τὸν λόγον ἀπεδέξατο, ἔπειτα ἡμῶν ὡς ὀξέως ᾔσθετο ὃ ἐπεπόνθειμεν ὑπὸ τῶν λόγων (*Pl. Phæd.* 89; *remarked what impression the discourse had made upon us*). (*b*) Οἱ μὲν παθόντες, ἄδηλον ἦν, εἰ ἀδίκως ἐτετιμώρηντο· ἡ μέντοι ἄλλη πόλις ἐν τῷ παρόντι περιφανῶς ὠφέλητο (*Thuc.* 6, 60). (*c. Xen. Anab.* 1, 10, 16.) (*d*) Εἰκὸς μέν, ἔφη, οὓς ἄν τις ἡγῆται χρηστούς, φιλεῖν, οὓς δ' ἂν πονηρούς, μισεῖν (*Pl. Rep.* 1, 334). Ἆρ' ἂν ὀλίγα τοιαῦτα Εὔανδρον ἐν τῇ ἀρχῇ διαπράξασθαι προσδοκᾶτε; ἐγὼ γὰρ μὲν οὐκ ἂν οἶμαι (*Lys.* 26, 7).[2] (Other irregularities in the construction of the members denoted by *μέν* and *δέ*, see under *Anacoluthia*, § 216, R. 1.)

Rem. 6. The particle *δέ* in the more ancient poetical language (Homer) is frequently used with a certain emphasis (akin to *δή*) in the apodosis after relative sentences or conjunctions. In Attic this is rare (especially in prose), and occurs only where the apodosis after a conjunction or a relative adverb of comparison (*ὡς, ὥσπερ*) is made to stand out with special emphasis by a demonstrative word or a personal pronoun denoting an opposition to some other term, and in the same manner after a participial construction containing an opposition to the leading

---

[1] Βίᾳ μέν, ὅμως δ' ἀπέχονται (*Pl. Rep.* 10, 607; *they refrain perforce, but still they do refrain*).

[2] Τούτους οὖν πάντας φιλοσόφους φήσομεν; Οὐδαμῶς, εἶπον, ἀλλ' ὁμοίους μὲν φιλοσόφοις (*Pl. Rep.* 5, 475; the antithesis φιλοσόφους δ' οὔ lies in what precedes).

sentence: Εἰ οὖν ἐγὼ μὴ γιγνώσκω μήτε τὰ ὅσια μήτε τὰ δίκαια, ὑμεῖς δὲ διδάξατέ με [§
(*Xen. Hell.* 4, 1, 33). Ἐπεὶ δὲ γῇ ἔκειτο τλήμων (Ἰοκάστη), δεινὰ δ' ἦν τἀνθένδ' 188.]
ὁρᾶν (*Soph. Œd. R.* 1267; cf. *Thuc.* 5, 16). Ἐπιτιμῶ ταῖς μοναρχίαις, ὅτι, δέον τοὺς μονάρχους τὴν φρόνησιν ἀσκεῖν μᾶλλον τῶν ἄλλων, οἱ δὲ χεῖρον παιδεύονται τῶν ἰδιωτῶν (*Isocr. Paneg.* 71).

REM. 7. Especially note the use of τὸ δέ (the article as pronoun) to attach a sentence which, in opposition to some less correct statement which has just been made, says what is the true state of the case (*but in truth; whereas really*): Οἴονταί με ἑκάστοτε οἱ παρόντες ταῦτα αὐτὸν εἶναι σοφὸν, ἃ ἂν ἄλλον ἐξελέγξω· τὸ δὲ κινδυνεύει, ὦ ἄνδρες Ἀθηναῖοι, τῷ ὄντι ὁ θεὸς σοφὸς εἶναι καὶ ἐν τῷ χρησμῷ τούτῳ τοῦτο λεγεῖν, ὅτι ἡ ἀνθρωπίνη σοφία ὀλίγου τινὸς ἀξία ἐστίν (*Pl. Apol.* 23). The expression originates in the omission of a sentence merely intimated by τό (τὸ δὲ ὧδε ἔχει· κινδυνεύει κ.τ.λ., *Pl. Theæt.* 166).

a) The Greeks not unfrequently use two sentences connected by §
μέν and δέ, when the scope of the discourse does not refer to each 189.
sentence by itself, but to the connexion of the two and their con- (320.
joint matter; which relation would be more distinctly expressed by K.)
making the sentence with μέν a *subordinate* sentence, appended by a conjunction to that with δέ. Two sentences connected in this manner are put either interrogatively (inquiring whether both can subsist together; whether the one beside the other is probable), or negatively (so that the negation of both precedes), or they are joined in the infinitive, accusative with infinitive, or by εἰ (ὡς, ὅτι) to a statement denoting something absurd or wrong. Sometimes in this manner a clause which asserts something actual, and a hypothetical clause with ἄν are connected, it being asked whether the actual state of the case and the supposition accord and can be conceived to subsist together: Τί οὖν; οἱ μὲν ἄρα νίκης ἕνεκα πάλης καὶ δρόμου ἐτόλμησαν ἀπέχεσθαι λεγομένου πράγματος ὑπὸ τῶν πολλῶν εὐδαίμονος, οἱ δὲ ἡμέτεροι παῖδες ἀδυνατήσουσι καρτερεῖν πολὺ καλλίονος ἕνεκα νίκης; (*Pl. Legg.* 8, 840.) Ἆρ' ἐξ ἴσου οἴει εἶναι σοὶ τὸ δίκαιον καὶ ἡμῖν (τοῖς νόμοις), καὶ ἅττ' ἂν ἡμεῖς σε ἐπιχειρῶμεν ποιεῖν, καὶ σοὶ ταῦτα ἀντιποιεῖν οἴει δίκαιον εἶναι; ἢ πρὸς μὲν ἄρα σοι τὸν πατέρα οὐκ ἐξ ἴσου ἦν τὸ δίκαιον καὶ πρὸς τὸν δεσπότην, εἴ σοι ὢν ἐτύγχανεν, ὥστε, ἅπερ πάσχοις, ταῦτα καὶ ἀντιποιεῖν, πρὸς δὲ τὴν πατρίδα ἄρα καὶ τοὺς νόμους ἐξέσται σοι; (*Pl. Crit.* 50.) (By ἄρα, *then*, the thing inquired about is denoted as the result of a reasoning and a consideration, sometimes in one clause, sometimes in both.) Ἔδει Αἰσχίνην, εἰ ἀδικοῦντά με ἑώρα τὴν πόλιν, ταῖς ἐκ τῶν νόμων τιμωρίαις παρ' αὐτὰ τἀδικήματα χρῆσθαι, εἰ μὲν εἰσαγγελίας ἄξια πράττοντά μ' ἑώρα, εἰσαγγέλλοντα, εἰ δὲ γράφοντα παράνομα, παρανόμων γραφόμενον· οὐ γὰρ δήπου Κτησιφῶντα μὲν δύναται διώκειν δι' ἐμέ, ἐμὲ δέ, εἴπερ ἐξελέγξειν ἐνόμιζεν, αὐτὸν οὐκ ἂν ἐγράψατο (*Dem.* 18, 14. *For it cannot be supposed* (οὐ) *that he can indeed prosecute Ctesiphon, but would not have impeached me, if*—; or, *that if he can prosecute Ct., he would not also have im-*

[§ 189.] *peached me.* In this way the connexion of an affirmative and a negative clause is often negatived.)[1] Οὐ δεινόν, ἄλλοις μέν τισι θεῶν ὕμνους καὶ παιᾶνας εἶναι ὑπὸ τῶν ποιητῶν πεποιημένους, τῷ δ' Ἔρωτι, τηλικούτῳ ὄντι καὶ τοσούτῳ θεῷ, μηδὲ ἕνα πώποτε πεποιηκέναι μηδὲν ἐγκώμιον; (*Pl. Conv.* 177.) Πάνυ θαυμαστὸν Κύρῳ ἐδόκει εἶναι, εἰ οἱ μὲν βάναυσοι ἴσασι τῆς ἑαυτοῦ τέχνης ἕκαστος τῶν ἐργαλείων τὸ ὄνομα, ὁ δὲ στρατηγὸς οὕτως ἠλίθιος ἔσοιτο, ὥστε οὐκ εἴσεται τῶν ὑφ' ἑαυτῷ ἡγεμόνων τὰ ὀνόματα (*Xen. Cyr.* 5, 3, 47. In the first member after the præteritum, the indicative retained, in the second the optative put; see § 132 *a* and *b*). Δεινὰ ἂν εἴην εἰργασμένος, εἰ, ὅτε μέν με οἱ ἄρχοντες ἔταττον, τότε μέν, οὗ ἐκεῖνοι ἔταττον, ἔμενον (fact), τοῦ δὲ θεοῦ τάττοντος, ἐνταῦθα δὲ φοβηθεὶς θάνατον λίποιμι τὴν τάξιν (*should now desert, Pl. Apol.* 28). On the double μέν and δέ, see § 188, R. 4.

REM. 1. In the same manner is denoted the prohibition of acting in two cases so that the actions do not accord: Μὴ τοίνυν, ἂν μὲν εἴπῃ τις (*brings forward, proposes*) παράνομα, ὀργιζόμενοι φαίνεσθε, ἂν δὲ ποιῇ, μὴ λέγῃ, πράως διάκεισθε (*Dem.* 21, 183).

REM. 2. Sometimes some inaccuracy appears in the construction of the two members when they ought to be dependent (e.g. οὐ δεινόν, εἰ —), in case the first is somewhat long, and the connexion is become less perspicuous, so that e.g. the second member is added as an independent question or statement, or changed in some other way (anacoluthia). See e.g. *Lysias* xii. § 36. *Xen. Cyrop.* iv. 2, 46.

b) Sometimes, partly in an apodosis, partly (especially with ὥστε) before that which is the main thing to be affirmed or denied, a co-ordinate member with μέν (and δέ following) is inserted, containing a remark by-the-bye of something which obtains at the same time, which should more accurately have been attached by a conjunction (*while, whereas, although, as*) or in a participial construction: Ἐπεὶ εἶδον οἱ Ἕλληνες τό τε Φαρναβάζου ἱππικὸν ἔτι συνεστηκὸς καὶ τοὺς Βιθυνοὺς ἱππέας πρὸς τούτους ἀθροιζομένους, ἀπειρήκεσαν μέν, ὅμως δὲ ἐδόκει καὶ ἐπὶ τούτους ἰτέον εἶναι οὕτως, ὅπως δύναιντο (*Xen. An.* 6, 3, 30; *they thought, although they were weary, yet* —). Οὕτω μοι δοκεῖς καλῶς λέγειν, ὦ Σώκρατες, ὥστε πρόσθεν μὲν οὐ προσιέμην δανείσασθαι, εἰδώς, ὅτι, ἀναλώσας, ὅ, τι ἂν λάβω, οὐχ ἕξω ἀποδοῦναι, νῦν δέ μοι δοκῶ εἰς ἔργων ἀφορμὴν ὑπομενεῖν αὐτὸ ποιῆσαι (*Xen. Mem.* 2. 7, 11; *that although hitherto I never took to borrowing, nevertheless I think that I* —).

§ 190. When the nature or quality of an action or a relation is first denoted in a merely general way by a demonstrative pronoun in the neuter (τοῦτο, τόδε, τοιόνδε, τοιοῦτον, ταὐτόν, as object or as subject to γίγνομαι), by a demonstrative adverb, by an adjective of reference (τοὐναντίον, τὰ ἀντίστροφα), or a similar expression, in order to be then more precisely assigned in a new sentence, the latter in Greek is attached without any connecting particle, in the same mood, even in the infinitive. (Apposition of an entire sentence.) Τί δέ; οἱ κόσμιοι

---

[1] Οὐχ ὁ μέν, ὁ δ' οὔ (ἀλλ' ἅπαντες). Denial of a partitive representation, because the truth demands a universal statement.

αὐτῶν οὐ ταὐτὸν τοῦτο πεπόνθασιν, ἀκολασίᾳ τινὶ σώφρονές εἰσιν; (*Pl. Phæd.* 68.) Δέδοικα, μὴ τοὐναντίον, οὗ βούλομαι, ποιῶ, σφόδρα ἀκριβῶς διεκνύναι πειρώμενος διοχλῶ πάλαι τοῦτ' αὐτοὺς ὑμᾶς εἰδότας (*Dem.* 19, 329). Ὡς οἱ τὴν δικαιοσύνην ἐπιτηδεύοντες ἄκοντες ἐπιτηδεύουσι, μάλιστ' ἂν αἰσθανοίμεθα, εἰ τοιόνδε ποιήσαιμεν τῇ διανοίᾳ, δόντες ἐξουσίαν ἑκατέρῳ ποιεῖν, ὅ, τι ἂν βούληται, τῷ τε δικαίῳ καὶ τῷ ἀδίκῳ, εἶτ' ἐπακολουθήσαιμεν θεώμενοι, ποῖ ἡ ἐπιθυμία ἑκάτερον ἄξει (*Pl. Rep.* 2, 359). Ἡ αὐλητικὴ οὐ δοκεῖ σοι τοιαύτη τις εἶναι, ὦ Καλλίκλεις, τὴν ἡδονὴν μόνον διώκειν; (*Pl. Gorg.* 501.) Ὁρῶμεν, ὅσοι ἂν μακρότερον τῇ φιλοσοφίᾳ ἐνδιατρίψωσι, τοὺς μὲν πλείστους καὶ πάνυ ἀλλοκότους γιγνομένους, τοὺς δὲ ἐπιεικεστάτους δοκοῦντας ὅμως τοῦτό γε ὑπὸ τοῦ ἐπιτηδεύματος, οὗ σὺ ἐπαινεῖς, πάσχοντας, ἀχρήστους ταῖς πόλεσι γιγνομένους (*Pl. Rep.* 6, 487). [§ 190.]

With declarative object-sentences, denoted by ὅτι or ὡς (see § 159, R. 3), as also with dependent questions, it should be remarked, that in Greek the subject of the object-sentence is often drawn (by an attraction) as object into the principal sentence, and then the accessory sentence attached, whereby the object, which *till then was incomplete*, is fully and properly represented[1]. This attraction often takes place although the principal verb (a verb of saying, thinking, or knowing) cannot otherwise in itself be constructed with an object-accusative of the kind denoted by the substantive, e. g. not λέγειν τινά for περί τινος. Κῦρος ᾔδει βασιλέα, ὅτι μέσον ἔχοι τοῦ Περσικοῦ στρατεύματος (*Xen. An.* 1, 8, 21). Γνώσῃ τὸν Ἡσίοδον, ὅτι τῷ ὄντι ἦν σοφὸς λέγων πλέον εἶναί πως ἥμισυ παντός (*Pl. Rep.* 5, 466). Φίλιππος ἔφη πυνθάνεσθαι τοὺς Ὠρείτας, ὡς νοσοῦσι καὶ στασιάζουσιν ἐν αὐτοῖς (*Dem.* 9, 12). Οἶσθα Εὐθύδημον ὁπόσους ὀδόντας ἔχει; (*Pl. Euthyd.* 294.) Τὰς τῶν πατέρων ἁμαρτίας ἀφίετε διὰ τοὺς παῖδας, οὓς οὔπω ἴστε εἴτε ἀγαθοὶ εἴτε κακοὶ ἡβήσαντες γενήσονται (*Lys.* 20, 34). (Ἀνεμνήσθην τοῦ Κόννου, ὅτι μοι κἀκεῖνος χαλεπαίνει ἑκάστοτε, ὅταν αὐτῷ μὴ ὑπείκω. *Pl. Euthyd.* 295.) § 191.

Rem. 1. Sometimes the subject of the accessory sentence is drawn into the principal as the subject to a passive or intransitive verb, which otherwise should stand impersonally: Περὶ τοῦ μήθ' ἑαλωκότος μήτ' ἐγνωσμένου, πότερον δέδρακεν ἢ οὐ καὶ πότερ' ἄκων ἢ ἑκών, πάνδεινον γράφειν, ὡς ἐκδοτέον τοῖς ἐγκαλοῦσιν (*Dem.* 23, 79; *about a man —, of whom it is not yet known whether —*). (Οἱ Λακεδαιμόνιοι σχηματίζονται ἀμαθεῖς εἶναι, ἵνα μὴ κατάδηλοι ὦσιν, ὅτι σοφίᾳ τῶν Ἑλλήνων περίεισιν, *Pl. Prot.* 342 = κατάδηλοι ὦσι σοφίᾳ — περιόντες, by § 177.) As the subject of the accessory sentence becomes the accusative to the principal verb, so it may sometimes become the objective genitive to a substantive: Ἦλθε τοῖς Ἀθηναίοις εὐθὺς ἡ ἀγγελία τῶν πόλεων, ὅτι ἀφεστᾶσιν (*Thuc.* 1, 61; *the tidings that the cities have revolted*).

Rem. 2. A somewhat similar attraction sometimes takes place in sentences with μή and ὅπως after verbs denoting fear and apprehension: Ἰσχυρῶς ἔδεισαν οἱ Ἕλληνες τὸν Ἰάσονα, μὴ τύραννος γένοιτο (*Xen. Hell.* 6, 4, 32).

[[1] E. g. as in *nosti Marcellum, quam tardus sit*, the proper object is, not *Marcellum* alone, but *Marcellum quam tardus sit*.]

§ 192. *a*) The particle ὅτι, which denotes a declarative object-sentence, is often also put before a person's own speech, when it is given in *orat. recta* and introduced by a *verbum declarandi*: Ἠρώτησεν ὁ Κῦρος τὸν Ὀρόντην· Ἔτι οὖν ἂν φίλος καὶ πιστός μοι γένοιο; Ὁ δὲ ἀπεκρίνατο ὅτι· Οὐδ' εἰ γενοίμην, ὦ Κῦρε, σοί γ' ἂν ἔτι ποτὲ δόξαιμι (*Xen. An.* 1, 6, 8). Τῷ ταῦτα εἰπόντι ἐγὼ ἂν δίκαιον λόγον ἀντείποιμι, ὅτι· Οὐ καλῶς λέγεις, ὦ ἄνθρωπε, εἰ οἴει κίνδυνον ὑπολογίζεσθαι τοῦ ζῆν ἢ τεθνάναι ἄνδρα, ὅτου τι καὶ σμικρὸν ὄφελος (*Pl. Apol.* 28). (Ἀπεκρινάμην, ὅτι οὔ, *I answered, No.*)

b) A report of a person's speech commenced in the *oratio obliqua* (in the infinitive, or with ὅτι or ὡς) often (even in a sentence dependent on the *oratio obliqua*) passes suddenly into the *oratio recta*, so that the words of the speaker are given in their own proper form: Κῦρος ἀπεκρίνατο, ὅτι ἀκούει, Ἀβροκόμαν ἐπὶ τῷ Εὐφράτῃ ποταμῷ εἶναι, ἀπέχοντα δώδεκα σταθμούς· πρὸς τοῦτον οὖν ἔφη βούλεσθαι ἐλθεῖν· κἂν μὲν ᾖ ἐκεῖ, τὴν δίκην ἔφη χρῄζειν ἐπιθεῖναι αὐτῷ, ἂν δὲ φεύγῃ, ἡμεῖς ἐκεῖ πρὸς ταῦτα βουλευσόμεθα (*Xen. An.* 1, 3, 20). Μετὰ τοῦτον ἄλλος ἀνέστη, ἐπιδεικνὺς μὲν τὴν εὐήθειαν τοῦ τὰ πλοῖα αἰτεῖν κελεύοντος, ἐπιδεικνὺς δέ, ὡς εὔηθες εἴη ἡγεμόνα αἰτεῖν παρὰ τούτου, ᾧ λυμαινόμεθα τὴν πρᾶξιν (*Xen. An.* 1, 3, 16). Λέγοντος ἐμοῦ ταῦτα ἀποκρίνεταί μοι Πολυκλῆς, ὅτι ὁ συντριήραρχος αὐτῷ οὐχ ἥκοι ἐπὶ τὴν ναῦν· οὔκουν παραλήψομαι μόνος τὴν τριήρη (*Dem.* 50, 37; *therefore* [said he] *I* (Polycles) *will not undertake the trireme by myself*, i. e. *therefore he would*, &c.).

Rem. On the use of ὅτι in the signification, *that, the circumstance that*, see § 170 a. R., and below, § 197. On the sense *because*, see the Lexicon [and Appendix]. Note also the *breviloquentia*, by which ὅτι and ὡς obtain the signification, *for proof that, to show that*: Ὅτι δὲ οὕτω ταῦτα ἔχει, λέγε μοι τὸ τοῦ Καλλισθένους ψήφισμα (*Dem.* 18, 37). Ὡς δ' εἰκότα ποιοῦμεν, καὶ τάδ' ἐννοήσατε (*Xen. Hell.* 2, 3, 34; *consider also what follows*).

§ 193. The verbs δοκῶ, δοκεῖ μοι, οἶμαι are often put before a sentence or are inserted in it, without grammatical connexion, to denote the thing said as opinion or conjecture; in the same manner we have οἴει (οἴεσθε) with a question, and εὖ ἴσθι (ἴστε) with an assurance; also φημί, φασίν, εἰπέ μοι are inserted in the same way. Ἀγαθοὺς ἄρα ἄνδρας οὐκ ἐβούλετο Περικλῆς ποιῆσαι τοὺς υἱεῖς; Δοκῶ μέν, ἐβούλετο, ἀλλὰ μὴ οὐ διδακτὸν ᾖ (*Pl. Menon*, 94; *but I fear it is not*; see § 124 a. R. 2). Νεώτερος πρεσβύτερον οὔτε ἄλλο βιάζεσθαι ἐπιχειρήσει ποτὲ οὔτε τύπτειν, ὡς τὸ εἰκός· οἶμαι δέ, οὐδὲ ἄλλως ἀτιμάσει (*Pl. Rep.* 5, 465).[1] Ἀνόνητα δὴ πονῶν ὁ ἀνὴρ οὐκ, οἴει, ἀναγκασθήσεται τελευτῶν αὑτόν τε μισεῖν καὶ τὴν τοιαύτην πρᾶξιν; (*Pl. Rep.* 6, 486.)

Rem. The expression δῆλον ὅτι, which originally introduces a declarative object-

---

[1] Ὅμηρος Ὠκεανόν τε θεῶν γένεσίν φησι καὶ μητέρα Τηθύν· οἶμαι δὲ καὶ Ἡσίοδος (viz. φησίν. *Pl. Crat.* 402), but more frequently where the verb is omitted in this manner: οἶμαι δὲ καὶ Ἡσίοδον (viz. φάναι). Ταῦτα ἐγώ σοι οὐ πείθομαι, ὦ Μέλητε, οἶμαι δ' οὐδὲ ἄλλον ἄνθρωπον οὐδένα (*Pl. Apol.* 25).

sentence, is then also appended after a sentence with the sense of a mere adverb, [§ 193.] *assuredly*: Ἐλάττω ἐκ τῆς πόλεως ἀπεδήμησας ἢ οἱ χωλοί τε καὶ τυφλοὶ καὶ οἱ ἄλλοι ἀνάπηροι· οὕτω σοι διαφερόντως τῶν ἄλλων Ἀθηναίων ἤρεσκεν ἡ πόλις καὶ ἡμεῖς οἱ νόμοι δῆλον ὅτι (*Pl. Crit.* 53, *and, of course, we Laws likewise*). (Δηλονότι.) The expression εὖ οἶδ' ὅτι (οἶδ' ὅτι, εὖ ἴσθ' ὅτι) is usually inserted in the sentence before the verb, so that the proper signification clearly appears (e. g. Εἴ τις ἔροιτο· Εἰπέ μοι, τῆς νῦν οὔσης Ἑλλάδος ταυτησὶ ἔσθ' ὅ, τι ᾤκεῖτ' ἂν ὑπὸ τῶν νῦν ἐχόντων Ἑλλήνων, εἰ μὴ τὰς ἀρετὰς ὑπὲρ αὐτῶν ἐκείνας οἱ Μαραθῶνι καὶ Σαλαμῖνι παρέσχοντο οἱ ἡμέτεροι πρόγονοι; οὐδ' ἂν εἷς εὖ οἶδ' ὅτι φήσειεν, *Dem.* 19, 312); but it remains with the infinitive and participle (with the signification of an adverb of assurance); e. g. ὥστε πάντας ὑμᾶς εἰδέναι τὰ μετὰ ταῦτα καὶ ἐλεεῖν εὖ οἶδ' ὅτι τοὺς ἀτυχεῖς καὶ ταλαιπώρους ἀνθρώπους, *Dem.* 19, 309. (Μονώτατος γὰρ εἶ σὺ πάντων αἴτιος, καὶ τῶν κακῶν καὶ τῶν ἀγαθῶν, εὖ ἴσθ' ὅτι, *Arist. Pl.* 183.)

a) Conditional propositions are denoted by εἰ, ἐάν (ἤν, ἄν, see § 125, R. 1); εἴπερ, ἐάνπερ, εἴγε (*if that is: if at least; wenn sonst, falls dann, wenigstens wenn*[1]) put the condition with a peculiar prominence. § 194. A plurality of cases in which something equally holds good, are denoted by εἴτε — εἴτε [*sive — sive*] (εἴτ' οὖν, *or be it that*), ἐάν τε — ἐάν τε, more strongly by εἴτε (ἐάν τε) καί — εἴτε καί (e. g. εἴτε καλὸς εἴτε πλούσιος εἴτε καὶ γενναῖός ἐστιν εἴτε καὶ τἀναντία τούτων, *Pl. Menon*, 71. Ἐάν τε καὶ ἀντιφιλῆται ἐάν τε καὶ μισῆται, *Pl. Lys.* 212).

Rem. 1. More rare combinations are εἴτε — ἤ, εἰ — εἴτε (the latter poetical). On εἰ and εἴτε, as interrogative particles, see § 199 *b* and *c*.

Rem. 2. Especially note the use of εἰ, εἴ πως, ἐάν πως, in the sense, *whether perchance* (= to try *whether* —). Διαλύσας τὸν ξύλλογον ὁ Ἀρχίδαμος Μελήσιππον πρῶτον ἀποστέλλει εἰς τὰς Ἀθήνας, ἄνδρα Σπαρτιάτην, εἴ τι ἄρα μᾶλλον ἐνδοῖεν οἱ Ἀθηναῖοι, ὁρῶντες ἤδη σφᾶς (τοὺς Λακεδαιμονίους) ἐν ὁδῷ ὄντας (*Thuc.* 2, 12). Οἱ Λακεδαιμόνιοι προθυμίᾳ τε πάσῃ ἐχρῶντο καὶ παρακελευσμῷ, εἴ πως ὠσάμενοι τοὺς Ἀθηναίους ἕλοιεν τὸ τείχισμα (*Thuc.* 4, 11). Βούλει οὖν δεώμεθα τοῦ ἀντιλέγοντος ἀκολουθῆσαι ἡμῖν, ἐάν πως ἡμεῖς ἐκείνῳ ἐνδειξώμεθα, ὅτι οὐδέν ἐστιν ἐπιτήδευμα ἴδιον γυναικὶ πρὸς διοίκησιν πόλεως (*Pl. Rep.* 5, 455).

Rem. 3. In animated and concise discourse, the condition is sometimes expressed in an independent sentence, as an assumed position or as a question: Παρὰ πᾶσιν ἀνθρώποις ὁρῶ διωρισμένα καὶ τεταγμένα πως τὰ τοιαῦτα: Ἀδικεῖ τις ἑκών· ὀργὴ καὶ τιμωρία κατὰ τούτου. Ἐξήμαρτέ τις ἄκων· συγγνώμη ἀντὶ τῆς τιμωρίας τούτῳ (*Dem.* 18, 274). Sometimes to one condition there is added another, of a more special and precise character: Εἰ ἐτύγχανόν σε ἐρωτῶν, τίς ἐστι τῶν ζωγράφων Ζεῦξις, εἴ μοι εἶπες, ὅτι ὁ τὰ ζῷα γράφων, ἆρ' οὐκ ἂν δικαίως σε ἠρόμην, ὁ τὰ ποῖα τῶν ζῴων γράφων καὶ ποῦ; (*Pl. Gorg.* 453; — *and then thou shouldest say* —.)

b) A negative condition is denoted by εἰ μή, which also indicates an exception: *if not, except if, unless* (εἰ μὴ ἄρα, *unless after all, unless perchance*, sometimes ironically; of a case which is possibly to be excepted also εἰ μὴ εἰ, *nisi si*, εἰ μὴ ἄρα εἰ: Ὁ χρηματιστικὸς τὴν τοῦ

[[1] M. therefore rejects (I think correctly) Hermann's '*wide difference*' between εἴγε (as assuming the *truth* of the condition), and εἴπερ (as leaving it *doubtful*).—T. K. A.]

[§ 194.] τιμᾶσθαι ἡδονὴν ἢ τὴν τοῦ μανθάνειν οὐδενὸς ἀξίαν φήσει εἶναι, εἰ μὴ εἴ τι αὐτῶν ἀργύριον ποιεῖ. *Pl. Rep.* 9, 581). **Εἰ δὲ μή**, without a verb, denotes, not only the opposite to an affirmative condition preceding (*if not*), but to the preceding condition and discourse generally, even if that be negative (*in the opposite case*) *otherwise*: Ἴσως οὐδεὶς οὐδέν σε κακὸν ἐρεῖ, ἂν μή τινα λυπῇς· εἰ δὲ μή, ἀκούσει πολλὰ καὶ ἀνάξια σαυτοῦ (*Pl. Crit.* 53, = ἂν δέ τινα λυπῇς). Πρὸς τῶν θεῶν, ὦ Κῦρε, μὴ οὕτω λέγε· εἰ δὲ μή, οὐ θαρροῦντά μ' ἕξεις (*Xen. Cyr.* 3, 1, 35). Conversely, εἰ δέ especially after εἰ μὲν βούλει (βούλεσθε) for εἰ δὲ μή: Λέγω πάλιν, ἅπερ τότε, εἰ μὲν βούλεσθε, ὡς παίζων, εἰ δ', ὡς σπουδάζων (*Pl. Legg.* 3, 688). (Εἰ μὴ διὰ τὴν Ἀρχιδάμου μέλλησιν, *Thuc.* 2, 18, *if it had not been for A.'s delaying; but for that.*)

Rem. When what seems to be the natural and desirable condition, what one must expect and assume, and upon which the consequence follows as matter of course, has first been put with εἰ μέν; and then, by εἰ δὲ μή, its opposite, and what would then follow, the apodosis to the first condition is often entirely omitted (e. g. εὖ ἔχει, *then is it well*, or generally, *well and good*): Εἰ μὲν τοίνυν, ἔφη ὁ Σωκράτης, καὶ διαγιγνώσκειν σε τοὺς ἀγαθοὺς καὶ τοὺς κακοὺς ἐδίδαξεν· εἰ δὲ μή, τί σοι ὄφελος ὧν ἔμαθες; (*Xen. Mem.* 3, 1, 9.) Ἐλθόντων τῶν Λακώνων ἔλεξε Χαρμῖνος· Εἰ μὲν σύ τι ἔχεις, ὦ Μηδόσαδες, πρὸς ἡμᾶς λέγειν· εἰ δὲ μή, ἡμεῖς πρὸς σὲ ἔχομεν (*Xen. An.* 7, 7, 15).

c) With verbs which express a feeling of approbation and joy (pride), or of disapprobation and surprise (shame), the Greeks often use a sentence with εἰ, instead of an object-sentence with ὅτι (*that, for that, because*), even when an actual fact is denoted, this being considered as the condition on which the feeling depends: Μὴ τοῦτο μεῖον δόξητε ἔχειν, εἰ οἱ Κυρεῖοι, πρόσθεν σὺν ἡμῖν ταττόμενοι, νῦν ἀφεστήκασιν· ἔτι γὰρ οὗτοι κακίονές εἰσι τῶν ὑφ' ἡμῶν ἡττημένων (*Xen. An.* 3, 2, 17). Τηλικούτων κακῶν αἴτιος γεγενημένος Δημοσθένης οὐκ ἀγαπᾷ, εἰ μὴ δίκην δέδωκεν, ἀλλ' εἰ μὴ καὶ χρυσῷ στεφάνῳ στεφανωθήσεται, ἀγανακτεῖ (*Æsch.* 3, 147; *D. does not think himself well off to have escaped the punishment; is not satisfied with having —*). Οἱ ἐπίτροποι οὐκ ᾐσχύνθησαν οὐδ' ἠλέησαν τὴν ἐμὴν ἀδελφήν, εἰ δυοῖν ταλάντοιν ὑπὸ τοῦ πατρὸς ἀξιωθεῖσα (*accounted worthy of a dowry of two talents*) μηδενὸς τεύξεται τῶν προσηκόντων (*Dem.* 27, 65; *nothing of what she has a right to*). [So often after θαυμάζω, &c.]

d) Καὶ εἰ, *even if, even in the case that*: Ἐὰν τοῦτο ποιήσῃς ἅπαξ ἢ δίς, ἢ λύγξ, καὶ εἰ πάνυ ἰσχυρά ἐστι, παύσεται (*Pl. Conv.* 185), εἰ καί (*if even*, wenn gleich) sometimes more inclining to the affirmation of the condition, almost = *although*, but often only distinguished from καὶ εἰ by its less emphatic character: Εἴ τις ἦν ἠδικημένος, εἰ καὶ τὸν ἄλλον χρόνον ἡσυχίαν εἶχεν, οὐκ ἂν ἠμέλησε τοῦ καιροῦ τοῦ παρόντος (*Isocr. de permut.* 33). (Εἰ τὰ μάλιστα, *if after all —*.) (The concession of an opposite fact is (properly speaking) expressed by καίπερ with the participle, see § 175 e.) [1]

---

[1] About sentences with conjunctions of time, there is nothing particular to be remarked; nor, again, about sentences with causal conjunctions, ὅτι, *because*, ἐπεί, ἐπειδή, *as, since*; (ἐπεί also with the ground or reason following, in the sense, *for*;) ὅτε, *then*, ὅπου, ὅπου γε, *when that is* (ὡς, *in that, for*, with the reason annexed). [Καίπερ (= *quanquam*) a *verb. fin.* *Pl. Conv.* 219 (καίπερ . . . ᾤμην) and *Theoph. Char.* 2]

Relative sentences are sometimes less accurately joined to the principal sentence. On this point it should be remarked: § 195.

a) A preceding relative sentence with a relative in the neuter, occasionally assigns merely the action, opinion, or utterance, upon occasion of which something is remarked in the principal sentence, so that the relative obtains the signification, *as regards this, that* —: Ὃ δὲ ὑμεῖς ἐννοεῖτε, ὅτι ἧττον ἂν στάσις εἴη ἑνὸς ἄρχοντος ἢ πολλῶν, εὖ ἴστε, ὅτι ἄλλον μὲν ἑλόμενοι οὐχ εὑρήσετε ἐμὲ στασιάζοντα, ἐὰν δὲ ἐμὲ ἕλησθε, οὐκ ἂν θαυμάσαιμι, εἴ τινα εὕροιτε καὶ ὑμῖν καὶ ἐμοὶ ἀχθόμενον (*Xen. An.* 5, 9, 29). Ἃ δὲ ἠπείλησας, ὡς, ἢν ὑμῖν δοκῇ, Κορύλαν καὶ Παφλαγόνας ξυμμάχους ποιήσεσθε ἐφ' ἡμᾶς, ἡμεῖς δέ, ἢν μὲν ἀνάγκη ᾖ, πολεμήσομεν ἀμφοτέροις, ἢν δὲ δοκῇ ἡμῖν, καὶ φίλον ποιήσομεν τὸν Παφλαγόνα (*Xen. An.* 5, 5, 22). On δέ after ἡμεῖς, see § 188, R. 6. (Cf. ὅτι, § 170 a. R.)

b) Ὅστις, ὃς ἂν sometimes stands, (not only without an expressly corresponding demonstrative, but also without its being possible for such a one to be understood agreeably with the form of the principal sentence,) in the sense of εἴ τις, in general expressions of opinion about a certain manner of acting (where also an infinitive or acc. with inf. might be used): Παντάπασιν ἀπόρων ἐστὶ καὶ ἀνάγκῃ ἐχομένων καὶ τούτων πονηρῶν, οἵτινες ἐθέλουσι δι' ἐπιορκίας τε πρὸς θεοὺς καὶ ἀπιστίας πρὸς ἀνθρώπους πράττειν τι (*Xen. An.* 2, 5, 21). Νόμιζε τὸ καλῶς ἄρξαι τοῦτ' εἶναι, ὃς ἂν τὴν πατρίδα ὠφελήσῃ ὡς πλεῖστα ἢ ἑκὼν εἶναι οὐδὲν βλάψῃ (*Thuc.* 6, 14). Ἐγὼ καὶ τοῦτο ἡγοῦμαι μέγα τεκμήριον ἄρχοντος ἀρετῆς εἶναι, ᾧ ἂν ἑκόντες οἱ στρατιῶται ἕπωνται καὶ ἐν τοῖς δεινοῖς παραμένειν ἐθέλωσιν (*Xen. Œcon.* 4, 19). (Ὅ, τι put first, *whatever, so often as any thing*: Εἰ ταῦτα ἐγὼ λέγω περὶ ὑμῶν ἄλλως γιγνώσκων, ἐμαυτὸν ἐξαπατῶ· ὅ, τι γὰρ μὴ τοιοῦτον ἀποβήσεται παρ' ὑμῶν, εἰς ἐμὲ τὸ ἐλλεῖπον ἥξει, *Xen. Cyr.* 1, 5, 13.)

c) Sometimes a relative sentence which calls attention to a particular circumstance, is annexed to a person who, though thought of during the speech, and given in the context, is not expressly named: Πῶς οὖν ἄν τις μᾶλλον ἐλεγχθείη παράνομα εἰρηκὼς ἢ τοῦτον τὸν τρόπον; ὃς (*thou who*) τὴν τιμωρίαν, ἣν οὐδὲ κατὰ τῶν ἐξεληλεγμένων διδόασιν οἱ νόμοι, ταύτην κατὰ τῶν ἀκρίτων ἔγραψας (*Dem.* 23, 36). Καλοῦμαί σε (*I sue thee for*) τῶν δώδεκα μνῶν, ἃς ἔλαβες ὠνούμενος τὸν ψαρὸν ἵππον. Ἵππον; οὐκ ἀκούετε; ὃν πάντες ὑμεῖς ἴστε μισοῦντα ἱππικήν (*Arist. Nub.* 1224; *me, who, as ye all know —; I to buy a horse, I, who —?*).

d) To a relative pronoun pointing in a general way to what goes before, a more particular statement of the thing meant is sometimes appended by an infinitive, or acc. with inf., as apposition to the relative, or by a conjunctional accessory sentence: Ὃ καὶ δεινότατον ἂν εἴη συμβαῖνον, τοὺς μὲν πολλὰ καὶ μεγάλα ποιήσαντας ὑμᾶς ἀγαθὰ μὴ τυχεῖν ταύτης τῆς δωρεᾶς, τὸν δὲ ὑπερπλήθη ἐξημαρτηκότα φαίνεσθαι ἐξουσίαν παρ' ὑμῶν τοῦ παρανομεῖν εἰληφότα (*Dem.* 26, 7). Οὕτω ἐξηρτήμεθα τῶν ἐλπίδων, ὥστ' οὐδ' οἱ κεκτημένοι τοὺς μεγίστους πλούτους μένειν ἐπὶ τούτοις ἐθέλουσιν, ἀλλ' ἀεὶ τοῦ πλέονος ὀρεγόμενοι περὶ τῶν ὑπαρχόντων κινδυνεύουσιν· ὅπερ ἄξιόν ἐστι δεδιέναι, μὴ καὶ ἡμεῖς ἔνοχοι γενώμεθα ταύταις ταῖς ἀνοίαις (*Isocr. de Pac.* 7).

Rem. In consequence of this, and by a *breviloquentia*, the relative pronoun in the neuter (ὅ, ὅπερ) occasionally comes to have merely the signification of a connecting particle (*while, whereas*): Διαφερόντως τόδε ἔχομεν (*we possess in a preeminent degree the characteristic property*), ὥστε τολμᾶν τε οἱ αὐτοὶ μάλιστα καί, περὶ ὧν ἐπιχειρήσομεν, ἐκλογίζεσθαι· ὃ τοῖς ἄλλοις ἀμαθία μὲν θράσος, λογισμὸς δὲ ὄκνον φέρει (*Thuc.* 2, 40; *which in others is otherwise, since —*, or simply, *whereas, on the contrary*). (In the poets ὃ καί, ἃ καί, *wherefore also*.)

CHAP. VII.]

[§ 195.] (237) *c*) The sentence annexed by the relative, has sometimes itself an accessory sentence, or an accessory definition in the participle, to which the relative also belongs, and to which it often attaches itself in point of case: Βούλου καὶ τοὺς ἄλλους μὴ τὰς εἰθισμένας ἄγειν σοι δωρεάς, ἀλλὰ τοιαύτας, αἷς κἂν σφόδρα χρῇ καὶ μηδεμίαν ἡμέραν διαλείπῃς, οὐ κατατρίψεις ἀλλὰ καὶ πλείονος ἀξίας ποιήσεις (*Isocr. ad Nic.* 54 = ἅς, κἂν σφόδρα αὐταῖς χρῇ, οὐ —). Ἐπέπληξέ τις, ὅτι τοὺς φύλακας οὐκ εὐδαίμονας ποιοῖμεν, οἷς ἐξὸν πάντα ἔχειν τὰ τῶν πολιτῶν, οὐδὲν ἔχοιεν (*Pl. Rep.* 5, 466. = οἵ, ἐξὸν αὐτοῖς π. ἐ. τ. τ. πολιτῶν, οὐδὲν ἔχοιεν). Sometimes the relative alone belongs to the accessory sentence or participle: Οἱ Ἀλεῖς, οὓς ἵνα διαλλάττωσι, κατασχεῖν τοὺς πρέσβεις Φίλιππός φησι, τοιαύτης τετυχήκασι διαλλαγῆς, ὥστ' ἐξελήλανται καὶ ἀνάστατος ἡ πόλις αὐτῶν γέγονεν (*Dem.* 19, 39). Ἆρα νῦν οὕτω τῇδε τῇ ἡμέρᾳ εἰλήφαμεν, ὃ πάλαι καὶ πολλοὶ τῶν σοφῶν ζητοῦντες πρὶν εὑρεῖν κατεγήρασαν; (*Pl. Theæt.* 202.)

Rem. On relative sentences as expression of the purpose and definition or cause, see § 105 a, c, d, and § 115 a, R.

§ 196. *a*) The particle *γάρ* in an independent sentence often assigns a relation or a circumstance which has been pointed at by a preceding demonstrative pronoun (*ὅδε*, *the following*, *τοσοῦτος*, more rarely *οὗτος*) or adverb (*ἐνθένδε*, *hence* = *from this*; *from the following circumstance*, *ἐκεῖθεν*), and which might equally well have been annexed in an accessory sentence with *ὅτι* (or *ὅσῳ* after *τοσοῦτον*): *Δηλοῖ δέ μοι καὶ τόδε τῶν παλαιῶν ἀσθένειαν οὐχ ἥκιστα· πρὸ γὰρ τῶν Τρωικῶν οὐδὲν φαίνεται πρότερον κοινῇ ἐργασαμένη ἡ Ἑλλάς* (*Thuc.* 1, 3). *Ὡς οἱ περὶ τὸν Κλεόμβροτον τὸ πρῶτον ἐπεκράτουν τῇ μάχῃ, σαφεῖ τούτῳ τεκμηρίῳ γνοίη τις ἄν· οὐ γὰρ ἂν ἠδύναντο αὐτὸν ζῶντα ἀπενεγκεῖν, εἰ μὴ οἱ πρὸ αὐτοῦ μαχόμενοι ἐπεκράτουν ἐν ἐκείνῳ τῷ χρόνῳ* (*Xen. Hell.* 6, 4, 13). *Ὅτι ἐγὼ τυγχάνω ὢν τοιοῦτος οἷος ὑπὸ τοῦ θεοῦ τῇ πόλει δεδόσθαι, ἐνθένδε ἂν κατανοήσαιτε· οὐ γὰρ ἀνθρωπίνῳ ἔοικε τὸ ἐμὲ τῶν μὲν ἐμαυτοῦ ἁπάντων ἠμεληκέναι, τὸ δὲ ὑμέτερον πράττειν ἀεὶ ἰδίᾳ ἑκάστῳ προσιόντα ὥσπερ πατέρα ἢ ἀδελφὸν πρεσβύτερον* (*Pl. Apol.* 31). (In English, *namely*, or omitted [or *that* substituted for it].)

Rem. Such a sentence is often added to the elliptical expressions τεκμήριον δέ, σημεῖον δέ, μαρτύριον δέ (viz. τόδε ἐστίν), δῆλον δέ (viz. ἐκ τοῦδέ ἐστιν), sometimes also to κεφάλαιον δέ (*the main thing is*), τὸ δ' αἴτιον (*the reason is*): Κᾶρες καὶ Φοίνικες τὰς πλείστας τῶν νήσων ᾤκισαν. Μαρτύριον δέ· Δήλου γὰρ καθαιρομένης ὑπὸ τῶν Ἀθηναίων καὶ τῶν θηκῶν ἀναιρεθεισῶν, ὅσαι ἦσαν τῶν τεθνεώτων ἐν τῇ νήσῳ, ὑπὲρ ἥμισυ Κᾶρες ἐφάνησαν (*Thuc.* 1, 8). Μέγιστον δὲ τεκμήριον τοῦ τρόπου τοῦ Εὐαγόρου· τῶν γὰρ Ἑλλήνων πολλοὶ καὶ καλοὶ κἀγαθοὶ τὰς ἑαυτῶν πατρίδας ἀπολιπόντες ἦλθον εἰς Κύπρον οἰκήσοντες (*Isocr. Evag.* 51). Sometimes *γάρ* is omitted: Κατὰ τοὺς προτέρους νόμους πολλὰ καὶ δεινὰ περὶ τοὺς τριηραρχοῦντας ἐγίγνετο· τὸ δ' αἴτιον· ἐν τοῖς πένησιν ἦν τὸ λειτουργεῖν (*Dem.* 18, 108).

b) With *γάρ* a remark is sometimes inserted parenthetically, which introduces the principal sentence *following*, and serves to explain what is said in it: Καρτερᾶς γενομένης ναυμαχίας, οὐκ ἔλασσον ἔχοντες ἐν τῷ ἔργῳ οἱ Χῖοι καὶ οἱ ξύμμαχοι (ἤδη γὰρ καὶ ὀψὲ ἦν) ἀνεχώρησαν ἐς τὴν πόλιν (*Thuc.* 8, 61). Sometimes (especially in Herod. and Thucydid.) the principal sentence attaches itself very closely to the parenthesis, something in the parenthesis being necessary to be understood in the principal sentence: Καὶ — ἦν γάρ τι καὶ ἐν Συρακούσαις βουλόμενον τοῖς Ἀθηναίοις τὰ πράγματα ἐνδοῦναι — ἐπεκηρυκεύετο (viz. τὸ βουλόμενον τ. Ἀ. τ. π. ἐνδ., *the party which* —) ὡς τὸν Νικίαν καὶ οὐκ εἴα ἀφίστασθαι (*Thuc.* 7, 48). (Hence ἀλλὰ γάρ, ἀλλ' οὐ γάρ, *but then, but then — not,* as a transition to something new.) [§ 196.]

§ 197. A peculiar interchange and partial intermixture of different constructions takes place, where a circumstance appended to a preceding statement, is marked as the greatest, the utmost that is to be said about it, or as being, in some other respects, the most remarkable feature of the case. This may happen (1) so that the circumstance is alleged in a sentence with ὅτι as a matter of judgment or reflection upon the case: Τὸ δὲ *μέγιστον* (viz. *ἐστίν*), ὅτι (the verb almost always omitted); or (2) so that the characterizing adjective is put foremost, as apposition to the sentence which states the circumstance: Τὸ δὲ *μέγιστον, οὐδ' ἑώρακα πώποτε τὸν ἄνδρα.* (Cf. § 19, R. 3.) Instead of the adjective in the apposition, there might, further, be a relative sentence as a premised remark: Ὃ δὲ *μέγιστον* (viz. *ἐστίν*), *οὐδ' ἑώρακα πώποτε τὸν ἄνδρα*[1]; but, by an interchange between this form and the first, we have (3): Ὃ δὲ *μέγιστον, ὅτι οὐδ' ἑώρακα πώποτε τὸν ἄνδρα,* where, therefore, both sentences have the form of accessory sentences and a principal sentence is wanting. Lastly, we have either (4) the adjective alone (which is rare), or (5) the relative sentence quite detached, as an intimation of that which is to follow, and then follows an explanatory sentence with *γάρ* (as in § 196, a): Τὸ δὲ *μέγιστον· οὐδὲ γὰρ ἑώρακα πώποτε τὸν ἄνδρα,* or Ὃ δὲ *μέγιστον· οὐδὲ γὰρ κ. τ. λ.* (1) Τὸ δὲ *πάντων ὑπερφυέστατον, ὅτι ἐν μὲν τοῖς ἰδίοις οἱ ἀδικούμενοι δακρύουσι καὶ ἐλεεινοί εἰσιν, ἐν δὲ τοῖς δημοσίοις οἱ μὲν ἀδικοῦντες ἐλεεινοί, ὑμεῖς δὲ οἱ ἀδικούμενοι ἐλεεῖτε* (*Lys.* 27, 12). (2) Τὸ δὲ *πάντων δεινότατον, ὑμεῖς μὲν Δημοσθένην οὐ προὔδοτε οὐδ' εἰάσατε κριθῆναι ἐν τῷ τῶν Ἑλλήνων συνεδρίῳ, οὗτος δὲ ὑμᾶς νῦν προδέδωκεν* (*Æsch.* 3, 161). (3) Ὃ δὲ *πάντων καταγελαστότατον, ὅτι τῶν γεγραμμένων ἐν ταῖς ὁμολογίαις τὰ χείριστα τυγχάνομεν φυλάττοντες* (*Isocr. Paneg.* 176). (4) Τὸ δὲ *μέγιστον καὶ περιφανέστατον πάντων· ὁ γὰρ ἀδικηθεὶς καὶ ἐπιβουλευθεὶς ὑπ' ἐμοῦ, ὥς φησιν, οὐκ ἐτόλμησε τεττάρων ἐτῶν ἐπισκήψασθαι εἰς ὑμᾶς* (*Lys.* 3, 39; *to make complaint to you*). (5) Ὃ δὲ *πάντων σχετλιώτατον· οὓς γὰρ ὁμολογήσαιμεν ἂν πονηροτάτους εἶναι τῶν πολιτῶν, τούτους πιστοτάτους φύλακας ἡγούμεθα τῆς πολιτείας εἶναι* (*Isocr. de Pac.* 53). (Ὃ δὲ *πάντων μάλιστα ἀγανακτῆσαι ἔφη· συντυχεῖν γὰρ ἀπιὼν Ἀτρεστίδᾳ παρὰ Φιλίππου πορευομένῳ καὶ μετ' αὐτοῦ γύναια καὶ*

---

[1] *Ὧι δὲ μάλιστα ἡμῶν προέχουσιν, ἵππους τε πολλοὺς κέκτηνται καὶ σίτῳ οἰκείῳ καὶ οὐκ ἐπακτῷ χρῶνται* (*Thuc.* 6, 20).

CHAP. VII.]

παιδάρια ὡς τριάκοντα βαδίζειν. *Dem.* 19, 305. The character of the circumstance not expressed by a single adjective.)

Rem. As a sentence with ὅτι (in the third form), so a sentence with εἰ or with a temporal particle may be connected with a characterizing relative sentence: Ὃ δὲ πάντων δεινότατον, ὅταν τις ἴδῃ τοὺς τὴν ἡγεμονίαν τῆς Ἑλλάδος ἔχειν ἀξιοῦντας ἐπὶ τοὺς Ἕλληνας καθ' ἑκάστην ἡμέραν στρατευομένους (*Isocr. Plat.* 45; *but the worst of all is, when* —).

a) Of interrogative sentences, it is to be remarked, that in Greek a pronominal interrogative may be referred to a participle, so that the question relates to the circumstance expressed by the participle, see *Participle*, § 176 a, and § 181 a. In the same way an interrogative pronoun may stand in an accessory sentence with a conjunction; or with the word which *characterizes* a substantive notion with the article (an adjective, a participle, or a preposition with a case),—to inquire with what accessory definitions, or for what more precisely assigned descriptions of persons or things something holds good. (In English the accessory sentence or characterizing notion must be expressed as an interrogative principal sentence.) Πότ' οὖν, ὦ ἄνδρες Ἀθηναῖοι, πότε, ἃ χρή, πράξετε; ἐπειδὰν τί γένηται; (*Dem.* 4, 10; literally, *when what takes place?* = *what must take place, in order that you* —? [*before you will* —?]) Βοηθούντων ἡμῶν εἰς Ἄργος, οὐχ ἕτοιμον μάχεσθαι Λακεδαιμονίοις; ἵνα τί γένηται; (*And.* 3, 26; *with a view to what result?*) Οἶσθά τινας ἀνθρώπους ἀχαρίστους καλουμένους; Καὶ μάλα, ἔφη ὁ νεανίσκος. Καταμεμάθηκας οὖν, τοὺς τί ποιοῦντας τὸ ὄνομα τοῦτο ἀποκαλοῦσιν; (*Xen. Mem.* 2, 2, 1.) Τοὺς πῶς διακειμένους λάβοιεν ἂν οἱ τοιοῦτοι μαθητάς; (*Isocr. Antid.* 222.)[1]

Rem. 1. Two interrogative pronouns may be connected in one sentence: Τίνας ὑπὸ τίνων εὕροιμεν ἂν μείζονα εὐεργετημένους ἢ παῖδας ὑπὸ γονέων; (*Xen. Mem.* 2, 2, 3.) Εἷς τρόπος ὀρθὸς παντὸς ἐπαίνου, λόγῳ διελθεῖν, οἷος οἵων αἴτιος ὢν τυγχάνει περὶ οὗ ἂν ὁ λόγος ᾖ (*Pl. Conv.* 195).

Rem. 2. On the construction of a demonstrative pronoun with the interrogative, see § 100 b.

Rem. 3. A sentence with οἷος, ὡς is added to expressions of praise, blame, or wonder, to assign the reference to a certain quality of the person or thing mentioned, in the sense: *upon the reflection*, or, *considering, how*, &c. (almost = ὅτι τοιοῦτος, ὅτι οὕτως): Κῦρος ἀπῄει κατοικτείρων τήν τε γυναῖκα, οἷον ἀνδρὸς στέροιτο, καὶ τὸν ἄνδρα, οἵαν γυναῖκα καταλιπὼν οὐκέτ' ὄψοιτο (*Xen. Cyr.* 7, 3, 13). Εὐδαίμων μοι Σωκράτης ἐφαίνετο καὶ τοῦ τρόπου καὶ τῶν λόγων, ὡς ἀδεῶς καὶ γενναίως ἐτελεύτα (*Pl. Phæd.* 58).

---

[1] Hence ἵνα τί; (viz. γένηται) *wherefore? to what end?* ὅτι τί; (ὁτιὴ τί;) *for what reason?* (lit. *because what?*)

REM. 4. Note particularly the originally elliptic use of οἷος, and especially ὅσος, with adjectives which denote a surprising, or, generally, a strikingly and uncommonly high degree, θαυμαστὸς ὅσος (*marvellous how great, surprisingly great*; originally, ἐφ' ᾧ θαυμάζειν δεῖ, ὅσος ἐστίν or ὅτι τοσοῦτός ἐστιν), ἄφθονος, ἀμήχανος, ὑπερφυὴς ὅσος, ἀμήχανος οἷος, ἀφόρητος οἷος. Μόγις καὶ μετὰ ἱδρῶτος θαυμαστοῦ ὅσου (*Pl. Rep.* 1, 350). (Ὑπερφυής τις ὡς μεγάλη βλάβη, *Pl. Gorg.* 477.) In the same manner adverbs of the same kind take ὡς after them: Θαυμαστῶς (ὑπερφυῶς) ὡς χαίρω. [§ 198.]

b) For the indirectly interrogative pronoun ὅςτις (also ὅς: Θεμιστοκλῆς φράζει τῷ ναυκλήρῳ ὅςτις ἐστὶ καὶ δι' ἃ φεύγει, *Thuc.* 1, 137. Δι' ἃς αἰτίας τὰ περὶ τὴν ἀκοὴν ξυμβαίνει παθήματα, λεκτέον, *Pl. Tim.* 67) not unfrequently the direct interrogative τίς is put in a more animated way: Αἱ γυναῖκες ἠρώτων αὐτούς, τίνες εἶεν (*Xen. An.* 4, 5, 10). Οὐ πάνυ ἡμῖν φροντιστέον, τί ἐροῦσιν οἱ πολλοὶ ἡμᾶς, ἀλλ' ὅ, τι ὁ ἐπαΐων περὶ τῶν δικαίων καὶ ἀδίκων (*Pl. Crit.* 48), and in the same manner ποῖος, πόσος, πῶς, for ὁποῖος, ὁπόσος, ὅπως. Οὐκ οἶδα, ὁποίᾳ τόλμῃ ἢ ποίοις λόγοις χρώμενος ἐρῶ (*Pl. Rep.* 3, 414).

REM. Ὅσος and οἷος, in exclamations of wonder, occur in the form of direct interrogation: Ὦ πάππε, ὅσα πράγματα ἔχεις ἐν τῷ δείπνῳ! (*Xen. Cyr.* 1, 3, 4.)

a) A direct question without any interrogative pronoun, or pronominal adverb, may stand in concise and animated expression, without a particle to denote the question (e. g. with a single verb in the second person), especially with an expression of doubt or wonder, or after λέγε, εἰπέ μοι. Οὐκ οἶσθα, ὅτι ταῦτα λέγουσι μὲν πάντες, ποιεῖ δ' οὐδείς; —Μὴ ἀποκρίνωμαι; (*Pl. Rep.* 1, 337; *am I not to answer?*) Ἐμὲ μόνον οὐ γιγνώσκεις, ὦ Κῦρε, τῶν συγγενῶν; (*Xen. Cyr.* 1, 4, 27.) Εἶτα (*and then*) τούτων μὲν ἐπιμελεῖσθαι παρεσκεύασαι, τὴν δὲ μητέρα οὐκ οἴει δεῖν θεραπεύειν; (*Xen. Mem.* 2, 2, 13.) Τί οὖν; ἐν ταῖς ὀλιγαρχουμέναις πόλεσι πτωχοὺς οὐχ ὁρᾷς ἐνόντας; (*Pl. Rep.* 8, 552.) Often such a question is attached by ἤ, *or*, sometimes as an expression of the conjecture and opinion of the person asking: Τί μένομεν; ἢ οὐκ ἐπιστάμεθα, ὅτι βασιλεὺς ἡμᾶς ἀπολέσαι περὶ παντὸς ἂν ποιήσαιτο; (*Xen. An.* 2, 4, 3.) Σὺ δέ, ἔφη ὁ Χαρμίδης, ὦ Συρακόσιε, ἐπὶ τῷ μέγα φρονεῖς; ἢ δῆλον, ὅτι ἐπὶ τῷ παιδί; (*Xen. Conv.* 4, 52.) (οὐ δή, οὐ δήποτε, οὐ δή που, οὔ τί που, *surely not!* see in Lexicon [Appendix].) An indirect simple interrogative sentence must always be denoted as such. § 199.

b) 1. A *simple direct* question is denoted by the particles ἦ (with emphasis, sometimes doubt), ἆρα (ἆρά γε), ἆρ' οὐ (also ἆρα alone of a conjecture, especially ἆρ' οὖν: *perchance —?*), μή (mostly expressive of doubt, or at least uncertainty), ἆρα μή (stronger), μῶν (from μὴ οὖν), μῶν οὐ, μῶν μή (strongly inclining to denial), and the elliptical expression ἄλλο τι ἤ (*is it any thing else than —, is the case otherwise than* —, *ought not* —). or, with ἤ omitted, ἄλλο τι (ἄλλο τι ἢ οὐ —, ἄλλο τι οὐ, *should perhaps?*), and lastly οὔκουν (*not then?*). (See the Rem.)—2. A *simple dependent* question is most generally denoted by εἰ, *if, whether* (εἰ ἄρα, *whether then, whether after all; whether perchance*), and more emphatically by ἆρα, *whether then*, rarely by μή, viz. after verbs denoting *look to*, and *consider* (§ 124, R. 1); with the same verbs also ἐάν (*whether, perchance*, cf. § 194 a, R. 2). (For the particulars of the special meanings of these particles, see the Lexicon [and Appendix].) Ἦ καὶ σχολὴ ἔσται, ὦ πάτερ, σωμασκεῖν τοὺς στρατιώτας; (*Xen. Cyr.* 1, 6, 17.) Ἆρ', ὦ Ἀντίσθενες, εἰσί τινες ἀξίαι φίλων ὥσπερ οἰκετῶν; (*Xen. Mem.* 2, 5, 2.) Ἆρά γε, ὦ παῖ, ἐν τοῖς στρατηγικοῖς καὶ οἰκονομίας τί σοι ἐπεμνήσθη ὁ διδάσκαλος; (*Xen. Cyr.* 1, 6, 12.) Ἆρ' οὐ (ἆρ' οὖν οὐ) πάντα, ὅσα ὑπὸ μυθολόγων ἢ ποιητῶν λέγεται, διήγησις οὖσα τυγχάνει ἢ γεγονότων ἢ ὄντων ἢ μελλόντων; (*Pl. Rep.* 3, 392.) Εἰπέ μοι, εἰ δεοίμεθα φίλου ἀγαθοῦ, πῶς ἂν ἐπιχειροίημεν σκοπεῖν; ἆρα (*ought not* —?) πρῶτον μὲν ζητητέον, ὅστις ἄρχει γαστρός τε καὶ φιλοποσίας; (*Xen. Mem.* 2, 6, 1.) Ἆρ' οὖν συμβαίνει μέγιστον κακὸν ἡ ἀδικία καὶ τὸ ἀδικεῖν; (*Pl. Gorg.* 479. On συμβαίνει, see § 177 b, R. 3.) Μὴ τὸν Ἀχιλλέα οἴει φροντίσαι θανάτου καὶ κινδύνου; (*Pl. Apol.* 28.) Μὴ ἀρχιτέκτων βούλει γενέσθαι; (*Xen. Mem.* 4, 2, 10.) Ἆρα μὴ ἄλλο τι τὸν θάνατον εἶναι ἡγούμεθα ἢ τὴν τῆς ψυχῆς ἀπὸ τοῦ σώματος ἀπαλλαγήν; (*Pl. Phæd.* 64.) Ἆρ' οὖν, ἔφασαν, μὴ καὶ ἡμῖν ἐναντιώσεται ὁ ἀνὴρ περὶ τῆς τῶν στρατιωτῶν ἀπαγωγῆς; (*Xen. An.* 7, 6, 5.) Ἀλλὰ μῶν καὶ πρὸς ἡμᾶς τοῦτο τείνει ἐν τῷ παρόντι; Παντάπασι μὲν οὖν, ἦν δ' ἐγώ (*Pl. Rep.* 5, 451). Τί δέ; οἱ τὴν ἡδονὴν ἀγαθὸν ὁριζόμενοι μῶν μὴ ἐλάττονος πλάνης ἔμπλεοι τῶν ἑτέρων; (*Pl. Rep.* 6, 505.) Νῦν οὖν, ἐπειδή σοι ἡ σοφία μόνη εὐδαίμονα καὶ εὐτυχῆ ποιεῖν τὸν ἄνθρωπον δοκεῖ, ἄλλο τι ἢ φαίης ἂν ἀναγκαῖον εἶναι φιλοσοφεῖν καὶ αὐτὸς ἐν νῷ ἔχεις αὐτὸ ποιεῖν; (*Pl. Euthyd.* 282.) Ἄλλο τι οὖν, ἦν δ' ἐγώ, μάθημα ἀναγκαῖον πολεμικῷ ἀνδρὶ θήσομεν λογίζεσθαί τε καὶ ἀριθμεῖν δύνασθαι; (*Pl. Rep.* 7, 522.) Φέρε γάρ, ὁ ἀγαθὸς ἀνὴρ καὶ ἐπὶ τὸ βέλτιστον λέγων, ἃ ἂν λέγῃ, ἄλλο τι οὐκ εἰκῇ ἐρεῖ ἀλλ' ἀποβλέπων πρός τι; (*Pl. Gorg.* 503.) A. Οὔκουν καὶ λῦπαι ὡσαύτως αἱ μὲν χρησταί εἰσιν, αἱ δὲ πονηραί; B. Πῶς γὰρ οὔ; (*Pl. Gorg.* 499.)—Οὐκ οἶδα, εἰ συγχωρήσετε. Ἠρώτησα, εἰ συνεξελθεῖν βούλοιτο. Σκοποῦμαι τοῦτο, εἰ ἄρα, ὥσπερ τῶν οἰκετῶν, οὕτω καὶ τῶν φίλων εἰσὶν ἀξίαι (*Xen. Mem.* 2, 5, 2). Ἡ ψυχή μου, διὰ τὸ ὑβρίσθαι καὶ ὀργίζεσθαι, ἀεὶ τοῦτο κυοῦσα διῆγεν (*brooding over the thought*), ἆρά ποτε ἔσται ἀποτίσασθαι τὸν καὶ θεοῖς ἐχθρὸν καὶ ἀνθρώποις (*Xen. Cyr.* 5, 4, 35). Ὁρῶμεν, μὴ Νικίας οἴεταί τι λέγειν καὶ οὐ λόγου ἕνεκα ταῦτα λέγει (*Pl. Lach.* 196). Εἰ τοῦτο μὴ ἱκανὸν δικαιοσύνης ἐπίδειγμα εἶναι σοι δοκεῖ, σκέψαι, ἐὰν τόδε μᾶλλον ἀρέσκῃ· φημὶ γὰρ ἐγὼ τὸ νόμιμον δίκαιον εἶναι (*Xen. Mem.* 4, 4, 12). (Ἦ γάρ; *Is it not so?*)[1]

Rem. From οὐκ οὖν comes οὐκοῦν as one word, denoting literally, *not then*, or, *therefore not*, whence *at least not*, in which sense the word is not unfrequently used (in answers: *no*) (οὐκοῦν—γε), and then the orthography is by most supposed to be οὔκουν (οὔκουν εἰκός γε). This orthography ought then to be retained in the interrogative signification likewise, which in many editions is not the case. The interrogative signification often passes almost into that of a simple affirmative inference (*therefore*), and then most commonly the note of interrogation is omitted, and the particle is assumed = οὖν. In this case it is always written οὐκοῦν. Ἀλλ', ὦ Χειρίσοφε, ἔφη ὁ Ξενοφῶν, δοκεῖ μοι βοηθεῖν ἐπὶ τοὺς καίοντας τὴν γῆν ὡς ὑπὲρ τῆς ἡμετέρας. Ὁ δὲ Χειρίσοφος εἶπεν· Οὔκουν ἔμοιγε δοκεῖ· ἀλλὰ καὶ ἡμεῖς, ἔφη,

[1] Πῶς οὐ (δεινόν, πολλὴ ἀφροσύνη, κ.τ.λ.): *Is it not —? Can one deny that it is —?*

καίωμεν, καὶ οὕτω θᾶττον παύσονται (*Xen. An.* 3, 5, 6).—A. *Ἀλλὰ πρὸς τῷ μαθεῖν καὶ ἀπότισον ἀργύριον.* B. *Οὐκοῦν ἐπειδάν μοι γένηται, εἶπον* (*Pl. Rep.* 1, 337; *yes, when I have got any money: then shall it not be when — ? but surely not till I have — ?*). [§ 199.]

c) 1. A *disjunctive direct* question is denoted by *πότερον* (*πότερα*)—*ἤ*, or, in concise and pointed discourse, without any particle in the first member. 2. A *disjunctive dependent* question is denoted in the same way or by *εἰ — ἤ, εἴτε — εἴτε.* *Ἢν ἄρχων τις τύχῃ σοι καὶ ἁμάρτῃ, πότερον ἐᾷς ἄρχειν ἢ ἄλλον καθίστης ἀντ' αὐτοῦ;* (*Xen. Cyr.* 3, 1, 12.) *Πότερά σοι δοκοῦσιν οἱ ἀπεργαζόμενοι εἴδωλα ἄφρονά τε καὶ ἀκίνητα ἀξιοθαυμαστότεροι εἶναι ἢ οἱ ζῷα ἔμφρονά τε καὶ ἐνεργά;* (*Xen. Mem.* 1, 4, 4.) *Οὐδενὶ τρόπῳ φαμὲν ἑκόντας ἀδικητέον εἶναι ἤ τινι μὲν ἀδικητέον τρόπῳ, τινὶ δὲ οὔ;* (*Pl. Crito*, 49.) *Ἄρτι, ὦ Τερψίων, ἢ πάλαι ἐξ ἀγροῦ;* (*Pl. Theæt.* 142.) *Παυσανίας ἐβουλεύετο, πότερον μάχην ξυνάπτοι ἢ ὑπόσπονδον τόν τε Λύσανδρον καὶ τοὺς μετ' αὐτοῦ πεσόντας ἀναιροῖτο* (*Xen. Hell.* 3, 5, 22). *Δοκεῖ μοι χρῆναι παρὰ τῶν πρεσβυτῶν πυνθάνεσθαι, ὥσπερ τινὰ ὁδὸν προεληλυθότων, ἣν καὶ ἡμᾶς ἴσως δεήσει πορεύεσθαι, ποία τίς ἐστι, τραχεῖα καὶ χαλεπὴ ἢ ῥᾳδία καὶ εὔπορος* (*Pl. Rep.* 1, 328). *Ὁ Κλέαρχος ἐβουλεύετο. Πρόξενον καλέσας, εἰ πέμποιέν τινας ἢ πάντες ἴοιεν ἐπὶ τὸ στρατόπεδον ἀρήξοντες* (*Xen. An.* 1, 10, 5). *Νῦν ἔμαθον, ὃ λέγεις· εἰ δὲ ἀληθὲς ἢ μή, πειράσομαι μαθεῖν* (*Pl. Rep.* 1, 339). *Δίδωμι ὑμῖν σὺν τοῖς ἄλλοις Χαλδαίοις βουλεύσασθαι, εἴτε βούλεσθε πολεμεῖν ἡμῖν εἴτε φίλοι εἶναι* (*Xen. Cyr.* 3, 2, 13).

Rem. 1. Sometimes *ἆρα — ἤ* is put where the question in the first member is not yet denoted as disjunctive: *Σκεψώμεθα τὸ διδόναι δίκην ἆρα μέγιστον τῶν κακῶν ἐστιν, ὡς σὺ ᾤου, ἢ μεῖζον τὸ μὴ διδόναι, ὡς αὖ ἐγὼ ᾤμην* (*Pl. Gorg.* 476). (*Ἦ — ἤ* for *εἰ — ἤ* in the Epic poets.)

Rem. 2. An affirmative answer is most simply expressed by *ναί*, *yes*, more strongly by *πάνυ γε* (*yes, certainly; to be sure*), *πάνυ μὲν οὖν* [*παντάπασι μὲν οὖν*] (*of course; unquestionably*), *πάντως δή, πάντως δή που, μάλιστα, καὶ μάλα, σφόδρα γε, ἔστι ταῦτα* (*it is so*), *φημί* (*I say 'yes;' so say I*), or by repetition of the verb or another emphatic word, with the predicate (*Ὁμολογεῖς; Ὁμολογῶ*), often with the addition of *μέντοι* (*Οὐ πολλὴ ἂν εἴη ἀλογία φοβεῖσθαι; Πολλὴ μέντοι*) or *γάρ* (*Ἔλεγες; Ἔλεγον γάρ*) or *ἀλλά* (which gives emphasis to the affirmation: *Ὁμολογοῦμεν ταῦτα; Ἀλλ' ὑπερφυῶς ὡς ὁμολογῶ*) or by *ἔγωγε* with the verb understood from the question (*Λέγεις; Ἔγωγε. Δοκεῖ σοι; Ἔμοιγε*). Sometimes the affirmation is expressed in the form of a question by *Τί γάρ; ἀλλὰ τί; τί μήν;* (*what else? doubtless* it is, *must*, &c.) *πῶς γὰρ οὔ;* (*how should it be otherwise? necessarily*) *πῶς* (*τί*) *οὐ μέλλω;* (*μέλλει;* with verb understood from the question: *how* (*what*) *else should I* (*he*), *than — ?*) *τί γὰρ οὐ μέλλει;* (*καὶ πολλά*, *yes, and much so*; *ἑώρων γάρ*, *yes, for I saw it.*) An answer in the negative is denoted by *οὔ*, *no*, *οὐ δῆτα, οὐδαμῶς* (as answer to a demand, *μή, μὴ γάρ, μηδαμῶς*), *ἥκιστα, ἥκιστά γε, πῶς; πόθεν;* (*whence should that come?*)

CHAPTER VIII.

The Negations.

a) The simple negative particles in Greek are *οὐ* (*οὐκ*) and *μή*. The difference between them, expressed generally, is, that with *οὐ* it § 200.

CHAP. VIII.]

[§ 200.] is stated absolutely, that something *is not*, or *does not* (reality is denied *objectively*), while by μή is denoted merely a *subjective* representation (a *conception* of the mind) in a negative form, without its being said that something is or is not, the representation being put as a *wish*, *will*, *purpose*, *condition*, or as a merely general representation of persons, things, or actions of a certain kind. This distinction, however, is not always accurately and precisely carried out, so that more special rules must be given. (In some cases the usage is not fixed.) Whatever holds of οὐ and μή, applies also to all negative words formed by composition with them, as οὐδέ, οὔτε, οὐδείς, οὐδαμῶς, &c., and μηδέ, μήτε, μηδείς, μηδαμῶς, &c.

b) Οὐ is used in all principal sentences (affirmative or interrogative) in the indicative (with or without ἄν), and in the optative with ἄν. In general οὐ is to be regarded as the simple mode of denial; which is also used in accessory sentences, whenever the following rules do not assign that μή can or should be used (e. g. οὐ stands in declarative object-sentences with ὅτι or ὡς, without regard to the nature of the principal sentence: Μηδεὶς ὑπολαμβανέτω με λέγειν, ὡς οὐ χρῆν εἰςπράττειν τοὺς ὀφείλοντας, *Dem.* 22, 51).

REM. Μή, however, is used in a peculiar manner with the indicative of the future in the prohibitive question with οὐ μή, see § 124 a, R. 4. In some quite occasional passages, where μή is otherwise put in a principal sentence with the indicative or optative with ἄν, this irregularity rests in part on some peculiarity of the sentence. Σχολῇ γὰρ ἄν τι ἄλλο φθορὰν μὴ δέχοιτο, εἰ τό γ' ἀθάνατον καὶ ἀΐδιον φθορὰν δέξεται, *Pl. Phæd.* 106, where μὴ δέχοιτο is put as one notion = *escape*, which is then virtually negatived by σχολῇ, *scarcely*. (In the declarative object-sentences οὐ is retained from the *oratio recta*.)

§ 201. *a*) In principal sentences, μή is used only with the imperative, with the subjunctive in *demands* or *requirements*, and *prohibitions*, together with questions about what one *is to do* [*deliberative subj.*], and with the optative (or indicative) in *wishes*: Μὴ ὀργίζου, μὴ ὀργιζώμεθα, μὴ ὀργισθῇς. Μὴ ἀποκρίνωμαι; Μὴ γένοιτο ταῦτα. Δειξάτω Ἄφοβος, μὴ διπλάσια μηδὲ τριπλάσιά μοι γεγενημένα, ἀλλ' αὐτὰ τὰ ἀρχαῖά μοι πάντα ἀποδεδομένα (*Dem.* 27, 59. Μή to δειξάτω). Μήποτε ὤφελον λιπεῖν τὴν Σκῦρον (*Soph. Phil.* 969). (Μή, μηδαμῶς, in prohibition: *no*. See § 199, R. 2.)

b) Μή is used in all sentences of intention [*final sentences*], and in object-sentences after verbs which denote a *working*, an *endeavour*, *fear*, and *apprehension* (object-sentences of the action), with the subjunctive, the optative, and, in some cases, the future indicative. See the examples to § 122, 123, and 124 with the Rems., together with § 131. When the object of a *fear* or *apprehension* (φοβοῦμαι, μή —, ὅρα, μή) is itself negatively expressed, this last negative is usually οὐ (*vereor, ne — non*). Οὐ δέδοικα, μὴ οὐκ ἔχω, ὅ,τι δῶ ἑκάστῳ τῶν φίλων, ἂν εὖ γένηται, ἀλλὰ μὴ οὐκ ἔχω ἱκανούς, οἷς δῶ (*Xen. An.* 1, 7, 7). Ἀλλὰ μὴ οὐ τοῦτ' ᾖ χαλεπόν, ὦ ἄνδρες, θάνατον ἐκφυγεῖν, ἀλλὰ πολὺ χαλεπώτερον πονηρίαν (*Pl. Apol.* 39. See § 124 a, R. 2)[1]. [§ 201.]

a) Μή is used in all *conditional* sentences with εἰ, ἐάν, εἴτε, ἐάν τε. Εἰ μέν σοι δοκεῖ, ποίησον, εἰ δὲ μή (εἰ δὲ μὴ δοκεῖ), ἔασον. Ποιητέον ταῦτα, εἴτε βούλει εἴτε μή. Ταῦτα διανοηθεὶς Κλεώνυμος, εἴτ' ὀρθῶς εἴτε μή, τὰς διαθήκας ταύτας διέθετο (*Isæ.* 1, 11). § 202.

REM. Sometimes, however, οὐ is found in a sentence with εἰ (ἐάν). This happens now and then where the negative, taken in close connexion with the verb, forms a negative notion, which is emphatically opposed to the affirmative; or where the emphasis in the condition lies in some single word other than the verb: Πάντως οὕτως ἔχει, ὦ Μέλητε, ἐάν τε σὺ καὶ Ἄνυτος οὐ φῆτε ἐάν τε φῆτε (*Pl. Apol.* 25). Εἰ μὲν οὖν οὐ πολλοὶ ἦσαν, καθ' ἕκαστον ἂν περὶ αὐτῶν ἠκούετε, νῦν δὲ συλλήβδην περὶ πάντων (*Lys.* 13, 72; the emphasis on πολλοί). Μὰ Δία, τούτων μὲν οὐδὲν ἴσον ἐστίν, εἴγε ἀφ' ἡμῶν τῶν ἐν μέσῳ οὐδεὶς οὐδέποτε ἄρξεται (*Xen. Cyr.* 2, 2, 3)[2]. But especially οὐ is frequently put in one or other of two sentences connected (§ 189) by μέν and δέ, which are governed by εἰ, where this does not so much concern each sentence by itself, or even in both of them: Δεινὸν ἂν εἴη, εἰ οἱ μὲν Ἀθηναίων ξύμμαχοι ἐπὶ δουλείᾳ τῇ αὐτῶν χρήματα φέροντες οὐκ ἀπεροῦσιν, ἡμεῖς δὲ ἐπὶ τῷ αὐτοὶ σώζεσθαι οὐκ ἄρα δαπανήσομεν (*Thuc.* 1, 121). Εἶτ' οὐκ αἰσχρόν, ὦ ἄνδρες Ἀθηναῖοι, εἰ τὸ μὲν Ἀργείων πλῆθος οὐκ ἐφοβήθη τὴν Λακεδαιμονίων ἀρχὴν ἐν ἐκείνοις τοῖς καιροῖς, ὑμεῖς δ' ὄντες Ἀθηναῖοι βάρβαρον ἄνθρωπον φοβηθήσεσθε; (*Dem.* 15, 23.) (Here μή is more rare.)

b) After conjunctions of *time* with ἄν (ὅταν, &c.), μή is always used; where the conjunctions have not ἄν, it is used where a past instant which has several times occurred [*indefinite frequency*] is denoted (*each time, so often as, when*), otherwise οὐ. Likewise usually (but not always) μή is put with ὅτε, ὁπότε, and ὅπου, in the sense *when, seeing that, because*: Τότε κάλλιστα λογίζεται ἡ ψυχή, ὅταν μηδὲν τούτων αὐτὴν παραλυπῇ, μήτ' ἀκοὴ μήτε ὄψις μήτε ἀλγηδὼν μήτε τις ἡδονή (*Pl. Phæd.* 65). Ἀεί, ὁπότε μὴ ἄλλο τι σπουδαιότερον πράττοιεν, ταύτῃ τῇ παιδιᾷ ἐχρῶντο (*Xen. Cyr.* 2, 3, 20). Ἦ που χαλεπῶς ἂν τοὺς ἄλλους πείσαιμι ἀνθρώπους, ὡς οὐ ξυμφορὰν ἡγοῦμαι τὴν παροῦσαν τύχην, ὅτε γε

---

[1] Rarely φοβοῦμαι, μή — μή: Ἐθαύμαζε Σωκράτης, εἴ τις φοβοῖτο, μὴ ὁ γενόμενος καλὸς κἀγαθὸς τῷ τὰ μέγιστα εὐεργετήσαντι μὴ τὴν μεγίστην χάριν ἕξοι (*Xen. Mem.* 1, 2, 7).

[2] εἰ μὴ Πρόξενον οὐχ ὑπεδέξαντο (*Dem.* 19, 74; *if they had not omitted to receive P.*).

[§ 202.] *μηδ' ὑμᾶς δύναμαι πείθειν* (*Pl. Phæd.* 84).[1] (On the contrary: Ἦν ποτε χρόνος, ὅτε θεοὶ μὲν ἦσαν, θνητὰ δὲ γένη οὐκ ἦν. *Pl. Prot.* 320. Ἕως μὲν οἱ σύμμαχοι οὐκ εἶχον, ὅποι ἀποσταῖεν, ἔκρυπτον τὴν πρὸς ὑμᾶς ἔχθραν. *Xen. Hell.* 3, 5, 10. Ἐπεὶ μαχόμενοι οὐκ ἐδύναντο λαμβάνειν τὸ χωρίον, ἀπιέναι ἤδη ἐπεχείρουν. *Xen. An.* 5, 2, 5.)

REM. Causal sentences with ὅτι, διότι, *because*, ἐπεί, ἐπειδή, ὡς, *then*, have οὐ.

§ 203. In relative sentences, *μή* stands (*a*) where the relative (pronoun or adverb) has *ἄν* with it, and (*b*) where a *certain kind* and *class* is denoted generally by a circumlocution (*he that —, those who —, such — as, if one —*, not merely indefinitely: *people who —, things which —*), and therefore also with exceptions (*ὅσοι μή*). In relative sentences to an indefinite and not general notion (*any one, people, things, who* or *which —*) *μή* is commonly used where the relative-sentence expresses (*c*) an *effect* or *purpose* (*τοιοῦτος ὃς μή*) or (*d*) serves to complete a *condition* (*εἴ τις, ὃς μή*) or a representation expressed in the *infinitive*, which is put by the speaker as merely thought, not as actual. In relative sentences to definite singular subjects, *μή* is put only sometimes (*e*), when a quality is expressly put prominently forward in relation to the principal sentence as *cause* and *ground* or *antithesis*. But this prominence is often wanting. In all other relative sentences the particle is *οὐ*. (*a*) *Μία κλίνη* (*one bier*) *κενὴ φέρεται ἐστρωμένη τῶν ἀφανῶν, οἳ ἂν μὴ εὑρεθῶσιν εἰς ἀναίρεσιν* (*Thuc.* 2, 34). (*b*) *Ἃ μὴ οἶδα, οὐδὲ οἴομαι εἰδέναι* (*Pl. Apol.* 21). *Τοὺς νεκρούς, ἔνθαπερ ἔπεσον, ἑκάστους ἔθαψαν· οὓς δὲ μὴ εὕρισκον, κενοτάφιον αὐτοῖς ἐποίησαν μέγα* (*Xen. An.* 6, 2, 9). *Τί γάρ; ὅστις δαπανηρὸς ὢν μὴ αὐτάρκης ἐστίν, ἀλλ' ἀεὶ τῶν πλησίον δεῖται καὶ λαμβάνων μὴ δύναται ἀποδιδόναι, οὐ δοκεῖ σοι καὶ οὗτος χαλεπὸς φίλος εἶναι;* (*Xen. Mem.* 2, 6, 2.) *Εἰς τὰ πλοῖα τούς τε ἀσθενοῦντας ἐνεβίβασαν καὶ παῖδας καὶ γυναῖκας καὶ τῶν σκευῶν ὅσα μὴ ἀνάγκη ἦν ἔχειν* (*Xen. An.* 5, 3, 1). *Ἡ θάλασσα ἐπῆλθε τῆς πόλεως μέρος τι καὶ ἀνθρώπους διέφθειρεν, ὅσοι μὴ ἐδύναντο φθῆναι πρὸς τὰ μετέωρα ἀναδραμόντες* (*Thuc.* 3, 89). (*Ὅσον μή, ὅσα μή, καθ' ὅσον μή, ὅ,τι μή, so far as — not*)[2]. — (*c*) *Ψηφίσασθε τοιαῦτα, ἐξ ὧν μηδέποτε ὑμῖν μεταμελήσει* (*Andoc.* 3, 41). *Κατοικίσαι τὴν πόλιν εἰς τοιοῦτον τόπον, οὗ ἐπεισαγωγίμων μὴ δεήσεται, σχεδόν τι ἀδύνατον* (*Pl.*

---

[1] Τό γε δυστυχέστατος εἶναι ἀνθρώπων οὐδαμῇ ἐκφεύγω, ὅτε δὴ προαγομένης μὲν τῆς πόλεως ἐπὶ ταύτας τὰς συμφορὰς οὐδεὶς ἐμοῦ δυσδαιμονέστερος ἦν, μεθισταμένης δὲ πάλιν εἰς τὸ ἀσφαλές. ἁπάντων ἐγὼ ἀθλιώτατος (*And.* 2, 9).

[2] But: Ἐπειδάν τις ἐγγὺς ᾖ τοῦ οἴεσθαι τελευτήσειν, εἰσέρχεται αὐτῷ δέος καὶ φροντὶς περὶ ὧν ἔμπροσθεν οὐκ εἰσῄει (*Pl. Rep.* 1, 330, *about things:* not; *about the*, or, *those* (definite) *things, about all the things*). Rare: Οἱ πολλοὶ τῶν ἱκετῶν, ὅσοι οὐκ ἐπείσθησαν, ὡς ἑώρων τὰ γιγνόμενα, διέφθειραν αὐτοῦ ἐν τῷ ἱερῷ ἀλλήλους (*Thuc.* 3, 81).

Rep. 2, 370). Τοσοῦτον μέρος τοῦ λόγου διελθεῖν χρή, ὅσον μὴ λυπήσει τοὺς παρόντας (*Isocr. Antid.* 12). Ἡ καλῶς οὖν οὗτος ὁ ἔπαινος ἔχει, τὸ ὁρῶντα τοιοῦτον ἄνδρα, οἷον ἑαυτόν τις μὴ ἀξιοῖ εἶναι ἀλλ' αἰσχύνοιτο ἄν, χαίρειν τε καὶ ἐπαινεῖν; (*Pl. Rep.* 10, 605.)[1] (*d*) Ἄξιοι οὗτοί εἰσι φθονεῖσθαι, εἰ λήψονται, ἃ μὴ προσήκει αὐτοῖς (*Isæ.* 6, 61). Οὐχ ὁρᾷς, ὡς σφαλερόν ἐστι τό, ἃ μὴ οἶδέ τις, ταῦτα λέγειν καὶ πράττειν; (*Xen. Mem.* 3, 7, 16.)[2] (*e*) Ταλαίπωρός τις σύ γε ἄνθρωπος εἶ καὶ οὐδὲ Ἀθηναῖος, ᾧ μήτε θεοὶ πατρῷοί εἰσι μήτε ἱερὰ μήτ' ἄλλο μηδὲν καλὸν καὶ ἀγαθόν (*Pl. Euthyd.* 302). Πῶς ἂν ὀρθῶς ἐμοῦ καταγιγνώσκοιτε, ᾧ τὸ παράπαν πρὸς τὸν ἄνθρωπον τουτονὶ μηδὲν συμβόλαιόν ἐστιν; (*Dem.* 33, 34). Τῇ πόλει, ὑπὲρ ἧς τὰ ὅπλα μὴ τίθεσαι, μηδὲ συμβουλεύειν ἀξίου (*Æsch.* 1, 29).[3] [§ 203.]

a) In simple dependent questions the negation is commonly expressed by οὐ: Ἠρώτησα, διὰ τί οὐκ ἔλθοι. Πρωταγόρας ἐρωτᾷ, εἰ οὐκ αἰσχύνομαι τἀγαθὰ δεινὰ καλῶν (*Pl. Prot.* 341). But in questions with εἰ it is also μή: Τηρητέον τοὺς ἄνδρας ἐν ἁπάσαις ταῖς ἡλικίαις, εἰ φυλακικοί εἰσι τούτου τοῦ δόγματος καὶ μήτε γοητευόμενοι μήτε βιαζόμενοι ἐκβάλλουσιν (*Pl. Rep.* 3, 412). Also μή stands in dependent questions denoting a purpose (how something *can* take place), especially with ὅπως, see § 123, R. 1. Τῷ τῶν Περσῶν βασιλεῖ οὐδὲν προυργιαίτερόν ἐστιν ἢ σκοπεῖν, ἐξ ὧν μηδέποτε παυσόμεθα πρὸς ἀλλήλους πολεμοῦντες (*Isocr. Paneg.* 134). Οὐ σκοπεῖς, ὅ,τι μὴ λυπήσεις τοὺς ἄλλους ποιῶν (*Dem.* 21, 135). § 204.

b) In the second member of a dependent disjunctive question (*whether — or not*) the negative may be either οὐ or μή. In a dependent question denoting a distinction and separation (*what — and what not*) μή is used when the verb is understood, but either οὐ or μή when it is repeated: Σκοπῶμεν, εἰ πρέπει ἢ οὐ (*Pl. Rep.* 5, 451). Σκεπτέον, πότερον δίκαιον ἐμὲ ἐνθένδε πειρᾶσθαι ἐξιέναι, μὴ ἀφιέντων

---

[1] Also τοιοῦτος, ὃς οὐ, where the representation of a consequence and purpose is not made, or not prominent: Τοιούτων δεησόμενοι πάρεσμεν, ἐν οἷς κίνδυνος οὐδεὶς ἔνεστιν (*Isocr. Plat.* 2). With negative preceding it is always οὐδεὶς (μηδεὶς) τοιοῦτος ὅστις (ὃς) οὐ —, οὐδεὶς οὕτως —, ὅστις (ὃς) οὐ. Νόμον τίθεμεν, οἴκησιν καὶ ταμιεῖον μηδενὶ εἶναι μηδὲν τοιοῦτον, εἰς ὃ οὐ πᾶς ὁ βουλόμενος εἴσεισιν (*Pl. Rep.* 3, 416). Μηδὲν τῶν σωμάτων οὕτως ἂν φαίην εἶναι φαῦλον, ὅ, τι γυμνασθὲν οὐκ ἂν εἴη βέλτιον (*Isocr. Antid.* 210).

[2] Οἱ Κερκυραῖοι καὶ αὐτοὶ ἀναγκασθήσεσθαι ἔφασαν, Κορινθίων βιαζομένων, φίλους ποιεῖσθαι, οὓς οὐ βούλονται (*Thuc.* 1, 28. Οὐ retained from the *oratio recta*).

[3] But also: Θαυμαστὸν ποιεῖς, ὃς ἡμῖν (ταῖς οἰσί) ταῖς καὶ ἔριά σοι καὶ ἄρνας καὶ τυρὸν παρεχούσαις οὐδὲν δίδως (*Xen. Mem.* 2, 7, 13). Οὔκουν δικαίως (γυναῖκα καλῶ Ἀμυνίαν), ἥτις οὐ στρατεύεται; (*Arist. Nub.* 692.)

[§ 204.] Ἀθηναίων, ἢ οὐ δίκαιον (*Pl. Crito*, 48). Νῦν ἔμαθον, ὃ λέγεις· εἰ δὲ ἀληθὲς ἢ μή, πειράσομαι μαθεῖν (*Pl. Rep.* 1, 339). Τοῦτ' αὐτό, εἰ χαίρεις ἢ μὴ χαίρεις, ἀνάγκη δή πού σε ἀγνοεῖν, κενόν γ' ὄντα πάσης φρονήσεως (*Pl. Phil.* 21). Οὐ δεῖ ὑμᾶς ἐκ τῶν τοῦ κατηγόρου λόγων τοὺς νόμους καταμανθάνειν, εἰ καλῶς ὑμῖν κεῖνται ἢ μή, ἀλλ' ἐκ τῶν νόμων τοὺς τοῦ κατηγόρου λόγους, εἰ ὀρθῶς καὶ νομίμως ὑμᾶς διδάσκουσι τὸ πρᾶγμα ἢ οὔ (*Antiph.* 5, 14). — Οἱ εἰδότες ἑαυτοὺς τά τε ἐπιτήδεια ἑαυτοῖς ἴσασι καὶ διαγιγνώσκουσιν, ἅ τε δύνανται καὶ ἃ μή (*Xen. Mem.* 4, 2, 26). Ἀλλά τοι περί γε φυλακῆς τῆς χώρας οἶδ' ὅτι σοι ἤδη μεμέληκεν καὶ οἶσθα, ὁπόσαι τε φυλακαὶ ἐπίκαιροί εἰσι καὶ ὁπόσαι μή, καὶ ὁπόσοι τε φρουροὶ ἱκανοί εἰσι καὶ ὁπόσοι μή εἰσιν (*Xen. Mem.* 3, 6, 10). Ὁ νομοθέτης διαρρήδην ἀπέδειξεν, οὓς χρὴ δημηγορεῖν καὶ οὓς οὐ δεῖ λέγειν ἐν τῷ δήμῳ (*Æsch.* 1, 27).

§ 205. An infinitive (both simply, with and without article, and also an accusative with inf.) is negatived by *μή* (*a*). But in the accusative (nominative) with the infinitive (*b*) the particle is usually *οὐ* after *φημί* and the verbs which absolutely and without any special accessory meaning denote *to think* (*οἶμαι, ἡγοῦμαι, νομίζω, ὑπολαμβάνω*, also *δοκῶ, ἀκούω*), and sometimes with other *verba declarandi et sentiendi* (e. g. *λέγω, ὑπισχνοῦμαι, ἐλπίζω, εἰκός ἐστιν, ὁμολογῶ*), but only when the governing verb is not itself in a form (imperative) or construction (*εἰ*, &c.) which requires *μή* for its negation; for then the infinitive thereby governed is negatived by *μή* (*c*): (*a*) Αἰσχρὸν μὴ βοηθεῖν. Παρεσκεύασμαι μηδενὶ ὑπείκειν. Δέομαι σοῦ μὴ περιορᾶν ἐμὲ ἀπολλύμενον. Ταῦτα ὑμᾶς μὴ ἀγνοεῖν ἠβουλόμην. Διεπραξάμην μηδένα ἡμῖν ἐναντιωθῆναι. Δέδοκται τὰς ναῦς μήπω ἐκπλεῖν. Οὕτως ἀναίσχυντοί εἰσιν ὥστε μηδενὸς ἀπέχεσθαι τῶν κέρδος φερόντων (but ὥστε οὐδενὸς ἀπέχονται). Πάντα ποιοῦσιν ὑπὲρ τοῦ μὴ δοῦναι δίκην. Τὸ μηδεμίαν τῶν πόλεων ἁλῶναι πολιορκίᾳ, μέγιστόν ἐστι σημεῖον τοῦ διὰ τούτους πεισθέντας τοὺς Φωκέας ἀπολωλέναι (*Dem.* 19, 61). Ὁ ὑπὲρ τοῦ ταῦτα μὴ γενέσθαι ἀγών (*Dem.* 18, 201). Σειρῆνες τοὺς ἀνθρώπους ἐπᾴδουσαι κατεῖχον ὥστε μὴ ἀπιέναι ἀπ' αὐτῶν (*Xen. Mem.* 2, 6, 11). (*b*) Πολλούς φασι γιγνώσκοντας τὰ βέλτιστα οὐκ ἐθέλειν πράττειν (*Pl. Prot.* 352). Ἐγὼ οἶμαι, εἰ τοιαύτην μὴ δύνασαι φέρειν μητέρα, τἀγαθά σε οὐ δύνασθαι φέρειν (*Xen. Mem.* 2, 2, 10). Εὐθύδημος ὑπέλαβεν οὐκ ἂν ἄλλως ἀνὴρ ἀξιόλογος γενέσθαι, εἰ μὴ ὅτι μάλιστα Σωκράτει συνείη (*Xen. Mem.* 4, 2, 40). Ξενοφῶν ἐδεῖτο τῶν στρατιωτῶν πάσῃ μηχανῇ μὴ ἀπολείπεσθαι (*to strive with all their might not to be left behind*). Οἱ δὲ σφάττειν ἐκέλευον· οὐδὲ γὰρ ἂν δύνασθαι πορευθῆναι (*Xen. An.* 4, 5, 16; supply ἔφασαν, contained in ἐκέλευον). Κινδυνεύω (= δοκῶ) ἁπλῶς οὐδὲν εἰδέναι (*Xen. Mem.* 4, 2, 39). Φορμίων ἤλπιζεν οὐ μενεῖν τῶν Πελοποννησίων τὴν τάξιν (*Thuc.* 2, 84). Ὁμολογῶ οὐ κατὰ Μέλητον καὶ Ἄνυτον εἶναι ῥήτωρ (*Pl. Apol.* 17). Καὶ ταῦτα εἰκὸς οὐχ ἧττον οὕτως ἔχειν (*Pl. Soph.* 254).[1] — (*c*) Νόμιζε μηδὲν εἶναι τῶν ἀνθρωπίνων

---

[1] After verbs more specially denoting an assertion or concession (e. g. *συγχωρῶ*), an assurance (*μαρτυρῶ, ὄμνυμι*), a conviction (*πείθομαι, γιγνώσκω, πιστεύω*), *οὐ* is a

βέβαιον (*Isocr. Dem.* 42). Περικλῆς οὕτως ἐκόσμησε τὴν πόλιν, ὥστ' ἔτι καὶ νῦν [§
τοὺς εἰσαφικνουμένους εἰς αὐτὴν νομίζειν μὴ μόνον ἄρχειν ἀξίαν εἶναι τῶν Ἑλλήνων 205.
ἀλλὰ καὶ τῶν ἄλλων ἁπάντων (*Isocr. Antid.* 234, because νομίζειν as infinitive after ὥστε would have μή).[1]

Rem. 1. From the οὐ belonging to the infinitive treated of in the paragraph, we must distinguish an οὐ which, though it stands with the infinitive, belongs, strictly speaking, to the governing verb: Οὐκ ἐπὶ τούτῳ κάθηται ὁ δικαστής, ἐπὶ τῷ καταχαρίζεσθαι τὰ δίκαια, ἀλλ' ἐπὶ τῷ κρίνειν ταῦτα, καὶ ὀμώμοκεν οὐ χαριεῖσθαι, οἷς ἂν δοκῇ αὐτῷ, ἀλλὰ δικάσειν κατὰ τοὺς νόμους (*Pl. Apol.* 35; *he has sworn, not that he will —, but that —*; ὀμώμοκε μὴ χαριεῖσθαι, *he has sworn not to —*). (Χρή — οὐ — ἀλλά —, and χρή — μή — ἀλλά with slight difference.) (Οὔ φημι ἰέναι = φημὶ οὐκ ἰ., and οὐκ ἀξιῶ = ἀξιῶ μή, e. g. Οἱ Σάμιοι οὐκ ἠξίουν περιιδεῖν Θρασύβουλον σφᾶς διαφθαρέντας, *Thuc.* 8, 73.)

Rem. 2. When, agreeably with the Greek idiom (see § 209, b), the negation of the preceding verb is repeated with the infinitive, οὐ is retained from the principal verb: Ὁ νόμος οὐκ ἐᾷ εἰσιέναι, οὗ ἂν ᾖ ὁ τετελευτηκώς, οὐδεμίαν γυναῖκα ἄλλην ἢ τὰς προσηκούσας μέχρι ἀνεψιότητος (*Dem.* 43, 63).

Rem. 3. Even with an infinitive after ὥστε, the negative is οὐ, when ὥστε follows after an acc. with inf. governed by φημί, οἶμαι, &c.: Οὕτω καταφρονεῖς τῶν δικαστῶν καὶ οἴει αὐτοὺς ἀπείρους γραμμάτων εἶναι ὥστε οὐκ εἰδέναι, ὅτι τὰ Ἀναξαγόρου βιβλία γέμει τούτων τῶν λόγων; (*Pl. Apol.* 26.)[2]

Rem. 4. Οὐ with the infinitive after other verbs than those mentioned, or after those in a form and construction in which they ought themselves to have μή, is a rare anomaly, for the most part occasioned by the circumstance, that the negation is more strongly urged in reference to a single notion: Οὐκοῦν τιθῶμεν ἀπὸ Ὁμήρου ἀρξαμένους πάντας τοὺς ποιητικοὺς μιμητὰς εἰδώλων ἀρετῆς εἶναι, τῆς δ' ἀληθείας οὐχ ἅπτεσθαι; (*Pl. Rep.* 10, 600.)

a) An adjective or participle without article as attributive or appo- §
sition (therefore also in the double-genitive or double-accusative) is 206.
negatived by μή when the substantive notion to which it is attached belongs, in this negative form, to a sentence or a single notion (e. g. an infinitive) which should itself be negatived by μή; otherwise οὐ is used. After ὡς, ὥσπερ, *as though*, when the principal verb is an imperative, μή is always used with the participle, but otherwise usually

---

rare exception. Examples of μή with infinitive after φημί, οἶμαι, &c.: Φαίην ἂν ἔγωγε, μηδενὶ μηδεμίαν εἶναι παίδευσιν παρὰ τοῦ μὴ ἀρέσκοντος (*Xen. Mem.* 1, 2, 39). Ἐμοί τε ἔδοξε καὶ τοῖς ἄλλοις πᾶσι τοῖς ἰδοῦσι, μήποτε φῦναι μηδὲ γενέσθαι γυναῖκα ἀπὸ θνητῶν τοιαύτην ἐν τῇ Ἀσίᾳ (*Xen. Cyr.* 5, 1, 7). Mixed: Ὅθεν δὲ αὐτὸ (τὴν πολιτικὴν τέχνην) ἡγοῦμαι οὐ διδακτὸν εἶναι μηδὲ ὑπ' ἀνθρώπων παρασκευαστὸν ἀνθρώποις, δίκαιός εἰμι εἰπεῖν (*Pl. Prot.* 319).

[1] Οἶμαι δεῖν οὐ — φημὶ χρῆναι οὐ (as after οἶμαι and φημί) and οἶμαι χρῆναι μή.

[2] Otherwise a very rare exception: Ἤδη γὰρ ἧπται καὶ κατείργασται πυρί (Ἴλιος); Ὥστ' οὐδ' ἴχνος γε τειχέων εἶναι (*Eur. Hell.* 108 = ἐστίν).

οὐ, although the principal sentence would require μή: Ἄθλιον μὴ ὑγιεῖ ψυχῇ συνοικεῖν (*Pl. Gorg.* 479). Ἀπάγου τήν τε γυναῖκα καὶ τοὺς παῖδας μηδὲν αὐτῶν καταθείς (*Xen. Cyr.* 3, 1, 37. Μή because of the imperative). Οἶμαί σε, ἐάν τι αἴσθῃ σεαυτὸν μὴ εἰδότα, ζητεῖν τοὺς ἐπισταμένους (*Xen. Mem.* 3, 5, 23. Because of ἐάν). Οὐχ οἱ μὴ δόντες, ἃ μὴ δοκεῖ, δεινόν εἰσιν οὐδὲν εἰργασμένοι, ἀλλ' οἱ δόντες μέν, πάλιν δὲ ὕστερον, μηδὲν ἐγκαλοῦντες, ἀφαιρούμενοι (*Dem.* 20, 117. Because it would be οἱ μὴ ἀφαιρούμενοι, as οἱ μὴ δόντες. See the following §). Δόξω τὴν πόλιν ἐλαττοῦν, εἰ Θηβαῖοι μὲν ἕξουσι Θεσπιὰς καὶ Πλαταιάς, ἡμεῖς δὲ ἕξιμεν μηδεμιᾶς ἀνάγκης οὔσης ἐξ ὧν τυγχάνομεν ἔχοντες (*Isocr. de Pac.* 17). — Ὡς οὖν μὴ ἀκουσομένων ἡμῶν, οὕτως διανοεῖσθε (*Pl. Rep.* 1, 327). — Εἰ ὡς οὐ τὰ βέλτιστα ἐμοῦ πολιτευσαμένου Κτησιφῶντος καταψηφιεῖσθε, ἡμαρτηκέναι αὐτοὶ δόξετε (*Dem.* 18, 207).

Rem. Sometimes, however, a participle or adjective stands with οὐ, although the principal verb requires μή, the representation being less closely attached to the verb, but put more independently by itself, e. g. Ἄτοπόν ἐστι περὶ τῶν δικαίων ὑμᾶς διδάσκειν αὐτὸν οὐ τὰ δίκαια ποιοῦντα (*Dem.* 15, 25; *without oneself doing what is just*, where αὐτὸν οὐ τὰ δίκαια ποιοῦντα might be expressed otherwise without a negative), especially where the participle contains an independent actual fact: Εἰ ἄρα καὶ ἐδοκοῦμέν τι ἀνεπιεικέστερον πρᾶξαι οὐ μετὰ τοῦ πλήθους ὑμῶν εἰσελθόντες (*in coming into the city against the will of your people*), τὰ ὅμοια οὐκ ἀνταπέδοτε ἡμῖν (*Thuc.* 3, 66).

b) Μή stands with the participle when this assigns a condition with the principal verb (= εἰ μή with a *verbum finitum*): Οὐδεὶς ἂν τοῖς σοφισταῖς διελέγετο μὴ ὑπισχνουμένοις εἰς τὰ πολιτικὰ δεινοτέρους ποιεῖν τοὺς συνόντας (*Pl. Soph.* 232). Τίς ἂν πόλις ὑπὸ μὴ πειθομένων ἁλοίη; (*Xen. Cyr.* 8, 1, 2; *by men not obeying*, i. e. *by men if they do not obey.* Otherwise: Λέγω ἐν οὐκ εἰδόσιν, *among people who are ignorant of it.*) Μὴ δηλωθεισῶν τῶν αἰτιῶν πολλοῖς ἂν ἴσως ἄτοπος ὁ λόγος εἶναι δόξειεν (*Isocr. Antid.* 1). (Τί χρήσαιτ' ἄν τις ἰσχυρῷ ἢ ἀνδρείῳ, μὴ σώφρονι; *Xen. Cyr.* 3, 1, 16 = μὴ ὄντι σώφρονι.)

Rem. 1. In other constructions, an adjective or participle without article is regularly negatived by οὐ. (Γλαύκων ἐπεχείρει δημηγορεῖν, οὐδέπω εἴκοσιν ἔτη γεγονώς. *Xen. Mem.* 3, 6, 1. Οἱ σοφισταὶ κατηγοροῦσι τῶν μαθητῶν, ὡς ἀδικοῦσι σφᾶς αὐτοὺς τούς τε μισθοὺς ἀποστεροῦντες καὶ ἄλλην χάριν οὐκ ἀποδιδόντες. *Pl. Gorg.* 519, *by depriving them, and not* —. Οἶδα, ὅτι οὐ γράψαντος Ἀθηναίων οὐδενὸς πόλεμον Φίλιππος πολλὰ ἔχει τῆς πόλεως. *Dem.* 8, 58; *without any one of the Athenians having* —. Ἔγνων τῶν πολιτῶν τινας οὐκ εὐνοϊκῶς πρὸς ἐμὲ διακειμένους. *Isocr. Antid.* 4. Αἰσθάνομαι οὐδὲν διαπεπραγμένος, ὧν ἠβουλόμην.) Now and then, however, μή occurs exceptionally with a participle of the circumstance, or a participle which, by §§ 177 and 178, stands with the subject or object: Οὐχ ὁρᾷς, ὅτι οἱ Ἀθήνησι δικασταὶ πολλοὺς ἤδη μηδὲν ἀδικοῦντας ἀπέκτειναν; (*Xen. Mem.* 4, 8, 5.)

Ἔξοιδα, παῖ, φύσει σε μὴ πεφυκότα Τοιαῦτα φωνεῖν μηδὲ τεχνᾶσθαι κακά (*Soph. Phil.* [§
79). (Αἰσχύνομαι μὴ ποιῶν = εἰ μὴ ποιῶ.) 206.]

REM. 2. Δόξα ὀρθὴ δεινῶν πέρι καὶ μή (*Pl. Rep.* 4, 430; = περὶ τοῦ, τί δεινὸν καὶ τί μή, by § 204 b).

An adjective or participle with the article denoting generally a §
certain kind and class is usually negatived by *μή* (*a*), yet sometimes 207.
by *οὐ* (*b*). But if it means some persons or things indefinitely of a certain class (*persons who —, things which —*; see § 180 b, R. 1), or individual definite persons or things which are characterized, then *οὐ* is used (*c*). (*a*) *Αἱ μὴ καλαὶ ἐπιθυμίαι. Μένων τὸν μὴ πανοῦργον τῶν ἀπαιδεύτων ἐνόμιζεν εἶναι* (*Xen. An.* 2, 6, 26). *Τῶν στρατιωτῶν οἱ μὴ δυνάμενοι διατελέσαι τὴν ὁδὸν ἐνυκτέρευσαν ἄσιτοι καὶ ἄνευ πυρός* (*Xen. An.* 4, 5, 11). *Τὰ ὁρατὰ καὶ τὰ μή* (viz. *ὁρατά*. *Pl. Phæd.* 79). *Τῇ πόλει πολλάκις μετεμέλησε τῶν μετ' ὀργῆς καὶ μὴ μετ' ἐλέγχου γενομένων* (*Isocr. Antid.* 19). (Τὸ μηδέν = τὸ μηδὲ ἕν, not τὸ οὐδέν.) — (*b*) *Νομίζετε δημοτικωτέρους εἶναι τοὺς μεθύοντας τῶν νηφόντων καὶ τοὺς νοῦν οὐκ ἔχοντας τῶν εὖ φρονούντων* (*Isocr. de Pac.* 13). *Τὸν οὐκ ὀρθῶς χρώμενον τῇ ῥητορικῇ μισεῖν δίκαιον, ἀλλ' οὐ τὸν διδάξαντα* (*Pl. Gorg.* 457. But shortly before: Οὐχ ἡ τέχνη αἰτία τούτου, ἀλλ' οἱ μὴ χρώμενοι, οἶμαι, ὀρθῶς). (*c*) *Οἶδα ἤδη ἀνθρώπους, τοὺς μὲν ἐκ διαβολῆς, τοὺς δὲ καὶ ἐξ ὑποψίας, οἳ φοβηθέντες ἀλλήλους, φθάσαι βουλόμενοι πρὶν παθεῖν, ἐποίησαν ἀνήκεστα κακὰ τοὺς οὔτε μέλλοντας οὔτε βουλομένους τοιοῦτον οὐδέν* (*Xen. An.* 2, 5, 5; *to persons neither going nor wishing —*, indefinitely). *Οὐκ ᾐσχύνοντο οἱ τότε πολιτευόμενοι ἐπὶ τοὺς οὐδὲν πώποτ' εἰς ἡμᾶς ἐξαμαρτόντας στρατιὰν ἐκπέμποντες* (*Isocr. de Pac.* 84; meaning the Sicilians). *Βοιωτοί, οἱ πρόσθεν οὐδ' ἐν τῇ ἑαυτῶν τολμῶντες Ἀθηναίοις ἀντιτάττεσθαι, νῦν ἀπειλοῦσιν ἐμβαλεῖν εἰς τὴν Ἀττικήν* (*Xen. Mem.* 3, 5, 4). *Αἱ οὐκ ὀρθαὶ πολιτεῖαι αὗται* (*Pl. Pol.* 302).[1]

REM. 1. (To §§ 201—207.) It is not uncommon for οὐ to stand in sentences which would require μή, when the negation concerns only a single part of the predicate, e. g. the object or an adverb, whereby a negative antithesis is annexed to the affirmative form, to make it more forcible (οὐκ — ἀλλά, ἀλλ' οὐ, καὶ οὐ, or simply οὐ, οὐχ ὅπως — ἀλλά, οὐ μήν, *yet not*, sometimes also οὐ μόνον). But we also find μή. Ἀνάγκη τὸν τοιοῦτον ζῆν οὐκ ἀνθρώπου βίον ἀλλά τινος πλεύμονος (*Pl. Phil.* 21; *of a mollusc*). Χρὴ τὴν σώφρονα πόλιν τὸν ἐν τῷ συμβουλεύειν μὴ τυχόντα τῆς ὀρθῆς γνώμης οὐχ ὅπως ζημιοῦν ἀλλὰ μηδ' ἀτιμάζειν (*Thuc.* 3, 42). Ἐπαιδεύθην οὕτως ὑπὸ τῆςδε τῆς ἐμῆς τε καὶ ὑμετέρας πατρίδος τοῖς πρεσβυτέροις οὐ μόνον ἀδελφοῖς, ἀλλὰ καὶ πολίταις καὶ ὁδῶν καὶ θάκων καὶ λόγων ὑπείκειν (*Xen. Cyr.* 8, 7, 10). Διαφέρει ἡ ἐμὴ τέχνη τῷ καὶ τὰς ψυχὰς τῶν ἀνδρῶν ἐπισκοπεῖν ἀλλὰ μὴ τὰ σώματα (*Pl. Theæt.* 150). (Δέομαι ὑμῶν, ἐὰν ἐπιδείξω Μειδίαν τουτονὶ μὴ μόνον εἰς

---

[1] Hence in Thucydides (3, 95): διὰ τῆς Λευκάδος τὴν οὐ περιτείχισιν, *their not having drawn a wall round L.*

CHAP. VIII.]

ἐμὲ ἀλλὰ καὶ εἰς ὑμᾶς καὶ εἰς τοὺς νόμους ὑβρικότα, βοηθῆσαι καὶ ἐμοὶ καὶ ὑμῖν αὐτοῖς. *Dem.* 21, 7. Here μὴ μόνον εἰς ἐμέ is an essential part of the condition.)

Rem. 2. Later writers (e. g. Plutarch, Lucian, Arrian) often use μή in different kinds of accessory sentences where the older writers have οὐ, as in object-sentences with ὅτι (διότι) or ὡς, and in causal-sentences with ὅτι, *because*, and ἐπεί. Also they, much more frequently than the older writers, use μή with participles which merely denote a circumstance, without having an occasion in the form of the sentence (see § 206 b, R. 1).

By οὐδέ or μηδέ (*and — not, and — even not*) a negative continuation is added, often with intensive force (*not even*). (Ἀσωπὸς ποταμὸς ἐῤῥύη μέγας καὶ οὐ ῥᾳδίως διαβατὸς ἦν. *Thuc.* 2, 5.) The connexion of two or more members into a whole is effected by οὔτε — οὔτε, μήτε — μήτε. (Ἐγὼ θρασὺς οὔτ' εἰμὶ μήτε γενοίμην. *Dem.* 8, 68.) A negative and an affirmative clause are coupled by οὔτε — τέ, μήτε — τέ, more rarely by τέ — οὔτε: Ὤμοσαν οἵ τε Ἕλληνες καὶ ὁ Ἀριαῖος καὶ τῶν σὺν αὐτῷ οἱ κράτιστοι, μήτε προδώσειν ἀλλήλους σύμμαχοί τε ἔσεσθαι (*Xen. An.* 2, 2, 8).

Rem. Where the negative closely coalesces with the verb into one notion, we also find τέ — οὐ (μή) for οὔτε: Ἀλλὰ μὴν καὶ τοῦ σώματος αὐτός τε οὐκ ἠμέλει τούς τ' ἀμελοῦντας οὐκ ἐπῄνει (*Xen. Mem.* 1, 2, 4). Οὔτε — οὔτε — οὐδέ (οὐδέ γε, οὐδ' αὖ), *neither — nor — no, nor yet* (*and also not*). Instead of the regular distributive connexion by οὔτε — οὔτε (μήτε — μήτε), the second member has occasionally οὐδ' αὖ (μηδ' αὖ), *and on the other hand also not*, or δέ for τέ: Οὔτ' ἄρα ἀνθρώπους ἀξίους λόγου κρατουμένους ὑπὸ γέλωτος ἐάν τις ποιῇ (*represents*), ἀποδεκτέον, πολὺ δὲ ἧττον, ἐὰν θεούς (*Pl. Rep.* 3, 388). Rare (poetical) connexions are οὐ — οὐ, οὔτ' — οὐ, or (where the verb is the same) the omission of the first οὔτε. (Τροφήν τε οὐδεὶς ἐδίδου καὶ αἱ Φοίνισσαι νῆες οὐδὲ Τισσαφέρνης ἧκον. *Thuc.* 8, 99.)

a) A *simple* negative (οὐ or μή), combined with a predicate into a negative expression, is cancelled by a foregoing negative: Οὐκ ἐμοὶ μόνῳ οὐ διεδέξατο Πολυκλῆς τὴν ναῦν (*Dem.* 50, 68; *succeeded to me in the ship*). Οὐδὲ τὸν Φορμίωνα Ἀντίμαχος οὐχ ὁρᾷ (*Dem.* 36, 46; *and A. sees Ph. very well*). Μὴ οὖν, ὅτι καὶ Λακεδαιμονίους καὶ Φωκέας ἐξηπάτησε Φίλιππος, διὰ ταῦθ' ὧν ὑμᾶς Αἰσχίνης ἐξηπάτησε, μὴ δότω δίκην (*Dem.* 19, 77; *let not Æsch. escape the punishment*).

Rem. 1. There are, however, some passages in which (by a kind of anacoluthia) an οὐ is inserted after an interposed sentence, merely to repeat the negative which stands immediately before the interposed sentence: Ὁρᾷς, ὅτι ἡ σωφροσύνη οὐχ ὥσπερ ἡ ἀνδρεία καὶ ἡ σοφία ἐν μέρει τινὶ ἑκατέρα ἐνοῦσα ἡ μὲν σοφήν, ἡ δὲ ἀνδρείαν τὴν πόλιν παρείχετο, οὐχ οὕτω ποιεῖ αὕτη, ἀλλὰ δι' ὅλης ἀτεχνῶς τέταται (*Pl. Rep.* 4, 432). Οὐδ' ἃς προσεδόκων κἀλογιζόμην ἐγὼ πρώτας παρέσεσθαι δεῦρο, τὰς Ἀχαρνέων γυναῖκας, οὐχ ἥκουσιν (*Arist. Lys.* 61).

Rem. 2. Οὐ μὰ τὸν Δί', οὐ — (in answers): *No, by Zeus, not —*. (Also, without further addition, merely: Οὐ μὰ τὸν Δί', οὐ μὲν δή.)

[PART II.

b) A composite negation, which follows after another, simple or composite, with the same predicate, does not cancel the former, but continues it, either heightening and confirming it (e. g. *οὐ — οὐδέ*, *non — ne — quidem*, *οὐδέ — οὐδέ*, *neque — ne — quidem*, *οὐ μέντοι οὐδέ*, *οὐ μὴν οὐδέ*, *yet also not*), or distributively (e. g. *οὐδείς — οὔτε — οὔτε*) or repeating it with the indefinite pronominal notion (pronoun or adverb), often several times (e. g. *οὐδέ — οὐδεὶς οὐδέν*, *οὐδεὶς οὐδενὶ οὐδέν*): Μὴ λανθανέτω σε μηδὲ τοῦτο (*Xen. Cyr.* 5, 2, 36). Τί δὲ σύ; πῶς ποιήσεις; οὐδὲ γὰρ οὐδὲ τὸν σὸν ἑταῖρον δεῖ παρελθεῖν (*Pl. Phæd.* 278). Κλέαρχος ἐπὶ μὲν τοὺς πολεμίους οὐκ ἦγεν· ᾔδει γὰρ ἀπειρηκότας τοὺς στρατιώτας· οὐ μέντοι οὐδ' ἀπέκλινε, φυλαττόμενος, μὴ δοκοίη φεύγειν (*Xen. An.* 2, 2, 16). Ἐξ οὗ τὴν πόλιν οἰκοῦμεν, οὐδεὶς οὔτε κίνδυνος οὔτε πόλεμος περὶ τηλικούτων τὸ μέγεθος ἡμῖν γέγονε, περὶ ὅσων νυνὶ βουλευσόμενοι συνεληλύθαμεν (*Isocr. Archid.* 7). Ἄνευ τούτου οὐδεὶς εἰς οὐδὲν οὐδενὸς ἂν ὑμῶν οὐδέποτε γένοιτο ἄξιος (*Pl. Phil.* 19). [§ 209.]

REM. This last repetition of the negative with the several pronominal words is only used where the negative is emphatically urged as universal; otherwise it is said: Οὐδεὶς πώποτε κάλλιον θάνατον ἤνεγκεν ἢ Σωκράτης (*Xen. Mem.* 4, 8, 2). Οὔτε τῶν πολιτῶν τῶν Φλιασίων οὐδεὶς πάνυ τι ἐπιχωριάζει τὰ νῦν Ἀθήναζε οὔτε τις ξένος ἀφῖκται χρόνου συχνοῦ ἐκεῖθεν (*Pl. Phæd.* 57).

With sundry verbs which contain a negative notion, and are constructed with the infinitive or acc. with inf., *μή* is attached to the infinitive, to give prominence to the negation (only the affirmative part of the verb being in the speaker's thoughts). (*Μή* with *τίς* becomes *μηδείς*.) Such verbs are those which denote a denial and a contradiction (*ἀρνοῦμαι, ἐξαρνοῦμαι, ἔξαρνός εἰμι, ἀντιλέγω*), a prohibition (*ἀπαγορεύω, ἀπεῖπον, ἀποψηφίζομαι, ἀποχειροτονῶ*), a desisting from or a retracting of an opinion or resolution (*ἀπογιγνώσκω, ἀποδοκεῖ, μεταγιγνώσκω, ἀνατίθεμαι*, also *ἀπεύχομαι*), an acquittal (*ἀπολύω, ἀφίημι*), a shunning or hindering and holding back or freeing from something (*εὐλαβοῦμαι, φυλάττομαι, κωλύω, διακωλύω, ἐμποδὼν εἰμι, ἐναντιοῦμαι, εἴργω, ἀπέχω, ἀφαιροῦμαι, ἀποστερῶ, σώζω*, &c.), lastly, a doubting of something (*ἀπιστῶ, ἀπροςδόκητός εἰμι*). Τῶν ἀποκτεινάντων Εὔφρονα οἱ μὲν ἄλλοι ἠρνοῦντο μὴ αὐτόχειρες γενέσθαι, εἷς δὲ ὡμολογήκει (*Xen. Hell.* 7, 3, 7). Ἀστυάγης ἀπηγόρευε μηδένα βάλλειν πρὶν Κῦρος ἐμπλησθείη θηρῶν (*Xen. Cyr.* 1, 4, 14). Μαντινεῖς ἀπεψηφίσαντο τοῖς ἱεροῖς χρήμασι μὴ χρῆσθαι (*Xen. Hell.* 7, 4, 33). Τιμόθεος Ἀριοβαρζάνει ἀπέγνω μὴ βοηθεῖν (*Dem.* 15, 9). Παυσανίας κριθεὶς ὑπὸ τῶν Σπαρτιατῶν ἀπελύθη μὴ ἀδικεῖν (*Thuc.* 1, 128). Εὐλαβεῖσθε ταῦτα μὴ πολλῶν ἐναντίον λέγειν (*Pl. Euthyd.* 304). Οἱ διακωλύσαντες § 210.

[§ 210.] ταῦτα μὴ γενέσθαι τίνες ἦσαν; (*Andoc.* 3, 21.) Οἱ Ἀθηναῖοι οὐ παρῆσαν ταῖς ναυσίν, ἀπιστοῦντες τὸν Σιτάλκην μὴ ἥξειν (*Thuc.* 2, 101).

Rem. 1. Μή, however, is sometimes omitted (e. g. Ὀκνήσουσι, μὴ ἀποδύξῃ ἡμῖν τὰς σπονδὰς ποιήσασθαι, *Xen. An.* 2, 3, 9: εὐλαβοῦμαι ἐμπεσεῖν, *Pl. Rep.* 10, 608), especially with verbs denoting a *holding back*, &c., and with κωλύω and its compounds, this is the most usual. On the genitive of the infinitive of the verbs which denote *holding back*, &c., with or without μή, see § 156, R. 3. With ἀντιλέγω, μεταγιγνώσκω, ἀνατίθεμαι the omission of μή gives a different sense: μεταγιγνώσκω ποιεῖν, *resolve, with abandonment of my former purpose, to do.*[1]

Rem. 2. Verbs which denote denial, contradiction, and doubt, may also be followed by an οὐ in a sentence with ὡς, which οὐ belongs to the affirmative part of the principal verb (ἀρνοῦμαι ὡς οὐ = ἀρνοῦμαι μή, λέγω, ὅτι οὐ): Οἱ Ἀθηναῖοι οὐδαμοῦ ἀντεῖπον, ὡς οὐκ ἀδικοῦσι τοὺς ἡμετέρους (τῶν Λακεδαιμονίων) ξυμμάχους (*Thuc.* 1, 86).

§ 211. *a*) After a principal verb, either directly negative or denying in the form of interrogation, the negative (both the usual one and the superfluous one mentioned in the preceding paragraph) is usually put twice by *μὴ οὐ*, the principal negative being repeated: Οὐδεὶς οἷός τ' ἐστὶν ἄλλως λέγων μὴ οὐ καταγέλαστος εἶναι (*Pl. Gorg.* 509; *can help being ridiculous*). Ἀδύνατα ἦν (= οὐ δυνατόν), Ἀθηναίων Ὠρωπὸν ἐχόντων, μὴ οὐ μεγάλα βλάπτειν τὸ χωρίον τὴν Εὔβοιαν (*Thuc.* 8, 60). Εἰ ἀληθῆ ταῦτα, τίς μηχανὴ μὴ οὐχι πάντα καταναλωθῆναι εἰς τὸ τεθνάναι; (*Pl. Phæd.* 72 = οὐδεμια μηχανή.) Τίνα οἴει ἀπαρνήσεσθαι (= οὐδεὶς ἀπαρνήσεται) μὴ οὐχὶ ἐπίστασθαι τὰ δίκαια; (*Pl. Gorg.* 461.) (Ἥττων εἰμὶ καὶ τοῦ ἑτέρου ὑμῶν, ὥστε πολλοῦ δέω μὴ οὐ δύο γε φεύγειν. *Pl. Euthyd.* 297. Πολλοῦ δέω as denial.) Οὐδὲ τὸ χρηματίζεσθαι Εὐθύδημος καὶ Διονυσόδωρός φατον διακωλύειν οὐδὲν μὴ οὐ παραλαβεῖν τὴν σφετέραν σοφίαν (*Pl. Euthyd.* 304, *hinder not the receiving*). Εἰ γενησόμεθα ἐπὶ βασιλεῖ, τί ἐμποδὼν μὴ οὐχὶ πάντα τὰ δεινότατα παθόντας ὑβριζομένους ἀποθανεῖν; (*Xen. An.* 3, 1, 13.) Οὐδεὶς ἐδύνατο κρύπτειν τὸ μὴ οὐχ ἡδέως ἂν καὶ ὠμῶν ἐσθίειν τῶν Σπαρτιατῶν (*Xen. Hell.* 3, 3, 7).

Rem. Rarely μή alone (Οὐ δυνήσονται μὴ πείθεσθαι τοῖς Θηβαίοις, *Xen. Hell.* 6, 1, 1), except with article prefixed (τὸ μή, see § 156, R. 4); for here, after a denial, both τὸ μή and τὸ μὴ οὐ are used. With the genitive of the infinitive (τοῦ μή) οὐ is not added. (Ὥστε μὴ οὐ after a principal verb negatived.)

b) In the same manner *μὴ οὐ* stands with the infinitive after expressions denoting a disapprobation of an action thought of (therefore a demand that it should be forborne), e. g. *δεινόν, αἰσχρόν, αἰσχύνη ἐστίν, ἀνόητον, πολλὴ ἄνοιά ἐστιν*, also *αἰσχύνομαι*: Πᾶσιν

---

[1] Ἀμφισβητῶ, *maintain* (in controversy with a different opinion), e. g. ἀμφ. τὴν ἐμὴν τέχνην μείζονος ἀγαθοῦ αἰτίαν εἶναι, ἀμφ. μὴ ἀληθῆ σε λέγειν.

αἰσχύνη ἦν μὴ οὐ συσπουδάζειν (*Xen. An.* 2, 3, 11). Πολλὴ ἄνοια μὴ οὐχὶ ἕν τε καὶ ταὐτὸν ἡγεῖσθαι τὸ ἐπὶ πᾶσι τοῖς σώμασι κάλλος (*Pl. Conv.* 210.) (More rarely simple μή: Σοῦ προθύμου ὄντος αἰσχρὸν γίγνεταί ἐμέ γε μὴ ἐθέλειν, *Pl. Gorg.* 458.) [§ 211.]

c) Μὴ οὐ is also sometimes put (but in Attic prose rarely) with participles, or other accessory definitions denoting an exception from the negative or quasi-negative statement of the principal sentence: Αἱ πόλεις πολλαὶ καὶ χαλεπαὶ λαβεῖν αἱ τῶν Φωκέων μὴ οὐ χρόνῳ καὶ πολιορκίᾳ (*Dem.* 19, 123). More usually: Οὐ γὰρ ἦν πρᾶξαι μηδὲν μὴ διδόντα δῶρα (*Thuc.* 2, 97). (In the poets here and there with the participle merely in the sense *without* (doing, &c.) where the preceding principal verb is negatived: [Οὐ γὰρ ἂν μακρὰν ἴχνευον αὐτός, μὴ οὐκ ἔχων τι σύμβολον (*Soph. Œd. T.* 221).[1] Ἥκεις γὰρ οὐ κενή γε . . . μὴ οὐχὶ δεῖμ' ἐμοὶ φέρουσά τι, *Œd. C.* 361].)

Of special negative expressions, which at the same time denote relations of connected sentences and clauses, the following are to be remarked: (1) οὐ μόνον, *not only* (ἀλλά), (2) μὴ ὅτι, *not to say; not merely* (μὴ ὅτι ἰδιώτης τις ἀλλ' ὁ μέγας βασιλεύς); when a negative follows in the predicate common to both members, μὴ ὅτι denotes (*not to say not*, i. e.) *not only not* (non modo): Ἀπατούριος μὴ ὅτι δικάσασθαι ἀλλ' οὐδ' ἐγκαλέσαι μοι ἐτόλμησεν (*Isæ.* 10, 1); the common negative may also be put first (οὐ — μὴ ὅτι, ἀλλ' οὐδέ): Τὸ ἱμάτιον ἢ ἄλλο τι, ὧν κέκτησαι, οὐδενὶ ἂν μὴ ὅτι προῖκα δοίης ἀλλ' οὐδὲ ἔλαττον τῆς ἀξίας λαβών (*Xen. Mem.* 1, 6, 11). After a negative clause μὴ ὅτι is (*not to say*, i. e.) *much less* (non modo): Οὐδ' ἀναπνεῖν, μὴ ὅτι λέγειν τι δυνησόμεθα (*Xen. Conv.* 2, 26).[2] (3) For μὴ ὅτι, in the sense *not only* and *not only not* sometimes, but more rarely, οὐχ ὅτι is used: Τῇ τῶν Σκυθῶν βασιλείᾳ ἀδύνατα ἐξισοῦσθαι οὐκ ὅτι τὰ ἐν τῇ Εὐρώπῃ, ἀλλ' οὐδ' ἐν Ἀσίᾳ ἔθνος ἓν πρὸς ἓν οὐκ ἔστιν (see § 209 a, R. 1), ὅ, τι δυνατὸν Σκύθαις ὁμογνωμονοῦσι πᾶσιν ἀντιστῆναι (*Thuc.* 2, 97). Οὐχ ὅτι στρατηγὸς ἀλλ' οὐδ' ὁ τυχὼν ἄνθρωπος (*Dem.* 23, 155). (4) In the sense *not only not*, we have also οὐχ ὅπως: Οὐχ ὅπως εὖ ποιήσας, ἀνθ' ὧν εὖ ἔπαθες, ἀξιοῖς ἡμᾶς ἀποπέμψασθαι, ἀλλ' ἀποπορευομένους ἡμᾶς οὐδὲ καταυλισθῆναι, ὅσον δύνασαι, ἐπιτρέπεις (*Xen. An.* 7, 7, 8). § 212.

REM. For particular constructions of the negative particles with adverbs of time or of place (e. g. οὔποτε, οὔπω, οὐκέτι, &c.), or with words which serve for transition, or to give a certain emphasis to the denial (e. g. οὐ γάρ, οὐ γὰρ ἀλλά, οὐ μήν, οὐμενοῦν, οὐδήπου, οὐ δῆτα, οὔτι). see the Lexicon [and Appendix]. (So for μόνον οὐ, ὅσον οὐ, *only not*, i. e. *nearly, almost.*)

The word οὐδείς (μηδείς) and some verbs and phrases of denial (e. g. ἀπαυδῶ) are sometimes by a less accurate turn of the sentence so put that in a subsequent adversative member the affirmative notion contained in them (πάντες, ἕκαστος, κελεύω, &c.) is understood. Λέγουσί τινες, ὅτι οὐδεὶς ἑκὼν δίκαιος, ἀλλ' ὑπὸ ἀνανδρίας ἢ γήρως ἤ τινος ἄλλης ἀσθενείας ψέγει τὸ ἀδικεῖν (*Pl. Rep.* 2, 366).[3] § 213. (472, b)

[[1] But see Schneidewin *in l.* and on v. 13. Comp. *App.* 296.—H. B.]

[2] Also (with a single noun): μή τί γε (Ἄκροι πεττευταὶ τοσοῦτοι οὐκ ἂν γένοιντο, μή τι δὴ βασιλεῖς γε, *Pl. Pol.* 292).

[3] Ἀμελήσας, ὧνπερ οἱ πολλοί (viz. ἐπιμελοῦνται), χρηματισμοῦ τε καὶ οἰκοδομίας καὶ στρατηγιῶν (*Pl. Apol.* 36).

CHAP. VIII.]

CHAPTER IX.

Certain particular Irregularities of Construction.

(APPENDIX TO THE FIRST AND SECOND PARTS.)

§ 214. (*The Verb understood.*) In co-ordinate connected sentences, or in accessory sentences of the same kind which mutually correspond, the verb is often understood, to be supplied in one sentence from the other: Σὺ μὲν τιμῆς, ἡμεῖς δὲ ἡσυχίας ἐπιθυμοῦμεν. Οὐδὲ ταῦτα οἱ παραγενόμενοι πάντα, πλὴν τὸ καθ' ἑαυτὸν ἕκαστος οἶδεν (*Thuc.* 7, 44). Ἱκανὸν τοῦτό μοι τεκμήριον, ὅτι ὡς ἀληθῶς μοι εὔνους εἶ, καὶ μήν, ὅτι γε οἷος παῤῥησιάζεσθαι, αὐτός τε φῂς καὶ ὁ λόγος, ὃν ὀλίγον πρότερον ἔλεγες, ὁμολογεῖ σοι (*Pl. Gorg.* 487).

REM. 1. Sometimes merely the infinitive of the preceding verb is understood after a new verb: Τῇ αὐτῇ ἰδέᾳ ἐκεῖνά τε εἶχον οἱ Ἀθηναῖοι καὶ τὰ ἐνθάδε νῦν πειρῶνται (*Thuc.* 6, 76). Οὔτε πάσχοντες κακὸν οὐδὲν οὔτε μελλοντες (*Isocr. Panath.* 103).

REM. 2. In some constructions, especially where the opposition between the other clauses of the sentence makes it plain how the words must be connected, the principal verb may be understood from the leading sentence in the accessory sentence (even the infinitive or participle, as in §§ 177, 178, may be thus understood from the verb finite in the principal sentence), rarely *vice versâ*, i. e. from the accessory in the principal sentence: Ἀργεῖοι πολεμοῦσι μέν, ἐξ οὗπερ τὴν πόλιν οἰκοῦσι, πρὸς τοὺς ὁμόρους, ὥσπερ Λακεδαιμόνιοι· τοσοῦτον δὲ διαφέρουσιν, ὅσον ἐκεῖνοι μὲν πρὸς ἥττους αὑτῶν, οὗτοι δὲ πρὸς κρείττους (*Isocr. Phil.* 51). Φιλεῖν οἴεσθε δεῖν, οὕσπερ ἂν καὶ ὁ βασιλεύς (viz. φιλῇ. *Isocr. Nic.* 60). Ἀνεχώρησαν καὶ οἱ Ἀθηναῖοι, ἐπειδὴ καὶ τοὺς Λακεδαιμονίους εἶδον (viz. ἀναχωροῦντας, *Thuc.* 3, 16). Εἰ δή τῳ σοφώτερός του φαίην εἶναι, τούτῳ ἄν (viz. σοφ. εἶναι φαίην), ὅτι οὐκ εἰδὼς ἱκανῶς περὶ τῶν ἐν Ἅιδου οὕτω καὶ οἴομαι οὐκ εἰδέναι (*Pl. Apol.* 29).[1]

REM. 3. Sometimes the verb is understood, from the preceding sentence, in a sentence which is not grammatically connected with it, as in an appended remark in hypothetical form with ἄν (§ 139 c), or in an explanation and statement of the reason with γάρ. Τοὐναντίον ὑπομνήσω ὑμᾶς ἢ οἱ πολέμιοί σφισιν αὐτοῖς παρακελεύονται· οἱ μὲν γάρ, ὅτι περὶ πατρίδος ἔσται ὁ ἀγών, ἐγὼ δέ, ὅτι οὐκ ἐν πατρίδι (*Thuc.* 6, 68).

REM. 4. Sometimes in two connected (or opposed) sentences, the verb of the first member supplies to the second a verb of kindred meaning capable of being comprehended under the same general notion (zeugma): Πλάτων ὅδε, ὦ ἄνδρες

[1] Σύ νύν μ', ἀδελφέ, μή τις Ἀργείων κτάνῃ, *Eur. Or.* 1037; κτάνε from κτάνῃ.

Ἀθηναῖοι, καὶ Κρίτων καὶ Κριτόβουλος κελεύουσί με τριάκοντα μνῶν τιμήσασθαι, αὐτοὶ δὲ ἐγγυᾶσθαι (viz. βούλονται, *Pl. Apol.* 38).

(*Ellipsis of the Verb.*) *a*) The verb ἐστίν or εἰσίν (third person in the indicative) is often omitted in short and pithy sayings, not only in the principal sentence, but also in simple and concise accessory sentences, e. g. declarative object-sentences, interrogative sentences, relative sentences (especially with ὅσος). Note in particular the frequent omission of ἐστίν with the gerundive (see § 84 a), and with adjectives in the neuter, and certain substantives with which it forms an impersonal expression to which an infinitive is attached, e. g. ὥρα, ἀνάγκη, ἐλπίς, οὐ σχολή. Οὐκ ἀσφαλεῖς αἱ μεγάλαι εὐτυχίαι. Ὥρα, εἴ σοι βουλομένῳ ἃ λέγω (*Pl. Rep.* 2, 358. On βουλομένῳ σοί ἐστιν, see § 38 d). Ἔνιοι τῶν πρεσβυτῶν τὸ γῆρας ὑμνοῦσιν, ὅσων κακῶν σφισιν αἴτιον (*Pl. Rep.* 1, 329). Ἀπὸ τῶν ἡρώων ἀρξάμενοι, ὅσων λόγοι λελειμμένοι, μέχρι τῶν νῦν ἀνθρώπων (*Pl. Rep.* 2, 366). Ἄξιον καὶ τῶν προγόνων τῆς ἀρετῆς μεμνῆσθαι. Οὐ σχολὴ κάμνειν (*Pl. Rep.* 2, 406). (Ἰωνία, Πελοπόννησος, νῆσοι, ὅσαι ἐντὸς Πελοποννήσου καὶ Κρήτης, *Thuc.* 2, 9. Ἀλκιβιάδης ἠρώτα, ὅπου Ἀγάθων, *Pl. Conv.* 212. Omission of ἔστι in the sense *is* in respect of place, *is to be found, lies,* &c.) (On οὐδεὶς ὅστις οὐ, see 105 b, R.) § 215.

Rem. 1. In the first or second person εἰμί is rarely omitted, viz. in quite simple principal sentences: Σοὶ οὐκ ὀλίγοι τῶν νέων πλησιάζουσι, καὶ δικαίως· ἄξιος γὰρ τά τ' ἄλλα καὶ γεωμετρίας ἕνεκα (*Pl. Theæt.* 143, *for thou art worthy*). (With the adjective ἕτοιμος it occurs more frequently: Λεκτέον, ἐπειδὴ καὶ σὺ ἕτοιμος ἀκολουθεῖν, *Pl. Pol.* 277.)

Rem. 2. The subjunctive third person singular ᾖ is now and then omitted after the relative with ἄν: Παρὰ τούτων κομίζονται, ὧν ἂν αὐτοῖς χρεία (*Pl. Rep.* 2, 370).

b) Other verbs are omitted only in proverbs and similar expressions, where the object or some other accompanying definition points to the verb to be supplied: γλαῦκ' εἰς Ἀθήνας (ἄγειν). Ἄνω οἱ ποταμοί. Also a verb denoting *to do*, or *to be done, to happen*, is omitted in certain frequent forms of interrogation with τί, e. g. Ἀλλὰ τί; (βούλει ποιῶ), and especially Τί δέ, εἰ —; as also an imperative which denotes in general an action or speech, with μὴ οὕτω, μή μοι οὕτω, and with μή μοι with an accusative (§ 32). (Μή, πρὸς σὲ γονάτων, § 77, 3 d.)

Rem. 1. Especially note the omission of the notions of doing, or being done, with οὐδὲν ἄλλο ἤ (Οὓς φαμεν μανθάνειν, οὐδὲν ἄλλο ἢ ἀναμιμνήσκονται, *Pl. Phæd.* 76), whence this expression is sometimes used quite adverbially in the sense *only, merely*. (Τί ἄλλο ἤ —, *what else than — !* Ἄλλο τι ἤ — ἄλλο τι —, see § 199 b.)

Rem. 2. Quite distinct from the ellipsis of a single word in definite form, in the Greek as in other languages, are the phrases (derived from the language of common life) in which originally an entire clause of the thought present to the mind is omitted, but intimated by a single particle referring to it, or by some

[§ 215.] other word, or by the general form of the speech; as in Greek by τὸ δέ (§ 188, R. 7), by the use of ἀλλά in the beginning of a speech, or in certain constructions with other particles (οὐ γὰρ ἀλλά, &c.), by ὡς with the indicative future in replies with assurance (Ὡς οὔτις ἀμφὶ τῷδ' ὑγρὰν θήσει κόνιν, *Eur. Phœn.* 1664; *think, say, do, what thou wilt; for* —), &c. Of such ellipses the Lexicon must supply the explanation.

§ 216. (*Anacoluthia.*) Anacolutha, or sentences which deviate from the strict continuation, in regular grammatical connexion, of the form in which they set out, are not rare in the Greek authors, though more frequent and harsh in certain authors who either (as Plato) imitate the freedom of oral discourse, or (as Thucydides) write, on the whole, in an embarrassed and perplexed style. They are caused, partly, by the circumstance, that instead of the form for which the beginning was calculated, in the further progress of the sentence, some other form is chosen as being more convenient and more impressive, or is induced through the use of other expressions; partly, by the intervention of side-remarks and parentheses, especially when these are carried to a greater length than usual, whereby the connexion of the discourse is obscured, or its continuation in the same form rendered difficult. Where the *anacoluthon* is caused in this last way, i. e. by an interruption through interposed matter, the last part is often attached to what goes before by repetition of some words from the beginning, or by repetition, in a different grammatical form, of what has been already said—often, at the same time, by the particles οὖν (*then; as I was saying*), δή (*well then*) or δέ, sometimes not so. Ἐπεὶ δὲ θορύβου τε ᾔσθετο Ξενοφῶν καὶ σημαινόντων ἀλλήλοις τῶν περὶ Σεύθην, κατέμαθεν, ὅτι τούτου ἕνεκα τὰ πυρὰ κεκαυμένα εἴη τῷ Σεύθῃ πρὸ τῶν προφυλάκων, ὅπως οἱ μὲν φύλακες μὴ ὁρῷντο, ἐν τῷ σκότει ὄντες, οἱ δὲ προσιόντες μὴ λανθάνοιεν, ἀλλὰ διὰ τὸ φῶς καταφανεῖς εἶεν —, ἐπεὶ δ' ᾔσθετο, προπέμπει τὸν ἑρμηνέα κτλ. (*Xen. An.* 7, 2, 18 sqq. Repetition without change, merely because of the numerous interposed clauses. The δέ of the commencement repeated with it.[1]) Τὰ δ' αὖ τῶν στρατιωτῶν ὁπότε ἐνθυμοίμην ὅτι τῶν μὲν ἀγαθῶν πάντων οὐδενὸς ἡμῖν μετείη, εἰ μὴ πριαίμεθα. ὅτου δ' ὠνησόμεθα, ᾔδειν ἔτι ὀλίγους ἔχοντας, ἄλλως δέ πως πορίζεσθαι τὰ ἐπιτήδεια ἢ ὠνουμένους, ὅρκους ἤδη κατέχοντας ἡμᾶς,—ταῦτ' οὖν λογιζόμενος ἐνίοτε τὰς σπονδὰς μᾶλλον ἐφοβούμην ἢ νῦν τὸν πόλεμον (*Xen. An.* 3, 1, 20. Repetition with change, and οὖν). Ταῦτά τε εὖ λέγεις, ὦ Σιμμία, καὶ τὰς πρώτας ὑποθέσεις, καὶ εἰ πισταὶ ὑμῖν εἰσιν, ὁμῶς ἐπισκεπτέαι

[1] Repetition of a conjunction alone: Δέδοικα, μή, ἂν ἅπαξ μάθωμεν ἀργοὶ ζῆν καὶ ἐν ἀφθόνοις βιοτεύειν καὶ Μήδων δὲ καὶ Περσῶν καλαῖς τε καὶ μεγάλαις γυναιξὶν ὁμιλεῖν, μὴ ὥσπερ οἱ Λωτοφάγοι ἐπιλαθώμεθα τῆς οἴκαδε ὁδοῦ (*Xen. An.* 3, 2, 25).

σαφέστερον (*Pl. Phæd.* 107. Plato began as if he meant to say ἐπισκεπτέον, but then he has been led to say ἐπισκεπτέαι, because of the clause εἰ καὶ πισταί εἰσιν). Βουλόμενος δὲ Κῦρος κατάσκοπόν τινα πέμψαι ἐπὶ Λυδίας καὶ μαθεῖν ὅ,τι πράττοι ὁ Ἀσσύριος, ἔδοξεν αὐτῷ ἐπιτήδειος εἶναι Ἀράσπας ἐλθεῖν ἐπὶ τοῦτο (*Xen. Cyr.* 6, 1, 31).[1] Κακῶν δ' αἴτιον φάναι θεόν τινι γίγνεσθαι, ἀγαθὸν ὄντα, διαμαχετέον παντὶ τρόπῳ μή τέ τινα λέγειν ταῦτα ἐν τῇ αὑτοῦ πόλει, εἰ μέλλει εὐνομήσεσθαι, μή τέ τινα ἀκούειν (*Pl. Rep.* 2, 380; properly φάναι ought to have been followed merely by οὐκ ἐατέον, or a similar expression, but the whole is repeated and its sense developed more in detail). Κατανοῶν δὲ ὁ Κῦρος, ὡς εὖ μὲν αὐτῷ εἶχον οἱ στρατιῶται πρὸς τὸ δύνασθαι στρατιωτικοὺς πόνους φέρειν, εὖ δὲ τὰς ψυχὰς πρὸς τὸ καταφρονεῖν τῶν πολεμίων, ἐπιστήμονες δ' ἦσαν τὰ προσήκοντα τῇ ἑαυτῶν ἕκαστος ὁπλίσει, καὶ πρὸς τὸ εὖ πείθεσθαι δὲ τοῖς ἄρχουσιν ἑώρα πάντας εὖ παρεσκευασμένους, — ἐκ τούτων οὖν ἐπεθύμει τι ἤδη πρὸς τοὺς πολεμίους πράττειν (*Xen. Cyr.* 3, 3, 9; after κατανοῶν it ought properly to have gone on in the participle thus: καὶ πρὸς τὸ εὖ π. δέ — ὁρῶν, but this is detached from the form with which the period commenced, and is put as a new principal sentence, whence the resumption is made by the words ἐκ τούτων οὖν). Ἔπειτα δέ — ἀναμνήσω γὰρ ὑμᾶς καὶ τοὺς τῶν προγόνων τῶν ἡμετέρων κινδύνους, ἵν' εἰδῆτε, ὡς ἀγαθοῖς τε ὑμῖν προσήκει εἶναι σώζονταί τε σὺν τοῖς θεοῖς καὶ ἐκ πάνυ δεινῶν οἱ ἀγαθοί· ἐλθόντων μὲν γὰρ Περσῶν παμπλήθει στόλῳ ὡς ἀφανιούντων αὖθις τὰς Ἀθήνας, ὑποστῆναι αὐτοῖς Ἀθηναῖοι τολμήσαντες ἐνίκησαν αὐτούς (*Xen. An.* 3, 2, 11; the sentence commenced by ἔπειτα is quite abandoned, and its purport attached by the words γάρ (ἐλθοντων γάρ) to the parenthetic sentence. Cf. *Pl. Rep.* 4, 428 A, where after ὥσπερ εἰ the corresponding demonstrative clause does not simply follow). [§ 216.]

REM. 1. A particular kind of anacoluthon consists in an inaccurate use of the co-ordinate connexion by τέ — καί, οὔτε — οὔτε, μέν — δέ (besides the lesser deviations assigned in § 185 a, R. 5, § 188, R. 5, and § 208, R. 1). Sometimes, namely, there are attached to the first member such interposed sentences and remarks, that the connexion of the speech is broken, and the second member is then given in a different form: Οὔτε τοὺς πονηροὺς ὁρῶ φίλους ἀλλήλοις δυναμένους εἶναι· πῶς γὰρ ἂν ἢ ἀχάριστοι ἢ ἀμελεῖς ἢ πλεονέκται ἢ ἄπιστοι ἢ ἀκρατεῖς ἄνθρωποι δύναιντο φίλοι γενέσθαι; Οἱ μὲν οὖν πονηροὶ πάντως ἔμοιγε δοκοῦσιν ἀλλήλοις ἐχθροὶ μᾶλλον ἢ φίλοι πεφυκέναι. Ἀλλὰ μήν, ὥσπερ σὺ λέγεις, οὐδ' ἂν τοῖς χρηστοῖς οἱ πονηροί ποτε συναρμόσειαν εἰς φιλίαν· πῶς γάρ, κτλ. (*Xen. Mem.* 2, 6, 19; after

[1] So, not unfrequently, a sentence begins with a participle in the nominative referred to the properly acting subject, though afterwards this comes to stand in a different case, especially with δοκεῖ, ἔδοξεν (e.g. *Pl. Apol.* 21).

[§ 216.] Οὔτε τοὺς πονηρούς, κτλ., we should expect *οὔτε τοῖς χρηστοῖς τοὺς πονηρούς* or some similar form). In this manner it is not uncommon for the co-ordinate connexion of two members to be broken, which members should belong to a preceding principal sentence, and then the second member enters as a principal sentence (sometimes with no particular inducement in the connexion of the sentence, but with the view of adding something to the second member, or to give it an easier form): especially in this manner after a circumstance denoted by a participle the second member follows as *verbum finitum*: Γενομένης ἐκκλησίας ἐλέχθησαν τοιοίδε λόγοι ἀπό τε ἄλλων, τῶν μὲν πιστευόντων τὰ περὶ τῆς στρατείας τῆς τῶν Ἀθηναίων, τῶν δὲ τὰ ἐναντία λεγόντων, καὶ Ἑρμοκράτης ὁ Ἕρμωνος παρελθὼν αὐτοῖς ἔλεγε καὶ παρῄνει τοιάδε (*Thuc.* 6, 32; we should expect ἀπό τε ἄλλων — καὶ ἀφ' Ἑρμοκράτους τοῦ Ἕρμωνος). Ἐπεὶ παρεσκευάζετο ἤδη Κῦρος ὡς ἀπιών, παρῆν ὁ Γαδάτας ἄλλα τε δῶρα πολλὰ καὶ παντοῖα φέρων καὶ ἄγων καὶ ἵππους δ' ἦγε πολλούς, ἀφελόμενος τῶν ἑαυτοῦ ἱππέων (*Xen. Cyr.* 5, 4, 29). Οἱ Βοιωτοὶ ἐστράτευσαν ἐπὶ τὸ Δήλιον καὶ προσέβαλον τῷ τειχίσματι, ἄλλῳ τε τρόπῳ πειράσαντες καὶ μηχανὴν προσήγαγον, ἥπερ εἷλεν αὐτό, τοιάνδε (*Thuc.* 4, 100). Οἱ Ἀθηναῖοι νόσῳ ἐπιέζοντο κατ' ἀμφότερα, τῆς τε ὥρας τοῦ ἐνιαυτοῦ ταύτης οὔσης, ἐν ᾗ ἀσθενοῦσιν ἄνθρωποι μάλιστα, καὶ τὸ χωρίον ἅμα, ἐν ᾧ ἐστρατοπεδεύοντο, ἑλῶδες καὶ χαλεπὸν ἦν (*Thuc.* 7, 47 = καὶ τοῦ χωρίου — ἑλώδους ὄντος). (Often in poets, e.g. δυσχλαινίᾳ τ' ἄμορφος ὀμμάτων τ' ἀπὸ φόνου σταλαγμοὶ σὴν κατέσταζον γένυν. *Eur. Hec.* 240, and in Herodotus.) (Εὐφρονίου υἱὸς ὅδε ἐστίν, ἀνδρός, οἷον καὶ σὺ τοῦτον διηγεῖ, καὶ ἄλλως εὐδοκίμου καὶ μέντοι καὶ οὐσίαν μάλα πολλὴν κατέλιπεν. *Pl. Theæt.* 144 = καταλιπόντος. Transition from an adjective to an independent sentence.)[1] Sometimes, where a leading term common to both members precedes them both, the connexion is disturbed by the insertion of a new leading term instead of this in the second member: Οἱ Λακεδαιμόνιοι ἐς τὴν Ῥόδον τὴν γνώμην εἶχον πλεῖν, ἐλπίζοντες νῆσόν τε οὐκ ἀδύνατον καὶ ναυβατῶν πλήθει καὶ πεζῷ προσάξεσθαι, καὶ ἅμα ἡγούμενοι αὐτοὶ δυνατοὶ ἔσεσθαι, Τισσαφέρνην μὴ αἰτοῦντες χρήματα, τρέφειν τὰς ναῦς (*Thuc.* 8, 44; where it might have been simply said: ἐλπίζοντες νῆσόν τε προσάξεσθαι καὶ αὐτοὶ δυνατοὶ ἔσεσθαι. So frequently in Thucydides. Often the new leading term is necessary, so that the partition by τέ — καί or μέν — δέ ought properly to have been applied to the two leading terms, not to the accessory definitions, e.g. here ἐλπίζοντές τε — καὶ ἅμα ἡγούμενοι. Hence τέ seems to be transposed.) Ἐν τῇ ὑστεραίᾳ ἐκκλησίᾳ μετέγνωσαν Ἀθηναῖοι (*the Athenians changed their mind and determined*; § 210, R. 1), Κερκυραίοις ξυμμαχίαν μὲν μὴ ποιήσασθαι (*to make indeed no public offensive and defensive alliance with the C.*), ὥστε τοὺς αὐτοὺς ἐχθροὺς καὶ φίλους νομίζειν (εἰ γὰρ ἐπὶ Κόρινθον ἐκέλευόν σφισιν οἱ Κερκυραῖοι ξυμπλεῖν, ἐλύοντ' ἂν αὐτοῖς αἱ πρὸς Πελοποννησίους σπονδαί) ἐπιμαχίαν δὲ ἐποιήσαντο, τῇ ἀλλήλων βοηθεῖν (*Thuc.* 1, 44).

Rem. 2. Sometimes an anacoluthon is caused by the circumstance that the writer, as he proceeds, has in his thoughts an expression, the sense of which is contained in what goes before, though the expression itself is not there used, and continues the passage conformably with this (the construction πρὸς τὸ σημαινόμενον, *according to the thing signified*, not according to the words, especially in poets and in complicated prose): Καὶ περὶ Πύλον ὑπ' ἀμφοτέρων κατὰ κράτος ἐπολεμεῖτο. Ἀθηναῖοι μὲν δυοῖν νεοῖν ἐναντίαιν ἀεὶ τὴν νῆσον περιπλέοντες τῆς ἡμέρας (τῆς δὲ

---

[1] Οἱ ξύμμαχοι Ὀρχύμενον ἐπολιόρκουν, βουλόμενοι ἄλλως τε προσγενέσθαι σφίσι καὶ ὅμηροι ἐκ τῆς Ἀρκαδίας ἦσαν αὐτόθι ὑπὸ Λακεδαιμονίων κείμενοι (*Thuc.* 5, 61, = καὶ ὅτι ἦσαν).

νυκτὸς ἅπασαι περιώρμουν)· Πελοποννήσιοι δ' ἐν τῇ ἠπείρῳ στρατοπεδευόμενοι [§ καὶ προσβολὰς ποιούμενοι τῷ τείχει (*Thuc.* 4, 23; as if ἀμφότεροι ἐπολέμουν preceded). 216.] Καὶ τοῖς Συρακουσίοις κατάπληξις οὐκ ὀλίγη ἐγένετο, εἰ πέρας μηδὲν ἔσται σφίσι τοῦ κινδύνου· ὁρῶντες οὔτε διὰ τὴν Δεκέλειαν τειχιζομένην οὐδὲν ἧσσον στρατὸν ἴσον τῷ προτέρῳ ἐπεληλυθότα τήν τε τῶν Ἀθηναίων δύναμιν πανταχόσε πολλὴν φαινομένην (*Thuc.* 7, 42). Ἡ οἰμωγὴ ἐκ τοῦ Πειραιῶς διὰ τῶν μακρῶν τειχῶν ἐς ἄστυ διῆκεν, ὁ ἕτερος τῷ ἑτέρῳ παραγγέλλων ὥστ' ἐκείνης τῆς νυκτὸς οὐδεὶς ἐκοιμήθη, οὐ μόνον τοὺς ἀπολωλότας πενθοῦντες ἀλλὰ πολὺ ἔτι μᾶλλον ἑαυτοὺς τὰ ἔσχατα πείσεσθαι νομίζοντες (*Xen. Hell.* 2, 2, 3 = πάντες διηγρύπνουν). Ὅτῳ γὰρ ὤφθην εὐτυχοῦσ', αἰδώς μ' ἔχει, ἐν τῷδε πότμῳ τυγχάνουσ', ἵν' εἰμὶ νῦν (*Eur. Hec.* 970 = αἰδοῦμαι). Οὐ λειπτέον τὴν τάξιν ἀλλὰ καὶ ἐν πολέμῳ καὶ πανταχοῦ ποιητέον ἃ ἂν κελεύῃ ἡ πόλις καὶ ἡ πατρίς, ἢ πείθειν αὐτὴν ᾗ τὸ δίκαιον πέφυκε (*Pl. Crito*, 51, as if ποιεῖν δεῖ, not ποιητέον, had preceded). Ἐννέπω σε ἀφ' ἡμέρας τῆς νῦν προσαυδᾶν μήτε τούσδε μήτ' ἐμέ, ὡς ὄντι γῆς τῆσδ' ἀνοσίῳ μιάστορι (*Soph. Œd. R.* 350, as if it had first been said ἐννέπω σοι, *I command thee*, not σέ, *I command that thou*).

Rem. 3. Now and then an interchange takes place between a remark to a leading sentence inserted with ὡς, and a principal sentence with object-sentence annexed: Ὡς ἐγώ, ἀπὸ τοῦ αὐτομάτου χθὲς ἥκοντος πλοίου, ἤκουσά τινος, ὅτι Κλέανδρος ὁ ἐκ Βυζαντίου ἁρμοστὴς μέλλει ἥξειν πλοῖα ἔχων καὶ τριήρεις (*Xen. An.* 6, 2, 18 = either Ὡς — ἤκουσά τινος, Κλέανδρος μέλλει —, or Ἤκουσά τινος, ὅτι — without ὡς).

PART III.

THE ORDER AND POSITION OF WORDS AND SENTENCES.

§ 217. (431, sqq.) *a*) The position of words in Greek, as in Latin, is, in detail, less tied down to fixed and definite rules than in English and other modern languages, and rests, in great measure, on the emphasis which is meant to be laid on the several words according to the sense of the passage, and at the same time on the consideration of euphony. The simplest order is, that the subject, with all that belongs to it, stands first, and then the predicate, viz. either the verb last, with all remaining definitions (object, &c.) between, or the verb first, and then the other definitions: *Τισσαφέρνης διαβάλλει Κῦρον πρὸς τὸν ἀδελφόν*. These definitions are arranged among themselves according to their importance and their connexion with the verb. Interrogative sentences begin with the interrogative pronominal word or particle, accessory sentences with the conjunction or the relative word.

b) For the sake of emphasis, a deviation from the simple order of the words takes place, such that the word which expresses the most important notion is advanced to the beginning, or sometimes kept back to the end of the sentence: *Ἐπηγάγοντο δὲ τοὺς Θηβαίους καὶ ἀνέῳξαν τὰς πύλας Πλαταιέων ἄνδρες, Ναυκλείδης τε καὶ οἱ μετ' αὐτοῦ* (*Thuc.* 2, 2). *Παρεσκευάζοντο δὲ καὶ οἱ Λακεδαιμόνιοι* (*Thuc.* 2, 7). Kindred or opposed terms are made to stand out prominently by juxta-position.

Rem. 1. One or more words conveying a notion on which there is a special emphasis may also stand before the interrogative word, as also before a relative which refers to a demonstrative following, and before a conjunction if the subordinate sentence begins the period: *Περὶ δὲ τοῦ πολέμου τί ὑμῖν δοκεῖ; Περὶ δὲ τοῦ πολέμου ἃ ἔλεγες, ὁμολογῶ ἀληθῆ εἶναι. Οἱ δὲ τῶν Ἀργείων ἄνδρες, ἀκούσαντες, ἐπειδὴ ἀνήνεγκαν τοὺς λόγους ἔς τε τὰς ἀρχὰς καὶ τὸν δῆμον, ἐψηφίσαντο Ἀργεῖοι καὶ ἄνδρας εἵλοντο δώδεκα* (*Thuc.* 5, 28). But in prose the *verb* may never stand before the relative or conjunction.

REM. 2. Between two connected words, sometimes a third is inserted which is less prominent, or which belongs at the same time to both: Διὰ τὴν Δαρείου τελευτὴν καὶ Ἀρταξέρξου. [§ 217.]

a) A genitive or an adjective to a substantive without article stands first with some emphasis, and because of the opposition: *εὔζωνος ἀνήρ, τῆς πατρίδος σωτήρ*, otherwise usually afterwards: *ἀνὴρ ἀγαθός*. For the order of the adjectives, of the genitive, and other additions to substantives with the article, see the doctrine of the article (Part I. Chap. II.). Sometimes the definitions belonging to a substantive are detached from it by the circumstance, that the substantive itself, or its definitions, are drawn off, with emphasis, to the beginning or end of the sentence, provided no obscurity or ambiguity is thereby occasioned, especially with the verb in the middle place: *Ἐρῶ, ἃ παρὰ σοφωτάτων ἤκουσά ποτε ἀνδρῶν καὶ ἐμπειροτάτων. Τούτων τῶν ἀνδρῶν οὐδὲ τὰ ὀνόματα οἶδα.* (Τῶν βαρβάρων τινὲς ἱππέων, *Xen. An.* 2, 5, 32. Τῶν ἀφ' Ἡρακλέους τινὶ πεφυκότων, *Isocr. Phil.* 76. Other peculiarities of position in the partitive genitive may be seen in § 50 a, R.) § 218.

b) Adverbs belonging to the verb stand either next to it (before it, if it closes the sentence), or, in case of special emphasis, in the beginning or at the end of the sentence; sometimes they are inserted without emphasis between other accessory definitions which are made prominent. Adverbs belonging to adjectives usually stand before them; adverbs of degree, and *οὕτω*, rarely stand after them (*πεφυκὼς οὕτως, Pl.*, *βελτίων πολύ, ὕστερον οὐ πολλῷ, γενναῖος πάνυ, καλὸς λίαν. Pl.*). (*Μάλα γέ τινες ὀλίγοι, Pl. Rep.* 7, 531. Μάλα καὶ ἄνδρες ἄλκιμοι, *Xen. Hell.* 6, 2, 37.)

c) On the placing of prepositions, see § 80.

a) The indefinite pronoun *τίς* and the indefinite correlative adjectives (*ποιός, ποσός*) and adverbs (*πώς*, &c.) can never begin a sentence. § 219.

b) The particles *ἄρα, αὖ, δέ, δή, γάρ, μέν, μήν, νύν, οὖν, τέ, τοί, τοίνυν*, which in various ways connect sentences, form transitions, or give prominence to particular notions, never stand at the beginning of a sentence, but always after one or more words, to which, in part, they closely adhere; so *ἄν*. See the Lexicon [and Appendix], and on *δέ, τέ, μέν*, § 185, R. 4, and § 188, R. 1; on the position of *ἄν*, § 139. So *γέ* always after the word to which it gives prominence (limiting and restrictive), or after the first of several, when it thus belongs to a set of words taken together (*κατά γε τὸν σὸν λόγον, Pl. Gorg.* 471: *εἴπερ γε, ὦ φίλε, ἄδικος, Pl. ibid.*).

REM. But in the parenthetic insertion of *φημί* (see *c*) the words mentioned under *a* and *b* are sometimes put first, the interposed matter coalescing, so to say, with the rest of the sentence: Τί οὖν, ἂν φαίη ὁ λόγος, ἔτι ἀπιστεῖς; (*Pl. Phæd.* 87.) Ἔδοξε, πού φησι, τῇ βουλῇ ἢ τῷ δήμῳ (*Pl. Phæd.* 258).

§ 219.] *c*) The verb *φημί* is put, when a person's own words are reported, by preference after one or more words of the speech reported: *Καὶ ὁ Σωκράτης, "Ἵνα τοίνυν, ἔφη, μὴ ἀμφίβολον ᾖ, ὁρίσατέ μοι, μέχρι πόσων ἐτῶν δεῖ νομίζειν νέους εἶναι τοὺς ἀνθρώπους* (*Xen. Mem.* 1, 2, 35. More rarely: *Καὶ ὁ Σωκράτης ἔφη· "Ἵνα —*, for *εἶπεν· "Ἵνα —*). When to the *φημί* thus used its subject is given, this stands by preference after it: *Τί οὖν, ἔφη ὁ Σωκράτης, ποιητέον σοι δοκεῖ;* more rarely *ὁ Σωκράτης ἔφη.* (Separated: *Εἰ δὲ μὴ ταύτῃ γε, ἔφη, πείθῃ, ὦ Σιμμία, ὁ Σωκράτης, σκέψαι, ἐὰν τῇδέ πῄ σοι σκοπουμένῳ συνδόξῃ. Pl. Phæd.* 73.)

Rem. The position of the words in poetry has various freedoms for which no rules can be given in this place.

§ 220. (444. 445) In Greek, as in Latin, accessory sentences of every kind may be inserted into every principal sentence, by which means, as also by the position of the relative clauses before the demonstrative, a manifold and diversified variety is obtained in the structure of the period: in which the main thing to be considered is, that every accessory sentence should be inserted in its proper place, i. e. precisely where the thought or statement contained in it naturally presents itself to one's mind, and, especially in the historical style, that the succession of time and the causal connexion of the several parts of the action and of the circumstances, should be carefully observed.

Rem. When a dependent sentence, especially interrogative, is drawn to the beginning, either by a pronoun referring to what goes before, or by the emphasis and an antithesis, either the whole leading sentence, if it be short, or some words of it, may be inserted before the interrogative word or the conjunction: *Τὰ τῶν πολεμίων, σαφῶς, ὅπως ἔχει, ἐρῶ.*

APPENDIX.

ON THE USE AND MEANING OF THE PARTICLES.

THE office of the particles is either (1) adverbial, i.e. as they are used to denote certain modifications, qualifications, or affections of the assertion, or of one or more of its terms (viz. affirmation and denial; absoluteness and conditionality: concession and opposition; confirmation and limitation; parity and disparity, &c.), or (2) conjunctional, as they serve for connexion of sentences or terms of sentences. The two uses at so many points run over into each other, that it will be more convenient, for the purpose of this Appendix, to comprise the subject under one general view. As the principal uses of conjunctions have been already described in Chapter VII., the adverbial, which is also the original, use will here principally come under consideration. § 221.

καί, connected by its origin with the form *κο-* of the relative and interrog. pronoun, is therefore cognate with *que* and *τε*, which are forms of the *same* pronoun, but as indefinite. Hence the primary force of the combination *τε — καί* is *any-where* (*some-where*), *any-how*, &c. — *where, how* (so), &c.: of *καὶ — καί*, *where, how*, &c. — *where* (there), *how* (so). Of *καί*, as conjunction, see § 185. As adverb, *etiam, also, too*, it denotes increase by accession. § 222.

The adverbial *καί* corresponds to another *καί* sometimes expressed, but as often left to be understood. *Καὶ ὁ Σωκράτης ταῦτα ἔλεξεν, Socrates, too, said this*, i. e. *καὶ οἱ ἄλλοι* (or the like) *καὶ ὁ Σ.*, originally *where the others, there S.* So in *οὐ μόνον ἀλλὰ καὶ* —, the full construction is *οὐ μόνον, ἀλλὰ* [*καὶ* —,] *καὶ* —, *not only* —, *but* [*where* —,] *there* —.

In *ὥσπερ* (or other relatives) *καὶ* —, *καὶ* —: *εἴπερ καὶ — καὶ* —: the original parataxis *καὶ — καί* is taken into the syntactic form, i. e. *καὶ ὁ Σ. καὶ οἱ ἄλλοι*, united with *ὥσπερ οἱ ἄλλοι, οὕτως ὁ Σ.*, gives the form *καὶ ὁ Σ. ταῦτα ἔλεξεν, ὥσπερ καὶ οἱ ἄλλοι*, *S.* also *said this, as did* also *the others*.

Where both clauses are expressed, the *καί* is often omitted in one or other: the first, when in conceiving the first clause the speaker has not the second clause or its *καί* distinctly present to his thoughts; thus, *ὁ Σ. ταῦτ' ἔλεξεν, ὥσπερ καὶ οἱ ἄλλοι*: the second, when he means to make the first more weighty than the other, *καὶ ὁ Σ. ταῦτ' ἔλεξεν, ὥσπερ οἱ ἄλλοι*. Often, also, the *καί* seems to be drawn over by a kind of attraction from the clause in which the thought would rather seem to demand its presence, to the other: thus, *στρατεύονται μεθ' ὧνπερ καὶ οἰκοῦσι*, for *with those they live with, they* also *take the field*; *ὁ Σωκράτης, εἴπερ τις καὶ ἄλλος*, where we should say, *καὶ ὁ Σ., εἴπερ τις ἄλλος*.—In like manner it is often with- § 223.

[§ 223.] drawn from the (preceding) temporal or conditional secondary sentence to the (following) primary, to denote immediate sequence: it may then be rendered *immediately, forthwith:* Αὐτὰρ ἐπεὶ δείπνησε —, καί οἱ πλησάμενος δῶκε σκύφον. *Od.* 14, 112. *after he had supped —, he* also (forthwith) *filled the cup and presented it to him.* So in Hom. εἰ — καί, and ὅτε — καὶ τότε. Ὡς δὲ ἔδοξεν αὐτοῖς, καὶ ἐχώρουν εὐθύς. *Thuc.* 2, 93. for ὡς καί, *simulatque: simulac decretum est ab iis continuo discesserunt.* (In these instances the original relative and demonstrative force of καί is distinctly perceptible.)

As the relative clause is often omitted, e. g. καὶ ὁ Σ. ἔλεξεν (viz. ἅπερ οἱ ἄλλοι), so is often the demonstrative clause: Πῶς οὖν, ἔφη, τῷ ἀῤῥύθμῳ σώματι ἁρμόττοντα τὸν θώρακα εὔρυθμον ποιεῖς; Ὥσπερ καὶ ἁρμόττοντα, ἔφη (sc. οὕτω καὶ εὔρυθμον). *Xen. Mem.* 3, 10, 11.

§ 224. In the single clause, it depends upon the nature of the unexpressed clause whether the καί heightens (aggravates) or lowers (extenuates): *even* = after all, in addition to all the rest, or *even* = but (so much as) independently of all the rest. In rendering this particle it is sometimes necessary to add to, or even substitute for, the literal rendering of the καί, some other particle or adverb. Thus:

a) *really, indeed:* Ἤνπερ καὶ φρονῶν φαίνῃ, ὅσαπερ λέγεις πρὸς ἡμᾶς, *if you make it good that* [besides professing] *you* also (really) *entertain the sentiments you profess* (or, *that you do' entertain*).

b) *even him-* (her-, it-) *self: aye —: and that —:* Καὶ ἂν Διῒ πατρὶ μάχοιτο. So καὶ λίην, καὶ κάρτα, καὶ πάνυ, καὶ πολύς, καὶ πᾶς.

c) *still, yet,* with comparatives and in some other cases: καὶ μᾶλλον, *yet more,* καὶ ἀμείνονας ἵππους, still *better* horses, πολλοῦ γε καὶ δέω, *I* still *want much of* = far from it: καὶ ἄλλοτε, καὶ πάλιν, καὶ τρίς, &c., ἔτι καὶ νῦν, καὶ ὀψέ (*late though it be,* yet still), καὶ ἔπειτα, καὶ δή: καὶ ὥς, καὶ οὕτως, *still even so, for all this.*

d) *even already* (without going further): Ἀλλ' ἀρκέσει καὶ ταῦτα, *this already* (of itself) *will suffice.* καὶ αὕτως (Hom.) *even* (already) *as it is.* To this head may also be reduced: καὶ πρίν, καὶ χθές, καὶ πάλαι, καὶ πρότερον, καὶ αὐτίκα, καὶ ἄρτι, καὶ ἤδη, καὶ δή.

e) *only, but* (so much as): Εἰ πώποτ' ἔκλεψα τῶν σῶν ἄξιόν τι καὶ τριχός, *worth but a hair.* Ὀκνῶ καὶ λέγειν, *I fear but* (even) *to say it.*

f) Often it is best rendered by the emphatic present or past (*do, did*), or emphatic auxiliary: εἰ δέ τις καὶ οἴεται, *but if a man* does' *think.* Τί γὰρ ἂν τις καὶ ποιοῖ ἄλλο; *why, what else* should' *one do!* Especially the καί following an interrogative: Πῶς καὶ διώλετ', εἰπέ, *how* did' *he perish!* "Τί χρὴ λέγειν asks, *What is one to say?* not, Whether there is any thing to say: but τί χρὴ καὶ λέγειν not only asks *what,* but doubts whether any thing at all is to be said (fully: *quid dicendum est, si omnino aliquid dicendum est?*)"[1] Or, more strongly, *at all, on earth:* Τί χρὴ καὶ προσδοκᾶν, *what on earth is one,* or, *what is one at all,* to *expect?* Ἔστιν ἄρα δικαίου ἀνθρώπου βλάπτειν καὶ ὁντινοῦν ἄνθρωπον; *Plat. Rep* 1, 335, B, *any human being at all, be who it may?* Ἵνα καὶ ἴδῃς ὅσα καὶ εἴδη ἔχει ἡ κακία, *ib.* 4, 445, C, *how' many forms* (*after all*). In

[1] Hermann ad Vig. p. 837, 320. But Krüger says, that the καί emphasizes the term to which it is prefixed, as being the particular point about which one requires to have full information Similarly Klotz: "si dico τί χρὴ καὶ λέγειν; proprie hoc quæro, *quid sit dicendum etiam si solum de dicendo cogitemus.*"

like manner, the frequent combination ἵνα καί, especially with εἰδῶ, ἴδης, &c., may be explained, *that* if *there is anything* (or, as there is something) to *know*, *I may know it*. [§ 224.]

§ 225. In καὶ γάρ, *nam etiam*, the καί belongs to the next following word, from which it is separated by the necessity of placing γάρ second in the sentence: Καὶ γὰρ πρὸς τούτους αὐτῷ ἐπεποίητο συμμαχίη, *Hdt.* 1, 77, *for with these also*. Καὶ γὰρ νῦν ὁμολογῶ, i. e. καὶ νῦν, *Plat. Gorg.* 467, B. Sometimes it is *namque*, and then the καί is not idle, but denotes the reciprocal correspondency of the clauses: ἀκούσατε, ἔφη, καὶ γὰρ ἄξιον, *for*, let me *also* tell you, *it is worth hearing*.

§ 226. In εἰ καί, the καί is *even*, and refers not merely to the εἰ, but to the whole concessive sentence = *etsi*, *quamquam*: Εἰ καὶ μητρὶ διαφορὰν ἔχει, *if it even be that he has a quarrel with their mother*, if it be ever so much the case that —: in καὶ εἰ, the καί refers only to the condition, = *etiamsi*. Κεἰ μὴ πέποιθα, *even if* (*for all that*) *I have no confidence*. Εἴ τι καὶ ἀγροικότερον εἰρῆσθαι, *Pl. Gorg.* 486, C, *if it be even somewhat rude* (as it is), i.e. though I own it is somewhat rude: but καὶ εἰ ἀγροικότερόν τι εἰπεῖν ἐστιν, *ib.* 509, A, *even if it be somewhat rude* (which I do not allow). — Both forms are abbreviated into the participial construction: thus, τὰ αὐτὰ ἂν ἔπραξε καὶ πρώτη λαχοῦσα, *Pl. Rep.* 10, 620 = εἰ καὶ or καὶ εἰ πρώτη ἔλαχεν. See § 175, e.

τε, *also*, *so*, denoting parity of the term appended. See § 222, and for the use as conjunction, § 185.

§ 227. The adverbial use of this particle is almost entirely confined to the ancient epic style, having disappeared, except a few traces, from the later language. Its meaning is so faint that, for the most part, it does not admit of being rendered otherwise than by an exaggerated analogy: it does little more than intimate the correspondency of the clauses which it accompanies. In its origin, τε is cognate with enclitic τις: in its use, it almost exclusively accompanies other particles which connect protasis and apodosis or other parallel members, and sometimes appears in both, oftener only in one. Τε — τε, *any*-where, -how, -way, -time, &c. . . . *some*-where, -how, &c.: hence it is the slightest possible intimation of *as — so*, *alike — alike*: Κραιπνότερος μὲν γάρ τε νόος, λεπτὴ δέ τε μῆτις, *Il.* 23, 591, *as on the one hand the mind is more rapid, so also on the other is the counsel slight*. Εἴπερ τε νοήσῃ, ἀλλά τε οἱ βράσσων τε νόος λεπτὴ δέ τε μῆτις, *Il.* 10, 224, *although* in-any-wise *he has the wit*, *yet* likewise *slower* alike (*on the one hand*, μέν om.) *the wit*, *scanty* alike *on the other hand the counsel*. Οὐ μὴν οἱ τόγε κάλλιον οὐδέ τ' ἄμεινον, *yet is this not for his honour*, *and* (as *not for his honour*) so *not for his good either*. Ὅς κε θεοῖς ἐπιπείθηται, μάλα τ' ἔκλυον αὐτοῦ, *whoso obeys the gods* (as *he obeys them*) so *do they hear him*. In sentences correlated by demonstr. and relative, τε is used only when the dem. and rel. do not come close together, or when the dem. is not expressed: in other combinations it is frequent: thus we have, εἴπερ τε — ἀλλά τε, or simply τε: εἴπερ — τε: and εἴπερ τε with second clause omitted. Μέν τε — δέ τε or ἀλλά τε (sometimes the μέν τε, sometimes the second τε, omitted), also (μέν omitted) τε — δέ τε: δὲ — τε: τε — δέ: τε — αὐτάρ. Again, ἤ τε, *so surely*: καί τε (*as* —) *so also*: γάρ τε, *for* (*as* —), *so*: and sometimes ἤτε, or ἤτε — ἤτε.

§ 228. Hence the usage of τε attached to relative words in dependent sentences to give force and clearness to the correlation: thus, ὅστε, *he*, or, *that*, *who* (Hom., lyr. poets, and lyrical parts of Tragedy, sometimes Herodot.), also ὅστις τε, οἷος τε, ὅσος τε (*just such*, or *so great*, *as*), ὥστε, *so as*, *so that*, ὡσεί τε, ἅτε, ὅπως τε, ἠΰτε, ὅτε τε (*then when*), ὅθι τε, ἵνα τε (*there where*). Of these the Attic prose has retained οἷός τε

[§ 228.] εἰμι, *I am in such sort as to —, in a condition to —* : ὥστε, ὡσεί τε, ἔστε (ἐς ὅτε) *quoad*, ἅτε, *quippe*, ἐφ' ᾧτε, *on condition that* (Herod. also ἐπεί τε, *postquam*). Corresponding forms in Lat. (τε = *que*, — *pe*) are *namque* (γάρ τε, comp. καὶ γάρ, *etenim*), *atque* (= *ad-que* καί τε). *quippe* (ἅτε), also *quisque* with its adverbial forms, as *ubique*, &c., *uterque*, *usque*, and the suffix —*cumque*.

§ 229. δέ, *on the other hand* (comp. μέν, *on the one hand*, § 232).

Opposition is denoted by the particles which originally denote *on the other hand*, viz. αὖ or αὖτε, and αὐτάρ (= αὖτ' ἄρα), which, shortened, is ἀτάρ. Synonymous with these is δέ, which, both as adverb or mere particle, and as conjunction, in virtue of its origin (cognate with the second numeral δύο, the δείς in οὐδείς, and the pronoun of the second person), means *in the second place*. For the conjunctional use, see §§ 188, 189. The adverbial use appears in

a) καὶ δέ, *and on the other hand, and also* (*moreover*). In Homer the particles usually stand together; in Attic, the word that has the emphasis comes between. Καὶ δ' ἄλλῳ νεμεσῶτον, and *of another* also *ye take it amiss*. Καὶ σὺ δ' αὐθάδης ἔφυς, *Eur. El.* 1122, and *thou* too *art self-willed* (not Ægisthus only). Καὶ οἵ τε ἄλλοι .... ὑπηρέτουν, ... καὶ ἡ τῶν Θηβαίων δὲ πόλις ... ξυνέπεμπε, *Xen. Hell.* 5, 2, 37, *and Thebes also* —.

Rem. Καί being both *and* and *also*, the Greek was obliged to have recourse to δέ to express *and also*.

b) *in the demonstrative sentence or the apodosis of a condition:* Οἵη περ φύλλων γενεή, τοίη δὲ καὶ ἀνδρῶν, *as is the nature of the leaves, so is*, on the other hand (also) *that of man*. Οἳ δ' ἄρα Μηθώνην .. ἐνέμοντο, ... τῶν δὲ Φιλοκτήτης ἦρχεν, *Il.* 2, 716. (comp. οἳ δ' Ἄργισσαν ἔχον ...., τῶν αὖθ' ἡγεμόνευε ... Πολυποίτης, *ib.* 738). Ἐγὼ μὲν οὓς ἂν τῶν λόγων ἀλγῶ κλύειν, Λαερτίου παῖ, τοὺς δὲ καὶ πράσσειν στυγῶ, *Soph. Phil.* 86, *I also*, on the other hand, *hate to do*. — Αἰ δέ κε λίσσηαι ἑτάρους ..., οἱ δέ σε ... δεόντων, *Od.* 12, 54, *let them*, on the other hand (or, however), *bind thee*. Ἀλλ' εἰ σύγε Παυσανίαν αἰνεῖς, ἐγὼ δ' Ἀριστείδαν ἐπαινέω, *I*, on the contrary, *praise A*. Ἀλλ' εἰ μηδὲ τοῦτο βούλει ἀποκρίνασθαι, σὺ δὲ τοὐντεῦθεν λέγε, *do thou*, however, *say*. So, especially in Attic, δέ after an abbreviated protasis in the form of a participle: Θαυμάζω σου, εἰ ἐκείνους ῥᾳδίως χειρούμενος, τούτοις δὲ μηδένα τρόπον οἴει δυνήσεσθαι προσενεχθῆναι, *Xen. Mem.* 3, 7, 8, *that although* —, *yet* —. Cf. § 188. R. 6.

When in an alternative, two protases, each with its apodosis, are opposed to each other, the form may be μὲν — μέν (prot. and ap.), δὲ — δέ (prot. and ap.), or also μὲν — δέ, δὲ — δέ: thus, ὃς μέν τ' αἰδέσεται κούρας Διὸς ...., τὸν δὲ μέγ' ὤνησαν ...., ὃς δέ κ' ἀνήνηται .. λίσσονται δ' ἄρα ταίγε Δία, *Il.* 9, 509, *whoso reverences the virgins, him they benefit* (might also be τὸν μὲν ..) —: *but whoso repulses them, then they pray*, &c. For Attic instances, see § 188, Rem. 4.

c) *in the combination* οὐδέ, μηδέ, *also not, not even*. Here the particle δέ stands for itself and also for καί, as καί cannot follow οὐ and μή in this sense. Its usage, therefore, exactly agrees with that of καί; so that οὐδ' ὧς, *not so too, not so either*, stands on the same footing with καὶ ὧς, οὐδὲ γάρ, *neque enim*, with καὶ γάρ, *etenim*, οὐδὲ μὲν οὐδέ, *neque vero etiam*, with καὶ μὴν καί, *et vero etiam*, οὐδὲ γὰρ οὐδέ, *for also not*, or *for not even*, with καὶ γὰρ καί. The particle sometimes puts the things on a par (*also not*), sometimes exalts the latter (*not even*), ἐπεὶ οὐδὲ ἔοικε, *because it is* also *not seemly* (*therefore must it* also *not be*). Τὰ γὰρ πεπρωμέν' οὐδ' ὑπερβαίην ποτ' ἄν, *Eur. Ion*, 1388, *that which is fated for me can I* also *not escape*. Οὐδέ νυ τοῦπερ φείσατο, *Il.* 24, 235, *not even him did he spare*; οὐδ' ὄναρ, *not even in a dream*. Οὐδὲ γὰρ οὐδέ τις

ἄλλος, *Od.* 8, 32, *etenim ne alius quidem*. Οὐδὲ μὲν οὐδὲ Τρῶας ἀγήνορας εἴασ' Ἕκτωρ [§
εὕδειν, *Il.* 10, 299. *Not*, however, *the T.* either (any more than the others) —. 229.]
Not the Trojans moreover (either) *did H. suffer to sleep.*

μέν, *on the one hand, indeed.*

§ 230. This particle, bearing the same relation to the first numeral (μείς) μία, that δέ bears to the second and to the δείς in οὐδείς (not οὐδ' εἷς) means therefore *in the first place*, and a μέν is usually followed by a corresponding δέ. But as the δέ has not always a preceding μέν, so μέν not always a following δέ. This, however, is always implied in the thought. Φιλοτιμία μὲν ἐνέχεται, δεινῷ κακῷ, *Eur. Iph. A.* 527, *ambition* indeed (in the first place, as far as that goes) *he is liable to* (the suppressed opposition being, *but what of the rest, but what then!*) Καὶ ὁπόθεν ποτὲ ταύτην τὴν ἐπωνυμίαν ἔλαβες τὸ μανικὸς καλεῖσθαι, οὐκ οἶδα ἔγωγε· ἐν μὲν γὰρ τοῖς λόγοις ἀεὶ τοιοῦτος εἶ, *for in your discourse* (to begin with that, = it must be owned, at any rate), &c. (*Pl.*) Λέγεται δὲ καὶ ὅδε ὁ λόγος, ἐμοὶ μὲν οὐ πιθανός, *Hdt.* 3, 3, *to me* for my part (but what others may think I know not). Οὗτοι δὴ ἀφίκται, ἀλλὰ δοκεῖ μέν μοι ἥξειν τήμερον, *Pl. Crito*, 43 D, *it seems to me, for my part.* So οἶμαι μέν, ἡγοῦμαι μέν, δοκῶ μέν, οὐκ οἶδα μέν. Παρεγένου μὲν τῇ μάχῃ, *Pl. Charm.* 153 C, *you were present* surely (or, I suppose) —? (suppressed: *but if not, I have no more to say.*)

Rem. In Homer and Ionic, μέν is frequently used in the same sense as the cognate form μήν, μάν, § 231: in the later dialects, only so in the combinations μέντοι, μὲν οὖν, μὲν δή.

μήν Dor., and Ep. μάν.

§ 231. This particle, cognate with μέν, involves the same primary notion "first and foremost," "to begin with," but more strongly expressed, as here the whole statement stops at the μέν, as if the *one* thing were all: it insists upon one thing (the first) to the exclusion of the rest. Hence it is confirmative and concessive, and also oppositive and adversative (as Lat. *vero*). Accordingly, it stands in hortatory addresses and exclamations: εἰ δ' ἄγε μήν, πείρησαι, *but come now, do try* (in the first place, now, for once); ἕπου μήν, *do follow*: in questions, τίνος μὴν ἕνεκα μανθάνετε τοξεύειν; *to what end* (let me ask you one thing) *do you learn —!* especially τί μήν; thus, οἱ τὸ παράπαν ἡδονὰς οὔ φασιν εἶναι. "τί μήν;" i. e. τί μὴν ἄλλο φασὶν αὐτὰς εἶναι; *what else, I pray* (for one thing), *do they affirm them to be?* Ὁρᾷς οὖν ἐκείνην τὴν ὑψηλοτάτην πλάτανον; "τί μήν;" *Pl. Phil.* 44, *what else, I pray, do I but see it!* = to be sure I do: in argumentative assertions with latent interrogation, σώφρων μὴν (I suppose I may assert this one thing) ὅ γε τοιοῦτος καὶ οὐδαμῇ φιλοχρήματος, *Pl. Rep.* 485, and adversatively, ταῦτ' ἐπιεικῶς μέν ἐστιν ὑπό τι ἄτοπα, δηλοῖ μὴν —, *this is indeed somewhat strange; it shows, however* —. οὐ μὴν ἐρεῖς γε, *but then surely you don't mean to say* —: in asseverations, ὧδε γὰρ ἐξερέω, καὶ μὴν τετελεσμένον ἔσται, *and be sure of one thing* = assuredly; so ἦ μήν, the usual formula of swearing, ἐπομνύω σοι, ἦ μὴν ἐγὼ βούλεσθαι, *verily and truly* (for one thing, come what will): in announcing the coming of a new person: ὅδε μὴν Αἵμων, *here, however, comes H.!* (The notion *however*, which often renders μήν, is given by the suppressed opposition, "for one thing, *however it may be with the rest*," or the like.)

§ 232. καὶ μήν, καὶ μήν γε, the καί adverbial. Καὶ μὴν χάριν γ' ἂν ἀξίαν λάβοις ἐμοῦ (*well, be sure of one thing* —): "καὶ μὴν μάλιστα τοῦτ' ἀφικόμην, ὅπως —" (*well, sure enough* —), *Soph. Œd. T.* 1004, 5. Adversatively: ἀλλ' ἐκδιδάσκει πάνθ' ὁ γηράσκων χρόνος. "καὶ μὴν σύ γ' οὔπω σωφρονεῖν ἐπίστασαι," *yet, sure enough.* — καὶ μὴν

[§ 232.] πάρεισιν οἵδε, *Soph. El.* 1412. καὶ μὴν ὁρῶ τάλαιναν Εὐρυδίκην, *Ant.* 1165 (announcing the arrival of a new person). καὶ μὴν Τάνταλον εἰσεῖδον, *then or moreover* (for one thing) —, *Od.* 11, 582 (comp. Attic καὶ μενδή, § 236 c.) — καὶ μὴν καί, *and (for one thing) moreover.*

§ 233. ἀλλὰ μήν: ἀλλὰ μὴν κεκραξόμεσθά γ' ὁπόσον ἡ φάρυγξ ἂν ἡμῶν χανδάνῃ, *well then, we will cry* (if that be all), expressive of readiness to do something which one is challenged to do: ἀλλ' ἔστι μὴν οἰκητός, *Arist. R.* 258, *well, it is inhabited* (I see that for one thing, sure enough): εἰ εἰσὶ βωμοί, εἰσὶ καὶ θεοί· ἀλλὰ μὴν (*atqui*) εἰσὶ βωμοί· εἰσὶν ἄρα θεοί, *but there are altars.* ἀλλ' οὐ μήν, — but not —, *be assured of that*, especially in hasty rejoinders: τῆς δ' ἑκοῦσα παιδὸς οὐ μεθήσομαι. "ἀλλ' οὐδ' ἐγὼ μὴν τήνδ' ἄπειμ' αὐτοῦ λιπών," *no, nor will I; be assured of that* —. (For ἀλλὰ μὴν δή, which often occurs in some copies of Plato, the critical edd. restore ἀλλὰ μὲν δή.)

γε μήν, *quidem certe*, see under γε, § 250.

Rem. In Homer, μέν is often used in precisely the sense of μήν: thus ἦ μέν: οὐ (μὴ) μέν: οὐδὲ μέν = ἀλλ' οὐ μήν: καὶ μέν.

§ 234. δή.

This particle, related to δέ as μήν is to μέν, insists upon the δέ to the exclusion of the μέν: its general force therefore = "leave all that is before (or intermediate) and come to *that*," "come to *that* at once, and stop there." Hence its very frequent use in emphatic statements of place, time, degree: in peremptory determinations and conclusions, urgent demands, impatient questions, in putting something as generally acknowledged (= "everybody has come to that conclusion"), and in the expression of irony and derision. Except in the epic style, δὴ τότε, δὴ γάρ, it never begins a sentence, and it is usually attached almost like a suffix to the word which it qualifies: comp. τόσος δή with τοσόσδε, αὐτὸς δή with i(s)*dem*, πρὶν δή with pri*dem*, ἄγε δή with age*dum*.

1) With numerals, demonstratives, local and temporal adverbs, words of dimension, superlatives. τρεῖς δή, *three* (not short of, and not beyond): ἕκτον δὴ τόδ' ἦμαρ, *this is now the sixth day* (it has come to that), πάντως and πάνυ δή. πολλοὶ and πολλάκις δή. — ἐκεῖνος, οὗτος, οὕτω, ἐνταῦθα, ὧδε δή: τὰ αὐτὰ δὴ ταῦτα: so the personal pronouns, σὲ δή, *thee there* —: νῦν δή, τότε δή (Hom. δὴ τότε, δή ῥα τότ'): ἔτι, οὐκέτι, πάλαι, πρὶν, ἀεί, τέλος, ὄψε δή δαρόν τε δὴ χρόνον. — ἐν βραχεῖ δή. — πλεῖστα, κράτιστοι δή.

2) With relative, interrogative, indefinite pronouns. ὅς, οἷος δή. τίς δή, *who'ever!* (= when are we ever to get at him? who on earth?) πῶς, ὅσος δή; — ἄλλος δή, *alius nescio quis.* δή τις, *quidam nescio quis.* δή που, *somewhere or other.* ὅστις δή and δήποτε. δή που, *surely* (= *that* somehow), and οὐ δή που, *surely not*, see under που. — ὡς and ἵνα (final) δή, *precisely in order that.* ὡς (as) δή with irony *as if forsooth* (so very certain is *that!*), ἅτε, οἷα δή.

3) With particles of asseveration and negation. ἦ δή, *verily* (= *that*, whatever comes before it), comp. ἦ μήν (= *this*, whatever comes after it). οὐ δή, not (*that!*). μὴ δή (do not think of *that!*), μή τι δή (cf. ne*dum*), and μή τί γε δή, *to say nothing of* —, *much less*, — (= only not *that!*).

4) With nouns: τότε δὴ ὁ Κῦρος λέγει· Ὦ Κυαξάρη, ὥρα δὴ ἐξαπαντᾶν, *Xen.* ἐπειδὴ δοκεῖ λήθη τις εἶναι κανάπαυλα δή, *Soph. Phil.* 866, *a cessation at last* (it has come to that). Often with irony, τοὺς Ἀθηναίους φίλους δὴ ὄντας, *Thuc.* 6, 80, *friends forsooth* (so likely that!). εἰσήγαγε τὰς ἑταιρίδας δή, *the pretended concubines*

[APPENDIX.

(that, to be sure, was what everybody would acknowledge them to be!). Comp. δῆθεν. [§ 234.]

5) With verbs: ἄγε δή. θώμεθα δὴ φόρτιον. ἐπεὶ προθυμεῖ, χρὴ λέγειν. ἄκουε δή, *well then, hear*. οἶσθα δὴ τὸ πᾶν, *there thou knowest the whole*. σύμπεμψον τοίνυν μοί τινα. "λαβὼν δὴ ἴθι, ἔφη, ὅντινα ἐθέλεις," *take then* (without more ado: as matter of course: come to that at once). With irony, δεδιὼς περὶ αὐτοῦ, μὴ διαφθαρῇ δὴ ὑπὸ Ἀλκιβιάδου, *Pl. Prot.* 320.

With the whole sentence: νῦν δ' αὖ μόνα δὴ νὼ λελειμμένα, *since it has come to this, that we are left alone*.[1] ὁ μὲν χρόνος δὴ διὰ χρόνου προὔβαινέ μοι, *Soph. Ant.* 58, denoting the slowness of the passage of time. § 235.

In conclusions: ἐκ δὴ τούτων —, *from this then it follows* (comp. μήν of the steps of an argument). In resumption after interruption: ἐν τούτῳ δὴ ἄν τις γενόμενος, *Pl. Men.* 240, *well then* (to come back at last to that point) *if one be in* —. Both uses are exemplified in δεῖ δὴ (*of course then it is necessary*) πρᾳότερόν πως ἀποκρίνεσθαι. δημοκρατία δή (*Well then* —). In enumerations, denoting the accession of some weightier consideration, ὑγίεια καὶ ἰσχὺς καὶ κάλλος καὶ πλοῦτος δή (*denique*), *Pl. Men.* 87: so καὶ τὸ δὴ μέγιστον: or something special, ἄλλος τε καὶ δὴ καὶ —.

καὶ δή, in replies: βλέψον κάτω. "καὶ δὴ βλέπω." *well, I am looking* (that already): ταῦτα δή, *there, 'tis done!* in the supposition of a fictitious case, καὶ δὴ τεθνᾶσι, *well, they are dead* (suppose it). § 236.

μήν and δή exclude each other, therefore this combination never occurs in good authors: but μὲν δή is frequent, especially in dismissing a consideration: εἶεν· τὰ μὲν δὴ τόξ' ἔχεις, *the bow thou hast* (enough of that). τοιαῦτα μὲν δὴ ταῦτα, *hæc hactenus*. ἀλλ' ἦλθε μὲν δὴ τοῦτο τοὔνειδος τάχ' ἂν ὀργῇ βιασθέν, *but in fact* — or, *it may be enough to say that* (one consideration, μέν, and there an end, δή). Hence μὲν δή approaches nearly to μήν, and Plato renders Homer's καὶ μὴν Τάνταλον εἰσεῖδον by καὶ μὲν δὴ καὶ Τάνταλόν γε εἰσεῖδον, *Prot.* 315, *and moreover* (the enumeration begun with μέν cut short by δή). So οὐ μὲν δὴ λήξω. *Soph. El.* 103 = οὐ μὴν λήξω. βασιλικοὶ μὲν ἄνδρες, οὐ μὲν δὴ ἐπιστήμονές γε (where Stallb. would read μέντοι for μὲν δή), *Pl. Phæd.* 266. καὶ μὲν δὴ χαλεπὸν ἐπιχειροῦμεν, *Pl. Pol.* 287 (*porro etiam*). ἂν μὲν δὴ καὶ ὑποπίῃ, *Pl. Lys.* 89, *jam si adeo*. μάλιστα μὲν δὴ (*in fact*, or, *and that one consideration enough*) — ἔπειτα μέντοι (*but then*), *Soph. Phil.* 350.

δῆτα.

This more emphatic form of δή (comp. ἔπειτα from ἐπεί, τηνικαῦτα from τηνίκα), not found in Hom. and Dor., rare in Herodot., is frequent in Attic, where it accompanies all the parts of speech. § 237.

In replies: ξυμβόλαια δὲ λέγεις κοινωνήματα, ἤ τι ἄλλο; "κοινωνήματα δῆτα" (just so, *that* is the very thing!). *Pl. Rep.* 1, 333. In earnest iterations: οἴκτειρε δ' ἡμᾶς . . . "οἴκτειρε δῆτα," *yes, do pity*, *Eur. El.* 678. ἰώ. "ἰὼ δῆτα," (it is') *alas! indeed*, *Soph. Œd.* 541. ὥς μ' ἀπώλεσας θανών. ἀπώλεσας δῆτ', *how hast thou undone me!*

---

[1] The particle belongs to the whole sentence, but attaches itself to μόνα. So in *Æsch. Eum.* 3. (First Gæa, and after her, Themis) ἣ δὴ (*ut satis constat*) τὸ μητρὸς δευτέρα τόδ' ἕζετο μαντεῖον, it belongs to the sentence as a whole, but more closely to τὸ μητρός. Fully expressed, the meaning is: "who succeeded to the oracle which — everybody knows *that* — was her mother's before her, and to which therefore — as everybody must see — she had the fullest right." *Müller on the Eum.* § 91, n.

[§ 237.] *yes, undone indeed!* *Soph. El.* 1155. σκόπει δῆτα, *only look!* In wishes: ἀπόλοιο δῆτα, *oh that thou mightest but perish!* In questions: τί δῆτ᾽, ἐπειδὰν —; *quid tum demum dicetis, quum —?* τί δῆτα κλαίεις; *what are you weeping for?* τίς ἄρα ῥύσεται, τίς ἄρ᾽ ἐπαρκέσει θεῶν ἢ θεᾶν; ποτέρα δῆτ᾽ ἐγὼ ποτιπέσω βρέτη δαιμόνων; *am I then* (and what avails that)? *Æsch. Sept.* 93. οἶσθα δῆτά γε; thou *dost, surely, know!* ᾔδησθα γὰρ δῆτ᾽, *I suppose you knew* (ironically). ἦ δῆτα, *yes, verily.* οὐ δῆτα, *minime vero.* μὴ δῆτα δράσῃς ταῦτα, *only not this!* ὅτε δῆτα, *just when.* καὶ δῆτ᾽ ἐτόλμας, *and, forsooth, you had the audacity*, *Soph. Ant.* 445.

§ 238. δαί (Attic).

This particle occurs only in the combination τί δαί; πῶς δαί; and is used in forcible transitions, with indignation, wonder, or other emotions: *what then? how so?* τί δαὶ τἄλλα; *what then say you to the rest?* It occurs only in the familiar Attic style.

§ 239. —θε, —θεν.

The first only as a suffix in εἴθε, "would that," "if but" = in this (or, in that) case. The second as a suffix of case, οὐρανόθεν, *from heaven*, ἐντεῦθεν, *thence*, &c.: hence, in composition with δή,

δῆθεν.

This particle (not used by Hom.), originally = *from that* (as the *terminus a quo*) is almost always ironical (= something which all the world acknowledges, to set out with!), *forsooth, in pretence, of course* (derisively). τοῦτο τὸ ἄγος οἱ Λακεδαιμόνιοι ἐλαύνειν ἐκέλευον, δῆθεν τοῖς θεοῖς πρῶτον τιμωροῦντες, *Thuc.* 1, 127. ὡς ἐκπεφευγὼς τοὺς ἐχθρούς, οἵ μιν . . . ἠθέλησαν ἀπολέσαι δῆθεν (*as he pretended*), *Hdt.* 1, 11. τῆς ἐκεῖνος οὐδαμὰ βλάστας ἐφώνει, δῆθεν οὐδὲν ἱστορῶν, *Soph. Tr.* 381.

§ 240. δήπουθεν.

See above, δή τις, and δήπου, under που: hence this (Attic) particle originally = *from that in anywise*, or, *surely*; therefore, *I should hope*, or, *surely*. ἐγὼ δέ, ἢν ἱππεύειν μάθω, ὅταν μὲν ἐπὶ τοῦ ἵππου γένωμαι, τὰ τοῦ ἱπποκενταύρου δήπουθεν διαπράξομαι, *Xen. Cyr.* 4, 3, 20. ἑστάναι γὰρ ἐξέσται δήπουθεν αὐτῷ, *Dem.* οὔτε γὰρ μαγείρῳ μαχαίρας οὐδὲν ἔστ᾽ ὄφελος δήπουθεν, ἥτις μὴ τέμνει, *Pl.*

§ 241. θήν.

This stronger form of θέν (§ 239) is Homeric and Doric (Sicilian). In Hom. always ironical, = δήπου, especially with ἦ οὐ, οὐ μέν θην — γε, *yet surely, yet surely at least not.* In Theocritus ἐγὼ θήν, *I for my part*, τὺ θήν, *thou for thy part*, and = *denique.* πείρᾳ θὴν πάντα τελεῖται, *Adoniaz.* 63.

§ 242. ἤδη.

As δή to δέ, so is ἤδη to ἠδέ (which answers to ἠμέν, *as on the one hand, so on the other hand*).[1] It denotes, therefore, the absence of an interval, chiefly with reference to time, *this* (that) *instant, immediately.*

(*a*) As temporal particle, it answers to Lat. *jam*, *now*, in the senses, *forthwith, henceforth, already, at last, still*, the *now* being either that of the speaker, or of the person, &c. spoken of, not, as νῦν, simply "at this present time." Thus ἤδη ἀπῆλθεν, *he went away just now*; ἤδη ἀπελήλυθεν, *is just gone*; ἤδη ἀπελεύσεται, *will go directly.*

[1] The ἤ = *as, so*, not ἦ, *verily*, but the original of ἤ, *or, than*, whence also ἦμος and ἠΰτε, *when.*

νῦν ἤδη, ἤδη νῦν, *now this instant*. ποιήσας δὲ τοῦτο, τὰ ἄλλα ἤδη ἤρχετο διοικεῖν, *anon, without more ado*, Xen. Hell. 7, 1, 12. ἤδη οὐκ εἴχομεν, *we were not yet* (erewhile) *able*; ἤδη οὐχ ἕξομεν, *we shall henceforth not* (or, no more) *be able*. λόγοι ἔσφηλαν ἤδη (*ere now* = full oft) καὶ κατώρθωσαν βροτούς, Soph. El. 408. ἤδη ποτ' εἶδον (*in my time*), ἤδη πάλαι (*this long while*). [§ 242.]

(*b*) In the other instances, the temporal signification, though less strongly marked, is still discernible: ἀπὸ ταύτης ἤδη Αἴγυπτος, *at this point immediately Egypt begins*. δῆλον δὴ τοῦτό γε ἤδη καὶ παιδί (*even to a child*): so οὗτος —, τότ' —, ἐνταῦθ' —, οὕτως ἤδη. τὰ δὲ παννυχίδων ἤδη —, *and then the vigils*; *vigilias demum si commemorem*, Soph. El. 92.

Rem. δήν, *jam diu*, evidently connected with δή, ἤδη, *denique, dudum, donec*.

νῦν.

This is the Latin *nunc, at this present time* (the *now* of the speaker). Hence it usually occurs in connexion with the present, or present-perfect, or future, the latter in the sense, *as the case is now, he, &c. will* —, or, *he is now going to* —. With the proper past (imperf. or aorist indic.) either the sense is present, as νῦν δ' εἰς τὸ κείνου κρᾶτ' ἐνήλαθ' ἡ τύχη, *but as it is now, destiny has* —; or the immediate past is denoted, ἐν ᾧπερ νῦν ἐκάμνομεν, Eur. Hec. 1144. νῦν ἐμέλλομεν, *we were now about to* —. νῦν δὴ ἔλεγον, *just now*: νῦν δὴ λέγω or λέξω, *nunc cum maxime, at this very time*. § 243.

νῦν, *igitur, jam vero*, further serves to denote transition or argument: μὴ νῦν ἀτίμα θεούς, *then do not* —, Soph. Aj. 1108. εἰ νῦν ἐπίστω, *if then thou knowest*, Soph. Phil. 1224. In the formula of adjuration: πρὸς νῦν σε γονάτων, πρὸς νῦν θεῶν, *now by* —.

This νῦν is reduced to an enclitic (our unemphatic "now"); but, as a single word, only in the poets; in Ionic prose μέννυν, in Attic τοίνυν. Homer has it, e. g. δεῦρό νυν, *hither then*, Il. 23, 485.[1] § 244.

Connected, if not identical, with enclit. νυν is the enclit. νυ of Homer, used in asseveration with somewhat of irony: οὔ νύ τ' ἀοιδοὶ αἴτιοι, *nempe, scilicet*, Od. 1, 348. θνητὸς δέ νυ καὶ σὺ τέτυξαι, *but I suppose*, Il. 16, 622. So ἐπεί νυ, ἦ ῥά νυ, μή νυ τοι, οὔ νυ τι. Also καί νύ κεν in apodosis with præt. indic. to an hypothesis also with præt. indic., *and doubtless* —. In questions: τί νυ οἱ τόσον ὠδύσαο, Ζεῦ, Od. 1, 62, *why art thou* —? τί νυ σ' ἔτρεφον, Il. 1, 414, *why did I* —?

νή, ναί, μά.

νή (cf. *ne*) asseverates, but only in affirmative sentences: νὴ τὸν Δία. § 245.

This lengthened becomes ναί, *yea, verily* (cf. δή, δαί): often followed by μά, as ναὶ μὰ τὸν Δία, a stronger form of νὴ τὸν Δία. The μά in itself is neither negative nor affirmative, but simply = "by;" but unless the ναί is expressed, μά must always have a negative expressed or implied, either preceding or following: οὐ μὰ τὸν Δ., or μὰ τὸν Δ., οὐ —. μὰ τὴν τέλειον τῆς ἐμῆς παιδὸς δίκην, Ἄτην, Ἐρινύν θ' —, οὔ μοι φόβου μέλαθρον ἐλπὶς ἐμπατεῖν, Æsch. Ag. 1354.

ἦ.

This particle (always adverbial) expresses assurance: ἦ = ἀληθῶς, ὄντως, Hesych., *indeed, surely*. ἦ μήν, § 231, a strong asseveration, *assuredly* (come what will, &c.). § 246.

---

[1] Krüger says, that in Aristoph. the υ is long (but still to be written νυν encl., not νῦν), in the Tragic poets long or short.

[§ 246.] ἦ που, assurance with a mixture of doubt, real or pretended (hence ironically of self-evident conclusions), or confident conjecture, *sane opinor, surely.* ἀλλ' ἦ (often falsely written ἀλλ' ἤ), *at profecto.* ἦ ρα, ἤτοι. See under ῥα, τοι.

The same particle used interrogatively, asks a question with confidence or conjecture. In Hom. without other particles, when the speaker answers his own question by another: τίπτε τόσον — ἐβόησας —; ἦ μήτις σευ μῆλα — ἐλαύνει; ἦ μήτις σαυτὸν κτείνειν; *Od.* 9, 405. Frequent in Attic, especially in Tragedy: ἦ τολμήσατε; *aye, did ye dare?* ἦ κεῖνος ὤμοσεν; *then did he swear?* With other particles: ἦ δή; *ergo revera?* ἦ ταῦτα δῆτ' ἀνεκτά; *then is this to be borne?* ἦ που[1], *num forte?* expects an answer in the negative, ἦ που τετόλμηκ' ἔργον αἴσχιστον τόδε; *do you mean to say that —? Eur. Med.* 695. Ἦ ῥα Att. ἆρα; ἦ γάρ; See under ῥα, γάρ.

§ 247. περ.

Etymologically connected with πέρι, "through and out at the other end," περᾶν, &c., comp. περί, Lat. *per*, this enclitic particle has for its fundamental meaning the notion, *throughly, thoroughly, throughout.* Hence

a) (In Homer) its meaning sometimes seems to be confined to the word which it accompanies (cf. *pergratus perque jucundus*): μίνυνθά περ οὔτι μαλὰ δήν, *Il.* 13, 573, *a very little while*, = just a little while: πρῶτόν περ, ὕστατόν περ, *quite or just first, last:* γεινόμενόν περ, *just = precisely at the birth, Il.* 23, 79. ἀλλὰ καὶ αὐτοί περ πονεώμεθα, *ourselves precisely* (and not others), *Il.* 10, 70. οἴκαδέ περ σὺν νηυσὶ νεώμεθα, *home just* that (and nothing else), *Il.* 2, 236. τόδε πέρ μοι ἐπικρήηνον ἐέλδωρ, *just this* (and only this) *prayer, Il.* 8, 242. ὁ δὲ πείσεται εἰς ἀγαθόν περ, to *what is good* if to nothing else = at any rate, *Il.* 11, 789.

b) (also in Hom.) *for all that:* ἀλλ' οὐδ' ὣς ἑτάρους ἐρρύσατο ἱέμενός περ, *though quite desiring, all eager as he was, Od.* 1, 6. ἀγαθός περ ἐών, *all brave as thou art.* οὐδὲ θεοί περ — δύνανται, *not the gods either for all that* (they be gods), *Od.* 3, 236. μῆτερ, ἐπεί μ' ἔτεκές γε μινυνθάδιόν περ ἔοντα, τιμήν περ μοι ὄφελλεν Ὀλύμπιος ἐγγυαλίξαι, *all short-lived as I am,* (yet) *honour,* if nothing else —, *Il.* 1, 353.

c) With relatives and conjunctions (*this* usage is Attic as well as epic): ὅσπερ, *just what, precisely who, the same that:* ὅσοςπερ, *just so great as;* οἷος περ, *just of the same kind as;* also with ὡς, οὗ, οἷ, ὅθεν, ᾗ, ὅπου, ὅτε, ἔνθα, ἕως, ἐπεί, ἐπειδή, &c. εἴπερ, *if the case be just so, if really* (εἴπερ εἴργασται τόδε. ἴσμεν γὰρ οὐδὲν τρανές, *Soph. Aj.* 22): sometimes, *if ever so much;* ἐάνπερ, *if indeed* and *provided only that:* εἴπερ, ἐάνπερ καί, *albeit that even;* ὅτανπερ, *when* (provided only it be so).

d) The Attic poets sometimes allow themselves the use of περ as in Homer: γενναῖός περ ὤν, *all noble as thou art;* but in this sense καίπερ with the participle is usual (rarely with indic.), § 175, e. (Sometimes καὶ — περ with the emphatic word between. μῶν καὶ θεός περ ἱμέρῳ πεπληγμένος; *Æsch. Aj.* 1125.)

§ 248. γε (Dor. γα).

This is also enclitic, and connected in its origin with *quĭ* in *quidem*, and our *yea.* Its (original) meaning may often be conveyed by *yea,* with repetition of the word to which it is attached: thus, ὡς δ' ὅτ' ἀνὴρ χαλκεὺς πελέκυν ἐν ὕδατι βάπτῃ . . . τὸ γὰρ αὖτε σιδήρου γε κράτος ἐστίν, *for that in the case of steel* (yea, of steel) *is strengthening,* i. e. *of steel indeed* (for in the case of other things it may be weak-

---

[1] Elmsley, Herael. 55, Med. 678, 1275, and Stallbaum, Pl. Lys. 207 D, deny the interrogative use of ἦ που, which Hermann, Opusc. iii. 161, has vindicated.

[APPENDIX.

ening). *πῶς οὐχὶ Σίμων' ἐνέπρησεν, ἀλλὰ τὸν αὐτοῦ γε νεὼν βάλλει; his own temple* (that, of all things!). *εἰ δὲ μὴ ἑκόντες γε, ἀλλ' ἄκοντες, if not willing* (yes, if not that), *yet* —. *ἔγωγε ταῦτα ποιήσω, I* (yes, I: if none other). [§ 248.]

(*a*) When the force of the particle is confined to the *one* word which it accompanies, this force can often be rendered in English by added emphasis, sometimes by *indeed, at least*. In general, any word admitting of emphasis may be followed by γε. Especially pronouns, personal and demonstrative: ἔγωγε (the accent retracted), σύγε, οὗτός γε, ἐκεῖνός γε, ὅδε γε, αὐτός γε: relatives and correlatives, ὅς γε, ὅσος γε, τόσος γε, τοσοῦτός γε (οἷός γε rare in Attic): pronominal adverbs, ὧδέ γε, ὥς γε, ὥστε γε, ὥσπερ γ': νῦν γε: interrogatives, rare in Attic, but not unknown, *τίνος γ' ὑπ' ἄλλου; by whom else? Eur. Hec.* 774. *τίνα γ' . . εἶπας; Troad.* 241. *πῶς γ' ἂν ψέγοις; how indeed? Soph. Œd. C.* 981[1]; negative particles, οὐ — γε, οὐ δή που — γε: μή πω γε: conditionals, εἴ γε (in Trag. most usually εἰ — γε), *certe si, at least if, if indeed, if* (*that is*), &c.: *εἴπερ γε, if really, if really.*—With nouns of every kind, if with article, the γε often attached to it: thus, *τό γ' ἄκον πρᾶγμα, the involuntary deed* (as certainly it was), *Soph. Œd. Col.* 981: and often to the preposition, ἔκ γε τῆσδε γῆς, the emphasis on τῆσδε, *Soph. Tr.* 798: and with verbs, with various kinds of emphasis, *παῦσαί γε, do cease! χρή γε, oportet nempe! behoves, forsooth, aye! ζῶν ἢ θανών γε, living or even dead. ἆρ' οἶσθά γε; thou knowest, aye? ἦ μαίνεταί γε; is he mad even?*

But in all these cases, it should be considered in each particular instance whether the γε is limited to one word, or whether its use comes under the following head:

(*b*) It approaches to the nature of a conjunction, where, attached to one of two sentences or members of a sentence, it virtually belongs to both.

In a reply, containing something additional to the preceding expression, the γε is placed as near as may be to the beginning, with the emphatic word first: *εἴπω τι δῆτα κἄλλο; "Ὅσον γε χρῄζεις," yes,* (and) *as much as you wish, Œd. T.* 364. *τί μέλλεις κομίζειν —; "μαθοῦσά γ' —," why delayest thou to carry —? "yes,* (I will carry) *when I have learnt —," Œd. T.* 680. Τροίαν σ' ἑλεῖν δεῖ. "οὐδέποτέ γ'" (take Troy!) *Never! Phil.* 987. *στεῖχε —. "μήπω γε πρὶν ἂν —"* (yes, go:) *not yet, at least* (however, though) *until —, Phil.* 1409.

Frequent in replies with secondary predicate (participle); e.g. *καλῶς γ' ἐγὼ ποιῶν, "aye, and well too for me to do so," Pl. Rep.* 5, 474. *ὀρθῶς γε σὺ λέγων, Lach.* 192. *ταύτην γ' ἰδὼν θάπτουσαν, yes* (I did it) *because I saw, Soph. Ant.* 400. In explanatory additions: *κλῦθι — εἰ ἐτέον γε σός εἰμι, if, namely* (or, that is) *I am —*. In enumerations: *γενναῖοι ἢ σοφοὶ ἢ τίμιοι ἢ γέροντές γε ἢ νέοι, yes, or old, Pl. Hipp. Maj.* 301. *πρακτέον καὶ γυμναστέον καὶ ἐδεστέον γε καὶ ποτέον, Crito,* 47.

καί γε (only Attic), *et quidem: ἀλλὰ παρῆσάν τινες, καὶ πολλοί γε, Pl. Phæd.* 58. § 249.
καὶ ταῦτά γ' ἄλλα, Soph. Phil. 38. *κρεῖσσον κἀμέ γ', ὦ πάτερ, θανεῖν, even me too, Trach.* 1226. *καὶ — γε πρός, yes and — to boot. καὶ κατακτενῶ γε πρός, Eur. Phœn.* 619. *νὴ τὸν Δί' ἐς κόρακάς γε, καὶ σαυτόν γε πρός, Arist. Pac.* 19. *τὸν ἀδίκως γε ἀποκτείναντα* (sc. ἄθλιόν φημι), *καὶ ἐλεεινόν γε πρός, Pl. Gorg.* 469.

δέ γε: εἰ ἡμέρα ἐστὶν φῶς ἐστιν· ἡμέρα δέ γέ ἐστιν, but it is day. ἐγὼ δέ γ' ἄνδρ' ὄπωπα, Soph. Aj. 1150 (in rejoinder to 1140, *ἤδη ποτ' εἶδον ἄνδρ' ἐγώ, aye, but I too*). *οὐδέ γ' ἐς θυμὸν φέρω, no, not even.*

---

[1] "The particle does not increase the force of the interrogation, but the natural force of the interrogative word." *Klotz.*

[§ 249.] In εἴ γε, *siquidem*, the γε influences the whole clause; in εἰ — γε it distinguishes the interposed word. Τίνι ἄλλῳ τις ἂν εἴη σοφός, εἴ γε μὴ ἐπιστήμῃ; *Pl.* πρώτη θάνοις ἄν, εἰ δίκης γε τυγχάνοις, *Soph.* The same remark applies to ἐπεί γε, *quandoquidem*.

§ 250. γε μήν: ὅρα γε μήν, *look to it, however*, *Soph. Œd. C.* 587. λόγῳ γε μὴν εὔκλειαν, *in word at least, however*, *Soph. El.* 973. τοξικήν γε μήν, *archery, at least, for one thing*, *Pl. Conv.* 197. Εἴς γε μὴν δικαιοσύνην, *In respect, however, of justice*, *Xen. An.* 1, 9, 16: where γε μήν expresses an opposition more strongly than δέ, but with transition to something new: *ib.* § 20, φίλους γε μὴν ὅσους ποιήσαιτο: 7, 6, 15, Ἐπεί γε μὴν ψεύδεσθαι ἤρξατο Σεύθης.

γε δή, *qui-dem*, ἐπεί γε δὴ — ἐκτησάμην, *since it has come to this that —*. ὥσπερ γὰρ —, ταύτῃ γε δὴ —, *in this way, sure enough*, *Pl. Rep.* 330.

γε μὲν δή, preceded by ἐπεί, *Soph. Trach.* 484 (ἐπεί γε, *quandoquidem*), ὅρα γε μὲν δή,[1] *El.* 1242 (cf. γε μήν).

§ 251. γέ τοι (see under τοι), *at least though* (thus much at least is certain, that —). ταύτης δὲ (sc. τῆς) ἀπορίας καὶ σύ μοι δοκεῖς κεκοινωνηκέναι· μεταβαλλόμενος γέ τοι ἄνω καὶ κάτω οὐδ' ὁτιοῦν παύει, *Pl. Alc.* 2, 17. Therefore often preceded by δοκεῖ, and the like: τὸν ἄνδρ' ἔοικεν ὕπνος . . . ἕξειν· κάρα γὰρ ὑπτιάζεται τόδε. ἱδρώς γέ τοί νιν πᾶν καταστάζει δέμας, *at any rate a sweat —*, *Soph. Phil.* 823. ἆρά γε πρὸς τὸν θεὸν προσευξόμενος πορεύει; "Πάνυ μὲν οὖν." φαίνει γέ τοι ἐσκυθρωπακέναι = I guessed as much: *for sure enough you seem*, *Pl. Alc.* 2 init. Ἐπιθυμεῖ Σωκράτης ἀκοῦσαι Γοργίου; Ἐπ' αὐτό γέ τοι τοῦτο πάρεσμεν = (Like enough.) *for to be sure —*. — Φορᾶς γέ τοι φθόνησις οὐ γενήσεται, *the carrying indeed, as far as that goes*, *Soph. Trach.* 1212. Ἀλλὰ — γέ τοι, after a condition: ἐγὼ δὲ σὸς, κεἰ μὴ σὸς, ἀλλὰ — σός γέ τοι καλούμενος, *certe tamen*. Εἰ δ' ἐν πᾶσι τούτοις ἡττώμεθα, ἀλλὰ τό γέ τοι πῦρ τοῦ καρποῦ κρεῖττόν ἐστιν, *Xen. An.* 2, 5, 19. — Often with δή added: thus (in answer to a question), φασί γέ τοι δή οἱ τούτων κύριοι, *yes, at least this is quite certain that —*, *Pl. Crito*, 44. κείνου γέ τοι δὴ παῖς ἐκλῄζετο, *Soph. Œd. T.* 1171.

γε μέντοι, *yet — at least*. τούς γε μέντοι ἀγαθούς, *yet the brave withal*, *Xen. An.* 1, 9, 14.

τοι.

§ 252. This enclitic, derived from το — (connected with *tamen* and *though*), is originally demonstrative, and by individualizing restricts and excludes.

The original demonstrative force appears especially in rousing exclamations: σέ τοι, σὲ κρίνω, ναί σε, *thee there* (thee only), *Soph. El.* 1445, so *Aj.* 1228: and other pointed allocutions, σύ τοι, σύ τοι κατηξίωσας, *thou*, *thou* alone —, *Phil.* 1095: and with emphatic pronouns, ἐγώ τοι, ἔγωγέ τοι, *I, for my part*. ἐγώ τοι οὐκ ἀμφισβητῶ, *I, be sure of that —*, *Pl. Hipp. Maj.* 369. ταῦτά τοι, *this and this only*. ταῦτά τοί σ' ἔχθει πόλις, *therefore*, and reason enough *that*, — *Eur. Androm.* 212. It is frequent in replies, in the sense *be sure of that! never fear!* Ἀλλὰ — ταχύ τοι ἀποκρινοῦμαι, *Xen. An.* 6, 4 (al. 6), 34. εἰρήσεταί τοι, *it shall be spoken* (*rely upon that!*), *Eur. Ion*, 760. ὅρα κατ' ὄρφνην μὴ φύλαξιν ἐντύχῃς. "Φυλάξομαί τοι," *Eur. Hipp.* 567. — ἴσθι τοι τίσουσά γ' ἀξίαν δίκην, *be sure though*, *Soph. El.* 290.

This particle is especially frequent in gnomes, maxims, and general reflexions, in the sense, *sure enough that!* Μῆτί τοι δρυτόμος μέγ' ἀμείνων, ἠὲ βίηφιν, *Il.* 23, 315.

---

[1] Ellendt adopts Blomfield's ὅρα γε μέντοι on the ground that μὲν δή *de rebus adhuc faciendis non dicatur*: which is not true.

[§ 252.]

τοῖς τοι δικαίοις χὠ βραχὺς νικᾳ μέγαν, *Soph. Œd. C.* 884. κάρτα τοι φιλοίκτιστον γυνή, *Aj.* 577. ἡδύ τοι ἀνδρεῖόν τι καὶ καλὸν νῦν εἰπόντα καὶ ποιήσαντα μνήμην — παρέχειν ἑαυτοῦ, *Xen. An.* 6, 3 (al. 5), 24. ἥ τοι τῆς διανοίας ὄψις ἄρχεται ὀξὺ βλέπειν, ὅταν ἡ τῶν ὀμμάτων τῆς ἀκμῆς λήγειν ἐπιχειρῇ, *Pl. Conv.* 219.

§ 253.

καί τοι, properly "and that" (an accession qualified by *though*, or "also this" viz. "to be considered"): hence especially frequent in the corrective sense, *tamen certe*, or *attamen*, and *quamquam*. ἀλλὰ κἀμέ τοι (*me also, though*) ταὐτὸν τόδ' ὄψει δρῶντα κοὐ μέλλοντα ἔτι. καί τοι σ' ἐάσω, *yet*, or, *however, I will let thee go*, *Soph. Phil.* 1255. καίτοι τί φημι; *quamquam quid loquor, what am I saying though!* ὦ Θάνατε, Θάνατε, νῦν μ' ἐπίσκεψαι μολών· καίτοι σὲ μὲν κἀκεῖ προσαυδήσω ξυνών· σὲ δ' —, *Ai.* 854. Ἀλλὰ ἰόντων (*Well, let them go*) —, καίτοι ἔχω γε αὐτῶν καὶ τέκνα —, *and yet* (= take *this also* into the account). With secondary predicates: οὐδέ μοι ἐμμελέως τὸ Πιττάκειον νέμεται, καίτοι σοφοῦ παρὰ φωτὸς εἰρημένον, *quamvis a viro sapiente dictum*, *Pl. Prot.* 339. The force is explained by resolving καί τοι into καὶ — εἰρημένον, καὶ (οὐδ') ὧς (= τῶς, οὕτως). A stronger expression of this sense is καὶ ταῦτα: τοιαῦτα — ὕβρισεν, καὶ ταῦτα τηλικοῦτος, *and that too —! Soph. El.* 614: even with the finite verb, though rarely, καὶ ταῦτα κούφως ἐκ μέσων ἀρκυστάτων ὤρουσεν, *Æsch. Eum.* 112. Placed at the end of the sentence: Νῦν γοῦν ἐπεχείρησας, οὐδὲν ὢν καὶ ταῦτα, *being nothing worth* (yet), *even so* (for all that!), *Pl. Rep.* 341.

In καίτοι γε, the γε belongs to the whole sentence: καίτοι γε ὀφειλόμενόν που ἐστι τοῦτο ὃ παρακατέθετο, *and yet to be sure* (it is true that —), *Pl. Rep.* 331 fin. In καίτοι — γε, the γε belongs to the interposed word: καίτοι τοσοῦτόν γ' οἶδα, *though indeed thus much at least I know*, *Soph. Œd. T.* 1455.

Often followed by ἀλλ' ὅμως, which, again, illustrates the original force of καίτοι = καὶ ὧς (τῶς): καίτοι οὐδὲν ὅ τι οὐκ ἀληθὲς εἴρηκα ὧν προεῖπον· ἀλλ' ὅμως —, = *yet for all that:* the thing is *even so* (καὶ τῶς), yet *even so* (ὅμως), *Pl. Euthyph.* 3. καίτοι φασὶν Ἰφικράτην — ἐλθεῖν εἰς ἔχθραν· ἀλλ' ὅμως —, *Dem. Mid.* 41, Buttm.

§ 254.

μέντοι = *for one thing, this*. In rousing exclamations, like τοι: οὗτος, σὲ λέγω μέντοι, σὲ τὸν τεθνηκότα. — Usually it may be rendered *however, to be sure*, with an opposition to something preceding: ἔπειτα μέντοι, *anon however* (*though*). μάλιστα μὲν δὴ —· ἔπειτα μέντοι, *Soph. Phil.* 350. τὸ μὲν πρῶτον ὤκνει —, ἔπειτα μέντοι εἶπεν, *Pl. Charm.* 159.[1] In affirmative answers (§ 199 c, R. 2): φαμέν τι εἶναι δίκαιον αὐτὸ ἢ οὐδέν; "φαμὲν μέντοι, νὴ Δία," *we affirm it, to be sure* (true enough *that*), *Pl. Phæd.* 65. οὐ πολλὴ ἂν ἀλογία εἴη; "πολλὴ μέντοι νὴ Δία," *ib.* 68. — Εἰ γὰρ ῥέοι τὸ σῶμα καὶ ἀπολλύοιτο —, ἀναγκαῖον μέντ' ἂν εἴη —, *to be sure, it would be necessary*, *ib.* 87. Σὸς μέντοι Σιμωνίδης πολίτης· δίκαιος εἶ βοηθεῖν τῷ ἀνδρί, *to be sure, S. is your countryman, you are bound to stand up for him*, *Pl. Prot.* 339 fin. Δῆλον ὅτι Σεύθης — ἀπαιτήσει με, καὶ ἀπαιτήσει μέντοι δικαίως, *and for the matter of that* —, *Xen. An.* 7, 6, 17. So *An.* 4, 6, 15, 16, ἐπιδείξασθαι τὴν παιδείαν καὶ φυλάξασθαι μέντοι (*withal*) μὴ ληφθῶμεν κλέπτοντες . . . Ἀλλὰ μέντοι (*well, for the matter of that*, i. e. talking of stealing) καὶ ἐγὼ ὑμᾶς ἀκούω τοὺς Ἀθ. δεινοὺς εἶναι κλέπτειν τὰ δημόσια — καὶ τοὺς κρατίστους μέντοι (*and your best men withal*). — In questions with οὐ, *nonne?* having the force of an affirmation: οἱ ἀντίδικοι τί δρῶσιν; οὐκ ἀντιλέγουσι μέντοι; *they oppose each other, to be sure, don't they? Pl. Phæd.* 261. οὐ τῶν καλῶν μέντοι ἡ σωφροσύνη ἐστί; *Pl. Charm.* 159.

---

[1] Stallb. Pl. Phæd. 266, says, that a preceding μέν requires μέντοι to follow, not μὲν δή.

[§ 254.] καὶ μέντοι = καὶ μήν together with καίτοι (corrective): *Pl. Alc.* 1, 113. ἐμὲ δὲ αἰτιᾷ μάτην. καὶ μέντοι καὶ εὖ λέγεις,[1] *and yet, to be sure, you do' say well.* Similarly, ἀλλὰ μέντοι, οὐ μέντοι (οὐ not interrogative), οὐ μέντοι οὐδέ —. Comp. οὐ μὴν ἀλλὰ — with οὐ μέντοι ἀλλὰ (καί), *yet no! but* — = *attamen, verumtamen.* Βούλει οὖν — ἐπιχειρήσωμεν —; "Πάνυ μὲν οὖν. οὐ μέντοι ἀλλ' ἔγωγε ἐκεῖνο ἂν ἥδιστα — ἀκούσαιμι," *not so, though; but* —, *Pl. Meno*, § 22 init.

γε μέντοι is a frequent combination, where both particles severally claim the second place in the sentence: thus, τούς γε μέντοι ἀγαθοὺς εἰς πόλεμον ὡμολόγητο διαφερόντως τιμᾶν, *Xen. An.* 1, 9, 14, the sentence being compounded of τούς γε ἀγ. and τοὺς μέντοι ἀγ. So οἶμαί γε μέντοι, ἔφη. But when the first word does not admit γε, but does admit μέντοι, the order is changed: thus, λέγουσι μέν τι· οὐ μέντοι γε ὅσον οἴονται, *Pl. Rep.* 329. οὐ μέντοι ταχύ γε ἀπαγγελῶ, *Xen. An.* 2, 3, 9.

On γέ τοι, see § 251.

§ 255. ἤτοι, comp. of ἤ and τοι, is epic:[2] *verily, assuredly:* ὦ φίλοι, ἤτοι κλῆρος ἐμός: often ἤτοι μέν. Sometimes in oppositions: ἤτοι Νεστορίδην —, Τηλέμαχον δ' —, *Od.* 15, 6. ἤτοι Ὀδυσσεὺς ὕστερος, αὐτὰρ Τηλέμαχος πρόσθ' ἡγεμόνευεν, 24, 154.

In the alternative ἤ — ἤ, the Attics often add τοι to the first ἤ. ἤτοι κλύουσα παιδὸς ἢ τύχῃ πάρα, *Soph. Ant.* 1182, *Trach.* 149. ἤτοι ὅλου τοῦ εἴδους ἢ μέρους ἑκάστου, *Pl. Parm.* 131. Often with γε added: ἤτοι θεούς γε ἡγούμεθα ἢ θεῶν παῖδας, *Apol.* 27. ἤτοι ἐπιστάμενοί γε — ἢ ὕστερον, *Phaed.* 76. In *Rep.* 344, E, ἔοικας — ἤτοι ἡμῶν γε οὐδὲν κήδεσθαι, the first ἤ is suppressed, the sense being, *or* (*else*) *in that case, you do not care for us at all.*

§ 256. οὔτοι, *not — though, surely not:* οὔτοι — γε: οὔτἄρα: usually at the beginning of a sentence, or preceded by ἀλλά.

μήτοι (the prohibitive μή), *do not — though:* μήτοι τις ἡμᾶς — θορυβήσῃ, *Pl. Rep.* 438. μήτοι — γε: μήτοι γε in aposiopesis, *Xen. Cyr.* 2, 3, 24. Μὰ Δί', ἔφη ὁ ταξίαρχος, μήτοι γε ἐν μιᾷ γε ἡμέρᾳ, *not in one day though:* often (in the same sense μή τι γε) = *nedum*, αὐτοὺς ἐποίει, μήτοι καὶ ἀλλήλους γε, — ἀδικεῖν, *not to say one another, Pl. Rep.* 352. μήτοι θεούς γε, — εἰ δ' οὖν θεούς, μήτοι τόν γε μέγιστον τῶν θεῶν, *ib.* 388. Sometimes μήτοι γε δή.

§ 257. ῥα and ἄρ (Epic), ἄρα.[3]

a) ῥα enclitic, ἄρ the same inverted, and also ἄρα,[4] are often attached (in epic poetry) to relatives and demonstratives, particles and conjunctions, at the beginning of a sentence or clause of a sentence, with a notion of progress or sequence, which is

---

[1] Not simply καὶ μήν, as Buttm. in l.

[2] But Soph. Œd. C. 1366, ἢ τἂν οὐκ ἂν ἦ = ἢ τοι ἄν, and El. 498, ἤ τοι or ἤ τοι.

[3] The supposed derivation from ἄρω (Kühner, Nägelsb., Stallbaum) explains *some* of the facts (see *Il.* 14, 511, and the preceding vss.); more satisfactory is that (cf. Hartung) which connects the simple ῥα (ἄρ) with the verbal root, denoting easy or sudden motion, which appears in ῥέω, ῥέα, and ῥᾴδιος, *rapio*, *repente* (applied to mental action in *reor*, *ratus*), *rite*, and with the suffix in comparatives and comparative words, δεινότερος, πότερος, *alter*(*o*), δεῦρο, *ultro*, *intra*, ἡμέτερος, *longer*, *other*, *either*, *hither*, *our*, &c. *nostr*(*o*). On this view, ἄ-ρα is the pronominal root ἀ — (ἀ-πό, ἀ-νά, ἀ priv., ἀ-τὰρ, ἄ-τερ, &c.) compounded with ῥα.

[4] But in numberless passages, a slight alteration will give ῥα or ἄρ where the edited text has ἄρα, ἄρ'.

[APPENDIX.

sometimes perceptible, but often so slight that the particle might as well be absent, and seems only intended to help the metre or to close an hiatus. Thus we find, indifferently, *ὣς ἔφαν* and *ὣς ἄρ' ἔφαν*, never *ὣς ῥ' ἔφαν* or *ὣς ῥ' ἔφατ'*: *ὣς ἔφατ', οἱ δ' ἄρα* and *ὣς ἔφατ', οἱ δέ*: *οἱ δ' ὅτε δή ῥ' ἵκοντο* and *οἱ δ' ὅτε δὴ σχεδὸν ἦσαν*: *τῶν μὲν ἄρ' Ἀμφίμαχος* and *τῶν μὲν Ὀδυσσεύς*: *οἵ τ' ἄρ' Ἀμύκλας εἶχον* and *οἵ τ' ἔχον Αἴγιναν*: *δὴ τότε* and *δή ῥα τότ'*. — *Ὣς ἔφατ'· ἔδδεισεν δὲ —, καί ῥ' ἀκέουσα καθῆστο*, with reference to the preceding command, *ἀλλ' ἀκέουσα κάθησο*, *Il.* 1, 565-8. *τίς τ' ἄρ σφωε θεῶν ἔριδι ξυνέηκε μάχεσθαι; and who then —*, with ref. to *διαστήτην ἐρίσαντε*, *Il.* 1, 6. 8. — It frequently appears in one member of an alternative: *ἤ ῥα — ἤ*, — *εἴτ' ἄρα — εἴτε*, *οὔτ' ἄρα — οὔτε*; or correlation, *τόσσον — ὅσσον ἄρ'*, *ἦμος — τῆμος ἄρ'*: or opposition, *μέν ῥα — δέ* (*ἀλλά*, *αὐτάρ*): *οὐκ — ἀλλ' ἄρα*. Also *ὅττι ῥα*, *ἐπεί ῥα*, *οὕνεκ' ἄρα*, *ὅτε ῥα*, *ὅτε* and *τότε δή ῥα*. *γάρ ῥα*. *ἦ ῥα* (*verily*): *οὐκ* and *οὐδ' ἄρα*, *εἰ μὴ ἄρ'*. [§ 257.]

b) This use is less frequent with other words: it is found, however, in primary sentences after some monosyllabic verbs: *ἦ ῥα, so spake he; βῆ ῥ' ἴμεν* and *αὐτὰρ ὁ βῆ ῥ' ἰέναι*, *Il.* 21, 205 (even not at the beginning of a sentence, *μετὰ δὲ κλειτοὺς ἐπικούρους βῆ ῥα μέγα ἰάχων*, *Il.* 17, 215): more frequently in apodosis, *αὐτὰρ ἐπειδὴ —, βῆ ῥ' ἴμεν*, and *ἀλλ' ὅτε δή ῥα —, γνῶ ῥ' ἄνδρας*, *Il.* 10, 357. *αὐτὰρ ἐπειδὴ τεῦξε σάκος —, τεῦξ' ἄρα οἱ θώρηκα*, *Il.* 18, 609. *αὐτὰρ ἐπεὶ —, εἶατ' ἄρ'*. *Il.* 22, 127. *οἱ δ' ἐπεὶ οὖν —, στῆσαν ἄρ'*, *Il.* 24, 349. Similarly, *ἤτοι ὅγ' ὣς εἰπὼν, κατ' ἄρ' ἕζετο*, *Il.* 1, 101: and with the participle, *τὸν δ' ὡς οὖν —, κινήσας ῥα κάρη*, *Il.* 17, 198. Rarely with substantives: *Αἴας ῥα πρῶτος*, *Il.* 14, 511. *ἀσπὶς ἄρ' ἀσπίδ' ἔρειδε*, *Il.* 16, 201. With preposition: *τοῦ δ' ὡς οὖν —, μετ' ἄρα δμωῇσιν ἔειπεν*, *Od.* 17, 493.

c) *ἄρα* (not *ῥα*) denotes subjective consequence, *so then —! why, then —! it appears*, or, *turns out!* always with a feeling of surprise, of finding oneself mistaken and, agreeably or disagreeably, undeceived. This use is known to Homer: *Ἕκτορ, εἶδος ἄριστε, μάχης ἄρα πολλὸν ἐδεύεο*, *Il.* 17, 142. *σχέτλιε, Πηλέος υἱὲ, χόλῳ ἄρα σ' ἔτρεφε μήτηρ*, *Il.* 16, 203. *οἷσιν ἄρα Ζεὺς ἐκ νεότητος ἔδωκε καὶ ἐς γῆρας τολυπεύειν*, *Il.* 14, 85. *νηλεὲς, οὐκ ἄρα σοίγε πατὴρ ἦν ἱππότα Πηλεύς*, &c., *Il.* 16, 33. — So *Hdt.* 1, 111, *πυνθάνομαι — ὡς ἄρα Μανδάνης τε εἴη παῖς, that after all* (or, *who would have thought it!*) — In this sense, *ἄρα* is very frequent in the Attic writers of poetry and prose. *οὐκ ἐνενοήσαμεν ὅτι εἰσὶν ἄρα τοιαῦται φύσεις, οἵας ἡμεῖς οὐκ ᾠήθημεν*, *Pl. Rep.* 375. *ὦ παῖδες, ὡς ἄρα ἐφλυαροῦμεν, ὅτε —, how, as it now appears, we did trifle —!* *Xen. Cyr.* 1, 4, 11. *ἐμοὶ, ὦ ἄνδρες, θυομένῳ — οὐκ ἐγίγνετο τὰ ἱερά. καὶ εἰκότως ἄρα οὐκ ἐγίγνετο· ὡς γὰρ ἐγὼ νῦν πυνθάνομαι —, and with good reason, as the result has shown*, *Xen. An.* 2, 2, 3. *μάτην ἄρ' ἡμεῖς, ὡς ἔοικεν, ἥκομεν, why then it appears —*, *Soph. El.* 762. *ὅτ' οὐκέτ' εἰμί, τηνικαῦτ' ἄρ' εἴμ' ἀνήρ*, *Œd. C.* 391. *οὕτω κοινόν τι ἄρα χαρᾷ καὶ λύπῃ δάκρυά ἐστιν!* *Xen. Hell.* 7, 1, 32. Hence the use of the imperfect, *ὅδ' ἦν ἄρα —, this then is he —!* (he was so all along, as it now turns out), *Soph. Phil.* 966. *καὶ ἐνενόησα τότε ἄρα καταγέλαστος ὤν, ἡνίκα — ἔφην —. οὐδὲν εἰδὼς ἄρα τοῦ πράγματος —. ἐγὼ μὲν γὰρ ὑπ' ἀβελτερίας ᾤμην —. τὸ δὲ ἄρα, οὐ τοῦτο ἦν —, ἀλλὰ —. εἰ δὲ ψευδῆ, οὐδὲν ἄρ' ἦν πρᾶγμα, ... ἀλλὰ γὰρ ἐγὼ οὐκ ᾔδη ἄρα —*, *Pl. Conv.* 198 C—E. Sometimes in the middle of a sentence: *πολλὰ καὶ ἀγαθὰ τὴν πόλιν πεποιηκότες ἄρα ἀδίκως ὑπ' αὐτῆς ἀπόλλυνται, ὡς ὁ τούτων λόγος*, *Pl. Gorg.* 519. *ὡς δὲ ταῦτα γελοῖά ἐστι, κατάδηλον ἔσται, ἐὰν μὴ πολλοῖς ὀνόμασι χρώμεθα ἄρα, ἡδεῖ τε καὶ ἀνιαρῷ καὶ ἀγαθῷ καὶ κακῷ*, *Pl. Prot.* 355.

On *ἄρα* in sentences with *μέν — δέ*, see § 189 *a*.

In interrogations it denotes surprise, perplexity, or impatience: *τίς ἄρα ῥύσεται; τίς ἄρ' ἐπαρκέσει θεῶν ἢ θεᾶν;* *Eur.* § 258.

[§ 258.] In exclamations, ἄρα, τίς ἄρ' ἦν; (in disappointment at not finding the person who was expected;) *Soph. Œd. C.* 118, πῶς πότε — πῶς ἄρα; *Phil.* 684, ὡς οὐκ ἄρ' ᾔδη —! *how ignorant, it seems, I was! El.* 1176. So εἰ and εἰ μὴ ἄρα —, *if* (or, *unless*), *which I do not expect*, &c.: ποταμὸς δ' εἰ μέν τις καὶ ἄλλος ἄρα ἡμῖν ἐστι διαβατέος, οὐκ οἶδα, *if it should turn out that there is* —, *Xen. An.* 2, 4, 6. εἴτε — εἴτ' ἄρα, *whether — or* (should such unexpectedly be the case). With ὡς, "that," it is often ironical: ὡς ἄρα οἱ πρόγονοι μεγάλα εὖ παθόντες οὐδένα ἐτίμησαν, *that it should seem forsooth* —, *Dem.*

§ 259. Peculiarities: ταῦτα δὴ καὶ οἱ ἄλλοι πάντες ἄρα ξυνέφασαν, *Pl. Conv.* 177. The force may be expressed by, *they could but assent*: ταῦτα ἀκούσας ὁ Κῦρος ἐπαίσατο ἄρα (*in his surprise*) τὸν μηρόν, *Xen. Cyr.* 7, 3, 6. Σακῶν δὲ ἰδιώτης ἀνὴρ ἀπέλιπεν ἄρα (*to the surprise of everybody*) τῷ ἵππῳ τοὺς ἀλλοὺς ἐγγὺς τῷ ἡμίσει τοῦ δρόμου, *Xen. Cyr.* 8, 3, 25. ὥστε ἐπεὶ ἐδεδειπνήκεσαν, καὶ τὰ πάντα πολλὰ ὄντα διαπεπόμφει ὁ Κῦρος ἀπὸ τῆς τραπέζης, εἶπεν ἄρα ὁ Γωβρύας· Ἀλλ' ἐγώ, ὦ Κῦρε, πρόσθεν μὲν ἡγούμην — (*said in his surprise*, or, *could not help saying*), *Xen. Cyr.* 8, 4, 7. In some places, the sense *as it turned out* subsides into *in fact*, or, *it should be remarked that*: "Σάκᾳ δὲ . . . οὐδὲν δίδως;" ὁ δὲ Σάκας ἄρα —, *now Sacas*, it should be observed, *was*, &c. (or, it would turn out upon enquiry, that —). So, in explanation of a preceding speech, οἱ δ' ἄρα τῶν βασιλέων οἰνοχόοι . . . . , *Xen. Cyr.* 1, 3, 9.

§ 260. γάρ, (*nam*) *namely, for.*

Being a form of γε with the suffix ῥα, ἄρ, this particle denotes an *affirmation* (γε) which is *explanatory* (ῥα) of something else: sometimes the notion of explanation predominates, sometimes the affirmation.

a) It is little more than merely explanatory = *namely*, after demonstratives and short sentences, such as σημεῖον δέ, δῆλον δέ· δείκνυμι δέ, σκέψασθε δέ, &c. (in which there is always a demonstrative, e. g. ἐνθένδε, ἐντεῦθεν, &c. implied.) See examples in § 196, and R., to which add· οὐκοῦν τοσοῦτον μὲν ἡμῖν εἰς τὸ πρόσθεν πεπέρανται; ὃ γὰρ ἔσμεν, ἐπιεικῶς ὡμολόγηται, *Pl. Alc. pr.* 132, *thus much, namely* —. δοκεῖ τοίνυν μοι, ἔφη, χαριέστερον εἶναι μῦθον ὑμῖν λέγειν. Ἦν γάρ ποτε, where the demonstrative is not expressed: *to tell you a story. Namely* —, *Pl. Prot.* 320.

b) The affirmative force predominates in replies: ἔλεγες; ἔλεγον γάρ, *why yes, I did.* αἱ μητέρες τὰ παιδία μὴ ἐκδειματούντων. Μὴ γάρ, ἔφη (*Pl.*), *why yes* (you say true): *they ought not* = *why no.*

c) Very often, especially in Herodot. and Thucyd., the explanatory clause with γάρ is premised to the thing explained: see § 196 *b*, and on the ellipsis in ἀλλὰ γάρ, ἀλλ' οὐ γάρ, see under Ἀλλά. — On καὶ γάρ, see under Καί, § 225.

d) The γάρ in interrogations may be referred to *a*) = "is this, *namely*, what you mean to say?" or *b*) = "*aye*, is it so?" In many places it may be referred to a preceding assertion: thus, ὄλωλε γάρ; = ὄλωλεν; οὕτω γὰρ λέγεις. — To this head belong the interrogative replies equivalent to assertions: πῶς γάρ; *for how* can it be so? = *how so! by no means*: πῶς γὰρ οὔ; *for how* can it be *not* so? = *to be sure, undoubtedly*: ἦ γάρ; οὐ γάρ; *is it not so!* (which are sometimes inserted in the middle of a sentence (especially by later Atticists): καλήν γε (οὐ γάρ;) τὴν ἀμοιβὴν ἀποδώσομεν.

§ 261. Τί γάρ; sometimes, like *quid?*, is a formula of transition to a new question. Οὐκοῦν πρῶτον μὲν ἀναβατικωτέρους ἐπὶ τοὺς ἵππους ποιήσεις αὐτούς; Δεῖ γοῦν, ἔφη. Τί γάρ; ἐάν που κινδυνεύειν δέῃ, πότερον —; *Xen.* In reply to a preceding question, it is a form of assent, ἄλλο understood (cf. τί μήν under μήν, § 231) = "(yes;) *for what*

[APPENDIX.

(else is it, if not as you say)?" It may be rendered, *why not? certainly, undoubtedly*, or, after a negative assertion or question, *certainly not*. τοῦτο μὲν ἄρα παντὶ δῆλον, ὅτι οὐκ αἰσχρὸν τὸ γράφειν λόγους. Τί γάρ; *why should it be?* = of course it is not. Μενέλαε, προσφθέγγει νιν ἀνόσιον κάρα; "τί γάρ; φίλος μοι πατρός ἐστιν ἔκγονος."

In γὰρ ἄν, οὐ γὰρ ἄν, there is sometimes a reference to a suppressed condition: οὐ φιλεῖς με, ὦ θύγατερ, οὐ γὰρ ἂν ἐμὲ ἀπεκρύπτου τὰ σὰ πάθη, *for (if you did) you would not* —. τούτου ἐνδεᾶ ἐφαίνετο· βίᾳ γὰρ ἂν εἷλον τὸ χωρίον, *for* (had it been otherwise —), *Thuc.*

ἆρα.

This (Attic) particle represents the Epic ἦ ῥα, or rather ἦ ἄρα,[1] and is described by ancient grammarians as σύνδεσμος ἀπορηματικός, denoting perplexity together with surprise; most commonly in interrogations, but sometimes also in exclamations.

In questions, the meaning is, *surely it should seem* (or, *it turns out*, &c.)? or, *aye, then —?* or, *I wonder whether —?* the interrogative force residing, not so much in the particle itself, as in the tone of the utterance: τί φῶ; ἆρ' ἔστιν; ἆρ' οὐκ ἔστιν; ἢ γνώμη πλανᾷ; καὶ φημὶ κἀπόφημι, κοὐκ ἔχω τί φῶ, *Soph. Œd. C.* 315. ἆρ' Ὀδυσσέως κλύω; *can it be that —? Phil.* 964. Ἆρα, ἔφη, ὦ ἄνδρες, νῦν μὲν καιρὸς διαλυθῆναι; *I should think it would be time —? Xen. Cyr.* 7, 5, 40. Sometimes in the middle of a sentence: Ἄδμητον ἐν δόμοισιν ἆρα κιγχάνω; *I wonder whether —? Eur. Alc.* 495. Very often it introduces an interrogation dependent on a preceding verb, but always in the form of *oratio recta*: σκεψώμεθα ἆρα λύπη ὑπερβάλλει τὸ ἀδικεῖν; (as if it were εἰ ἄρα). *Pl. Gorg.* 475. δεῖ ἄρα — σκοπεῖν, ἆρα τεχνικός ἐστιν —; *Pl. Lach.* 185. ἐπισκέψασθαι, ἆρα ἃ νῦν δὴ διήλθομεν — ἁρμόττει; *Pl. Rep.* 462. (Cf. § 199 c, R. 1.)

In ἆρά γε, the interrogator believes, or pretends to believe, that the thing is as he says: Ὁ δὲ δὴ ἀὴρ ἆρά γε . . . ὅτι αἴρει τὰ ἀπὸ τῆς γῆς, ἀὴρ κέκληται, *I should say that —? Pl. Crat.* 410.—Ἆρ' οὖν —; *I presume, then —?* either where no answer is expected, but the speaker passes on to some further view of the subject, or where the question is grounded on what goes before (according to the two leading uses of οὖν, § 264, a, b).

Ἆρ' οὐ —; expects an affirmative, ἆρα μή —; a negative answer. ἆρ' οὐ μωρόν ἐστι; = *can it be, that it is not foolish?* meaning, that it would be surprising if the thing were *not* so. ἆρα μὴ δοκεῖς; *surely you do not imagine?* = *can it be, that there is reason to apprehend your imagining?* (Cf. § 199 b.)

In the poets, ἆρα sometimes occurs in exclamations, in the same sense as ἄρα: οἴμοι ταλαίνης ἆρα τῆσδε συμφορᾶς, *Soph. El.* 1170. τοιοῖσδε χρησμοῖς ἆρα χρὴ πεποιθέναι, *Æsch. Choeph.* 281.

οὖν, Ionic ὦν.

This word is explained (by Hartung) as accusative αὖν of αὖς, a Cretan and Laced. form of αὐτός. Hence its original force = "the same," "all one." (Others make it = ἐόν, ὄν, so that the primary sense is *ut nunc est.*)

a) Originally οὖν appears only as an adjunct to pronouns and conjunctions. In Homer it occurs only so; chiefly with ἐπεί and ὡς (also οὔτ' οὖν, and γοῦν): αἵ τ' (*the cranes*) ἐπεὶ οὖν χειμῶνα φύγον καὶ ἀθέσφατον ὄμβρον, κλαγγῇ ταίγε πέτονται, *at what same time*, i. e. *no sooner have they* —, *Il.* 3, 4. τὸν δ' ὡς οὖν ἐνόησε, *ib.* 21 and 30,

[1] Or, possibly, εἰ ἄρα, when, as is most usual, it is interrogative. Cf. the instances where it depends on a verb of considering, &c.

[§ 264.] and frequently: *αἴτ'* (*the fawns*) *ἐπεὶ οὖν ἔκαμον —, ἑστᾶσι*, *Il.* 4, 243. In Attic writers, *ὅστις, ὅσπερ, ὅσος, ὁποῖος*, &c., *οὖν*, with their adverbial forms *ὅπῃ, ὥσπερ*, &c. *οὖν*, all in the sense of the Lat. *—cunque*: e. g. *γυναῖκα πιστὴν δ' ἐν δόμοις εὕροι μολὼν οἵανπερ οὖν ἔλειπεν*, *such exactly* (*περ*), *whatever that might be* (Clytæmn. is speaking of herself), *Æsch. Ag.* 565. *πῶς λέγεις; ἔστι γὰρ ὁτιοῦν πρᾶγμα ὁτῳδὴ ὁπωσοῦν ἔχοντι ἄμεινον ἀγνοεῖν ἢ γιγνώσκειν*; fully, *anything, no matter what it may be, to any person soever, no matter in what condition*, *Pl. Alc.* 2, 143. *ὅπερ οὖν οὐδεὶς ἂν οἰηθείη*, *just what* (*without more ado about it, without question*), *ib.*[1] *τοὐδέ σοι μέλειν ἐφίεθ' ἀνὴρ κεῖνος, ὥσπερ οὖν μέλει*, *Soph. Aj.* 970. *εἰ δ' ἔστιν, ὥσπερ οὖν ἔστιν*, *Pl. Phædr.* 242, with the same notion of *indifference*, not caring to argue the point further.[2]

b) In its *consecutive* use, *οὖν* = *thus, then, accordingly, such being the case*: *ἔδοξεν οὖν μοι*. Hence frequent in resumptions, after interposed matter, *κατανοῶν δὲ ὁ Κῦρος ὡς . . . . , ἐκ τούτων οὖν* (*I say*, or, *so then*) *ἐπεθύμει*, *Xen. Cyr.* 3, 3, 9. — In poetry, often between the preposition and its noun, *ἐν οὖν ῥοπῇ τοιᾷδε*, *Soph. Tr.* 82.

§ 265. In Herodot. *ὦν* (*οὖν*) is frequently placed between a preposition and its verb: thus, *ἤν τις ψαύσῃ παριὼν ὑὸς, αὐτοῖσι ἱματίοισι κατ' ὦν ἔβαψε ἑωυτόν*, 2, 47. (On the death of any person of note) *τὸ θῆλυ γένος πᾶν τὸ ἐκ τῶν οἰκίων τούτων κατ' ὦν ἐπλάσατο τὴν κεφαλὴν πηλῷ*, *ib.* 85. (In embalming) *παρασχίσαντες παρὰ τὴν λαπάρην, ἐξ ὦν εἷλον τὴν κοιλίαν πᾶσαν*, *ib.* 86. (In making boats) *νομεῦσιν οὐδὲν χρέωνται, ἔσωθεν δὲ τὰς ἁρμονίας ἐν ὦν ἐπάκτωσαν τῇ βίβλῳ*, *ib.* 96. (In sacrificing) *καὶ ἔπειτα βρόχῳ περὶ ὦν ἔβαλε τὸν αὐχένα*, 4, 60: usually, as in these instances, with the aorist, in descriptions of a customary process: the force seems to be, *without more ado, straightway*;[3] comp. the Homeric *οὖν* in the relative member.

§ 266. With *ἀλλά, ἀτάρ, δέ*, it has a force resembling that of *ὅμως*: *but, however* (= *all one for that*), *ἀλλ' οὖν τοσοῦτόν γ' ἴσθι*, *Soph. Ph.* 1289. *ἔστω δ' οὖν ὅπως ὑμῖν φίλον*, *Œd. C.* 1207. *καὶ ἐλέχθησαν λόγοι ἄπιστοι μὲν ἐνίοισι Ἑλλήνων, ἐλέχθησαν δ' ὦν*, *but spoken they were, all the same*, *Hdt.* *εἰ δ' οὖν, φιλεῖ γὰρ τοῦτο μὴ ταύτῃ ῥέπειν*, with aposiopesis, viz. *ἄλλῃ ῥέπει*, *Soph. Ant.* 722.

In alternatives, *εἴτ' οὖν — εἴτε*, the *οὖν* implies that, whichever side be taken, it comes to the same thing: *οὐκοῦν δαιμόνια μὲν φῄς με καὶ νομίζειν καὶ διδάσκειν, εἴτ' οὖν καινὰ, εἴτε παλαιά· ἀλλ' οὖν δαιμόνιά γε νομίζω κατὰ τὸν σὸν λόγον*, *Pl. Apol.* 27 (comp. *ἤτοι — ἤ*, § 255): with *οὖν* in the second member, *λέγοντες εἴτ' ἀληθὲς, εἴτ' ἄρ' οὖν ματήν*, or, *for aught I care —*, *Soph. Phil.* 345: in both members, *καὶ τοῦτο τοὔνομα ἔχοντα, εἴτ' οὖν ἀληθὲς εἴτ' οὖν ψεῦδος· ἀλλ' οὖν δεδογμένον γέ ἐστι τὸν Σωκράτη διαφέρειν τινὶ τῶν ἄλλων ἀνθρώπων*, *Pl. Apol.* 34 fin. So *οὔτ'* (*μήτ'*) *οὖν*: *οὔτε γὰρ θρασὺς, οὔτ' οὖν προδείσας εἰμί*. *Soph. Œd. C.* 90. *μήτ' ἄροτον αὐτοῖς γῆς ἀνιέναι τινὰ μήτ' οὖν γυναικῶν παῖδας*, *ib.* 275. Homer also has *οὔτ' οὖν*: *ἔνθ' οὔτις τὴν νῆσον ἐσέδρακεν ὀφθαλμοῖσιν, οὔτ' οὖν κύματα μακρὰ — εἰσίδομεν*, *Od.* 9, 147. *νῦν δ' ἐπεὶ — ἱκάνεις, οὔτ' οὖν ἐσθῆτος δευήσεαι οὔτε τευ ἄλλου*, *Od.* 6, 192.

---

[1] Buttmann *in l.* explains it as answering to a *γάρ* in the independent form of sentence: *τοῦτο γὰρ οὐδεὶς ἂν οἰηθείη*, and similarly Homer's *ἐπεὶ οὖν ἔκαμον* = *αἵδε γὰρ, ἐπεὶ ἔκαμον*. But this will hardly explain the other facts.

[2] Not as Stallb. *in l.*, *οὖν*, *hic quoque nativam servat ratiocinandi et concludendi potestatem*, which, in fact, is not the native force of the particle.

[3] Compare the cognate *αὐτίκα* and *αὔτως* = *αὔτως*. Hartung says that it denotes a *cool, offhand* way of going to work; but this is evidently not always the case.

γοῦν = γε οὖν (therefore placed like γε), *yes, without more ado:* ἔχεις διδάξαι δή μ', ὅποι καθέσταμεν; —"τὰς γοῦν 'Αθήνας οἶδα, τὸν δὲ χῶρον οὔ," *Soph. Œd. C.* 24 (the feeling of certainty with indifference). τούτω δ' οὐ πάλιν αὖτις ἀποίσετον ὠκέες ἵπποι ἄμφω ἀφ' ἡμείων, εἰ γοῦν ἕτερός γε φύγησιν, *Hom. Il.* 5, 259, with the γοῦν in the condition (cf. § 264 a), where the Attics would place it in the apodosis, comp. εἰ καὶ τυραννεῖς, ἐξισωτέον τὸ γοῦν ἴσ' ἀντιλέξαι, *Soph. Œd. T.* 408. § 267.

γὰρ οὖν, with adverbial γάρ, in answers, denotes assent with indifference: φημὶ γὰρ οὖν. οὐ γὰρ οὖν, *Pl. passim.* With γάρ, "for," as in οὐ τήν γε μὴ θιγοῦσαν, εὖ γὰρ οὖν λέγεις, *Soph. Ant.* 772, *for, of course:* οἰκουμένη γὰρ οὖν στέγη πυρὸς μέτα πάντ' ἐκπορίζει, *Phil.* 298.

μῶν = μὴ οὖν; *surely* (without more ado) *not —?* μῶν 'Οδυσσέως ἐπησθόμην; *surely not Ulysses!* (= I hope not.) With οὐ: μῶν οὐχ ὁρᾷς; *surely it cannot be that you do not see this! Œd. C.* 1729. But the separate force of the particles having become obscured, so that μῶν has subsided into a mere particle of interrogation, the Attics also say μῶν οὖν; = *num igitur!* and μῶν μή —; Μῶν δοῦλος ὤν (ἄρχει σου ὁ παιδαγωγός); then, μῶν μὴ καὶ οὗτοί σου ἄρχουσιν οἱ διδάσκαλοι; and μῶν μή τι ἠδίκηκας τὸν πατέρα ἢ τὴν μητέρα; *Pl. Lys.* 208.

οὔκουν, = *not, all one for that; assuredly not, by no means.* When the οὐκ is assertive, and the οὖν illative, *not therefore,* it should be written οὐκοῦν, or rather οὐκ οὖν; but in this sense the combination is rare: it is more frequent, when the οὐκ is interrogative, e. g. οὐκ οὖν μ' ἐάσεις; *will thou then not let me alone!* and then it is usual to write οὐκοῦν, as also when the οὖν is not illative, and the combination represents *assuredly not,* but in an interrogation, *will thou not assuredly* (or, *without more ado*) *let me go!* (In both these cases it would be better to write οὔκουν; see § 199 b, R.) But this negative interrogation is virtually a strong affirmation, and is often used as such, and then it is written οὐκοῦν: e. g. οὐκοῦν ὅταν δὴ μὴ σθένω, πεπαύσομαι, prop. *shall I not — have done! = Aye, no doubt —. I shall have done: Soph. Ant.* 91, with a bitter irony which sometimes accompanies this use of the particle. Hence οὐκοῦν οὐκ —; is it *not then* (or, *not assuredly*) the case that — *not!* οὐκοῦν οὐκ ἂν εἴη τὸ μὴ λυπεῖσθαί ποτε ταὐτὸν τῷ χαίρειν; "πῶς γὰρ ἄν;" = *is it not then the case, that the absence of grief will not be identical with rejoicing,* or, *well then, to be sure, the — will not be —? Pl. Phil.* 360, where the second οὐκ is assertive. Sometimes also, where it is interrogative, οὐκοῦν καὶ ἡ σωφροσύνη — ἆρ' οὐ τούτοις μόνοις προσήκει; *Pl. Phædo,* 68. § 268.

μὲν οὖν, prop. *for one thing,* with the same adjunct notion of indifference, *it is all one, it makes no difference,* &c. (But from this must be distinguished the cases where μέν is followed by a corresponding δέ, and the οὖν is illative, *on the one hand therefore —.*) Hence in affirmative answers, πάνυ μὲν οὖν = *quite, for one thing* (however it may be with the rest) *decidedly* (so): so κομιδῇ μὲν οὖν, παντάπασι μὲν οὖν. With Attic urbanity, this formula of assent is used with a corrective force = *immo vero:* ἐγὼ οὔ φημι; φημὶ μὲν οὖν ἔγωγε, *I deny! nay, rather* (= *for one thing, decidedly*) *I assert it. Pl. Gorg.* 466. 'Εγὼ σοὶ οὐκ ἂν δυναίμην ἀντιλέγειν —. "οὐ μὲν οὖν τῇ ἀληθείᾳ — δύνασαι ἀντιλέγειν," *nay, rather say, you cannot gainsay Truth, Pl. Conv.* 201. In this sense, μὲν οὖν is sometimes used in continued discourse: δείσασα γὰρ γραῦς οὐδέν· ἀντίπαις μὲν οὖν, *Æsch. Eum.* 38. μάταιος ἄρ' ἦν, οὐδαμοῦ μὲν οὖν φρενῶν, *Eur. Hipp.* 1009. — It is often used in continuation of a preceding statement: ὃ μὲν οὖν (*now what* = as far as that goes, enough said) ἐγώ φημι τὴν ῥητορικὴν εἶναι, ἀκήκοας . . . . ἴσως μὲν ουν (*however,* or *now*) ἄτοπον πεποίηκα . . . § 269.

. APPENDIX.]

ἄξιον μὲν οὖν (*however*) ἐμοὶ συγγνώμην ἔχειν ἐστί . . . . ἐὰν μὲν οὖν (*then, on the one hand*) καὶ ἐγὼ — μὴ ἔχω —, ἐὰν δὲ ἔχω —, *Pl. Gorg.* 465.

§ τοίνυν.

270. This particle is compounded either of enclitic τοι (§ 252) (*for that matter*), or the stronger form τῷ, *in that case*, with νυν (§ 243). Its use is in transitions and inferences: *then* (to proceed), *then* (in brief), *well then, why then* (especially in lively replies). In the beginning of a speech: ἐγὼ μὲν τοίνυν, *I, for my part, sure enough*, *Xen. An.* 5, 1, 2. In continuation: Ἔτι τοίνυν τάδε ὁρᾶτε, *moreover now* —, *ib.* § 10. συνεπόμνυμι μηδὲ ἃ οἱ ἄλλοι στρατηγοὶ ἔλαβον εἰληφέναι, μὴ τοίνυν μηδὲ (*nay, for that matter, in short, not even*) ὅσα τῶν λοχαγῶν ἔνιοι. *Xen. An.* 7, 6, 19. In answers: ἄπειμι τοίνυν, *well then* (to cut the matter short) I am going, *Soph. Œd. C.* 444. In unwilling reply: τῶν Λαΐου τοίνυν τις ἦν γεννημάτων; *well then* (if you must needs have it), *ib.* 1167. — τὰ λῷστα τοίνυν ταῦτά μ' ἀλγύνει πάλαι, *why then* (*to dispose of that matter briefly*) *this which you call 'best' has been troubling me all along*, *ib.* 1067.

§ τοίγαρ.

271. The position of this particle in the beginning of a sentence shows that its first element is not the enclitic τοι, but the ancient τῷ, *in that case, therefore*. Hence, τοίγαρ = *ergo, proinde*. It is used in expressions of assent: *why* (γάρ) *then* (τῷ), τοίγαρ ποιήσω, *Soph. Tr.* 1249: in inference, *Soph. Aj.* 666 (after citing a proverb), τοίγαρ τὸ λοιπὸν εἰσόμεσθα, *why then* (such being the case) —. The rendering in each instance varies with that of γάρ: thus often in the beginning of a reply, *yes*, (and) *therefore*: e. g. τοίγαρ δι' ὀρθῆς τήνδε ναυκληρεῖς πόλιν, *Soph. Ant.* 994.

τοιγάρτοι is the same with addition of τοι enclitic, *why therefore to be sure*. τοιγάρτοι νῦν, ἅτε μέγιστα ἠδικηκὼς τῶν ἐν Μακεδονίᾳ, ἀθλιώτατός ἐστι πάντων Μακεδόνων (ironically, after a recital of wicked acts), *yes, and therefore no doubt* —, *Pl. Gorg.* 471.

τοιγαροῦν, *why then, such being the case*: ἀλλὰ θεοῖς γ' ἔχθιστος ἥκω. "τοιγαροῦν τεύξει τάχα," *why then for that very reason* (they are the more likely to grant thy request), *Soph. Œd. T.* 1519. ὀρθῶς ἔλεξας· τοιγαροῦν τὸ σὸν φράσον, *such then being the case, tell me*, *Phil.* 341. ξύμφημι κἀγώ· τοιγαροῦν σῴζου τόδε. Frequent in prose: e. g. (Cyrus never left a man's zeal in his service unrewarded) Τοιγαροῦν κράτιστοι δὴ ὑπηρέται παντὸς ἔργου Κύρῳ ἐλέχθησαν γενέσθαι, *accordingly, and reason good this* —, *Xen. An.* 1, 9, 18. (He never broke promise) καὶ γὰρ οὖν (*and therefore in fact*) ἐπίστευον αὐτῷ —. Τοιγαροῦν ἐπεὶ —, *accordingly*, (it is no wonder that) *when* —, *ib.* 1, 8, 7—9.

§ που.

272. This enclitic particle (an adverbial form of τις, *quis*, κος, whence Ion. κου, κως, &c.) properly = *somewhere*. Apart from the notion of place, it means, *somehow*, *in some sort* or *degree*; in conjectures, = *perhaps*, *I suppose*, used in conversation when the speaker puts something in a half-questioning manner (*surely*), intending to build something on the affirmative answer of the person addressed: τὸ γάρ που κακῶς ποιεῖν ἀνθρώπους τοῦ ἀδικεῖν οὐδὲν διαφέρει, for, *I presume* — (it being possible that the other would say there was some difference), *Pl. Crito*, 49. Also when, with a degree of uncertainty, a speaker repeats another's words: thus (Socr. having proposed a definition of σχῆμα, Meno says), "Ὅτι σχῆμά πού ἐστι, κατὰ τὸν σὸν λόγον, ὃ ἀεὶ χρόᾳ ἕπεται, *because figure, I take it* —, *Pl. Men.* 75. Hence with Attic urbanity, it is used in matter of certainty, especially to intimate that, before the speaker proceeds with his argument, he waits for the other to affirm the

[APPENDIX.

point, or call it to mind: *ὁ γὰρ σκυτοτόμος τέμνει που τομεῖ καὶ σμίλῃ καὶ ἄλλοις*
ὀργάνοις (*I suppose you will grant*, or, *remember that*), *Pl. Alc. pr.* 51. Οὔ τί που [§ 272.]
οἴει —; *You do not, I trow, at all imagine* ("mirantis et indignantis," *Stallb.*). Cf.
οὐ δήπου. (Sometimes it is put before an interposed φημί, or the like, to which it
belongs: ἔδοξέ πού φησι, *It says, I suppose, "It seemed good, &c.," Pl. Phædr.* 258.)

The same, with greater emphasis, is δήπου (*we may say that at once, I suppose*). §
Ἐγὼ γάρ που ἀπεκρινάμην τὸ διὰ παντὸς ὀρθῶς ἔχον· ὀρθῶς δὲ δήπου ἔχει τὸ κατὰ τὴν
τέχνην γιγνόμενον, *my answer, I presume you perceive, was as to what is done rightly* 273.
(in wrestling) *at all points: and rightly done — surely you will grant this — is*
what is done by strict rule of art, Pl. Alc. pr. 107. τῶν Λαΐου δήπου τις ὠνομάζετο,
I suppose we may be pretty sure that —, Soph. Œd. T. 1042. —

Sometimes in a direct interrogation, distinct from the latent interrogation of the
particle itself: καὶ ἔστι δήπου τὸ δίψος δίψος τοῦ; *Pl. Rep.* 439; even when the
interrogation is virtually negative: καὶ τούτου γε δήπου τις ἂν ἐπιθυμήσειεν; equiva-
lent to οὐ γὰρ δήπου τούτου γέ τις ἐπιθυμήσειεν, *Pl. Conv.* 200. In οὐ δήπου (γε), the
negation is expressed interrogatively: οὐ δή πού σέ γε — ἄγουσιν, *surely they are*
not —! Soph. Ant. 381. οὐ γὰρ δήπου σοῦ γε —, *Pl. Apol.* 20. ("οὐ δήπου est sus-
picantis: οὔ τί που mirantis et indignantis," *Stallb.*)

Stronger still is δήπουθεν (see § 240); used when the speaker, with a kind of
defiance, disputes the possibility of an opposite assertion: ἑστάναι γὰρ ἐξέσται δήπου-
θεν αὐτῷ, *for I presume there can be no doubt that —, Dem. Mid.* c. 26.

REM. Cf. μέν in interrogation: Ἕλλην μέν ἐστι, καὶ ἑλληνίζει; *Pl. Men.* 82,
where μέν assumes the fact as unquestionable: που in the same question would
mean, that the speaker waits for the other's assent. (Buttm. in l. and *Index*, s. v.)

ποτέ (enclitic). §

This temporal adverb of τις (*quis*, κος, Ion. κοτέ), *at some time; once* (ποτὲ μέν — 274.
ποτὲ δέ, *one while — another while, modo — modo*, or ἐνίοτε, or ἄλλοτε δέ): *at any*
time, ever. With other designations of time: νῦν ποτε, ἤδη ποτέ, πάλαι ποτέ, πρίν
ποτε, πρόσθε πού ποτε, πώποτε, ἔτι ποτέ. The notion of time is less prominent in
the following: μέθες μέθες με. "ποῖ μεθῶ;" μέθες ποτέ, *do let me go* (*utique, in any*
wise), *Soph. Phil.* 816. τίσασθε, τίσασθ' ἀλλὰ τῷ χρόνῳ ποτέ, *at last, tandem aliquando*,
or simply by the emphasis, *do avenge me!* So μόγις οὖν ποτε ἡμῖν ἄνθρωπος ἀνέῳξε
τὴν θύραν, *at last.* Ἐκκάλυπτε νῦν ποθ' (*now at last*) ἡμῖν οὕστινας λέγεις λόγους,
Eur. Iph. A. 872. Κἀπειδὴ ἀφίκετό ποτε ὁ Ἵππαρχος.

In interrogations, it expresses impatience for an answer (*tandem*), or wonder, or
emotion in general. τί ποτε λέγεις; *what do you say!* τί ποτε πέπονθας; *what* (*in*
the world) *ails you?* πῶς ποτε δράσεις; = *how will you do it!* τί ποτε (Hom.
τίπτ'), *what can be the reason that —?* Ποίῳ ποτ' ἐχρήσαντο τεκμηρίῳ; *Xen.* And
so in indirect questions: Ἐθαύμασα ὅτῳ ποτὲ τρόπῳ τοῦτ' ἐγένετο: and with indefinite
pronouns, ὅστις ποτε, who-*ever*, &c.: and with εἰ, εἴποτε, *if ever*, and *if perchance.*
With δή. ὅστις δήποτε, *whosoever*, ὅπου δή ποτε. So εἰ δή ποτε. τί δή ποτε; τοῦτο
πέπρακται νυνὶ ὅπως δή ποτε, *no matter how*: and with οὖν. Ἐμισθώσατό με ὅστις δή
ποτ' οὖν, *Æsch.* Οὐ δή ποτε in negations interrogatively expressed, *surely never —!*
οὐ δή ποθ' ἡμῖν ξυγγενὴς ἥκεις ποθέν; *surely it can never be that —! Soph. El.* 1202.
Cf. οὐ δή που.

Ἀλλά. §

This adverbial form (distinguished by its accent from pl. neut. ἄλλα) derives its 275.

[§ 275.] force from the proper signification of ἄλλος = "what there is else remaining *after the removal or exclusion* of some:" i. e. the notion introduced by ἀλλά is presented as being exclusive of some other preceding notion; or ἀλλά corresponds to a preceding οὐ, expressed or understood.

a) οὐκ ἐγώ, ἀλλὰ σύ. οὐκ ἐάσομεν, ἀλλὰ κωλύσομεν: the second notion excludes the first, to which it stands in direct opposition.

b) αἰσχρὰν γυναῖκ' ἔγημας, ἀλλὰ πλουσίαν. σοφὸς σὺ μάντις, ἀλλὰ τἀδικεῖν φιλῶν. Here the first notion is not expressly excluded, and the ἀλλά introduces, not its direct opposite, but something different. But here also ἀλλά has, in fact, its proper force with reference to a suppressed οὐ; for in this form of sentence the speaker implies, that the first notion, which he concedes, is *not* the point, *but* the second is. In the full expression of the thought, there is an opposition by μέν and δέ, with an οὐ in the δέ clause, to which οὐ the ἀλλά corresponds. Thus, τὸ σῶμα δοῦλον, ἀλλ' ὁ νοῦς ἐλεύθερος, *the body is enslaved* — this indeed (μέν) I grant, but (δέ) *not* this is the point — *but* (that) *the mind is free.* Often, to mark the concession more strongly, the μέν is expressed in the first clause: τοῦτο τὸ πρᾶγμα ὠφέλιμον μέν ἐστιν, ἀλλὰ δύσκολον, which, however, is by no means simply equivalent to ὠφ. μέν ἐ., δύσκολον δέ, nor does the ἀλλά correspond to the μέν, but to the negation in the suppressed δέ clause. In μέν — δέ, it is intimated that both considerations are taken into the account: in μέν — ἀλλά, the former is conceded only to be set aside. When the second member is negative, the μέν *must* be expressed, ὠφέλιμον μέν, ἀλλ' οὐ καλόν: without μέν, this would = *advantageous*, and not *handsome*; see *c*. — The first also may be negative, e. g. οὐκ ἀρνοῦμαι μέν, ἀλλ' (ἀλλ' ὅμως) ἐρωτῶ; but then the ἀλλά corresponds, not to the expressed, but to the implied negation, viz. *not* my not-denying is the point, *but* my asking.

c) But the Greek often introduces with ἀλλά a negation in direct opposition to a preceding affirmation: thus, ἐκεῖθεν ἀλλ' οὐκ ἐνθένδε ἡρπάσθη, *Pl. Phædr.* 229. See other exx. in § 187, to which add: Χαραδριοῦ τινα αὖ σὺ βίον λέγεις, ἀλλ' οὐ νεκροῦ οὐδὲ λίθου, *Pl. Gorg.* 494. κινδυνεύει τὸ ἑκόντα ἐπὶ τὸ ἄρχειν ἰέναι, ἀλλὰ μὴ ἀνάγκην περιμένειν, αἰσχρὸν νενομίσθαι, *coming forward to rule instead of* (and not rather) *waiting till one is forced*, *Pl. Rep.* 347. τίς μηχανὴ — δικαιοσύνην τιμᾶν ἐθέλειν, ἀλλὰ μὴ γελᾶν ἐπαινουμένης ἀκούοντα; *ib.* 366. φιλοσόφους ἀλλ' οὐ φιλοδόξους κλητέον, *ib.* 480. ἔπειτ' ἀπὸ ταῤῥοῦ τοὺς θεοὺς ὑπερφρονεῖς, ἀλλ' οὐκ ἀπὸ τῆς γῆς; *Arist. Nub.* 226. The natural expression would be οὐκ ἐνθένδε ἀλλ' ἐκεῖθεν, &c., but to give greater emphasis to the affirmation by more forcible repudiation of its opposite, *which is assumed as having been asserted*, or *likely to be so*, the order is inverted, so that the ἀλλά seems to belong, in a manner, to the preceding clause, and to look backward rather than forward: *thence* (quite another thing that!), *not hence.* But the true explanation (which reduces this to the form *a*) is this: ἐκεῖθεν ἡρπάσθη· οὐκ (ὡς σὺ λέγεις, or, ὡς ᾠόμεθα, or the like) ἐνθένδε, ἀλλ' οὐκ ἐνθένδε, *thence* — not as people might suppose, "hence" — *but* "*not hence.*" This explanation accounts for the irony which commonly appears in this use. Comp. ὑμεῖς — μάλιστ' ἂν οὕτως — εὐδοκιμοῖτε καὶ οὐκ ἐπαινοῖσθε —· ἡμεῖς τ' αὖ μάλιστ' ἂν οὕτως εὐφραινοίμεθα οὐχ ἡδοίμεθα, *Pl. Prot.* 337, followed in each instance by an explanation: τὸ μὲν γὰρ εὐδοκιμεῖν . . . . , τὸ δὲ ἐπαινεῖσθαι . . . . , &c. Here is no irony: had such been the case, the full form would have been, εὐδοκιμοῖτε καὶ οὐκ ἐπαινοῖσθε ἀλλ' οὐκ-ἐπαινοῖσθε, = "and the case would be, not a being praised, but a not being praised;" whence, the negative statement being suppressed, the form would be εὐδοκ. ἀλλ' οὐκ ἐπαινοῖσθε.

Rem. This use of ἀλλ' οὐ must be distinguished from the *but not* —, which is opposed to a preceding μέν; see *b*: e.g. *profitable indeed, but not handsome,* ὠφέλιμον μέν, ἀλλ' οὐ καλόν, which is better expressed, οὐ μέντοι (or μὲν δή) καλόν γε.

οὐ μόνον — ἀλλὰ καὶ —, *not only —, but also* — (the ἀλλά in direct opposition to οὐ, the καί = καὶ —, καὶ —), sometimes with the addition πρὸς τούτῳ, or τούτοις. § 276.
When the καί is omitted, the notion contained in the first member is entirely put aside. Thus, in οὐ μόνον ἐκινδύνευσεν, ἀλλὰ καὶ ἔπαθεν, *not only was he in danger, but he* (*both* was in danger, *and*) *also suffered*, an equal stress is laid on both notions: but in the same sentence without καί, on arriving at the second notion, we think it so important, that we reject the intention with which here also we set out, viz. of putting the notions (ἐκινδ. and ἔπαθε) on the same level by (καὶ —,) καὶ —.

a) When ἀλλά follows conditional clauses with εἰ, εἰ μή, &c., it may be rendered by *yet, yet at least* = *saltem, certe*. This case comes under *b*, viz. the ἀλλά refers to § 277.
a suppressed apodosis with μέν — δέ. Εἰ σῶμα δοῦλον, ἀλλ' ὁ νοῦς ἐλεύθερος: the suppressed apodosis is ἔστω μὲν δοῦλον, to which ἀλλά refers in the manner explained above. So εἰ μὴ πάντα, ἀλλὰ πολλά γε ἴστε. (Comp. *si mihi bona republica frui non licuerit, at carebo mala.*) This ἀλλά is often followed by οὖν (*even so, all one for that,* &c.; see § 266). Εἰ καὶ μὴ καθ' Ἑλλάδα τεθράμμεθ', ἀλλ' οὖν ξυνετά μοι δοκεῖς λέγειν (*Eur.*). ἢν καὶ τὴν φύσιν καταδεεστέραν ἔχωσιν ἀλλ' οὖν ταῖς γ' ἐμπειρίαις . . . προέχουσιν (*Isoc.*).

Rem. ἀλλά γε, in direct combination, perhaps never occurs (in fact this would = *no yes*); but γε, as in the preceding instances, heightens the antithetic word.

b) By an ellipsis of the conditional clause, ἀλλά comes to stand in the middle of a sentence: αὐτή γε νοῦν σχὲς ἀλλὰ τῷ χρόνῳ ποτέ (*Soph.*), the suppressed clause being, εἰ μὴ πρότερον. So, frequently, ἀλλὰ νῦν γε, ἀλλὰ νῦν γ' ἔτι (*Dem.*). βούλομαι αὐτὸν διδάξαι, ἄν πως ἀλλὰ νῦν γε παιδευθῇ (*Lys.*). ὦ θεοὶ πατρῷοι ξυγγένεσθέ γ' ἀλλὰ νῦν, *Soph. El.* 411. In like manner ἀλλ' οὖν: τοὺς πρώτους χρόνους ἀλλ' οὖν προσεποιοῦνθ' ὑμῖν φίλοι εἶναι (*Æsch.*), (*if they were not really so*) *at any rate they pretended.*

Often ἀλλά stands at the beginning of a speech, either in opposition to something advanced or supposed to be advanced by another, or to some unexpressed thought § 278.
of the speaker: viz. in quick, abrupt replies; in starting an objection, or in approbation and assent (§ 199 c, R. 2), in exclamations, exhortations, &c., especially when the discourse is suddenly interrupted and something new is introduced. Εὐριπίδη, Εὐριπίδιον, ὑπάκουσον, εἴπερ πώποτ' ἀνθρώπων τινί. "ἀλλ' οὐ σχολή" (*I hear,*) *but* —. ἀλλ' ἐκκυκλήθητ' (*If so,*) *why then, do let yourself be rolled out* (on the eccyclema). "ἀλλ' ἀδύνατον." ἀλλ' ὅμως, *Nay, do though!* ἀλλ' ἐκκυκλήσομαι, καταβαίνειν δ' οὐ σχολή, *Why then, I will* —, *Arist. Ach.* 404. τίνα καὶ ἀναβιβάσωμαι δεησόμενον ὑπὲρ ἐμαυτοῦ; τὸν πατέρα; ἀλλὰ τέθνηκεν. ἀλλὰ τοὺς ἀδελφούς; ἀλλ' οὐκ ἐστίν. ἀλλὰ τοὺς παῖδας; ἀλλ' οὔπω γεγένηνται, *My father? Nay, but he's dead. Well then, my brothers! Why, I have none. My children then!* — (*Andoc.*). In Xen., Clearchus begins a speech with, 'Αλλ' ὤφελε μὲν Κῦρος ζῆν, ἐπεὶ δὲ τετελεύτηκεν —, *Well, I would Cyrus were alive* —. And the same author even begins his Sympos. with 'Αλλ' ἐμοὶ δοκεῖ —, where the ἀλλά refers to considerations which he has been turning over in his mind; *Well, after all, it does seem to me* —.

ἀλλ' ἄρα: εἰπέ μοι, ἔστι σοι ἀγρός; "οὐκ ἔμοιγε." ἀλλ' ἄρα οἰκία προσόδους ἔχουσα; (*you don't say so!*) *well then* —?

ἀλλ' ἦ; a question with surprise or perplexity, the ἀλλά denoting difference from § 279.

[§ 279.] what the enquirer expected: *ἀλλ' ἦ δόλον τιν', ὦ ξέν', ἀμφί μοι πλέκεις; why how (is this)?* — *Æsch. Choeph.* 214. *ἀλλ' ἦ, τὸ λεγόμενον, κατόπιν τῆς ἑορτῆς ἥκομεν καὶ ὑστεροῦμεν;* (*Pl.*) *οὗτος, ἀλλ' ἦ παραπαίεις;* (*Luc.*)

In *ἀλλὰ δή, δῆτα, μέν, μὲν δή, μέν τοι, τοι, μήν*, both particles have their distinct force, which is not affected by their concurrence in the same sentence.

ἀλλὰ — γάρ (comp. § 196 b) is often elliptical, the sentence to which *ἀλλά* belongs being left to be gathered from the context. *'Αλλ', ἡδὺ γάρ τοι κτῆμα τῆς νίκης λαβεῖν, τόλμα*, where the sentence is completed by *τόλμα* (*Soph.*). *ἴσως 'Ερινύς ἐστιν ἐκ τραγῳδίας, βλέπει γέ τοι μανικόν τε καὶ τραγῳδικόν. "ἀλλ' οὐκ ἔχει γὰρ δᾷδας,"* i. e. *ἀλλ' οὐκ 'Ε., οὐκ ἔχει γὰρ δ.* (*Arist.*). *ἀλλ' ἔστ' ἔμοιγ' υἱὸς καλός τε κἀγαθός· ἀλλ' οὐκ ἐθέλει γὰρ μανθάνειν*, where *ἀλλὰ — γάρ* seems to be a mere colloquialism = *attamen*, as the context contains nothing from which the sentence with *ἀλλά* may be completed (e. g. *but what's the use of that?*). In familiar discourse, the two particles may come together: *εἰ ἐγὼ Φαῖδρον ἀγνοῶ, καὶ ἐμαυτοῦ ἐπιλέλησμαι· ἀλλὰ γὰρ οὐδέτερα ἔστι τούτων, εὖ οἶδα ὅτι οὐχ ἅπαξ ἤκουσεν* (*Pl.* = *ἀλλὰ Φαῖδρον οὐκ ἀγνοῶ· οὐ γὰρ ἐμαυτοῦ ἐπιλέλησμαι· οὐδέτερα ἔστι τούτων*).

§ 280. In the combinations *οὐ μὴν ἀλλά, οὐ μέντοι ἀλλά*, and (much less frequent) *οὐ γὰρ ἀλλά*, there is always an ellipsis (§ 215 b, R. 2), which may sometimes be supplied by repeating the preceding verb to *οὐ μήν*, &c. *ὁ ἵππος πίπτει εἰς γόνατα, καὶ μικροῦ κἀκεῖνον ἐξετραχήλισεν· οὐ μὴν* (supply *ἐξετραχήλισεν*) *ἀλλὰ ἐπέμεινεν ὁ Κῦρος μόλις πως, the horse came down on his knees, and was within a little of throwing C. over his head; not* [that he did throw him], *however*, but *C. managed somehow to keep his seat* (*Xen.*). *μὴ σκῶπτέ μ', ὠδέλφ', οὐ γὰρ ἀλλ' ἔχω κακῶς* = *οὐ γὰρ ὥστε σκώπτειν, for it is no jeering matter this, but I am indeed in a miserable condition.* But sometimes the notion of opposition is too vague to be supplied, and the combination may be regarded as a colloquialism, *οὐ μὴν* (and *μέντοι*) *ἀλλά* = *veruntamen, attamen*, *οὐ γὰρ ἀλλά* (*etenim*: nearly = *καὶ γάρ*). *τούτων ἀληθῆ μέν ἐστι τὰ πολλά, οὐ μὴν ἀλλ' ἴσως οὐχ ἡδέα ἀκούειν* (*Dem.* where only *ἡδέα could* be supplied).

§ 281. *ἀλλ' ἤ.* The union of these two particles after negations, direct or implied, is explained by a union of two constructions. *Οὐδένα ὁρῶ ἀλλὰ σέ*, may be strengthened by the insertion of *ἄλλον*, *I see none other, but* (I see) *thee.* But this sense may also be expressed, with a slight difference, by *οὐδένα ἄλλον ὁρῶ ἢ σέ, I see none-other-than thee;* and with omission of the *ἄλλον*, *οὐδένα ὁρῶ ἢ σέ.* The two forms combined (which was the more natural by reason of the affinity which the particle *ἀλλά*, in respect of its origin, has for *ἤ*) result in the forms, *οὐδένα ἄλλον ὁρῶ ἀλλ' ἢ σέ, I see none other except that (I see) thee:* in which, if we would express the force of both particles, we must say, *I see none other than thee, but (I see) thee*, or, *I see none other, but I see (thee, and none other) than thee;* and with omission of *ἄλλον*, *οὐδένα ὁρῶ ἀλλ' ἢ σέ.* The combination originating in this simplest form of sentence finds its way into more complex enunciations.

In the neuter, it may often be doubted whether the wording is *οὐδὲν ἀλλ' ἤ* = *ἀλλὰ ἤ* or *οὐδὲν ἄλλ' ἤ* = *ἄλλο ἤ.*

In the ellipsis of the verb (*γίνεται*, or the like) to *οὐδέν* (§ 215 b, R. 1), there is no doubt that the word is *ἄλλο*: thus, *οὓς φαμεν μανθάνειν οὐδὲν ἄλλο ἢ ἀναμιμνήσκονται* (*Pl.* = *οὐδὲν ἄλλο ποιοῦσιν ἢ* —): whence *οὐδὲν ἄλλ' ἢ* (not *ἀλλ' ἤ*) *προσκυνεῖν ὑπελάμβανον*, whether it be, *I (did) nothing other than suppose him to be praying*, or, *I supposed him to be (doing) nothing other than praying.* In many other cases, the form *ἄλλο* is easily supposable: e. g. in *ἐγὼ γὰρ δι' οὐδέν, ἄλλ' ἢ διὰ σοφίαν τινὰ τοῦτο*

[APPENDIX.

τὸ ὄνομα ἔσχηκα (*Pl.*), it is as natural to suppose the word to be ἄλλο, *by none other* [§
thing than by —, as that it is ἀλλά. Only where an ἄλλος is expressed in the first 281.]
member, it may seem more natural to assume the form to be ἀλλ' ἤ: thus, οὐδὲν ἄλλο σκοπεῖν, ἀλλ' ἢ τὸ ἄριστον (*Pl.*). Madvig, however, conceives the true reading to be, *in all cases*, ἄλλ' ἤ; see § 91, R. 2. To the examples there cited, add: οὐδὲν γὰρ, ἔστ' ἀλλ' (ἄλλ', Brunck) ἢ κοάξ, *Arist. Ran.* 227. ἀργύριον μὲν οὐκ ἔχω, ἀλλ' ἢ μικρόν τι. *Xen. An.* 7, 7, 53. ὡς δ' οὐχὶ φιλεῖ σ' οὐδ' ἔστ' εὔνους, τοῦτ' αὐτό σε πρῶτα διδάξω, ἀλλ' ἢ διὰ τοῦτ' αὖθ' ὁτίη σου τῆς ἀνθρακιᾶς ἀπολαύει, *Arist. Eq.* 779. μηδαμοῦ ἀλλόθι — ἀλλ' ἢ ἐκεῖ (*Pl.*). μηδαμῶς ἄλλως — ἀλλ' ἢ — (*Isocr*). In questions implying negation: τίς ἂν εἰς ἄλλο τι ἀποβλέψας ἢ δειλὴν ἢ ἀνδρείαν πόλιν εἴποι, ἀλλ' ἢ εἰς τοῦτο τὸ μέρος; *Pl. Rep.* 429. τίνος ἕνεκα κἂν τις — ζῴη ἀλλ' ἢ τῶν τοιούτων ἡδονῶν ἕνεκα; *Pl.*

Sometimes ἀλλ' ἤ results from confusion of οὐκ — ἀλλά with the elliptical οὐδὲν ἄλλο (γίγνεται, &c.) ἤ. Thus, οὐ δ' οἵδε γ' εἷλκον οὐδὲν 'Αργεῖοι πάλαι, ἀλλ' ἢ κατεγέ- § 282.
λων τῶν ταλαιπωρουμένων = οὐδὲ εἷλκον ἀλλὰ κατεγελων, and οὐδὲν ἐποίουν ἄλλο ἢ κατεγέλων, *Arist. Pac.* 476. μή μοι μυρίους μηδὲ δισμυρίους ξένους, μηδὲ τὰς ἐπιστολιμαίους ταύτας δυνάμεις, ἀλλ' ἢ τῆς πόλεως ἔσται, *Dem. Phil.* 45, 19, which Krüger explains as a union of the two constructions, *an army must consist, not of mercenaries, nor* —, *but of citizens*, and, *not of mercenaries*, &c., *nor of other than citizens*, = μηδὲ λέγε ἄλλας δυνάμεις ἢ τῆς πόλεως.

ἀλλά without ἤ: οὔτι μοι αἴτιος ἄλλος, ἀλλὰ τοκῆε δύω (*Hom.*). ἔπαισε δ' αὐτόχειρ νιν οὔτις ἀλλ' ἐγώ, *Soph. Œd. T.* 1355. (ἀλλ' ἤ is colloquial, therefore does not occur in Tragedy.) ἐν δὲ τῷ μέσῳ ἄλλη μὲν πόλις οὐδεμία οὔτε φιλία, οὔτε 'Ελληνίς, ἀλλὰ Θρᾷκες καὶ Βιθυνοί, *Xen. An.* 6, 2 (al. 4), 2. μηδένα ἕτερον εἶναι τὸν Νικομήδου φονέα ἀλλ' 'Αρίσταρχον, *Dem. Mid.* 554. And in interrogation: ἦ ἔχετέ τι ἄλλο τέλος λέγειν, εἰς ὃ ἀποβλέψαντες αὐτὰ ἀγαθὰ καλεῖτε, ἀλλὰ (Steph. ex conj. ἀλλ' ἤ) ἡδονάς τε καὶ λύπας, *Pl. Prot.* 354.

ἤ without ἀλλ': τί ποιῶν ἢ εὐωχούμενος ἐν Θετταλίᾳ; *Pl. Crito*, 53 E. ἀλλὰ τί οὖν τούτων ἐστὶν αἴτιον, ἢ ὅτι —; *Xen. Œcon.* 3, 3. σκοπῶ εἰ ἄρα τι ἐστὶ τοῖς θεοῖς ἔργον, ἢ ἀνθρώπους θεραπεύειν, *Xen. Mem.* 4, 3, 9 (meaning, that he inclines to think that *the gods have no (other) work than* —).

ἤ, *or*, *than*.

The original force of this particle (radically cognate with *ve*, *ve-l*, and possibly a § 283.
mutilated form of the relative—comp. the use of the Lat. *quam* in comparison), is *how*, *in what manner*, *as*, in correlation (comp. ἢ μέν — ἢ δέ, ἠδέ, § 242), but always with the notion of *other-ness*: ἢ ἐγώ, ἢ σύ, prop. *other-how I*, *other-how thou*. Hence

In *alternatives*: ἤ — ἤ is both *aut* — *aut* and *vel* — *vel*: ἢ ἀμφαδὸν ἠὲ κρυφηδόν. ἢ τέον ἢ Αἴαντος — γέρας, ἢ 'Οδυσῆος. Often the first ἤ is omitted, then ἤ = *aut etiam*, usually with a *descensus a majore ad minus*, viz. to something conceived as *less likely*: ἕξομεν κλέος καλῶς θανόντες ἢ καλῶς σεσωσμένοι, *having nobly died*, *or* — if that be possible — *nobly saved*, *Eur. Or.* 1145. ὑπὲρ ὧν ἐκεῖνος ᾤετο δεῖν ἀποθνήσκειν ἢ νικᾶν, *aut*, si fieri posset, *vincere*. — In Attic, the disjunction is often rendered stronger by τοι (usually followed by a γε) attached to the first ἤ, rarely to the second: ἤτοι ὅλου τοῦ εἴδους ἢ μέρους (*Pl.*). ἤτοι ἐπιστάμενοί γε — ἢ ὕστερον ἀναμιμνήσκονται (*Pl.*). ἤτοι πρότερόν γε ἢ ὕστερον (*Pl.*). And without the first ἤ: ἔοικας, ἦν δ' ἐγώ, ἤτοι ἡμῶν γε οὐδὲν κήδεσθαι, *Like enough, said I* (viz. that you do think so), *or else* (sure enough) *you don't care for us*, *Pl. Rep.* 344 (Stallb. *in l.*).

When the first member of the alternative is not expressed, ἤ = *or* (*else*), *alias*, *alioquin*. αὐτὴ μὲν ἐκμοχθοῦσα κερκίσιν πέπλους, ἢ γυμνὸν ἕξω σῶμα (= *as I must either do this, or else* —), *Eur. El.* 306. τοῦτο δὲ οὔτ' ἀπόλλυσθαι οὔτε γίγνεσθαι δυνατόν, ἢ (supply ἀναγκαῖον, *or else needs must* —) πάντα τε οὐρανὸν πᾶσάν τε γένεσιν συμπεσοῦσαν στῆναι, *Pl. Phædr.* 245. (Cic. renders it, *vel concidat omne cœlum omnisque natura.* See further, § 186, R.)

§ 284. In *alternative* (double) questions, Hom. has ἤ — ἤ —; (rare in Attic poetry): in later writers, especially Attic, πότερον — ἤ —; or the particle is omitted in the first clause, see § 199 c: and on ἆρα — ἤ —; *ib.* R.: also on ἄλλο τι ἤ, ἄλλο τι ἢ οὐ, *ib.* b. On ἤ — ἤ for εἰ — ἤ, in dependent questions, *ib.* c, R. 1. Sometimes, after a question put quite generally and indefinitely, a second is put with ἤ (*an*) with corrective or restrictive force = *or, which I suppose is nearer to the truth —?* πόθεν ἥκει; ἢ δῆλον ὅτι ἐξ ἀγορᾶς; (*Pl.*) ἀλλὰ τίς σοι διηγεῖτο; ἢ αὐτὸς Σωκράτης, *Pl. Conv.* 173 (Stallb. *in l.* and Elmsl. on Soph. Œd. C. 66).

Rem. When the second member of the disjunctive question is negative, this is expressed by ἢ οὐ, if the predicate, and by ἢ μή if only a part of the sentence, is negatived.

§ 285. In *comparison*, after comparatives, and words implying comparison or opposition, ἄλλος, ἕτερος, ἐναντίος, &c., ἤ = *than* (*quam*, Germ. *als*, both illustrating the connexion of ἤ with the relative: our "than" is demonstrative, = "then"); see § 89, sqq. On μᾶλλον ἢ οὐ, § 89, R. 2, cf. Herm. on Soph. Aj. 1260, where it is explained, that the last of the exx. above given (*Thuc.* 3, 36) is equivalent to οὐ τοὺς αἰτίους ἀλλὰ μᾶλλον τὴν πόλιν ὅλην. — (This union of two constructions resembles that which we have noticed above in οὐδεὶς ἄλλος — ἀλλ' ἤ.)

§ 286. οὐ and μή.

For the distinction and use of these particles, see § 200 sqq., and the §§ there referred to (cf. Index):[1] on οὐδέ, μηδέ, οὔτε, μήτε, see § 208. 216. 229 c.

All the applications of μή may be derived from the *prohibitive.*

Μὴ τύπτε, μὴ τύψῃς. It is not, on the whole, indifferent which form is used. "Μή with imperative, enjoins the giving over something that a person is doing (or thinking of doing): with aor. subj., the not beginning it is ordered. Moreover, the present is used of a continued act, as μὴ βάλλετε: the aor. of a quickly transient, momentary act, μὴ βάλῃς, when a single throwing of the weapon is in question." *Hermann. ad Viger.* § 268, p. 809. The reason why the imperative phrase (in second pers.) must always be μὴ τύπτε, not μὴ τύψον, is, because the direct actual prohibition of a thing prohibits it, not as a single momentary act, but *once for all.* In μὴ τύπτε, μή expresses the prohibiting, τύπτε the act prohibited: in μὴ τύψῃς, there is an intermediate verbal notion, viz. an imperative: e. g. μὴ λέγε, μὴ ἐννόει, μὴ βούλου, or the like (or rather, the μή itself is the expression of such a verbal notion, "I will not have it," &c.), on which the subjunctive, as a form of the future, is dependent: e. g. "do not let the thought come into your mind, that you will strike." And because

[1] Οὐ appears to be cognate with αὖ, ἀ-πό, *ab*, *aut*, *haud*, therefore primarily denotes separation or removal, reversal or contrast. Μή, although it coincides to a considerable extent with *ne*, appears to have a different origin from that particle (Sanscrit *mâ*, Persian *me*, both *prohibitive*). It seems to stand on the same line with the pronoun of the first person, μέ, and with μά, μείς, μέν, &c.: but perhaps its peculiar force, as the particle of subjective denial, is best derived from the *labial* expression of rejection, dislike, impatience, &c., possibly with some notion of the first pers. pronoun in it, "*I* will not have it," or the like.

such a form of prohibition is more distinctly related to the future, therefore (cf. § 128) the subj. *aor.* is used, not the subj. present. (Besides, μὴ τύπτῃς would be a circuitous way of expressing what is better said by μὴ τύπτε.) But μὴ τυψάτω is allowable, § 142, R. 1, though rare: for here, as in μὴ τυπτέτω, the verb has relation to a suppressed imperative, just as we are obliged to express the third pers. imperative by the verb *let:* μὴ (*let — not*) τυπτέτω (*strike*). [§ 286.]

The construction of μή with the indicative and subj. in independent sentences is always to be referred to this principle of an unexpressed imperative. Thus in the question μὴ γράψεις; "*do not say* (think, &c.), you will write" = "surely you will not write?" (μή introduces a question to which we wish, but are not confident of receiving, an answer in the negative: with μῶν, we express a confidence that the answer will be, "no"). But λέξεις δὲ μηδὲν τῶν ἐμοὶ δεδογμένων, *Eur. Med.* 804: *but you will* (not) *tell—do not think of it!—aught of what I have resolved upon;* an assertion having the force of an express prohibition. 'Αλλ' οὖν προμηνύσεις γε τοῦτο μηδενί, *Soph. Ant.* 84, with the same emphasis of entreaty or dehortation expressed by the following μηδενί, *do not think of doing so* (no, not) *to anybody!* The principle is the same for the subjunctive, which is in its origin only another form of the future:[1] but in the usage of the language, μηδὲν λέξῃς, μηδενὶ προμηνύσῃς has come to be merely the expression of a prohibition, as above explained; whereas the fut. indic. asserts that which will be. Καὶ τἀμὰ τεύχη μήτ' ἀγωνάρχαι τινὲς θήσουσ' 'Αχαιοῖς μήθ' ὁ λυμεὼν ἐμός. *Soph. Aj.* 569 ("admodum notabilis hæc ratio particulæ cum fut. indic. positæ," *Ellendt.;* but the explanation is obvious on the principle here given, viz.), "and *as for my arms, do not imagine* (*that*) *either —:*" it is an emphatic negation.— So with subj. μὴ δοκῶμεν, *and let us not think*, where μή = the imperative "*do not let.*" ὦ ξεῖνοι, μὴ δῆτ' ἀδικηθῶ, *Soph. Œd. C.* 172. § 287.

With the proper optative, e.g. μὴ νῦν ὀναίμην, *Soph. Œd. T.* 644. μὴ δῆτα — ἴδοιμι ταύτην ἡμέραν, *ib.* 830, the suitableness of μή, as expression of not wishing, is obvious.

With the adj., as also infin. and particip. of the verb, "μή, non reapse negat sed jubet cogitari negatum," Frank. *Diss. de Partic. negant.* i., p. 8. Τὸ μὴ καλόν, "the (do not call, think it, &c.) good:" αἰσχρὸν (τὸ) μὴ βοηθεῖν (*if one does not —*), μὴ βοηθῶν, ὁ μὴ βοηθῶν. See § 205, 6. For μή with inf. after verbs of denying, &c., see § 210. Comp. under μὴ οὐ.) § 288.

In sentences dependent on verbs denoting fear, anxiety, consideration, &c. (see § 124, and R. 1, 2), the μή is evidently in its place as the expression of *not wishing*, and has the same force as in the independent sentence. φοβοῦμαι μὴ εὑρήσομεν: without φοβοῦμαι, (*do*) *not* (*say*) *we shall find*, i. e. *I hope we shall not:* in φοβοῦμαι, the nature of the unwillingness is expressed: *I am afraid* (we shall). And so with the subj., δέδοικα μὴ ἐπιλαθώμεθα. Φροντίζω μὴ κράτιστον ᾖ.— Hence the absence of δέδοικα, &c., is not necessarily elliptical. Μὴ ἀγροικότερον ᾖ τὸ ἀληθὲς εἰπεῖν, *do not say it is,* = *I fear it may be.*— In the usage of the language, φοβοῦμαι μὴ ἔστι is, *I fear it is:* φοβοῦμαι μὴ ᾖ, *I fear it may turn out to be:* φοβοῦμαι μὴ ἔσται, *I fear* (I think with fear) *it certainly will be.*— The same principle holds for the optative § 289.

---

[1] Thus, *Od.* 16, 437, οὐκ ἔσθ' οὗτος ἀνήρ, οὐδ' ἔσσεται, οὐδὲ γένηται (cf. *Pl. Rep.* 472, οὔτε γὰρ γίγνεται, οὔτε γέγονεν, οὐδὲ οὖν μή ποτε γένηται) ὅς κεν Τηλεμάχῳ σῷ υἱέϊ χεῖρας ἐποίσει: comp. *Od.* 6, 201, οὐκ ἔσθ' οὗτος ἀνὴρ διερὸς βροτός, οὐδὲ γένηται, ὅς κεν Φαιήκων ἀνδρῶν ἐς γαῖαν ἵκηται.

under the same circumstances, § 131, e. g. ἔδεισαν μὴ προσαγάγοιεν = the præteritive enunciation of φοβοῦνται μὴ προσαγάγωσιν.

§ 290. With ὁρᾶν, and the like, μή seems to have more interrogative force. 'Ορῶμεν, μὴ Νικίας οἴεται, *you do not say N. thinks? (surely he does not think?) let us see whether he does.* "Ορα μὴ τίθης, *see whether you are putting:* ὅρα μὴ τιθῇς, *see whether it may not turn out that you are putting:* ὅρα μὴ θήσεις, *see whether you will be putting.*

§ 291. In sentences of intention, § 122, ἵνα, ὅπως, &c., μή, and object-sentences after verbs of endeavour, &c., § 123, the μή has the same force as in the prohibitive sentence, e. g. τὴν γέφυραν λῦσαι ὡς μὴ διαβῆτε, the primary sentence being, "Μὴ διαβῶσιν, *let them not cross.*"

§ 292. The use of μή in conditional (εἰ μή), § 202, temporal (ὅταν, ὁπότε μή), and, generally, relative sentences (ὅς, ὅσος, &c., ὃς ἄν, &c., μή), *ib.* and 203, is determined by the thought, "no notion of," "not to be supposed," or the like. Thus, εἰ μὴ δώσουσιν = "in case there be no notion of their giving;" but εἰ οὐ δώσουσιν, "in case of their not-giving:" i. e. the difference is the same as that between μὴ δώσω = *don't suppose I shall give*, and οὐ δώσω, *I shall not give:* of which the former is obviously more suitable to the hypothetical form of statement with εἰ, ἐάν. Hence also with ὅς, ὅσος, &c., ὅτε, ὁπότε, &c., the principle is that μή is used when there is room for supposition in each case that the thing does (will, &c.) occur, or that it does (will, &c.) not, but the supposition of its occurrence is negatived. Thus, ὃς οὐκ οἶδεν, "a person who (as matter of fact) knows not," ὃς μὴ οἶδεν, "who (as matter of necessary supposition) knows not:" in the one case, the εἰδέναι is denied directly; in the other, there is implied a previous consideration, μὴ οἶδεν, "do not suppose he knows," whence ὃς μὴ οἶδεν, "the sort of person that does not know:" ἃ μὴ οἶδα, οὐδὲ οἴομαι εἰδέναι, "what I know not," = "if there are things that I do not know," or, "say I do not know them." And just so with ὅτε and other adv. forms of the relative. — With ἄν (ὃς ἄν, ὅταν, &c.) the negation is necessarily μή, in virtue of the notion of contingency conveyed by that particle.

§ 293. In § 124, R. 4, the use of οὐ μή with second pers. fut. indic. denoting peremptory prohibition, is distinguished from that (*ib.* R. 3) which, with subjunct. or also fut. indic., expresses a strong negation in the form of an assertion. In the latter, the μή is usually explained as referring to a suppressed verb or verbal notion, e. g. δέδοικα, δέος ἐστί, which is negatived by οὐ: comp. the full expression οὐ γὰρ ἦν δεινὸν μὴ ἁλῷ ποτε, *Hdt.* 1, 84, with καὶ τῶνδ' ἀκούσας οὔ τι μὴ ληφθῶ δολῷ: while the former, e. g. οὐ μὴ ληρήσεις, is explained as, "will you not not-trifle?" = "will you not have done with your nonsense?" But both phrases are referable to the same origin, and (considered in themselves) admit alike of the interrogative or of the assertive notion, i. e. on the one hand, οὐ μὴ ληρήσεις may be, "no, don't think you will (shall) talk nonsense," a union of οὐ ληρήσεις, with μὴ ληρήσεις (= μὴ ληρήσῃς): on the other, οὔ τι μὴ ληφθῶ (= ληφθήσομαι), "shall I not-be-taken?" i. e. "shall I not be safe from being taken?" (Cf. Herm. Cens. Elmsl. in *Eur. Med.*) In the practice of the language, however, the οὐ μή of prohibition with second pers. is best understood interrogatively; in other cases, οὐ μή is assertive. Thus, in the exx. given in § 124, R. 4, and *Eur. Bacch.* 340, οὐ μὴ προσοίσεις χεῖρα, βακχεύσεις δ' ἰών, μηδ' ἐξομόρξει μωρίαν τὴν σὴν ἐμοί; where the groundwork of the sentence is οὐ βακχεύσεις; *will you not go, play the Bacchanal?* into which μὴ προσοίσεις χεῖρα, *do not imagine you shall lay your hand upon me*, is inserted, and μηδ' ἐξ., &c., is added as opposition. But in *Soph. Œd. C.* 173, οὔτοι μή ποτέ σ' ἐκ τῶνδ' ἑδράνων, ὦ γέρον, ἄκοντά τις ἄξει, the

[APPENDIX.

interrogative form is evidently not intended, and the sense is, "*no, assuredly! do not imagine, do not fear*, &c. (= *μή*) *that any shall carry thee off, &c.*" [§ 293.] The usage of the language would rather require *ἄξῃ* (*ἀγάγῃ*), but the thought prominent at last in the speaker's mind is *οὐκ ἄξει*: hence the future indic. = "do not imagine that the thing shall be; *it shall not be.*" So *Œd. C.* 848, *οὔκουν ποτ' ἐκ τούτοιν γε μὴ σκήπτροιν ἔτι ὁδοιπορήσεις* —, where, though the verb is in the second person, *οὐ — μή* is assertive, not prohibitive; *you shall not have these — do not imagine it — as props in your wayfarings*, and the assertion is stronger than with *ὁδοιπορήσῃς*. *Soph. El.* 1052, *ἀλλ' εἴσιθ'· οὔ σοι μὴ μεθέψομαί ποτε, οὐδ' ἢν σφόδρ' ἱμείρουσα τοῦτο τυγχάνῃς*, the fut. indic., as in the preceding instance, because the action is negatived for all future time. *Arist. Ran.* 508, *μὰ τὸν Ἀπόλλω, οὐ μή σ' ἐγὼ περιόψομαι ἀπελθόντα*, an asseveration beginning in the usual form, *μὰ τὸν Ἀ. οὐ*, and strengthened by the prohibition of imagining the contrary.[1]—In the dependent sentence, *ἐθέσπισεν — ὡς οὐ μή ποτε πέρσοιεν*, *Soph. Phil.* 607, represents *οὐ μή ποτε πέρσουσι* of *oratio recta*. So acc. c. inf., *σαφῶς γὰρ εἶπε Τειρεσίας, οὐ μή ποτε σοῦ τήνδε γῆν οἰκοῦντος εὖ πράξειν πόλιν*, *Eur. Phœn.* 1606.

The usage of *μὴ οὐ* is derived from that of *μή* prefixed to a verb negatived by *οὐ*. § 294.

In the independent sentence, this combination does not occur with the indicative, i. e. not *μὴ οὐ γράφεις; you do not say you are not writing!* but only *μῶν οὐ*: thus, *ἐν οἷς τί χρῆν ποιεῖν ἐμέ; μῶν οὐχ ὅπερ ἐποίουν; Soph. Œd. C.* 1727. But with the subjunctive in a form of sentence which may be considered as elliptical (cf. § 289), we have *μὴ οὖν, ἔφη, οὐ δύνωμαι ἐγὼ . . . ἐξηγήσασθαι; you do not say I am not to be able —? Xen. Mem.* 4, 2, 12. *ἡμῖν δὲ . . . μὴ οὐδὲν ἄλλο σκεπτέον ᾖ*, where the supposed ellipsis is *ὅρα*, *Pl. Crito*, 48. — In the dependent sentence, *δέδοικα μὴ οὐκ ἀποθάνῃ, ἐδεδ. μὴ οὐκ ἀποθάνοι, δέδοικα μὴ οὐ τέθνηκεν*, require no further explanation.

With the inf., see § 211, comp. § 210. Here observe that (1) *οὐκ ἀρνοῦμαι οὕτως εἶναι* represents the simple assertion *οὕτως ἔστιν*, with negation of denial, *οὐκ ἀρνοῦμαι*. § 295. (2) In *ἀρνοῦμαι μὴ οὕτως εἶναι*, there is a union of *ἀρνοῦμαι οὕτως εἶναι* with *μὴ οὕτως ἔστιν, you do not say that it is so?* or with *φημὶ μὴ οὕτως εἶναι*: the phrase is therefore stronger than (1), viz. = both *I deny that it is so*, and, *I have no notion that it is so*; and, the whole phrase being negatived, *οὐκ ἀ. μὴ οὕτως εἶναι* = *I do not deny that it is so*, and, *I would not have you imagine that it is not so*, which is equivalent to *contendo ita esse*. (3) Lastly, *οὐκ ἀρνοῦμαι μὴ οὐχ οὕτως εἶναι* may be referred to a union of *οὐκ ἀρνοῦμαι οὕτως εἶναι* and *μὴ οὐχ οὕτως ἔστιν, you do not say*

---

[1] The pres. subj. is rare: *οὐ μὴ δύνωμαι* (*Xen.*), and *οὐ μὴ οἷός τ' ᾖς* (*Pl.*), are not conclusive instances, since these verbs have no aor., and, besides, *δύνασθαι* and *οἷόν τ' εἶναι* have in themselves the future signification which is required in this phrase. In *Soph. Œd. C.* 1023, the text is uncertain: *οὓς οὐ μή ποτε χώρας φυγόντες τῆσδ' ἐπεύχωνται*, al. *ἐπεύξωνται*, for the *ἐπεύχονται* of the MSS. Ellendt receives *ἐπεύχωνται*, in the sense, "are *now* giving thanks to the gods," viz. "because Theseus surmises the persons to be already taken: with *ἐπεύξονται* or *ἐπεύξωνται*, he would imply, that they would be taken;" and so Hermann in l.; but Schneidewin reads, *οὓς οὐ δή ποτε*, and *ἐπεύχονται*. As regards the *principle*, there is no reason why the vulg. should not be retained, viz. *μή* and *ἐπεύχονται*, "they are not — never imagine it! — giving thanks —."

[§ 295.] *that it is not so?* In this construction, the leading verb must be expressly or virtually (by interrogation) negatived, or must contain a negative notion, δεινόν, αἰσχρόν, αἰσχύνη, &c. (cf. § 211 b): thus, οὔτε μὴ μεμνῆσθαι δύναμαι αὐτοῦ, οὔτε μεμνημένος μὴ οὐκ ἐπαινεῖν (*Xen. Apol.* fin.), where μὴ μεμνῆσθαι is the necessary infinitive form of οὐ μέμνημαι, and μὴ οὐκ ἐπαινεῖν of μὴ οὐκ ἐπαινέσω: *you do not imagine I am not to praise him? Impossible* (not to do so).[1]

§ 296. With the participle, μὴ οὐ (rare in Attic prose, § 211 c) will be found to involve the same relation to μὴ οὐ with the indicative = *you do not suppose, &c., that — not —?* Thus, οὐκ ἂν ἀξιώπιστος εἴην μὴ οὐχὶ πρότερον αὐτὸς φανεὶς οἷός εἰμι: with οὐ only, this sentence, reduced to its simplest form, is οὐ πρ. φανείς —, οὐκ ἀξ., "a person not first showing himself what he is, is a person not worthy of credit:" with μή only, οὐκ ἀ. ἂν εἴην, μὴ πρ. φανείς: both expressions are united upon the basis of the expression μὴ οὐ πρ. ἐφάνην, *you do not suppose I have not first showed myself?* so that the whole is not simply = *without first showing myself*, which would be sufficiently expressed by μή alone, but together with this, *as it is not to be supposed that I should not.* So *Soph. Œd. T.* 13, δυσάλγητος γὰρ ἂν εἴην τοιάνδε μὴ οὐ κατοικτείρων ἕδραν, without οὐ,[2] the sense would be, εἰ μὴ κατοικτείροιμι, with it δυσάλγ. must be resolved into a negative expression, and we have then οὐ κατοικτείρων, οὐκ εὐάλγητος: οὐκ εἴην ἂν εὐάλγ. μὴ κατοικτείρων: and, as the basis of their union, μὴ οὐ κατοικτείρω, *you do not imagine that I do not take pity? Soph. Œd. C.* 359, ἥκεις γὰρ οὐ κενή γε, τοῦτ' ἐγὼ σαφῶς ἐξοῖδα, μὴ οὐχὶ δεῖμ' ἐμοὶ φέρουσά τι: the negation is οὐ κενή, and this is taken up and enlarged upon in the last clause, which, however, is formed as if the negation were οὐχ ἥκεις: *thou comest not empty* — (not) *without being the bearer — I am sure it cannot be otherwise — of some terror to me.* — With ellipsis of the participle, αἱ πόλεις πολλαὶ καὶ χαλεπαὶ λαβεῖν αἱ τῶν Φωκέων, μὴ οὐ χρόνῳ καὶ πολιορκίᾳ (*Dem.* in § 211, c). The ellipsis is ἁλοῦσαι, or the like, and χαλεπαὶ λαβεῖν = οὐκ εὐάλωτοι, and the explanation is the same as in the former instances. — With the gen. absolute: εἰνάτῃ δὲ οὐκ ἐξελεύσεσθαι ἔφασαν μὴ οὐ πλήρεος ἐόντος τοῦ κύκλου, *Hdt.* 6, 106. The elements are, οὐ πλ. ἐστιν ὁ κ., οὐκ ἐξελευσόμεθα: οὐκ ἐξ. μὴ πλ. ἐόντος τοῦ κ.: μὴ ἐξελευσόμεθα, οὐ πλ. ἐ. τοῦ κ., "do not imagine we shall go out with the moon not at the full."

§ 297. ἄν, and enclitic κε, κεν (not Attic).

Ἄν is probably cognate with the preposition ἀνά (Hermann, *de Part.* Ἄν, Opusc. t. iv., makes ἐβουλόμην ἂν εἰ ἐδυνάμην = ἐβουλόμην ἀνὰ τοῦτο εἰ ἐδυνάμην, *secundum hoc*); and κε, κεν with κατά, therefore also with καί (Hermann), and pre-eminently with the enclitic τις in the form κος (κου = που, κως = πως). — In the earlier

---

[1] "*Per* μή *certo, per* μὴ οὐ *dubitantius negatur,*" Hermann. ad Vig. p. 797. But in many places, the meaning is rather that of wondering or indignant repudiation of the opposite notion, e.g. οὐδ' ἐθέλω προλιπεῖν τόδε, μὴ οὐ τὸν ἐμὸν στοναχεῖν πατέρ' ἄθλιον, *Soph. El.* 131; *I will not forego or desert this sad duty — you do not imagine that I should not bewail,* &c.? Hence (as H. also suggests) its force may be rendered by *mirum foret, ni* —.

[2] Omitted by Schneidewin on grounds which seem to be insufficient, since, according to the explanation in the text, the οὐ before κατοικτ. does not serve for "merely external correlation" to the οὐ involved in the primary clause. In *Œd. T.* 221, οὐ γὰρ ἂν μακρὰν ἴχνευον αὐτός, μὴ οὐκ ἔχων τι σύμβολον, the μή is better omitted (with Schn.), since Œd. does not mean to allege that he has a clue, and οὐκ ἔ. τι σ. carries on the notion of αὐτός, "left to myself alone."

(not Attic) Greek, *κεν* and *ἄν* often appear in correlation (cf. *τε — καί*. § 222), the [§ 297.]
former in the protasis, the latter in the apodosis, *εἴπερ γάρ κε βλεῖο —, οὐκ ἄν — πέσοι βέλος*. *Il.* 13, 288, but often so that the apodosis stands first: thus, *αὐτὸν δ' ἂν πύματόν με κύνες πρώτῃσι θύρῃσιν ὠμησταὶ ἐρύουσιν, ἐπεί κέ τις — ἐκ θυμὸν ἕληται*, *Il.* 22. 66. *ὡς ἂν ἔπειτ' ἀπὸ σεῖο — οὐκ ἐθέλοιμι λείπεσθ', οὐδ' εἴ κέν μοι ὑποσταίη θεὸς αὐτός*. *Il.* 9, 444. The force of *κεν — ἄν* is, *in some* (or, *any*) *way* (*sort, case*, &c.) —, *in that way* (*sort, case*, &c.). More frequently *κεν* appears in both clauses (cf. *τε — τε*, § 227): *εἰ δέ κε μὴ δώωσιν, ἐγὼ δέ κεν αὐτὸς ἕλωμαι* = *if in any way — then in some way*. *ὁ δέ κεν κεχολώσεται ὅν κεν ἵκωμαι*. But the one or the other particle is often omitted: *αἴ κ' αὐτὸν γνώω νημερτέα πάντ' ἐνέποντα, ἕσσω μιν χλαῖναν*. And very often the protasis or condition to which *ἄν* or *κεν* refers, is not expressed. Thus, *πληθὺν δ' οὐκ ἂν ἐγὼ μυθήσομαι οὐδ' ὀνομήνω*, viz. (*εἴ κε —*) "if I try," or, "if another can:" *καί κέ τις ὧδ' ἐρέει*. viz. "(if in any wise so be,) *then may-hap* —." Ἄν, and in apodosis *κεν*, always thus looks back to a supposition expressed or understood.

But *ἄν*, though it properly belongs to the apodosis, is often drawn into the pro- §
tasis, viz. with the particle *εἰ* in *ἐάν, ἤν*, with *ὅς*, and its adverbial forms (*ὃς ἄν, ὅταν*, 298.
ὡς ἄν, &c.); also *εὖτ' ἄν, ἐπεὶ ἄν*, and *ἐπήν*, &c. In all these cases, the *ἄν*, together with its verb, is apodosis to a suppressed condition: thus, *ὄψεαι ἢν ἐθελῃσθα* = *thou shalt see, if*, when the time comes, then *thou shalt be willing* (i.e. if in the event it shall appear that thou art willing). So with the relative forms. *Οὓς ἂν ἴδῃς κάλεσον*, = *whom*, if so and so (e.g. if there be any to be seen), *you shall see* . . . *ὡς ἂν ἐγὼν εἴπω, πειθώμεθα* = *in what way* (whatever the way may be,) *I shall speak*, or, *in what way* (supposing that I speak,) *I shall speak*: i.e. the groundwork of the sentence is, *if I speak, I shall speak so* (*εἴ κ' εἴπω, τὼς ἂν εἴπω*), and this thrown into the relative form becomes *ὡς ἂν εἴπω*. So *ἐκ γὰρ Ὀρέσταο τίσις ἔσσεται* . . . . , *ὁππότ' ἂν ἡβήσῃ*: the groundwork, "when the time shall come (*ὅτε κεν —*), *τότ' ἂν ἡβήσῃ*," in the relative form, *ὁππότ' ἂν ἡβήσῃ*. Or, as all relatives imply correlation, the relative with *ἄν* may be explained as condensed from demonstr. with *ἄν* together with relative with *κεν*, viz. *τότ' ἂν* (*ἔσσεται*) *ὅτε κεν ἡβήσῃ*. So *Il.* 15. 232. *τόφρα γὰρ οὖν οἱ ἔγειρε μένος μέγα, ὄφρ' ἂν Ἀχαιοὶ φεύγοντες νῆάς τε καὶ Ἑλλήσποντον ἵκωνται* = *τόφρα ἂν* (*ἐγερεῖς*) . . . . , *ὄφρα κεν ἵκωνται*. — Hence, where *ἄν* appears in the protasis, the apodosis rarely (perhaps never) has *κεν*: i.e. it would be difficult to produce a sentence of the form *ἢν δὲ μὴ δώωσιν, ἐγὼ δέ κεν αὐτὸς ἕλωμαι*. In *νῦν γάρ χ' Ἕκτορ' ἕλοις, ἐπεὶ ἂν μάλα τοὶ σχεδὸν ἔλθοι*, *Il.* 9, 304, the *κεν* in the first clause corresponds with an unexpressed *εἴ κε θέλοις, εἴ κεν ἔλθοι*, or the like, not with *ἐπεὶ ἄν* in the latter clause, which resolves itself into some such correlation as *διὰ τοῦτο ἂν* (sc. *ἕλοις*) *ὅτι κεν μ. σχ. ἔλθοι*.

Sometimes *ἄν* and *κεν* appear in the same clause: thus, *ἵσταντο φάλαγγες. ἃς οὔτ' ἄν κεν Ἄρης ὀνόσαιτο μετελθών, οὔτε κ' Ἀθηναίη*, *Il.* 13, 127, where *ἄν* (see next paragraph) is attracted by *οὔτε*, and the sentence may be resolved either into *ταὶ ἂν ἔσονται* (*αἱ φ.*) *ἃς οὔτε κεν Ἄρ., οὔτε κ' Ἀθ.*. or, independently of the relative, *οὔτε, εἴ κεν Ἄρης ἔλθοι* (or *ἐθέλοι*, &c., or *εἴ κεν Ἄρη λέγοις*, &c.), *Ἄρης ὀνόσαιτο ἄν*. (See other instances under *ὄφρα*.)

With respect to position in the sentence, *κε* never recedes far from the beginning. §
Εἰ δ' Ὀδυσεὺς ἔλθοι —, αἶψά κε — ἀποτίσεται, *Od.* 17, 540. *ἀλλ' ἤτοι νῦν μέν κε* 299.
νεμεσσηθεὶς ὑποείξω, *Il.* 15, 211. *καί κέ τις ὧδ' ἐρέει*, *Il.* 4, 176 (not *καί τίς χ' ὧδ' ἐρέει*, like *μαθὼν δέ τις ἂν ἐρεῖ*, *Pind. Nem.* 7, 68[1]). But *ἄν*, besides its attraction by the relative or conditional word, though its proper place is with the predicate, usually

---

[1] Hermann remarks, that *ἦ κε μέγ' ὠμώξειεν ὁ Πελοπίδης Ἀγαμέμνων*, *Hdt.* 7, 159,

[§ 299.] attaches itself to the emphatic word of the clause. Thus, *πατρὸς δὲ καὶ μητρὸς οὐκέτι μευ ζωόντων, ἀδελφεὸς ἂν ἄλλος οὐδενὶ τρόπῳ γένοιτο*, *Hdt.* 3, 119 (see § 139 b). Hence it likes to attach itself to words by which the simple form of the sentence is altered, such as *οὐκ, οὔτ', οὐδ', οὔποτε*, &c., *τίς, τί, πῶς, ἆρα*, &c., adverbs of time, place, manner, such as *ἐνταῦθα, τότε, τάχα, ἴσως, εἰκότως, ῥᾳδίως, ῥᾷστα, μάλιστα, μόλις, σχολῇ. ἡδέως (ἄσμενος), σφόδρα, καί (κἄν, etiam, vel)*, &c., and the inferential *οὖν, τί οὖν ἄν τις εἴποι* —, the principle being the same in all, viz. that that term of the apodosis which is to have the greatest prominence in reference to the conditional sentence (expressed or unexpressed) draws the *ἄν* after it, because *ἄν* has the same reference. For other remarkable attractions (hyperbaton) of *ἄν*, see § 139 b, R.

§ 300. For the usage of the particle *Ἄν*. see the Index. — In the cultivated Attic prose, the use of *ἄν* with fut. indicative (Homer, Pindar, and lyrical parts of Tragedy) is rejected, partly in consequence of the rejection of *κε*, partly because the provinces of the indicative future and the subjunctive are more clearly discriminated (whence also the omission of *ἄν* with the subj. in conditional and relative sentences, which is frequent in the early and extra-Attic Greek, is rare in Attic, e. g. *εἰ ποιήσῃς, ὅτε λέξῃς*). Thus, *αὐτὸν δ' ἂν πύματόν με κύνες πρώτῃσι θύρῃσιν ὠμησταὶ ἐρύουσιν, ἐπεί κέ τις — ἐκ θυμὸν ἕληται*, *Il.* 22, 66, an apodosis with *ἄν*, followed by its protasis with *κε*: here the Attic, rejecting the *κε*, gives the protasis in the *different* form, *ἐπειδὰν ἕληται*; consequently, the *ἄν* of the apodosis falls away. In the elliptical sentence, *πληθὺν δ' οὐκ ἂν ἐγὼ μυθήσομαι*, where *ἄν* points to an unexpressed *εἴ κε* —, e. g. "if I shall try," the Attic retaining *ἄν* for the like reference uses the optative. In the passages (of Attic prose) where *ἄν* appears with fut. indic., there is some negligence of construction. Thus, *Pl. Apol.* 29, *ὡς εἰ διαφευξοίμην, ἤδη ἂν ὑμῶν οἱ υἱεῖς ἐπιτηδεύοντες ἃ Σωκράτης διδάσκει πάντες παντάπασι διαφθαρήσονται* (so all the best MSS.): the writer meant to say, *ἤδη ἂν ὑμῶν οἱ υἱεῖς ἐπιτηδεύοιεν* . . . . , *καὶ π. π. διαφθαρήσονται*, but, changing the construction, puts the participle in place of the finite mood. The other two undoubted instances in *Pl.*, are *Rep.* 615, *οὐχ ἥκει, οὐδ' ἂν ἥξει δεῦρο*; *Phædon.* 61, *οὐδ' ὁπωστιοῦν ἄν σοι ἑκὼν εἶναι πείσεται*: in both, the irregularity is caused by the aptness of *ἄν* to attach itself to *οὐδ'* and *οὖν*. So *Thuc.* 2, 80, *ῥᾳδίως ἂν σχόντες — κρατήσουσι*, the adv. *ῥᾳδίως* drawing *ἄν* after it, as if the writer had meant to say, *σχοῖεν, καὶ σχόντες κρατήσουσι*. Just so *Xen. Cyr.* 6, 1, 45, *ἄσμενος ἂν πρὸς ἄνδρα οἷος σὺ εἶ ἀπαλλαγήσεται = ἡδέως ἄν*, "he would gladly come forward (or the like), and will —." *Ib.* 7, 5, 21, *πολὺ ἂν ἔτι μᾶλλον ἢ νῦν ἀχρεῖοι ἔσονται = πολὺ ἂν — τοῦτο γένοιτο —, ὅτι —*. *Æsch. de f. leg.* 196, *οὕτω γὰρ ἂν μάλιστα μεμνήσομαι καὶ δυνήσομαι εἰπεῖν. = ἂν εἴη, ὅτι —*. And in questions: *τί ποτ' ἂν ἐκ τούτων ἐρεῖ; Eur. Bacch.* 595. *ἆρά γε τοῦτ' ἂν ἐγώ ποτ' ἐπόψομαι; Arist. Nub.* 465. *τί ποτ' ἂν ἐρεῖ; Æsch. Ctes.* 155: here the *ἄν* does not belong to the verb, but to an unexpressed optative, *λέγοις, φαίης*, or the like, followed by *ὅτι*.

With imperf. and aor. indic., *ἄν* is always = "in that case," with reference to a preceding "if:" *εἰ ἐβουλόμην, ἔλεγον ἄν. — οἱ μὲν ὄνοι, ἐπεί τις διώκοι, προδραμόντες ἂν εἱστήκεσαν* (*præcurrere et deinde restitare solebant*, Porson: instead of the vulg. *ἀνειστήκεσαν*, for which others *ἕστασαν* without *ἄν*), *Xen. An.* 1, 5, 2, *so often as* —, (in that case) *they would* — (*ἄν rei fieri solitæ*): cf. *Soph. Phil.* 287—295, which is the locus classicus for this usage.

So in all the usages of *ἄν* with optative; *μένοιμ' ἄν* (viz. *εἰ θελοις*, or the like).—

---

was suggested by reminiscence of *ἦ κε μέγ' οἰμώξειε γέρων ἱππηλάτα Πηλεύς*: else the speaker would have said, *ἦ μέγ' ἂν ᾤμ.*

[APPENDIX.

But ἄν with subjunctive always accompanies a conditional or relative word; and here the "in that case" refers to a latent condition, as explained above, whence it closely accompanies, or even coalesces with, the conjunction or relative. When with the temporal particles, ἐπεί, ἕως, μέχρι οὗ, &c., the ἄν is omitted, the event is put by itself without the "in that case," or "if so be," involved in ἄν. Ἔσπεισται μέχρι οὗ ἐπανέλθωσιν οἱ πρέσβεις (*Th.*), ἐν τῷ φρονεῖν γὰρ μηδὲν ἥδιστος βίος. ἕως τὸ χαίρειν καὶ τὸ λυπεῖσθαι μάθῃς (*Soph.*). (On πρίν, πρὶν ἄν with subj., see § 306.) [§ 300.]

It follows from the foregoing principles, that ἄν cannot appear in the indicative or optative protasis, unless the protasis be itself in some respect conceived as apodosis to some other proposition. Thus, ἔδωκας ἄν, ἃ ἂν ἤθελες αὐτός, "you would have given what (if so and so) you would have wished." ὁπόταν ἥκοι ἐπὶ τὸ δεῖπνον, λέγοιμ' ἄν (*Xen.*) = ὁπότε (if so and so, ἥκοι ἄν,) λέγοιμ' ἄν. (This, however, may be considered as indirect form of ὁπόταν ἥκῃ, λέξω: comp. the ex. of opt. with ἐπειδάν in a depend. sentence which has passed from the subj. into the opt., § 132 b, R.) With εἰ, the ἄν will usually follow the verb: Εἰ λῷον καὶ ἄμεινον εἴη ἂν τῇ πόλει οὕτω κατασκευαζομένῃ (*Dem.*): here the basis of the sentence is, λ. καὶ ἄ. εἴη ἂν τῇ π. οὕτω κ., = εἰ οὕτω κατασκευάζοιτο, and this whole assertion is made conditional with εἰ. So from the assertion δοῦλον ἀκρατῆ (= εἰ ἀκρατὴς εἴη) οὐ δεξαίμεθ' ἄν, we have the condition εἴ γε μηδὲ δοῦλον ἀκρατῆ δεξαίμεθ' ἄν. Ἀγαπητόν, εἰ καὶ ἐξ ὑποβολῆς δύναιντ' ἂν ἄνδρες ἀγαθοὶ εἶναι (*Xen.*), the fundamental assertion being καὶ εἰ ὑποβολὴ εἴη, ἐξ ὑ. δύναιντ' ἄν. — Εἰ τοίνυν τοῦτο ἰσχυρὸν ἂν ἦν πρὸς ὑμᾶς τεκμήριον . . . , κἀμοὶ γενέσθω τεκμήριον, *Dem.* c. Timoth. 1201, "if this, had it been alleged, would have been —." — Οὐ γὰρ ἂν καλῶς ἔχοι, εἰ ὅτι τελέως ἀνὴρ ἀγαθὸς ἐγένετο, διὰ τοῦτο οὐδὲ μειόνων γ' ἂν τυγχάνοι ἐπαίνων (*Xen.*); here the assertion μειόνων γ' ἂν τυγχάνοι, εἰ καὶ δικαίων μὴ τυγχάνοι, negatived by οὐδέ, is put hypothetically with εἰ. Οὗτοι δ' εἰ μὲν εἶχον χείρον' ἂν ἡμῶν, οὐδὲν ἂν ἦν δεινόν (*Dem.*), i. e. εἰ εἶχον, χείρον' ἂν ἡμῶν εἶχον, and εἰ χείρον' ἡμῶν εἶχον, οὐδὲν ἂν ἦν δεινόν. § 301.

With the final particles, ὡς, ὅπως (poet. ὄφρα) ἄν with subj., refers to a condition implied either in the protasis or in the apodosis. Thus, ὡς ἂν μάθῃς, ἄκουσον, *ut discas, audi* (i. e. *ut discas, si forte discas*, Herm.); or, and this more frequently, *ut discas, disces autem si audias*. This will be evident upon reducing ὡς ἂν μάθῃς to its original correlation: ὥς κεν ἀκούσεις, τῶς ἂν μαθήσῃ. — νιυκλήρου τρόποις μορφὴν δολώσας, ὡς ἂν ἄγνοια προσῇ, *Soph. Ph.* 129 = "that it may be so, as, if I do this, it will be so;" therefore almost equivalent to *so shall* —.[1] ἐάσωμεν . . . ἔκηλον αὐτόν, ὡς ἂν εἰς ὕπνον πέσῃ, *ib.* 815 = "that he may —, as he will, if we leave him quiet." ὡς ἂν σκοποὶ νῦν ἦτε τῶν εἰρημένων, *Ant.* 215 = "(you say well: do it then;) so shall ye be —." Creon not only insists that they shall make this their object (ἦτε), but that it shall result (ἔσεσθε).[2] ἴσθι πᾶν τὸ δρώμενον, ὅπως ἂν εἰδὼς ἡμὶν ἀγγείλῃς σαφῆ, "acquaint yourself with all that is doing, that you may —," and, "so shall you —." — With the optative, ὡς ἄν, ὅπως ἂν = *quomodo*, or *ut*. προμηθοῦνται ὅπως ἂν εὐδαιμονοίης, derived from the direct interrogation πῶς ἂν (εἰ δυνατὸν εἴη) εὐδαιμονοίης; — Ἵνα with ἄν, subj. or opt., is never final, § 122. πατρὶς γάρ ἐστι πᾶσ' ἵν' ἂν (*ubicumque*) πράττῃ τις εὖ, *Arist.* § 302.

---

[1] I cannot assent to M.'s statement, § 122, note, that ἄν does not perceptibly alter the meaning.

[2] Comp. ὅπως with fut. in the phrase ὅπως οὖν ἔσεσθε ἄνδρες ἄξιοι τῆς ἐλευθερίας, *Xen. An.* 1, 7, 3.

§ 303. *ὄφρα* (Hom.).

The derivation is either the relative form *ὅ-φι* with *ῥα*, or *ὃ πάρα*, and the meaning, *until that, while that;* but *ὄφρα* also assumes the force of a final particle, the point of time to be reached being conceived as the goal or intent of the action. In this sense, *ὄφρα ἴδω, ὄφρα πυθοίμην* expresses the same thing as *ὡς, ὅπως, ἵνα*. The appearance of *κε* and *ἄν* with this particle results from the correlation *ὄφρα κε —, τόφρ' ἂν* (or *κε*) —. *Ὗε δ' ἄρα Ζεὺς συνεχές, ὄφρα κε θᾶσσον ἁλίπλοα τείχεα θείη*, *Il.* 12, 25 (as the direct expression of the purpose would be *τόφρ' ἂν* (or *κεν*) *ὕσω, ὄφρα κε θείω*). So, *ὄφρα κε τερπόμενος ὄπ' ἀκούῃς Σειρήνοιϊν*, *Od.* 12, 51, "(let them bind thee = they shall bind thee the while, *τόφρ' ἂν* (or *κεν*) *δήσουσι*) that thou the while mayest hear, &c." *Μή με πω ἐς θρόνον ἵζε, διοτρεφές, ὄφρα κεν Ἕκτωρ κεῖται* (r. *κῆται*) *ἐνὶ κλισίῃσιν ἀκηδής*, *Il.* 24, 553. In this correlation, the *ἄν* is often attracted to the relative clause, especially when the demonstrative clause is imperative: *μνήσασθε δὲ θούριδος ἀλκῆς ὄφρ' αν ἐγὼν Ἀχιλῆος ἀμύμονος ἔντεα δύω.* So *τὸν ξεῖνον δύστηνον ἄγ' ἐς πόλιν, ὄφρ' ἂν ἐκεῖθι δαῖτα πτωχεύῃ.* In a few passages, where the correlation is expressed, we have *ὄφρ' ἂν μέν κεν —, τόφρα*: viz. *ὄφρ' ὂν μέν κεν ὁρᾷ . . . τόφρ' ἀναχωρείτω*, *Il.* 11, 187. and *ib.* 202. *ὄφρ' ἂν μέν κεν δούρατ' ἁρήρῃ, τόφρ' αὐτοῦ μενέω*, *Od.* 5, 361, and *ὄφρ' αν μέν κ' ἀγροὺς ἴομεν —, τόφρα — καρπαλίμως ἔρχεσθαι*, *ib.* 6, 259.[1]

§ 304. *ἕως. τέως.*

The earlier form is probably *ἧος* or *ἦος* (comp. *ἦμος*). Its correlative is *τέως*, but also *τόφρα* is so used. *τόφρα γάρ ἂν ποτιπτυσσοίμεθα μύθῳ . . . . ἕως κ' ἀπὸ πάντα δοθείη*, *Od.* 2, 77. *ἕως* (*ἧος*) *ὃ ταῦθ' ὥρμαινε, τόφρα οἱ ἔγγυθεν ἦλθεν — Νέστορος υἱός*, *Il.* 18, 15. Sometimes *ἕως* in Homer is demonstrative, e. g. *ὡς Ἕκτωρ εἵως μὲν ἀπείλει*, in the same sense as *τέως μὲν* (*for a while*) *ἡσύχαζον, ἐπεὶ δέ —*, *Xen.*: and sometimes in Attic prose, *τέως* is used for *ἕως*. (*Buttmann, Index ad Dem. Mid.*)

§ 305. *ἔστε.*

Comp. Homer's *εἰς ὅτε, εἴσοκε*, and Lat. *usque*. The Attics use it instead of *ὄφρα*, and in the sense *usque* with a preposition, *ἔστε ἐπὶ τὸ δάπεδον* (*Xen.*).

Rem. The same sense is expressed by *ἕως οὗ, μέχρις οὗ, ἄχρις οὗ*. These two prepositional adverbs, in which there is no perceptible difference of meaning, are derived from *μακρός, ἀκρός* ("to the length of where," "up to where"). Hom. has also *μέσφα* (related to *μέσος*) in the sense of *μέχρι*, *Il.* 8, 508.

§ 306. *πρίν.*

This particle, whether explained as a locative form of the root *προ*, or as an ancient comparative (*πριον-*, comp. *prius* and *pris* in *priscus*, &c.), is properly an adverb (and so used especially in poetry: *ὧν πρὶν οὐκ ἀκήκοας. ὃς πρὶν ᾤχετο. ἐν τῷ πρὶν χρόνῳ*, &c.), and is still in fact such even when it is used as a conjunction in the connexion of sentences, and ranks, as such, with the temporal particles *ὅτε, ἐπεί, ἕως*, &c. (§ 127. 138.)

---

[1] Thiersch holds, that *ὄφρα* with *κεν, ἄν*, is not final, "in order that," but "while," "until;" but in several of the passages cited, an intention is clearly implied. Rost makes *ὄφρ' ἂν* to be = *ut, si forte*, and *ὄφρα κε* to imply that the event is confidently expected. Quite an erroneous distinction. The difference at most is that between *ὄφρα κε — τόφρα κε*, and *ὄφρα κε — τόφρ' ἄν* (§ 297); and *ὄφρ' ἂν δύω* is "so shall (or, may) I the while put on," *ὄφρα δύω*, "while that I put on."

Thus, in Homer, *οὐδ' ὅγε πρὶν λοιμοῖο βαρείας κῆρας ἀφέξει, πρίν γ' ἀπὸ πατρὶ φίλῳ δόμεναι ἑλικώπιδα κούρην*, *Il.* 1, 97, with correlation, *nor will he sooner hold off —, sooner there must be a giving —:* the first *πρίν* looking forward, = "before the giving;" the second looking back, = "before the holding off." *ἥμεθ' ἀτυζόμεναι . . . , πρίν γ' ὅτε δή με σὸς υἱὸς ἀπὸ μεγάροιο κάλεσσεν*, *Od.* 23, 43: here the *πρίν* properly belongs to the first clause, *we sat — before, and then indeed*, which in the relative form becomes — *before* (the time) *when at last*, or *πρὶν ἢ ὅτε*. So with *ὅταν*: *ὅμοσον μὴ μυθήσασθαι, πρίν γ' ὅταν . . . γένηται*, = *μὴ πρὶν μυθήσασθαι, ἢ ὅταν*, or *ἀλλ' ὅταν*. — In good Attic authors, we find *πρὶν ἄν* with subj., *πρίν* with opt., only after a negation expressed or implied, probably because this form of sentence is conceived as resting on the *correlation* of *πρίν — πρίν*, which necessarily involves a negation of one clause. This correlation is sometimes even expressed: e.g. *οὐκ ἀποκρινοῦμαι πρύτερον . . . . πρὶν ἂν πρῶτον ἀποκρίνωμαι ὅ τι ἐστίν* (*Pl.*) = "I will not answer sooner . . . . , (but) before (doing so) I will first answer," combined with the form *οὐκ ἀποκρινοῦμαι πρίν, ἢ* (or *ἀλλ'*) *ὅταν ἀποκρ.* So (*εἰ*) *μὴ ἀνείη . . . . πρὶν ἐξελκύσειεν εἰς τὸ τοῦ ἡλίου φῶς*, which is the indirect form of *οὐκ ἀνήσει* (*πρίν*, or *πρότερον*), *πρὶν* (*ἀνιέναι*) *ἐξελκύσει*, and *οὐκ ἀνήσει πρὶν* (*ἢ ὅτε*) *ἐξελκύσει*. Or, the *πρίν* may be conceived to belong to the latter clause, but with relation to the first, as in Homer's *τὴν δ' ἐγὼ οὐ λύσω· πρίν μιν καὶ γῆρας ἔπεισιν*, "I will not let her go: before (ere, sooner than, that shall be) old age shall come upon her." With the indicative, an affirmative sometimes precedes, but this is comparatively rare (mostly confined to Trag. and Thuc., who usually has *πρὶν δή, πρίν γε δή*). Thus, *οἱ Λακεδαιμόνιοι ἡσύχαζον, πρὶν δὴ ἡ δύναμις τῶν Ἀθηναίων σαφῶς ἤρετο* (*Thuc.*) — a phrase contracted from *ἡσύχαζον πρίν, καὶ τότε δή —*, or *ἡσ. πρὶν ἢ ὅτε δή*. *Παραπλήσια . . . ἔπασχον, πρίν γε δὴ οἱ Συρακόσιοι ἔτρεψαν* (*Thuc.*). Here no correlation is implied: but in the negative sentence, *οὐκ ἰέναι ἤθελεν πρὶν ἡ γυνὴ αὐτὸν ἔπεισεν* (*Xen.*), the form may be either *οὐκ ἤθελε πρίν, πρὶν ἔπεισεν*, or *οὐκ ἤθ. πρίν, ἢ* (or *ἀλλ'*) *ὅτε ἔπεισεν*. So *πρίν* with inf. may follow either a negative or an affirmative assertion, according as there is or is not correlation. *Οὐδέ τις ἔτλη πρὶν πιέειν, πρὶν λεῖψαι*, *Il.* 7, 480, the elements being, "they will not drink first, (but) first they will make a libation," "they will not drink before (libation made), before (drinking, there must be) libation:" but *στῆτ' αὐτοῦ πρὶν πεσέειν* = *στῆτ' αὐτοῦ πρὶν ἢ πεσεῖτε*, *Il.* 6, 82. (Both forms, infin. and subj., are united by *ἤ*, "or," after a negation, in *Il.* 14, 504.) [§ 306.]

REM. In Attic, *ἤ* is rarely expressed after *πρίν*; and *ἄν* with the subj. is sometimes omitted, as also with *μέχρι οὗ, ἕως*, especially in Trag. and Thuc. *οὐ χρὴ ἀρχῆς ἄλλης ὀρέγεσθαι, πρὶν ἣν ἔχομεν βεβαιωσώμεθα* (*Thuc.*), the thought being, "before (we do that), let us (= I counsel, that we first) make sure what we have." *Μὴ στέναζε, πρὶν μάθῃς*, *Soph. Phil.* 917, "before (you groan), (I advise you to) learn," combined with *μὴ στ. πρὶν μαθεῖν*: but *πρὶν ἂν μάθῃς* would be, "not sooner, but when, if so be, you shall have learnt." — On the other hand, *ἄν* is sometimes inserted with optative: *ἀπαγορευόντων μὴ ἀποκτείνειν τὸν ἄνδρα πρὶν ἂν ἐγὼ ἔλθοιμι* (*Antiph.* 5, 113), as indirect form of *μὴ ἀπόκτεινε πρὶν ἂν ἐγὼ ἔλθω*.

ὡς. §

This adverbial form of the relative *ὅς*, the same as *ut* (i.e. *quut* from *qui*), derives its various usages partly from the correlation *τῶς* (*ὧς, οὕτως*) — *ὡς*, *in the manner — in which, so — as*; partly from the corresponding interrogative form *πῶς*; (*κῶς*; from *κός* = *τίς*; *quis?*) and indirect interrogative *ὅπως*. 307.

a) *as, sicut, quemadmodum*, in comparison, *οὕτως ὡς ἔχω*, *just as I am.* *πρέπει ὡς τύραννος* (sc. *πρέπει*) *εἰσορᾶν* (*Soph.*): *ἐχίδνης ἰὸς ὡς* (sc. *δαίνυται*) *ἐδαίνυτο* (*Soph.*):

[§ 307.] and frequently in Homeric similes, ὡς δὲ —, ὣς —, *and as —, so.* Strengthened by περ, e.g. ἡ ψυχὴ ἐκβαίνουσα ὥσπερ πνεῦμα ἢ καπνὸς διασκεδασθεῖσα οἴχεται. — In wishes and asseverations, as in Engl., "so heaven help me, as —:" οὕτως ὀναίμην τούτων ὡς ἀληθῆ ἐρῶ, cf. *ita me dii ament ut ego lætor* (*Ter.*). — With ὁ αὐτός, ἴσος, &c., *the same as*, for ὅς. τὸ αὐτὸ σχῆμα ὥσπερ τὸ πρῶτον (*Xen.*). τοῦτον δὲ εἶναι τὸν πλάστην τὸν αὐτὸν ὥσπερ τότε. Similarly, πιστὸς ὥς τις καὶ ἄλλος implies the comparison, *as faithful as* —.

b) *As, ut*, in the sense *quantum, quantum quidem*, in interposed sentences of a limiting or restrictive kind (where the speaker qualifies a statement by remarking, that he puts it, or wishes it to be understood, *in that way in which* it holds, is allowable, &c., under the circumstances described in the parenthetic clause): e.g. "he will come to-day, *as I hear*, ὡς ἀκούω: *as they say*, ὡς λέγουσιν: *as it seems*, ὡς ἔοικεν." The correlation is, *e.g. I speak this* (*so*) *as I hear*, &c. Σὺ δ', ὡς ἔοικας, νομίζεις. — Of the same kind is the ὡς with inf. in the phrases ὡς εἰπεῖν, ὡς ἔπος εἰπεῖν (where we use the demonstrative, "*so* to say"), = οὕτω λέγω ὡς ἔξεστιν εἰπεῖν, or the like: ὡς συντόμως εἰπεῖν, ὡς συνελόντι εἰπεῖν. Elliptically, ὡς πλήθει, *ut summatim dicam* (*Pl.*), — and ἐπίσταμαι ἰδιώτας ὄντας ὡς πρὸς ἡμᾶς ἀγωνίζεσθαι, and ἢ ὡς with inf. after a comparative. So ὥς γ' ἐμοὶ κριτῇ, for which we have also ὥς γ' ἐμοὶ χρῆσθαι κριτῇ. ὥς γ' ἐμοὶ ἀκροατῇ: — ὡς ἐμῇ δόξῃ (*Xen.*). — ὥς γε ἐντεῦθεν ἰδεῖν: ὥς γε οὑτωσὶ δόξαι (*Pl.*). So ὡς with a preposition and its case, πυργοὶ μὲν ὡς ἀπ' ὀμμάτων πρόσω (*Soph.*). ὡς ἐκ τῶν δυνατῶν, ὡς ἐκ τῶν ὑπαρχόντων (*Thuc.*): ἄπιστον τὸ πλῆθος λέγεται ἀπολέσθαι ὡς πρὸς τὸ μέγεθος τῆς πόλεως (*Thuc.*). To the same head may be referred the ὡς which we should express by *for*. Thus, ἦν δὲ οὐδὲ ἀδύνατος, ὡς Λακεδαιμόνιος, εἰπεῖν (*Thuc.*), *for a Lacedæmonian.* πιστὸς ὡς νομεὺς ἀνήρ (*Soph.* (*Ed. T.* 1118), *faithful, for a herdsman, that is* (viz. considered as a mere herdsman, as far as such a person is likely to be faithful). φρονεῖ γὰρ ὡς γυνὴ μέγα, *she has, for a woman, a high spirit.* (Here the force of the particle will be perceived by substituting an interrogation with πῶς; *e.g.* "for *how* should a Lac. be δυνατὸς εἰπεῖν;" — πῶς ἂν γυνὴ φρονοῖ μέγα; &c.) And with the same construction, the dative: μακρὰν γὰρ ὡς γέροντι προὐστάλης ὁδόν (*Soph.*), *long, for an old man.* ταχεῖαν, ὡς ἐμοί, σκέψιν ἐπιτάττεις (*Pl.*). — Ὡς τὰ πολλά, ὡς ἐπὶ τὸ πολύ, ὡς ἐπὶ τὸ πλῆθος, and the like, may be explained in the same way.

c) *As*, in the sense *quasi, tanquam*, also *quippe, utpote.* In this use of ὡς with nouns and participles, there is involved a notion of cause, as when we say, "*as* the case is so and so, therefore —:" i.e. the relation is partly that which is expressed by "*how* —? as —," partly by "why —? because —." This use of ὡς also differs from a), as the things are not compared in their own nature, but put together as like in some thought, feeling, or purpose of the speaker or some other person. Thus, ὡς πολεμίους ἐφυλάττοντο ἡμᾶς, *as* (they thought us) *enemies*, (therefore) *they were on their guard against us* (so as they would be against enemies). εἴπερ ὡς φίλοι προσήκετε, *if, as* (you wish to be) *friends* (therefore) *you are come* (in the way that friends do come). ὡς φύλακα συνέπεμψεν αὐτόν, *as* (he wished him to be) *a guard*, (therefore) *he sent him with* (us) (so as one sends a guard). ὁ δ' ὡς ἀνὴρ γενναῖος οὐκ οἴκτου μέτα κατῄνεσ', *as* (he was) *a noble-spirited man*, (therefore) *he complied* (in the way in which such an one acts). Especially with the participle (as, indeed, in the case of subst. and adjj., the participle ὤν, ἐσόμενος, &c., may always be supplied). Thus, ἀγανακτοῦσιν ὡς ἠπατημένοι, *as* (they think themselves) *deceived*, (therefore) *they are indignant* (in the way that people are, who find themselves deceived). παρεσκευάζετο ὡς μαχούμενος, *as* (he said to himself) *he would fight*, (therefore) *he made ready* (as one does who is going to fight). ᾐτιῶντο ὡς πείσαντα, *as* (they said)

[APPENDIX.

he had been the mover, (therefore) &c. See § 175 d. (Ἅτε, ἅτε δή, in the same [§
connexion, denotes the objective reason, § 175 c.) Hence with the gen. absol. 307.]
ὡς ἠπατημένων ἡμῶν ἠγανάκτουν, *as* (they said) *we were deceived, they were indignant* (so, as in the case of our having been deceived); see § 181, R. 2: and the acc. absol., see § 182, with R. 1. — In like manner, ὡς with the finite verb, in the sense *as* = "as assured that —," especially followed by a negation. δέομαι οὖν σου παραμεῖναι ἡμῖν, ὡς ἐγὼ οὐδ' ἑνὸς ἥδιον ἀκούσαιμι ἢ σοῦ. And so with fut. indic. ὡς οὔτις ἀμφὶ τῷδ' ὑγρὰν θήσει κόνιν, *Eur.* Cf. § 215 b, R. 2. ὡς, ἂν σοὶ πειθώμεθα, οὔτε ὁ γεωργὸς γεωργὸς ἔσται, = *since*, or *for* —, *Pl.*

As if, with the finite verb, in the ironical ὡς δή —, e.g. ὡς δὴ σὺ βραχέα ταῦτα δ' ἐν καιρῷ λέγεις (*Soph.*), *as if forsooth* — ! This might also be referred to the sense *how*, see under *e*. Comp. οἷα δή —, ἅτε δή.

With εἰς, ἐπί, πρός c. acc.: e.g. παρεσκευάζετο ὡς ἐς μάχην (*Thuc.*), ἀνάγεσθαι ἔμελλεν ὡς ἐπὶ ναυμαχίαν (*Xen.*). Here the sense *quasi* is unsuitable, and it is better to understand the phrase in the same manner as ὡς μαχούμενος, *with the intention of going to* —. In the same way, κατέλαβε τὴν ἀκρόπολιν ὡς ἐπὶ τυραννίδι = ὡς τυραννήσων. — Ἀπαγγέλλετε τῇ μητρὶ χαίρειν, ὡς ἀπ' ἐμοῦ = ὡς ἀπαγγέλλων, or ἄγγελος ἀπ' ἐμοῦ.

Ὡς with numerals, ἔδωκεν ὡς μυρίας δραχμάς (*Lys.*), *some ten-thousand drachmæ*, scarcely differs from εἰς: thus, in the enumeration *Xen. An.* 1, 2, 3, ὁπλίτας εἰς πεντακοσίους καὶ χιλίους . . . , ὁπλ. ὡς πεντακοσίους . . . , (ἄνδρας) εἰς ἑπτακοσίους. It is usually referred to the sense *quasi*, but is rather to be explained as ὅσον: comp. the particles in the phrases, "*how* many?" "*as* many *as*," and ἕως, ὧδε, *usque*.

Rem. Ὡς with the accus. (but only of personal objects, or objects conceived as persons) is distinct from the preceding ὡς εἰς, &c. It is a pronominal form (like Lat. *quo*, comp. *usque*), denoting the direction *whither*, the *terminus ad quem* of a motion, and used quite as a preposition. αἰεὶ τὸν ὅμοιον ἄγει θεὸς ὡς τὸν ὅμοιον (*Hom.*), *like to like*. οὐχ ἥκει πρὸς σὲ κηρύσσων ὅδε, ἀλλ' ὡς ἐμέ (*Eur.*). πορεύεται ὡς βασιλέα (*Xen.*). ἥκοντος ὡς τὴν Μίλητον, and ὡς Ἄβυδον (*Thuc.*).

d) With superlatives, especially adverbs, ὡς τάχιστα = *quam celerrime*. Cf. ὅτι (= ὅ,τι) τάχιστα: both combined, ὡς ὅτι σμικρόταται. Comp. also ἀπέχθειαι — οἷαι χαλεπώταται, *Pl.* χωρίον οἷον χαλεπώτατον, *Xen.* Here the full construction is ὡς δυνατὸν, or οἷόν τε, or δύνανται, &c., τάχιστα. See § 96. Also with some positives: ὡς ἀληθῶς = ὡς οἷόντε ἀληθῶς, *as true as possible*. So ἤγγειλαν ὡς ἐτητύμως (*Soph.*), and ὡς ἠπίως ἐννέπειν (*Soph.*),[1] and ὡς τάχος = "in what way speed is possible." So ὡς ἀτεχνῶς, ὡς πάνυ, ὡς μάλα. ὡς αὔτως (ὡσαύτως), ὡς ἑτέρως. Hence we may explain ὡς ἕκαστοι as representing ὡς ἕκας (ἑκάς).

e) *how*, *quomodo* (and *quantopere*). In the sense of ὅπως, in indirect interrogation: thus, (πῶς ἔχει τὸ πρᾶγμα;) αὐτὸς ἂν εἴποι ὡς ἔχει τὸ πρᾶγμα, *how the affair stands*. ὡς δ' οἶδα ταῦτα τῇδ' ἔχοντ', ἐγὼ φράσω (*Soph.*), *how I know* —. And in exclamations: ὡς ἀστεῖος ὁ ἄνθρωπος, (*see*,) *how polite the man is* — ! ὡς οὐδὲν ἄρα ἴσμεν, (*to think*) *how ignorant we are!* ὥς μ' ὑπῆλθέ τις φόβος (*Soph.*). So εὐδαίμων μοι Σωκράτης ἐφαίνετο — ὡς ἀδεῶς καὶ γενναίως ἐτελεύτα (*Pl.*), *when I thought how fearlessly* —, though this may also be explained as § 198 a, R. 3.[2] ἃ πρὸς τὸν

---

[1] Not as Ellendt s. v. ὡς explains, = οὕτως ὥστε ἐτητύμως ἀγγελθέντα (ἠπίως εἰρημένον) δοκεῖν.

[2] *Xen. An.* 2, 5, 39, οὐκ αἰσχύνεσθε —, οἵτινες ὀμόσαντες ἡμῖν —, τοὺς ἄνδρας αὐτοὺς οἷς ὤμνυτε ὡς ἀπολωλέκατε, an anacoluth.: ὡς either = (*to think*) *how* — ! or ὅτι τοιούτως, *that you have so* —.

[§ 307.] Θυέστην ὡς ὠμὰ διεπράττετο, *Pl. Crat.* 395, may be explained as a parenthetic exclamation, *how ruthless!*[1] θαυμαστὰ γὰρ τὸ τόξον ὡς ὀλισθάνει, *Soph.*, whence the adverbial phrases θαυμαστῶς ὡς, § 198 a, R. 4. — In wishes, ὡς ὄλοιτο! *how (I wish) he might perish!* unless this is rather to be referred to the ancient use of ὥς demonstr. = οὕτως. But comp. πῶς ἄν in wishes, § 120, R. 1. — Possibly, ὡς δή ironical: *how much forsooth it is the case that —!* but see under *c*.

f) In object-sentences, § 123, ὡς for ὅπως with fut. indic. ἐπιμελεῖσθαι ὡς ἔσονται, *how they shall be:* with subj., ἐπιμελοῦνται ὡς ἔχῃ οὕτως, prop. *how it may be so* (the latter usage is rare). — In final sentences with subj. and opt., § 122, 131, a, b. τὴν γέφυραν λύσει ὡς μὴ διαβῆτε = either (considering, planning, &c.) *how you shall not cross*, or with the notion of intention as explained under *c*. So Κῦρος φίλων ᾤετο δεῖσθαι ὡς συνεργοὺς ἔχοι, *Xen.* On ὡς ἄν, see § 302: but ὡς ἄν with opt., τὰ βασίλεια οἰκοδομεῖν ὡς ἂν ἀπομάχεσθαι ἱκανὰ εἴη, = *in the manner in which —*, § 137. — With the past tense of the indic., ὡς is used in the same manner as ἵνα, see § 131 b, R. 3, to denote *an unattained result:* τί μ' οὐ λαβὼν ἔκτεινας εὐθύς, ὡς ἔδειξα μήποτε ἐμαυτὸν ἀνθρώποισιν ἔνθεν ἦν γεγώς, (*so*) *as I should never have shown —*, = *so had I never shown*, approx. to the final *that I might never —*. See under ἵνα.

g) To the same head belongs the use of ὡς instead of ὅτι after *verba declarandi et sentiendi*, § 159, R. 3, as we sometimes in the like case use *how*, or *how that* (and in vulgar Engl. *as how*). μαθὼν τὸν Σμέρδιος θάνατον ὡς κρύπτοιτο γενόμενος καὶ ὡς ὀλίγοι ἦσαν οἱ ἐπιστάμενοι αὐτὸν Περσέων, *when he learnt the death of S., how* (that) *the fact of its having taken place was concealed, and how* (that) *few —*. With verbs of fearing, considering, &c., ὡς with fut. indic. is rare: μὴ δείσητε ὡς οὐχ ἡδέως καθευδήσετε (*Xen.*).

h) When ὡς with inf. denotes effect or consequence (more commonly ὥστε), it may be explained as representing the correlation τοσοῦτος — ὅσος, τοιοῦτος — οἷος. Thus, εὖρος ὡς δύο τριήρεις πλέειν ὁμοῦ, *a breadth* (so great, or such) *as for two triremes to sail abreast:* and ἢ ὡς with inf. after a comparative, μείζω ἢ ὡς (ὥστε) φέρειν. So μείζονα ἡγησάμενος εἶναι ἢ ὡς ἐπὶ Πισίδας τὴν παρασκευήν (*Xen.*, suppl. εἶναι). In Herod. and Att. poets, sometimes also in Xen., ὡς for ὥστε occurs with the finite mood, with the correlation οὕτω — ὡς, τοιοῦτος — ὡς expressed: see the exx. in § 166 c, R. 2. — Ὡς also occurs (and ὥσπερ) where we should expect ἤ after a comparative, μᾶλλον ὥς μοι προσήκει (*Lys.*). The full construction is ἢ ὡς. Thus, μαλακώτεροι γίγνονται ἢ ὡς κάλλιον αὐτοῖς (*Pl.*).

i) Lastly, ὡς = ὅτε, ὡς ἴδεν, *when he saw, ut vidit:* and hence, like other temporal particles, it denotes *cause*, see *c*. "Crœsus, as it was summer, did so and so," ὡς θέρος ἦν (*Xen.*).

The comparative ὡς is strengthened with περ, ὥσπερ, *just as:* οὕτως, τοιοῦτος, ὁ αὐτός, ἴσος — ὥσπερ. On the ellipsis ὥσπερ (ὡς) ἂν εἰ —, see § 139 c.

Rem. On ὡς, in the sense ὅτι οὕτως, see under *c*.

§ 308. ὥς, demonstr. *thus, so.* Frequent in Hom. ὣς ἔφατ', &c., and in comparisons, ὡς δ' —, ὥς —, *and as — so.* Also οὐδ' ὥς, *not even so*, which is also used in Attic prose. Plato has also ὡς — ὥς: ὡς πρὸς ἀστρονομίαν ὄμματα πέπηγεν, ὣς πρὸς ἐναρμόνιον φορὰν ὦτα (κινδυνεύει) παγῆναι, *Rep.* 530: and ὣς φήσομεν, *ib.* 415, *Stallb.*, *so we shall say.* ὣς οὖν ποιήσετε καὶ πείθεσθέ μοι, *id. Prot.* 338, *thus then ye shall do —*.

§ 309. ὥστε = ὡς with the particle τε, § 227.

---

[1] Heindorf. *in l.* and in Phædon., p. 152, explains it, "per*quam* sæva," which is not amiss, though many of his exx. are of a different kind. (It may also come under *d*.)

[APPENDIX.

a) It is used in comparisons by Hom. and the Tragedians, πάντες ὥστε τοξόται τοξεύετε, *Soph.*, and now and then in the older Attic prose. [§ 309.]

b) In the sense (*so*) *that*, it refers to a preceding οὕτως, or the like, expressed or understood. ἡ δ' ὧδε τλήμων, ὥστε τῷ μιάστορι ξύνεστι, *Soph.* ὥστ' οὐδὲν αὐτοῖς προὔργου θύειν — μάτην (*Pl.*) = *quocirca, igitur*, i.e. *the case is such that* —. θνητὸς δ' Ὀρέστης, ὥστε μὴ λίαν στένε (*Soph.*).

c) With infin. ἔχεις ἔγκλημα ὥστε θυμοῦσθαι, *such as* (is reason enough = ἀρκούντως ὥστε) *to be angry*, § 152. — *So that*, see § 166, a, b. (In the passage cited in § 141, R. 1, ἀδύνατον ὑμῖν ὥστε Πρωταγόρου τοῦδε σοφώτερον ἐλέσθαι (βραβευτὴν τῶν λόγων), ὥστε is not superfluous: this construction occurs only with ἀδύν. and the like, and implies the looking out, &c. for a way *so as to* — *;* i.e. it is impossible for you to be in such a condition as to —: it combines ἀδύνατον ἐλέσθαι and οὐκ ἔσεσθε οἷοί τε ἐλέσθαι.)

d) With the participle, in Herodot. where the Attics have ὡς, or ἅτε: ἦν γὰρ ἀδύνατος, ὥστε σηπομένου τοῦ μηροῦ. — Cf. § 166, note.

ὅπως. §

This is properly the dependent interrogative adverb corresponding with πῶς, *how*, as ὁ-πόσος with πόσος, ὁ-πότε with πότε &c. Thus, ἔστω δ' οὖν ὅπως ὑμῖν φίλον (*Soph.*): the direct interrogation is πῶς ὑμῖν φίλον; indirect or dependt. (σκέψασθε) ὅπως ὑ. φ.: hence, (say for yourselves,) *how you like to have it*, (and) *so let it be* = *so* be it, *as* you like. In most of its usages it coincides with ὡς, differing from it (originally) only as implying a question *how?* 310.

a) As correlated to ὧδε, οὕτως. Frequent in poetry, but less so in prose. Ὅπως ἕκαστος ὑμῶν — βούλεται, τοῦτον τὸν τρόπον φερέτω τὴν ψῆφον (*Isocr.*) = ὅντινα τρόπον. χρὴ τοὐμὸν σῶμα θάπτειν οὕτως ὅπως ἂν ἡγῇ νόμιμον εἶναι (*Pl.*) Ποίει ὅπως ἄριστόν σοι δοκεῖ εἶναι (*Xen.*). Like ὡς in comparisons, it frequently follows the term compared: Ἔρωτι — ὅστις ἀντανίσταται, πύκτης ὅπως ἐς χεῖρας, οὐ καλῶς φρονεῖ (*Soph.*).

b) The sense ὅτι, after *verba declarandi*, &c., is even more rare (viz. like ὡς, especially after a negative verb of this kind: οὐ λέγω ὅπως), and where it does occur, the sense is still that of a depend. interrogation: τοῦτον ἔχοι τις ἂν εἰπεῖν ὅπως οὐ δίκαιόν ἐστιν ἀποθνήσκειν; (*Xen.*) = πῶς οὐ δ., "*how it is not just — ! can any one say how!*" τοῦτ' αὐτὸ μή μοι φράζ' ὅπως οὐκ εἶ κακός (*Soph.*), *don't tell me* (that you are not a villain); *how are you not a villain!* Comp. § 159, R. 3.

c) The force of ὅπως is just the same in οὐκ ἔσθ' ὅπως —, *there exists not the way in which*, = it cannot be but that —, § 102 b, R. 2: 122, R. 2, and in the elliptical οὐχ ὅπως — ἀλλά —, "I say not how —" = *not only* —, *but* —, § 212. — It should be observed, however, that this phrase (and οὐχ ὅτι) is sometimes *not only*, sometimes *not only not*. Thus, οὐχ ὅπως ἔτρεσεν, ἀλλ' (or ἀλλὰ καὶ) ἔφυγεν, should prop. = *I say not how he was frightened* (he was frightened, and not only that) *but he also fled*. οὐχ ὅπως ἔφυγεν, ἀλλ' οὐδὲ ἔτρεσεν —: here the negation in οὐδέ extends to both members, *he did not — I say not, flee — but* (*not*) *even tremble*. Ἔφυγεν, οὐχ ὅπως ἔτρεσεν, *he fled*, (I say not how =) *much more, he was afraid; fugit, nedum extimuerit.* But in the usage of the language, οὐχ ὅπως in the first clause is often *non solum non*, even when the adversative clause is positive: thus, οὐχ ὅπως χάριν αὐτοῖς ἔχεις, ἀλλὰ καὶ — κατὰ τουτωνὶ πολιτεύῃ (*Dem.*), *you not only are* not *grateful to them, but you even* —, viz. because the first clause is, *to say nothing of your being grateful* — (you are not grateful, and not only so) *but* —*;* in other words, οὐχ ὅπως has become a

[§ 310.] phrase of negation, as if it were one word, like οὔπως. On the other hand, in οὐχ ὅπως τοὺς πολεμίους ἐτρέψαντο οἱ Ἕλληνες, ἀλλὰ καὶ τὴν χώραν αὐτῶν ἐκάκωσαν (*Xen.*), the οὐχ ὅπως is not treated as a negation of ἐτρ., but retains its proper force, *I say not how they routed —; they not only did that, but also —.* With the infinitive: μὴ ὅπως ὀρχεῖσθαι, ἀλλ' οὐδ' ὀρθοῦσθαι ἐδύνασθε, *not only not to dance, but not even to stand upright* (*Xen.*). (τοὺς Θηβαίους) ἡγεῖτο οὐχ ὅπως ἀντιπράξειν — ἀλλὰ καὶ συστρατεύσειν (*Dem.*), *that they would not only not act against him, but would even join with him in the expedition: = that far from acting against him*, &c.

d) With the superlative, ὅπως ἄριστα: to be explained in the same way as ὡς, viz. ὅπως δυνατόν ἐστι, &c. ("how can it be best done?")

e) After such verbs as σκοπεῖν, βουλεύεσθαι, μηχανᾶσθαι, σπουδάζειν, φροντίζειν, and the like: *to see how*, &c.: see the rules and exx. in the §§ referred to in the Index. Hence the ellipsis, ὅπως οὖν ἔσεσθε, (*see then*) *how ye shall be.* — Also after verbs of fearing and of prohibition, § 124 b, e. g. δέδοικα ὅπως μὴ γενήσεται, *I fear (considering with myself) how it shall not be.* Ἀπείρηταί μοι, ὅπως μηδὲν ἐρῶ —, the prohibition being, ὅρα ὅπως μηδὲν ἐρεῖς.

f) As final particle, ὅπως and ὅπως μή with subj. and opt., § 122 and 131 b. εἰς καιρὸν ἥκεις ὅπως ἀκούσῃς = *your intention being how you may hear.* On ὅπως ἄν with subj., see under Ἄν, § 302. It results from the proper interrog. signification of ὅπως that this particle (not ὡς or ἵνα) can be used with fut. indic. in the final sense, see the exx. at end of § 122. (To do so and so) ὅπως μαχοῦνται = *with this view and intention, how they shall fight.*

g) Its use with histor. tenses of indic. to denote an unattained result is rare. Ἐχρῆν σε Πήγασον ζεῦξαι ὅπως ἐφαίνου τραγικώτερος = *that you might have appeared*, prop. *how you would have —.* See the expl. under ἵνα.

§ 311. ἵνα.

The root is either the pronoun of the third person ἵ or ἴ, or perhaps more probably the relative ὅ- with the vowel lightened (attenuated) into ι. The original meaning is "where," "in which (or, what) case," &c. (comp. ἐν in ἔνθα, *where*, and the first element of *in*-de, *un*-de, last of alio-*quin*.)

a) *ubi* and *quo.* ἵν' οἴχεται, *where* (*whither*) *it is gone, Hom. Od.* 4, 821: and demonstratively, ἵνα γάρ σφιν ἐπέφραδον ἠγερέεσθαι, *for there* (= it was there that) —, *Il.* 10. 127. This use is almost entirely confined to the poets. ἱκόμην ἵν' ἱκόμην. οὐδ' ὁρᾷς ἵν' εἶ κακοῦ, *Soph.* (ἵνα with gen.) With ἄν: σε προσθέσθαι πέλας χώρας θέλουσι, μηδ' ἵν' ἂν σαυτοῦ κρατῇς, *Soph.*. *and not where* (if they place thee) *thou shalt be thine own master.* (Brunck and Elmsl. κρατοῖς, wrongly, since ἵν' ἄν is never final = ὅπως ἄν.)

b) With subj. and optat. it forms sentences of intention, *that, in order that.* ἐξαύδα, μὴ κεῦθε νόῳ, ἵνα εἴδομεν (= εἰδῶμεν) ἄμφω, prop. *in that case* (or, as the case in which) *we shall both know it.* See § 122. 131. ἵνα τί; ellipsis, § 198 a, note.

c) More frequently than ὡς, it is used with the historical tenses of the indicative to denote *an unattained result*, i. e. something which *would be* (or *would have been*) *attained* on the supposition made by the speaker (in the form of a wish, a question *implying* a wish, or of a declaration of what *should be*, or *should have been*). Here, "I wish he had come, in which case (= so that) I should (might) have seen him," implying, "but he did not come, so I did not see him." See the exx. in § 131 b, R. 3. Thus, "he does (did) so and so, ἵν' ᾖ (εἴη) τυφλός, as the case wherein he may (as he purposes) be blind;" but "he should have done so, &c., ἵν' ᾖ (imperf. indic). τυφλός, as the case in which he would have been blind." The force of the latter clause rests upon the convertible proposition, "where this (e. g. the doing) is, there that (e. g. the being blind) is," and "where that is, there this," so that the one being denied, the other is also denied. [§ 311.]

The absence of ἄν from the relative clause is explained by the kindred meaning of the two particles, ἵνα and ἄν: comp. εἰ ἐβουλόμην λέγειν, ἤκουσας ἄν, "if I had wished to speak, you would *in that case* have heard," with ἐβουλόμην ἂν λέξαι, ἵνα ἤκουσας, "I wish I had spoken, *in which case* you would have heard." Where ἄν does occur in the relative clause, it is drawn in by some other consideration: thus, καίτοι οὐ προσῆκεν ἀλλ' εὐθὺς λέγειν — ἵνα μᾶλλον ἂν ἐπιστεύετο ὑφ' ὑμῶν (*Isæus*), the ἄν attaches itself to μᾶλλον as a set phrase (see ἄν, § 299).

ὅτι. § 312.

This is the Lat. *quod*, our *that:* not originally the neut. of ὅστις, but the ancient form of neut. acc. of ὅς, ὅτ, covered with the vowel ι. Hence Hom. has indifferently ὅ and ὅτι.

a) *that*, after *verba declarandi, sentiendi*, &c. οὐκ ἀΐεις ὅ με βάλεν Αἴας; *Hom.* prop. *hear you not this — which* (= that) *Ajax has wounded me?* λέγει (ἀκούει, οἴεται. &c.) ὅτι νοσεῖς: ἔλεγεν ὅτι ἐνόσουν, ὅτι νοσοῖμι. § 159, R. 3, 4; 178 a, R. 5. On the moods in object-sentences with ὅτι, see § 108. 130 a, b; 137. On the difference between ὅτι and ὡς (ὅπως), § 159, R. 3. "Ὅτι and ὡς are very rare after verbs denoting a purely subjective or uncertain view (e. g. οἴεσθαι, δοκεῖν, νομίζειν, φάναι = 'to declare one's own opinion:' but we find φάναι ὅτι, *Pl. Gorg.* 487; ὡς, *Dem.* 4. 48. *Xen. Hell.* 6, 3, 7; οἴεσθαι ὡς, *Xen. Mem.* 3, 3, 14. In later writers, δοκεῖν ὅτι, *Polyb.* 28. 9, 14; ἐλπίζειν ὅτι, *Arr. An.* 1, 4, 7. Cf. *Thuc.* 8, 54. νομίζειν ὡς, *Thuc.* 3, 88). But after λέγειν, to *tell* (with reference to the substance of the narrative), and εἰπεῖν (with reference to the expression), ὅτι and ὡς are not uncommon." *Krüger.* Also, it follows from the original meaning of ὡς, that this particle is preferred to ὅτι where the "as" or "how" is of more importance than the "that:" hence, πείθειν ὡς, *to get one to believe*, and ἀκούειν, πυνθάνεσθαι, ἀγγέλλειν, *to bring a report*, ἀποδεικνύναι, &c. ὡς; and after verbs of *calumniating, reproaching, accusing*, &c.

On ὅτι in the sense (*the circumstance*) *that* —, (*in regard*) *that* —, § 170 a, R.: (*to prove*) *that* —, § 192 b, R. Τὸ δὲ μέγιστον ὅτι, § 197. And on μὴ ὅτι (= μὴ εἴπω ὅτι), οὐχ ὅτι (= οὐκ ἐρῶ ὅτι), see § 212, and cf. under ὅπως, § 310 c.

Rem. We also find, οὐ μόνον ὅτι: thus, καὶ μὴν ὑπεραποθνήσκειν γε μόνοι ἐθέλουσιν οἱ ἐρῶντες, οὐ μόνον ὅτι ἄνδρες, ἀλλὰ καὶ γυναῖκες (*non modo — sed etiam*, *Pl.*). Likewise οὐχ ὅσον and οὐχ οἷον: οἱ μὲν οὐχ ὅσον οὐκ ἠμύναντο, ἀλλ' οὐδ' ἐσώθησαν, *Thuc.*, which might have been expressed by οὐχ ὅπως. or by μὴ (οὐχ) ὅτι, ἠμύναντο. Οὐχ οἷον ὠφελεῖν δύναιντ' ἂν τοὺς φίλους, ἀλλ' οὐδ' αὐτοὺς σώζειν, *Polyb.*

b) *because*, for διὰ τοῦτο ὅτι, whence also διότι. Ἆρα τὸ ὅσιον, ὅτι ὅσιόν ἐστι, φιλεῖται ὑπὸ τῶν θεῶν, ἤ, ὅτι φιλεῖται, ὅσιόν ἐστι; *Pl.* Διὰ τί δὲ ἄλλο ἄλυποι ἀλλήλοις εἰσὶν οἱ ἐμπλέοντες, ἢ διότι ἐν τάξει — κάθηνται; *Xen.*

Rem. The poets have in the same sense, οὕνεκα = οὗ ἕνεκα, i. e. τούτου ἕνεκα, ὅ —, and ὁθούνεκα = ὅτου ἕνεκα.

With the superlative, though written as the conjunction, ὅτι τάχιστα, the word is ὅ τι, acc. neut. governed by δύναμαι, or nom. neut. subject to δυνατόν ἐστι, or the like. — Also in the elliptical ὅτι μή (*except*), the full construction is οὐδὲν ὅ τι μή.

APPENDIX.]

§ 313. **ὅτε**, *when.*

This adverbial form is not a compound with **τε**, but its second syllable is an ancient case suffix: cf. *quum*, *quando*. Like other temp. adverbs, it is also used in a causal sense, § 127, R. 1, whence **ὅτε μή** = *quando non* and *si non.*

On **μέμνημαι, ὅτε**, see § 178 a, R. 5, and note. — With **μέν** and **δέ**, *sometimes — sometimes*, the accent conforms itself to that of **ποτέ**, viz. **ὁτὲ μέν — ὁτὲ δέ.**

The correlative of **ὅτε** is **τότε**, *then.* The corresponding interrogative **πότε**, *when?* indef. **ποτέ**, *at some* (any) *time*, § 274, and relative (depend.) interrogative, **ὁπότε**. Hence **ὁπότε**, as implying the question *when?* is indefinite. Cf. **παρήγγειλεν ὑπομένειν ὅτε οἱ πολέμιοι ἐπικέοιντο** (*Xen.*), and **εἰώθει γοῦν ὁπότε δεῦρ' ἐμβάλλοι**, *whenever —*, *Xen.*

§ 314. **ὅπου**, *where.*

As **ὅτε, πότε; ὁπότε, ποτέ** (encl.) of *time*, so **οὗ, ποῦ, ὅπου, πού** (encl.) of *place.* The correlative (**τοῦ** being lost) is **ἔνθα**, demonstr. or **ἐνταῦθα.** — In prose, **ὅπου** has taken the place of **οὗ**, as the simple relative *where.* — Sometimes, but rarely, it is *since, siquidem, quandoquidem:* and then the apodosis is often **ἦπου**, in the sense, *if —, then surely.* **ὅπου γὰρ Ἀθηνόδωρος καὶ Καλλίστρατος — οἷοί τε γεγόνασιν, ἦπου — ἡμεῖς — ἂν δυνηθείημεν** (*Isocr.*), *if A. and C. have been able, surely we should be able.*

§ 315. **ἐπεί (ἐπειδή).**

Properly a particle of time, *when, after, postquam*, but, like most particles of time, also denotes cause, *since, quoniam, quandoquidem.* **ἐπεὶ τάχιστα**, *as soon as ever.* — Both are also *since* (*ex quo*) of *time.* **Οὐ πολὺς χρόνος ἐπειδὴ χιτῶνας λινοῦς ἐπαύσαντο φοροῦντες** (*Thuc.*). With **ἄν: ἐπειδάν, ἐπάν, ἐπήν**; the first by far the most frequent, and the second somewhat more so than the third.

In the sense "*for if not*," "*for otherwise*," "*for if so*" (where **εἰ δὲ μή**, or **εἰ δέ** after a negat. proposition might have been used), there is an ellipsis: *since* (*if you doubt it*, or, *if you think so*, &c.) —. **Νόσον γὰρ ὁ πατὴρ ἀλλόκοτον αὐτοῦ νοσεῖ, ἣν οὐδ' ἂν εἷς γνοίη πότ' οὐδ' ἂν ξυμβάλοι εἰ μὴ πύθοιθ' ἡμῶν, ἐπεὶ τοπάζετε**, *Aristoph.*

§ 316. **εἰ**, *if.*

This is an ancient dative of the pronoun of the third person, **ἵ** or **ἴ**, comp. Lat. *si* (*sibi*). Its original force is "in this that," "in the (case, hap, event) that," "on the (condition) that."[1]

For the use of **εἰ, ἐάν, ἤν**, in conditional propositions, see the Index.

From such expressions as **σκέψαι εἰ —**, *consider if —*, results the sense *whether* in

---

[1] This (the reflexive) pronoun is closely connected with the relative pronoun, so that, in point of sense, the conditional particle may be said to be directly derived from the relative. Thus in Sanskrit, from relat. *yas, yâ, yat*, **ὅς, ἥ, ὅ**, we have *yadi* = **ὅτε**, "when," and *yadi* = "if;" and in German, "wenn" is both *when* and *if.* Accordingly, the usages of the relat. (and interrog.) and of the conditional particle very often run over into each other. Thus, **ὅτε** and **ὅπου** approach to the sense of condition: **εἴ τις** is more nearly = **ὅς τις** than "if any:" **θαυμάζω εἰ** represents **θ. ὅτι** (see § 194 c); the **εἰ** of wishing may also be expressed by **ὡς** and **πῶς** (the relat. *utinam*), and the interrogative **εἰ** (*whe-ther*) by **πότερα.**

[APPENDIX.

depend. interrogation, § 199 b. εἰ (ἐάν) is thus used only in indirect, and, indeed, properly only in double questions, denoting a wavering between two considerations: but often only one member is expressed, the other being present in the mind of the speaker. Where both are expressed, the second is introduced by ἤ, § 199 c. Σκέψαι εἰ ὁ Ἑλλήνων νόμος κάλλιον ἔχει, *whether it be not* (*Xen.*). δέομαι ὑμῶν τούτῳ τὸν νοῦν προσέχειν εἰ δίκαια λέγω ἢ μή (= μὴ δίκαια) *Pl.* Comp. πρὶν δῆλον εἶναι . . . πότερον ἕψονται Κύρῳ ἢ οὔ (= οὐχ ἕψονται). — The same thing is expressed by εἴτε — εἴτε, § 199 c. In poetry we also find εἴτε — ἤ, εἰ — εἴτε, and — εἴτε with the first εἴτε omitted. [§ 316.]

REM. Εἴτε — εἴτε is also conditional, viz. where several cases are put conditionally, *both if — and if:* but here also in English we use the interrogative *whether — or*. See § 194 a.

The use of εἰ in wishes, εἰ γὰρ ὤφελον πρότερος ἰδεῖν, is elliptical: *if it were so*, it would be well. Thus we say, *O if it were so!* (i.e. *how happy I should be!*) — Hence with suffix θε, § 239, εἴθε, *utinam*. See exx. in § 129, and R. 2. § 317.

εἴ γε (= *si quidem*) *if at least, if, that is* (εἰ — γέ when the γέ distinguishes the interposed word, εἴ γε when its influence extends to the whole clause). Οὐδείς, εἴ γε σὺ ἀληθῆ λέγεις, *nobody*, if, that is (or, *if, at least*) *what you say is true*.

εἴπερ is εἰ strengthened by πέρ. It calls attention to the condition, and so adds emphasis to it. The force of πέρ may be rendered in the condition by *always supposing that* —, in the apodosis by, *then it quite follows that* —.

καὶ εἰ, is *even if:* the καί emphasizes the condition, marks it as improbable, extreme, or as the most unfavorable that can well be conceived. In εἰ καί, the καί gives emphasis, not to the condition, but to the thing supposed. καὶ εἰ λέγω, *even supposing I say*, i.e. *go so far as to suppose that I say*. εἰ καὶ λέγω, *supposing I even say*, i.e. *suppose I go so far as to say*. For (see § 222) καί adverbial implies a correlation καί — καί: therefore the first is καὶ (ἄλλως), καὶ εἰ λέγω; the second, εἰ καὶ (ἄλλως), καὶ λέγω. This is the principle of the distinction, but in practice the difference is often so slight, that no reason appears why one form should be chosen rather than the other.

εἶτα. ἔπειτα.

These particles, perhaps, are related to εἰ, ἐπεί, as δῆτα to δή. τηνικαῦτα to τηνίκα; and thus they may be considered as denoting the demonstrative apodosis of a suppressed condition (*if*) or relative (*when*). Thus Ellendt remarks that εἶτα may sometimes be explained by a sentence with εἰ or εἰ καί. *Soph. Phil.* 1337, ἀλλ' εἰκάθω δῆτ'; εἶτα πῶς ὁ δύσμορος εἰς φῶς — εἶμι; i.e. (and *if* I yield) *then how* — ! § 318.

Others make εἶτα cognate with ἔτι (corresponding forms in Sanskrit *ati, éta*), and ἔπειτα = ἐπ' εἶτα (*Kühner*). — In Latin, the sense is expressed by *deinde*:—

a) In enumerations, πρῶτον (μέν) —, εἶτα, ἔπειτα (δέ) —. (b) In the usage with participles, see § 175 a (comp. 181, R. 2). (c) In interrogations, expressed with vehemence or indignation; as in the ex. given above. Εὖ ἴσθι, ἔφη, ὅτι, εἰ νομίζοιμι θεοὺς ἀνθρώπων τι φροντίζειν, οὐκ ἂν ἀμελοίην αὐτῶν. Σ. Ἔπειτ' οὐκ οἴει φροντίζειν; (*Xen.*) It may be explained = *post talia* (Gronov.), *quum ita sit, ergo:* the Lat. uses *deinde* in the same way: *quæ nunc* deinde *mora est, aut quid jam, Turne, retractas?* Virg. Æn. 12,889. *Hercules solus domat. Cur* deinde *latebras aut fugam vecors petam?* Sen. Herc. 1407. — Often κᾆτα, κἄπειτα, which are more emphatic: κἄπειτα τοιοῦτον ὄντα οὐ φιλεῖς αὐτόν; (*Xen.*) — Εἶτα, ἔπειτα, *and then*, § 185 a, R. 6.

ἔτι.

This particle is cognate with Lat. *et*, *at*, prep. *ad*, *at*-que = *ad*-que. Its meaning is, *further* (on), *yet*, *still*. Comp. also Lat. *item*. ταῦτα μὲν οὖν πάντα ὁμοίως ἀμφοτέρων ἐστίν· ἀλλὰ τὸ μάχεσθαι οὐκέτι (οὐκ ἔτι, *non item*) ἀμφοτέρων (*Xen.*). ἀνεστράφησαν οἱ ἀμφὶ βασιλέα, πεζοὶ μὲν οὐκέτι, τῶν δὲ ἱππέων ὁ λόφος ἐνεπλήσθη (*Xen.*).

INDEX I.[1]

---

[1] The numbers refer to the paragraphs and remarks: n. = marginal note. The particular words which come under a general rule (especially of case-government) are, except in a few instances, not specified in this Index; e.g. for ἀΐσσειν χεῖρα (22, R. 2), ἐβασίλευσα, *became king* (111, R. d), see in Index II. "intransitive verbs" and "aorist of verbs denoting office and public station;" and so in other instances.

B.

Γ.

H.

M.

N.

INDEX II.

A.

THE END.

GILBERT AND RIVINGTON, PRINTERS, ST. JOHN'S SQUARE, LONDON.